THEATRE OF LIFE

Esme Howard

Washington. 1925.

THEATRE OF LIFE

BY
LORD HOWARD OF PENRITH

LIFE SEEN FROM THE STALLS

1905—1936

LONDON
HODDER AND STOUGHTON LIMITED

First printed 1936

*Made and Printed in Great Britain for Hodder & Stoughton Limited,
by Wyman & Sons Limited, London, Reading and Fakenham*

TO ISA

HIEME ET ÆSTATE ET
PROPE ET PROCUL USQUE
DUM VIVAM ET ULTRA

CONTENTS

Contents

LIST OF ILLUSTRATIONS

Isabella Howard-
Washington- 1925-

CHAPTER I

THE INTERNATIONAL ADMINISTRATION OF CRETE.
A FOOTNOTE TO HISTORY

(1903–1906)

WARNING to those about to read these pages. I, the writer, have been advised that I have given far more space than is fitting or proper in a book of this size to so small a scene in the Theatre of Life as was Crete during the years 1903 to 1906, and that no one will care to wade through so many pages of such trifling matter.

I plead guilty at once. It is always the quickest way to deal with criticism, but this I may say in extenuation.

What I have set down I have written because, quite frankly, the memory of it amused and interested me. If it should seem that I have dealt in too great detail with events of little importance I would ask the reader to bear in mind that Crete was then not so insignificant politically as it is to-day. Before 1914 all European countries dreaded the shadow of war, and most of them believed that the great future war of Europe would spring from some Balkan source. Which that source would be none could tell—there were plenty to choose from, Greek, Bulgarian, Serbian, Montenegrin, Rumanian, and, of course, Turkish. There was, in fact, no part of this area from which the spark might not fly out that would set alight to all the piles of dry wood lying around. Crete had been for many years a source of trouble and anxiety, and the temporary compromise arrived at by the Great Powers in giving the Cretans a Greek Prince as Governor, while retaining the suzerainty of Turkey, with a semi-Western Constitution, all somewhat nebulous

THEATRE OF LIFE

of them, the British, French, Italian and Russian Consuls-
Generals, supported by some troops and ships of each,
satisfied no one.

There seemed therefore no little possibility of the spark
flying out from the friction continually caused by all these
diverse ill-assorted elements trying to keep the peace in
this fascinating but unruly island, while over all hung the
pall of the cloud of war that might easily spread throughout
the whole of Europe. Let but the reader put himself
into the place of a Consul-General of one of the Protecting
Powers or of a Military or Naval Officer with the knowledge
that some little blunder on his part might set that spark
alight, and the curious fascination which that period still
has for me may perhaps in some degree communicate
itself to him and make little affairs of daily life in Crete
appear to be of great pith and moment, just as they did
to us during the International Occupation.

Longfellow tells us that :

Things are not what they seem

That I entirely deny. For the moment that is just what
they are, and that is why even after they have lost the
mirage of appearances they still may retain some of its
colours.

* * * * *

I knew, of course, of Sir Arthur Evans's wonderful
discoveries at Knossos, and I knew that St. Paul had landed
somewhere in Crete on his way to Italy, at a place called
Fair Havens.

I had also read while in the Diplomatic Service in the
" Confidential Print " dispatches and telegrams from our
Consuls and Consuls-General at Canea, Sir Alfred
Biliotti, Mr. R. Graves and others, interminable reports
of insurrections, murders, depredations, devastations of
olive yards and vineyards, and frequent repetitions of
names ending in—akis—. It all seemed complicated and
very tiresome, which was the view that the Foreign Office

as a rule took it, but it also seemed that for one in the midst of it it might be a place of unexpected adventures, and therefore more interesting than most settled countries where diplomats overfeed each other and where ladies quarrel over questions of precedence. And so it proved.

As soon as I knew Crete was to be my fate, I set to work to read it up in the *Encyclopædia Britannica*, ever a standby for the searcher after truth, and such books on Crete as I could discover, as well as, of course, the more recent Foreign Office "Confidential Print."

From all these sources of original research I discovered, without going back to the Minoan tradition, that Crete was about 160 miles long and 35 broad in the broadest place, and that it holds three separate ranges of high mountains. In the west the White Mountains, or Lefka Oree (I spell it as pronounced) 7,832 feet ; in the centre the Psiloriti, or ancient Ida, the birthplace of Zeus, 8,193 feet ; in the east the Lasiti Mountains, 7,185 feet ; not to mention other smaller ranges.

The northern coast is greatly indented and possesses one of the finest and largest landlocked harbours in the Mediterranean—Suda Bay—but the southern shore is generally flanked by high precipices rising in places abruptly two thousand feet or more out of the sea, into which small rivers discharge themselves through narrow canyons one or two thousand feet deep which are almost always in semi-darkness at the bottom.

It will be readily understood that a country with such high mountains in so small an area has not much space left for cultivation. Yet what cultivatable land there is produces wonderful grapes from which strong wine is made (the original Malmsey or Malvoisie) splendid olives, oranges, lemons and all kinds of fruit a fair amount of wheat and oats on the high lands, corn woods and also woods of valona oak, the cups of the acorn of which are largely exported for curing leather. The population amounted to about 300,000 at the time of which I am writing. Of the inhabitants some 265,000 were Greeks and Orthodox Christians, and 35,000 were

Moslems of all nationalities. There were also some hundreds of Roman Catholics, principally Maltese, and a few Jews. The Orthodox Greeks were, approximately, as nine to one to the Moslems who, moreover, were mostly of Cretan origin and of Greek speech.

It is necessary to remember some of this dry data in order to get a picture of the conditions on the Island.

The mountainous and difficult terrain, the almost exclusively Greek character of the population, and the fine physique of the Cretan mountaineers as well as the utter incapacity of Turkish rule, go to account for the constant insurrections against the Turks which broke out all through the nineteenth century, but principally in 1833, 1841, 1858, 1866–68, 1878, 1889, and, lastly, 1896, 1897 and 1898. This last insurrection led to the intervention of Greece on behalf of the insurgents, the entrance on the scene of the six Great Powers—Great Britain, France, Italy, Germany, Austria and Russia—the withdrawal of Greek troops, and the later withdrawal under pressure of the Powers of the Turkish troops and authorities. This was followed by the establishment of an autonomous Government under a Greek High Commissioner acting on behalf of the Powers while the Porte retained a shadowy suzerainty which was finally reduced to the flying of one Turkish flag on an island in Suda Bay, where the Powers kept ships permanently during the period of the International occupation. These were known as the " *Stationnaires.*" Their principal duty was to protect the flags of the Protecting Powers—Great Britain, France, Italy and Russia, and particularly that of the Suzerain Turkey—from the nationalist and patriotic ardour of the Cretans who, after the first joy over the evacuation of the Turkish troops in 1898 had evaporated, were eager to see the end of all foreign intervention in their island and to obtain union with Greece. It will be easily understood that with the above-mentioned record for insurrections, the Cretans had acquired the insurgent habit, in fact it was often told me that the maidens of Crete would not look at a man until he had been

" to the mountains " with his rifle and taken part in an insurrection of sorts.

Crete was truly an isle of unrest, and the Protecting Powers hardly realised what a hedgehog they had laid hold of when they made themselves responsible for its administration. This they did, it must be admitted, not for any sentimental reason, but quite frankly to end the Greek occupation, which was looked on as likely to lead to a new combined attack by the Balkan Christian nations on the decadent Turkish Empire. Some of the Powers were perhaps inspired by a desire to prevent the occupation of Crete by any of the other great European Powers, because the possession of Suda Bay, one, as above mentioned, of the finest harbours in the Mediterranean, made it an object of desire.

In the opinion of the Cretans, Crete was the centre of all political ambitions of the world on account of Suda Bay, and it is hardly exaggerating to say that many of the representatives of the Powers in Crete, whatever the real feelings of their own Government towards Crete and Suda Bay, were convinced that the other Protecting Powers, as well as Austria and Germany, which had withdrawn from this curious partnership out of deference to Turkey, were all hotfoot after Suda Bay.

In addition to these elements of suspicion and unrest, there was the High Commissioner, Prince George of Greece, whose dominating ambition was to obtain from the Powers their consent at the earliest possible date to the union of Crete to Greece, and the equally strong determination of all the Powers to continue to shelve the troublesome question for as long as possible and, at any rate, not to accept the Greek solution for the moment.

Finally, Prince George, a very cheery, friendly sailor, made no secret of his dislike for a constitutional regime. He told me once that he had no use for parliamentary government, that being a sailor he only understood strict discipline, and that he intended to govern Crete as if the island was a battleship and he the captain, whatever the Powers might think of the Constitution with which

B

they had endowed the island. This, however, was not at all the point of view of the islanders who, being pure Greeks, had strong views about democratic Government ; nor, indeed, that of the Powers, except Russia.

The Prince had certainly gathered round him a personal following of the mountaineers by constantly—in a metaphorical sense—waving the Greek flag, and also of such of the inhabitants of the towns and plains as will always cling like limpets to the sources of honour and wealth. But the discontent with his administration which, even by the time I reached the island, had grown to alarming proportions, was already known to the Protecting Powers, and causing them no little uneasiness.

My own particular rôle in this witches' cauldron was rendered none the more easy from the fact that I was given to understand at the Foreign Office before taking up my new post that the Prince was the favourite nephew of King Edward and Queen Alexandra, and that it must be my particular job to let him down gently.

Such, then, very briefly, was the *Hexenkuche*[1] for which I was destined. I did not, of course, realise it all or even any great part of it at the first start, but I understood enough to convince me that the Theatre of Life would now supply me with considerable entertainment for quite a number of years. I therefore set out from Syracuse for Canea—the capital of Crete—full of the most pleasurable anticipation.

My ship arrived at Canea on a glorious morning of July, 1903, and I was up on deck shortly after sunrise. I fell in love with Crete and Canea at first sight. The ship was too large to enter the little harbour, and we lay far enough out to take in the whole picture of the town and its hinterland.

Across half a mile of sparkling turquoise sea lay the old town and harbour with its fine Venetian fortifications, its white-domed churches, Catholic and Orthodox, and its whiter minarets backed by the rocky White Mountains, on whose reddish rocks the snow still glittered here and

---

[1] Witches' kitchen.

CRETE

CANEA, FROM HALEPA, LOOKING WESTWARD

there in the sunlight, with occasional cypresses and date palms breaking the line of the middle distance which was, for the most part, grey with olives and dark green with orange gardens.

Boats were streaming out from the harbour, rowed by Cretans in their high boots, wide, blue baggy trousers, red sashes and baggy red Greek fezes with long tassels, and a motley crowd of passengers such as one can only see in the Levant. Lastly came a boat manned by four Cretans with the Union Jack at the stern, and two splendid Albanians in their white fustanellas, red sashes complete with silver-handled pistols and daggers, red velvet waistcoats embroidered with gold, and red Turkish fezes ; while in the stern sat three Englishmen : Robert Graves, the Consul-General, whom I was coming out to relieve ; Captain Clarke, an R.A.M.C. officer, who had been originally appointed to Crete with the British forces and had remained on in Canea ; and Paul Wilkinson, the Vice-Consul.

I could not tear myself away from the pleasure of drinking all this in, and forgot to get my cup of coffee before leaving the ship. The two Albanians, the Consular cavasses, soon got my luggage together, and we landed at the quay of the picturesque little harbour and passed the Customs. I was duly presented to the staff of the Consulate and the dragomans, and at last, to my satisfaction, for the loss of breakfast was beginning to make itself felt even in these novel and delightful surroundings, we drove out to Halepa, a suburb about a mile away, where Graves's house was situated.

This was an old Turkish house with some modern additions but most primitive sanitary arrangements. However, it stood in a charming old garden with paved walks and rose arbours, scarlet geraniums climbing up it, and some palms and datura trees. Besides these, there was from the drawing-room a fine view to the west over Canea Bay and the town to the rocky promontory beyond, while to the south, on the left, rose the jagged mass of the White Mountains. I at once settled to take the house over from Graves, with his servants : Manoli, the Maltese cook ; Zacharia, the Greek boy ; Mahommed, the Moslem groom, etc. The two Albanian cavasses were a standing institution at the Consulate and there could be no question of changing them. The old one, Sherif Agha, had been there for years, and was one of the most faithful of men. Given an order, he would execute it at no matter what cost, and this made it necessary to be very careful about the orders one gave him. Graves told me that he had given him strict orders not to allow anyone to touch the Consulate mail pouch, which it was Sherif's duty to fetch from the post office on mail days and bring up to Halepa. On one occasion one of the British officers stationed at Canea was expecting an important letter. He saw Sherif carrying the mail pouch, and went to him asking him to let him see if there was a letter in it for him. Sherif understood no languages but Albanian and Greek, and simply shook his head. This irritated the Englishman, who tried to snatch the pouch. Sherif then, without any warning, in the words of the old ballad :

> . . . took him by the middle so small
> and tumbled him into the sea,

which, as the post office was on the quay, happened to be handy. Graves had some difficulty, I believe, in smoothing down the ruffled feathers of the officer in question. On another occasion when Shakir, the youngest of the two cavasses, thought that some horseman in the streets of Canea had intentionally bumped against Graves's horse, he sprang at the offender and pulled him out of the saddle on to his back in the road.

It was certainly necessary to keep an eye on these retainers, but at least one felt that wherever one went, it was possible to rely absolutely on their fidelity.

The next fortnight passed quickly enough. Graves instructed me in my duties and drew for me a good sketch of the political situation, which we discussed at length. He introduced me, of course, to Prince George, who was frank, cheery and charming, and to the three

Councillors who made up the Cabinet and have left no impression on my mind. Also to M. Papadiamantopoulos, the Private Secretary of Prince George, a lean, tired, hungry-looking gentleman who was said to be the real ruler of Crete and to make Prince George's policy for him. There followed many other official calls, which were all duly returned.

There was not a spare moment during the time Graves remained in Crete. Nothing could be more kind and helpful than he was, and I remember his friendliness and hospitality with the deepest gratitude. When he and Captain Clarke left I settled down to a bachelor existence for the rest of the summer. Isa could not come out to me yet as she was expecting our firstborn, and was spending the summer at Vallombrosa, a famous mountain resort and monastery near Florence where many diplomats from Rome went for the hot season.

Curiously enough, there were both at Vallombrosa and in Rome that summer many who later became Foreign Ministers and were in office at the outbreak of the Great War, e.g. Berchtold, Austria ; Jagow, Germany ; Sazonow, Russia ; and San Giuliano, Italy. Of these, Sazonow and San Giuliano remained our close friends afterwards— both were most agreeable companions. Jagow left no great impression on my mind, and Berchtold simply that of a pleasant Society man and carpet knight.

Beside the ever-dominant need of dealing in what may be termed a spirit of sympathetic procrastination with the Cretan desire for union with Greece, which formed the subject of fully fifty per cent. of my interminable conversations with the High Commissioner, I found that there were several secondary matters to occupy the time and attention of the Consuls, of which the principal was the financial state of the island, which was rapidly approaching bankruptcy owing, according to general belief, to the incapacity of the three Councillors appointed by the High Commissioner.

The financial situation concerned the Consuls not only generally but directly, for the Government collected and held the proceeds of a three per cent. surtax on imports which had been earmarked by the Powers for the service of a special fund, called the Foreign Indemnities Fund, the object of which was to meet the claims for losses incurred by foreigners and foreign-protected subjects during the insurrections of 1896–97–98 against the Turks. Every fortnight the representatives of the four Protecting Powers and the Austro-Hungarian Consul-General and the German Consul met in the great council-room of the Konak, the old Turkish Government office, in order to discuss what was to be done about this and any other matters which concerned them collectively. At these meetings the Consuls-General were provided with high-backed arm-chairs, but the German, who was but a Consul, was only allowed a chair without arms.

The Consuls and the Government sent each other notes on the subject of the Indemnity Fund without getting any nearer a solution until at last in the spring of 1904 the Consular Corps decided, somewhat tardily, that they had better undertake the examination of these foreign claims many of which were, obviously, grossly exaggerated. This duty was assigned to my German colleague, Dr. Seeliger, and me, principally because we were the youngest, did not mind roughing it and could ride. The work took us nearly to the spring of 1905 when the Venizelos insurrection broke out and put a stop for the time being to our indemnities work.

Dr. Seeliger and I rode all over the country examining olive and valona woods which had been cut down, houses that had been burned, orange groves and vineyards destroyed, and hearing hundreds of witnesses. We slept in monasteries, gendarmerie barracks and in the bigger towns in the houses of prominent citizens, sometimes of our Vice-Consuls. Whenever I visited Candia where the British troops were stationed I stayed in their camp on the Venetian ramparts. We enjoyed our work greatly and, I believe, accomplished it impartially and thoroughly. We made a picturesque cavalcade riding over mountain passes accompanied by our dragomans, our armed cavasses,

CRETE

DEMARCH OF ANNOIA AND SECRETARY

our Moslem grooms with a relay horse, and often by local landowners who had suffered from depredations and wished to show us the extent of their losses.

Every Cretan was ready to talk politics, from the Abbots of the principal monasteries down to the humblest peasant. All were friendly and all offered us what they could, generally a bunch of grapes or a glass of wine. In this fashion Dr. Seeliger and I toured the island and got to know more about the feelings of the people than if we had sat at home for years and read many books about Crete. It was a very pleasant duty and we finally became experts at valuing an olive wood which had been cut down or a vineyard which had been destroyed.

When our work was done the whole amount allotted to various claimants only came to a little over two million francs while the Indemnity Fund allocated to cover the damages was but one million. Nevertheless the claimants were well satisfied at getting anything after having waited in vain for so many years, and I have vivid recollections of one very dirty old Cretan lady, who declared she was the widow of an American citizen (though she spoke nothing but Greek) and was therefore under my charge in Crete, flinging herself into my arms and clasping me to her ample bosom when I told her that she had been allotted a few hundred francs.

The climax of the Indemnity tale, however, was reached when the Consuls were told by the Government that they might remove the proceeds of the 3 per cent. Surtax Fund from the Bank of Crete and look after it themselves.

This embarrassed us greatly for we did not know where to keep it, but we hired a little villa about a quarter of a mile from the Bank of Crete and turned the cellars into a strong room. We all then went down to the Bank of Crete and counted out coins, gold, silver and copper, for a solid three days and sealed up the bags containing all this wealth with our six seals.

Then on one great day in 1906 a strange procession was seen moving away from the Bank of Crete.

Twelve soldiers of the armies of the four Protecting

Powers, three men of each army, marched with fixed bayonets before and behind and on either side of two small asses laden with large sacks containing smaller sacks of specie. Behind them in tall hats and frock coats as befitted so solemn an occasion walked the Consuls General of the Protecting Powers and the Austrian Consul General and the German Consul. Behind them again their dragomans with tape and sealing wax and seals and, to bring up the rear, the respective cavasses, armed to the teeth. When they reached the little villa, which had now been christened the Bank of Public Utility, the sacks of specie were off-loaded and taken down to the strong room which was locked up and sealed by the Representatives of the Powers and guards were placed over it.

Thus the long duel between the Cretan Government and the Consuls for the possession of the Indemnity Fund ended satisfactorily at last and shortly after the Consuls were able to distribute their shares to their respective nationals. That procession with asses was a truly characteristic Cretan ending to an apparently interminable struggle.

Other questions of a general order which required the collective attention of the Consuls of the Protecting Powers and necessitated constant meetings at the house of their *doyen*, or Dean, arose out of the relations of the International officers and troops among themselves and with the Cretan gendarmerie.

Fortunately for me the British contingent was stationed at Candia and until the Venizelist insurrection of 1905 broke out the presence of British soldiers in the island raised no questions of any kind. There was, however, a constant complaint on the part of my colleagues which was that the British War Office positively refused to allow even a small body like a corporal's guard to be stationed at Canea. It had in fact been quite definitely decided that British soldiers could not be placed under the orders of an International officer.

This caused my colleagues to say that the Cretans never believed in the solidarity of the four Powers. There was no doubt, much truth in this, but until the Venizelist insurrection it seemed to have only an academic interest.

Then again we had to look after Moslems and protect their properties, or see that the Cretan gendarmerie did this, and make complaints to the Government of any attack on Moslems or Moslem property.

We had also to see that the Cretan flag, with which the Powers in their generosity had endowed the islanders, was not insulted by the latter, who were at all times anxious to put up the Greek flag in its place.

This was to be stopped at all costs and latterly we had even to protect from the Cretans themselves with small squads of International soldiers, every Cretan flag flown on public buildings. The Turkish flag that still floated on the island in Suda Bay gave us no trouble, being protected by the *Stationnaires*.

Further I was constantly being asked by His Majesty's Government whether the British detachment could now be withdrawn and if not, why not ? We were supposed to keep our Governments informed of the minutest details of the political situation in the island, of the financial conditions, of the incidence of taxation, as questions were asked in Parliament as to whether this pressed unfairly on the Moslems, etc. In addition there was the ordinary consular work which was not inconsiderable—especially on account of the large Maltese colony. The Maltese were generally very hard working and well behaved but they were congenitally litigious. I should have been constantly engaged in trying cases between them if one of my predecessors, Sir Alfred Biliotti, wearied at having his time continually taken up by petty lawsuits between Maltese, which ran into two or three hundred a year if I remember right, had not adopted the admirable plan of obliging both parties to the suit to make a suitable deposit before he would try a case at all. When it was over, the party against whom he gave the verdict lost the deposit. This system, though not perhaps quite in accordance with English practice, had the most satisfactory result of curing the

Cretan Maltese so completely of their passion for litigation that, during the three and a half years I was in Crete, I never had to try a case of any kind.

For entertainment I played tennis periodically with Prince George and with the naval officers at Suda Bay, or rode with Isa over the plain behind Canea, where we used to have paperchases on horseback with the International officers followed by tea in a large tent. Occasionally I went up to the mountains to shoot, or try to shoot, quail and red-legged mountain partridges, or else snipe and duck in the swamps by the sea. We also had our bathing hut on the sandy bay beyond Canea.

Further we had our little dinner parties, and once a week the High Commissioner came to our house to play whist or bridge. We had private theatricals and concerts, etc., in fact the usual forms of entertainment of " polite society." It was all very pleasant when there were no rifts in the international lute which, however, occurred not infrequently. But the best entertainment consisted, after all, in the daily round, the common task which was so full of unexpected and curious incidents so complicated, at times so dramatic and also ludicrous that no theatre in a Western capital could offer a spectacle more absorbing, no drama present problems more amusing to unravel.

I may perhaps describe shortly one of these, the sad tale of a Cretan patriot, one Dr. Jannaris, a graduate of the University of Athens who spoke English well and had been appointed Professor of Modern Greek in the University of St. Andrews, a Chair established and endowed, if I am not mistaken, by the late Lord Bute.

After some years Dr. Jannaris returned to Crete and became an ardent Venizelist and opponent of the High Commissioner. Some time later he was tried for using unsuitable language about the High Commissioner and condemned to two years imprisonment by the Cretan High Court.

This created a great stir among his friends in Scotland ; questions were asked in Parliament and Prince George was attacked in the Liberal Press. I was told to interest myself unofficially in the case and do what I could to get a mitigation of the sentence. I talked to the Prince and found him very immovable. The law must take its course. Finally, however, I persuaded him to allow me to go to the prison and endeavour to get from Janneris a suitable apology to the High Commissioner who then promised he would procure his release.

Then began a long negotiation. Jannaris at first proved as stiff-necked as the Prince had been. He told me that he would never trust the Prince's word and went so far as to say on one occasion :

" You think he is a Dane and can be trusted because he has blue eyes, but I tell you he is a Greek."

As Jannaris himself was a Greek and very proud of it I could not suppress a smile. I became very sorry for him, because prison life was telling on him and he was the victim of boils. Finally, after many journeys to and fro between the Palace and the prison, I at last persuaded him to give the Prince a trial. Together the Prince, who had really a very kind heart, and I drew up a mild apology which at first Jannaris refused to sign. But after one or two more weeks of prison life and having made some insignificant alterations just to show his independence, he signed and also promised that he would leave Crete, where indeed there was nothing for him to do, and would take no further part in Cretan elections. Prince George accepted this somewhat grudgingly and remarked that I had probably been bamboozled, being no match for a Greek. Again I smiled.

Jannaris did leave at once for Greece and did not actually take part in the elections, but as soon as the Venizelist insurrection started in 1905 Jannaris returned hot foot and joined the insurgents at Therisso, where he apparently intrigued against one of the insurgent leaders, Constantine Manos, and endeavoured to supplant him.

He was, of course, amnestied with the other insurgents in the autumn of 1905 and I never heard of him any more.

Had I been bamboozled ? I don't know, but I was devoutly thankful to have avoided by his release what threatened to grow into a serious scandal especially if Jannaris's health had been really undermined by the prison in Canea, which was not exactly a health resort.

In October of 1903 the Foreign Office generously allowed me some leave, to which I was not by strict regulations entitled, in order to be with Isa at the time of the birth of our first child. I arrived in Rome where she was established in the Via Gregoriana, near the Pincio, in the upper apartment of a little house which I had inhabited more than once and which I was fond of on account of the view across the city to the great dome of St. Peter's. It is hard to say when this view of the dome is more beautiful, whether at sunset when it stands up dark purple before a sky of crimson and orange or at sunrise when, with the rising morning sun upon it, it floats suspended in a garb of silver-blue, like the clear coolness of a northern sea on a summer's day, like something ethereal, unsubstantial.

So it was on the evening before and on the morning of the great event. Isa and I had walked on the terrace roof and watched the sun set in a blaze of glory behind the dome and then she went to her room. I sat up waiting for many anxious hours till the nurse told me I had better go and rest. Early before dawn I was called, and sat by the open window watching the stars fade out of the sky and the colours of dawn gradually appear to give form to the roofs and domes of the city below me. The hours seemed endless. At last as the sun rose St. Peter's dome took on its early morning silver-blue garb. Though the sun was bright behind me, a heavy black storm cloud began to rise from the sea to the west, while around the dome, showing up against the blackness of that cloud, circled the innumerable pigeons of St. Peter's, also silver-blue with the sunlight upon them. Their flight fascinated me and after the long and anxious watch almost produced a hypnotic sleep. Nothing seemed to be moving and I grew seriously alarmed, but I did not dare to stir. The sun was already well up when Isa's maid, Alda, our good and faithful friend for thirty years, came out of her room.

" *Ma che cosa succede ?* " I asked, now in an agony.

" *O,*" she replied quite calmly and, as I thought, with some little contempt in her voice, " *Tutto è gia finito da ore. Cè' un bellissimo bambino e la Signora sta benino.*"

" *Grazie a Dio. Ma perche non m'avete avertito prima ?* "

" *O Lei,*" and here, it seemed, the contempt became rather more marked, " *L'abbiamo dimenticato.*"[1]

It was impossible to resist a smile at this crude lesson of the absolute worthlessness of the mere man at such a time and on such an occasion. I went down humbled but grateful to *S. Andrea delle Fratte*, whose curious tower raised itself below the window, to offer up my heartfelt thanks with the first Mass that I could attend there.

In this way were St. Peter's dome, silver-blue in the dawn, and the pigeons also, silver-blue against a black cloud, engraved for life on my inward eye. It was October 17th and as warm as a fine August morning in England.

Immediately after this I left for Crete and before Christmas Isa joined me with the boy Esme who was afterwards, to distinguish him from me, known as Esmetto, and was during twenty-four years for the whole family the constant mainspring of all that human affection can give.

In August the High Commissioner had started on the second of his tours of the capitals of the Protecting Powers with the avowed object of asking for the immediate union of Crete with Greece. He described the restless condition of the island and said that the only remedy that could cure this was union, but he added that, if this could not be immediately accorded, some advance in this

---

[1] Translation : " What is happening ? " " O, it's all over long ago. There is a beautiful boy and the signora is doing very well." " Thank God, but why did you not tell me sooner ? " " O, we'd forgotten you ! "

direction would have to be granted and that the concession to Crete of an administration under Greece, retaining the suzerainty of Turkey, like that of Bosnia and Herzegovina under Austria, would probably satisfy the aspirations of the islanders for a few years more. This would, of course, have implied the withdrawal of the troops of the Protecting Powers and the occupation of the island by Greek troops, as well as government with a Greek Governor with practically despotic powers. It was doubtless this which appealed to Prince George. The Porte, having got wind of this, at once notified the Powers that if Greece sent troops to Crete it would do so also, which naturally meant a new Greco-Turkish war with all which that implied in the Balkans.

Apart from this result which the Powers could not look forward to with equanimity, there was another complication in the Bosnia-Herzegovina proposal which was, perhaps, not so generally understood in the European capitals but soon became clear to us in Crete itself.

Ever since 1901, when, after Prince George's failure to obtain European consent to union, M. Venizelos launched his proposal for an autonomous administration for Crete *à la Roumélie Orientale* (which would have entailed a much freer and more democratic Constitution with a High Commissioner as a really Constitutional Governor), there had been war to the knife between M. Venizelos and Prince George.

The latter, as already stated, believed in governing the island as a captain does a ship, whereas M. Venizelos believed in the most ample form of democratic government. Prince George considered—no doubt with reason —that had he accepted the Eastern Roumelian solution he would have been most bitterly attacked as being desirous of postponing union *ad infinitum* to perpetuate his Governorship of Crete, of which, by the way, he was genuinely anxious to be rid if he could escape with some kudos, mainly, I am inclined to think, because life on the island bored him. He therefore not only rejected the Venizelos suggestion in 1901, but allowed M. Venizelos to be publicly attacked as a traitor to Greece whose aim was to set up Crete as a quasi-independent State in which he, Venizelos, would play the leading rôle. This was doubtless suggested to Prince George by some of his political adherents in the island such as M. Koundouros, who had, from the moment Crete had become free from the Turks, been at daggers drawn with Venizelos and his liberal ideas—and in Crete being " at daggers drawn " generally ended by being no figure of speech.

Prince George therefore, when the storm burst over the Eastern Roumelian scheme, dismissed Venizelos, who was unquestionably much the ablest councillor in the Government, from his office, letting it be known to all and sundry that he, the High Commissioner, considered him as a traitor to his country.

M. Venizelos on the other hand assured me personally, and subsequent events have confirmed his assurances, that his aim was always to bring about union as soon as this was practical, but in the meantime by good government in the island to see to it that when Crete did come to Greece " she should come with a coat on her back," whereas, according to him, Prince George's policy seemed to be to keep her in rags and misery so that she should be in a state of constant unrest and possibly insurrection and drive the Powers, out of sheer weariness, to grant his request.

It was generally admitted that M. Venizelos was not only by far the most brilliant man in Crete but that he was also among the most ambitious. For this last reason, if for no other, it always appeared probable that he would never be satisfied with the narrow limits of Crete alone, which Prince George declared to be his aim.

After his dismissal M. Venizelos practically retired from politics and was clearly biding his time, while Prince George definitely attached to himself the party of Koundouros and others who were the bitter opponents of the Venizelists. These latter were already in the end of 1903 beginning to murmur openly at the entry of the High Commissioner into the political arena and to say that with the dice thus loaded against them, they had no chance at the ballot boxes and the only thing that remained to them was to go to the mountains with their rifles.

The fact was that, reduced to its simplest terms with all exterior political complications left out, the Cretan question resolved itself into a duel to the death (politically speaking, naturally) between the High Commissioner and Venizelos.

This situation was complicated by the fact that the French and Italian Consuls were much impressed by the ability of M. Venizelos and were therefore regarded by the Prince almost as his personal opponents. He had to an equal degree alienated them by his brusque and quarter-deck manner of speaking when he was annoyed.

Seeing that his moments of annoyance were frequent and explosive, the rift in the relations between the Palace and the two above-mentioned Consulates grew until finally relations were almost broken off. This state of things must naturally have coloured the Consuls' reports on the political situation and not have helped the Prince's cause.

With my Russian colleague, a most delightful and agreeable Finn, M. Nicholas de Etter, with whom Isa and I were quickly on terms of close friendship, the Prince's relations were always exceedingly cordial and, to a rather less degree, the same may be said as regards myself. He often, indeed, did not hesitate to speak to me as a serjeant-major might to a raw recruit. Once, however, I was able, to my own great satisfaction to give him the retort courteous but merited. He had just returned from one of his tours in Europe and was telling me about his visit to Sandringham :

PRINCE GEORGE : " King Edward asked me what I thought of you."

I : " I hope, Sir, you didn't give me too bad a character."

PRINCE GEORGE : " Oh, no ! I said you were all right, but I told him you had no more character than my boot," with which he slapped his riding boot hard as if to show me how such spineless creatures should be treated.

I : " But I think, Sir, that you do your boot great injustice. I expect that at this very moment it is probably itching to kick me out of the house and is only restrained by the astonishing courtesy of your Royal Highness."

We both laughed together and enjoyed the little dialogue, but I couldn't help feeling that if this had been said to either my French or my Italian colleague we should have heard a great deal about it at the next Consular meeting.

After Isa arrived with the baby and had settled in, our life passed pleasantly enough. The spring was enchanting. We rode our Syrian Arabs over the fields full of iris and red and purple anemones, under olive groves and up valleys with running water, the banks of which were covered with myrtle and oleander and cystus ; we visited quaint villages with great plane trees in their central squares in which blue coated Cretan men danced in circles on feast days while the women, mostly in black, sat and watched ; we went to see Arthur Evans' wonderful excavations at Knossos, the cradle of all European civilisation ; I made an excursion with some British officers to the top of Mount Ida, the birthplace of Zeus, and so the centre, or one of the principal centres, of Greek Mythology. It is over eight thousand feet high and the highest point of the Island, and the sunrise which we saw from the top was more than a reward for the trouble of the ascent. I have, in fact, endless delightful reminiscences of that spring and summer. Visits of the British Fleet to Suda Bay with exchanges of dinners and luncheons with naval officers, always the most cheery of companions. How many sailors do I not remember from these days ?

Tupper, Captain of the *Venus* ; Waymouth, Captain of the *Minerva* ; Captain Craddock, a most singularly attractive man who afterwards perished in the tragic battle of Coronel, and two old friends, " Rosy " Wemyss, afterwards First Sea Lord, who signed the Armistice for Great Britain, and my kinsman, Colin Keppel, one and all of them of the salt of the earth.

One little incident amused us. Admiral Lambton, having arrived with the Fleet at Suda Bay, asked me and

C

any guests I had staying with me to dine on the flagship instead of paying the ordinary official call. It happened that I had a touch of influenza and so neither I nor Isa went. My eldest brother Harry and his daughter Joan went in our places. They sat on either side of the Admiral, who plied my brother with questions about Crete, to all of which Harry, not being a man of many words, simply murmured :

" I don't know."

At last the Admiral in exasperation turned to Joan and said :

" Who is this idiot that the Government have sent out here as Consul-General ? " which delighted her and the rest of the company when the situation was explained, which, of course, she did not fail to do forthwith.

So the time passed pleasantly. The green and the flowers of spring gave way to the heat of summer, but we never suffered at Halepa, for in the day we had a breeze off the sea and at night a breeze off the mountains. Every day an old Cretan with a little mule went up to the mountains and came back in the night with a load of frozen snow to cool our drinks. We had nearby on the shore, only a few yards from the sea, a spring of delicious water, to which we sent our small donkey with barrels twice a day for fresh drinking water for the house. We were never short of fresh meat, fish, vegetables or fruit, though perhaps a French *chef* would have complained of a lack of variety.

On one occasion the Duke and Duchess of Connaught called in at Suda Bay in an English man-of-war on their way back from India. They were accompanied by their two daughters, Princess Patricia and Princess Margaret, who afterwards married the Crown Prince of Sweden and whom we saw much of in Stockholm during the war. We became, I think I may say, real friends. She was a woman for whom it was impossible not to feel the highest respect and devoted affection. We dined on board their ship and they paid us a visit, delighted, as Princess Margaret told me years after, with our drawing-room decorated entirely with peach or almond blossom. I remember I took them afterwards to see the ceremony of the Dancing Dervishes, of which, on account of its stately grace, I never tired. The dervishes were always most courteous in allowing me to bring visitors of distinction to see them.

There were many causes of friction between the different International contingents, not the least of which was that as already mentioned, the British War Office absolutely refused to allow any British detachment, however small, to be under the command of a foreign officer. So long as the military contingents of each Protecting Power remained within their own " *secteur* " or territory all was well. Unfortunately, however, it had been decided from the first that a small international " *secteur* " was to be created round Canea, the capital. On account of the unbending attitude of the War Office about the command, no British detachment could be quartered in Canea, and this was a constant source of complaint by my colleagues and certainly led to the Cretans believing that we did not altogether support the policy of the other Protecting Powers.

In the absence of the High Commissioner on his tour in Europe and while the Cretans still hoped for a satis- factory reply to His Royal Highness's request for union, everything went on, for Crete, fairly quietly. The Powers as usual were in no hurry to answer. The first indication of the sort of line His Majesty's Government would take up with regard to the Prince's Memorandum of complaints and *desiderata* was conveyed to me in a copy of a Note dated November 30th, 1904, which Lord Lansdowne addressed to the Ambassadors in London of the three other Protecting Powers. As this was the first general indication I had received of H.M. Government's policy and is to-day perhaps the best summary of the views of the Conservative Government of that time on the matter, it is of interest to reproduce the principal points of this Note.

The High Commissioner, wrote Lord Lansdowne, declared that annexation to Greece was the only complete solution of the question, but he fully realised that the Powers would not grant this at present. He believed, however, that unless annexation or some measure pointing towards it were not at once conceded, the Cretans would proclaim union with Greece and it was, therefore, absolutely necessary that the Powers should take measures to remove the prevailing discontent and satisfy to some extent Cretan national aspirations.

The Prince had consequently submitted his proposal for the Boznia Herzegovina plan to be applied *mutatis mutandis* to Crete.

The Secretary of State for Foreign Affairs now submitted the following suggestions and considerations to the other Protecting Powers.

1. Annexation to Greece could not be permitted as being a violation of pledges to the Sultan.

2. The Boznia Herzegovina solution was equally impossible for various reasons;[1] the utmost that could be done to meet Prince George's views would be to give him an undertaking that the Powers would not themselves annex the island or permit it to be annexed by any other Power save with the consent of the inhabitants. This undertaking to be subject to the consent of Germany and Austria.

3. Military situation. International troops could not permanently garrison Crete for in any case His Majesty's Government would not consent to the retention of a British garrison for an indefinite time and desired the existing arrangement to end as soon as possible. His Majesty's Government thought that each Protecting Power might immediately withdraw half its contingent and the remainder two or three years later.

4. Financial situation. This presented considerable difficulties. The Cretan Government having no credit and the Revenue not being sufficient to permit much needed public works, His Majesty's Government suggested as a remedy a loan, based on continuation of the existing surtax, the proceeds of which could be used for public works.

[1] The principal of these was that it would have made the High Commissioner almost independent of the popular will.

5. His Majesty's Government concluded by stating that it should be clearly explained to the High Commissioner that the terms offered represented the utmost that the Protecting Powers could sanction and that if they were rejected the responsibility for the consequences must rest with the Cretan Government.

I still remember how my heart sank when I read this document, the futility of which must have been as apparent even to those who drafted it as it was to us in Crete. There was no question that if these suggestions were adopted we were certainly heading for an insurrection. Yet unless some minor concession could have been made to national aspirations that would have tided over the crisis what, things being as they were in the Balkans, could the Powers have done about Crete unless they were prepared to spend considerable sums of money on public works and so keep the Cretans quiet? It was a case of *panem aut circenses* only the *circenses* in Crete were insurrections. In spite of all this the optimist or cynic who drafted the Note wrote that the Protecting Powers, desiring to avoid the complications which would result were a crisis to occur in the affairs of the island, would gladly avail themselves of any opportunity for improving Prince George's position and inducing him to retain, for a time at all events, his position as High Commissioner.

Needless to say the remaining Protecting Powers accepted the suggestions with alacrity and some trifling alterations. The final text of the reply of the Powers was, however, still held up for months awaiting the approval of Germany and Austria who had been consulted.

Meanwhile the island was rapidly becoming a prey to electoral fever, for new elections were to take place on April 2nd and candidates were nominated on February 16th.

M. Venizelos told my French colleague that his Party had not yet decided whether to take part in the elections or not. If they abstained it probably meant trouble. Other leaders declared openly that the situation was intolerable and that they would change it.

CHAPTER II

CRETE: INSURRECTION

(1905)

BY the middle of March it was known that the Venizelists had decided on making an armed demonstration in the mountains and were only waiting for supplies of arms and ammunitions to be smuggled in from Greece. Their reliance on the importation of arms from Greece gave the proposed insurrection a sinister look. It appeared that the insurgents were financially backed from Athens.

It was also generally stated that the Venizelists proposed to hoist the Greek flag and put union with Greece first on their programme. I supposed that their object in this was: First, to prevent the High Commissioner from acting against them by force of arms since, as he actually told me later, it was impossible for him to order the gendarmerie to march against the Greek flag. To that extent, therefore, their calculations were successful. Second, in order to gather adherents in the island and financial support in Greece.

This calculation also proved well founded.

On March 23rd, an armed band of several hundred met at the village of Therisso in the White Mountains and were joined during the night by MM. Venizelos, Constantine Foumis, Constantine Manos and other political leaders.

A gendarmerie patrol was attacked and one gendarme severely wounded. The gendarmes behaved well.

The High Commissioner telegraphed direct to the British officer commanding at Candia instructing him to take over various duties in the town so as to liberate gendarmes for the country districts.

VILLAGE OF THERISSO IN CRETE

HEADQUARTERS OF THE VENIZELIST INSURRECTION OF 1905

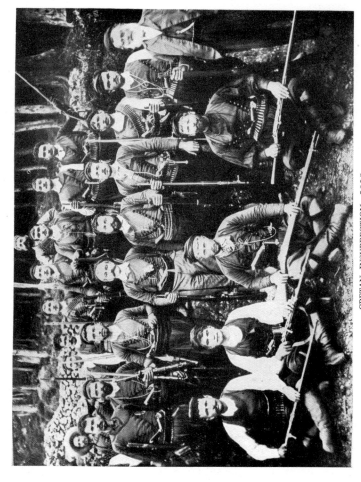

CRETAN INSURRECTION, 1905

CONSTANTINE MANOS AND HIS BAND OF LAKIOTES

(Fourth from left, 2nd row, is Constantine Manos)

The insurgents proclaimed union with Greece and were about to establish a Provisional Government.

Scenting trouble in the future if the High Commissioner were allowed to give orders to the officer commanding British troops at Candia I requested my Government, if they considered it desirable, that he should consult me before taking action, to send him instructions accordingly.

The fat was now in the fire.

The next day, March 24th, the great question of the extent of military co-operation between the International contingents on the one hand, and between them and the gendarmerie on the other, naturally came up for discussion since there was no prearranged plan of any kind. The officer commanding British troops in Candia telegraphed to me that he had temporarily taken over all gendarmerie duties there to release gendarmes for duty elsewhere. I concurred but asked for instructions from the Foreign Office with regard to permitting British troops to be used against insurgents in the interior of the island.

The High Commissioner desired that they should be so used and the Russian and Italian Consuls had already given their consent, but my French colleague and I felt we could not agree without instructions.

Differences of opinion on this matter of military co-operation which continued during the greater part of the insurrection thus sprang up on the first day.

The following day the High Commissioner sent to me and my colleagues for transmission to our Governments a telegram stating that the forebodings which he had had " the pleasure " of submitting to them were being realised. The Cretan gendarmerie were not able to do police work and repress disturbances at the same time. On the other hand, since he could not, as he had explained in his Memorandum, make use of the international troops and as he had now waited for the reply of the Powers, respecting the representations made during his last voyage, for more than four months, he requested the four Governments to tell him what he should and what he could do.

Three replies to my various inquiries were sent by the Secretary of State the following day.

1. If other Powers agreed to troops co-operating with gendarmerie British troops might do likewise but, as far as practicable, they should confine operations to the protection of life, property and order in centres of population and should be as little as possible involved in interior of the island.

Both the officer commanding at Candia and I read this as meaning they should *not* take any offensive measures against insurgents in the interior.

2. The Consuls, if they all had similar instructions, were at once to present the famous joint reply to Prince George's Memorandum. It was based on Lord Lansdowne's Note of November 30th to the other Protecting Powers and was as likely to help in present circumstances as a bucket of water to put out a burning oil well.

3. I was instructed to communicate to the High Commissioner, in reply to his telegram asking what he should and could do, the substance of the Foreign Office telegram permitting co-operation of troops with the gendarmerie within the limits stated.

This last, I knew, would not at all satisfy the High Commissioner, who had already told me in the most vigorous language that he would never give the gendarmerie the order to march against Cretans who had raised the Greek flag, though they might act to protect life and property where possible—which, of course, meant in the plains and cities. He considered that if the Powers desired the insurrection to be ended speedily it was clearly their business, and should be done with the International troops. Within less than a week, therefore, the situation had resolved itself into this :

Troops were to protect life and property in the towns and centres of population, " as far as practicable," and gendarmerie to do the same over a rather wider area, while both avoided risking a real clash with the insurgents, who were thus free to act as they liked over the greater part of the island without let or hindrance, a liberty which they very soon realised they possessed, and of which they did not fail to take advantage.

Meanwhile the High Commissioner grew more and more irritable and denunciatory of all and sundry, using most undiplomatic language to me in his own unconventional way : " If I could only get Uncle Edward (King Edward) and Nicky (the Russian Emperor) in a room together, I'd bang their heads together till they settled the Cretan question." He was tall and powerful enough to have done it too. This, I need hardly say, I did not report home.

He very soon found that instead of sending out circular telegrams to the four Powers through my colleagues and me, one copy to each of us, it saved time and trouble to call us to the " Palace " and dictate these missives.

I well remember our amusement the first time this happened.

We were ushered into the Prince's little study, a small, square room looking out on to the dusty main road, and saw four " occasional " chairs ranged behind four " occasional " tables—" occasional " is, I believe, the correct word used in Tottenham Court Road for these articles of furniture. The tables were of that small kind which fit into each other like a nest of Australian " billies." The largest one was on the right for the doyen of the Consular Corps, and the others grew smaller as the precedence of the Consul who was to sit at it grew less. This I felt would have delighted our Austrian colleague, who was such a stickler for precedence.

Presently the door was flung open and the High Commissioner entered in all the majesty of his height, six feet four inches, and his avoirdupois, which was considerable. In his right hand he carried a large round ruler like a marshal's baton.

" *Asseyez-vous, messieurs.*"[1] he said, pointing with the baton to the chairs. " *Et écrivez, si vous savez écrire ; j'en doute.*"

Had any of us laughed he would, perhaps, have laughed

[1] " Be seated, Gentlemen, and write if you know how—I doubt it."

too, for he had a saving sense of the ridiculous. But we all remained grave, feeling the matter was, after all, serious. Having dictated his message of appeal or sarcastic reference to the valuable assistance the Powers were giving him in dealing with the insurrection, the Prince said : "'*Bon jour, messieurs*," and stalked out of the room as aloof and stately as he entered it.

By the beginning of April it was clear that the insurrection was steadily gaining ground. It had spread already to the Russian "*secteur*" of Rethymo and the British "*secteur*" of Candia. It was also clear that unless the leaders would give way or the Cretan Government would come to terms with them there was no chance of an early settlement. Neither of these alternatives being in the least likely to occur, the probable end of the insurrection, in view of the lack of armed opposition to the insurgents on a serious scale could be looked for only after several months, when the rank and file lost heart owing to their action being unproductive of any definite result and also to the discomforts of a winter spent in the mountains. This was indeed the way the end actually came in November, when insurrection in the mountains ceased to be a form of exciting picnic even in Crete.

In the meantime we Consuls had our hands full. Every week, almost every day, brought an incident of some kind, now comic, now tragic, which had to be dealt with.

It was not long before the insurgents began coming down to the coast and raiding and sometimes occupying the smaller custom-houses.

On one occasion Captain Tupper, of the *Venus*, was asked by the Consular Corps to recover a custom-house which had fallen into the hands of one Birakis, a rather enterprising insurgent leader. Birakis allowed the captain to land with some of his men, and after an apparently quite friendly parley in which, however, he declared that the insurgents were adamant about union with Greece, he not only handed over to him the custom-house, but also all the money in the till, amounting to what, for the insurgents, must have seemed quite a goodly sum.

The action of the captain of the French *stationnaire*, sent out on a similar mission to a distant custom-station, gave rise, on the other hand, to much scandal in Government circles, and particularly annoyed—it must be admitted with good reason—the High Commissioner and the French Consul-General.

The captain, having arrived at the little port, asked the insurgent commandant on the spot if he could see one of the insurgent chiefs whom he knew personally and whose house was in the neighbourhood. The leader was sent for and appeared, and the inhabitants of the district were not unnaturally surprised to see the French captain and some of his staff ride off with him into the hills to be entertained at his house and, later, to see the captain and the insurgent leader dining comfortably together in the public square of the village where the custom-house was situated.

This of course spread like wildfire over the island, and for some days the whole population believed the Protecting Powers were about to take the insurgents under their wing.

Meanwhile the French captain had been successful in persuading the insurgents to withdraw from the village.

The Russians, on the other hand, took a very different line, and when their *stationnaire*, the " Khrabry," went to recover a custom-house and landed men, who were straightway fired on, they withdrew their men, but bombarded the unfortunate village, causing much damage and loss of life.

The Italians, as a general rule, objected to taking any action at all, not because my Italian colleague, Baron Fasciotti, had any special affection for the insurgents, but because the Italian Government frankly favoured a policy of masterly inactivity as far as internal Cretan dissensions were concerned, Baron Fasciotti was short and stout, extremely intelligent, and rapid in judgment if not always correct, very energetic, and always ready

for an argument.   He contributed greatly to the liveliness
of our daily Consular Conferences, but it was unfortunate
that the High Commissioner and he took so undisguised
a personal antipathy to each other, since this did not
help to make the International machine go round more
smoothly.

The British attitude has already been described, and
amounted to this : Help to keep order and protect the
Moslem minority in accordance with pledges but within
safe limits, and never risk the life of a British soldier.

Colonel Panton, who had come from Egypt to command
the contingent at Candia, carried out these instructions
admirably and with notable success.   We both, I think,
understood each other's particular difficulties and worked
together in complete harmony.

His " *secteur* " was, it may be said, a model one, but
it must in fairness to the others be admitted that it was,
perhaps, the least difficult to handle.

Yet even here insurgents from time to time occupied
villages, carried off cattle, raided Moslem farms and
destroyed olive and orange plantations, etc., and I often
received distracting appeals from Moslems for protection.

There was, as may be imagined, frequently little
harmony at our daily consular meetings, the different
attitudes   of the Governments being reflected in the
views of their representatives.   Owing to the departure
of M. de Etter, the Russian, and the deaths, in 1905,
of the French and Italian Consuls-General, M. Drouin
and Count Negri, I had become dean of the Consuls
of the Protecting Powers, and had, therefore, to act as
chairman at our interminable conferences.

The questions we discussed at these conferences were
not merely daily incidents resulting out of insurgent
attacks and how to meet them in accordance with the
expressed wishes of all the Governments concerned
(with the exception of Russia) that our troops should
be exposed to no unnecessary danger, but also the establishment of martial law in our respective " *secteurs* " to
deal with all offences of a political character, such as

carrying arms, and all disturbances of the public peace. Further, we had to deal with vexed questions of law: such as who should give authority for International vessels to search ships in Cretan waters for arms, since we had ample evidence of arms being landed from Greece. Discussions over the International Command and a variety of other minor matters kept us continually busy. The Command question was finally settled by a compromise, under which the foreign contingents in each " *secteur* " acted independently under their own commanding officers, but troops in the International " *secteur* " in and around Canea, of whatever nationality, were under the orders of the " *Commandant Supérieur.*"

It was always the aim of the insurgents to cultivate the myth that the Protecting Powers really sided with them in every way. Thus one day, before the insurgents took to coming regularly into the plain of Canea, Isa, with some friends, wives of Internationals, went for a picnic to the garden of a Moslem Bey, two or three miles out of the town, and found it occupied by insurgents. They were most polite, and only insisted on the ladies being photographed in a group with them. Some ladies agreed, and a smiling and happy group of insurgents and International ladies was the outcome which, no doubt, made the tour of the island and produced the effect desired. Fortunately, Isa wisely refused to appear in the group, or I should never have heard the end of it.

Again, M. Constantine Foumis, one of the triumvirate of Therisso, who before he went to the mountains had been on quite friendly terms with us, knowing that I was interested in my garden, used periodically to send me down some plants in old biscuit tins, which were found with his card and compliments on my doorstep by the servants in the morning. The news of this would probably be all round the market at Canea that day.

But the thing that caused me most trouble because it roused, as it was no doubt intended to do, suspicion in the Prince's mind of double-dealing on my part, was the stationing for hours together on the road between my house and the " Palace " of the empty carriage of M. Constantine Manos, another of the Therisso triumvirate. This had its effect not only in the " Palace," where I was able to remove suspicion, but probably also in the market-place, where I was not.

There was, in fact, no end of these political tricks, which were part and parcel of the daily life of Crete, and perhaps of all the Levant, where they help greatly to enliven the inhabitants.

Of all the International officers perhaps the most unhappily placed was Captain Monaco, the excellent Italian commander of the gendermerie, to whom his Consul-General insisted on giving orders of every kind, which were often opposed to those given him by the Prince. This led, naturally, to frequent bouts between the High Commissioner and Baron Fasciotti, of which poor Captain Monaco bore the brunt. He used at times to come for sympathy and support to Isa, and confide to her that his life was becoming insupportable, which indeed it must have been. His one desire was to leave Crete as soon as possible.

The doings of the Cretan Chamber, which had been elected in March, the Venizelists abstaining from voting, also gave the Consular Corps matter for discussion, and sometimes entertainment.

On April 22nd, 1905, I sent a messenger to the meeting-room of the Chamber, which served also on occasions for lectures, concerts and theatricals, etc., in order to report on the proceedings of that body when they received the negative answer of the Powers to their Proclamation of Union. I received a hasty message, scrawled in pencil, that the Chamber was filled with peasants from the mountains armed with sticks ; that at one moment, during a violent altercation, a rush was made for the Government benches ; that the " peasants' sticks were up "; that the members of the Government escaped through the windows ; that one councillor, who was stouter than the rest, had, like the Duc de Mayenne in Dumas's famous novel, *Les Quarante Cinq* (or was it

La Dame de Montsoreau ?), stuck in the window, and received from the peasants the same chastisement from behind that M. de Mayenne received from Chicot without ever being able to recognise who administered it.

But the Assembly gave us little trouble. It naturally proclaimed Union with Greece, and also passed a Budget of sorts without discussion, but then, somewhat illogically, considering Union had been proclaimed, went on to pass various internal reforms, including the removal of the Italian officers of the gendarmerie and their replacement by Cretans.

The Powers notified the Chamber through the Consuls that Union with Greece could not be allowed, and none of its other acts were enforced. It was not, in fact, taken seriously.

One of the tragic incidents of the insurrection has left an indelible impression on my mind.

A young gendarme was waylaid by insurgents and killed not far out of Canea. The Government decided to give him a public military funeral. So he was laid out in the gendarmerie barracks in a room which had been temporarily converted into a *chapelle ardente*.

It was thought right that the Consuls of the Protecting Powers should pay their respects to one who had lost his life in the cause of law and order.

With Isa, therefore, I set out for the barracks on a very hot August morning. We were shown into the humble, shabby barrack-rom, now the *chapelle ardente*.

It was filled with women relatives of the boy on the bier, who were chanting the wailing dirges of the Greek Church for the dead. The body, dressed in full uniform, lay on a bier surrounded by guttering candles ; the face was already showing signs of decomposition, and the air was heavy with the scent of candles and flowers mixed with the smell of putrefaction.

The wailing of the voices, the heat and the odours in the room, both of the dead and of the living, made so strong an impression that for weeks afterwards that potpourri would return suddenly to my nostrils, no matter where I was, and produce a sensation of physical sickness and faintness. I don't think I ever suffered from that unpleasant form of hallucination again, but it was very marked while it lasted.

Although no immediate change seemed likely in the attitude of the insurgents at the beginning of July, the Consuls, with the approval of their Governments and the High Commissioner, drew up a Proclamation to the insurgents, on the following basis, on July 12th:

First.—A categorical reaffirmation of the impossibility of altering the political status of the island in present circumstances. Consequently the continuation of the insurrection could have no other result than the complete ruin of the country.

Second.—The readiness of the Powers to approve such extensive internal reforms as might be recognised as necessary for the progress and prosperity of the country.

Third.—A period of fifteen days, dating from July 15th, to be allowed for the insurgents to lay down their arms.

Fourth.—An amnesty to be granted to all those who had laid down their arms within the period stated, except to those guilty of violations of common law or desertions from the gendarmerie.

Fifth.—Failing submission on the part of the insurgents, the Powers reserved the right to apply martial law in such manner and in such parts of the country as they thought the situation required.

We then invited the insurgent leaders to meet us at 9.30 a.m. on July 15th, to discuss a settlement on these lines. We had indeed little hope of any immediate result, but believed that the publication of this Proclamation, and especially the offer of an amnesty—for which we had the greatest difficulty in securing the consent of the High Commissioner—would make the submission of the insurgents easier later on.

We met Messrs. Venizelos, Manos and Foumis at the little monastery of Aghia-Monì, a short way out of the village of Mournies, at the foot of the White Mountains, where an Italian detachment was stationed and which was on the boundary of the *cordon militaire* drawn round the Plain of Canea for its protection.

The insurgent leaders were accompanied by several hundred armed adherents. The insurgents behaved in a most correct, even friendly, way and added greatly to the picturesqueness not to say theatrical setting of the meeting.

I had of course met M. Venizelos previously, but rarely. It amused and pleased me later at the Paris Conference in 1919, where M. Venizelos had become one of the great of the earth and dictated the Allied policies in the Near East, to reflect how I had played the heavy father to his part of the insurgent chief in the little parlour of a monastery under the White Mountains in Crete.

M. Manos, who lived in Candia, I knew well. He was a Greek from the mainland, had been educated at Oxford, had been reader in Greek to—if I am not mistaken—the ill-fated Empress of Austria, had married an English lady, and with all these connections was therefore really more " European " in his ways than the others, in addition to which he was unusually good-looking and was careful to dress in Cretan costume which enhanced his good looks. Politically he was, above all, a super-nationalist. He fell, I believe, fighting in the Greek Army at the end of the Great War.

M. Foumis was a Cretan lawyer who had taken part in the insurrection against Turkey and had been a member of the first Autonomous Government of Crete. Being a Venizelist, he was both a champion of the cause of Union and a liberal in politics.

Of M. Venizelos—the great man of the trio—I have already spoken.

As *doyen* I read our Proclamation to the three insurgents in French and also a short speech emphasizing the folly of continuing the insurrection for the purpose of obtaining Union which was unobtainable, while as regards their other *desiderata* everyone was only too willing to meet and discuss internal reforms in a friendly spirit.

D

M. Venizelos replied at some length. His speech dealt mainly with political grievances and complaints against the Government of the High Commissioner.

As a result of our long discussions I felt that the leaders could not yet give way on account of their followers who insisted on Union, or at least a solution *à la Roumélie-orientale*, and that it would be some time before the latter would be persuaded by anything but active military operations to take a more reasonable point of view.

When I made my report of our meeting to the High Commissioner, it seemed to me that His Royal Highness was not altogether displeased that the insurgents had rejected our terms and especially the offer of an amnesty, which he had opposed from the first.

The question of the command of the gendarmerie which had been raised in our Consular meetings by the Italian Consul-General, whether, that is to say, the Commandant, being an Italian officer, should obey instructions given him by the Consul-General or take orders only from the High Commissioner, occupied us continually, since it may well be imagined that the dual control exercised in a constantly opposite sense was beginning to have a serious effect on the gendarmerie especially after the Chamber had passed a measure removing the Italian officers and replacing them by Cretans.

At the beginning of August all the Consuls-General of the Protecting Powers were instructed to request the High Commissioner to refuse assent to this measure, and to another permitting arms to be carried by all and sundry. On August 12th, His Royal Highness called a private meeting of the Deputies in order to hear the reply of the Greek Government to a letter which the Chamber had addressed to the latter asking whether they should not set up a Provisional Government in the interior and organise a counter-insurrection to that of Therisso in favour also of Union with Greece. The Greek Government fortunately advised them to allow the insurrection to be confined to the opposition at Therisso. Prince

George also told the Deputies that the Powers had instructed him to refuse to sanction the two measures passed by the Chamber : (1) annulling the law prohibiting the possession of arms ; (2) abolishing the posts of Italian officers in the gendarmerie.

This however did not settle the question of the Command, which continued to cause friction.

Towards the end of August there were signs of a definite reaction against the insurgents in different parts of the island. Bands of insurgents who had been allowed to do as they pleased in parts of the interior were being turned out of villages by the inhabitants who, having hitherto lived up to a good old Cretan maxim, " During an insurrection no one pays taxes," were probably beginning to find that the insurgents' demands for cash were quite as onerous as those of the Government which, when the insurrection ended, would certainly demand arrears.

In view of this new turn of events I went, with the High Commissioner's consent, to consult with Dr. Sphakianakis at Candia.

This gentleman was the Nestor of Crete. He was the principal Cretan leader of the insurrections of 1896-7-8 against the Turks and was universally respected as a perfectly honest, intelligent and patriotic man. He was also a friend of M. Venizelos. I therefore supposed that Dr. Sphakianakis might prove the best person in the island to act as our intermediary for a settlement with the insurgents.

I saw the Doctor at Candia on August 28th, and impressed on him that it was useless for the insurgents to carry on in hopes of gaining the assent of the Powers to Union or the Eastern Roumelian scheme and that we—the Consuls—could not make another advance to the insurgents who had slammed the door in our faces at Mourniès, but I requested him, if he ever received a hint from the insurgents of a desire to give way, to let me know at once. This he said he would do and as I was leaving Candia he wrote to me offering his mediation and asking whether all parties could not first agree to :

(A) Appointment of an International Commission instructed :

    1. To inquire into the causes of the present crisis.

    2. To study administrative and financial, etc., conditions.

    3. To propose such changes and reforms as were considered necessary.

(B) Reiteration of the offer of amnesty (finding a formula which would also allow the gendarmes who had deserted to avoid punishment).

(C) Declaration on the part of the insurgents that they would submit to the decision of the Powers and return to their homes.

He said that if the Consuls agreed to these points he would make a suggestion in this sense to M. Venizelos as a personal proposal of his own and endeavour to persuade him to accept it.

Two of these conditions seemed to me unacceptable : viz., that the insurgents should submit only *after* a Commission for reform of the Administration had been appointed and, secondly, that a formula should be found for amnestying the deserting gendarmes, but the letter generally seemed to me hopeful enough to submit to my colleagues without delay, which I did. These proposals of Dr. Sphakianakis became the foundation stone of the arrangements finally arrived at with the Venizelists for ending the insurrection.

Isa had left for Italy with Esmetto in May or June to avoid the heat as she was expecting another child. Again she went to Vallombrosa till the autumn. I was naturally anxious to be on the spot for the critical time and again the Foreign Office were kind. All matters with regard to the insurrection seemed to be in the doldrums, and as Dr. Sphakianakis had said there appeared to be nothing that could be done for the moment I asked for a short leave from September 19th or 20th. This was granted and Mr. Charles Marling,[1] First Secretary at Athens, took charge.

[1] Afterwards Sir Charles Marling, Minister at the Hague.

I joined Isa in Rome where she had a fine apartment in the Palazzo Chigi, Piazza Colonna, now the Italian Foreign Office, kindly lent to her by her brother-in-law and sister, Count and Countess Colleoni. Even in September, which is the worst month of the year in Rome, the great lofty rooms were cool, but we did not, down in the centre of the town, enjoy the breezes from the sea and still less the views over the city to St. Peters which we had from our little apartment in the Via Gregoriana.

September is the quietest season of the year in Rome and we were left practically alone, but I was more than thankful to have a rest from the daily worries of Crete, and Isa and Esmetto were always the best of company for me.

On October 5th Francis was born and Cardinal Merry del Val, then Cardinal Secretary of State, was good enough to be his godfather.

As soon as I was satisfied that all was well, I hurried back to Canea and found that Mr. Marling had received and forwarded to the Foreign Office a letter addressed to me by Dr. Sphakianakis, dated September 30th, in which the Doctor set forth the terms, received from " a very good source," which was no doubt M. Venizelos, on which the insurgents were prepared to give up the struggle.

He stated that the latter now recognised that no change was possible in the International status of Crete or in the person of the High Commissioner. Having accepted the views of the Powers on these points they considered themselves entitled to expect that the reforms which the Powers had undertaken to introduce into the administration and finances should be thorough and effective. They believed that this could not be achieved by a Cretan Assembly elected to revise the Constitution and preferred that the case should be confided to a Commission appointed by the Powers. They attached special importance to this and, should it commend itself to the Powers, they would be ready to lay down their arms as soon as the Commission was appointed and a General Amnesty, including deserters from the gendarmerie, proclaimed.

They would bind themselves to accept the findings of the Commission.

The final condition on which they particularly insisted was that the *possession* of arms should not be prohibited but only the *carrying* of them.

Then followed a list of financial reforms.

On October 16th, Mr. Marling, who had always together with his colleagues opposed an amnesty for the deserting gendarmes, received a hint from another source that the insurgents might be satisfied if the deserting gendarmes " were allowed to escape from Crete," a plan which Lord Lansdowne, telegraphing to me on October 21st, declared that H.M. Government strongly favoured if it led to a conclusion of the insurrection. His Lordship suggested that instructions might be given to the International troops not to prevent any deserters from leaving the island.

On October 21st the four Consuls-General of the Protecting Powers received identic communications from MM. Venizelos and Manos stating that, as the Powers opposed the insurrection by force of arms, they considered their programme at present unrealisable and were disposed to lay down their arms. There were, however, two questions to be settled before they could submit.

First.—The manner of laying down their arms of which they desired to retain possession.

Second.—The extent to which amnesty would be granted to all insurgents alike, including deserting gendarmes. By this it appeared that if the gendarmes were to be punished the leaders desired to share the penalty inflicted.

The Consuls replied :

1. That the insurgents would be required to hand over from 800 to 1,000 breach-loading rifles in good condition and cartridges therefor.

2. As regards the second point we adopted a proposal of Baron Fasciotti, the Italian Consul-General, to the effect that all those who had committed offences against common law as well as prisoners sentenced by military

tribunals, whether International or Cretan, must be excluded from the amnesty unless they were guilty of political offences only.

Sir Francis Elliot, H.M. Minister in Athens, telegraphed on October 30th that the Greek Government, having been informed by the Venizelist representative in Athens of the difficulty regarding the gendarmes, had offered, subject to the approval of the Powers, to cause to be chartered, at the expense of the Government but without its appearing officially in the matter, a steamer large enough to take all the insurgents who wished to leave the island ; the Consuls-General should designate the port of embarkation and the Greek Government would also send a man-of-war to keep an eye on the transport and prevent insubordination on the part of the passengers, who would have to be disarmed before embarkation.

This proposal for the " escape " of the gendarmes and others not included in the amnesty was approved.

In the interval, however, another hitch occurred. The Consuls, in order to make their reply more palatable to the insurgent leaders, had inserted at the end a paragraph stating that they considered that, in view of the submission of the insurgents, it would be opportune to undertake, through persons appointed by the Powers, an early inquiry into the administrative and financial reforms to be introduced into Crete and that the effective enforcement of such reforms would be supervised by such agents (French " organes ") as they might consider best suited for the purpose.

The High Commissioner strongly objected to this, which he characterised as a personal insult to himself, taking it to mean that a Commission would be sent to undertake the study of and to make suggestions for the necessary reforms without consulting him and possibly, even, that a special permanent Commission would be appointed to supervise the enforcement of these reforms, and he added that he would have to consider whether his further stay in Crete was possible in these circumstances.

On November 9th I received a letter from the three

insurgent leaders accepting all conditions imposed by the Powers but asking a delay of a fortnight, as from November 3rd, in order to collect the number of rifles demanded. M. Venizelos also asked for an interview with the Consuls in order to settle certain details with regard to surrender. The Consuls replied on the following day that the delay would be granted and that they could meet M. Venizelos on the 15th.

On that day M. Maurouard, Baron Fasciotti and I (M. de Bronewsky, the Russian Consul-General, being indisposed) met M. Venizelos again at the Monastery of Aghia Monì. He was alone, and whether for this reason or because he was sincerely anxious to come to terms at once, he spoke much more reasonably and was in a less *exalté* mood than at our last meeting on July 15th. He begged us to believe that he did not wish to make any new conditions and had no wish to start fresh negotiations. We accepted this statement in the spirit in which it was evidently offered and went on to discuss arrangements to be made for surrender of arms, etc., which were fixed at 700. Various other minor matters were also decided between us, among others the place, Palaia Suda, from which the " escape " of the deserting gendarmes was to take place, undisturbed by International troops or Cretan gendarmerie. At the end of the meeting M. Venizelos spoke earnestly and impressively about the hopes entertained by himself and his party that the High Commissioner would, in future, act with complete impartiality towards every party in Crete. They wished to feel that he was their Prince as well as the Prince of their political opponents. He added that the transfer of M. Papadiamantopoulos would be regarded as symbolic of a change in the administration.

A *procès-verbal* of our meeting, which lasted till late in the evening, was drawn up and signed by all present and, thankful that all seemed now satisfactorily settled, I got on my horse and with the paper in my pocket galloped back to Halepa to make my report to the High Commissioner of the arrangements. Here I was to encounter one more obstacle.

The Prince raised no objection to the arrangements, but when I told him that the Consuls, considering all arranged, had given M. Venizelos a safc conduct to come to Canea the following day in order without delay to transact business connected with the settlement, he suddenly turned upon me :

" What," he said, " have you given Venizelos a safe conduct without asking me to sign it ? "

I said that as he had already approved the amnesty, I could not suppose that he would have any objection to this.

He gave me to understand, however, in his own vigorous way, that he considered this another personal affront, but on second thoughts his manner changed and he said, with a smile :

" After all, perhaps it's for the best, for if he comes into the town to-morrow I can give orders to the gendarmerie to arrest him and he will be lodged in jail to-morrow night."

Then, having had nothing to eat since the morning—it is strange how too much or too little food may affect the most serious issues—and having been hard at work all day and arrived, as we thought, at a solution satisfactory to our Governments and good for the future peace of the island, to see everything shattered at one fell swoop was too much for my temper.

" If," I said, " M. Venizelos is arrested or imprisoned to-morrow by Your Royal Highness's command, I will guarantee that within a fortnight you will cease to be High Commissioner of the Powers in Crete."

Whether he was bluffing or not with this threat, or whether it was just a spasm of ill-temper, I never dis-covered ; I could not say to-day how much my outburst was ill-temper or bluff.   In any case he never mentioned the matter again, and M. Venizelos came and went un-touched.   But during the whole of the next day, until I learnt that he had returned freely to Therisso in the evening, I was desperately anxious and nervous, for had the threat been carried out it was not difficult to foresee that the fury of the Venizelists against the High Commissioner could not have been calmed for months more, or that an attempt might even have been made on his life which, apart from the personal sorrow I should have felt if anything had happened to him, would have had disastrous consequences.

I cannot, however, in fairness to Prince George, let it be believed that he was always unwilling to listen to reasonable argument, even if he would not be convinced by it, for two days after the little passage of arms above described I thought I had better attempt to give him a general review of what I felt, after two and a half years in Crete, to be necessary for the future peace and prosperity of the island.

I ventured to hitch this on to a reassuring communication from Lord Lansdowne, which I was instructed to make respecting the famous paragraph in the Consuls' Note to the insurgents about the appointment of a special Commission for Crete.

Availing myself of a sentence at the end of Lord Lansdowne's message: " The cordial co-operation of His Royal Highness would be invaluable," I said that, speaking from my two and a half years' experience, it seemed to me that the force of public opinion in the liberal countries was such that the Protecting Powers were obliged to insist on strict constitutionalism and impartiality on the part of their High Commissioner in Crete, otherwise it would be most difficult if not impossible to give him the support of their troops in case of another insurrection.

If His Royal Highness considered it his duty as a Greek Prince to use his influence for or against this Party or that at elections, he ought clearly to inform the Governments of the Powers whose mandatory he was before embarking on so dangerous a policy.

The moment had come, I believed, when by conciliating rather than actively opposing the Venizelist opposition, he might easily win them over to himself. It seemed that M. Venizelos really wished to wipe out the past if he was sure there would be fair play as between the parties in the future.

The High Commissioner was identified with the cause of Hellenism in Crete ; would there not be a real danger to that cause if he, a constitutional Governor, should continue to use his influence both as a Greek Prince and High Commissioner to crush the Venizelist Party ? Moreover, this seemed unnecessary for, as he had often told me, the Cretans were to a man in favour of Union, and therefore, if M. Venizelos was, as His Royal Highness said, against Union, the people themselves would certainly cease to support him.

If, on the other hand, His Royal Highness would, as he could do, reconcile all parties in Crete and make them work together for the welfare of the island, he would earn the gratitude not only of his own country and of the island, but also of the Powers whose mandatory he was.

His Royal Highness listened in a very friendly spirit to these rather didactic observations which, he declared, were but the result of my ignorance of the true state of things. He denied that he had ever used his influence against the Venizelists, which caused me to ask what had occurred during his so-called " electoral tour " in 1903.

He replied quite frankly that he had only during that tour given advice to peasants and others who had asked him how they should vote. He ended by declaring that he believed that M. Venizelos was a traitor to Hellenism, that it was his duty as a Greek Prince to oppose him, and that if he obtained a majority at the elections for the General Assembly, he, Prince George, would forthwith dissolve that body.

In reporting this converstaion to Lord Lansdowne, I concluded my dispatch by saying that Prince George evidently believed it to be his duty to intervene in the coming elections as before, and that if he did so I feared that nothing would save the administration from ship-wreck.

Every possible influence should therefore be brought to bear on him to save him from such a course.

After this interview, from which I gathered that it would be as difficult to move Prince George from his truly impossible views of his duties as a constitutional ruler of Crete under the Protecting Powers as to persuade an Ethiopian to change his skin or a leopard his spots, I came regretfully to the conclusion that it would be necessary, in his own interests, in those of Crete, of Greece, and of the Powers, to bring about a change of High Commissioners as soon as possible. I felt sorry for this, because, apart from his political vagaries, Prince George was, personally, a most likeable character, and I truly wished him well.

Before we could, however, finally settle the arrangements with regard to the amnesty, there occurred a final flutter in the Palace dovecote.

Seven hundred and sixty-four rifles had been collected from the insurgents by various detachments of International troops on November 19th at different agreed points, but there was a slight hitch in the embarkation of the " escaping " gendarmes because the Greek steamer on which M. Venizelos was relying to transport them from Palaia Suda to Greece never arrived. In all haste my colleagues and I arranged, with the help of the Austrian Consul-General, for the Austrian-Lloyd mailboat which called at Canea and Candia on its way to the Piræus, to pick up these passengers, a mixed crowd of deserters and intransigent insurgents, among whom were many common criminals. This was done on the 23rd, and we gave another sigh of relief, believing that all was settled at last, when a final bolt shot out of the blue.

The above arrangements had much retarded the Proclamation of Amnesty. That same day, the 23rd, I submitted to the High Commissioner a draft Proclamation which the four Consuls had drawn up in accordance with the terms agreed upon between us and His Royal Highness.

Prince George sent for me that very evening and

expressed surprise that the Consuls should have proposed to sign the Proclamation of Amnesty, which was a prerogative belonging to him under the Constitution, and the Cretan authorities could not recognise an amnesty as valid which was not signed by him.

I explained that we had prepared our draft in the belief that as we, in the name of the Powers, had declared martial law and were acting by virtue of it, and had also in the name of our Governments conducted negotiations with the insurgents, it seemed to us proper that the Proclamation should be signed by us. At the same time I readily admitted the force of His Royal Highness's arguments, and promised to submit the matter to my colleagues the following day. At the Consular meeting next morning it was decided that, the International military tribunals not being under the authority of the High Commissioner, he could not issue an amnesty for offences falling under their competence, but we all agreed that the amnesty for all offences falling within the competence of the Cretan courts ought to be signed by His Royal Highness.

We had a collective audience with the Prince that afternoon and explained our views, together with the manner in which doubtful cases should be treated. To all this His Royal Highness apparently agreed. We then handed the Prince the text, in French, of the draft Proclamation for *his* signature, and left the Palace to draw up *our* Proclamation covering sentences passed by the military tribunals, much relieved to find that we had arrived, as we believed, at complete agreement.

Having been informed that the Prince's Proclamation had gone to the printing office, we hastily sent ours there also, only to be informed at the office that it would have to be submitted to M. Papadiamantopoulos before going to press.

The same evening the High Commissioner came round unannounced to my house after dinner and protested most vigorously against the Consuls signing any Amnesty Proclamation at all.

He had, he said, understood at our meeting that we intended to issue merely an " explanatory declaration," and in any case he was the only authority in Crete who had a right to issue any Proclamation of Amnesty, and he refused to allow a Proclamation by the Consuls to appear in the official gazette.

I said that whatever I felt about this point my colleagues were decidedly of opinion that in matters dealt with by the International military tribunals they were the proper authorities to issue such Proclamations. The Prince replied that he had as High Commissioner formerly amnestied persons sentenced by the International military courts during the years 1897–98, and that he alone was competent to do so now. If, however, we were especially instructed to do so by our Governments, that was another matter.

I said I would at once consult my colleagues as to whether we should telegraph or not to our Governments for instructions, and drafted a telegram accordingly.

The next morning I found my colleagues very indignant that the High Commissioner, evidently at the instigation of M. Papadiamantopoulos, should have suddenly changed his attitude after apparently accepting our proposal.

At the same time we were informed that many insurgents who had gone to their homes, being alarmed at the non-appearance of any Proclamation regarding sentences of the military courts, were returning to the mountains until they received satisfactory assurances on this point. M. Venizelos sent us an urgent message from Mournies asking for explanations.

Considering that the insurgents had fulfilled their part of the programme and that a final settlement was urgent, if only as a matter of good faith, we decided not to telegraph for instructions but to issue our restricted Proclamation at once. In order, however, not to encroach on the High Commissioner's prerogatives we caused it to be posted only on the Consulates or buildings occupied by International troops. This was done at once, and at the same time M. Venizelos was invited to come and meet us in Canea in order to receive explanations with regard to certain points which he wanted to have cleared up.

Thus at last the final hectic measures were taken, and the Cretan insurrection of 1905 terminated, if not in a spirit of good will all round, at least without leaving any too bitter aftermath behind it. The experiment of endeavouring to obtain internal reforms by the old methods so commonly adopted during the Turkish regime was never again repeated during the International regime.

As regards the Prince's complaint respecting the Proclamation, I must admit that I should have been willing to accept his point of view though, as a matter of fact, there was no real analogy between the remission of sentences passed by the military tribunals of 1897–98 and the present amnesty because, when we came to Crete in 1901 the 1897–98 military tribunals had long ceased to exist, whereas ours were still working. If, however, the argument as to the sentences of 1897–98 emanated from the fertile brain of M. Papadiamantopoulos, the plan of posting the Consuls' Proclamation on the Consulates and International buildings issued from the equally ready mind of Baron Fasciotti who, as I look back on those times now, seems to have been more than a match for the private secretary in ingenuity and resource.

CHAPTER III

CRETE. RECONSTRUCTION

(1905–6)

A CURIOUS sidelight on internal politics in Crete was thrown by the elections for the mayorality of Canea.

Mechmet Bey, an influential Moslem, who was retiring from the post of mayor, was sought for by all parties—Moslems, Venizelists and Governmentals—as their candidate at the next elections, which were to take place in January. He called on me early in December and told me that he had entirely declined to declare himself for any party and, unless he could stand as an independent, would withdraw from the contest.

Shortly after this I received information that the High Commissioner himself had sent for Mechmet Bey and endeavoured to persuade him to declare himself for the Government. I informed His Royal Highness later of this rumour that I had heard, and asked him if I might contradict it in his name.

Prince George replied that he had sent for Mechmet Bey in order to induce him not, in any case, to stand as a Venizelist, which Mechmet Bey had assured me he had no intention of doing, since he wished to be entirely independent of parties.

If, His Royal Highness went on, the Bey stood either as an independent or as a Government candidate there would probably be no opposition, whereas if he stood as a Venizelist there would be a struggle which might end in reprisals against Moslems, and this His Royal Highness particularly wished to avoid.

It was the warning thus given to the Mayor that,

according to Prince George, the Venizelists had construed into " pressure " and " intimidation " on his part. The Prince said his whole object had been to avoid a contest, because he knew that if Mechmet Bey was, *or appeared to be*, on the Venizelist side, other Christian parties would at once start one or two candidates of their own. This, declared the Prince, was unfortunately what had happened because Mechmet Bey, while announcing himself as independent, had sided rather with the Venizelists, and a certain hostility towards the Moslems had already sprung up among the Governmentals.

This explanation appeared to me to be somewhat disingenuous. It was clear that the High Commissioner had, at the instance of the Government, sent for Mechmet Bey and tried to persuade him to declare himself on the Government side, which he refused to do, stating himself to be independent of parties, as before. The whole question at issue was, in my opinion, simply one of loaves and fishes. If the mayor was at any rate morally bound to either party, that party would secure the lion's share of municipal posts. Hence the struggle over Mechmet Bey. The sequel of the story was curious. The Government party entered a protest against his candidature on the ground that he could neither write nor read Greek, a *conditio sine qua non* under the Constitution. It seemed that this was really the case, but the regret at his having to retire from public life was so general and the pressure brought to bear on the Government that he should have some public appointment so strong, that in the following year the High Commissioner with, I could not but think, his tongue in his cheek, appointed him Councillor for the Interior, which included Education, an excellent post indeed for a man who could not write or read the language of the country. All this was so curiously and typically Cretan that I cannot help recording it here.

Early in November Lord Lansdowne had a long conversation at Windsor about the affairs of Crete with the King of Greece. He told His Majesty that the High Commissioner had apparently withdrawn his opposition

E

to the proposal for the appointment of a Special Commission of inquiry and report, and he informed the King that the British delegate would be Sir Edward Law, whose appointment would, it was believed, be regarded as a guarantee that no injustice would be done to the High Commissioner. (Sir Edward had previously served on a financial mission in Greece and was a *persona grata* to all the Greek authorities.)

Having given so full an account of the Cretan Insurrection of 1905, fuller, perhaps, than it deserves, it may not be altogether amiss if I conclude this part of my Cretan experiences with a short synopsis of the cause of the insurrection, taken from a long dispatch which I wrote to Lord Lansdowne on November 12th. In this dispatch the insurrection was attributed to four principal causes :

First.—Personal, i.e. the quarrel between Prince George and M. Venizelos.

Second.—Internal political causes, more particularly the necessity for ending the system of " the spoils to the victor " after every electoral struggle.

Third.—Economic : proper control of finance and public expenditure.

Fourth.—National, i.e. desire for union with Greece, for which, the Moslems excepted, the whole population was practically unanimous.

I concluded by saying that the best way temporarily to tranquillise the people would be, while introducing such financial and administrative reforms as might immediately improve the economic condition of the country, to give at the same time some pledge that union with Greece would not be indefinitely postponed.

The fixing of a date at which the International troops would be withdrawn from the island, conditionally on the good behaviour of the Cretans, and the place of these troops taken by Greek troops or a native militia organised by Greek officers would, I believed, be the best way of securing peace and quiet in the island for some time to come.

At the same time I warned the Government that any step of this kind must be taken prudently for the sake of the Moslem inhabitants, for whom during my residence in Crete I had acquired a considerable respect. Any sudden and unexpected move towards Union would certainly result in a *sauve qui peut*. Moslem properties would be thrown on to a market quite unable to absorb them, and a slump in land values would take place, which would be most unfortunate. The Moslems ought to have at least two or three years' grace to prepare for the change, but the International Occupation of Crete could not be prolonged indefinitely for the sake of thirty thousand Moslems.

Looking back now I see no reason to alter, in the light of subsequent events, any part of that dispatch.

If the Powers wanted Crete to cease from troubling or being a menace to peace in the Near East, there was clearly only one policy to follow : i.e. to move gradually, neither too rapidly nor too slowly, towards union with Greece by substituting Greek troops for Internationals, by substituting an impartial High Commissioner for one who was so definitely committed to one political party in the island, the new High Commissioner being, of course, a Greek but, for choice, not a member of the Royal family, and lastly, by helping Crete on to her legs again financially and economically as far as this was practically possible.

This is what was done in the course of the next few years with the excellent result that Crete is, politically speaking, no longer on the map,[1] but only a delightful centre of interest for archæologists and tourists, while Suda Bay has become what it is eminently suited for : a port of call for refuelling air liners plying between Europe, India and Africa.

In December, 1905, the Conservative Government in the United Kingdom went out of office and Sir Edward Grey succeeded Lord Lansdowne at the Foreign Office. I could not help feeling personally glad of the change,

[1] This was written before the Venizelist rising of 1935.

for while Lord Lansdowne had always been most courteous to me, as he was to everyone—he had the courtly
manner of the old school—and had even been good
enough to express approval of my work in Crete, yet on
the one or two occasions on which I was asked to talk to
him I felt he dwelt on Olympian heights from which he
would not readily descend.   I now look back with regret
to Landsowne House, that fine old eighteenth century
building in Berkeley Square, which formed such a noble
setting for the distinguished-looking Secretary of State.
I preferred it to almost any other of the old pallazzi, as
they would be called in Rome, of the fast disappearing
London of my youth.   Lord Lansdowne, who might in
truth have been called the last of the Whigs, has passed
and his house followed him only a few years later, but the
name is still attached to an amorphous block of flats.

With Grey on the other hand it was different.   Though
he had a reputation for aloofness and austerity, we had
known each other for so many years, had often stayed
together in the houses of mutual friends, and shot and
fished together in England and Scotland, that I felt I
could write to him freely about any matter which was
troubling me.   His answers, if any, were always brief,
but I knew him well enough to be sure that he had read
what I had written, and I had sufficient confidence in his
judgment to be sure that he would always do what was
fair and square and practical.

All things considered, therefore, the New Year began
well so far as I personally was concerned.

But the Old Year could not even complete its course
without one more incident between the High Commissioner, with the Cretan Government behind him,
and the International troops. This time the French
military authorities were involved. A Cretan who was
an office keeper in the Municipality of Canea attempted
to kill and severely wounded a French soldier.   It transpired afterwards that a warrant was out for his arrest for
a murder committed in Greece.   As the man had been
recommended for a permit to carry a revolver by the

prefects of two provinces including that of Canea, Colonel
Lubanski, commanding the French troops in Crete and
acting as President of the Military Tribunal of Canea,
ordered the arrest of both prefects and various other
Government authorities suspected of protecting the
criminal. The Prince, while expressing his regret at the
incident and at the fact that the criminal had not yet been
arrested, was not unnaturally highly indignant at these
arrests. He countermanded the fêtes, including a review
of the International Contingents, usually held on
December 22nd, to commemorate his landing in Crete as
High Commissioner.

He also sent round word to Isa to ask her not to invite
the French Consul-General or the French military
authorities to the weekly evening parties we gave which he
often attended.

Isa replied that she could not put off those whom she
regularly invited, but that we should be delighted for
him to come and play bridge any night to meet guests
whom he himself selected.

Relations between the French and the Palace continued to be much strained for a considerable time and
all hopes of a pleasant Christmas and New Year faded
quickly away.

The Powers set themselves now with laudable zeal to
appoint members of the " Reform Commission," as it
was called, which was to inquire into the administration,
political and financial, of the island and propose necessary
reforms.

Every other question dropped into the background and
was quietly settled. The Cretan authorities arrested by
Colonel Lubanski for complicity in the assault on a
French soldier were released, the removal of Mechmet
Bey's name from the list of candidates for the Mayorality
of Canea remained a subject of correspondence with the
Foreign Office and of discussion with the High Com-
missioner, some trouble was caused by the return to
Crete of escaped insurgents who had not been definitely
amnestied, but all hopes and fears were now centred in

the expected Commission whose advent was warmly greeted by the Venizelists and as coldly anticipated by the Government party.

Sir Edward Law, who was at one time Financial Secretary to the Indian Government and, as already mentioned, had served in Greece as a financial adviser, was appointed as British member of the Cretan Commission, and was instructed to proceed to Crete by the end of January. Sir Francis Elliot, H.M. Minister at Athens, informed the High Commissioner, who was at Athens for the New Year, of this choice and he expressed particular gratification thereat. This at least was as satisfactory as it was unusual. At the same audience, however, His Royal Highness " expounded," as Sir Francis wrote to the Foreign Office, " with great volubility and emphasis his complaint against the Powers and the Consuls, that they did not understand the situation in Crete, that they did not consult him and ask his opinion, and that they were unfairly biased in favour of M. Venizelos." I fear it gave me a certain unholy satisfaction to learn that for once someone else besides myself was enjoying the " volubility and emphasis " of His Royal Highness's complaints.

The municipal elections took place early in January and went off, all things considered, fairly satisfactorily, and disturbances were reported at two or three places only. At Cambanù, in the Italian *Secteur*, late in the evening the crowd, supporters of the Government, tried to rush the polling station and seize the arms. The small Italian detachment guarding the place kept them back with the butt ends of their rifles for a time, but when a Cretan ex-gendarme drew a revolver and wounded one of the Italians severely in the arm, his comrades fired at the crowd killing two and wounding others.

As it was late and as the small Italian detachment was greatly outnumbered it withdrew to another post, but was obliged to leave the wounded man under the care of the Mayor.

As soon as the Italian detachment had left, the crowd,

which had departed after being fired on, returned, broke into the house and stabbed to death most brutally the unfortunate wounded Italian.

The Cretan and Italian versions of this unpleasant incident were practically in agreement with only one or two minor discrepancies. All the Protecting Powers instructed their representatives in Crete to support the Italian demand for an indemnity, but expressed to the Italian Government hopes that custom-houses would not be seized. This, however, was done on January 25th.

In order to make the general situation still more pleasant the High Commissioner gave an interview to an Athens newspaper, the *Patris*, in which he spoke of the ex-leaders of the insurrection as impostors and traitors, and stated that they had imposed a new yoke on Crete which was now to be governed through the Consuls by the enemies of Union. His Royal Highness concluded by urging the population of Crete to end this state of things at the coming election.

This declaration on the part of the High Commissioner naturally caused great excitement in Crete, and was clearly opposed to the assurances of impartial government given by the Powers to the Cretans on more than one occasion. My colleagues and I believed it might well lead to disturbances and even bloodshed at the coming elections, and therefore sent an identic dispatch to our respective Governments saying that we considered it imperative that a firm assurance should be obtained from the Prince that he would observe a line of conduct at once impartial, conciliatory and constitutional.

The Prince, on being asked by Sir Francis Elliot whether he would not issue a denial of this interview, said at first that it was published so long ago (about ten days) and that it was no use reviving a matter that was already forgotten, but that if the Powers would ask him to do so he would make a declaration on these lines stating at the same time that he had always been the victim of the partiality of the Consuls for his opponents.

On January 22nd, in forwarding the text of the now notorious interview to Sir Edward Grey, I felt I must make my own sentiments about the continuance in office of the High Commissioner quite clear to H.M. Government, and wrote that his undisguised hostility towards a large body of public opinion in Crete made it necessary to consider how far we could continue to support him as High Commissioner.

After the murderous attack made by an employé of the Canea custom-house, who was also wanted for homicide in Athens, on a French soldier in December, 1905, the Consular Corps asked the Commandant of Gendarmerie for information respecting the previous records of lesser Government employés in Canea. Captain Monaco sent us lists of these employés, among whom were no less than thirty-two persons all of whom had been condemned for terms of varying length for such crimes as homicide and murderous attacks, cattle lifting, brawling and assault.

A short time before a customs officer was appointed who, in 1903, i.e. only two years before, had been condemned to fourteen months imprisonment for violent assault.

I ventured to speak to M. Koundouros, the Councillor of the Interior, about the dangerous character of some of these minor officials. He replied with some warmth that they were all known to him as patriots who had shed their blood for their country.

They were, doubtless, all political supporters of his, and M. Koundouros's warm defence of these patriots confirmed my views about the manner in which Government patronage was too often distributed in Crete.

The Consular Corps thought it their duty, after having received information from an International picket set to guard one of the custom-houses that the custom officers themselves opened the safe and helped themselves to the contents of boxes and parcels, to call the attention of the Government to this as also to the lamentable condition of the prisons where similar criminals had been installed as warders.

While we had no confidence in the willingness of the then Cretan Government to reform such abuses we hoped that the Commission of Enquiry, which arrived on February 10th, would examine these matters closely and help us to endow Crete with an honest and capable administration.

Sir Edward Law, on his arrival, held himself aloof from the Consular body. He gave me the impression that we were as much on trial as anyone else and that he did not wish to have over friendly relations with me or my colleagues until he had got his bearings. He indeed refused all invitations to come to my house.

He had, doubtless, seen the High Commissioner in Athens, and had been impressed by the extreme force and vigour of his accusations against the whole Consular body, whom by this time His Royal Highness regarded as little better than insurgents.

The attitude of the Delegates of the Commission, however, changed very rapidly, and the first identic message they sent to their respective Governments on February 28th, 1906 (they arrived on February 10th) was to the effect that if serious disturbances were to be avoided it would be necessary for the Prince to discharge all his present Councillors and to choose his new ones from a list presented to him by some absolutely impartial person to be suggested by the Powers.

When the proposal of the Delegates was communicated to Prince George, it was explained that the object of it would be to establish a " Ministry of Conciliation," which would be a guarantee that the coming elections, fixed for May 20th, would be fairly conducted. He opposed the idea saying that this would be construed by the adherents of the Government as rewarding the wicked and punishing the good.

Meanwhile things in the Italian (Western) " *secteur* " were going from bad to worse and the confusion appeared to be greater than even during the insurrection. So bad indeed did matters become that a joint conference of Military Commanders and Consuls was called to discuss what could be done to restore order.

It was generally agreed that more troops would be required to enable the Powers to co-operate in pacifying the Italian " *Secteur* " before the elections.

I wrote to the Secretary of State on March 3rd :

> It seems that the only way of avoiding civil war or at least dangerous disturbances which the High Commissioner prophecies as certain if a Ministry of Conciliation is formed and which M. Venizelos assures me must occur if it is not, is by such a display of military force as will overawe the turbulent elements of the population in this part of the Island.

After a good deal of correspondence between the Protecting Powers on the subject of a " Government of Conciliation " during the electoral period, nothing was done mainly because the Russian Government would not concur unless Prince George agreed to the proposal, which of course he would not do.

The Prince, therefore, clearly won the first game of the rubber and was accordingly elated.

" I will tolerate no surveillance or control whatever," were the words he used on the subject.

Seeing that this triumph of the Government Party might lead to real trouble, especially in the Italian " *secteur*," the Consular Corps set themselves to elaborate a plan for securing peace in that " *secteur*," but failed in reaching an agreement largely because of the opposition of the Italian Consul-General to any British, French or Russian officers being appointed to act as " military attachés " to gendarmerie columns sent to keep order in that part of the island. So our difficulties increased.

Jealousies on the part of the High Commissioner, jealousies on the part of the representatives of the Powers, jealousies on the part of the Cretans themselves blocked every road.

With the departure of the Commission at the end of March our work seemed only to have increased.

The report of the Delegates was, however, drawn up with great promptitude in Athens and forwarded to their respective Governments on March 30th.

The Report was divided into four parts.

The first dealt with administrative and general questions.

The second summarised the recommendations of the Commission on these questions.

The third consisted of various " Annexes."

The fourth treated of financial and economic matters.

For anyone interested in the history of Crete during the International Occupation as an example of " international co-operation " in Government, this long Report is of the greatest interest. As I have already stated, the Cretan *imbroglio*, while minute in itself, contained the elements of serious trouble in the Near East, and is not without value as an experiment in International administration. The study of this Report might well enable two or more Powers who have at any time to undertake a similar duty to avoid many pitfalls. This is no place to go at length into these matters, but I hope that some day a serious study will be made of the International occupation in Crete as a curious foot-note to history.

About the beginning of April I lost the services of Mr. Paul Wilkinson, the Vice-Consul at Canea, who had been invaluable during the past very busy months. He was a British subject born at Smyrna and spoke French, Greek and Italian as well as English. A hard worker, he never spared himself, and the amount of work in one small office where all dispatches and reports had to be written out in longhand and sometimes copied in duplicate or triplicate was at times overwhelming ; as second Vice-Consul I had also Mr. Gerald Lascelles, the son of our Ambassador in Berlin, who, unfortunately, owing to ill-health, was unable to do as much as Wilkinson. As also he knew no Greek he was badly handicapped in Crete. At this moment of " reconstruction " when we needed all the forces we could muster, the Government offered Mr. Wilkinson an independent post and, unwilling to stand in his way, I advised him to accept it. But it left me very short handed.

On March 30th, 1906, Sir Edward Law forwarded to

Sir Edward Grey the Report of the International Commission on Cretan affairs, together with a confidential covering letter addressed to the Governments of the Protecting Powers by the four Delegates collectively. They stated in this letter that the political status of Crete presented serious difficulties and dangers. It was so ill-defined and answered so little to the aspirations of the inhabitants that all administrative and financial reforms could but be expedients incapable of giving the island permanent peace and prosperity. On the other hand Crete was for the Four Powers an incessant source of anxiety, preoccupation and useless expense. They, therefore, gave it as their considered opinion that the only real remedy was to permit union with Greece as soon as possible.

Both Prince and people believed the actual situation to be provisional, both suffered and general bitterness resulted.

The Commissioners did not believe that the reforms proposed in the Report could have any permanent result. The only useful and radical reform was the one which the Commission could not propose in its Report, namely : Union.

As to Prince George, the delegates stated that while giving full weight to his many qualities, they were compelled to declare that he was quite unfitted to govern the Cretan people after a constitution had been given to Crete. His character, his education and his tendencies were in complete contradiction with his rôle ; his qualities were not those of the head of a Constitutional State. His prestige on landing in Crete was immense, but was now much impaired. Both Prince and people were tired of waiting for the accomplishment of that union of which he was to have been the artificer. Unable to put up with opposition, he was no longer leader of the Cretans but only leader of a party in Crete.

Nevertheless the delegates would not suggest the obvious conclusion to be drawn from the above conditions, namely, that if union could not be granted at once the Prince ought to be replaced by someone more willing and able to govern constitutionally, though this should only be done after his prestige had received some satisfaction in the shape of a definite step forward towards union.

The delegates then referred to the relations between the Consuls and the High Commissioner, and said that there were mistakes on both sides. The Prince had complained of almost all the foreign agents with whom he had to do in Crete. He hardly indeed accepted that surveillance which it was the duty of the Consuls-General to exercise but which ought to have been carried out much more discreetly. " He complained that some of them even forgot to observe those rules of good breeding (*convenances*) required in dealing with a Royal Prince."

They concluded by saying that the various reforms proposed in the report could only have some prospect of success if Crete, having peaceably accomplished the elections for the Constituent Assembly which was to pass legislation embodying the proposed reforms, were to enter into an era of tranquillity and calm.

The elections had been fixed for May 20th.

Those who wish to study the reforms proposed by the Commission must do so by consulting the report itself. They have no present value now that Crete has at last been united to Greece.

On the whole the findings of the Commission and the conclusions drawn in their covering letter concurred entirely with my own view except for the fact that I was, as before stated, reluctantly of the opinion that there could be neither peace nor prosperity of any kind in Crete so long as Prince George remained its ruler. As to the complaints made by the High Commissioner of the Consular Body, they left me, I must confess, very cold, for if we did not always remember to treat him as a Royal Prince he frequently forgot to treat us as officers having certain duties to perform which, it was true, were sometimes disagreeable to him.

About Easter, if I remember right, King Edward paid

a visit to Athens. He was accompanied as always on these journeys by Sir Charles Hardinge. I was sent for to Athens to see His Majesty and he spoke to me at great length about Crete, asking me all sorts of questions which showed how deep an interest he took in the matter. Sir Charles Hardinge was present at the interview. After I had told the King exactly what I felt about the situation, he suddenly asked me point blank :

" Well, what are we to do next ? "

I turned hopelessly to Hardinge, much embarrassed, and said that it was clearly a matter for His Majesty's Government to decide and Sir Charles would be better able to reply to that question than I. Sir Charles's answer was, no doubt, diplomatic and non-committal, for I cannot recall what it was. But at least after that interview I had the satisfaction of feeling that His Majesty had my view of the case which I believed was as unbiased as was humanly possible in the circumstances.

One other incident is impressed on my mind during that visit. There was a great State banquet at the Palace to which I was bidden. Everything connected with it I have forgotten but the then all-absorbing necessity of balancing myself through dinner on a chair of which one leg was so feeble that it felt like giving at any moment. The anxiety of endeavouring to eat one's way through a long meal while balancing in a tight uniform on a three-legged chair was such that I frequently wished myself back in Crete, and my attention was so concentrated on equilibrium that my mind is to-day a complete blank as to everything else connected with that dinner.

In the interval before the elections for the General or Constituent Assembly to be held on May 20th, the Consular meetings were kept busy as before over co-operation between International naval and military forces to prevent landing of arms and returning insurgents who had not been amnestied ; with protection of Moslems ; with Cretan indemnities and with arrangements for the elections, besides various minor incidents which cropped up from day to day.

Both the Cretan Government Party and the Opposition joined as soon as the Assembly met in passing a resolution in favour of union with Greece.

I was especially glad to hear that H.M.S. *Suffolk*, commanded by my old friend " Rosy " Wemyss, would be sent to Crete for the time of the elections. That made me look forward with eagerness to what might otherwise prove a stormy period.

All authorities in Crete, from the Prince to the Consuls, were agreed that, as the Italian " *secteur* " in the west, which included the White Mountains, was the storm centre, contingents of troops of all the Protecting Powers ought to co-operate in keeping order there during the elections. Prince George particularly urged me to allow British detachments to go to Sphakia and Cambanù where the Italian soldier had been murdered during the elections in January. He guaranteed that they would come to no harm since both parties looked upon them as having maintained a strictly impartial attitude during the late insurrection and after, and he promised he would himself insist that the Government side at least should take every precaution to avoid a disturbance. The Italian Consul-General was equally insistent that no Italian should be sent to Cambanù.

On the whole, having received assurances both from the High Commissioner and the Venizelists that the strictest orders would be given to their respective adherents to refrain from any disturbance whatever, I felt that the best prospect of peaceful elections in that part of the island lay in agreeing to the requests for a British detachment, and on May 15th arrangements were made accordingly, the French guarding twelve polling stations in the Italian " *secteur*," the Russians eight, the Italians eight and the British three. Canbanù was guarded by British at the express desire of the High Commissioner.

It may be supposed that these arrangements were not arrived at without much discussion. I had particular difficulty in persuading Colonel Panton to allow a British detachment to guard the station at Cambanù, and at one moment it seemed possible that the whole of our arrangements would fall through because no Commanding Officer was prepared to undertake the ungrateful task. When, however, the Colonel understood that the High Commissioner, the Opposition and the Italian Consul-General were all agreed in asking for a British detachment to be sent there he reluctantly agreed. That was the only disagreement, or approach to disagreement, between Colonel Panton and myself during all the time we worked together in Crete. He was always strictly impartial between both parties and was trusted by both, and consequently there was less trouble in keeping order in the British " *secteur* " than in some other parts of the island.

In view of the strong objection felt by Colonel Panton to our men going to Cambanù, I decided to accompany our detachment there and help the British officer in charge to keep order if that was necessary.

Captain Willett and Lieutenant the Hon. H. L. Pelham of the Sussex regiment and I embarked with their men on May 19th at Suda on the *Suffolk* under Captain Rosslyn Wemyss. After a delightful trip round the west end of the island we landed at Selino Castelli.

An early start and a perfect day enabled us to disembark immediately after lunch and then Pelham and I, having said good-bye to Wemyss and Willett, made our way up into the hills with Pelham's small detachment to the little village of Cambanù of sinister memories.

Pelham was a real good companion and I often wonder if he has as pleasant recollections of our Cambanù excursion as I have. The day was glorious and nothing could have been more enchanting than climbing that rough road winding about the rocky valleys and looking out over the sea.

We reached the Cambanù polling station well before dark, were received by the Mayor and authorities with speeches of welcome, prepared our mattresses on the floor of the school-house in the same room where the unhappy Italian had been so brutally done to death, and having slept the sleep of the just woke up at dawn to meet the first electors who were assembling before the school house. For the first and last time in my life I ventured on a speech in modern Greek, carefully prepared beforehand.

I said the usual thing that people say at such elections : that the eyes of the world were upon Cambanù that day, that the electors of Crete must understand that elections could not be conducted with pistols and daggers but with balloting pellets only. If they chose to act otherwise they would not be worthy of the great name of Greece, etc. etc. Above all they must remember, from the mayor downwards, that on this occasion at least all authorities and leaders of parties were united in desiring that there must be peace and order in Cambanù.

All began as quietly as if we were voting in Belgravia. It was soon clear that the electors were really impressed by the orders given them by their superiors.

Having, before leaving Canea, ordered my horse to be brought to me over the mountains to Cambanù I decided, seeing how quietly the elections were going, that it would be quite safe for me to ride home that afternoon and leave Pelham and his men to return next morning to the ship and so back to Suda.

It was a glorious ride over a high pass, the spring air was keen at that height and small alpine flowers were coming out in bloom. Views over the sea, south and west and, later, to the north, varied the outlook over the rugged crags at our feet and little streams from the melting snow made perpetual music by the path. As we rode down on the northern side I saw a long file of horsemen in Cretan costume coming up the narrow path towards me. Presently one got off and approached me on foot. As he came nearer I recognised M. Constantine Foumis, the insurgent leader who used to send me down ferns and alpine flowers from his mountain stronghold at Therisso. I had not seen him to speak to since the insurrection ended. I got off my horse and greeted him. He told me he was making his electoral tour and that all was in

F

perfect order, and promised me that when he passed by Cambanù he would impress on his followers there the necessity of avoiding any aggressive action.

That ride over the White Mountains in May and the meeting with the cavalcade of recent insurgents was the last characteristic picture of Cretan life that I was to carry away with me. Two or three days later, to my great content, I was able to telegraph to the Foreign Office that the first set of elections in the island had passed off in perfect tranquillity, the result being that the two parties were almost equal in the new Assembly.

The elections held in the Prefectures of Canea, Sphakia and Candia on May 20th, i.e. the Italian and British " secteurs," passed off perfectly quietly with one slight disturbance in the Italian " secteur." It was most gratifying to be able to report to H.M. Government that Captain Willett and Lieutenant Pelham had been presented with addresses signed by men of both parties thanking them for the way in which they had kept order, and also to report that complete tranquillity had prevailed throughout the British " secteur."

The Venizelists swept the Prefectures of Canea and Sphakia, and the Government party that of Candia except for a few Moslem Deputies who were expected to vote Venizelist in the Assembly.

So far the two parties were so evenly balanced that the Moslems would have the deciding vote.

The results of the Prefecture of Lasithi (French " secteur ") and Rethymo (Russian " secteur "), where the elections were to take place on May 27th, had still to come in.

On the same day the four Ministers of the Protecting Powers at Athens had an audience with the High Commissioner in Athens, where he had prudently remained during the elections, and made to him a joint verbal communication at the instance of their Governments, requesting him to use his influence to persuade the Assembly not to make any declaration in favour of Union.

His Royal Highness replied characteristically that

unless the Powers would give him some definite statement to make to the Assembly to satisfy them that real progress would be made in the direction of their desires, he did not see what arguments he could use to dissuade them from passing a resolution in favour of Union.

He also declared that if the Government Party found themselves in a minority after the final elections they would take to the mountains without waiting for the Assembly to meet.

This being the attitude of the Government Party it was, perhaps, as well that they later swept the board both in the Province of Rethymo and of Lasithi. They could, after these final elections, reckon on the support of seventy-eight Christian Deputies against thirty-six Christians and a doubtful sixteen Moslems.

This did not, indeed, represent the actual proportion of the two parties, because the method of voting, the "*scrutin de liste*," favoured the winners, but at best it was now clear that the Venizelists were not in a majority anywhere but in the Eastern or Italian "*secteur*" of the island and the capital, Canea.

On June 19th, the French Minister for Foreign Affairs submitted to the other Protecting Powers a plan of reform for Crete which, while giving certain satisfaction to the High Commissioner's view and based largely on the suggestions in the Report of the International Commission of February, would nevertheless, as it was hoped, not too greatly alarm the Porte.

These proposals formed the basis of discussion for the arrangements to be settled between the Powers regarding the future administration of Crete, and were in the main incorporated in the plan submitted by the four Powers to the High Commissioner on July 23rd (see pages 87 & 88).

The only real advance towards the ultimate Union of Crete with Greece lay, of course, in the establishment of a purely Greek-Cretan militia and, so far as possible, gendarmerie.

It was hoped that this would satisfy both the High Commissioner and the Cretan patriots for the time being.

Sir Edward Grey, however, speaking to the French Ambassador on the subject on June 20th, observed that he did not think the French proposals went far enough because they did not touch the question of the High Commissioner. Prince George's position in Crete had become disagreeable if not dangerous. The Powers could not dismiss him nor could he well resign until he could do so with some credit. His Majesty's Government had therefore endeavoured to find a way to make it easy for him to withdraw from the High Commissioner-ship, and that was why they had suggested that the King of Greece should nominate a new Commissioner with the consent of the Powers.[1]

When I read the dispatch reporting this conversation I was delighted, as always, with Grey's straightforwardness and clearness. There was no diplomatic circumlocution. It was, indeed, perfectly English in matter and manner—like everything he did. Mr. Asquith once said of him that listening to his speeches in the House of Commons was like " reading without tears." It was this quality which, I think, endeared him to all the foreign diplomats with whom he had to deal. Lichnowski, the German ; Imperiali, the Italian ; Cambon, the Frenchman ; Sazonow, the Russian ; all who came into contact with him held the same opinion of him. His judgment was sound on all points because he sought justice and what was fair, and because, as Bryce said of Spencer and Carnarvon, it was impossible to think of him doing anything mean or tricky.

If he represented the " old diplomacy " it were well there should be as much of it as possible.

It may be thought that the above conversation is a small peg on which to hang these reflections, but I re-member now the satisfaction with which I first read it and, therefore, I reproduce here the thoughts that occurred to me on rereading it years after in 1935.

---

[1] The Powers had themselves appointed Prince George. Placing the appoint-ment in the hands of the King of Greece was, therefore, a direct advance towards Union, one of those forward steps Prince George had always advocated.

I saw Prince George on his return from Athens about the middle of June and asked him when he would convoke the National Assembly. He said he was waiting for the message from the Powers to do so. He reiterated his declarations to the Ministers in Athens about the absolute necessity of some definite satisfaction being given to Cretan aspirations, without which he felt that the Deputies would not proceed in a regular manner with the work of reform, financial or administrative. They might simply break up, leaving everything *in statu quo*, or declare a general strike in consequence of their Proclamation of Union, or they might go to the mountains and establish a provisional government there.

A further question having arisen about the place of meeting of the Assembly, which many Government Deputies wished to transfer from Canea to Candia, alleging that they feared for their lives in Canea, which was a Venizelist stronghold, I found to my relief that the High Commissioner did not favour this plan, which would have probably resulted in the Venizelist Deputies refusing to go to Candia. He only requested the Consular body to make a declaration to him that the International authorities in Canea would do all in their power to protect all members of the Assembly and freedom of discussion at its meetings. This we were, of course, delighted to do.

I urgently requested His Majesty's Government to be allowed to inform the High Commissioner that they objected strongly to Candia as the seat of the Assembly, feeling that that body should be protected not by one Power only, as would be the case in the British " *Secteur*," but that all the Powers should be responsible for this, which would be the case in the International " *secteur* " at Canea. Colonel Panton shared this view.

Some days later, however, it seemed that the High Commissioner, having become suddenly imbued with a sense of his duties as a constitutional governor, felt he ought to defer to the wishes of the majority of the Deputies and transfer the seat of the Assembly from Canea to Candia.

It looked, therefore, as though we might in the near future have two Provisional Governments in the mountain instead of one.

The place of meeting of the Assembly continued to give trouble for some weeks, despite the fact that the High Commissioner himself went to Candia to persuade the backers of the Government party there to agree to Canea, and even succeeded with the leaders. The rank and file, however, most of whom hoped no doubt to move the capital to their part of the island, having had their appetites whetted by the prospect, declined to give up their hopes and still refused to come to Canea.

It was not until the Consuls, with the approval of their Governments, drew up a Proclamation for publication by the International military authorities, stating that if the Assembly met against the wishes of the Powers anywhere else than at Canea, the Governments of the Powers would not take its deliberations into consideration, that the mass of Government adherents gave in.

The next most important questions that occupied the Protecting Powers during the following weeks were the text of the Collective Note to be presented to the High Commissioner for communication to the Assembly and, so far had matters now advanced, the solution of that most difficult problem : the succession to the High Commissionership.

There is little use in giving a detailed account of these negotiations. It will suffice to say that the Assembly was opened at Canea on July 14th, in perfect tranquillity, but the Collective Note was, of course, not ready for communication to the Deputies. His Royal Highness in his speech referred to the mission of the Reform Commission to Crete, and stated that the four Ministers at Athens had told him that various proposals to satisfy Cretan aspirations were being considered by the Powers, but that it would be impossible to carry them into effect if the Cretans made " inopportune demonstrations." He said he relied on them to work for peace, but since it was desirable for them to decide freely what was expedient and right for them to do, he had no special recommendation to make as to their task. As soon as His Royal Highness left the Assembly, the Deputies joined, with the exception of the Mussulmans, in proclaiming annexation to Greece, and then suspended further sittings.

On July 24th the four representatives of the Protecting Powers at Athens presented to the King of Greece a copy of the Collective Note to be communicated to the High Commissioner to the Assembly. The British Chargé d'Affaires reported: " His Majesty received our communication in silence. He did not appear satisfied and he made no reply."

On July 23rd the Consuls presented the Collective Note to the High Commissioner, who " showed himself far from pleased by that communication in spite of our efforts to point out its friendly character." His Royal Highness stated that it gave satisfaction neither to the Cretans nor to him, and that he took a most gloomy view of the future and declined all responsibility for what might occur. He said he would not read it to the Assembly but merely transmit it by writing to the President for communication to the Deputies.

Shortly after, Prince George informed the Greek Government that he proposed to resign as the Collective Note of the Powers was so unsatisfactory. The Greek Government, at the end of July, sent over the President of the Greek Chamber, M. Bouffides, with the ostensible mission of persuading the High Commissioner to reconsider his threat of resignation. His real object, however, seems to have been to persuade M. Venizelos to join with the Cretan Government Deputies in rejecting the proposals of the Collective Note.

Stripped of unnecessary verbiage the famous Note, about which much sound and fury was blaring in the Greek and Cretan press, amounted, when presented to the High Commissioner on the twenty-third, to the following proposals :

1. Reform of gendarmerie and creation of a militia

in which Greek and Cretan elements could be progressively developed under Greek officers. Early withdrawal of the International troops.

2. Prolongation of the surtax and issue of a loan guaranteed thereon.

3. Extension to Crete of the Commission of Control of Greek finances and the appointment of a foreign expert to set up a service for the inspection of Cretan finances.

4. Recommendation that the Consuls in future should deal directly with the Cretan Councillors and not with the High Commissioner, and other minor matters such as the settlement of outstanding Cretan questions with the Porte and the safeguarding of Mussulman interests in Crete.

It somewhat amused me to find when we read the Note to the High Commissioner that he, so far from being grateful for being relieved of having to deal directly with the Consuls, strongly objected on the ground that this would be another blow to his personal prestige. He had himself so complained to the Commission of the way in which he had been treated by the Consuls that the delegates doubtless believed that this proposal would sweeten the rest of the Note. The result was just the reverse, and so it was, indeed, with every proposal contained therein.

It was truly difficult to avoid the conclusion, after hearing the Prince's remarks on the Note, after reading the Greek and Cretan press on the subject, and after hearing the different versions of the Bouffides Mission, that the King of Greece, the Greek Government, and Prince George and his party were stirring up popular opinion against accepting the proposals of the Note and against the Powers.

Meanwhile the Governments of the Powers went on exchanging hurried views as to the mode by which a change had best be effected in the person of the High Commissioner.

The visit of M. Bouffides, however, was not having

the result desired of persuading the Venizelists to reject the Note, lock, stock and barrel, for it appeared that he was being persuaded by M. Venizelos to accept its proposals and to try to get the Greek Government to do so also. It was a case of Mr. Hilliare Belloc's epigram " On Lady Poltagrue, a Public Peril " :

> The Devil having nothing else to do
> Set out to tempt my Lady Poltagrue ;
> My Lady seized by some peculiar whim
> To his extreme annoyance, tempted him.

The success of the tempter's tempter in this particular case seems to have been so great that the High Commissioner felt perhaps that it would be wiser in order to save the integrity of poor M. Bouffides to prohibit him any further intercourse with the island politicians, and doubtless with that object only, sent to the hotel for his baggage and immediately after lunch shipped him back to the Piræus on his own yacht.

Shortly after there appeared in the Greek press a *communiqué* from Prince George making, without, it is true, any enthusiasm, the best of the Note which, had it appeared at once, might easily have altered the course of things. At this distance of time it is impossible to guess the cause of this *volte-face* on his part, but it looks as if the King thought that the press campaign had gone too far and ought to be checked. After what the High Commissioner had said to the Consuls, and indeed to all that cared to hear about the Note, it seemed hardly credible that he should suddenly have changed his mind to this extent.

The Consular body, however, felt obliged to telegraph to the Powers that the Prince's entourage were disseminating rumours of His Royal Highness's approaching and final departure from Crete, that the Cretan Government Party were forming armed bands in the Western " *secteur*," and that leaders of the Party were said to be again buying arms in Athens.

It seemed that the High Commissioner, while outwardly agreeing with hints received from Athens that it would be well for him to leave, was engaged with his entourage in preparing opposition in the island to any such solution. Everything at least pointed to disturbances being deliberately fomented by some persons to prevent his departure.

By August 18th the succession to the High Commissionership was finally settled with the King of Greece.

The Powers at last accepted Sir Edward Grey's proposal that Prince George should retire and his successor be appointed by His Majesty. The four Ministers at Athens recommended M. Zaimis, a former Prime Minister and Minister of Foreign Affairs. The British Chargé d'Affaires at Athens reported that he had rendered conspicuous services in connection with finance and that he had the reputation of great integrity and trustworthiness. He was a man in whom all, except perhaps the super-Nationalists, had confidence. This proposal was accepted by the King of Greece, who had always desired that Greek national aspirations should receive the satisfaction of seeing the Governor of Crete nominated by the King of Greece rather than by the Protecting Powers.

I had asked for leave about the middle of August, being rather exhausted by the last year and a half in Crete. This the Foreign Office were kind enough to grant, and I handed over the Consulate with a moderately easy conscience on August 11th to Mr. Ronald Graham,[1] who came to relieve me.

I expected that once the change of High Commissioners was settled the island would have a period of rest, and I went off on leave hoping that Graham would not have any serious worries in my absence.

My hopes were not to be realised.

In his first interview with the High Commissioner, Mr. Graham reported that His Royal Highness, while welcoming him in very friendly terms, " referred almost immediately to the political situation in the island, which

[1] Afterwards Sir Ronald Graham, Ambassador in Rome from 1921 to 1933.

he depicted in the most gloomy colours. He considered that the present tension could not continue, and that the slightest incident might give rise to a general explosion. . . . The gendarmes might at any moment desert in a body to the hills. Nothing but his personal influence had prevented their having already done so."

On August 17th, however, Mr. Graham was able to report that perfect tranquillity prevailed in the island, though rumours were rife about the High Commissioner's departure and his replacement by M. Zaimis. The Prince himself was keeping unusually quiet, and hardly— so it was said— mentioned politics even to his own staff.

This calm before the storm did not, however, last long.

The Government Party leaders convoked a meeting for August 30th of the Deputies of Candia, Rethymo and Lasithi, at Candia, to protest against the departure of Prince George and to declare that they would not return to Canea for the Assembly unless they received a favourable reply from the Powers on this point.

The meeting was held and a telegram sent by those present to the King and Government of Greece, declaring that the departure of Prince George would be prejudicial to national interests and begging them to prevent it.

As I was to have no further direct connection with the affairs of Crete, the rest of Prince George's " reign " will be told with less detail.

Up to the moment of his departure, efforts were made by his personal adherents in the island, fomented, I think it may be said almost without doubt, by his private secretary and staff, to prevent his departure by almost any means, including force if necessary.

For weeks the Powers continued to exchange telegrams about the manner in which M. Zaimis was to be invested as High Commissioner and about the ceremonies to be observed for the departure of Prince George and for M. Zaimis's arrival in Crete—in fact, about questions of procedure.

The approaching change of Governors of the island naturally became known, and was discussed in the press, which inflamed public opinion and caused renewed uneasiness.

The Italian Consul-General indeed stated that party feeling was growing so bitter in the Italian " *secteur* " that he should withdraw the Italian troops from the interior unless more International troops could be spared to help them to maintain order.

On September 4th incendiary proclamations were issued in Canea and Candia in connection with Prince George's departure, defying the Powers, calling Cretans to arms, and inciting to acts of violence against the Opposition.

Prince George, however, acting on the advice of the King of Greece, who had been completely won over to the proposed nomination by His Majesty of M. Zaimis, issued a Proclamation on the fifth, counselling tranquillity and patience and faith in the goodwill of the Powers.

Meanwhile the Porte also, rather late in the day, got wind of the approaching change, and protested against the appointment of a Governor by the King of Greece.

Sit Edward Grey informed the Turkish Ambassador in London, with much more firmness than was usual in reply to such protests respecting Crete, that this appointment, made with the approval of the Protecting Powers, would not, in the opinion of His Majesty's Government, constitute an infringement of the *status quo*.

The Cretan Government Party were now becoming frantic, and suddenly called the Assembly together. The meeting of the Assembly at this juncture and for such an object would certainly have produced tempestuous scenes and probably disorders throughout the island, and the Consuls, therefore, took the serious step of prohibiting the meeting of the Assembly, which was approved by the Governments of the Powers.

In consequence of this action the Government leader in the Assembly sent a flamboyant telegram of considerable length to the Governments of the Protecting Powers, protesting against the departure of the Prince, on behalf of the Cretan people, who saw their rights abolished, their most sacred feelings wounded, etc., etc.

And so the game went on.

On the fifteenth, however, the Prince issued a manifesto to the Cretan people to the effect that the Powers, having now agreed to concede to the King of Greece the right of proposing the future High Commissioner in Crete, this step constituted such an advance towards the final solution that he could, in agreement with and by instructions from the King, leave the Island with an easy conscience. He, therefore, believed that his beloved Cretans, inspired by true and pure patriotism, would respect his inflexible decision to depart in accordance with the instructions of the King, and that they would accept with all loyalty the decision of the Protecting Powers.

This was a perfectly unequivocal statement and the Government Party bowed to the wishes of the King of Greece.

On the seventeenth the Foreign Office telegraphed to Mr. Graham that His Majesty's Government were sending H.M.S. *Barham* to Crete, to salute the Prince when he left the island. The desire of all was, it appeared, that he should leave Crete with as much of a halo of glory as could be arranged.

But the usual alarums and excursions continued. MM. Venizelos and Foumis, at a meeting with the Consuls, stated that they would probably be attacked and murdered when the Assembly met on September 8th, and that if they suffered violence at the hands of their opponents in the Assembly, their own friends outside would see to it that not a single Deputy of the majority left Canea alive.

Mr. Graham remarked dryly in reporting this conversation that whatever consolation this prospect might offer them, it afforded none to the Consuls, but he added that the Cretan appeared to be alarmist of the most confirmed type, especially when he hoped to produce an impression thereby.

That description of the Cretan politician I can

thoroughly endorse, and it was not the least of our difficulties that we had continually to sift the grains of truth
like pennyweights of gold from tons of worthless rumour
and fiction which contained them.

On the strength of the statement of the leaders of
the Opposition, the Consuls took it upon themselves to
postpone the meeting of the Assembly a few days until
all precautions could be taken to prevent disturbances.

For once the Greek press, influenced by the Prime
Minister, M. Theotokis, who was most anxious to see
Prince George's place taken by M. Zaimis, found that
the action of the Consuls was justified.

In view of the rising tide of agitation in Crete against
Prince George's departure, all the Powers agreed with
the Greek Prime Minister that M. Zaimis should replace
His Royal Highness as soon as possible, but still it seemed
impossible to reach an agreement as to minor details
regarding the ceremonial to be observed, and the days
passed. The time wasted over the manner of the in-
vestiture of M. Zaimis, and the manner of his reception
in Crete was, considering the urgency of the matter,
literally incredible.

Finally, on the evening of September 28th, the Consuls
sent the following identic telegram to their Governments :[1]

Prince George had fixed his departure for four o'clock p.m. from
Suda, but upon information which he gave us at our farewell
audience, that 2,000 to 3,000 armed men were on the heights around
Suda and some had even come down into the plain over which
passed the road to Suda, we suggested to His Royal Highness, after
consulting among ourselves, that he should embark at Canea. The
Prince agreed to this without demur and his departure was put
off till 6 p.m. We took all naval and military measures accordingly.
Towards 3 p.m. armed bands, advised we do not know how, of
the change of programme, forced the line of advanced posts of the
International troops and burst menacingly into the neighbourhood
of the Palace and the Consulates and engaged in a series of
conflicts with the International troops assembled at Halepa to do
honour to the Prince and keep order during his departure. Among

[1] Translated from the French.

Internationals a Cavass of the Russian Consulate was killed and a Russian soldier wounded. The greater part of the Cretan bands, whose losses are as yet unknown, were driven some way back late in the evening. Nevertheless as the situation continued threatening and nightfall might favour renewed attacks we thought better to suggest to the Prince that he should embark at Halepa. The Prince agreed and gave orders accordingly to the Commander of the Greek warship and departure took place without incidents. Troops are camping and patrolling the streets.

Mr. Graham gave a most graphic account of the events of that day in a dispatch to the Foreign Office, which is too long to transcribe here.[1]

From this it appears that a number of armed men entered Halepa and Canea unexpectedly, that Mr. Graham went to the Russian Consulate to warn his Russian colleague, M. de Bronewsky, and that both of them with a *cavass* went to the windows looking out over the street, where these new insurgents and the Italian, Russian and French guards of honour drawn up for the Prince's departure were already exchanging shots. I will let Mr. Graham tell the rest in his own words :[2]

I had just been pointing out to my Russian colleague some insurgents firing from behind an outhouse when a heavy fire was suddenly and unexpectedly opened on the Russian Consulate itself at from under 100 to about 200 yards. One of the first bullets, probably from a sporting rifle, struck the cavass at the window between those at which my Russian colleague and I were standing, blowing off the top of his head ; he only lived for a few minutes. M. de Bronewsky, who was but a few feet from him when he fell and was not unnaturally moved at the incident, produced a revolver from his pocket and accidentally discharged it, the ball striking a stove within a yard from my knee. I hastily imparted to him a rudimentary knowledge of how to handle these unreliable weapons. In the meantime a company of Russian infantry had doubled up to defend the Consulate and they beat off the insurgents in about half an hour. The shooting on both sides was remarkably bad.

Nevertheless the insurgents managed to hit the Russian Consulate-General, which was, indeed, almost the largest house in Halepa and very conspicuous, for a later report says that the house was riddled with bullets.

[1] See Appendix A. 2.   [2] *Ibid.*

In a final audience with the Consuls, which was of a painful character, Prince George declared that he was being driven from Crete against his will by diplomatic intrigues. He had been treated by the Powers, he said " *en canaille* "(like a scoundrel), and he requested Mr. Graham to inform His Majesty's Government that he was leaving Crete " like a thief and a rascal."

This last statement was, unfortunately, true, but it was hardly the fault of the International authorities who only desired that he should leave surrounded by all the pomp and circumstance that the occasion required. Once again and at the eleventh hour his staff tried to stage a " demonstration " that would retain His Royal Highness in the Island, and they had failed more lamentably than ever before.

Was the High Commissioner aware of their plans or did he really believe that this demonstration was spontaneous ? Who can tell ? The results in any case were disastrous for his political future, for, when he went out into the night by the back door of his house down the private steps to the sea, where a small boat was waiting to take him off to the ship that was to convey him to the Piræus, his political career was ended. This was probably for the best as far as he was concerned, for he was, as the International Commission to Crete of 1905 had reported, by nature quite unfit to act as a constitutional ruler of any kind, and there was no room for autocrats in Greece or her dependencies.

Yet I could not but feel sorry for him. He had gone to Crete as a man might go for a week-end to Deauville, with just luggage enough for two or three days at the outside. When, however, he got aboard his Channel steamer it was only to find that he was in for a cruise round the world, and he soon got tired of it. But still, having set out to acquire credit for the dynasty and for himself, he did not want to leave without something on the right side of the ledger. The trouble was that he was a singularly poor judge of men and was undoubtedly as ill-served by the staff of his own choice as any man could be. How far M. Papadiamantopoulos, who was as subtle as a serpent without it's wisdom, really led him or *vice versa* I could never discover, but in any case the two together ruined the position of the Prince in Crete.

Had he set himself, in the words of M. Venizelos, to arrange for Crete to be united to Greece with a coat on her back, he might have gone down in history as a real statesman. Instead he chose the more exciting path of trying to force the Powers by continual pin pricks to do what he wanted at a time which they all considered inopportune.

M. Zaimis went to Milos on a Greek warship, where he disembarked, and was from there transported to Crete by an International squadron.

In this way the interminable negotiations respecting his journey and arrival in Crete were finally settled.

M. Zaimis landed in Crete on October 1st, without any discordant note and at once made an excellent impression.

He continued to act as High Commissioner till the final annexation of Crete to Greece in 1912. During all his term of office Crete was comparatively quiet and slowly progressing.

Strangely enough as I write these lines (March, 1935) there comes the news that M. Venizelos is leading a new insurrection in Crete, this time against a Greek Government, and a Republican Government to boot, with M. Zaimis as President. The Cretan air must have renewed his youth and gone like good Cretan Malmsey wine to his head. It is exactly thirty years ago to the month, almost to the week, since he went up to the White Mountains to protest against the administration of the High Commissioner of the Protecting Powers. He told me later, in Paris in 1919, if I remember right, that whatever happened he would never play the insurgent again. I hope he will get as easily out of his last adventure as he did out of the former one.[1]

---

[1] Considering that his Party in the Insurrection of 1935 was completely defeated, it cannot be said that he suffered too much for his last escapade. M. Venizelos has since died and his great services to his country have been duly recognised. (Note added June, 1936)

During these exciting times I was enjoying a complete holiday, visiting with Isa in Cumberland and Scotland and shooting grouse and fishing.

The Foreign Office had told me that I need be in no hurry to return. From this, and from the fact that the Secretary of State had sent me when I left Crete a complimentary despatch on my work while there, I judged that it was his intention to move me to some other post.

It was not, however, till the end of September that I was called on to go to the Foreign Office and there told, to my great surprise, that I was to be sent to Washington as Councillor of Embassy, and that it was desired that I should take up my post without delay because Sir Mortimer Durand, the Ambassador, was leaving shortly and I should have to be in charge till his successor was appointed.

This was, naturally, a most gratifying appointment for me. It meant a definite return to the Diplomatic Service, and to have at once to act as Chargé d'Affaires at one of the principal Embassies showed, I suppose, that my chiefs had a confidence in me which I myself was far from feeling.

Officially I had no knowledge whatever of America and to be suddenly put in charge of the Embassy at Washington without any previous experience of it filled me with alarm. However this was not an occasion for raising doubts and difficulties, and I accepted with gratitude, only asking for time to return to Crete and pack up my goods and chattels. This was permitted.

I, therefore, set off early in October and travelled as quickly as I could to Crete. I was again as enchanted at the glamour of Canea and its setting of sea and mountains as on the first day of my arrival more than three years before, and almost regretted that I had to leave it.

About ten days sufficed to say good-bye to my friends, to pack up and, above all, to hear the complete story from Ronald Graham of all that had happened in my absence.

I called on M. Zaimis and, so far as was possible in one

interview, was much impressed by his calm and controlled manner—the very reverse of our late High Commissioner.

Lastly I said good-bye sorrowfully to our old Turkish
house at Halepa where, in spite of much toil and trouble,
I had spent so many happy hours with Isa and the two
little boys, Esme and Francis ; to my garden where I had
grafted many roses ; to my two Syrian Arab horses,
Mofred and Azra ; to the Dragomans, M. Moazzo and
M. Petykhakis (the latter is now Vice-Consul at Canea)
whose help had been most useful ; to the two most faithful
Albanian Cavasses, Sherif Agha and Shakir ; indeed to
all I could think of with whom the Consulate was connected and to my various friends.

Finally I had to say good-bye to Crete and this was
difficult because my feelings were so mixed.   Had I then
read Mr. Nevinson's *Good-bye America*, and Mr. Duggan's
equally admirable *Good-bye England*, I might have
written something of this kind :

Good-bye Crete, cradle of European civilisation where
Minos had drains with running water in his house
thousands of years before they were known in England.

Good-bye, land of rocks and precipices and fantastic
canyons and caves.

Good-bye, land where the Minotaur once lived and
where splendid ibexes still elude the eager hunter.

Good-bye, Crete, I am going home.

Good-bye, Island of unrest where any excuse is good
for a picnic in the mountains with a rifle slung behind.

Good-bye, White Mountains of jagged outline and
pleasant waterfalls.

Good-bye, olives and cypresses and vines and purple
grapes ; good-bye, cystus and bay and anemones, iris and
cyclamen.

Good-bye, little cities surrounded by Venetian forts
and villages with great plane trees.

Good-bye, wondrous ruins of ancient races that have
passed away.

Good-bye, precious stone set in a sapphire sea.

What if St. Paul (quoting the Cretan poet Epimenides[1]) did say in a moment no doubt of annoyance such as often came also to me, that all Cretans were liars, evil beasts and slow bellied—though what he meant by the latter term I have never discovered ? What if your people have not, or had not when I was with them, too much consideration for human life, though they never took it for pelf ; what if they loved politics as a game that can be played for the fun of it, as people in my country in good old days used to like cricket and football, and occasionally broke bones, or even skulls, in the playing—what of all that ?

Your folk were kindly and hospitable, ingenuously disingenuous, fine looking, and with the grand air of those who come indeed of a very ancient and noble stock, and they fitted in perfectly with their surroundings. May it be long before they become Hollywooded, sham picturesque, for tourists to gape at.

I hope I shall see them once more before I die.

Good-bye, Crete, I am going home.

---

[1] *Note.*—Epistle to Titus I, v. 12 : "One of themselves, a prophet of their own, said the Cretans are always liars, evil beasts, slow bellied." (Authorised Version.)

CHAPTER IV

UNITED STATES

(1907–1909)

TWO events which changed the course of the world's history happened while I was in Crete.

The first event which was destined to have a lasting effect on international politics was the Anglo-French Agreement of 1904, eliminating causes of disagreement between the two countries and generally known as the " *Entente Cordiale*."

In Crete the outward and visible signs of this new orientation in Europe were confined to the fraternization of the British and French sailors at Suda who one day paraded about Canea arm in arm, exchanged hats, drank to each other's health in wine shops and gave other indications of a friendly feeling which no one would have expected a few days before. So ready are the unsophisticated sons of our different countries and races to join hands in friendship on the slightest provocation if they are given a chance. For years, centuries even, we have been kept apart by exaggerated nationalism and ancient grudges, by politicians and pressmen, and by school books which deliberately taught the young to look at history from one angle only. Then suddenly the picture changes ; soldiers and sailors of both countries, who are always more ready to make friends than the man in the street, exchange hats and sing their own national songs in superb contempt for harmony, walking arm in arm through the streets of Canea—and doubtless at many other places where they met.

German propagandists then and now have endeavoured, unfortunately with too much success in England, to attribute this to a Macchiavellian desire to surround poor Germany with a ring of hostile bayonets—" *Einkreisungs-politik.*" It would be wiser on their part to recognise that it was owing to the fatal gift of German Governments for making enemies all round them that their neighbours at last found it would no longer pay to continue pin-pricking each other as heretofore.

The second event affected the Far East and occurred in 1905.

Most of us, officers or officials of the Protecting Powers in Crete, were so busy with the storms in our own tea cup that we had little time to follow events in the greater world beyond. But though we did not, perhaps, fully realise the significance of the Russo-Japanese War in its final result, i.e. the rise of Japan to a World Power and the dominating factor in the Far East, we naturally followed the major events of the war with the deepest interest.

One side of it particularly—the fate of the Russian Baltic Fleet under Rozhestvenski, which was practically annihilated at the battle of Tsushima by the Japanese under Admiral Togo, was brought home to us by the fact that one half of the Fleet under Admiral Nebogatoff called in to revictual at Suda Bay, on its way out to the Far East.

The behaviour of the men certainly impressed us all most unfavourably. On two or three occasions during the stay of the Fleet at Suda several hundred men at a time were given leave to visit Canea.

They made the most of their time to get hopelessly and completely drunk, and for the rest of the day the road to Suda was strewn with wretched lifeless creatures who were thrown like parcels one on top of the other into all the wheeled vehicles that Canea could provide for the purpose. Eyewitnesses told us that they had seen the old Canea landaus, which we hired to go out to dinner, collecting these bodies which were thrown in head first with their feet sticking up in the air. One or two boats taking them piled up from the shore to their ships upset and the miserable creatures were all drowned.

Prince George told me that the Russian officers were in despair about their crews, most of whom had never been to sea before, and sat about in groups talking about their cows and their pigs. Worse than this ; he told me that the Mayor of Canea had informed him after the Fleet left that he had at the request of the Commissariat officers signed papers declaring that the price of various commodities, particularly olive oil, which the Fleet had bought in large quantities, was very much higher than the price actually paid. His Royal Highness took him sternly to task for helping these Russian officers to perpetrate so gross a fraud on their own Government. The poor Mayor much taken aback said :

" But I saw that these gentlemen were friends of yours, were invited to your house and I thought that anything I did to please them would please your Royal Highness."

Prince George explained to him that he did not approve of swindlers of this or any other kind.

Altogether the visit of the Russian Fleet to Suda did not lead us to expect any other fate than that which befell it at Tsushima, which was indeed the decisive action of the war. After that both parties willingly accepted President Roosevelt's offers of mediation, which finally resulted in the Treaty of Portsmouth, August 23rd, 1905, whereby Japan definitely took her place as a great World Power.

Before leaving for the United States of America I went to spend a week-end at Sandringham with King Edward and Queen Alexandra and a large party. King Edward was, as always, most kind and asked me to his study to have a long talk about Cretan affairs and particularly Prince George. He deplored the latter's lack of vision and failure to understand his rôle as a Constitutional Governor, and he certainly bore me no ill will for the share I had unwillingly taken in the Prince's removal from Crete.

One little incident occurred which was so characteristic of the King that I cannot help relating it. The first night at dinner I was told that I must wear my miniature decorations. I put on my two or three medals but did not wear a humble grade of an Italian Order, that of SS. Maurice and Lazarus, conferred on all members of the British Embassy at the time of King Edward's visit to Rome in 1902, four years before. When the King and Queen entered the drawing-room where we were all assembled before dinner, he looked critically at me and said :

" Where's your Italian Order ? "

I said it was upstairs but that I thought it was not to be worn in England.

" Of course you must wear it," he said. " You'd better go up to your room and get it at once."

I had to scurry down a long passage, find the little medal, fasten it on as best I could and scurry back only to find that their Majesties had gone in to dinner and the other guests were seating themselves. I took my place, which was beside the late Princess Victoria, only just in time.

She looked at me rather critically and then said :

" What was the matter ? "

" I had forgotten to put on an Italian Order," I replied.

" Oh, for goodness sake put them all on," she laughed back at me, " or you'll get no peace."

I had always heard that King Edward's eye for a decoration in the wrong place was astounding, but that he should remember that I, a humble Secretary in the Diplomatic Service, had about four years before received the lowest grade of SS. Maurice and Lazarus, whom Signor Ruggero Bonghi once described on account of the enormous number of members of the Order as little better than omnibus horses, seemed to me almost incredible.

After that I have always been careful, in memory of King Edward, to put on the little cross of Maurice and Lazarus on every possible occasion, whether correct or not.

King Edward's delight in conferring a decoration, simply because he believed it would give pleasure to a recipient, was infectious. At the end of my audience with him at Sandringham he took a little packet from his table and said :

" By the way I've got something here for you," just as a kind uncle might give a tip to a schoolboy during his holidays ; I took it and opening the parcel found it contained the cross of the C.V.O., his own particular and personal decoration. I thanked him warmly and wore it at dinner that night, which caused him to say smilingly :

" I see you've got that on. That's all right."

This quality of delighting in doing simple little things that he thought gave particular pleasure to those about him was one of the special charms of Kind Edward and endeared him to his *entourage*. It was as much the way in which he conferred the favour as the favour itself which pleased. He was indeed as the Italians say " *Un gran simpaticone*."

I left England for America without my family, being charged, as usual by Isa, to go on before, find a house and prepare it to be ready for their arrival. My instructions from the Foreign Office, received before leaving, were simply to carry on ordinary business pending the arrival of the new Ambassador, whoever he might be, for his appointment was not yet decided. This was very satisfactory and somewhat allayed my fears and I hoped for the best.

I met on board ship Sir Horace Plunkett, the well-known agriculturist, who owned property in Ireland and a ranch in the Far West, where he had known and become very friendly with the President, Theodore Roosevelt. He came up to me on deck the first day out and said,

" I hear you are going to play poker with Teddy Roosevelt. You'd better look out for he's pretty smart."

I answered in the same vein that while I might indeed be taken in by Teddy's bluff I at least should never be caught bluffing because I did not believe in it — in diplomacy anyhow. I may say that I don't think that " Teddy " was ever otherwise than perfectly sincere and straight with the British Embassy while I was there.

His methods no doubt lacked those conventions and cir-
cumlotions to which we were accustomed in European
diplomacy. His way of conducting business with jests
rather than with solemn phrases to cover over disagreeable
or other unpleasant incidents delighted me from the first.
If that was Teddy's way of playing poker I was all
for it.

On arrival at New York I was at once invited to stay
with Mrs. Whitridge, the wife of a well-known lawyer,
and the sister of my friend Mrs. Armine Wodehouse,
who afterwards married Lord Sandhurst. They were
daughters of Matthew Arnold and both agreeable and
excellent hostesses. It was the first time I had stayed in
a good New York house and I found everything very
pleasant, indeed so far as comfort was concerned greatly
in advance of a London house of the same type. A few
important people had been asked to meet me at dinner
that first night, among whom I remember especially
Mr. J. P. Morgan, Senior, and old Sir Percy Sanderson,
our Consul-General, brother of Lord Sanderson, the
Permanent Under Secretary at the Foreign Office. Sir
Percy with his dignified mien, portly figure and long
white whiskers was exactly the American ideal of what an
English official ought to be.

I left New York for Washington the next day feeling I
had true friends in the Whitridges.

That is one of the first impressions anyone—unless he
be as prickly with prejudices as the " fretful porpentine "
—who enjoys private hospitality in any city, north, south,
east or west of the United States will always carry away
with him. He is made to feel that his hosts have been
really glad to see him and will be glad to see him again.
Friendly hospitality is indeed an outstanding feature of
the United States, and if sometimes the visitor is in danger
of being killed with kindness, he is yet always ready to run
the risk a second time. There are times when it is
pleasant, when one is weary of life and on very intimate
terms with one's hosts, to be treated as if one were not
there, but when one is a real stranger, a rather warmer

welcome is pleasant, and even the conventional transatlantic " Delighted to see you " helps to make a social
evening go.

Arrived at Washington, Sir Mortimer Durand, the
retiring Ambassador, although he was leaving Washington
in ten days, insisted on putting me up at the Embassy.
This was truly the height of hospitality and, though I felt
that my presence would be most inconvenient, I accepted
because it seemed that to refuse at such a time would have
appeared to be singularly ungrateful.

It was my first introduction to the old British Embassy
on Connecticut Avenue which housed such British representatives as Pauncefote, Bryce, Spring-Rice, Reading
and Grey of Fallodon. The reception rooms were large
and well proportioned and suited to receptions on a great
scale, and it was certainly popular with Washington
Society, which in 1907 had pleasant memories of entertainments there for about forty years back. But there
was a double line of trams in Connecticut Avenue which
made the street intolerably noisy, especially in summer
when open windows everywhere were a necessity, and the
bedroom floors were far from comfortable. It was from
the first a sad and even sinister house to me, partly perhaps
on account of the first impression I had of it, at the close
of the Durand régime.

Poor Sir Mortimer could not get over the shock of
his sudden recall for which the Foreign Office could or
would give no reason. After dinner when we retired
together to smoke, he would go over the past few years
wondering what could have gone wrong, or complaining
with justice that he had been over to England in the
summer and had been given no hint whatever that his
recall was contemplated. I heard afterwards that the
reason was simply incompatibility of temperament between
the President and Sir Mortimer. Sir Mortimer who had
lived all his life in the East could not appreciate the
President's Far Western lack of conventional methods,
and the President, who was very human, liked to
be appreciated. This led to something like coldness

between them which the Foreign Office having discovered thought better to end by withdrawing Sir Mortimer. I cannot say whether this reason was well founded or not, but at least the Foreign Office should not, in my opinion, have turned out of office suddenly without a word of apology or previous warning an old and tried servant. The way Sir Mortimer was treated seemed to me then and still seems to me to have been most unjust and uncalled for. Often in later years when I sat in his chair in that same room I wondered whether suddenly and unexpectedly the axe might fall and decapitate me as swiftly. Somehow, many of the dwellers in that old house—it was only built in the 1860's but seemed old in Washington—seemed to have been unfortunate. One or two died there, and others had been retired before their time, others again had left stricken with a mortal disease, and me also the house was not to spare, for some of the saddest days of my life were passed under its roof. So I never loved it, and though many Washingtonians looked on its passing with regret, I have a feeling of satisfaction that it was during my tenure of office as Ambassador that its days were numbered.

The first event of my new life in Washington to which I looked forward eagerly was my presentation to the President. Theodore Roosevelt at that time occupied the attention of the world almost as much as Bismarck did in his day. He certainly competed successfully with the Kaiser for " news value." I had heard so many and so different appreciations of him that I was naturally all agog to meet him and form my own estimate. A few days after my arrival in Washington, Sir Mortimer took me to the White House for the first formal presentation.

The White House naturally interested me. Its comfortable and yet dignified aspect, as an old Colonial country house set in a pleasant garden with lawns and trees and flowering shrubs—though these were, of course, not at their best in mid-November when I arrived— belonged to the good period, æsthetically speaking, of Virginia and at once inspired me with a sense of friendly

WASHINGTON : IN WHITE HOUSE GROUNDS

(*Left to Right*) Sir Esme Howard (British Ambassador), Hon. Charles E. Hughes (Secretary of State), M. Jusserand (French Ambassador)

Theodore Roosevelt
Feb 16th 1908

welcome. There was certainly nothing awe-inspiring or pompous about the White House, neither was there anything sinister. It was, I decided, a distinctly pleasant place.

Secondly I was glad to see that there were no rows of liveried lackeys—there was indeed as old Mrs. Leiter, a well-known hostess in Washington and the mother of the first Lady Curzon and other beautiful daughters, remarked to me sadly, a great lack of " uniformity " about the White House.

Mrs. Leiter was, of course, famous for such sayings, but this is the only one I actually heard drop from her lips. The best I ever heard, though only indirectly, was " Of course, my dear, you should never look a gift horse in the face."

Many of these, like Spoonerisms at Oxford, were doubtless invented, but many were beyond the reach of doubt and did much to enliven Washington Society of that day.

So of " uniformity " there was little at the White House, only perhaps a couple of coloured messengers it the hall and a coloured porter in the portico all dressed in black. We were, however, ushered into the presence of the President by an aide-de-camp in uniform and another was standing near him.

He spoke some time to the Ambassador, during which I was able to observe him. A square-set stocky man of middle height with large gold-rimmed spectacles and a large mouth which he opened wide when speaking, showing very large and gold-filled teeth, a square chin and a wide forehead, a short nose and very vivacious eyes behind his large spectacles, Mr. Roosevelt did not at first sight impress the visitor as an exceptional personality. It was only when he became animated in his conversation that one realised the tremendous vigour and vitality there was in the man. He seemed to be bursting with both mental and physical energy, and so he was. No one round him could tire him. He delighted in taking his staff out for afternoon walks and making them climb with him perpendicular rocks overhanging the Potomac, or insisting on poor old Generals accompanying him on long rides till they nearly fell out of their saddles. Occasionally he would invite certain Ambassadors like M. Jusserand, of whom he was very fond, to walk with him and make them ford Rock Creek when it was in flood. Once I heard that one of his guests was swept down the stream but was fortunately caught by an overhanging branch.

As I watched him I felt that unquestionably his main quality was energy.

When I was introduced he asked me where I had come from, and when he heard it was Crete he at once began to discuss, with knowledge of the subject, the discoveries at Knossos, which he had evidently followed closely. The political events in Crete he, however, cared little about. Next he asked me if I was one of the family of " Belted Will," and quoted from some book of Scott's giving an account of that Border hero of which I was quite ignorant. Then the interview ended but I was quite delighted, because he had come up to my expectations. He was as far from the conventional politician as a powerful hunter is from a hired hack—but I was to find out later that he knew as much of the wiles of the politician as a man could know. Nevertheless he had a just and a generous soul, he genuinely cared for the under dog and was a good friend. But he was also a good hater who did not hide his feelings and he was hated in return, especially by the " Old Guard," or as we should call them the " Die-hards," among the Senators. There is a story that when some Senator told him of the sudden death of one of the " Old Guard," the President only emitted an indistinct sound.

" You don't seem very sorry," said the Senator.

" Sorry ! Of course I'm sorry," said the President. " I'm sorry it's not Senator X," mentioning another of his still more active opponents among the " Old Guard."

I suppose there never was a President who afforded more copy to the pressmen. There was hardly a day when some new tale, true or not didn't much matter, was not telegraphed from one end of the United States to the other.

He adored his children and played with them like a child. There are probably few children who realise that they owe their " Teddy Bears " to him. They all descend from a little bear that was caught, if I remember rightly, while the President was shooting somewhere and which he at once adopted as a member of the family. This bear became a sort of mascot or token of the President in the illustrated papers and was known as the Teddy Bear. It was, of course, soon copied by the toy-makers and has rejoiced the hearts of millions of children ever since.

He loved natural history : trees, birds and beasts he knew well, and we have Lord Grey of Fallodon's word for it that he picked up the songs of English birds with extraordinary facility. He had, indeed, all the charm of an outdoor man.

I cannot pretend that I ever got to know him well, our stations in life were, of course, too far apart, but Isa and I saw him and Mrs. Roosevelt more intimately than most Secretaries because we became close friends of his sister Mrs. Cowles, who occasionally asked us to dine alone with the President and Mrs. Roosevelt so that we could enjoy his wonderfully racy conversation. Besides all his other qualities he had a great knowledge of English literature and his opinion of various writers and books was always interesting. I became frankly a great admirer, but this is anticipating somewhat.

The other men who dominated the Washington scene for me at that time were Senator Cabot Lodge, Chairman of the Senate Committee on Foreign Relations, Mr. Justice Oliver Wendell Holmes of the Supreme Court, and Mr. Henry Adams, a most gifted writer possessed of a mordant wit and a most delicate irony.

Senator Lodge was in appearance a fine gentleman of the old school. Tall and dignified, always carefully groomed and immaculately dressed, widely read and highly cultured, he represented on the one hand the highest rung of the ladder in Boston Society, for was he not related to the Cabots and came from

" Boston, the land of the Bean and the Cod,
Where the Lowells speak only to Cabots and the Cabots speak only to God "

while on the other he represented in politics the old Conservative New England element which drew its inspiration largely from the days of the American Revolution. This naturally gave him in politics an anti-British twist and made him, in his commanding position of Chairman of the Foreign Relations Committee of the Senate, a personage with whom it was necessary if possible to be on good if not friendly terms. Both Isa and I ended by being on a good footing in the Lodge household, and particularly liked Mrs. Lodge, though Senator Lodge, while always royally gracious, appeared to live too much in the stratosphere to be ever intimate with people like us who were neither Cabots nor intellectually brilliant. The only member of the British Embassy with whom he was ever intimate was, I believe, Springy (Cecil Spring Rice) who captured all classes of Washington society from the President downwards by his infectious and mordant wit.

By pure chance Mrs. Lodge and I became friends from the first time we met. It was in this wise.

At one of the first entertainments to which I was bidden after arrival in Washington, I had the good fortune to sit next to her. It was one of the great Sunday luncheons in the house of Mr. and Mrs. Boardman, where leading lights of all sorts were gathered together who could not spare time to lunch out on week days. These luncheons were an institution in Washington.

Mrs. Cabot Lodge realising that I was the new-comer at the British Embassy took me under her wing and began to tell me the names of all the personages around the table. After pointing out one or two Senators, Cabinet Ministers, etc., she started on the millionaires.

" There's so-and-so who's worth twenty million

dollars ; so-and-so said to be worth forty million," and so on.

I looked at her to see in what sort of spirit this information was offered, and saw a twinkle in her eye.

" Please stop, Mrs. Lodge," I said, " or I shall have to get under the table and hide there."

The twinkle developed into a real smile.

" I should like to go with you if you do," she answered.

From that moment there was a sort of understanding between us. I had guessed what was passing through her mind, which was clearly this :

" Here's another Britisher who will swallow anything about all Americans being worshippers of the golden calf. I'll try him and see the effect of my giving him solemnly the alleged fortunes of all the millionaires in the room."

The twinkle in the eye fortunately gave her away and I realised that her feelings about millionaires in the mass were much the same as mine.

This reassured her about the new boy of the British Embassy and the alliance we struck metaphorically under the Boardmans' hospitable table stood me in good stead afterwards.

Henry Adams was on quite a different plane from Senator Lodge though he was an intimate friend both of the President and Senator Lodge. He came from the famous old Boston family which had given two Presidents to the United States in the earliest days of the Republic and has continued to provide the Civil Service of his country with distinguished members ever since. Henry Adams' father had been United States Minister to London during the difficult period of the American Civil War, and the son tells his experiences of that time in perhaps one of the best biographies ever written which he characteristically called *The Education of Henry Adams*. His other claim to immortality as a man of letters is that admirable book *Mont St. Michel and Chartres*, which not only gives an arresting description of these two great mediæval Gothic monuments, but also shows a profound

H

knowledge of the mentality of the period.[1]   Both books are especially interesting as an example of his outlook on life and to read them is like almost hearing him talk in his own house when he would allow himself to be drawn into talking of serious matters.   There was in his conversation a constant play of humour and irony and wit combined with a strong feeling for spiritual values in the things that really matter, and this made him unquestionably one of the most delightful conversationalists I have ever met.   He had a large house in Lafayette Square, now unfortunately pulled down to make way for an apartment house.   Here he entertained from time to time at little luncheons and dinners the intellectual élite of Washington, whether of residents or passing strangers, and it was considered a great honour to be invited to these.   For merely successful business men or politicians he cared nothing.

I appreciated such invitations more than any others at Washington.   I owed them to a good friend and connection of mine, Carlo Milnes Gaskell, who was Henry Adams's greatest friend in England, and gave me a letter to him.   I owe to Carlo Gaskell also an introduction to the works of Anatole France, especially the series *L'Orme du Mail*, etc., and found in them just the same pleasant undercurrent of irony which was such a feature of Henry Adams's conversation.

Even now if I take up *L'Orme du Mail* and read the description of M. Bergeret and the Abbé Lantaigne, of the Sous-Préfet and Madame Worms-Clavelin and the rest, it reminds me vividly of Henry Adams's description of the world around him.   His general attitude to life was perhaps, fully explained by St. Gaudens' wonderful monument to Mrs. Adams in Rock Creek cemetery, which is probably the sculptor's masterpiece.   The seated veiled figure waiting—for what ?

The last personality I shall endeavour to give a short sketch of was very different but also very striking, Justice

---

[1] Henry Adams was the author of a well known History of America and Professor Emeritus of Harvard, but his two great works are the two mentioned above. His most entertaining *Letters*, 1858–1891, were published by the Riverside Press, Cambridge, Mass., 1930.

Oliver Wendell Holmes of the Supreme Court. He was of course, also a Bostonian and the son of a father of high repute in the literary world. A man of very distinguished appearance and very distinguished courtesy to all, he was also a great judge, whose decisions on the Supreme Court Bench are likely to be quoted for many years to come. Though he came of a true blue Conservative New England stock, his ideas on questions of social reform were too far advanced to be altogether in harmony with those of most of his colleagues. He was, in fact, a pioneer. He and his wife also did us the honour of extending to us their friendship and inviting us from time to time to intimate luncheons or dinners both at Washington and at their house in the country on the " North Shore," near Boston. where we used to spend our summers during this term of my service at the Embassy and later when I was Ambassador.

Justice Holmes began his career as an officer on the northern side in the Civil War and was actually left for dead on the field of battle. But he lived to be for many years a member of the Supreme Court and only died in 1934, at a very advanced age. His was a very noble character incapable of any meanness or trickery, and his judgments on passing events and on persons were always sound and valuable perhaps because like Mr. Adams's they contained a good admixture of irony.

The closest and most intimate friend, however, whom I made at that time and who has always remained the same for me, was James R. Garfield, Secretary for the Interior, one of the youngest members of the President's Cabinet and one of his special group of young men. He was the son of President Garfield, who was assassinated by a maniac in 1881. His was one of the finest characters I have ever known, and it was a real privilege to number him and all his family among my close friends.

He taught me, I think, more about American mentality than anyone else and I am always deeply grateful for the lesson.

This account of our Washington friends of that time

would not be complete without a mention of Mrs. Cameron, who also belonged to the literary *coterie* of Henry Adams and Cabot Lodge. She was the daughter of General Sherman who went " marching through Georgia " in the American Civil War, and whose equestrian statue by St. Gaudens stands close to the entrance of Central Park, New York, rivalling the Adams Memorial at Washington as one of that sculptor's most famous works. I have certainly never seen any equestrian statue which equalled it in producing a sense of steady unswerving forward movement.

Mrs. Cameron was a beautiful woman and a delightful hostess who dispensed eclectic hospitality in a pleasant old mansion in Lafayette Square near Henry Adams' house. Her house has now been, I believe, turned into a club. She was a witty and a brilliant talker as were nearly all those who lived and moved constantly in the Adams planetary system. Her beautiful and most attractive daughter Martha married, while we were in Washington for the first time, Ronald Lindsay, then Secretary now Ambassador in Washington. Martha Lindsay's early death deeply grieved all her friends and deprived the British diplomatic service of one who would have most delightfully adorned any of our Missions abroad.

Among many other friends I must especially note two families who have remained close and kind friends up to now, the Hennen Jennings and the Boardmans. Mr. Jennings had been a mining engineer in South Africa and had lived many years in London, and my introduction to the Boardman family dated from 1888 when I was a young Secretary in Berlin and Miss Mabel Boardman was acting as hostess of the American Legation for her uncle Mr. Phelps, the American Minister. She afterwards became one of the three Commissioners or Governors of the district of Columbia in which Washington is situated. She is, I believe, the only woman who has held this post. Through Mrs. Jennings and her son Coleman, and through Miss Boardman and her sisters, Mrs. Murray Crane and Mrs. Keep, whom we see whenever they come to England and with whom we correspond, we manage still to keep in touch with the Washington scene.

After the Durands left, the Embassy settled down quietly to its ordinary work of which there was always more than enough in Washington.

Suddenly a bolt fell upon us out of the blue sky.

There occurred on January 14th, 1907, a terrific earthquake at Kingston, Jamaica, in which and in the fires that followed it innumerable buildings not only in Kingston but also in Port Royal and St. Andrews were destroyed, and over one thousand people lost their lives, while numbers more were injured. The conflagration lasted several days.

The United States Government immediately fitted out a squadron of three men-of-war under Admiral Davis, the brother of Mrs. Cabot Lodge, with every kind of medical aid and comfort for the wounded as well as tents, food and all necessaries to meet such a calamity.

These arrived on January 17th and were welcomed most heartily by the inhabitants and the authorities.

A day or two later, however, news came trickling through that relations were strained between the Governor of Jamaica, Sir Alexander Swettenham, and Admiral Davis. The latter had it seemed, at the request of certain American citizens, who for some reason feared that the coloured population were about to run amok against the whites, landed marines without, as would of course have been correct according to the rules of International Law, requesting permission of the Governor. The latter politely, but somewhat curtly perhaps, pointed this out to the Admiral, who withdrew the marines on board. A day or two later the American colony of Kingston again sent an urgent message to the Admiral to land men to protect them from imminent danger. The Admiral sent hasty messages to the Governor to ask permission but, so it was reported, his messengers could not find His Excellency who was, it was said, engaged in passing buckets of water to help put out the fire which was still raging. The Admiral then yielded to the urgent appeals of his fellow citizens and again landed marines.

When the Governor was informed of this he at once wrote the Admiral what is vulgarly called a " snorter," and the Admiral not only withdrew his marines but his doctors and nurses, tents and medical comforts and sailed home on January 19th.

The effect of this incident in the United States can better be imagined than described. Every paper had enormous headlines, Governor Swettenham's letter was published and denounced as a gross and gratuitous insult from one end of the country to the other.

On the morning of the 20th, I awoke to find the papers full of these purple passages. Hardly had I finished breakfast when I was called to the telephone and told the President wanted to speak to me. I had scarcely been two months in charge at Washington and here already was what promised to be a first class quarrel. Now the President was calling me up on the telephone at an early hour of the morning. He was clearly anxious to make some communication to me if he took this unusual step. What could it be ? I went to the telephone with great misgivings, but I was much relieved when I heard the President's voice coming cheerful and friendly over the wires :

PRESIDENT : " Have you seen all the row there is in the papers this morning over that Jamaica business ? "

I : " Yes, Mr. President."

PRESIDENT : " Well, we've got to stop it. Will you send your Government a telegram at once asking them to let me have a friendly message of some kind expressing their regret at the language used by Governor Swettenham in his letter to Admiral Davis. The Admiral was, no doubt, mistaken in landing his marines a second time without the Governor's permission but that was no reason in the circumstances for the Governor to use such strong language about it. After all we and the Admiral were only doing what we could to help in a great calamity. Will you then telegraph in that sense to your Government to send me a message which I can publish and stop all this pother ? "

I : " I will send off the telegram this morning, Mr. President."

PRESIDENT : " That's all right. Then you'll see all this row will stop at once."

This seemed to me a new, unconventional and very pleasant way of dealing with deplorable incidents and with an immense feeling of relief I sat down to draft the telegram to Sir Edward Grey, which went off immediately.

Meanwhile it seemed that the same idea had occurred to him, for he had asked the American Ambassador in London to cable to Washington a message such as the President had asked for. This was published in the press the following day and all agitation in the newspapers stopped as if by magic. The President was as good as his word.

A few days after he asked me to go round to the White House and received me in the little study where the President used to work in the days before the new offices were built. The study opened out on to an ante-room, which was always filled with reporters, and the door was open between the two rooms. I reproduce the conversation as I remember it :

THE PRESIDENT : " Well, we stopped that newspaper row, didn't we ? "

I : " You did, Mr. President."

THE PRESIDENT : " Anyhow, your Government helped. I was really sorry for them being put in a position like that. The fact is I've been suffering a lot lately from prize idiots myself. You've heard of course about X. and Y."

I said I had read some of the correspondence lately published in the papers. It is unnecessary to enter here into the epistolary controversy between Mrs. Y.Z. and the President which began " My dear Theodore " and " My dear Y," and ended " Mrs. Z presents her compliments, etc." What it was all about few people seemed to care and certainly no one remembers, but when Mrs. Z.

published the letters they reverberated all round the echoing arches of the American Press. The President was a little irritated, but the public turned to some other sensation in a day or two.

So the President, thinking of these letters, said to me :
" I, too, have suffered lately from prize idiots," and then a sudden inspiration occurred to him and he said with the laugh of a boy scoring off another :
" I'll tell you what we can do. We'll get a divorce for Y. and send her down to Jamaica where she can marry Swettenham and then they will both live happily ever after."

I have already said that in principle I have always enjoyed the jokes of Royalties, and a President is temporarily a Royalty, so I shamelessly enjoyed this one, particularly as the President's mirth was really infectious and his informal way of treating diplomatic incidents was to me novel and pleasing. But I began to understand why a grave and reverend Signor like Sir Mortimer Durand, who had learnt his diplomacy in Eastern countries, could not appreciate him nor he Sir Mortimer.

I searched the papers next day to see if any of the reporters in the room adjoining, who must have heard every word of the President's discourse, had published any part of it. There was not a word, and yet it is easy to see what a scoop it would have made. I could only imagine that these reporters were put on their honour not to divulge anything they heard in the White House and that they carefully observed that rule. I may say that I never knew an American pressman give away any statement which had been made to him in confidence.

After this high wind in Jamaica nothing more disturbed the ordinary course of things at the Embassy during my first Chargéship, but I was thankful when the new Ambassador, Mr. James Bryce, arrived with Mrs. Bryce and relieved me of the responsibility of running the Embassy.

I had hardly ever met Mr. Bryce before but I knew of him, of course, as the author of the *American Commonwealth*, which was then and still is the standard work on the subject, and another standard work, *The Holy Roman Empire*. Also I knew of him as a Liberal statesman of the old school who had been more than once in the Cabinet and up to recently had been Secretary of State for Ireland, always one of the most thorny posts in the Government. I knew of him as Professor of Civil Law at Oxford, as a great Latin scholar and as a ready debater in the House of Commons. Altogether I looked forward to his régime with some trepidation as I feared it would be too highbrow for me.

What was, therefore, my relief and delight when after he had been in Washington two or three weeks he confided to me that he had also looked forward to his relations with a staff of career diplomats with forebodings, fearing that he would be criticised for all sorts of shortcomings in conventional etiquette and ambassadorial dignity, but he found we were all really quite friendly and easy to get on with.

Personally I may say that from the first I found him the most agreeable of Chiefs. He was full of information on every conceivable subject and a more delightful companion for an afternoon walk it would be impossible to imagine. The only difficulty was that he was always overflowing with curiosity about everything that met the eye or ear, natural history, geology, botany, anthropology, astronomy as well as history, geography and literature, all had their well stocked pigeon-holes in his mind. If I ever ventured an opinion, for which he had previously asked, since I never gave one unasked, he would speedily demolish it with such a mass of references and quotations that I was quickly snuffed out. The accuracy of his memory was amazing.

Yet with all this there was nothing the least superior in his manner. Far from it ; while really giving instruction, he always seemed to be seeking it. In the United States he enjoyed an exceptional position on account of his *American Commonwealth* and other books. All knew that even when he criticised he was truly friendly and, therefore, whatever he said in public speeches passed without question. It was Mr. Bryce speaking and that was enough. It was an enormous advantage to him that he could make a speech worth listening to on every conceivable subject from ice caps to deserts, from political Constitutions to astral bodies. Every city wanted to hear him, every University wanted to give him a degree. We never had before and never shall have again an Ambassador so universally known or so universally acceptable.

With all this mental energy, his physical energy was also stupendous. He had been a great mountaineer in his day and was the first known man to climb Mount Ararat, which he did alone, his porters, I believe, having deserted him half way up. Up to the last in the United States he never could see a mountain or hill of any kind without wanting at once to climb it and, having little or no sense of time or of what could be accomplished in a given time, he would often, to the despair of Mrs. Bryce, start off to climb some hill which would take at least four or five hours only two hours before dinner when guests were coming to dine.

Such was Mr. Bryce, and I found his companionship most delightful. One anecdote of him I must tell. Years after the time of which I am writing Lord and Lady Bryce, as they then were, came to stay with us at the Embassy in Madrid. He wanted, of course, to see everything, and after a tiring day at Toledo (he must have been seventy-seven years of age) he was suddenly taken with very severe internal pains during the night. I sent for the best Spanish doctor who, according to the traditions of the country, did not arrive for more than an hour.

Meanwhile Lord Bryce holding tight on to the bars at the head of the bed was groaning in pain. I asked if he would rather I left the room. He begged me to stay saying it was a distraction to talk to me. Then he begged me to excuse his groaning saying he had hardly ever been ill in his life and had never suffered severe pain before. From that he went on to speak of certain characters in history who while not lacking in physical courage could not support pain, whereas others showed no signs of suffering even when afflicted with the most grievous tortures. Again it was well known that there were some tribes of Indians, whom he named, who could support without a murmur excruciating agonies which other Indians would die under. Did some people actually feel more than others ? And so he went on for about forty minutes with one of the most interesting lectures on pain I have ever had in my life, and entirely forgot his own. Finally, to my infinite joy the doctor came and speedily relieved his sufferings.

I had found a most comfortable house, No. 2208 Massachusetts Avenue, with an exceptionally kind land-lord, Mr. Halstead, the American Consul General at Montreal, who allowed me to use all his bedroom furniture gratis which was, naturally, a great saving to me. We remained on the friendliest terms for years. Isa and the two children arrived about February and we were quickly comfortably installed. My work at the Embassy was not excessive, the main business at the time being the negotia-tion of a Claims Convention to settle up an accumulation of claims on either side, some dating back nearly a hundred years. This Mr. Bryce chose to take almost entirely on his own shoulders with the help of the very able head of the Chancery, Mr. George Young[1], who, being a glutton for work only handed out to me whatever he did not think he could do better himself, which was truly very little. So the spring passed happily enough. We saw the Japanese cherry-flowers in the Potomac Park which, with Rock Creek Park, forms a chain of public recreation grounds such as surely no other capital can boast. Potomac Park is a flat well planted peninsular between the wide Potomac river and a branch of the same, with views up and down the lakelike sheet of water, while Rock Creek Park consists of woodland several miles in length in the beautiful valley of Rock Creek with roads and riding paths which are enchanting in spring and autumn, and are the haunt of many of the bright coloured

[1] Now Sir George Young, Bt.

American birds, cardinals, blue birds, indigo birds, oriels and many others not to mention an occasional humming bird in summer. Further afield there were most pleasant excursions down the Potomac river to Mount Vernon, Washington's lovely old home, or up the river to the Potomac falls among rocks and forest trees which had hardly been touched.

On April 26th, 1907, there was to be a great celebration of the tercentenary of the first founding of Jamestown on the James River, the beginning of the real history of Virginia and indeed of the United States, which, of course, preceded by many years the landing of the Pilgrims on the Rock of Plymouth. The State of Virginia had planned a memorial exhibition in honour of the occasion. Foreign Governments were asked to send ships, the President was to deliver the inaugural address, foreign representatives of all degrees were to be invited to be present. The Bryces were going, and I also accepted the invitation. The evening before the 26th, all the Diplomats who had accepted went on board one of the large and commodious river steamers that plied on the Potomac, specially chartered for us, and after dinner we sat about on deck watching the pleasant wooded banks of the Potomac glide past in the semi-darkness of a perfect starlit night. We arrived at our destination about 7 a.m. on the James River opposite the island on which the original Jamestown stood, of which only a few ruined or semi-ruined buildings remained.

All were quickly up on deck, there being no baths on board to delay the unco-clean. The President's yacht *Mayflower* steamed up and down between the lines of the International squadrons at Hampton Roads, all ships being dressed and royal salutes fired. The American battleships covered a thin line of about four miles and there were besides British, German, Austrian, Argentine and other cruisers present.

At 9 a.m. our steamer drew up alongside a rickety pier, still in the course of construction, and after scrambling for strange vehicles, some of which must have been fully a hundred years old, harnessed both to horses, mules and even jackasses, we were driven over unfinished sandy roads between the unfinished buildings of the exhibition to the stand where the President was to give his opening address. Some distinguished foreigners and Senators could find no conveyances at all and had to trudge about a mile and a half in loose sand under a hot sun to the stand. This did not improve their tempers, but throughout the day it was a case of each for himself and the devil take the hindmost.

The President arrived at eleven, and the ceremony began with an apparently interminable prayer and a lengthy historical lecture by the President of the Exhibition. Then came Mr. Roosevelt's turn. With the strategic eye of a general he quickly saw that standing on the platform where he was he would not be seen by at least half the crowd. He leapt up on to the table in front of him, to the delight of all, and from there addressed the audience for about an hour on every possible subject —historical, political and moral. It was interesting, characteristic and entertaining.

By the time this was over we were all hungry and, having been given tickets for a " light lunch," we went in search of it. The Austrian and Russian Ambassadors whom I followed were led by mistake into a room on the first floor with a good luncheon spread for about fifty guests. The Baron von Hengelmüller, the Austrian, put his eyeglass into his eye and examined with care the names on the cards. A coloured manservant tapped him on the shoulder.

" Whose you lookin' for ? " he asked.

" I am the Austrian Ambassador," replied the Baron, with dignity.

" Ah knows nuthin' 'bout dat," said the darkie, " dis place for de President an' his friends. All odders down below wid de crowd."

The Ambassador lost control of himself and dropped his eyeglass which we helped him to recover. He was literally speechless, but the Russian Ambassador helped

him from the room and slowly we descended to the
ground floor where we found our colleagues and about
five hundred other persons struggling round a small
table at which extremely substantial ham sandwiches
and small cups of black coffee were being handed
out by an uninterested darkie. I found the French
Ambassadress, the ever-charming Madame Jusserand,
sitting exhausted on a heap of planks (for the whole
building was entirely unfinished) and Mr. and Mrs.
Bryce sitting on empty barrels. I managed with the help
of a French Secretary to get them ham sandwiches and
coffee. By the time my French friend and I had secured
a bite for ourselves it was half-past three. We obtained
a small carriage with two asses and drove back to the
pier, passing on the way the Austrian Ambassador, with
his arms crossed and his head bowed on his breast, like
Napoleon after Waterloo, driving hard in the wrong
direction away from the river. Arrived at the unfinished
pier we again found Madame Jusserand seated quite
exhausted on a pile of planks without the Ambassador,
and surrounded by a circle of coloured men who gazed
at her with great interest. She said her husband had
gone to a little summer hotel near-by for a cup of tea.
We persuaded her to join us and go there too. There
we found the Bryces also and, having refreshed ourselves
with tea and bread and tinned butter, we returned to the
pier and so to the ship well pleased.

M. Jusserand in after days referred to this famous
inaugural ceremony as the " Fast Day of Jamestown,"
but my French friend and I declared we had never
enjoyed any opening ceremony so much—which was
quite true.

Washington is indeed a most pleasant residence from
October to July. But the heat from July to October is
more than tropical, and I would far rather spend a
summer in the West Indies than in Washington. I speak
from experience, having sampled both. It is reported
that a citizen of Washington and one of a Middle Western
town, each zealous for the honour of his native city, made

a bet that an egg could more quickly be fried on the pavement of his home town without artificial heat than on that of the other man. Washington apparently won hands down and I can well believe it.

In the summer it was the custom in those days for all the Ambassadors and Ministers to go into summer quarters, leaving one or two Secretaries behind in Washington to hold the fort. Everyone who could did this, from the President down, and business almost ceased in Washington from July to mid-September or October.

The socially-minded went to such places as Newport or Long Island. Those who, like the Bryces, didn't care for Society chose quieter spots. In the summer of 1907 Mr. and Mrs. Bryce chose a little place, Intervale, in the White Mountains, so quiet that it nearly caused a mutiny among the unmarried Secretaries who naturally liked places where invitations to luncheons and dinners flowed in. This did not matter to Isa and me and the children. We had a nice house and large garden and a wood behind it. For recreation there were some bad tennis courts and a very poor golf course where Mr. Bryce and I sometimes played. I once sliced a ball badly and hit him in the back. He smiled in a pained way and said :

" I never suspected you of being capable of trying to win a hole in that way."

But his real recreation was walking up every mountain within a radius of about fifteen miles, generally followed by some panting members of his staff with their tongues hanging out.

In September, 1907, I went for a short tour in Eastern Canada, which I had hardly yet visited, and with the help of the Chief Justice, Sir Charles Fitzpatrick, who acted as my good fairy all through, I got to know a number of very interesting people in Toronto, Ottawa, Montreal and Quebec, among whom the most noteworthy were Sir Wilfrid Laurier, and the President of the Canadian Pacific Railway, the Chairman of the Bank of Montreal, the Director of the Allan Line, various lights in the

Catholic and in the Protestant educational world, and particularly Mr. Mackenzie King, who has always remained our good friend and was, when we returned to America in 1924 and revisited Canada, always most kindly and helpful.

I enjoyed Canada enormously. It had a distinct flavour of its own, different both from the Old Country over the seas and the great New Country to the south. It seemed to me to lie somewhere between, with much of the energy and hustling capacity of the American world and at the same time much of the steady self-control of the English.

French Canada also attracted me greatly. It was refreshing to find so wholly and sincerely Catholic a spirit in the New World. I suppose there were few parts of Europe, except perhaps Austria, which could be compared to Quebec in that respect.

Besides making all these acquaintances and learning what I could about the country, I spent—always with the help of Sir Charles Fitzpatrick—three days fishing in a camp north of Pointe-à-Pic or Murray Bay on the St. Lawrence and caught numerous trout. One morning, resting about midday after fishing from 6 a.m., I heard the rustling of wings and looking up saw a ruby-throat humming-bird investigating a red fly which was on my cast—for they are always attracted by red objects. I told this story years after at an annual meeting of the Royal Society for the Protection of Birds to illustrate the extraordinary power of the wing muscles of even the smallest birds which travel such immense distances, in order to drive home the cruelty of keeping wild birds in cages. I am afraid that many thought I was telling a fishing story, but it was perfectly true, and, besides, having seen thousands of humming birds I could not make a mistake.

My three weeks in Canada were to have ended with a party got up by Sir Charles going down the Saguenay River from Lake St. John in canoes and shooting the famous rapids. When we got to Lake St. John the water was terribly high and the Saguenay River was so threatening that none of the canoe guides would risk the rapids except one who was constantly drunk. But each one of the four of us, three men and one lady, was so afraid of appearing afraid that we all said we would go with the drunken canoeist, though another adventurous party had all been drowned a few days before.

The next morning when we were to start it poured with rain. We looked gloomily out of the windows pretending to hope that it would clear up. To pass away the time I went out in a canoe and fished for *ouananiche*, a kind of fresh-water salmon, and caught two. They are said to be the most sporting fish in the world and these lived up to their reputation.

When I got back to the hotel, as it was still pouring in torrents, we decided we had better return by the next steamer across the lake. Curiously enough the party, instead of being depressed as it was at breakfast, had become one of the liveliest imaginable. All gloom was banished on the way back to Pointe-à-Pic.

To conclude my tour I stayed for two or three days in the Citadel at Quebec with Lord Grey, the Governor-General, whose company was always of the best. The citadel is a most attractive house and is part of the French fortification which still dominates the old town.

This trip to Canada was very useful to me because, having much to do with Canadian questions, of which there were many to deal with at Washington, it was helpful to know personally leading men on the other side of the border. I was especially grateful to Sir Charles Fitzpatrick for assisting me in the way he did, and look back to his friendship as one of my pleasantest bonds with Canada.

As the Bryces did not take any leave that year I seized the opportunity of going in November to Tobago to see my friend Thorleif Orde and the plantation at Louis d'Or and sailed from New York for Trinidad after the Embassy had returned to Washington. Tobago I found as enchanting as ever but, unfortunately, after ten years of planting castilloa it had become clear that that tree would

I

never produce enough rubber to make planting it a paying proposition even at the enormously high prices obtaining in those days. Thorleif wisely during the past year or two had taken to planting cacao instead of rubber and now we were compelled to cut down the castilloa trees everywhere except the plantation roads and plant cacao instead. It went to my heart to condemn those trees now grown tall which we had planted together with such high hopes ten years ago. It was, moreover, most humiliating to have to report to the directors at home the failure of our rubber plantation.

It was doubly hard on Thorleif, however, who had dedicated his life to making the plantation a paying concern. Nevertheless cacao seemed then to offer good prospects also. The trees grew remarkably well at Louis d'Or and we hoped that in four or five years more we should be making fair profits. I therefore enjoyed my visit, the resumption of life as a planter and particularly the company of my friend, and I left far from hopeless over future prospects and promising to return again soon. My next visit was in 1929. So it is with the plans of mice and men.

I got back to Washington about the end of November, and on December 23rd Hubert was born there in our house on Massachusetts Avenue.

The winter passed pleasantly. We largely increased our circle of friends, and invitations to lunch and dine poured in. There was only one drawback to this—the public carriages of Washington called Herdics, from the individual who invented them as Hansoms were called after their inventor. These Herdics were like old-fashioned wagonettes, very uncomfortable, not over clean, and lit by a paraffin lamp which hung from the roof and took a delight in dripping oil on to the evening gowns of ladies. The Herdic horses seemed all to be centenarians which made me hope that they were well treated. The price for taking one of these vehicles out to dinner and back amounted to about 15s. or 16s., so that dining out became a serious expense in a budget already much cramped by an increasing family.

For an Englishman or any European, Washington life was extraordinarily expensive and the salaries were not in those days proportionate to the expense. Indeed, my house rent, which was by no means high for Washington, swallowed up two-thirds of my salary.

I found that after a year in the United States I was badly out of pocket. I decided that I could not manage another winter and asked for an exchange, much to my own sorrow, for I hated leaving Mr. and Mrs. Bryce and the many good friends I had in Washington. The Foreign Office demurred at first but finally was persuaded and informed me that I could be transferred to Vienna as First Secretary after Mr. Bryce's leave in the summer, during which they wished me to remain on as Chargé d'Affaires. This suited me well as there was extra pay for a Chargé d'Affaires that would enable me to stay on for those months without serious loss. So it was arranged.

That spring was particularly pleasing to me for Esmetto being now about five years old was able to take little walks with me along Rock Creek. His joy in finding new flowers and seeing new birds was so vivid that it communicated itself to me, and every Sunday morning after Mass we used to sally forth together, I often carrying him pick-a-back. That was a thing which, I suppose, a First Secretary of Embassy could hardly do in a major European capital without loss of—what shall I say ?—of face, but Washington was still kindly enough —and small enough in size but big enough in heart—not to take offence. Two or three excursions I made, mostly with Victor Sturdy, our Honorary Attaché, to Williamsburg, the old capital of Virginia in the Colonial days, a wholly delightful bit of old world America which is scarcely spoiled, the home of the William and Mary College and still adorned by the statue of the last British Governor of Virginia, Lord Botetourt ; to " Biltmore," George Vanderbilt's magnificent French Renaissance château in North Carolina ; to Charlestown, the capital of South Carolina, an old-fashioned city with many delightful reminiscences of Colonial days, and lastly to Savannah, the capital of Georgia, much less attractive, but with one of the most beautiful cemeteries I ever saw. This burial place is divided by avenues at right-angles, formed of very old ilexes from the branches of which hang long sprays of that grey moss known as Old Man's Beard. This waves to and fro in the wind, producing a curiously eerie effect. The trees are so thick that even on the brightest day there is a twilight in the long avenues from which one looks out at the open squares filled with brilliant southern flowers and birds (including innumerable humming-birds), making a most violent contrast with the gloom of the avenues. The place impressed me deeply and the memory of it still haunts me. It stood, a real symbol of the proximity of life and death, but here the dead were out in the sunlight with the flowers and birds and the quick wandered in the dark avenues hung with dead man's beard.

Two very typical events in the American scene I attended during my first term at Washington. The first of these characteristic events was as follows.

The adjournment of the House of Representatives at the close of a Session of Congress was, in those days and may be still, an interesting and entertaining spectacle for Europeans accustomed to a certain old-fashioned solemnity in such ceremonies. Here is an account from a letter written to my brother Stafford of what I saw in the House on March 4th, 1907 :

> The Senate had not finished its business by 12 o'clock (by which time all Bills must be passed and sent up to the President for signature if they are to become Law) so the clocks in the House were solemnly put back twenty-five minutes, a man bringing in a ladder up which he climbed in order to reach the clock and turn back the hands in full view of all present. During the twenty-five minutes the Members had a " recess " till all was finished, and amused themselves by singing Glees—remarkably well—and waving American flags large and small in time. Finally the member who occupied the Speaker's chair *pro tem* announced: " The gentleman from Missouri will now whistle." Then a young member got up on

the rostrum under the Speaker's chair and began whistling various airs in a curious way that sounded like whistling two notes at a time. He was loudly applauded. When the hands of the clock pointed to five minutes to midday, the Speaker resumed the chair and, after thanking the House for a complimentary resolution, he declared as the hands reached twelve that the fifty-ninth Congress was ended and brought down his " gavil "—which is like an auctioneer's hammer—smartly on the desk before him. Then everyone crowded onto the floor of the House and shook hands with everyone else.

The whole scene for its sheer youthful gaiety reminded me of the end of a term at Harrow ; it was like the animal spirits of boys let free. That is perhaps what I meant when, in speaking of books which to me represent certain countries, I said in my former volume that I had chosen Mark Twain's *Tom Sawyer* and *Huckleberry Finn* as representing America for me.

The second of these events was the Republican Convention held in June, 1908, in Chicago, which Mr. Bryce and I attended with one or two other members of the Embassy, including Captain Hood[1], our Naval Attaché.

For those readers who may not be familiar with American political machinery it is, perhaps, necessary to explain that these great Party Conventions are held every four years, about six months before the Presidential Elections take place, in order to select the Republican or the Democratic candidates. The Convention we attended in 1908 was called for the purpose of selecting the Republican candidate to succeed Mr. Roosevelt who declined to " run " for a third term, though he had a large number of supporters all through the country who were urging him to do so.

Instead of this he gave the whole weight of his support, which was enormous, to Mr. William Howard Taft, who was his Secretary for War during the latter part of his administration.

Mr. Taft was a first-rate lawyer and was, before joining President Roosevelt's Cabinet, Governor of the

[1] Admiral Sir Horace Hood, who went down with his ship at the battle of Jutland.

Philippines. After being President of the United States, he became Chief Justice of the Supreme Court of the United States. He was a man of the kindliest possible disposition, fond of relaxing from the pressure of hard work with the help of a good story or joke but he was, perhaps, too kindly to adapt himself to the hurly-burly of American politics. He never could take his gloves off no matter against whom he was boxing.

Shortly after my return to the United States in 1924 as Ambassador, I went into the Supreme Court and sat down just to hear what was going on. Mr. Taft was presiding. Presently I saw him call a messenger and give him a paper on which he had written something. The messenger, to my great surprise, came straight to me and handed me the paper on which was written, " Welcome to this Chamber from which all insomnia is banished. W. H. Taft." As he had not seen me for many years I was greatly astonished and flattered at being recognised.

The local Republican Committee of Chicago, hearing that Mr. Bryce was coming to the Convention naturally invited him to dinner, and he thought fit to consult me as to what he should do about it. He said that he felt they might be hurt if he did not accept while, on the other hand, to accept might suggest too much sympathy with one Party to be quite proper in a diplomat. We talked it over together, and finally came to the conclusion that it would be all right if he took them into his confidence and told the Committee he would be glad to accept on condition that some Democrats should also be invited. I was included in the invitation and naturally went with my Chief. Some amusing speeches were made after the dinner and jests of a friendly kind were indulged in at the expense of both Mr. Bryce and the Democrats. I remember particularly the reply of the leading Democrat, who said that he was extremely flattered at being asked to meet the British Ambassador on such an occasion, especially as he had been given to understand that his presence there was necessary in order to enable the Ambassador to keep up his reputation for comparative impartiality. What, however, rejoiced him still more as a Democrat was the fact that in order to establish the balance between the two parties he noticed that his Republican friends seemed to consider that three or four Democrats were equal in weight and importance to something like fifty Republicans. This brought down the House and it was clear that there need have been no fear of anything like unpleasantness between the respective members of the two Parties in Chicago on such an occasion.

The Republican Party was in 1908 so cloven in two by its progressive and " die hard " or " stand pat " factions that it was generally expected that at the Republican Convention there would be war to the knife between the two and that there might even be a split. President Roosevelt was, of course, the champion and leader of the Progressives or Liberals while the " old gang " in the Senate and Speaker " Joe " Cannon in the House represented the " stand patters."

What made the situation still more complicated was that there was a certain sympathy springing up between the Radicals among the Democrats and the Progressives among the Republicans, and consequently between the Republican and the Democratic " stand patters ", to the distress and bewilderment of the professional politicians or Party bosses. To explain the situation I sent home to my brother Stafford a cartoon from *Puck* of that date which seemed to give the most concise description of the state of the political parties. This cartoon was called " The Elephass and the Jackaphant." It was and still is the custom in political cartoons to depict the Republican Party as an Elephant and the Democratic Party as a Jackass. This cartoon explained itself. The bewilderment of the professional politician was highly entertaining to the outsider.

I remember, however, one night at dinner with the Bryces some American wit giving an even more cynical description of the two Parties which he said were now nothing but two empty bottles with the old labels still stuck fast upon them. As a matter of fact it seemed to me then that only their respective Party machines kept these Parties with any semblance of unity within themselves and the machines worked on the plan of the spoils to the victors.

A description of this Republican Convention which I wrote home to Stafford at the time was as follows :—

> I had a very interesting time in Chicago during the Republican Convention, though in comparison with other Conventions it was not an exciting one. Taft was sure of a nomination, for as someone said, the delegates (of the different States) were iron bound and copper riveted to him.

While the delegates on the floor of the hall, who had the right to vote, were thus all, or practically all, bound beforehand, this was, of course, not so with the spectators in the galleries who did their best to stampede the delegates for Roosevelt. The great interest of this Convention thereby lay in the possibility of their design being successful. On the second day an organised cheering boom for Roosevelt was started. Senator Cabot Lodge, the Chairman of the Convention, being an old political hand, apparently had no fear of this upsetting the prearranged plan of the Convention which was to nominate Taft. He let the galleries cheer themselves hoarse. There was one man not far from me who as soon as the cheering seemed about to die down brought out a huge megaphone and bellowed, " Roosevelt . . . Roosevelt ! " which was at once taken up in other parts of the building. I sat through thirty-two minutes of it carefully timed on my watch and then, seeing my friend with the megaphone about to rekindle the blaze after it seemed quite dead, I felt I had had enough and left. The cheer really did end five minutes later, but to the general sorrow it was not a record one for some other popular favourite had had a three-quarters of an hour cheer, if I am not mistaken, on a previous occasion.

Yet it must have been good while it lasted, for I wrote :—

> Men stamped about, yapped like dogs and miaoued like cats, shouted in megaphones, in fact did anything that could make a

noise. A greater pandemonium it would be impossible to conceive. Enthusiasm which was somewhat of the made-to-order kind reached its highest pitch when one of the Pressmen produced a large Teddy Bear (Price $25.00) and held it up. Then the cheering became deafening—but the delegates showed no signs of being moved and hardly cheered at all, so the Teddy Bear was passed in among them and came to a bad end being torn to pieces in a scuffle.

Then we had a stuffed elephant decorated with the American colours paraded about. He was sitting on his haunches and had a very tired look on his face.

The Texas delegation, however, got the prize for conventional (or should it be *un*conventional ?) wit when they paraded round the hall with a large banner bearing apparently the following legend :

So Texas 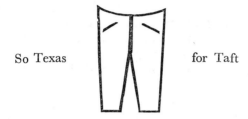 for Taft

which looked at first like a tailor's advertisement but when the banner drew near one read in smaller letters above :

As pants the harte for cooling streams

My letter continued :

In spite of the row, the talking of the spectators in the galleries of the hall, of whom there are said to have been from twelve to fourteen thousand, the business of the Convention was carried on with the greatest order and method. Everything was cut and dried and arranged in Committee the night before and the delegates had practically no word to say. The actual voting which was done openly was, however, exciting (for a stranger of course who did not know the ropes). The Clerk of the Convention stands at the edge of the platform and calls out the names of the States in alphabetical order " Alabama, sixteen votes." Then the head of the Alabama delegation gets up and answers " Alabama sixteen votes for Taft " or " ten votes for Taft," " six for Fairbanks " as the case may be. If it had been a near thing the excitement would have been too thrilling, as it was it was quite exciting enough.

Altogether it was a most interesting experience. There were crowds of professional politicians at the great hotel where they all congregated. As a body they were what one would expect : fat, coarse-looking men generally with the end of a cigar stuck into one side of their mouths. The body of delegates came later. They were mostly a lot of nice-looking old farmers and artisans, but the " bosses " were the fat, clean-shaven men with the cigars.

This gives a lightning impression of the 1908 Republican Convention as it struck me, a perfect stranger to such events. I dare say now the political bosses have entirely changed and look like the Hermes of Praxiteles. The man I most admired was, however, Senator Cabot Lodge, who, as Chairman, sat quite unmoved, cool and collected, through the worst part of the pandemonium. He evidently knew just how far he could let it go without upsetting the coach. My admiration for him increased greatly from that moment.

I wrote in the same letter dated " Manchester-by-the-Sea," July 4th, 1908 :—

I was waked about five this morning by the sound of much firing and thought at first there must be a revolution till I recovered my wits and remembered it was the fourth of July, Independence Day, when every self-respecting American boy does what in him lies to make life hideous with the noise of crackers and pistol shots and the smell of gunpowder. This generally results in several thousand casualties during the day every year, but it is all borne with a patience that can only be compared with the patience this long-suffering people show towards bosses, grafters and other abuses. Not being able to sleep I got up at six and wandered down into the little town. The streets and sidewalks were littered with the remnants of squibs and crackers. Small boys not older than five or six were busy lighting more with a determined air and in the centre of the town, where four roads cross, about a dozen men and and several older boys were standing on the sidewalk and with complete solemnity throwing cracker after cracker into the middle of the street causing a perfect cannonade and sending up clouds of gunpowder smoke. The papers protest yearly against this nuisance and against the accidents it causes but so far to no avail. One paper said yesterday that " Old George the Third was turning in his grave with delight at the thought that every fourth of July the darned Yankees kill more of each other than he ever did in seven years of warfare ! " When Americans themselves can write thus about this curious custom, they will, I hope, pardon a passing Britisher who takes note of it as something strange.

Perhaps, like many curious old customs, it is now past and gone. But this particular way of pursuing pleasure or method of celebrating a great national anniversary led me to ponder on the love of the human race for mere noise as a means of celebrating great occasions and expressing joy. This is surely not worthy even of the animal improperly termed " *Homo Sapiens*."

During my two terms as Chargé d'Affaires I had, of course, many opportunities of meeting one of the most distinguished men in Washington at that time, Mr. Elihu Root, the Secretary of State. He was not like Theodore Roosevelt, a sort of electro-magnetic disturbance, continually throwing off sparks of light, heat and energy ; he was not a great, almost Olympian, political manager like Cabot Lodge ; he was not a brilliant observer of the Theatre of Life like Henry Adams, nor perhaps a lawyer with a sense of the future changes required in the law to make it more just for rich and poor like Oliver Wendell Holmes, Justice of the Supreme Court. Mr. Root was indeed also a great lawyer but rather an exponent of the Law as it was. He was an ardent supporter of the movement for World Peace, though he was Secretary for War under Presidents McKinley and Roosevelt, and he received the Nobel Peace Prize in 1912. On the other hand, he was almost perfect as Secretary of State, so deliberate, so careful in his choice of words that at times when he was making a public speech one wondered when the next word would fall from his lips and remained perfectly satisfied with it when it did. Never excited over any negotiation or apparently the least annoyed or resentful on account of unexpected hitches or difficulties, perfectly courteous in argument and manner, and always almost cruelly logical and uncompromisingly to the point, he was in fact a wonderful man to do business with.

He and Mr. Bryce understood each other perfectly and managed to clear the slate of a number of questions which had remained tiresomely unsettled for years. Lest

it may be supposed from what I have written about the
two years I passed in the United States that at the
Embassy we spent most of our time in jaunts and
junketings I will but quote from one more letter written
to my brother Stafford from Washington on April 19th,
1908.

> We have got three Treaties signed and one has been ratified by
> the Senate. I fear there is no hope of getting the Newfoundland
> Arbitration Treaty signed in time to have it ratified by the Senate
> this Session. These things take ever so much more time than one
> expects.

Though all the main part of the work connected with
these Treaties and the great " Claims Treaty " which
Mr Bryce was negotiating in order to " clean the slate "
was, of course, dealt with by the Ambassador directly
with the Secretary of State, many minor matters connected with them had to be discussed and arranged
between the Assistant Secretary of State, " Bob " Bacon,
and myself, or George Young. All these Treaty
negotiations while not, perhaps, of any transcendental
importance, yet gave plenty of occupation in addition to
the ordinary current affairs of the Embassy.

" Bob " Bacon as he was familiarly known to almost
all in Washington was an altogether charming person—
one of the handsomest men I ever knew. A great rider
and hunter, which I especially appreciated as he used
to give me mounts for rides with him in Rock Creek Park,
he was a gentlemen through and through in his dealings
and it would have been difficult if not impossible to find
two men more satisfying to do business with than Mr.
Root and " Bob " Bacon. It was, no doubt, owing to
our very happy relations with the State Department, that
this period of my diplomatic life remains engraved so
pleasantly on my memory.

As a result I said good-bye with most sincere regret
to Washington, to my very kind Chief and Mrs Bryce,
and to the members of the Embassy staff, including the
messengers, Robert Williams and Charlie Browne, who
afterwards wrote an account of the old Embassy House,

and to my many friends, some of whom, like Jim Garfield, still remain to talk over old times.

I never dreamt of returning as Ambassador to Washington for that seemed to me to be far out of my reach. Indeed, I left hoping that, while I might return to see my friends again and again enjoy the unexpected and joyous shocks of the American scene at close quarters, I should never bear the burden of the responsibility of that Embassy on my shoulders. When Mr. Bryce was appointed Ambassador someone told me that he had done all he could to get out of it because " he did not care for stars and he feared stripes." If that was indeed his view it was one which I entirely shared.

I cannot close my account of these two interesting years without referring to two visits which Isa and I paid to Mrs Cowles, the sister of President Roosevelt at her charming old house, " Old Gate," at Farmington, Connecticut. Mrs. Cowles was very like the President in character, tremendously energetic, full of interests of all kinds and a most delightful hostess and companion. As her husband the Admiral had been American Naval Attaché in London she knew many of our friends, especially Ronald Munro Ferguson,[1] Edward Grey, Carlo Milnes Gaskell and, of course, " Springy " among others.

" Old Gate " was an old-fashioned, partly seventeenth century house, some of it built of logs cut by British prisoners taken when General Burgoyne surrendered at Saratoga Springs. The marks of their axes, for they do not seem to have been very dexterous craftsmen, were still quite visible on the columns supporting the portico that gave access to the garden. On the other hand, there is within the house some beautiful panelling, also carved by prisoners from Burgoyne's army, which is in the best tradition of English wood-carving of that period. The front of the house looked out on to the long double avenue of great elms which is characteristic of so many of the old New England settlements of Colonial times.

---

[1] Afterwards Lord Novar, Governor-General of Australia.

In 1906, before motors became common, that avenue was a place of refreshment and peace to me coming from Boston and New York. Also Sheffield, the son of the house, who was then a boy at school used, if home for the holidays, to take me for long walks in the woods and being a perfect companion and guide would show me caves where the first settlers hid from Indian raids. Once even he took me very secretly to show me his greatest treasure, unknown to anyone else—a humming-bird's nest—the first I ever saw, a thing even more exquisite than a wren's nest at home.

So " Old Gate," Farmington, which I often visited again later when I came back to the United States of America, became perhaps my most favourite spot on the Western Continent.

Shortly after my return from Tobago in November, 1909, I left America for London on my way to my new post.

CHAPTER V

BUDAPEST

(1909)

I MUST have reached England some time at the end of November or beginning of December, 1908, and on arrival was offered the Consulate-General at Budapest instead of the post of Councillor at the Vienna Embassy. Both had the same rank in the Diplomatic Service, but Budapest was semi-independent. Hoping for more interesting work than as Councillor acting immediately under an Ambassador in Vienna, I chose Budapest.

I rejoined Isa and my sons in Italy for a week or so at Christmas. They were staying with her brother-in-law and sister, Count and Countess Colleoni, at their country house, the Castello di Thiene, in the neighbourhood of Vicenza in Northern Italy. This was not a mediæval castle but rather a beautiful Venetian country house of the fifteenth century, built in the noble style of many of the palaces on the Grand Canal, with frescoes, by Paolo Veronese, in one of the drawing-rooms. The rooms were enormous and filled mainly with Venetian seventeenth and eighteenth century furniture and quantities of family portraits whose principal merit was that they covered great areas of wall space. We were all attached to Thiene and to its master and mistress who being unfortunately childless were, nevertheless, devoted to children and laid themselves out to making ours happy. So that particular Christmas is stamped on my mind on account of its festivities and, above all, on account of the largest Christmas tree I ever saw which soared up to the ceiling of one of those splendidly proportioned Italian rooms,

almost like a cedar of Lebanon to a starry sky. Covered
with lights and packets of presents for everyone in the
house, and coloured glass ornaments and gold and silver
tinsel, it was a glorious sight worthy of old Bartolomeo
Colleoni, whose statue in the Piazza San Giovanni e
Paolo of Venice—

Bronzo di Bronzo nell' arcion s'incastra[1]

—is one of the finest equestrian statues in the world.

The days passed quickly and I had to hurry on, for the
Balkan world was again in a turmoil.

Austria-Hungary had in September, 1908, notified the
interested European Powers that she intended to annex
the former Turkish Provinces of Bosnia-Herzegovina
which had been merely placed under her protection by
the Treaty of Berlin, 1878.

The British Government took the view that this was
a serious blow to the Turkish Government, whose
protestations of reform since the Young Turk Revolution
of 1908 British public opinion regarded as genuine.
Sir Edward Grey, who desired to see the new Turkish
Administration encouraged, wrote to Sir Edward Goschen,
the British Ambassador in Vienna, on October 5th, 1908,
that :

> A deliberate violation or alteration of the Berlin Treaty, under-
> taken without previous consultation with the other Powers of which
> in this case Turkey is most affected, could never be approved or
> recognised by His Majesty's Government.

As far as Turkey was concerned her " loss of face " in
this matter—for it was little else—was compensated
without great difficulty by a money payment.

Another delicate matter that arose out of this annexation
was the claim put forward by Russia for compensation in
the shape of the opening of the Dardenelles to her ships
of war, a claim which obviously could not be met without
the consent of all the Powers parties to existing Treaties

---

[1] Translation   " Bronze of bronze, sits morticed to his saddle." (d'Annunzio :
Sonnet.)

regarding the *status quo* of the Straits.   When, however, Russia a little later suddenly gave up supporting Serbia's claim to compensation nothing more appears to have been said about the Straits.

But the case was different as regards Serbia. The Serbs regarded the two annexed Provinces as a part—the principal part—of Yugo-Slavia *irredenta*, that is, of their own national heritage. As long as these Provinces remained even nominally Turkish, there was always a hope that when the Ottoman Empire broke up, these Provinces would in the scramble that must ensue, surely fall to Serbia to whom they belonged by right of race, language and history. Their unexpected annexation by Austria-Hungary seemed to put off indefinitely the accomplishment of this Yugo-Slav dream.

Therefore besides the Russian and Turkish troubles arising out of Æhrenthal's coup " there came upon us all," as Lord Grey puts it in his book[1] :

> . . . another and more formidable affair. Serbia demanded (territorial) compensation for the change in the *status quo* made by Austria. . . . We thought a demand by Serbia for territory would not be reasonable but that some economic concession to facilitate the transport of Serbian exports to the Adriatic might provide an innocent solution.

> Serbia was obstinate and headstrong, Austria was haughty, hard and stern.

The Austro-Hungarian-Serbian dispute therefore already threatened the peace of Europe early in 1909. Sir Edward Grey on February 27th of that year telegraphed to Sir Arthur Nicolson, British Ambassador at St. Petersburg, urging that war must inevitably ensue unless Serbia abandoned claims for territorial compensation and that Russia could count on no more than diplomatic support from Great Britain to obtain such redress for Serbia as was possible.

Sir Edward thought that Austria should be asked by the Powers in the interests of peace to grant economic

[1] *Twenty-five years.*" (Chap XI, p. 186) Hodder & Staughton, London.

K

concessions to Serbia, but first Russia must decide what action she would take, as unless Russia advised Serbia to accept economic concessions, the British Government could not usefully make representations to Serbia to do so.   On the other hand Russia could not be expected to advise Serbia to abandon territorial claims unless Germany would previously give a substantial assurance of support to a Serbian demand for economic concessions.   The telegram concludes with these significant words :

> If war were to take place it would probably in the end embroil the greater part of the Continent and even Russia must see that such a risk for the sake of Serbia's demands is utterly disproportionate to the end in view.

Sir Edward Grey comments in his book on the situation as follows :

> The probability is, that if Russia had told Serbia from the first that she must not expect more than economic concessions, the situation would never have become dangerous and Russia would have emerged with the credit of having done, at any rate, something for Serbia.   As it was Russia was stiff for a time and then suddenly threw up the sponge and collapsed unconditionally.

The net result of Count Æhrenthal's brilliant coup, which was to strengthen the prestige of the Austrian Empire was, therefore, in the light of after events :

1. To lay the powder train by which that Empire was finally blown to pieces.

2. To lead to a world war which destroyed not only the Austrian Empire but also monarchial institutions in Germany and Russia, producing in the latter country a revolution which for violence, destruction, famine and general cataclysm has never been equalled in the world's history.

3. To re-establish the Yugoslav nation within its ancient national boundaries so that the despised Serbs have become an element of greater strength and power in the councils of nations than the Archduchy of Austria or the Kingdom of Hungary.

Never did a statesman in a responsible position take a step so fateful for his own country, which step, even in the event of complete success, could only have gained so trifling a prize. The only person who, so far as I know, got anything out of the Bosnia-Herzegovina coup was Æhrenthal himself who, unless I am mistaken, was given a rise in the ranks of the Austrian nobility by being promoted from Baron to Count. Considering the magnitude of the results of his action this reward seems somewhat meagre.

After this the bitterness between Serbia and Austria-Hungary became so acute and grew so constantly in strength, fanned as it was by a national press on both sides, that it became clear that unless great efforts were made to establish better feelings on either side, an outbreak of hostilities was sooner or later inevitable.

Meanwhile, in spite of all his efforts to promote peace, Sir Edward Grey was often accused in Austria and Germany also of having tried to provoke a European war. This attitude towards him was to continue in the German and Austrian and even pro-German neutral press up to and during the War.

Truly, but in a sense too generously, he says that it was :

> . . . a symptom of that inveterate and ineradicable distrust which poisoned European diplomacy and made any healthy growth impossible.

Personally, I think it was rather a determined propaganda effort on the part of the Governments of the Central Powers to find a scapegoat for an action to which they knew they were already irretrievably committed by their own policies.

One more quotation from *Twenty-five years* comes in appositely here. Sir Edward Grey writes (page 192) :

> It is impossible to recount these events of 1908–9 without being struck by an ominous parallel with the crisis of 1914. In 1908 as in 1914, Austria acted without full consultation with her Ally—so the world was told by von Bülow in the first and by von Bethman Hollweg in the latter crisis. In 1908 as in 1914 Germany, while deprecating the headstrong character of Austria's action, thought it necessary to support her Ally. In 1908, as in 1914, Russia felt

herself challenged to support Serbia. There the parallel ends. In
1909 Russia preferred humiliation, in 1914 she faced war. . . .
Let the reader remember also that this humiliation was branded into
Russian feeling by the subsequent speech of the German Emperor
at Vienna—the exulting speech in which he spoke of having
supported Austria " in shining armour." Prestige amongst the Slav
nations of South-Eastern Europe was as necessary to Russia as to
Austria. Russia could not afford a second blow such as that of
1908–9. And yet in the crisis of 1914, especially after Serbia's
disarming reply to the Austrian Ultimatum, there was no ruler in
Germany great enough to feel that what was essential to the peace
of Europe was not the support of Austria " in shining armour " but
a wise and restraining hand.

There was the whole trouble. The German Emperor
instead of keeping a wise and restraining hand on the
incompetent Austrian statesmen of that day, encouraged
them in their fatal policy of expansion in Slav territory
to the south, thus inevitably bringing the " ramshackle
Empire " of the Hapsburgs into conflict with Russia.
This must have been known and understood in Berlin,
and yet the German Emperor made his speeches about
standing by his Ally " in shining armour " or about
Austria's services as a valuable second at Algeciras, both
of which were intended to show to the world that on
every front Germany and Austria formed a solid block
with, it must be admitted, the Austrians always playing
second fiddle.

If these speeches were intended to please Austro-
Hungarian vanity they failed signally in their object, for
public opinion in the dual Monarchy did not like a
descendant of the Holy Roman Empire to be considered
inferior to so upstart a State as Prussia. In fact, these
speeches of the Emperor William reminded me, when
their consequences were considered, of the utterances of a
well-known lady in London society in the eighteen-
nineties, who was known as the " Acrobat " because she
never opened her mouth without putting her foot in it.

I have thought it necessary to give the above very short
sketch of the political situation when I arrived in Budapest
at the beginning of 1909. I had hoped that in the midst

of the turmoil Budapest would be a particularly interesting post.   In this I was disappointed, for the whole
political interest in the dual Monarchy, so far as foreign
politics were concerned was, I soon discovered, centred
in Vienna.   Budapest counted only for Hungarian internal politics and for the moment, apart from the usual
party squabbles, there was nothing going on that could
interest the Foreign Office.

All that could be said for Budapest at that time was
that it was a good post for observation for anyone who
wished on his own account to study the complexes of
that portion of the dual Monarchy, and there were plenty
of them.

I arrived in Budapest early in January, 1909, after
spending a pleasant day or two at Vienna with our
Ambassador, Fairfax Cartwright and his charming Italian
wife, whom I had known in Rome as Donna Mary Chigi
and who belonged to the Siennese branch of that family.

I gathered from Cartwright that he was not deeply
interested in Hungarian affairs, and that I was not expected to make reports on matters outside the borders of
the Magyar Kingdom, unless something unusually important came to my knowledge.

Budapest at first sight did not impress me favourably.
Perhaps I had expected too much.   The weather was
grey, foggy and cold.   There was a slush of melting snow
under foot.   Big blocks of ice covered with dirty snow
were floating down the river.   On entering the hotel,
which was said to be one of the best hotels in the city,
I sat down disconsolately in my bedroom to write a
letter to Isa announcing my arrival, when a large bug,
the first friendly visitor that came to greet me, marched
slowly and deliberately over my writing paper.   Most
inhospitably I speared it with my pen and ringing the
bell, I held it so transfixed under the nose of the waiter
who came.

" *Was ist das?* " I asked, but he answered quite unconcerned with a strong Hungarian accent :

" *Och die !   Die Deutschen bringen die Insekten mit* "

(Oh ! those. The Germans bring those insects with them).

This taught me at once two things about the city in which I was now to spend some time. First that bugs were not considered anything unusual. Secondly, that Germans were not popular.

Of course a great deal of this anti-German attitude was merely traditional and dated back to the time of the Kossuth movement in 1848 for the independence of Hungary from Austria, when the Austrians being as usual defeated called in the help of Russia, which was in those days ready to oblige if it was a question of extinguishing the flame of liberty in any country.

Nevertheless the excess to which hostility to the German language was carried became very tiresome. It was not for some months that I realised that if one wanted to get an answer from a passer-by in the street it was generally useless to ask the question in German. The individual addressed would almost invariably pretend not to understand, but if you asked your question in French or English, he would generally ask you politely if you understood German and the conversation could then be carried on comfortably in that language.

My predecessor, Clarke-Thornhill, had already left when I arrived, and had placed the disposal of his apartment in the Andrassy Ut, the " Fifth Avenue " of Budapest, and of his furniture in the hands of Dr. Brühl, a Jewish lawyer, who was our Vice-Consul and became our very good friend. I took the lease on at once for a few months and bought all the furniture so as to enable Isa and the children to join me without delay, as I felt I could not spend my days alone in a bug-ridden hotel looking out at a river covered with ice floes themselves covered with dirty snow. In a few days the family arrived.

This did not, however, on this occasion contribute to my contentment, for the two eldest children almost immediately developed scarlet fever, and we were all interned in a half-furnished flat ; Isa, her maid and the patients on one side, and I and the rest of the company on the other. I could go to my office and that was all. It was an inauspicious beginning, but all in the day's work for a diplomat's family. Still, perhaps it unconsciously prejudiced me against Budapest, and that prejudice took some months to wear off.

Meanwhile I found that my office was entirely in the hands of the unpaid Vice-Consul, Dr. Brühl, and his nephew, Dr. Kaufmann.

Although both were above suspicion I could not but feel that it was a little too happy-go-lucky to leave an office of this sort which might at any moment have important political matters to deal with altogether in the hands of Hungarians, who not only had charge of all the archives but actually copied out all the dispatches I sent to the Foreign Office. It was also, I may say, quite in keeping with the English lack of suspicion and dislike of all change. I represented the state of affairs to the Foreign Office and before long got leave to hire two more rooms in the same building and to take on a suitable Englishman, if I could find one on the spot, to act as confidential clerk. Dr. Bruhl made no difficulties, the rooms were quickly found, and I was lucky in securing the services of an Englishman, Mr. F. Chambers, who had been employed with some commercial firm in Budapest and spoke Hungarian and German.

We found we had a sort of Augean stable in the archives, which had not been put in proper order for years past, and the first months of my time in Budapest were taken up in working with Chambers, both in our shirt sleeves, in sorting, indexing and packing these dusty archives for transmission to the Foreign Office. Thus I got to know Mr. Chambers very thoroughly and to have complete confidence in him. (He has remained in Budapest and speaking Hungarian fluently has been able to render useful service to his country there.)

If I have given up a paragraph or two to the altogether trifling and dull subject of the archives and the office of the British Consulate-General at Budapest in the year

1909, it is simply as an example of the curious lack of interest our Foreign Office took in those days in minor posts abroad.

Generally a certain sum was furnished annually to the incumbent which might have been adequate fifty years before, but was quite insufficient later. From time to time an inspector came out, but if the office had been passed on previous inspections it was just allowed to go on as before because the main object was always not to increase expenditure.

I have no right to complain, however, because whenever I found office accommodation inadequate and explained the necessity of greater security and convenience for the office, I generally obtained what seemed to be required after a struggle, which was, I believe, often put up for form's sake.

To return, however, to rather more interesting matters.

With the coming of spring Budapest became far more cheerful and attractive. The parks and gardens were well kept, for if Hungarians objected to hearing the German tongue they had no objection to German order and cleanliness in their public places. The view across the Danube to the old citadel of Buda is very striking, the Margarethen Insel in the river has been turned into an agreeable park. There was a pleasant club with lawn tennis courts where Budapest Society met on summer evenings, and there were restaurants in the park where the famous Gipsy bands played their wild and entrancing music especially well if there happened to be a rich man among the audience who treated them to champagne. Parliamentary life afforded both sport and amusement and even interest on one occasion. An old General having been appointed Prime Minister, principally because civilian Ministers fought so continuously with each other that little or no business could be transacted, a fair lady friend complained to him that she had been two or three times to attend a sitting of the Chamber and had not been fortunate enough to witness any disturbance worth mentioning. He said :

" Send me your card next time you are in the galleries and I'll arrange that for you."

So she did and the General at once began taunting the Opposition with such effect that the books of the Laws of Hungary, which lay on the table between the members of the Government and the members of the Opposition, were very soon hurtling through the air. One member of the Government was severely wounded in the eye. My French colleague, Vicomte de Fontenay, who had a French wit, declared that he believed that it was the first time in history that the *Corpus Juris* had become the *Corpus Delicti.*

Socially the Hungarians were delightful. Hospitable, full of life, if somewhat irresponsible, eager sportsmen and good riders, keen musicians, travellers, excellent linguists, often well versed in the literature of other countries, they certainly made life in Budapest agreeable for the not too serious diplomat. Unfortunately the Bosnia-Herzegovina crisis and its aftermath lasted long enough to prevent my taking advantage of the many invitations to visit Hungarian country houses which we received.

The two or three visits we did pay gave us a glimpse of a life nearer to English country house life than anything I had ever met with outside the British Isles. I do not propose to describe these country houses but one exception must be made for Keszthely, the château of Prince Festetics, where the stateliness of a feudal establishment was combined with the gorgeousness of an American millionaire's residence—a word which I find suitably defined in the Oxford dictionary as " a house of considerable pretensions."

All day long there stood in the court before the entrance four drags with four-in-hands waiting for any guests who wanted to drive—there were still no motors to speak of in Hungary in those days. There was a steam launch on Lake Balaton for guests who had other plans ; wonderful partridge and hare shooting in the season, and of course tennis, croquet, etc.

There were, I think, over a hundred horses in the stables and about forty different carriages—everything was on the same scale.

The house was modern and very large, built in the same style as most of the great Hungarian country houses.

The only thing that qualified my pleasure during my visit was that I had long ago given up playing cards, not caring either to win money or lose it. As cards formed the principal diversion in the evening, one who did not join in felt himself a drag on the festivity of the party.

Some excursions into the country I was able to make during my sojourn in Hungary. I went with my brother Stafford and his daughter Alianore to the Tatra Mountains, a most attractive part of Hungary, which since the War, as Slovakia, has been given over to Czechoslovakia ; also I made a very interesting tour in Transylvania and the Banat with my Italian colleague, Count Bosdari, and was particularly struck with the air of well being of the Transylvanian " Saxons," a colony of about a quarter of a million Germans from the Lower Rhine, whose ancestors settled there in the twelfth century on the invitation of the King of Hungary and had prospered exceedingly. As all the non-Magyar races were complaining bitterly about oppression by the Nationalist Magyar Government at Budapest, I asked the Mayor of the Saxon capital, Hermanstadt, how it was they seemed to get on so well.

He said : " We have never any difficulty. We have a solid party in the Lower House which is large enough to be worth cultivating by the Government in power and we always support the Government provided it doesn't trouble us and leaves us our old privileges and liberties."

These Transylvanian Saxons seemed to be a most sensible, hard working and worthy people. Their little capital was a pleasant, clean old-world, thoroughly German city with an interesting fortified church. It was indeed a last outpost of Western civilisation of an earlier type and contained among other things a fine old library possessing many treasures.

Yet the real interest of the Banat and Transylvania as a meeting place of East and West lay in the astonishing mixture of races for both in the Banat and in Transylvania perhaps six or eight different languages could be heard in the market square of most of the larger towns. This alone gave an idea of the difficulty of creating a united people in such a country, and I confess I could not so much blame the Magyar Government for endeavouring to enforce, somewhat drastically perhaps, the use of the one language, that of the ruling race. The Transylvanian Saxons were not, I understood, troubled in this way, being a solid block. But where, one asked oneself, was the use of perpetuating for all time the babel of languages which obtained for instance in and around Temesvar, the capital of the Banat?

With reference to the enforcement of the language laws, however, I had myself in Budapest a curious experience that made me sympathise with those who protested against them.

My fourth son, Edmund, was born in Budapest, and in order to complete the required formalities I went to the district registrar to register his birth. Considering that I was a foreigner the conversation was allowed to take place in German. All went well until the officer came to my Christian name "Esme."

REGISTRAR: "What is that name in Hungarian? Because all names have to be entered in Hungarian."

I: "I am sorry but as I don't speak Hungarian I cannot tell you."

REGISTRAR: "I have never heard it before and I must enter it in Hungarian."

I: "If you don't know its equivalent in Hungarian you can hardly expect me to do so. Why not put it down just as it is?"

REGISTRAR: "Impossible. You must find the Hungarian equivalent."

I: "But if there isn't one, what then?"

REGISTRAR: "Then I shall have to enter the child among the illegitimate births."

I : " Look here, Mr. Registrar, if you do that you will hear about it from the Hungarian Government because I am British Consul-General here, and I shall at once complain to your Government about your conduct."

This sobered the Registrar and in some way or other he overcame his scruples, but we did not part, I fear, the best of friends.

Had I known then what the name of Esme signified and that it was the Scottish equivalent of the French *Aimé* I might have avoided the altercation which became rather heated. It was not a case where ignorance was bliss.

Among other matters of little importance I cannot omit recording the visit of a curious and afterwards notorious personality. One day—I have forgotten the exact date— a man walked into my office bringing the usual printed form of introduction from the Foreign Office saying that he was going to Hungary to study some philanthropic Government institution and asking me to procure for him all the facilities required for this purpose. He was, as far as I remember, a short, decidedly foreign-looking person with a rather loud tie and a check waistcoat which impressed me. His name was Trebitch Lincoln. He was a Liberal M.P. who had been brought into politics with the assistance of one of the Rowntrees for whose philanthropic activities I had a great respect. I told Mr. Trebitch Lincoln that I would, of course, help him to obtain the facilities he required and would at once ask for an interview for him with Mr. Franz Kossuth, the Minister of Commerce, who was the member of the Government with whom we Consuls-General were authorised to deal, there being no Minister for Foreign Affairs in Budapest.

Mr. Lincoln and I talked for a while on matters of general interest and then he suddenly developed what I understood was the real purpose of his coming to Hungary which was to obtain a concession of some sort for prospecting for either minerals or oil or else financing a loan for Hungary in London ; I forget precisely what it was, but, at any rate, a speculative proposition. I told Mr. Lincoln that this matter was not mentioned in the Foreign Office letter he brought me and that I, therefore, was precluded from saying anything on the subject to the Hungarian Minister. I further told him that if he mentioned it to Mr. Kossuth I should have to say that he did so entirely on his own responsibility and that my Government was in no way interested in the matter. Mr. Lincoln said he quite understood this.

My surprise then was great when at the end of the interview with Mr. Kossuth, Lincoln suddenly—perhaps encouraged by Kossuth's amiability—developed this scheme. I at once told the Minister that I had nothing to do with it and that what Mr. Lincoln had said he had said entirely on his own responsibility. There was an immediate change in the Minister's manner and Lincoln evidently saw that he had made a big blunder. I don't remember that I ever saw Lincoln again but he left a very strong impression on my mind as being a rascally adventurer which was subsequently confirmed by his career as described in his book, " The Autobiography of an Adventurer."[1] I never saw a man whose rascality was so obviously worn on his sleeve for daws like myself to peck at. If I remember right I wrote to the Foreign Office about him something of this kind :

> I treated Mr. Trebitch Lincoln with all the respect due to an Elected of the People and with all the circumspection required in dealing with an obvious rascal.

[1] Trebitch Lincoln was born a Hungarian Jew, was converted to Lutheran Christianity, became a Curate in the Church of England, was elected an M.P. for Darlington in 1904. He went into oil ventures in 1911 and floated various Oil Companies. He went to New York and was for some time in gaol in America between 1914 and 1916. He was extradited to England in 1916 and condemned to 3 years' penal servitude for forgery and fraud. It may be added that he was strongly suspected of being a German spy. In 1920 he was mixed up with the Kapp Putsch and the book contains a chapter headed " International Intrigues in Budapest," where he seems to have been engaged in selling secret information to any party that would buy it. Afterwards he went to China and raised a Chinese Loan with the Knott Firm for 25 million gold dollars. His son was executed in England for having murdered a man at Reading. Lincoln became a Buddhist monk in 1932. At the close of his book he was still living in China and concluded the autobiography with these words : " The world revolution is on the march and the only real bulwark against it is England standing in the midst of the surging yellow Bolshevist wave."

One natural characteristic of the Hungarians no one who has even lived a short time among them could fail to note : their love of display. This shows itself in all classes and their often reckless spending, like Cyrano de Bergerac simply "*parceque le geste était beau.*" I remember one friend of ours among the magnates, whose balance at the bank, if it existed at all, was none too large, giving a ball for the coming-out of his daughter and paying for a special train from and to Paris for his friends who lived there. "*Le geste était beau,*" perhaps, but a number of such *gestes* seriously handicapped his daughter's chances in the matrimonial market.

It was, however, especially in the matter of clothes that the love of finery was so conspicuous. No official receptions or balls could be, I think, more gorgeously full of colour than those of the Palace or Burg at Budapest. Not only were the women more often than not beautiful in themselves but they were, so I was assured by good judges, most beautifully dressed. The men of course all wore as a uniform the magnificent Hungarian national costume with velvet tunics, high boots, velvet and fur coats hanging from one shoulder, jewelled swords, jewelled collars, jewelled brooches in their caps to hold the traditional eagles' feathers. These uniforms were of different colours according to the fancy of the wearer. often with rich embroidery. It must be added that Hungarians knew how to wear their clothes. Finery never made them shy or shame-faced. "*Panache*" came natural to them. When you saw the White Marble Hall of the Burg filled with visions of this kind it was a sight worth seeing, especially if the centre of all was the octagenarian Emperor Franz Joseph who, with his simplicity and kindly homeliness, seemed by contrast to give an added touch of dignity to the surroundings. Throw in a first-class Hungarian string band playing stirring Magyar music and the impression left on the mind was of a scene that could not be paralleled in any other capital. There was nothing mean or common about these people.

Again, if one wanted to study the Hungarian passion for
finery one had only to go to one of the market towns in
the Alföld—the great plain of Hungary—on a feast day.
To see the peasants gathered in hundreds in the church
or on the turf-square round about when there was no room
left in the church building was to be overwhelmed as it
were by the tide of colour. Men and women all in
beautiful and brilliant costumes, and all, as observed
above, not in the least shy in their fine feathers, but
enjoying the impression made on the stranger. I was
taken once by a Hungarian friend, Dr. Leipnik, editor
of the *Pester Lloyd,* to see one of these festas at a place
called, I think, Mezöhegyes which was famous for its
costumes. We were in truth the only two black beetles
in that crowd of gorgeous butterflies. I hope this still
continues, for it would be sad if a people who know so
well, as the French say, how to wear their clothes should
be reduced to the drab shapelessness of mass-produced
body-coverings which Western civilisation apparently
must bring in its train.

As spring and summer came on all my original
prejudices against Budapest disappeared. We took two
flats in a villa near the Varosliget Park where the children
could enjoy themselves, and on Sundays when I was free
we used all, to the great delight of the children, to drive
out into the wooded valleys behind Buda, which in May
were full of lilies of the valley.

One event of my sojourn there remains indelibly fixed
on my mind. In the summer of 1909 the Channel was
flown for the first time by Blériot. In America I had
of course heard of the trial flights of Wilbur Wright and
his brother, but flying then still seemed to be something
so remote as to be hardly within the realm of immediately
practical things. The crossing of the Channel by Blériot
in an aeroplane created therefore an indescribable
sensation, and in a sense almost consternation in England
for, unimaginative as we are, we nevertheless realised that
this must sooner or later revolutionise our whole attitude
towards the question of national defence.

Blériot came to Budapest in October, 1909, to give an exhibition of flying. The impression it made on me, though, it must be admitted the exhibition was of the humblest sort, was almost overwhelming. I felt like a child again when the world was new, and suddenly some astonishing and unexpected sight was unfolded before my eyes. It was an exhilaration, a renewal of youth. Perhaps even to-day the hearing for the first time of a great piece of music might produce the same effect—nothing else could.

Blériot at first hesitated about going up because there was a little wind, so we were entertained for some time by an Hungarian aviator who careered round and round the field in his aeroplane which would not rise. One of the Budapest papers said the next morning that since the field was the site of some famous and ancient victory of the Magyars it was not surprising that a patriotic aeroplane could not tear itself away from such holy ground. But at last Blériot came out with his plane and, after going round the field once or twice, rose slowly and circled over us at a height of a few hundred feet. My heart stood still as he rose. It was like a fairy tale coming true.

The next day we met Blériot at luncheon with my French colleague, M. de Fontenay. As a man he did not make a deep impression, but it was enough to have been the first to fly over the sea to England. That was a feat which will never be forgotten or wiped out by all the astonishing records of later years.

In May, 1910, King Edward died unexpectedly. All felt that a change was coming and that we had probably lost in him a great champion of the cause of World Peace. But looking back now on the events which led up to the War, and on the mentality of leading personages in Germany and Austria at that time as disclosed by documents since published, I think we may fairly assume that he would have been unable to stem the tide had he lived.

So far as I personally was concerned his death was a great blow for he had been, during the short time that he had known me, exceptionally friendly for a man of his high position, and I also felt, rightly or wrongly, anxious to help me on in my career. In any case I believed that I owed him a personal debt of gratitude, and my sorrow at his death was, therefore, a genuinely personal one.

He was extremely popular in Hungarian society where he was well-known, and when we held an English Memorial Service for him in one of the large Lutheran churches in Budapest it was attended not only by those who came officially, but in very large numbers by those who looked upon the late King as a real friend.

Before concluding this chapter on Budapest one or two personalities must be mentioned.

The first of these is Professor Arminius Vambéry, one of the greatest travellers, explorers, and orientalists of the nineteenth century. He told me once, I believe, that he knew thirty-two languages but only spoke fluently about eighteen.

We took a fancy to each other since he liked telling me of his experiences and I liked listening. He suffered from the handicap in Budapest of having been born a Jew and this despite his extraordinary achievements in exploration and travel he never could overcome. He had the most grateful admiration for King Edward, because when Prince of Wales he had in his kindly way helped him to greater social recognition. Vambéry had presumably in order to get a regular income, however small, accepted the position of librarian of the Club of the Magnates which was most select. On one of the first visits of the Prince of Wales to Hungary a dinner was given in his honour at this Magnates Club. The Prince, who like most men of his time, much admired the achievements of Vambéry asked him if he would be at the dinner. He replied ruefully that he would not because he would hardly be considered sufficiently high up in the social scale to be invited. The Prince said at once that that was a shame for the Club, and that he would put it right, and told Vambéry to meet him at the entrance to the Club when most of the members congregated there

L

to play cards. When they reached the card-room the Prince put his arm round old Vambéry's shoulder and went up to a group in which the President of the Club was talking to some friends, and said :

" Professor Vambéry is an old friend of mine and I am so much looking forward to seeing him at the Club dinner next——" whatever the date was.

Vambéry was at once asked and was treated with greater respect after that.

Another story of his was about his reception by Disraeli after his great journey on foot as a Persian Mohammedan pilgrim from Teheran across Central Asia and Afghanistan into India. Vambéry was a short, insignificant-looking man, lame and far from strong in appearance, and nothing but his knowledge of oriental ways and languages and his undaunted spirit could have carried him through such a journey in those old fanatical days.

On his return to Europe he was made much of in England and other European countries by the Geographical and learned Societies. In London he received an invitation to call on Disraeli, then Prime Minister, at his house in Carlton House Terrace. Vambéry told me Disraeli received him in a long gallery and asked him at once to be seated in the centre of the room and then began to walk up and down, stopping occasionally to look at his guest. Vambéry sat still, wondering what was to happen next. After a while the Prime Minister stopped in front of him and asked :

" Pray, Mr. Vambéry, what is your nationality ? "

" Hungarian," was the reply.

The pacing up and down began again and then another stop and another question :

" And what is your religion, Mr. Vambéry ? "

" Protestant."

" Indeed."

More pacing, and then a final question.

" And was your nationality always Hungarian and your religion always Protestant ? "

" No, Mr. Disraeli, I was born a Jew."

"Ah," said Disraeli, beaming, "I knew it. No one but a man of our race could have had the dauntless perseverance to go through all you have gone through and successfully overcome so many difficulties."

I forget whether this story appears in Vambéry's *Memoirs*, but in any case it is substantially as he told it to me.

One more story.

He had almost completed his journey, having arrived at Kandahar, of which a son of the Amir of Afghanistan was the Governor. This Prince, it appears, had a fondness for Western music and kept a military band which played Western military marches and popular airs. Vambéry, the pilgrim, was resting for a day or two in preparation for the last lap of his long journey on foot, and was sitting on a bench in the square in which the band was playing some well-known melody. He was enjoying this return to something that smacked of home and sat in the sun just thinking of home. The bench on which he sat was right opposite the Palace of the Governor. Presently a man came out of the Palace straight up to him, tapped him on the shoulder, and said :

"The Prince wishes to speak to you."

Vambéry was surprised and alarmed. What could this mean ? He said it was impossible that His Royal Highness should want to speak to him, a poor pilgrim on the way to some shrine in India.

"But he does," said the man, "and I have orders to bring you to him."

There was nothing to be done but to obey. On being shown into the presence of the Prince the latter, after dismissing the people about him, at once asked him in Persian who he was. Vambéry replied a Persian pilgrim travelling to India. The Prince told him not to attempt to disguise his real origin any longer because he had recognised him as a European. Not wishing him to come to any harm he had called him up to warn him that his origin had been discovered, but he had only to make a clean breast of everything and he would be assisted out of the country safely for the remainder of the journey. Vambéry saw it was useless to attempt to deceive him any more and told him what he was, whence he had come, and whither he wished to go. Then he summoned up courage to ask the Prince how he had seen through his disguise at that distance across the square. The Prince told him at once :

" I was," he said, " looking out of the window across the square when I noticed you sitting on the bench. You had your legs crossed and were listening intently to the band which seemed to please you. Suddenly I noticed you beginning to beat time with your foot to the tune the band was playing. No Afghan and hardly any Asiatic would do that, and I knew at once you must be a European and sent for you to warn you. For there are many fanatics here who, if they discovered what you are, would certainly try to kill you and then we should probably get into trouble."

Vambéry thanked the Prince, who then sent him on his way with a gift of food and apparently let his people know that this pilgrim was a friend of his and must be treated with respect as far as the Indian frontier.

Vambéry was fond of telling this story as an example of the ease with which the best possible disguise might be betrayed quite unconsciously.

Two other friends we made in Budapest—Count Albert and Count Alexander Apponyi and their wives. Count Albert was a statesman of considerable reputation but, above all, one of the greatest orators in Europe who used later to exercise a good deal of influence in the Assemblies of the League of Nations at Geneva by his silver tongue. He could speak almost equally well without any preparation not only in Hungarian and German but also in English, French, Italian and, I believe, in Latin. He had a noble character and, apart from a little childish vanity at times over his oratorical successes, he was a most delightful companion. I remember well once during the War, when he came to Stockholm on some business for Hungary, he approached Isa and me in church one Sunday after Mass, and held out his hand, saying :

" Here at least old friends can meet and shake hands and forget present misfortunes."

His cousin, Count Alexander, was a very different character. A scholar with a great knowledge of history, fonder of the library than of society, but most agreeable to talk to, I liked him well, and his wife who was an Italian, a Borghese of Rome, was an intimate friend of Isa.

Alexander Apponyi once told me an experience of his which so surprised me that it deserves to be recorded. Many years before he had, as a young man, been staying at Venice and met Richard Wagner at dinner at the house of some mutual friend. After dinner Wagner proposed that Apponyi should go home with him and offered to play something on the piano. Apponyi said this prospect alarmed him considerably as he was not particularly fond of music and especially not of Wagner's music at that time.

" I felt sure," he told me, " that he would sit down at the piano, begin composing, and I should never be able to leave till morning. So I told him that I was really not musical and not worthy of such an honour. ' Never mind,' said he, ' I'll play you something you'll like.'

So feeling he could not refuse such hospitality on the part of the great man, he reluctantly accepted. Wagner sat down at once to the piano and played divinely for an hour or more the dance music of Strauss, which he declared was the best thing of the kind ever written.

" I could never have believed," said Apponyi to me, " that Wagner was so catholic in his tastes."

One other friendship I owe to that time at Budapest, that of Dr. Ferdinand Leipnik, the editor of the *Pester Lloyd*, the leading Hungarian paper for foreign affairs. It was widely read for its appreciation of Balkan politics and indeed European affairs generally.

Shortly after I left Budapest in 1911 he was compelled to leave the staff of the *Pester Lloyd*, because, I believe, he did not then share the nationalistic or rather Imperialistic trend of Austrian policy in the Balkans and quite clearly foresaw that along that path lay the disruption of the dual Monarchy. I have often seen him since and corresponded fairly regularly and have always admired his accurate knowledge of the affairs around him and his diagnosis of the ills most countries are suffering from. But he was too detached from fashionable " nationalisms " in any country and too ironical in the expression of his opinions of them and their prophets to be " popular " as a journalist.

I found him invaluable as a guide in the Balkan labyrinth and later during the aftermath of the War.

About the middle of 1910 I suddenly realised that with a family now of four, with education expenses likely to come upon me at an alarming rate, I must either get a better post or reduce my expenses at Budapest, which was at that time a decidedly expensive place, though less so than Washington. I therefore drew the attention of the Private Secretary at the Foreign Office to this unfortunate state of things and even hinted that if they had any intention of promoting me to a Legation, I should very much like Berne. I had never asked for any particular post before and never did so again. But I thought that Berne might perhaps be given me as it was not much sought after, being considered rather uninteresting politically and socially by diplomats.

I was sure, however, it would suit us for a number of reasons and therefore plucked up my courage to say so. To my great surprise instead of a snub I was told early in 1911 that I should be transferred there in February, after just two years in Budapest.

We had both grown to like Budapest and as nearly always were sorry to leave our friends. " *Partir c'est mourir un peu* "[1] is very true. At the same time I was delighted to get promotion and to go to a place equidistant between England and Italy, which would enable us to see more of relatives in both countries.

[1] To say farewell is to die a little.

CHAPTER VI

SWITZERLAND : BERNE

(1911)

IN February, 1911, I started for Switzerland with high anticipations. As usual I went alone. Isa stayed behind in Budapest in order to wind up our affairs there and pack up. She was to bring the family to Berne as soon as I had found a house there. She wanted, however, to stay for another reason. There was to be a Court Ball at the Burg in Buda, and she was very anxious to see and be presented to the old Emperor, who was unlikely to attend such a function again. It was indeed the last ceremony of the sort he ever took part in. Isa was as delighted with the splendid picturesqueness of the ball as I was with the Emperor's Reception I attended there which I have mentioned in the previous chapter.

There was no official Legation House at Berne. My predecessor had lived all the time he spent there at the principal hotel, the Bernerhof, overlooking the Aar valley with a fine view to the Bernese Oberland mountains, which is one of the chief attractions at Berne. I found Berne from the first an attractive small city. That it was very small for a capital did not in the least prejudice me against it. On the contrary this was rather in its favour for one who was never a lover of town life. It implied two great advantages in my opinion, the first being that it was more easy to escape into the country, the second that social activities were unlikely to be onerous and excessive.

In both these points Berne came up to my expectations.

In respect of office accommodation, however, I found that the Legation at Berne was even worse off than the

Consulate-General at Budapest. The offices consisted of
two small rooms in a little villa belonging to an old German
(not German Swiss) widow. Papers were kept in ancient
cupboards, of which it would be easy to have duplicate
keys made even if such keys did not already exist. The
only reliable receptacle in the place was a small safe for
keeping ciphers.

As far as security was concerned I hoped for the best
for the time being, but I at once reported the state of
things to the Foreign Office and begged for a sufficient
allowance to be able to rent a satisfactory office.

Another matter which disturbed me was that on
arrival I found that I was literally entirely alone at the
Legation. The only Secretary, a most excellent fellow,
was unfortunately so ill with tuberculosis that he was
unable to come down from Davos to meet me and the
Chancery servant, a German like the landlady, was ill
with influenza. If it had not been for the kindness and
help of our Consul, M. de Muralt, who had lived in
Berne all his life and knew all the ropes, I should have
been entirely at sea as to what to do on arrival. Every
diplomatic post has its own peculiarities and a new
arrival will be careful to make inquiries as to the rules of
local etiquette. Even with M. de Muralt's help in
dealing with such matters I had never been so completely thrown on my own resources as I was here on my
first appointment as head of a Mission abroad.

Not only had I to decipher and cipher all telegrams,
but I had to copy my own dispatches for the Foreign
Office and my notes to the Swiss Government, to enter
them in the Registry, to put them in their envelopes,
which I had to address, stamp and lick, and finally, since
it was not etiquette for Notes to a Foreign Government
to be sent in otherwise than by hand, and I had no
Chancery servant to deliver them, I was compelled to
do postman myself and hand them in to the porter of
the Ministry of Foreign Affairs. Fortunately, in Berne
everyone from the President down did everything for
himself, so this did not appear to excite the surprise it

might have done, say, in London or Paris, or even Washington.

I did not object to doing these things at all, remembering always that I had been a successful donkey driver in the virgin forests of the Zambesi and might therefore hope to become a successful postman in Berne. But I fear that while the Chancery servant's influenza lasted the two rooms of the Chancery were never swept out, and that I neglected that part of my duties.

On the whole, I think it amused me to find myself not only the " Captain bold," but also :

> " The Bo'sun tight
> And the midshipmite
> And the crew of the Captain's gig,[1]

of my new post, but I did not want this state of things to continue indefinitely, and told the Foreign Office so in plain language.

What with these multifarious labours, with making the usual calls on all my colleagues and the councillors of the Swiss Government, and house-hunting, my time for the first month or six weeks was fully occupied.

I took a most attractive house with a large garden and every American convenience in the new part of the town, with a little public wood, the Dälhölzli, at the back. It was built by an American lady who had married a Swiss doctor, and was then moving into a larger house which she had also built, farther out on the banks of the Aar. This house combined everything I was looking for, and would have made a perfect Legation for the Government, but when later I proposed that it should be bought, another house, which was far less convenient, less well-built and situated between two tram lines, was preferred because it cost two thousand pounds less. Every occupant of the new Legation house has attacked me since for not insisting on my Elfen Strasse house, which was afterwards bought by one, I think, of the Balkan Governments. The decision was made on the

---

[1] " Yarn of the Nancy Bell," W. S. Gilbert (*Bab Ballads*.)

report of a young official of the Office of Works, who was the only person sent out to examine the question. Perhaps if I had fought it, I might have got it reversed, but I foolishly thought that it was so much in my own interests that the dearer house should be chosen that I hesitated to show the necessary fighting spirit. As I was transferred to Stockholm immediately after the purchase was decided on, it was only my unfortunate successors that suffered. They have not hesitated to tell me what they thought of me, and I could but agree with them. This is but another instance of the lack of interest sometimes shown by the Office of Works at that time in the minor diplomatic posts. However, as far as my own comfort, and I may add the security of His Majesty's Chancery Office was concerned, the requirements of both were amply met by the Elfen Strasse house, and I look back to my two years in Berne as among the happiest, very largely on that account, of my diplomatic life.

My first experience of the extreme simplicity which gave its tone to official life in Switzerland was gained on my presentation of Letters of Credence to the President of the Republic. Instead of a gilded coach which it was the custom in most capitals to send for a new envoy who was to present his credentials to the head of the State accompanied by some State officials in full uniform, I drove to the President's office in an old hired fly that smelt of straw, and I was alone. I liked this, which quite suited my own rather quiet tastes.

When later in Madrid I was driven to the palace to present my Letters of Credence in a carved and gilded coach, and a second similar and empty coach following, in case the first broke down, and a third one for the Secretaries of the Embassy, all escorted by countless servants in gorgeous liveries on foot, I mentally compared my progress through the streets on this occasion to that of the presentation of Letters in Berne, not wholly, be it remarked, in favour of Madrid.

The ceremony of the introduction to the President and the presentation of the Letters of Credence was marked with the same friendly simplicity. I realised from the first that this, one of the oldest Republics in Europe, and perhaps in the world, had preserved its primitive character, and it was this quality that first attracted me to Switzerland and to its form of government, about which I shall write a word or two later.

First, however, I must mention a, to me, perfectly novel experience which occurred very soon after my arrival in Berne.

One day M. de Muralt called me up on the telephone and said that a German had left a very confidential parcel at the Consulate for me. He had departed immediately, but said that he would call again to see me in a few days' time. He would give no further account of himself. I went down to look at the parcel, and on opening it found it contained maps.

I saw at once that these maps were apparently blue prints of the then much-discussed new forts on the islands off the German North Sea coast. Doing the packet up again, I carried it back to my office for further investigation. On arrival I found that with the maps there was an unsigned letter stating that the maps and charts were those of the latest fortifications on these Friesian islands, of which the most notorious was, I believe, Borkum at the mouth of the Elbe.

The letter asked me to submit the two or three maps enclosed to the competent British authorities, said that more could be obtained where these came from, and stated a price. The writer said he would return in a month or so and get his answer.

I was considerably troubled by being in any way mixed up with a matter of this sort, with which the head of a mission ought, of course, never to have anything to do. As, however, there was no one else in the Legation it was necessary for me to deal with it, and I forwarded the parcel as I received it to the Foreign Office by the next messenger, to be dealt with by the proper authorities.

I was not a little surprised to receive an answer by return that an official from the War Office would come out to Berne before the time mentioned by the writer as the date of his return and wait there to see him.

When this gentleman came he told me that these blue prints were evidently genuine, and certainly came from the map department of the German War Office ; and that these particular maps were not of great interest, but that the London authorities wished to see what the others mentioned in the letter were like. I told him it would be better for him not to see the German in question either at the Consulate or at the Chancery. We decided that the meeting should take place in my still empty house, No. 20, Elfen Strasse.

In due course the German turned up—an obvious Prussian officer, Herr von ——. He told me he had lost money and was obliged to recoup himself in this way. I told him to come to No. 20, Elfen Strasse, at a certain hour the next day, where he would meet a man come from London for the purpose. The next day, a little before the hour I had arranged with the German, I took the Englishman and established him in my study, where he put on a false beard and a wig. We then waited for the German to come. He turned up punctually, spent a considerable time in the study, and left the house forthwith. I found the Englishman doing a quick change in the study, and we returned to the town by another route. He told me he had been offered more maps, but did not give me any more information ; neither did I ask for more. He also said he was leaving that night for London. I hoped, though he seemed a pleasant fellow, I should not see him again in Berne, as he told me he had arranged for the next meeting with the German in Brussels.

My annoyance, therefore, was great when he turned up again some days later saying that the German had not met him in Brussels but had written to say that he was afraid to go there and was returning to Berne. He, therefore, asked the Englishman to take the first express from Brussels to Berne, where he gave an address at which he would be staying. The Englishman said

that as the express passed through Germany he smelt
a rat and preferred to take a long route through France.
He asked me if he could again have a meeting in 20,
Elfen Strasse. Extremely annoyed, I agreed, but said I
could not lend the house a third time. We then once
more went through the whole comedy of the false beard
and the rest, with the result that the German sold a
certain number of maps at a high price.

The sequel to this story was that months after the
Russian Military Attaché came to me and asked if my
Government had bought any German military maps of
the Friesian Islands from a certain Herr von ——. I
replied guardedly I did not know for certain, but I knew
that such maps had been offered by a man of, I thought,
that name. He said that he only asked because he had
bought for his Government some maps from the same
man, and had since discovered that he was a German
Government agent who sold false maps especially con-
cocted by the German War Office and printed on special
War Office paper, etc., in order to deceive foreign governments. A regular centre of this traffic in forgeries carried
on by the German Government was, as I was told, discovered later somewhere in Switzerland. The German
Government must have benefited largely by the guile-
lessness of their friends and neighbours.

Can such deception be considered an offence against
honour and gentlemanly conduct ? Perhaps. But looking
at the game of foreign politics as played at that time,
I cannot but feel that it was merely a successful bluff
which came well within the rules of the game. I have
thought that Mr. Bernard Shaw might write an amusing
comedy on the theme of the Governments of the Great
Powers balancing their Budgets by selling to each other
falsified plans of their own fortifications. One is tempted
to wonder if the world has not or will not shortly return
to such a system which resembles that Utopia where
families lived by taking in each other's washing.

Macchiavelli could hardly ever have imagined a more
virtuous and patriotic way of making both ends meet.

As the spring was fairly far advanced before Isa and the children could join me, I took a furnished châlet at Thun, to which they could go on arrival instead of attempting at once to take possession of the house in Berne. Thun is only about three-quarters of an hour from Berne, and it was not necessary for me to go into the Chancery daily, as I had now, pending the appointment of a regular secretary, an honorary attaché, George Herbert, a son of Lord Pembroke, who could hold the fort, so to speak, and telephone for me if anything urgent required my presence, which was unlikely. I was very sorry for him, since for a young bachelor Berne is not an amusing place.

I found I could well deal with the current work by going into Berne about twice a week and writing in Thun such reports on the country as I was asked for.

It was during this summer that I first began to take an interest in the workings of the Swiss Federal Constitution and political machinery, which I have since always regarded as a monument of human wisdom and successful practice in the science of Government. I hope to return to this topic later.

In the meantime the summer months passed delightfully. Friends and relations from Italy and England came to see us. It was the last summer that I was ever to know unspoilt by serious threats of war, war itself, or the pains of reconstruction after war.

Among the friends who came to see us were Mr. and Mrs. John X. Merriman, formerly Prime Minister of South Africa, and his wife, who had been so kind to my mother and myself on our first visit to Capetown in 1891, and afterwards again to me during the South African War. Both Isa and I found them, as I had done before, singularly attractive. His tall figure was now somewhat bent with years, but his face had retained all its refinement and his talk all its sparkle and charm. We went for several walks together on the hills behind Thun and Beatenberg, with their glorious views of the Bernese Oberland. He was still sad over the Boer War and the events that led up to it. We talked the subject all over together, he attributing the responsibility entirely to Rhodes and the gold bugs of Johannesburg and the financiers in England who supported them, whom he regarded with particular dislike ; I feeling that whatever their faults the die-hard attitude of Paul Kruger and his *entourage* towards any political reforms rendered a clash inevitable some day or other, though I never attempted to excuse the utterly illegal conduct of Rhodes in giving his support to the Johannesburg-Jameson plot of 1898. So we fought old battles over again, but never with the slightest shadow of vexation between us, and I have ever since looked back on our meetings at Thun with the greatest pleasure. On the great subject of the future of South Africa we were at least quite agreed that the breach between Dutch and English must be healed ; that they must learn to run the country together as an autonomous member of the British Commonwealth of Nations without interference from Downing Street.

Mrs. Merriman said one thing to Isa which touched us both greatly :

" Do you remember," she asked, " that when before the end of the Boer War we came over to London to plead the cause of an agreed peace with the Boers, and we were practically boycotted as pro-Boers, you and your husband came to the station to see us off when we left and brought me a bunch of roses. Well, we have never forgotten it, and we decided that we could not leave Europe this time without coming to Switzerland to thank you for that."

Isa and I were as much touched as they had been by the bunch of roses, and felt that that little courtesy had been well worth while. They were both delightful people, and we were sorry to say good-bye. We never met them again.

In 1912 Herr Forrer succeeded automatically to the Presidency of the Swiss Republic for the third time, which signified that he had been a member of the Federal Council for twenty-one years. He was to be President yet once again, which, of course, meant that he had been in the Government for twenty-eight consecutive years. How any man can remain so long a member of a democratic State, for democracy is notoriously unstable, is one of the miracles of the Swiss Government system which I shall endeavour to explain later, but for the present I shall confine myself to a few reminiscences of President Forrer, with whom I soon became very friendly. In Switzerland the President always has control of the Department of Foreign Affairs, and the foreign representatives therefore saw him much more frequently than they do the head of the State in other countries.

Herr Forrer when I knew him was already well on in years. He was of the Swiss stocky peasant build, with a fine massive head and waving white hair and curly beard, like the well-known picture by Albert Dürer of his own father. He was a Radical in politics, but was respected by all parties. Indeed, political parties in Switzerland when I was there hardly counted, except, of course, for questions of patronage, which in many democratically governed countries often creates the most formidable line of cleavage.

Herr Forrer always dressed like a good Swiss bourgeois in black broadcloth with an immaculate white shirt and small black tie. His hat was black and wide brimmed and of soft felt, and was as unchangeable as the rest of his garb. Had it not been for his air of the " Father of Albert Dürer," he might almost have passed as a Scottish Presbyterian Minister of the middle of the last century.

I frequently met President Forrer when I went for my early morning walk about 8 a.m., and he was on his way to his office. We could then talk freely on all sorts of subjects. He would also often accompany my boy Esme—aged seven— to a dame school which he attended, and would even wait for him if he was late. One day the President, as we walked together, said with a very serious mien :

" I must really warn you to look after your son."

I : " Why ? What has he been doing ? "

THE PRESIDENT : " Well, yesterday I was waiting for him to join me and walk down to his school, and he would linger behind. I said : ' Come along, Esme, or we shall both be late for school. What are you waiting for ? ' What do you think he answered ? ' *Ich warte für die kleine Lisa.*'[1] Then I said : ' But you will have years in which to walk about with the girls, and you won't be able to walk out much longer with the old President,' and then he answered : ' *Ja wohl aber, Herr President, ich hab' die Mädel so lieb.*'[2] So I thought I had better warn you because he is beginning young."

I : " I'm very grateful, and will certainly keep an eye on the young *Nix-nutz.*"[3]

Another morning when we were walking together he was carrying a very large brown-paper parcel under his arm, and we had the following little conversation :

THE PRESIDENT : " You will never guess, Herr Minister, what I've got in this parcel."

I : " I'm sorry, Herr President, that I cannot see through thick brown paper."

THE PRESIDENT : " Well, I'll tell you. I've got one of the sunniest gardens in Berne, where fruit and vegetables come to maturity long before they do elsewhere. This is a parcel of young turnips, which are a great delicacy at this time of year, and I'm taking them down as a present for my colleagues at the council meeting this morning."

By little incidents such as these, almost impossible in any other country, I learnt to appreciate the innate simplicity of manners of those who in Berne sat in the seats of the mighty. All this charmed and delighted me because here at least wealth practically counted for nothing. No one troubled about " how much money you could expose,"[4] and if you had more than your neighbour it was bad form to expose it.

---

[1] " I am waiting for little Lisa."
[2] " Yes, indeed, Mr. President, but I am so fond of the girls."
[3] " Good-for-nothing."
[4] Expression used by a negro bar tender in Trinidad.

M

I enjoyed my walks with Herr Forrer partly because of his utter lack of conventional ceremony, which was combined with the simple courtesy of a great gentleman, and partly because he had much of interest to tell me out of his long store of knowledge of the science of government and the ways of men.

In October, 1912, a most unusual event happened during Herr Forrer's presidency. The German Emperor came to Switzerland to attend the Swiss army manœuvres and was received at Berne and feasted at a great dinner. The Emperor had expressed a wish for some time to visit Switzerland and attend the manœuvres but there was no great anxiety on the part of the Swiss Government to receive so illustrious a guest. Nothing, I believe, in the way of an official reception of a crowned head in Berne had occurred for generations, and the idea of the visit of so hustling a Sovereign as William II agitated the Government Departments concerned very considerably. However, it was felt that it was better to get this visit over, and so at the appointed time the All Highest arrived with a great civil and military staff.

In attendance on the Emperor on the civil side were Count Eulenburg, Herr von Roeder, Baron Jenisch, and others. On the military side were Baron Huene, General von Plessen, General von Moltke, General Baron von Lyncker, and other smaller fry. The doyen of the Diplomatic Corps was the German Minister, Herr von Bülow, brother of Prince von Bülow, the former Chancellor. The Military Attachés of the Great Powers —who, of course, knew all about the Schlieffen plan to turn the great fortresses protecting the French frontier between Luxembourg and Switzerland by passing either over Swiss or Belgian territory in case of a war with France—made no secret of their belief that the Emperor had really come in order to give his Generals an opportunity of seeing for themselves what the Swiss army was like in time of manœuvres. They pointed to the concentration of German railways both at Bâle and at Aix as a positive proof that some such turning movement was and had been for a long time past in the mind of the German Government. Subsequent events naturally confirmed this opinion, and it may have been that the Emperor's visit to Switzerland proved the final argument against the German army taking the Swiss route. The Commandant of the Swiss army at that time, Colonel Sprecher von Bernegg, was said to be an extremely able soldier and he was certainly a first-class organiser who had learnt everything he knew in the German military schools and had the greatest possible admiration for Prussian military science. He must have got the organisation of the Swiss army up to a pitch of extreme perfection since, if I am not mistaken, the whole army of about 250,000 men was mobilised and in position on the Swiss frontier to prevent any violation of Swiss neutrality immediately after the Declaration of War in August, 1914, before any such large body of men on the German side were ready to move forward against France.

I, of course, was not invited to attend the manœuvres and saw nothing of them, but I heard a very pleasant story of an incident which occurred between the Emperor and President Forrer while they were watching the troops during a high wind. The President who was wearing his usual Presbyterian minister's garb had his old, broad-brimmed soft felt black hat carried away by the wind. The Emperor dashed after it and brought it back, smiling. The President said :

" *Danke Majestät. Ich hab' noch nie einen so schneidigen flügel-adjutanten gehabt.*"[1]

The Emperor during the whole time that he was in Switzerland made himself perfectly charming to everyone expect to one of the bears in the bear-pit. When he was taken down to pay the regulation visit to the bears with a large crowd watching, amongst whom I stood, he was given, like others, a big bunch of carrots to feed them with. He tried for some time but in vain, on account of his withered left arm, to detach one of these carrots and throw it down. The bear meanwhile was sitting up on its

---

[1] " Thank you, Majesty, I have never yet had so smart an A.D.C."

haunches waiting. It was evident that the Emperor was getting impatient and uneasy on account of the crowd that was watching him and noticing his futile efforts to detach the carrots. Then finally losing his temper, with the whole force of his tremendously strong right arm, he hurled the big bunch of carrots straight at the bear and caught it full on the chest. Bruin was quite pleased and munched his carrots contentedly, but from this little incident I gathered how extremely sensitive the Emperor was to anything that might draw attention to his withered arm. It seemed to me that this particular flaw in his physical outfit had probably much to account for with regard to his sudden and uneven temperament.

After the great dinner at the Federal Palace, at which I sat nearly opposite to the Emperor and was able to watch his cheerful conversation with President Forrer and Federal Councillor Müller who was in charge of military affairs, all the Heads of Missions were received by the Emperor in turn. I don't think I ever saw him in a better humour, and he kept me quite a long time talking about his visits to various country houses in England. By way of saying something I remarked that it was a great pity that a number of these houses would very soon have to be shut up. (This was shortly after Mr. Lloyd George's Budget bringing in the death duties.) The Emperor at once caught this up, saying :

" Yes, I suppose that is so, and whose fault will it be ? "

I answered : " That is a matter, sir, on which you will understand that my lips are sealed."

He replied, laughing : " I suppose you think, like most people, that my lips ought to be sealed too ? "—to which I returned an anodyne reply. This little interchange of remarks, not so long after the interview with the *Daily Telegraph* which cost Prince von Bülow his place as Chancellor, shows that when he wished to be pleasant nobody could be more so than William II. Anyway, he parted from me in the most friendly way and did not appear to bear any grudge for a remark which he might have thought reflected on his impetuosity.

As a matter of curiosity I give below the menu of the dinner offered by the Swiss Republic to the German Emperor. It would almost compare with the banquet of a Roman Emperor, and the wines, if I remember right, were particularly good. The simplicity of Berne did not extend to teetotalism.

DÎNER

Cantaloup frappé au Biscuit Dubouché
Consommé Juanita
Darnes de Saumon Chambord
Selle d'Agneau à la Châtelaine
Suprêmes de Poularde rosés Lamberty
Punch glacé au Marasquin
Jeunes Perdreaux, escortés de Cailles de Vigne
Compôte panachée, Salade Demidoff
Nids d'Artichauts Forestière
Bombe Favourite
Mille-Feuilles Petit Duc
Paillettes au Gruyère
Jardinières de Fruits
Friandises

Dézeley 1904
Château Margaux de Luze 1900
Saint Saphorin 1895
Clos Vougeot Grand Vin 1878
Veuve Clicquot rosé-doux
Pommery et Gréno nature 1906

Berne.   6 Sept. 1912.

We made an unexpected acquaintance during the Emperor's visit—that of General Beyers, of South Africa General Beyers had been an exceptionally successful guerilla warrior on the Boer side during the South African War. He had spent some time in London before coming to Switzerland, and came with a letter of introduction from the Foreign Office stating that he wished to see the Swiss Militia Army at work as it might be a useful experience for his work in South Africa in organising the military forces of the South African Government. He was like most of the South African Generals of that time, completely reconciled to the settlement arrived at after the war. I invited him to dinner and we had one or two long talks together, from which it seemed to me that there was no longer any doubt of his complete adherence to that settlement. I found him a pleasant companion and, so far as I could judge, a very intelligent man. He had been, if I am not mistaken, like many other of the South African leaders, a lawyer, and had received part of his education in Europe. It was noticed by some of the Military Attachés who were present during the manœuvres that the German Emperor paid particular attention to General Beyers, and I heard very shortly afterwards that he had invited the General to pay him a visit.

The visit took place soon after and I believe General Beyers was made much of. I heard no more about him until, shortly after the entry of Great Britain into the World War, I read in the paper that General Beyers was heading an insurrection against the South African Government, which the German papers naturally hoped would lead to the collapse of the Anglo-Dutch régime in South Africa and to the establishment of a Boer Republic under the wing of the great German World Power which was to be the child of a German victory.

It was impossible for me not to connect in my mind this unfortunate movement with the meeting of the German Emperor and General Beyers in Berne. The Boer insurrection lasted for a very short time and General Beyers was drowned endeavouring to swim the Klip river in flood in order to get away from the Government forces which were pursuing him.

A series of events of overwhelming importance occurred during my stay in Berne. In the autumn of 1911 there was formed, on the inspiration of M. Venizelos, the Balkan League by which all the Balkan States, Bulgaria, Greece, Serbia, and ultimately Montenegro joined in an alliance aimed against Turkey. The object of each was not only the liberation of its own co-nationals from the Turkish yoke but also, in the background, the materialisation of their age-long dream of the re-creation of the old

Bulgarian Empire, of the Pan-Serb or Yugo-Slav State and of a greater Greece. The fact that each of these seriously overlapped one of the others, and that the Yugo-Slav dreams could not come true without shaking the ramshackle Hapsburg Empire to its foundations, made no difference. It was in vain that M. Poincaré pointed out to M. Sazonow, the Russian Foreign Minister, in August, 1912, that the various agreements between the Balkan States, " contained the germ of war not only against Turkey but also against Austria,"[1] because these things sooner or later were bound to happen. In reading of them one feels again and again at work the force of necessity, the " 'ανάγκη " of the Greek tragedies.

To the amazement of the world war was declared against Turkey on October 8th, 1912, by Montenegro and the other Balkan States joined in at once, and again, to the amazement of the world, won victory after victory over the Turkish army.

General Conrad von Hoetzendorff, Chief of the Staff of the Austrian army, wished to attack the Serbs, who had reached the Adriatic, but was restrained by the old Emperor of Austria, backed up on this occasion by both Germany and Italy.[2] At the initiative of Sir Edward Grey a European conference was called in London to deal in such a way with these events as to bring about a peaceful settlement of the situation arising out of the break-up of Turkish power in Europe, and so to avoid the imminent danger of war between the European Great Powers which all had dreaded for years past.

It was, I think, while this conference was in progress in December, 1912, and all Europe was on tenterhooks as to the result, that M. de Muralt, the British Consul, who was also a banker in Berne, went to Berlin on business.

" There will be no war this time," he told me, on his return.

" Why not ? "

[1] *Europe in the 19th and 20th Centuries*, Grant and Temperley, p. 473. Longmans Green & Co.
[2] Ibid., p. 474.

" Well," said he, " a big German financier told me that the Emperor had called a conference of German financiers and asked them straight whether German financial houses could stand the strain of a war at this time. He was told that there was so much German capital out on deposit in foreign countries, especially France and England, that if this were embargoed as a result of a Declaration of War that would mean widespread ruin."

It was consequently decided that war must not be allowed to break out then, and every effort was made to restrain the Austrian war party.

This report of M. de Muralt returned very forcibly to my mind when, after the outbreak of war in 1914, due once more to the desire of Austria to curb the Pan-Serb movement, I learnt that the German financiers had withdrawn the greater part of their deposits in Paris and London some weeks before war was declared. It was difficult to avoid the conclusion that the withdrawal must have been arranged on the inspiration of the German Government which had already made up its mind to let Austria go all lengths in dealing with Serbia.

Before the German Government definitely gave Austria its support in the Ultimatum to Serbia in July, 1914, I, remembering the way in which they had blocked Austria the year before, could not believe that war was possible as the result of the Austrian Ultimatum. I felt certain that Germany would never allow it. That Germany could have prevented the War in 1914 as she did in 1912–13 I have and had then no doubt whatever. She had only to accept Edward Grey's invitation to a European conference and bring pressure to bear on her Ally. This she deliberately omitted to do and on her, therefore, rests the major responsibility for the catastrophe, for the Austrians could well have accepted the Serbian reply to their Ultimatum.

When in 1913 it became clear that the Balkan conflagration would not lead to a major European war all breathed more freely. But we felt that we had escaped by a hair's breadth and that the Austrian Pan-Serb conflict was only postponed, and not done with.

The year 1913 also saw a family event of the first magnitude—the last of its kind—for Henry was born on March 3rd at 20, Elfen Strasse, Berne.

My family therefore now consisted of two Romans, Esme and Francis ; one Washingtonian, Hubert ; one Budapester, Edmund ; and one Bernese, Henry.

My time in Switzerland was a particularly enjoyable one as I have already stated. I was free enough to be able to do a good deal of travelling, two or three days at a time being quite sufficient for my purpose, and I paid particular attention to the delightful small mediæval towns which are generally omitted from the programme of the ordinary Swiss tourists. Murten or Morat, the scene of the final defeat of Charles the Bold by the Swiss Federation was a particular favourite of ours. It was within a fairly easy drive of Berne and on half-holidays I was fond of taking the family there. There was something fascinating to me in the little walled city by the lake, the walls of which still showed marks of the cannon balls of Charles the Bold. It was, I think, after the Battle of Murten, which was decisive as far as the liberties of Switzerland were concerned, that the Swiss captured the camp of Charles the Bold with all the magnificent tapestries that are now to be seen in the National Museum at Berne. Other places which I also visited with particular pleasure were Fribourg, where I first met the Queen of Spain, whose son, the Prince of the Asturias, was being treated there by one of the Swiss doctors ; the village and Castle of Gruyère, and other places, all extremely picturesque in their way.

At Geneva, which we visited two or three times as guests of the late ever-hospitable Mrs Barton, who was known after the establishment of the League of Nations as the Queen of Geneva, we found an agreeable cosmopolitan and Italo-Franco-Swiss native society of old families with whom it will be remembered Count Cavour, the great maker of modern Italy, was closely connected.

Geneva as represented at Mrs. Barton's hospitable board was by no means the overpoweringly strict and serious society that one naturally connects with the city of Calvin.

Switzerland was also for us particularly agreeable because, being in the middle of Europe, we saw more of our relations and friends travelling between England and Italy than at any other post. It was, therefore, with real regret that I received notice in May, 1913, of my transfer to Sweden.

CHAPTER VII

SWITZERLAND ; THE SWISS DEMOCRACY

Let those, who despise the capacity of the Swiss, tell us by what wonderful policy or by what happy conciliation of interests it is brought to pass that in a body made up of different communities and different religions there should be no civil commotions though the people are so warlike that to nominate and to raise an army is the same thing.—DR. JOHNSON.

Boswell's *Life of Johnson*, 1826 Edition, Vol. I, p. 133.

I MIGHT go further and ask by what miracle it comes about that the Swiss, having the most complete and advanced form of democracy in the world, have at the same time the most stable Government in the world since, unbelievable though it may seem, their actual administration has not changed now for about sixty years, i.e. since the adoption of the Constitution of 1874. By this I mean not only that the form of Government has not changed but also that, though the members of the Federal Council—which corresponds to our Executive or Cabinet—have necessarily changed in the course of nature, the actual body itself has never been out of office for a day during all these years, but has gone on quietly, slowly, efficiently, doing its work as though on a continuous chain.

When I first realised this amazing fact I determined to learn all about it, as it always seemed to me that, since lack of stability was one of the principal weaknesses of democracies from the days of Athens to our own, there must be some special quality about the Swiss democracy which might perhaps be injected with advantage into our own more volatile species.[1]

[1] If anyone cares to pursue these studies I can confidently recommend the following books :

1. *The Rise of the Swiss Republic*, by W. D. McCracken, M.A., published by Henry Holt & Co., of New York. This is a compact and well-written narrative of the most interesting history of the Cantons and of the Confederation with an Appendix containing the present Constitution.

2. *The Swiss Democracy*, by Lloyd & Robson, published by T. Fisher Unwin,

After reading the works mentioned in the footnote and after many conversations with Swiss politicians on the working of their system of Government, I began to understand how it was that the Swiss, alone perhaps of all people in the world, succeeded in solving the problem of reconciling stability of tenure with genuine democratic government.

The English system works indeed sufficiently well so far as England is concerned by giving either party—so long as there are only two major parties—a reasonably long lease of administrative life, when returned with a good working majority. This is, however, because the English temperament is naturally ready for compromise and therefore Members of Parliament are generally willing to subordinate their own judgment on any question, on which the fate of the Ministry depends, to that of their Party leaders. This is not so in Latin countries or indeed wherever Representative Government on the English model invariably tends to split up Parliament into many Parties on account of which stability is too often unattainable and chaos ensues, leading to revolution or to some form of dictatorship more or less camouflaged—of late considerably less than more.

I may perhaps be allowed to quote here from an article I published anonymously in October, 1913, in the *Edinburgh Review* called " The Problem of Democracy and the Swiss Solution." I have seen no reason to change my mind on this subject in the years that have passed since 1913. On the contrary the introduction of open dictatorship in various countries and the failure of Parliamentary Government in others only confirms me in my opinion that ultimately all democratic countries will be compelled to adopt a system on lines approaching those

of London, 1908. An up-to-date account of the evolution of Swiss Government up to the time of publication.

3. *The Swiss Republic*, by Boyd Winchester, late United States Minister at Berne, published by J. B. Lippincott Co., of Philadelphia and London. This is a classic on the subject of Swiss history and development.

4. *La Démocratie Suisse*, par Felix Bonjour, published by Payat & Cie, of Lausanne, 1919.

of the Swiss Constitution in order to secure stability of government and not fall under a dictatorship of some kind.

I wrote in 1913 :

> It may be accepted as an axiom that a truly democratic Government should first and foremost express as far as is humanly possible the will of the people of the country. An ideal Constitution should make it impossible for Parliamentary representatives to impose on the country laws which the people do not want. Further, it should be very difficult, if not impossible, for a small majority to impose constitutional changes to which nearly one-half of the electors are opposed.
>
> Yet these obvious requirements of democratic government are conspicuously absent in most so-called democratic countries to-day and there consequently exists a very widespread discontent with Parliamentary government both in Europe and America.
>
> It is often uncertain on both sides of the Atlantic how far laws, which are easily carried through Parliament, are really wanted by the people and whether, if put to the popular vote, they would have even a bare majority in their favour. This doubt necessarily provokes bitterness among minorities in legislative assemblies and from that state of mind it is but a step to obstruction, followed by the closure, and in turn followed by increased discontent and finally by indifference to Parliamentary proceedings.
>
> A further consequence of the present methods of legislating is that attempts are made to defeat Governments by trickery, by snap votes, by plots and counter plots and all the mean and meaningless paraphernalia of party intrigue. The expression of the will of the people as an aim of Government is altogether lost sight of and Party opportunity and Party necessities become the sole motive of political action.

The first requirement of democratic government being the expression of the real will of the people, the second is that the political machine should work as smoothly and as stably as possible. For this end care should be taken so to constitute the legislative and executive bodies as to avoid as far as humanly possible political crises consequent upon, or the cause of, sudden change of Government, and to minimise the turmoil and excitement inevitably caused by general elections.

These two fundamental requirements of democracy, first that government should be an expression of the people's will and secondly that it should work both smoothly and stably and not be subject to frequent crises, seem to have been met more successfully by the Swiss system than by any other in the world.

The Swiss Confederation is made up of twenty-two Sovereign States or Cantons, which have united and have delegated to the Federal Government the duty of dealing with certain matters of common interest to all. All matters not specially so delegated to the Federal Government remain naturally within the jurisdiction of the Cantonal Governments.

My interest in Swiss political institutions lay rather with the Federal Government than with those of the Cantons and what follows is a very short synopsis of Federal institutions :—

The Executive is called the Federal Council and consists of seven members presided over by the President of the Republic who acts for one year, being only *primus inter pares*, the first among equals, a sort of Chairman rather than a leader of the Government.

Each Federal Councillor is at the head of one of the Government Departments. Federal Councillors may sit and speak in either Chamber but have no right to vote.

Each member of the Council is elected separately, as such, by both Chambers[1] sitting together in joint session.

Each is elected for four years.

The President and Vice-President are elected in the same way from among the Councillors and retain their respective offices for one year only, it being the almost invariable habit for the Chambers to choose as President the next Councillor in order of seniority. These posts are thus practically always filled by rotation and there is no more excitement over the election of a President and Vice-President in Switzerland than there is over the accession of an elder son to the estates of his father in a land where primogeniture is recognised. Indeed, there is much less for while all know practically for certain who

---

[1] The Upper Chamber, called the Council of States, has forty-four members, two for each State or Canton like the American Senate. The Lower or National Council has over 160 members, elected for three years in the proportion of one to every twenty thousand inhabitants.

he will be, they all know that his term of office will cover
one year only, so that if he is unsuccessful it will require
no political earthquake to turn him out.

Thus the Swiss Executive is not renewable all at once
but only gradually and partially as the term of office of
each member (i.e. four years) comes to an end. Nor is it
dependent for its existence like the British Cabinet on
the vote of a majority in the Federal Assembly. Yet the
Swiss Executive, like the British but unlike the American,
has the right and duty of initiating legislation and, of
course, of defending its proposals in the Assembly, though
if a measure is rejected by the Assembly the Federal
Council does not resign and that particular measure drops
for the time being. Nothing else happens ; there is no
political crisis, no general election, no change of Government.

Let us now consider what immense advantages in regard
to freedom of voting according to his conscience this
system confers on the individual member of Parliament.
By it he is saved from ever being placed in the dilemma
of having to choose between his own judgment on a
matter, or the risk of, by voting against his Party's Government on a measure he disapproves, helping to turn that
Government out, forcing on a General Election and
perhaps so helping into office a Party of whose principles
he disapproves. The Swiss Member of the Assembly
knows that whichever way he votes there will be no
change of Government, no General Election, and none
of the turmoil and serious interference with the steady
flow of business throughout the country which a General
Election in England on account of the uncertainties it
creates invariably carries with it. In this way, therefore,
the Swiss have succeeded in obtaining a real and working
stability of Government which both English and Americans or indeed any other democratic people in the world
are very far from enjoying. It is not necessary to mention
France, which for several years in succession had an
average, I believe, of three Governments a year. In
Spain, Portugal, Italy and many other countries matters

have been almost as bad until it appeared that Dictator-
ships seemed the only way of salvation.

A dictatorship, with God's help, we may yet avoid in
this country. What, however, we suffer from is " the
swing of the pendulum." Party Government as such
exasperates and wearies those electors who are not Party
men, the always uncertain element among us, so that
the country may often be compared to Florence, Dante's
sick woman in the Purgatorio, Canto VI, who finds no
rest upon her cushions of down, but seeks to escape pain
by turning from side to side.[1]

Some may ask how can a system like the Swiss be
brought into harmony with an hereditary Monarchy such
as ours, which without doubt an overwhelming majority
of British subjects all over the world wish to preserve.

There seems to me no difficulty, *mutatis mutandis*,
about this. In fact the increased stability of Parliamentary Government obtained by adopting some plan
approaching to the Swiss system would certainly give
increased stability to the monarchical idea.

Thus, if we write " Prime Minister " instead of " President of the Republic " and allow the King to nominate
him and his second in command on the petition of the
House of Commons—very much as the King now does
in the case of Bishops on the recommendation of the
Prime Minister—or if his term of office were to be fixed
at four to five years, subject of course to the House having
the right of recall, would that be very different in practice
to the working arrangement by which the Prime Ministers
are appointed in England to-day ? In other words the
Swiss system might be followed more or less closely,
provided always that stability was maintained.

Aiming, therefore, at stability and smooth operation
of Government and especially at the real necessity of
escaping the danger of a possible dictatorship, whether of
the Left or of the Right, to which may lead our present
Constitutional custom of allowing any victorious Party

---

[1] " *Che non puo trovar posa in su le piume*
Ma con dar volta suo dolore scherma."

at elections complete power to do what it thinks fit, subject only to a possible short hold up by the House of Lords, I have often wondered whether it would not be possible to incorporate into our political system some of those elements which have enabled Switzerland, in the midst of revolutions, wars and all kinds of chaotic conditions going on around her, to run along quietly as on a continuous chain of Government for sixty years or more.

Switzerland is also far ahead of other countries in that it has adopted and used as a practical part of its legislative machinery, the Referendum. By this, if a sufficient number of voters can be found to sign, within ninety days of the passing by the Federal Assembly of any measure a petition demanding that the law in question be submitted to a direct vote of the people before being finally placed on the Statute Book, the Federal Council must organise the popular vote, inform the Cantonal Councils and secure the prompt circulation to voters of the question " Do you accept the Federal Law relating to (here follows the title of the Law) ? ' Yes ' or ' No '."

After the votes are cast, each electoral district or commune draws up its report containing four columns.

1. The number of registered voters.
2. The number of actual voters.
3. The number of those voting " Yes."
4. The number of those voting " No."

This is simple enough for most men and women to understand, and it prevents a law which is really unpopular and therefore difficult to enforce from being placed on the Statute Book.

Messrs. Lloyd and Robson write in their book :[1]

Party names or organisations have not indeed entirely disappeared in Switzerland, but their meaning and importance are slight. Under the domination of the Representative system the hiearchy of influence runs Party, men, measures. Under the dominion of a sovereign People it runs Measures, men, party. Not that there is less political

[1] *The Swiss Democracy.* Lloyd and Robson, p. 231. Ernest Benn Limited, London

N

organisation in Switzerland than elsewhere. There is more. But citizens group themselves into leagues, societies or purely temporary associations for the promotion of particular acts or lines of policy. In Switzerland the initiators or enthusiasts for an idea which they wish to embody in a public policy can devote the whole of their energy to the simple task of educating the electorate. They cannot hope to carry through their project by cajolery or menace or log-rolling in the lobby of the Party Convention or of the House.

In order to succeed they must convert the people.

Concrete proposals, not Party, become the basis of organisation and of education under direct democracy. The political machinist can no longer pump his will down the machine and convert a notion or an aspiration into a law which the people is bound under penalty to obey.

Thus the Party system inevitably withers under the growth of direct democracy. If the vote of the entire people must confirm every important and contested Act, if the people can force any measure to the test of a vote which has legislative validity, the despotism of the machine is broken and Party resumes its modest place as a loose voluntary association of like-minded citizens working for a common policy which is wider and more continuous than that of separate Leagues that devote themselves to ripening some concrete proposal for legislative action.

This puts the matter in a nutshell. It is, I feel, true that under the domination of the Representative System, as we had it in England before the present National Government, the hierachy of influence ran to a great extent : Party, men, measures, while it should run—to be healthy for the country—measures, men, party as, speaking generally, it does in Switzerland under the regime of direct democracy.

Whenever I have spoken of this to British Statesmen or still more mere politicians, I have invariably been met with a pitying or slightly contemptuous smile. But Switzerland is such a small country, they always say, how can its example affect us ? To this I can only reply, Switzerland has had far greater difficulties to contend against than any other European country. She has everything within her borders that would make for her disruption ; three different nationalities, three official languages, two religions almost equal in influence, whose feelings towards each other in some parts were still so

violent that in the Protestant half of the Canton of Appenzell, for instance, Catholics were not allowed to reside as
late, so I have been told by old residents there, as the
eighteen sixties.

This small country also contains the greatest physical
barriers of Europe in the shape of the two Alpine ranges
which, in the days before railways, divided it in winter
at any rate quite as effectively as wide seas would have
done.

What then has held these parts together with an
almost supernatural power ?   What centripetal force has
cemented together these seemingly unsympathetic parts
into so solid and patriotic a whole when any ordinary
student of human nature would be amply justified in
concluding that natural centrifugal force would be such
that they could not possibly hold together ?   This is the
question that Dr. Johnson asked himself and apparently
never answered.

The answer is, I think, to be found in the text of the
League and Pact of perpetual peace drawn up on
August 1st, 1291, between the three Forest States of
Schwyz, Uri and Unterwalden, which was concluded in
order to protect them against the encroachments of the
Hapsburgs, of whom Rudolph, Count of Hapsburg,
Archduke of Austria and German Emperor, was their
most dangerous enemy.   This famous Pact, which
deserves to be far better known than it is and might well
have been used to inspire the founders of the League of
Nations, begins as follows :

> In the name of God, Amen.   Honour and the public weal are
> promoted when Leagues are concluded for the proper establishment
> of quiet and peace.
> 1. Therefore know all men that the people of the valley of Uri,
> the democracy of the valley of Schwyz and the community of the
> mountaineers of Unterwalden seeing the malice of the Age, in order
> that they may better defend themselves and their own and better
> preserve them in proper condition have promised in good faith to
> assist each other with aid, with every counsel and every favour
> with person and goods within the valleys and without with might
> and main against one and all who may inflict upon any one of them

any violence, molestation or injury or may plot any evil against
their persons or goods.

The remaining clauses of this inspiring document are
too long to be quoted here, but one must still be given
in extenso because it is short and very much to the point.
This is No. 12 :

> But if War or discord arise among any of the Confederates and
> one party of the disputants refuses to accept justice or satisfaction,
> the Confederates are bound to defend the other party.

In this it has always seemed to me lies the seed, the
germ of any real League for the preservation of peace.

All parties to it must join to make the continuation of
war impossible by those who in the words of this prototype
of Peace Leagues refuse to accept justice or satisfaction.
But in order to reach this happy solution there must be
some penalty for those who refuse and unless all sign the
Covenant or Pact or whatever it may be called to force
the contumacious party to accept an armistice as a preliminary to giving justice and satisfaction, we may be
sure that many nations, who feel themselves strong will
sooner or later take the bit between their teeth and go
their own way.

This is not the place to discuss what the penalty for
violation of such a general Pact " for the proper establishment of quiet and peace " should be, but in my opinion
there is only one kind of sanctions which all, once they
are sufficiently enlightened to see that War, whenever and
wherever entered upon, is Public Enemy No. 1, would be
willing to undertake and this is simply to cease all
financial, commercial or economic business of any kind
with the belligerent who will not, when summoned to do
so, agree to an armistice. It has long seemed to me that
neutrals who have prided themselves as morally superior
to belligerents but who were only too willing to make
enormous profits out of trading with both belligerents
and so assisting to prolong the war, were playing but a
sorry part. In real truth I rather prefer the so-called
imperialist statesman who believes he is working for the

greatness of his country, and certainly I much prefer the soldier or the sailor who is willing to die for the defence if not for the greatness of his country, to those statesmen who grow righteously indignant over any interference with their liberty of making money out of trade with both belligerents and so helping these to go on killing each other for the benefit of the pockets of impartial neutrals. It is indeed difficult not to feel anything but contempt for that kind of neutral.

Unfortunately neither the name of the place where this great League or Pact of the three Forest States—those smallest of all the Cantons—was signed, nor the names of those who signed it have been handed down to us. But the parchment itself is still preserved in the archives of the Canton of Schwyz.

That then is the real foundation of the Swiss Confederation and all the rest follows therefrom.

There was a story current in Berne that a Count von Müllinen, a descendant of one of the oldest Bernese noble families, was once sent on a diplomatic mission to the Emperor of Austria. When he was introduced to the Emperor the latter spoke of the cradle of his family, the Castle of Hapsburg, being within the boundaries of the Swiss Confederation. Count von Müllinen asked if His Majesty was aware that the Hapsburgs and the Müllinens had at one time been rivals.

" *Ja wohl*," said the Emperor, " *Meine Familie hat jedoch die bessere Carriere gemacht.*"[1]

I have often wondered whether the Count Müllinen, whom I knew well in Berne as the Keeper of the City Library, would wish to-day to change with one of the family which made the better career.

In one respect at least we seem to be moving empirically, as our habit is, towards one of the great discoveries of the Swiss, which is that a permanent National Government is much better for the country than the swing of the pendulum of parties.

On Saturday, June 8th, 1935, Mr. Stanley Baldwin

[1] " Yes, certainly, but my family made the better career."

making at Himley Park, near Birmingham, his first speech
after accepting for the third time the office of Prime
Minister, said :

> I want for a moment to look back four years, not so much
> at what has happened but at the circumstances in which the National
> Government (i.e. that presided over by Mr. Ramsay MacDonald)
> was returned to power. . . . The political instincts of our people
> never showed to greater advantage.
> They could never have been shown in a similar manner by any
> other democracy in the world.[1] For our people, when unemploy-
> ment was almost at its worst, rallied to the support of a Government
> they believed would put things right, and they knew that to put
> things right sacrifices would be demanded by the people.

Further on he said :

> Since the formation of the National Government the under-
> standing between the three parties represented in the Government,
> our own (i.e. Conservative), the National Liberal, and the National
> Labour, has been that we should work as three independent parties
> and extend to each other all the co-operation and help that is
> possible.

and the general impression left on the mind of the reader
of his speech is the slogan " National Government must
go on."

Thus we in England seem to be approaching the
practical working conclusions at which the Swiss arrived
long ago. But if we try to keep a National Government
in being with our old machinery, which is built up on the
assumption that there will always be two parties struggling
in Parliament for the upper hand, then it may be feared
that National or Coalition Government must sooner or
later disappear and Ministries will revert to type and
depend on the swing of the pendulum.

What has given the Swiss National Government, which
for so long has been made up of representatives of three
parties, its extraordinary long lease of life, avoiding
political crises and internal convulsions, has undoubtedly
been the fact that the members of the Executive are not

---

[1] I venture to think that in saying this Mr. Baldwin forgot the Swiss, who being
the most democratic people have adopted the system of National as opposed to
Party Government for many years past with the greatest benefit to themselves.

SWITZERLAND, 1912

LANDAMMANS BAUMANN'S ELECTION

dependent for their places on a majority vote given for the whole Cabinet or Council in regard to any particular measure but to the public record of each one and his reputation for zeal, efficiency and honour.

In these circumstances it will be readily understood that it was soon recognised as being for the public advantage that the principal parties in the Assembly should agree to something like proportional representation in the Federal Council, which apparently works so well that I remember one Councillor saying to me :

" You would be surprised if you attended our meetings to discover how little disagreement there is on any subject of National importance."

The reason for this is clear. All are thinking nationally and without an eye to the next General Election.

It remains to be seen whether in England a National Government can stand much longer on the foundations built for a Two-Party system. I personally doubt it and regret it with all my heart, for I feel that a National Government whose members think nationally as in Switzerland must surely be far better for the country at large than a form of Government like ours which in the nature of things must oscillate between two extremes. In this case we must make up our minds to the swing of the pendulum going one day unpleasantly far in one direction or the other.

There is much else to which attention might be drawn in the Swiss system of Government that might well be imitated elsewhere, but this book is not intended to contain long treatises on the systems of Government in different countries. I have only written about the Swiss Constitution at some length because it has appeared to me the most worthy of study of any with which I have come into direct contact and I should be glad if this short notice might lead to closer study of it.

In one thing I may say that Switzerland is singularly fortunate. It is still largely a country of peasant farmers. As Trotsky has most truly remarked in his history of the Russian Revolution, this makes the introduction of any advanced system of Communism practically impossible. Though Communism has increased considerably in the larger manufacturing cities because, as in other countries, the working men are beginning to feel even there the burden of our too-accentuated individualistic and capitalistic era, this tendency in countries like Switzerland will probably always be so far held in check by the large body of peasant proprietors as to prevent any revolution of the Russian type.

Early in June, 1913, I left Berne for London on my way to Stockholm to my new post. Isa and the children, being comfortably installed in our good house in the Elfen Strasse, were in no hurry to leave.

The Balkan Conference was in session when I arrived in London, and Edward Grey was so busy that he had no time to see a Minister passing from one secondary European post to another, so I had to be content with seeing my old friend, Eyre Crowe, the Permanent Under-Secretary for Foreign Affairs, who gave me all necessary information about my new post. He told me that I could just greet Grey before leaving if I attended the annual party given at the Foreign Office for the King's birthday. This I did, expecting to have perhaps a word or two with my chief.

As I shook hands with him at the top of the staircase of the Foreign Office, he looked me straight in the face and observed :

" I've seen that crested tit."

For a moment I thought either he or I must have gone mad, then there flashed across my memory a heated argument I had had with him after dinner at a country house in the south of England when I had sworn I that had seen a crested tit. He perfectly justly declared that there were no crested tits in Great Britain south of some place in Scotland.

When I had sufficiently recovered from my amazement at his unexpected statement that he had seen one, I replied that in that case I hoped he would believe me next time. All he said to this was :

" Not at all. The one I saw was in Scotland about four hundred miles north."

I could argue no more, even if I had wished to, for a queue was growing on the stairs waiting to shake the hand of the Secretary of State and no doubt wondering what was the serious diplomatic conversation between him and the new Minister to Stockholm, that is if the people knew the latter by sight.

Years after, when we were both attending an annual meeting of the Society for the Protection of Birds, being asked to say something I told this story as an illustration of his extraordinary memory for anything connected with birds, and I told it as having occurred at Littlecote, in Wiltshire. After the meeting was over he came up and said, laughing :

" You were wrong again. We were shooting at Cornbury, Oxfordshire, when you said you saw that crested tit, and I could take you now to the corner of the covert where you said you saw it."

Evidently the crassness of my ignorance made an indelible impression on his scientific ornithological mind.

This conversation was the only one I had with him before leaving for my new post, and it left me, for some reason which I cannot expect anyone but an Englishman to understand, and which, to tell the truth, I can hardly understand myself, with a feeling of greater personal friendship with him than I ever had before.

CHAPTER VIII

SWEDEN

(1913)

I MUST confess that I started for Sweden without enthusiasm. Switzerland I had enjoyed for many reasons, amongst others that it was on the road to everywhere, and I saw more friends and relations than at any other time of my career. The fact that there was little Society life there was, in my eyes, an advantage rather than the reverse, and though Berne was cold and foggy in winter, the winter was not too long, and it was comforting to reflect that in a few hours one could be in Italy or, at any rate, at Lugano or Locarno.

I dreaded Stockholm because I knew that the winter went on till April and was long and dark, and Stockholm, moreover, seemed practically at the end of the civilised world and not on the road to anywhere, so that it was unlikely that many acquaintances would come along that way. I knew it was a lovely city, surrounded by lakes, fjords and pine woods, but this did not compensate, in my opinion, for the absence of sun for months and for the presence of ice and snow for a much longer time than I cared to think about. So I left without enthusiasm and could I have foreseen the difficulties that awaited me during the four years of the War that I spent there, I should have felt even more low-spirited than I did when I boarded the steamer at Harwich for Gothenburg.

After a day at Gothenburg, which produced a pleasant impression of cleanliness, business and order, I took a night train for Stockholm, and was again pleasantly impressed by the comfort and cleanliness of the Swedish

sleeping-cars. Nothing seemed to hurry greatly in this
country, but everything went surely and pleasantly along
its ordered way. This impression remained with me to
the end and even through those evil days of the War.
It only made me laugh when Swedish friends tried to
make my flesh creep by depicting their fellow-countrymen
as slumbering volcanoes which might only too easily be
roused to sudden fury, as when they tore poor Axel
Fersen to pieces in the streets of Stockholm for, as far
as I could gather, no very special reason.

The agreeable impression grew on arrival at Stockholm,
which was certainly a lovely city on a fair and fresh
morning in June.

I found the Legation was situated in a first-floor
apartment in the Strandvägen, having a beautiful view
across a sheet of water to the Royal Palace, but hardly
large enough for me, my numerous family, and the
Chancery. It had, besides, the disadvantage of being
situated over a grocer's shop which smelt strongly of
cheese and bacon. This so outraged King Edward, when
a year or two before on a visit to Stockholm he had dined
at the Legation, that he had at once, on returning to
England, insisted that a proper Legation should be built
far from such perfumery.

So I was engaged in superintending for the second
time the erection or purchase of a new home for one
of our missions abroad. I could wish now I had been
a little firmer with the Office of Works, for both here
and in Berne it should have been possible to have a far
more satisfactory house. In Stockholm, however, I was
so glad when the time came to leave the neighbourhood
of the scented grocery and get installed in a house of
our own that I would readily have accepted something
much less adapted to its purpose than the very comfortable
villa which the Office of Works finally put up. The one
great drawback of the new house was that the architect,
not knowing Stockholm, had not recognised that the
dining-room is always looked upon as a sort of temple
in which the religious ceremony of eating and drinking

has to be carried on with all proper dignity, and that a large room of noble proportions is therefore considered as a necessity which no gentleman can decently do without. How much more, then, is this the case where it may fall to the lot of the incumbent of a Legation to entertain kings. Now, the mind of the architect of the Office of Works was not tuned up to the proper pitch in the matter of dining-rooms, and he only calculated for dinner parties of sixteen, a sadly bourgeois conception of the requirements of a Stockholm dining-room. But by the time we got to the point of building the dining-room we were already in the War, and I could not pay the proper attention to this most serious matter. That must be my excuse to future generations of Ministers, many of whom I have been told have criticised me with some bitterness for overlooking this defect.

To return, however, to the apartment on the Strand-vägen, what immediately reconciled me to the grocer's shop and would have reconciled me to far worse things, was the welcome accorded to me by old Frida Anderson, the housekeeper, who had been with successive Ministers for over thirty years, and looked on a new Minister as a person to be not only protected from all evil but also coached in his duties. She was absolutely loyal, faithful and respectfully motherly, and so reminded me of my old German nurse Binchen, that I adored her from the first moment I saw her. Besides Frida, there was also Strandberg who, while being Chancery servant, acted at first for me as butler, valet, and in household matters confidential adviser, and was as perfect in his way as Frida. These two almost made up to me for the absence of my family.

With their help the first months at Stockholm passed far more pleasantly than I had anticipated.

The Secretary to the Legation, William Erskine, and his charming wife, left Stockholm very shortly after my arrival for another post, leaving me, as usual in a new post, without any regular diplomatic assistant in the Chancery, though I was lucky in having an active honorary attaché, C. F. Madeley, who knew Stockholm well, spoke Swedish fluently, and was a general favourite in Swedish society. He was, therefore, extremely helpful. Not having, however, anyone whom I could leave in charge of the Legation, I was compelled to decline a most tempting invitation for a short trip on the yacht of Mr. and Mrs. Löffler, in the Baltic, which would have included a visit to St. Petersburg and Moscow. I thus lost my only chance of seeing those cities before they were bolshevised out of all recognition, which has been a standing grievance ever since.

During that summer I made friends with two men, both of whom were unusual in character and had had unusual careers, and who therefore at once interested and attracted me. One was Dr. Axel Munthe, the doctor of the Queen of Sweden, and author of a book, *Letters from a Mourning City*, which I had read years before and had never forgotten. He was also the author-to-be of that book which has fascinated more readers in all parts of the world than any other published in my lifetime—I refer, of course, to *San Michele*. He talked very much as he wrote in *San Michele*, and I always found his conversation most entertaining.

The other man who, like Axel Munthe, has remained a close friend up to this day, was of a very different kind. One morning I was sitting writing in my study when a visiting-card was brought to me :

MR. ALWYNE MAUDE,
Breidablik, Drottningholm.

Some Anglo-Swede, I thought, probably come on business. He was shown in and sat on the edge of his chair. He was obviously not a business man.

He explained that he had known me some forty-five or fifty years ago at Greystoke, when I was a child in the nursery, he being about nine years older. He used to spend his summers with his uncle and aunt, Sir Henry and Lady Vane, at their place Hutton-in-the-Forest, about five miles from Greystoke. I was delighted to find someone who could talk about Cumberland, and from these somewhat slender and distant memories we built up rapidly a house of friendship which has stood the test of time. I learnt that having been born into Court circles, for his father, Colonel Sir George Maude, had been for years the Controller of the Royal Stable under Queen Victoria, he had first been a smart young man about Town, next an art student, then had married on little or nothing, and had started farming in Tennessee in Hughes' Co-operative Colony, called Rugby. When that failed he was found by a lady friend of his smart days wandering homeless about the streets of New York, and helped on to his legs again. He studied music at Munich and something else at Oxford, and after the death of his first wife he married a most charming and beautiful Swedish widow with a house called " Breidablik," in the Royal Park at Drottningholm on the Mälaren Lake.

Here I felt was just the sort of man that interested me. He had gone through more experiences of life than I had, had met perhaps stranger people than I, was in spite of present easy circumstances a bohemian in many respects and a man who interested himself as much in cows as in pictures and in the rearing of babies—for he had brought up his own with bottles in the wilds of Tennessee —as in the symphonies of Beethoven or Brahms.

He was besides a passionately eager gardener and had built up what house agents would call a " garden of distinction " at Drottningholm. He had, moreover, a certain inconsequent whimsicality in his outlook and method of expression which pleased me greatly.

No two men could be more unlike than these two Stockholm friends of mine, but they both had one thing in common, which endeared them to me, a great compassion for suffering whether in man, woman or child, bird or beast. Both at times might allow this compassion to carry them to somewhat unreasonable lengths, but when you see suffering inflicted it is probably better to boil than to remain genteelly lukewarm. All my unfortunate diplomatic training goes to warn me against boiling, and I feel that more can be accomplished by those who can control their indignation, righteous or otherwise, than by those who cannot. Nevertheless I esteem those who having passed the first heat of youth are still capable of reaching boiling point at times.

Axel Munthe I saw seldom, for he was nearly always in attendance on the Queen of Sweden, and she being an invalid rarely came to Stockholm, but I made during that summer some short excursions with Alwyne Maude, such as one into Dalecarlia which I remember with great pleasure. It was in the sitting-room of the hotel at Eiljen Lake that he discovered and played to me on a poor old tinkling hotel piano Sibelius' little " Élégie," which has ever since been to me the musical expression of the Swedish landscape.

I had very little work but, during the summer I took regular lessons in Swedish, which is not difficult to learn, at least to read, and soon I could enjoy going to the theatre. The Swedes are a remarkably artistic race and wonderful craftsmen, first-rate workers in metals, whether silver, gold, iron or bronze. Excellent architects, musicians and singers. After the Russians I think that they come next for full melodious bass voices. They are also good average actors. When I was in Stockholm they had two or three artists of the first rank such as Anders Zorn, Liliefors and Carl Larsen.

So that what with familiarising myself, as I always tried to do, with the language and literature and habits of the people among whom I was probably destined to spend some years, the summer passed fairly quickly. My former Secretary in Berne, Robert Henry Clive, joined me in October, of which I was extremely glad, for he was a man of rapid intelligence and grasp of detail, which has led to his being promoted at an unusually early age to the important Embassy in Tokyo.

I arranged to join my family in England about the middle of November. We spent a very happy month at Thornbury which was lent to us by my brother Stafford. The autumn was mild and fine and has remained especially

engraved on my memory by the numbers of missel-
thrushes or of red wings, which sang on the bare tree-
tops just before Christmas with all the abandon of Spring.
Also Esmetto, Francis and I had many good gallops
along the grass-covered sea wall which has kept the
Severn in bounds since the time of the Romans.

Starting after Christmas we left for Stockholm
via Copenhagen and Malmö and arrived there before
January 1st in order to attend the New Year reception
at Court. But though we were to spend five years at
Stockholm we were fated never to see a reception at the
Palace.

We arrived in Stockholm on December 29th. It was
real winter, dark, cold and snowy. The next day the
Dowager Queen Sophie died, which added to the gloom,
since all connected with the Court, including of course
the Diplomatic Corps had to dress like undertaker's
assistants. The funeral was impressive by reason of the
darkness of the sky, the whiteness of the falling snow and
the overpowering mass of black crepe which seemed to
be contending with the snow for the mastery of the
landscape.

This meant that the Court would be shut up for half
a year. At the end of the period of mourning the crisis
that led to the declaration of war by Austria against
Serbia had already become acute.

Owing to the War no reception was held at Court
during 1914 or indeed for two years more, so that Isa had
no opportunity of meeting the King till three years after
her arrival at Stockholm. A very minor matter this was
in such a universal earthquake as the World War, but it
seriously restricted our contacts with Stockholm society
and to that extent perhaps our general usefulness. The
stress of the War practically and very properly put an
end to all ordinary social gaieties. In fact, for the first
two years of the War no dinner parties of a formal kind
were given at all.

So beyond the regular visits to Cabinet Ministers, high
Court functionaries and heads of Foreign Missions and

their wives, Isa and I were unusually free to follow our own inclinations and look after the children, which suited our taste. As in most places, we found some friendly families who liked to be on good terms with the British Legation, but on the whole, as I was to find out when the War broke out, the general feeling among all the upper classes in Sweden was pronouncedly and frankly one of real admiration and respect if not actually affection for Germany and everything German. My predecessor, Cecil Spring Rice, warned me of this before I arrived in Sweden and experience amply justified his warning to a degree which I certainly did not anticipate. The impression on my mind even in those early days was that the spirit of Potsdam literally dominated the scene and that the British were looked down on with some pity as a people whose sun was rapidly setting owing to their own faults, lack of organising ability, love of amusement and ease and general carelessness with regard to the serious things of life among the principal of which was military science.

The Germans on the other hand were the greatest people on earth and no one—especially such triflers as the British—could hope to succeed against them.

After the Balkan Peace of 1913 which resulted from the Conference in London, Europe breathed again, though all felt it was but a rotten peace and the old causes of disturbance lay festering under the surface.

Austro-Yugoslav friction was just as great as ever.

As Messrs. Grant and Temperley state in their excellent historical handbook, *Europe in the Nineteenth and Twentieth Centuries*, p. 485. (*Longmans.*)

Serious as was the threat to Austro-Hungary both internal and external from the Roumanian danger, it could not compare with that from Serbia. The Government of that country had promised in 1909 to live in good neighbourly relations with Austro-Hungary and to repress hostile propaganda towards her. They were not anxious either in 1913 or 1914 for a new war because they had much to gain by delay. Ammunition and rifles were deficient, their new territory needed consolidating and Russia would not be ready for

O

war until 1917. But the four million Serbian Serbs called to the eight million Serbo-Croats under the Hapsburgs. Even had the Serb Government desired to do so, they could hardly have suppressed the incessant propaganda and habitual intercourse between their own Serbs and those beyond the Danube and the Dwina. . . . Pan-Serb agitation, which had been at blood-heat in 1908 was at boiling point during 1913 and 1914. A feverish and furious agitation ran through Serbia, Bosnia, Dalmatia, Croatia.

In 1910 an attempt was made on the life of the Governor of Bosnia. In 1912 the Governor of Croatia was almost assassinated. In 1913 two young Bosnians only gave up at the last moment a plan to murder their Governor, and in the same year another attempt was made by a student on the life of the Governor there. In 1914 a new plot was discovered in Zagreb just in time to prevent the assassination of the Governor and an Austrian Archduke.

Having spent two years at Budapest fairly recently (1909--11) I was naturally only too well acquainted with the exasperation these constant attempts at assassination aroused both in Hungary and Austria.

Nevertheless, when after a comparatively quiet spring in 1914, we learnt that the Archduke Franz Ferdinand and his wife had been assassinated by a Serb terrorist on June 28th I still refused to believe that this outrage would lead to war because I had faith that Germany would prevent Austria from committing a crowning folly that must almost inevitably lead to a chain of declarations of war sooner or later—the end of which it was impossible to foresee. For Russia, however unready she might be, as the champion of Slav nationalities in the Balkans, could not possibly allow Austria to swallow up Serbia, Germany could not allow Austria to be attacked by Russia without defending her Ally, France must then come to the assistance of Russia and Great Britain—if Germany acted on the Schlieffen Plan and attacked France through Belgium, which both Britain and Prussia had sworn to preserve from aggression—Great Britain also must be drawn in, if she was not to be branded forever as unfaithful and untrue to her solemn pledges.

At first it did not seem as though Austria would go to all extremes. Indeed a spirit of optimism prevailed and I went with Isa and my old friend Carlo Placci for a short and very delightful tour in Norway, visiting for the first time the lovely Sogne and Hardanger Fjords and Christiania (as it was then called) and Bergen. That was the last pre-War trip and greatly we enjoyed it ; I *would* not doubt that Germany would join a conference for mediation between the two countries in the conflict and insist on a peaceful settlement as soon as matters became really serious.

This is not the place to give a long account of the negotiations that preceded the final catastrophe ; they can be found in many memoirs and histories of the time.

In any case, however, I believe it can be confidently stated that Austria fully intended to present Serbia with an ultimatum which she knew must be unacceptable by any State unwilling to give up its national independence, and that, as Messrs. Grant and Temperley say in their book, which is written in a spirit of real truth and moderation, Germany gave a blank cheque to Austria and publicly avowed that she did so. So it seems to me that the responsibility for the outbreak of war may be considered as evenly divided between the statesmen of Austria and Germany, while it is not possible to acquit the Serbs of a considerable measure of blame for the terrorism and criminal agitations which were allowed to continue, if not actually encouraged by the Government, for years before 1914.

We had returned to Stockholm near July 20th and knew little or nothing about what was going on in negotiations beyond what the newspapers gave us. But we returned to be at our post when President Poincaré and M. Viviani, the French Foreign Secretary, arrived at Stockholm officially on their way back to France from a visit they had been paying to the Czar in St. Petersburg. On our Norwegian tour one sight comforted us, and this was that of the Emperor William's beautiful white steam yacht lying most peacefully like a swan—Lohengrin's swan we compared it to—in the Sogne Fjord. The Kaiser was on board. We, like many others, argued that surely, if the European situation was as critical as the papers described it, His Majesty would hardly be enjoying the quiet and repose of the Sogne Fjord. There were those who after the storm burst declared that this lingering in foreign waters at so serious a moment was with the deliberate intention of throwing dust in the eyes of the world, so that men should say " Surely if the Kaiser believed in war being near he would have hurried back to Berlin long before he did." In any case his presence in Norway had a calming effect on Scandinavian nerves.

On July 25th, President Poincaré, accompanied by M. Viviani, French Minister of Foreign Affairs, arrived at Stockholm in a French cruiser, *La France*, on a short visit to the King of Sweden on their way home from a visit to the Czar at St. Petersburg.

The political atmosphere was, as may be imagined, tense to a degree when we all sat down to a State dinner in the Palace that evening. I was sitting between M. de la Margerie, the head of the French Foreign Office, and Herr von Reichenau, the German Minister at Stockholm. I remember M. de la Margerie was enthusiastic about the splendour of the Russian Imperial Guard who had been passed in review by the Czar and the President. My German neighbour was not communicative.

Unless I am mistaken the Serbian reply to the Austrian Ultimatum had been published the day before. Those of my colleagues to whom I had been able to speak about it had all agreed that short of sacrificing national independence the Serbian Government could not have gone further to meet Austrian demands. It seemed to us impossible, that unless Austria was determined on war, she should not accept the Serbian reply and we felt confident that in a day or two we should hear that another war cloud had been dispersed. Still the general feeling of all at that ever memorable banquet was one of tense anxiety.

In spite of this M. Viviani, I well remember, made a

speech which impressed us all as one of the most eloquent, graceful and from every point of view perfect speeches ever delivered on such an occasion. It almost made us forget the circumstances, though what he said I have completely forgotten. Then of a sudden a whisper went through the assembled guests. The news had come that Austria had rejected the Serbian reply and had broken off diplomatic relations. We all knew that this must mean war.

The Court banquet broke up at once. The President and his suite hurriedly bade the King of Sweden farewell and left with a haste that gave us at least almost the impression of a *sauve qui peut*. The French were not unnaturally alarmed at the prospect of their passage home being intercepted by the German Fleet. It is impossible to describe the excitement and consternation at the close of that Belshazzar's feast, for that was what all felt it to be. The only question all were asking was, who was cast for the rôle of Belshazzar ?

Although the hour must have been almost 10 p.m. when we hastily broke up, it was of course on July 25th at Stockholm still daylight. I found myself going slowly down the great stairs of the Castle of Stockholm side by side with my Austro-Hungarian colleague, Count Hadik, whom I was personally fond of. The Hungarians were generally among the pleasantest colleagues. I turned to him and said in French :

" This is a most serious step your Government has taken. Who can see the end of it ? "

I can see him smile now as he turned to me and said :

" *Bah ! il était temps de donner un coup de pied a ces cochons-là.*"[1]

And suiting the action to the word he kicked out one of his highly polished Blücher boots as he walked down the great wide stone staircase. There was little I could say, for had I said what I felt, it would have been to tell him that no country had ever committed such a crowning act of folly. It seemed inevitable, whether she was

[1] " Bah ! it was time to give a kick to those swine."

victorious with German help or utterly defeated, as was the case, that the Dual Monarchy would perish. But I knew only too well the bitter exasperation created, especially among Hungarians by the Yugo-Slav propaganda and terrorism of recent years, and I could at least understand his feelings.

We reached the bottom of the stairs in silence. Then he turned to me and said :

" Well, whatever happens we shall remain friends, shan't we ? "

I said : " Of course, whatever happens."

But we hardly ever had the opportunity of speaking together again, for naturally during the War the heads of Missions whose countries were at war could not have any communication with each other.

The remaining hectic days before England came into the War over the violation of Belgian territory by Germany in accordance with the Schlieffen Plan prepared by the German General Staff since 1905, need not be recounted here.

When the news of Edward Grey's proposal for an eleventh hour Conference to stave off the war danger which he made on July 26th came through to us, my hopes mounted again for I still believed that Germany would, as she had done in 1913, agree to a Conference with that end in view. But when the Conference suggestion was rejected by Germany, then indeed I felt all hope was lost, and from that moment the German Government became for me the party most responsible for the outbreak of war—more responsible than Austria, because they had not the same excuse for exasperation with Serbia and because they could, by a stiff attitude towards Vienna, where after all it was only General Conrad and the military who were pushing on towards war, even at that late hour have forced the Austro-Hungarians to hold their hand.

It has frequently been stated that if earlier in the crisis Grey had told Berlin definitely that England would take up arms in defence of Belgium, Germany would have withdrawn her support of Austria. Not only is it very doubtful whether Grey could, *before the violation of Belgian neutrality*, have got united Cabinet support for such a declaration, but from reading the Swedish and German Press, after the declaration of War, I gathered that the great bulk of public opinion in Germany rather welcomed than otherwise the entry of Great Britain into the War. The Germans had not the slightest doubt about their ultimate victory and they said openly and with gusto that the presence of Great Britain among the defeated nations would give Germany an opportunity of annexing all the best parts of the British Empire. In reading these articles I certainly got the impression that the feeling was rather one of satisfaction than otherwise. It was as if they said :

" At last we have got them, these Carthaginians who without any military qualities, but simply by trade and for trade, have acquired a vast Empire which they are both unfit and unworthy to hold."

One after another the inevitable steps leading to World War were taken. On July 25th, Austria-Hungary declared a partial mobilisation, Serbia having mobilised on the same day. On the 28th she declared war on Serbia. On the 30th Russia began a general mobilisation. On the 31st Austria-Hungary made her partial mobilisation general, having been advised to do so by General von Moltke, Chief of the German General Staff.

On the 31st also Germany received news of Russia's general mobilisation, and at midnight of that day sent her an Ultimatum requiring that her mobilisation be stopped within twelve hours and an Ultimatum to France requiring her to remain neutral. Without awaiting the Russian reply Germany declared War on Russia on August 1st.

On August 1st France decreed general mobilisation and Germany declared war on France late on August 3rd.

The British Government asked for pledges from Germany and France that in case of war Belgian territory would not be violated. This Germany refused to give, and from that time it became practically certain that Great Britain must take part in the war. At 2 p.m. on

August 4th, Grey, having received information that Belgian territory had been entered by German troops, instructed the British Ambassador at Berlin to ask for his passports unless he received a satisfactory reply by midnight respecting Belgian neutrality. At midnight England was at war with Germany.

When I got up early in the morning of August 5th, I found a telegram waiting for me in the Chancery with the words "War. Germany."

It came almost as a relief after all the uncertainties of the last days and the overpowering fear that perhaps my country might not live up to her plighted word.

Strange to say it was rather with a thankful heart because now in any case we should be spared that dreaded dishonour, that I sat down to take the steps required on receipt of such a telegram—i.e. to repeat it to our Embassy in Berlin, to instruct our Consuls in Sweden of the measures they should take and so on.

The excitement of uncertainty was over and we were now for better for worse face to face with realities. I had not yet the vaguest conception of what those realities would be, but *alea jacta erat.*

CHAPTER IX

SWEDEN : THE WAR

(1914)

" Warre and Battel is a thing very beastly."
SIR THOMAS MORE'S Utopia[1]

IT would obviously be useless to attempt within the space of this book to give an account even of the main events of the Great War except in so far as they affected the situation and the work of the British Legation in Sweden. Within this compass even it will be entirely impossible to give an accurate review of our activities. These were naturally mainly concerned with the blockade of Germany, and that covered such an immense area of technical knowledge, of statistical information and, of course, of bitter controversy, that it would be out of the question to convey in a book which aims at giving personal recollections rather than historical or technical information, anything more than the most general impression of what went on around us in those tremendous years from the beginning of August, 1914, to November, 1918.

There was frankly nothing heroic about our work, nothing to make us exult in it as Herr Hitler tells in *Mein Kampf* (pp. 180–9), he exulted when he marched singing *Deutschland über Alles* as a young recruit over the stricken fields of Belgium.

Our work consisted in carrying out two main objectives :
First. Keeping Sweden out of the War.
Second. Preventing her from assisting Germany to obtain a mass of overseas supplies which the Germans

---

[1] *Of Warfare*, p. 131, Ralph Robinson's translation, 1551. Republished *English Reprints*, A. Murray, London, 1868.

needed for the prosecution of the war and, therefore, for the slaughter of our sailors and soldiers at the front and of those of our Allies.

As regards the first of these objectives, many of those who always preached an extreme blockade policy and looked upon others who took anything else into consideration almost as traitors, believed that we ought regardless of consequences from the first to have brought such pressure to bear on Sweden (and other neutrals) that all exports from them to Germany would have been stopped.

Thus Admiral Consett, Naval Attaché to the Scandinavian Countries during the War, for whom I have always felt the highest regard and friendship as a most valuable and devoted servant of his country, wrote in his book " The Triumph of the Unarmed Forces," page 109 (published 1923).[1]

> To Sweden's threat to join Germany the proper reply was " Join." To Germany's threat to invade Denmark the proper reply was " Invade."

Looking at the situation simply from the blockade point of view he was doubtless right, but we had to take other matters into consideration, and for me as head of the Legation at Stockholm the principal of these was the continual and lively fear of the Russians that Sweden might join Germany, and the fact that, during the first years at least, the French Government strongly backed up Russian representations in this matter. We were not fighting the War alone and were compelled to take into account the views of our Allies.

To those who would object and ask what harm could the entry of Sweden into the War on the side of Germany have done to the Allied cause I should answer by requesting them to look at the map of the Baltic Sea.

They will then see that it is but a step across the entrance of the Gulf of Bothnia from Stockholm or one of the Swedish ports rather more to the North to Finland into

---

[1] Williams & Norgate, London.

which Sweden could easily have thrown a large part of her army which the Russians in 1916 estimated at 400,000 well trained and well equipped men. These stiffened by perhaps some 50,000 Germans and an equal number of Finns, trained in Germany and backing a Finnish rising, would probably have crushed with ease the Russian garrison in Finland and have been at the very gates of St. Petersburg in a very short time. I think I am not wrong in saying that the Russian General Staff calculated that they would have to withdraw at least two Army corps from the Polish front to deal with this danger, and these army corps with their requisite arms the Russians positively could not spare from that theatre of war. We must also bear in mind that as mentioned by Mr. Winston Churchill in *The Crisis* the Schlieffen Plan on which the German General Staff had built their hopes of crushing France was weakened owing to their having to withdraw from the French front a large number of troops to meet the Russian attack in Galicia in 1915. Had the numbers of the Russian army in Galicia been greatly reduced to meet a powerful attack in Finland the Germans would have been able to increase proportionately the numbers of men on their Western Front and so been in a better position to carry out the original Schlieffen Plan. In fact the entry of Sweden into the War would have completely changed the whole aspect of the War in the Eastern theatre.

So much was this the feeling of the Russian General Staff that, in reply to an enquiry from the British Foreign Office as to what the Russians believed the consequences of Sweden entering the War would be, the Russian Government telegraphed that the Russian Chief of Staff had laconically answered " The consequences for Russia would be incalculable and disastrous." This telegram, which was repeated to me by the Foreign Office, burned itself into my memory in letters of fire. I do not suppose Admiral Consett could have seen the telegram when he wrote that to Sweden's threat to join Germany (a threat to the best of my knowledge never actually made) the proper answer would have been " Join," but as this statement in his work may still cause many to believe that the actions of our Legation at Stockholm were criminally weak, I feel it necessary even after all these years to give the above explanation in order to show that there was another side to the picture.

Speaking of Finland, which continued to cause us much anxiety right up to the end, when the Bolshevik revolution broke out in Finland with especial violence, I must mention one entertaining episode.

One morning in the autumn of 1914 I went to the Swedish Foreign Office to make some communication to Herr Wallenberg, the Swedish Minister for Foreign Affairs. He was engaged with someone else and I waited in the room adjoining.

Presently the German Minister came out, and staring coldly at me passed on through the room. As I entered Herr Wallenberg's room he said :

" The German Minister has just been here."

I : " I saw him go out."

HERR WALLENBERG : " Would you like to know what he came to say to me ? "

I : " Certainly—if it does not inconvenience you to tell me."

HERR WALLENBERG : " He offered us Finland if we would join Germany in the War."

I : " That's very interesting ; but it would interest me still more to know what your Excellency replied ? "

HERR WALLENBERG : " By all means. I asked him a question. I said ' Herr Minister, have you ever sat down with a hedgehog in your coat tail pocket ? ' and he pursued the matter no further."

Herr von Reichenau represented for me the incarnation of the spirit of Potsdam. I met him in the street one day between the declaration of War by Germany on Russia and the British declaration of War on Germany. We were not at war and there was no reason to refuse to salute him. I took off my hat. He stopped and said :

" Now, no doubt you English have got what you want and you will play as always the *tertius gaudens*."

I answered as politely as I could.

" You are making a great mistake, Herr von Reichenau, because in this War there will be no *tertii gaudentes*."

I had no idea at the time how true this prophecy would be.

On another occasion in September he told the Swedish Foreign Minister that the German troops would positively be in Paris on a certain day.

" Very interesting," said Herr Wallenberg quite gravely.   " In the morning or in the afternoon ? "

It was no wonder they did not like each other.

Poor Herr von Reichenau's Potsdam spirit was such that even the Swedes could not put up with it, and a few months later they persuaded his Government to recall him and replace him by a far more able, suave and, if I may say so, dangerous diplomat, Herr von Lucius.

I never spoke to Herr von Reichenau again after that last encounter in the street.

The question of Swedish neutrality in the War was that which was, as already stated, during the first months of the War the main cause of anxiety to the Allied Legations, and each Minister endeavoured from the first to obtain assurances on this score from Herr Wallenberg, the Swedish Minister for Foreign Affairs.

On August 2nd His Excellency in reply, no doubt, to a question from me stated that Sweden was determined to maintain her neutrality as long as possible ; but if Great Britain joined with Russia Sweden might be forced to take the other side because public opinion, if Sweden were forced into the War, would always compel the Government to take the side against Russia.   He went on to say that if England entered the War he feared that circumstances might arise that would oblige Sweden to do so, but he added that it would be very useful if he could receive from the British Government a categorical assurance that they would not occupy any Swedish port as long as Sweden remained neutral.

On the following day he repeated this message still more emphatically.

On August 4th Sweden declared her complete neutrality for the period of the War.

In the meantime, however, we had been having increasingly persistent rumours of German pressure on the Swedish Government to take some more active step to defend herself against a violation of her neutrality by the Allies.

I was, therefore, not surprised when my friend Dr. Axel Munthe called on me on the morning of August 2nd or 3rd to say that he had been told that a Cabinet Council was to be held very shortly in order to decide whether the Swedish Army should be mobilised or not, and that he believed that if the Allies would give the Swedish Government categorical assurances that, as long as Swedish neutrality was maintained, Swedish integrity and independence would not be violated by them, this would help greatly to prevent mobilisation. What the Swedes mainly feared now was the seizure by England of a Swedish port so as to get command of the Straits into the Baltic.

I naturally informed the Foreign Office of this, and they at once set machinery in motion to get France and Russia to join them in giving the Swedes the assurances in question. These same assurances were to be given also to the Norwegians, Dutch and other Governments.

On August 4th I received instructions to give the Swedish Minister for Foreign Affairs a message in this sense.

In hot haste I prepared a Note to hand to Herr Wallenberg and telephoned to ask him if he could receive me at once, as I had an urgent message to give him. He told me to come without delay.

When I entered his room I handed him the paper, he read it over once, twice, thrice, gravely and in silence and I wondered what impression it had made. Then his face broke into a smile and he said :

" I am no wine bibber, but if I were I would gladly

drink a bottle of Champagne to the health of His Majesty's Government this evening because with this paper I shall be able to prevent the mobilisation of the Swedish Army at the Council Meeting to-morrow."

Then with a twinkle in his eye he added :

" I hope you will excuse me but I am an old business man (he was a great banker). I like to have important documents signed," and he gave me back the Note.

I had in my haste forgotten to sign it. That error was quickly set right and I left the Swedish Foreign Office much relieved, though I did not then realise all that the mobilisation of the Swedish Army at that time might have carried with it.

But I have been very deeply grateful to Axel Munthe ever since. When I reminded him of this episode years after the War had ended, he had forgotten all about it and he said :

" I suppose there will be those in Sweden who will say I committed an act of treachery to my country."

To which I answered :

" Possibly—there are fools in every country—but I think the majority will say that you served your country well and perhaps saved her from untold ills."

Very soon after this episode he came to say good-bye to my great regret, saying that the pro-German atmosphere of Stockholm was too much for him and he was off to give his services as a doctor to the French among whom he had passed the early years of his medical career.

" There are plenty of Swedes offering their services to Germany and I don't see why one or two shouldn't help the other side."

So he went and was in Rheims during the bombardment. Indeed he was actually in the Cathedral when a shell shattered the great West Window under which he was standing at the time and covered him with a shower of jewelled glass, leaving some pieces of that marvellous French blue glass in his pockets, of which pieces he has since given me one.

I always felt, when I learnt of the destruction of some

great monument of irreplaceable beauty like the Cathedral of Rheims, more deeply distressed than over the loss of thousands of lives which was part of the beastly course of the War. Men could be replaced in course of time, the Cathedrals of Rheims and Amiens and their jewelled windows could not. I trembled above all for Chartres and for St. Marks in Venice. Had these been destroyed by the brutish violence of barbarian invaders I should, I believe, have felt it as much as a major defeat.

On August 7th the French and Russian Minister presented the Swedish Government with similar Notes, but the tension was already relaxed because what Sweden had really feared was the occupation of a Swedish port by Great Britain.

CHAPTER X

SWEDEN: "TERTII GAUDENTES"

I HAVE designedly applied to the Neutral Powers during the War the term " *Tertii Gaudentes* " which Herr von Reichenau believed at first would be applicable to Great Britain. I have done so because during the four years' ever-tightening blockade of the Central Powers I became convinced that one object of neutral Powers is to make all the money they can out of war by trading with belligerents and thus, intentionally or not, helping to prolong war to the latest hour possible.

I do not accuse the neutrals of the Great War only of this rather unsavoury rôle, but neutrals in all wars at all times, including my own country.

The history of International Maritime Law informs us that the Dutch, the great traders of the seventeenth century, first promoted the two fundamental principles or *desiderata* of neutrals in maritime warfare. These were first " Free ships, free goods " or " the neutral flag covers the goods " and second, " Neutral goods free even under an enemy flag."

Great Britain and some other countries constantly opposed these principles but they were finally embodied in clauses 2, 3 and 4 of the Declaration of Paris, signed on April 16th, 1856, by the seven Powers that took part in the Congress which met after the Crimean War.

These principles which had been loosely recognised for centuries before were then defined as follows :—

2. The neutral flag covers enemy goods with the exception of contraband of war.

3. Neutral goods, with the exception of contraband of war, are not liable to capture under enemy's flag.

4. Blockades, in order to be binding, must be effective, that is to say maintained by a force sufficient really to prevent access to the coast of the enemy."

Nos. 2 and 3 of this Declaration were contrary to the interests of the strongest naval Powers and therefore of Great Britain, which had always maintained the reverse since if recognised as a part of international law they would obviously greatly hamper any belligerent Power in carrying on a naval blockade, the object of which was to prevent the enemy from obtaining overseas supplies. Nevertheless the British Government subscribed to Nos. 2 and 3 because of No. 1, which read :

1. " Privateering is and remains abolished."

Privateering by means of " letters of marque " had been recognised by almost universal custom and had been made great use of, particularly by the United States Government, which in those days preferred to avoid the expense of regular naval vessels to carry out this part of a navy's duties.

Great Britain, however, had always considered with some justice that privateering was an irregular form of maritime warfare and was especially anxious to see it abolished. In this other European Powers concurred. When, however, the United States Government was invited to adhere to the Declaration of Paris it did so in so far as clauses 2, 3 and 4 were concerned, while with regard to No. 1, the privateering clause, it only did so with reservations which again Great Britain would not accept.

The Declaration of Paris concluded with the words :

> The present Declaration is not and shall not be binding except between those Powers who have acceded or shall accede to it.

This being so it was not binding as between the United States and the other signatories.

I have merely made this reference to the Declaration of Paris, which has often been described as the Magna Charta of International Maritime Law in War, in order to show that Maritime Law was in 1914, as regards most important questions, still in a state of flux.

It rested indeed on two indefinite, shifting and often conflicting foundations, custom and international conventions, neither of which was universal or even embraced all the leading Maritime Powers.

What happened therefore in wartime after the Declaration of Paris and after the Declaration of London in 1909, was simply that, just as before, the belligerents who believed themselves to be fighting for their very existence only respected those conventions (which were never universal) in so far as they believed it was dangerous not to do so. These Conventions, in fact, introduced no new principles, but merely, so to speak, endeavoured to codify principles which had been in existence for centuries, but which, like all international law which was neither universal nor enforceable by sanctions, rested, as stated above, on indefinite and shifting foundations.

It is, I think, obvious that as long as there are wars this will always be so. It is clear that no nation having the power to stop supplies going to the enemy which supplies are likely to result in its own defeat, will let them pass freely because of some Declaration signed years before. To believe this is to believe what is contrary to human nature.

It may be that as Basset Moore says in his *Digest of International Law*, Vol. VIII, p. 382.

> ˙ Neutrals have the right to continue during war to trade with the belligerents subject to the law relating to contraband and blockade. The existence of this right is universally admitted, although on certain occasions it has been in practice denied.

Yet if a right, though universally admitted is in practice at times denied, it seems to me to rest as before stated on extremely uncertain foundations. The reason for this is evident. War is a game in which the stronger wins. Germany believing herself to be the strongest at the opening of the War committed a gross violation of the rights of neutrals and of Treaties to which she was a party, by invading Belgium with whom she was at peace for no other reason than that she believed that this would enable her to crush France at the outset. As she had gained this initial advantage by an illegal act, it was too much to expect that the Allies should allow her to supply her needs from overseas, on account of some rules of Maritime Law which had not been universally accepted.

Regarding the *dictum* that neutrals have the right to continue to trade with the belligerents subject to the law relating to contraband and blockade we may also well ask what was the law of contraband. The Declaration of London signed in 1909, but never ratified by the Parliament of Great Britain, endeavoured indeed to define " contraband." In the face of the practical issues of the War, however, it was found that the academic list then drawn up by " experts " in time of peace did not at all conform to the requirements of war. Therefore it was jettisoned step by step by Great Britain and her Allies and Associates as it became obvious that various goods listed as " free " were really of enormous value for the manufacture of munitions and the prosecution of war. I give only a few mentioned by Admiral Consett in his valuable chapter on the " Rules of Naval Warfare,"[1] namely, raw cotton, nitrates, metallic ores, ammonia, oil seeds, rubber, etc., to which I would add above all lubricating oils, for it is obvious that in this mechanised age all life comes to a standstill without these.

When the Declaration of London was being negotiated public opinion in England was divided on the subject into two schools of thought. There were those who held that with the growth of foreign navies, especially the German, which seemed to constitute a real menace to our seaborne commerce in case of war, the rules of the Declaration of Paris enforced by those of the Declaration of London would, if adhered to, secure seaborne supplies to belligerents, and would therefore be of great value to

---

[1] *Triumph of the Unarmed Force.*   Williams & Norgate, London.

an island like ourselves if threatened by an effective blockade.

On the other side were those like Admiral Consett, who declared that our seaborne supplies would always be protected by our Fleet and that, therefore, the rules of the two Declarations hampering, as they did, the seizure of goods going by sea to the enemy would be merely a thorn in the side of Great Britain and would deprive her of her best means of attack.

There was much to be said for both sides and while the first school of thought in favour of the free supply to belligerents won the day in the negotiations for the Declaration of London, the second school won in Parliament where the ratification of the Declaration was rejected by the House of Lords after a tremendous campaign in the country.

With regard to these questions and to the alleged right of neutrals to trade with belligerents, I confess that I came during the War, and as a direct result of the blockade work with which we in Sweden were almost entirely and continuously engaged, to the conclusion that it is useless to try to apply an ethical standard to any transaction necessary for the prosecution of war.

" Warre and battel is a thing very beastly " and Moltke was right when he said that the most humane war is that which is ended soonest. Ethical considerations do not and cannot come into the business of war, and I cannot indeed perceive that neutrals who sell to belligerents the supplies needed for carrying on their " beastly " business and thereby line their own pockets, have any right to consider themselves morally superior to belligerents. On the contrary in as much as they are really those who, so far as they can, make money out of the follies or the necessities of others they are hardly less responsible for war than the belligerents and certainly far less interesting.

For these reasons I have no sympathy with the *Tertii Gaudentes*. I cannot but feel on the contrary that if neutrals had long ago followed principles exactly the reverse of those supported so actively by the Dutch in the seventeeth century and later by the Americans and others, including the British when it suited us, and had they, instead of insisting on securing so far as possible the right of free trading with all and sundry, agreed to sign Declarations that neutrals would at once cease to trade with any belligerents, whoever and wherever they might be, the neutral Powers would not only have made a great step forward towards that which we all desire, the end of war, but incidentally by inspiring confidence in the stability of peace they would have promoted world trade to a greater degree than they did by Declarations such as that of Paris or of London which practically recognise the legality of war as such.

This chapter is not the place to discuss this novel and indeed wholly topsy turvy view of what the International Law of War should be—I hope to come back to it later and explain it more clearly.

Meanwhile as far as the ethics of a blockade are concerned, I believe there are none. Germans have denounced the wickedness of the Allies in starving women and children and the cry has been taken up in England, the United States and elsewhere. Yet I have never heard of any German who denounced the German military authorities in France in 1871 for refusing to allow French women and children to leave Paris during the siege when they had to eat rats from the sewers and grass from the ramparts of the city.

All complaints about this or that measure in wartime-which is taken simply because it is considered necessary for victory, are beside the mark. This, of course, does not apply to sadist cruelty for its own sake.

" Warre and battel is a thing very beastly." What we have to aim at is less to humanize it by Pacts, Covenants and Declarations which simply recognise its legality, than to take such measures as will altogether abolish it by making war so great a risk that it is no longer worth while.

Sceptics and pessimists say this cannot be done and that we had better face the facts and return to a pre-War mentality, relying for a very uncertain security on our own armaments and on alliances which, however, we know by past experience will not prevent wars.

I, on the contrary, as the result of experience of the power of blockade—when once it became powerful and ceased to be hampered by the Declarations of Paris and London—am entirely convinced that anything like a universal blockade is a contingency that no country— even the most powerful—would face if it believed that it would be the inevitable result of having recourse to armed force.

In this opinion I am confirmed by quotations from General Ludendorff, given by Admiral Consett, p. 268 of his book :

> A three years' war was only possible [says Ludendorff] because we had in Germany abundant coal, and so much iron and food that *together with* what we could obtain from occupied territory and *neutral countries* we could, by practising the most rigid economy, manage to exist in spite of the hostile blockade. The importance in war of coal, iron, food, was known before this war ; but how absolutely decisive they would become was only demonstrated to all the world as hostilities proceeded.[1]

To the three indispensables for carrying on war in these days Ludendorff might have added many more, such as mineral oils and especially lubricating oils, hardening metals, without which iron alone is of little importance, cotton, nitrates and all materials for making explosives, and dozens of other articles which are in one way or another required for warfare.

I remember that I was early awakened to a realisation of the fact that England was dependent on Sweden and Norway for certain absolutely indispensable imports. The German Government not long after the War began placed all timber on its contraband list and neutral vessels carrying timber to belligerents were warned that these cargoes would be seized. The result of this was that for

[1] *Triumph of the Unarmed Forces*, p. 268. Admiral Consett. Williams & Norgate.

some time we in Stockholm were bombarded with telegrams from the Foreign Office to leave no stone unturned to get cargoes of pit props moving again. It seemed we were desperately short of pit props and no pit props meant no coal; no coal, no steam and the result may be imagined.

We finally obtained our pit props from Norway and from Canada. But let us imagine the plight of a belligerent relying on his own coal but having to import pit props and being confronted with a universal blockade.

Similarly we were dependent on Sweden for certain hardening metals, for a certain kind of iron ore which was the best for high speed steel, for ball bearings of a kind required not only for our larger guns, but also for many of our great industrial concerns throughout the Midlands, without which we should, I believe, have been practically hamstrung. This defect was, if I remember right, only remedied quite late in the War. For these things we had to bargain with the Swedish Government, and Germany had to do likewise. But we, fortunately, had not, like Germany towards the end, an almost universal blockade against us or we could certainly never have held out for Ludendorff's maximum of three years.

Germany could indeed manage to exist for three years with what she obtained from neutral countries during the first two years and what she obtained from occupied territories, but the blockade was in the end too much for her, imperfect though it was, and it was that which von Tirpitz feared, the " silent pressure of sea power " which really decided the issue.

It is astounding that this is still so little realised that in Messrs. Grant and Temperley's account of the War,[1] while taking into consideration the amount of space given to the War in a book so necessarily compact, no mention of the blockade is made until quite at the end the causes of the German defeat are examined. Even then, however, no detailed account of the systematic working of the blockade is given.

[1] *Europe in the Nineteenth and Twentieth Centuries,* Part V.   Longmans Green & Co.

When this comes to be written it will perhaps be more generally understood that no country, not even the most carefully prepared for war and the most self-sufficing can hope for victory if it is beset from the first by all the difficulties created by a universal blockade. War, in fact, in such circumstances will have ceased to be worth while. But the *Tertii Gaudentes* must first agree to abandon their unsavoury role of enriching themselves by prolonging war.

CHAPTER XI

SWEDEN : THE BLOCKADE

TO return from the general to the particular. I had not at the start the least idea of the sort of work that would be expected of the Legation in war time.

The first two or three weeks were largely occupied by helping British tourists who were stranded in Scandinavia to return home. Everything had, of course, to be done by telegraph and our Government had to charter special steamers for their conveyance from the least exposed port of the North Sea. Credits had to be opened and tickets arranged. We were naturally much less busy with this sort of work than our colleagues in Christiania and Copenhagen, but still our Chancery was stormed from time to time by indignant travellers who seemed to think that H.M. Government had nothing more important on hand in those days than to look after their safety and comfort. But after a few weeks the tourist spate ended and we waited to learn what next would be expected of us. All we knew was that the Rules of the Declaration of Paris (of course) and also those of the Declaration of London were to be observed.

The first indication received that we were likely to be called on to play some part was a telegram from the Foreign Office which I remember well. It ran :

> s.s. —— [name forgotten] with cargo copper due arrive Gothenburg such and such a day stop you should watch it.

I should watch it ! How was I able to watch it ? What in the name of all that was holy did the gentleman sitting in the Foreign Office expect me to do ? Gothenburg was hundreds of miles away. I could spare no one from the Chancery of the Legation. We had at Gothenburg a most worthy elderly Consul who had lived his whole life in Gothenburg, was greatly respected by all and spoke English with a strong Swedish accent. I felt he would probably faint if asked to watch cargoes of copper and other things—which was likely to prove an unpopular task.

When in doubt I always consulted my Secretary, Harry Clive, who was, I considered, far brighter than myself at unravelling conundrums of any kind. After talking it over together we decided, if I remember right, that he should go down to Gothenburg, discuss the situation with our worthy old Consul, Mr. Duff, and report to me. We could then send a telegram to the Foreign Office stating our difficulties and asking for special help to deal with cases of this sort.

As I anticipated, Mr. Duff showed himself most unwilling to undertake any business of this kind which was entirely out of his usual line. Neither could he suggest anyone that would be likely to do so.

I had already had some very unpleasant communications from certain of our Vice-Consuls in smaller ports, who like the majority of our unpaid Vice-Consuls, were natives of the country and traders doing business in their own cities. I therefore quickly came to the conclusion that it was useless to rely on many of these to do our war work for us, indeed it was not fair to ask them to do so. So on Clive's return from Gothenburg reporting that Mr. Duff did not see his way to watching imports and exports I informed the Foreign Office accordingly and asked them to send out at once one or two men who could assist the Legation in this particular line. We were very lucky in obtaining soon after the services of Mr. Owen Philpots, the son of a well known headmaster of a public school in England who had considerable knowledge of Germany and the Scandinavian countries. He was a hard and conscientious worker, with a special aptitude for his work, but with a congenital carelessness which once or twice caused us serious inconvenience.

On one occasion, being at Gothenburg, he had managed to procure copies of the manifests of one or two ships whose cargoes were strongly suspected of enemy destination ; he left these copies in his greatcoat pocket when he went to dinner at his hotel. He was disturbed to find when he came out that they were missing. One or two mornings later after breakfast he started as usual for the Consulate and found himself surrounded by some hundred urchins all armed with kodaks who took snapshots of him at every step. Losing his temper at last he seized one of them, dragged him to the Consulate and temporarily confiscated his kodak. As a result an angry crowd collected round the Consulate which had to be protected by the police.

What had caused the commotion was that a smart reporter of a violently pro-German and activist paper called *Vidi* had gone through the pockets of Philpots' greatcoat, found the documents and had them photostated. Part of them appeared in the next issue of the paper with a portrait of *Spionen Philpots* (The Spy Philpots) and an offer of Kr.50 for the best snapshot of the offender. Dozens of small street boys were then collected, provided with kodaks and told to compete for the prize.

It all sounds ridiculous now, but at the time it was very serious and troublesome, as many papers clamoured for Philpots' removal from the country. By withdrawing him from Gothenburg I managed most fortunately, however, to avoid this for later on in the War he secured papers and letters which conclusively proved enemy destination in a famous case before the Prize Courts and so obtained the condemnation of a cargo worth hundreds of thousands of pounds. Like many other most charming people, his untidiness remained phenomenal and his roll-top desk was always piled up with apple peel, cigarette ends, bits of string and sealing-wax, as well as confidential telegrams and reports. Finally his sister, Miss Bertha Philpots, a wonderful woman, who afterwards became Mistress of Girton College, joined the Legation, kept her brother tidy and acting as my private Secretary kept me in order too.   They made a wonderful couple and were greatly liked by all who came across them except the " black listers " who had reason to dread Philpots' powers of detecting wolves in sheeps' clothing.

In the beginning of 1915 it was clear that if the Allies followed the rules of the two Declarations and adhered faithfully to the contraband lists of the Declaration of London, Germany would be able to provide herself freely through neutral countries even though her own ports were strictly blockaded.   Thus the seaborne supplies that Germany desired to import were almost immediately directed to Scandinavian, Dutch or, until Italy came into the War, Italian ports, every effort being, of course, made to disguise their real destination.   Little by little measures were taken to stop this spate of goods through neutral countries.

In reply to a declaration made by Germany that the English Channel, the north and west coasts of France and the waters round the British Isles were a " war area " and that all enemy ships found in that area would be destroyed and neutral vessels there might be exposed to danger, the British Government issued the Reprisals Order of March, 1915.

This was practically the beginning of the end for the régime of the Declarations.

The first two articles of this Order simply tightened up the blockade with regard to all vessels trading directly with a German port.

The third and fourth articles went much further. The third laid it down that every merchant vessel on the way to a port not a German one but carrying goods with an enemy destination might be required to discharge such goods in a British or Allied port.

The fourth declared that every merchant vessel having on board goods of enemy origin, or which were enemy property, might be required to discharge such goods in a British or Allied port.

From that time forward our work increased by leaps

and bounds until at last from having only three men in the Chancery and sending out perhaps a dozen telegrams in the year we ended by having a party of thirty six working daily from 9.30 a.m. till 8 or 9 at night and even later, and the numbers of our out and in telegrams went into thousands.

How did this happen? Well, it soon dawned on neutral shippers that it didn't pay them to have their vessels taken into a British port and to have the cargo examined and there were few that got through the Blockade line, which ran north from the British Isles up to beyond Iceland, without examination.

It being dangerous on account of submarine attacks to halt in the open sea in order to examine papers and overhaul cargo, vessels carrying goods to neutral ports adjacent to Germany were required to go into some British port for the purpose. There were often many such vessels waiting their turn, so that they frequently waited many days, sometimes even weeks. To avoid the loss occasioned by these delays ship owners begged to be given before sailing some documents that would pass them through the blockade line. From this sprang up a whole system of inquiry as to the *bona fide* nature of cargoes before these documents, " navicerts " and " letters of assurance " as they were called, were issued. A ship owner or shipping agent in, let us say, New York, who was sending a vessel with cargo for Gothenburg would go to the Allied Office in New York and submit the manifest and bills of lading of the cargo. This was then telegraphed to the Contraband Department in London, which telegraphed it to the Legation in question for inquiry and report as to the Consignees, their *bona fides* and reliability and as to the quantities of such goods already imported into the country. This information we had to get together as soon as possible and forward to London which would then give instructions to the shipping office as to what part of the cargo would be allowed to pass without being taken into a British port for examination. The documents so released to the masters of vessels were termed " Letters of Assurance," as regards the cargo and " Navicerts " for the ships.[1]

Neutral States naturally protested against this systematic regulation of the goods for import, but as America took no strong action to prevent it, the control of export goods at the port of embarkation gradually became a general rule with the co-operation of the ship owners, and also of the shippers.   Indeed, I believe that the first Letter of Assurance was issued at the request of a Danish firm for a lot of corsets in August, 1914.

It must not be supposed that the systematic blockade from neutral ports of embarkation came into force at once.   The system grew very gradually as it appeared necessary to stop certain commodities which, from the amounts imported by some neutral countries, were far in excess of the average pre-war imports and the excess of which, therefore, was assumed to be intended for an enemy destination.   It was really not until the middle of 1916 that the blockade began to be water-tight.   Up to that time Sweden and other neutrals undoubtedly exported goods of all kinds and especially foodstuffs to Germany and Austria.[2]

His Majesty's Government also endeavoured to negotiate agreements with neutral countries adjacent to Germany, regulating by a system of quotas their imports of contraband goods.   These agreements were called rationing agreements.

My old schoolfellow and colleague, Mansfeldt Findlay, our Minister in Norway, was early successful in arranging an agreement of this kind which worked satisfactorily for both parties.   We in Sweden on the other hand were up against the true blue legalism of a great international lawyer, Professor Hammarskjöld, the Prime Minister, who took his stand on the Declarations of Paris and London, the complete freedom of the seas or nothing. It was impossible to move him from this position in which

[1] See Appendix C1.
[2] *Vide* statistics given in Admiral Consetts' book, *The Triumph of the Unarmed Forces.*   Williams & Norgate.

he thought the honour and independence of his country were engaged.

Three times he sent for me to protest against our actions under the Reprisals Order. Twice, not wishing to argue with a pundit of International Law, I merely told him I would report what he said. The third time, however, feeling it was time to end this very unusual procedure on his part, for as a Foreign Representative I was expected to deal only with the Foreign Minister, I retaliated by asking him if he was really such an upholder of neutral rights as he wished me to believe. He replied that he certainly was. I then asked him if he considered the violation of Belgium by Germany a gross violation of neutral rights or no. He replied it undoubtedly was. I asked if he had, as a champion of neutral countries, ever protested against that ? He said no, it did not concern Sweden directly. Then I spoke my mind clearly :

" Mr. Prime Minister, being the champion of neutral rights that you are, I am surprised that you should not have at least protested. You will understand that by that action Germany gained such immense initial advantages over France and England in this war that they might well have been as decisive as Germany expected and hoped. Germany took off her gloves from the beginning and you expect us to keep ours on. Allow me to say that we cannot follow your reasoning and opinions in this respect. The ordinary rules of warfare came to an end when Germany entered Belgium. That act of hers killed the Declaration of Paris and the Declaration of London at one blow as well as other provisions guaranteeing neutral seaborne trade with belligerents."

" Great Britain," I continued, " will not, like her antagonist, torpedo unarmed merchant vessels and cause the deaths of those on board, but the Swedish Government must be prepared to see everything possible, short of this murder on the high seas, done to prevent goods reaching Germany and her Allies through neutral countries. The old rules of maritime warfare no longer obtain ; it is therefore no use protesting about these matters any longer or quoting these rules to me."

Professor Hammarskjöld was, I thought, surprised at the unusual vehemence of my words which, however, exactly expressed my feelings at that time and since.

He remained silent for a while in thought, then shaking his head he said sadly :

" I am afraid you are right."

He never sent for me again and I was relieved to have to deal with Herr Wallenberg only.

Before this conversation took place there had been some correspondence between the two Governments with the object of facilitating imports into Sweden of goods on our contraband list provided Great Britain and her Allies could obtain satisfactory guarantees against re-export to enemy countries.[1]

The Allied Governments were at that time prepared, as will be seen from consulting the two Notes referred to in the footnote, and anxious to reach an agreement with Sweden which would have been far less drastic than that which the Swedish Government ultimately accepted after years of real shortage, such as probably no other neutral Government suffered.

From an early period of the War the blockade policy of the Allied and later of the Allied and Associated Governments was largely based on a system whereby neutral Governments became parties to the blockade in so far as they, at the request of the Allied Governments, made permanent their prohibitions of export, which were imposed at first for the purpose of preserving domestic supplies only, or even enlarged them or added to them.

The Allied procedure for carrying out this policy was hardly thought out at one time but really grew up step by step and had already been adopted as a working basis for agreements with several neutral countries some time before the following proposals were made to the Swedish

---

[1] *Vide* Sir Edward Grey's Note to the Swedish Minister of January 20th, 1915, and of March 19th, 1916.

Government at the end of January, 1915, and in March, 1916.

1. When the Swedish Government placed on their list of prohibited exports any raw material or article wanted for *bona fide* home consumption in Sweden, the Allied Governments would not interfere with such imports except in so far as was necessary for examination in an English or French port of ship's papers, etc., provided that the goods in question were consigned not to order, but to a consignee in Sweden specifically named.

2. It would be understood that in case of goods destined for Sweden, which though on the Allies' contraband lists, were not on the Swedish list of prohibited exports, the Allied Governments reserved the right to treat such goods as absolute and conditional contraband.

3. It was to be understood that paragraph 1 would not be carried into effect unless the Swedish list of prohibited exports included not only the raw materials in question, but also half finished products made from those raw materials in so far as their inclusion might be necessary in order to prevent evasions of the prohibitions of exports of such raw materials and half finished products made from the same, which were especially proper for purposes of war.

As an illustration of this last requirement, Sir Edward Grey drew attention to the fact that articles of every kind made of copper or containing a high percentage of copper, brass or bronze, were being smelted down in Germany and used for the manufacture of implements of war, that in the occupied territory in France and Belgium every article of this sort was requisitioned, removed and despatched to Germany, and he quoted an advertisement that appeared in the *Berliner Tageblatt* of January 10th :

> For the war industry, wanted to purchase at highest prices for immediate cash payments : Old metals, scrap metals, such as copper, brass, red metal, zinc, lead, etc., also finished and half finished goods, etc., etc.

Sir Edward stated that in mentioning these facts His Majesty's Government did not mean in any way to reflect on the perfect loyalty of the Swedish authorities in enforcing their prohibitions of export, but that all he desired to point out was that " the most rigid application of these prohibitions " still afforded " loopholes for a free flow of contraband traffic."

So freely indeed did the traffic flow that in the following year many Swedes complained that every available scrap of these metals had been exported to Germany, that in fact dealers made hay—and sold it—while the sun shone, so that there were literally no stocks left in the country to fall back on.

Another matter which was occupying our earnest attention was the transit trade across Sweden to Russia.

The Foreign Office Letter of Instructions of June 26th, 1915, to the British Delegation appointed to negotiate for an agreement with the Swedish Government, refers especially to this subject, stating that that Government had recently refused to allow goods to pass through Sweden in transit without being subject to the Swedish prohibitions of export. This naturally cut off Russia from her only chance of obtaining goods on the Swedish prohibited export list without a special dispensation in each case from the Swedish Government.

The object of His Majesty's Government was therefore stated in the Letter of Instructions to be to secure one of two solutions, either (*a*) that the grant of dispensations in respect of goods which are passing across Sweden in transit shall not be made the pretext for granting dispensations (i.e. for export to other countries) in respect of goods which have been imported into Sweden for home consumption, or (*b*) that some route may be recognised for the passage across Sweden of goods in transit to or from Russia, without coming under the Swedish prohibitions. Of these two alternatives His Majesty's Government stated they would prefer the former.

The objects at which the Commission were instructed to aim were :

I. " Free interchange, as far as may be practicable, between Sweden and the United Kingdom of their respective products.

II. " Security that goods imported into Sweden, whether of British or neutral origin, shall, in the case of as many commodities as possible and particularly of those of military importance, not be re-exported from Sweden to Germany or her Allies.

III. " The limitation of the amount of goods imported by Sweden to that which she requires for her consumption subject to certain exceptions.

IV. " The free passage of goods in transit across Sweden to or from Russia.

V. " The removal so far as military exigencies may permit, of Swedish grievances in respect of matters of trade."

The method by which objects Nos. II and III were to be secured were by the establishment of a body somewhat like the " Netherlands Overseas Trust," a reliable institution from our point of view, to which all imports were consigned and which controlled their distribution. This, however, the Swedish Government refused to accept at the outset, always insisting that its own export prohibitions gave us security enough, a solution which past experience forbade us to accept.

The British Delegation consisted of :

Mr. Lancelot Hugh Smith, of the well known family of bankers and city men, head of the Delegation.

Mr. Eric Hambro, son of Sir Everard Hambro of Hambro's Bank, which had many connections with Scandinavia.

Mr. Robert L. Vansittart of the Foreign Office, now Sir Robert Vansittart, Permanent Under Secretary of State and head of the Foreign Office.

Mr. H. M. Cleminson, a well-known solicitor, who was particularly engaged in shipping affairs and now Secretary to the British Chamber of Shipping.

Lancelot Smith, Robert Vansittart and H. M. Cleminson continued struggling to arrive at an agreement up to the end of the year, and Hambro went over to London from time to time to explain the situation.

It was in reality a hopeless case from the first. The

Swedish delegates—I do not pretend to criticise, but only try to state facts—from the first took up the high line that Sweden could allow nothing that would appear to call in question in the slightest degree her liberty of action on her own territory, and they would not, therefore, hear of the establishment of any such body as the Netherlands Overseas Trust in Sweden for keeping watch over goods coming from Allied and neutral ports overseas. On our part, however, the placing of such goods on the Swedish prohibition list was not enough to satisfy us. They frequently referred to Sweden's ancient glories and independence. As my French colleague used to say: "*Ils se grisent volontiers de l'odeur des bottes de Charles XII*"[1]. But except for one or two occasions the negotiations were carried on in a most friendly spirit, and towards the end the main object was not so much to arrive at any agreement, which by September all understood was hopeless, but rather to find some way of ending off these long negotiations without a bad breach.

After protracted conferences with the object of arranging a friendly if unsuccessful conclusion, they finally drew up the following very anodyne communiqué to the Press at the end of December, 1915:

> Negotiations entered into at Stockholm at the beginning of July between Sweden and Great Britain with the object of arriving at an arrangement respecting certain economic questions have not led to the desired result and will not be pursued.
>
> It has been declared on both sides that the termination of the negotiations will not affect the friendly commercial relations between the two countries.

One scene has remained peculiarly vivid in my memory. The Swedish delegates complained very grievously about the interference by His Majesty's Government with Swedish cablegrams from the Americas passing in transit over British territory, and begged this might be stopped. This seemed a not unreasonable demand to us of the English Delegation (I say " us " for I sat with the

---

[1] "They like to intoxicate themselves with the smell of the jack boots of Charles XII."

others) and we forwarded it to the Foreign Office. In reply I was instructed to tell the Minister for Foreign Affairs that the Foreign Office had discovered that certain Swedish representatives abroad were in the habit of sending messages for their German colleagues to the Swedish Foreign Office for transmission to Berlin. In view of this very unneutral act of Swedish officials we could not accede to the request to allow their cablegrams to pass without examination.

When I made this communication Herr Wallenberg looked very serious and, stroking his beard as he always did when thinking hard, he said :

" I am sorry to say this has happened. I only found it out a short time ago and gave immediate orders that it should be stopped, and you can give your Government my word of honour that it shall not occur again."

I believe that after this it did not occur again during his period of office.

But our Delegation was also instructed to inform the Swedish members of the Commission of the reason why we could not accede to their request, and I shall never forget the effect this statement produced at the Council table.

Most of them, including the two principal delegates Admiral Lindman and M. de Trolle, denied quite truly all knowledge of it, but the two Foreign Office gentlemen of the Delegation, who must have been aware of this breach of neutrality, were struck dumb and were evidently nervous. Had they denied it, I should of course have been compelled to tell the Swedish Delegation what Herr Wallenberg had said to me.

It was not till later that we learnt of the cypher telegrams sent by Count Luxberg, German Chargé d'Affairs at Buenos Aires, through the Swedish Legation advising his Government to spare certain merchant steamers if possible, or if not to sink them without leaving any trace (*spurlos versenkt*).

The period of these negotiations in 1915 was also one of continued Russian defeats and retreats in the Eastern theatre of War, and the Russian Minister, M. de Nekludoff was more insistent than ever that nothing should be done which might give Sweden any excuse for entering the War on the side of Germany. It was at this time that the Chief of the Russian General Staff sent the telegram previously mentioned, saying that the result of Sweden's entrance into the War would be disastrous and incalculable. M. de Nekludoff particularly begged that our negotiations with Sweden might not be broken off in anger.

I was very sorry to see our Delegation depart. We had got to know each other very well in those five months and during the summer, when I had again for the sake of my children, taken the delightful old Rosen house at Drottningholm, our Delegates constantly came on Sundays, if work allowed, to spend a good part of the day with us.

Lancy Smith, who had been on a mission to America about the time that the famous library of Louvain in Belgium was burnt by the Germans, told us that he had met Theodore Roosevelt the ex-President at dinner. Speaking of Louvain, one of the guests expressed surprise that President Wilson should not have protested to the Germans against the destruction of such a treasure as Louvain. " Teddy " Roosevelt burst out with all his old fire and energy :

" I wouldn't have protested against the burning of Louvain. I should have asked them what the hell they were doing there anyhow."

I felt it was a misfortune that he was not in the White House during that crisis.

We often got some relaxation by sitting out in the garden and playing absurd paper games, writing limericks, etc. I even remember one by Robert Vansittart (who is no mean poet) which caused the greatest indignation in my family because of its unworthy reference to my old spaniel " Bobbo " greatly beloved of the children.

> There was an old spaniel called Bobbo
> Who suffered from inverted gobbo[1],
> So when he was ill
> And needed a pill
> The doctor charged twice for the jobbo.

[1] Gobbo is a hunchback in Italian.

I apologise humbly to him now for remembering these lines rather than many of his excellent verses. This is due to my own deficiency in poetical judgment.

How much Isa and I should have enjoyed that summer with the children in those very pleasant surroundings of wood and rock and water, of fine old oaks and firs, and heather and ferns and grasses, had it not been for the ever-present shadow of the hellish War. The children naturally forgot and helped us to forget—they were a great help in time of trouble.

The other matter, apart from the regulation of imports into Sweden, which formed the subject of long and weary discussions between the delegates, was that of goods in transit to Russia. This was one of exceptional delicacy on account of the strong anti-Russian feeling which pervaded all classes in Sweden. Even those who were most bitterly opposed to joining Germany in the War would not hear of the Government taking any steps to assist Russia.

That country after recovering from the first great spectacular defeat at Tannenberg, in 1914, was during 1915 in full retreat and suffering defeat after defeat. The result of this was that while the Swedish activists were particularly jubilant and again busy about their War propaganda, the Russians were at once most urgent that nothing should be done to irritate Sweden, while at the same time they pressed us continually to come to some arrangement with the Swedish Government to permit the passage to Russia over Swedish territory of goods on the Swedish export prohibited list particularly rubber and certain metals.

The Swedes with much justice naturally objected to allowing goods to be transited to Russia without compensation, which they could not obtain in quantities satisfactory to themselves and—as they always proclaimed —necessary for their own requirements.

As a result of this state of things there sprang up, in order to satisfy the ever more pressing demands of Russia, a system of bargaining between Sweden and

Great Britain whereby the former permitted the passage to Russian consignees of certain goods in exchange for export to Sweden of agreed quantities of other goods always, of course, under the understanding that these latter were for home consumption in Sweden and would not be re-exported. This was clearly a very clumsy makeshift for a more general arrangement, but as the Swedish Delegation refused to grant transit facilities on any other basis we were glad to get anything we could that would to some extent satisfy the perpetual clamour of our Russian friends.

As may be imagined, this bargaining business by which every transit consignment became the subject of separate negotiation, enormously increased the work of my already much overworked Chancery. To deal with this we set up a special Transit Dept. in the Legation, which worked fairly smoothly until we found that certain of the Swedish agents of Russian consignees, not infrequently with the consent of the latter, diverted to Germany the goods for which we had paid in exports to Sweden. We drew the attention of the Russian Minister to these abuses, until at last having discovered a flagrant case of a whole cargo of rubber which had gone that way, we decided that, as the Swedish Government would not allow us officially to control these transit shipments with the help of Swedish officials on account of the supposed infringement of Swedish Sovereign rights, we must initiate and exercise some system of private control. We therefore organised a Swedish Company to which all goods for Russia would be consigned and which would look after such goods while in passage over the Swedish railways as far as the frontier station of Haparanda at the top of the gulf of Bothnia.

I found a pro-English Swedish gentleman of good family, Herr Axel de Bildt, who was willing to undertake the formation of this company which was called the " Transito Company " and remained in being until the end of the War, rendering to all parties concerned most important services. In fact without it, the transit traffic could not have been continued and the Russians, to that extent, helped to be of good cheer in their pressing need. Indeed had this line of supply been altogether closed to them, they might possibly have broken down morally if not physically before they actually did, a prospect which our French Allies always feared even more than we did.

But the path of the Transito Company was not a path of roses either for Axel de Bildt or for me.

A violent campaign raged about its head for months. He was socially boycotted and the Legation was bitterly attacked for setting up an independent body in Sweden contrary to the alleged interests and the sovereign rights of the State. That perfume from the jack boots of Charles XII became peculiarly inebriating. Bildt received anonymous threats and pressure was put on him from the highest quarters to drop his Transito, but he stuck to it like a man. On the other hand I received continual whispered warnings from unexpected and hitherto unknown well-wishers to the Allied cause, who had never been particularly conspicuous before, that Transito was helping to send over to Germany all kinds of goods intended for Russia. How this could happen it was difficult to say, for the Transit Department of the Legation, most ably presided over by Mr. G. Sampson,[1] received an account from London of every consignment forwarded to Transito and received at Gothenburg, and followed it on to Haparanda, finally receiving a receipt from the Russian Government officials in charge there.[2] What happened to it after that we could not alter and if some Russian officials chose to make a little profit by diverting a part of the cargo to German agents who were always waiting at the frontier to pick up any scraps that might be going, it was beyond our power to prevent them from doing so.

The storm continued to rage round Transito for months

---

[1] Afterwards an official of the Lena Goldfields Co., and imprisoned by the Soviet Government.

[2] We could not follow up these goods once they had crossed the Russian frontier

so furiously that at the time my Russian colleague got seriously alarmed and begged me to drop it. I was entirely opposed to this since I had first initiated Transito in response to his prayers for Russian transit, which in turn would not be carried on unless we could devise some means of preventing leakage to Germany.

There are times when even in diplomacy it is necessary to stick to one's guns, and it seemed to me rightly or wrongly that this was one.

But the Transito business did not make life in Stockholm any the more pleasant until even the most vociferous of activists found that it was after all not doing them any particular harm, and settled down to it quietly.

The whole situation with regard to Transito sometimes had its unexpected and even pleasant sides as well as its difficult and disagreeable ones. One morning I was told the Crown Princess of Sweden wanted to speak to me on the telephone. She was perhaps the most generally popular woman in Sweden and made herself so greatly beloved that when some years later unexpected news of her death reached a great Socialist demonstration, which was composed of elements far from Royalist in their sympathies, it was unanimously decided to break up the meeting, furl the flags and go home as an expression of their respect and regard for one who had endeared herself equally to all classes.

She was an English Princess, being the daughter of the Duke of Connaught, and Isa and I, who had known her before we came to Sweden, had every reason to respect and admire her character and conduct during the difficult years of the War and to become indeed personally much attached to her. I should always have been willing to do anything I could for her.

I went to the telephone wondering why she called me up at an early hour.

She said she had a great favour to ask. I replied that it would certainly be granted if in any way possible. She said that her chauffeur had just reported that there were no spare tyres to her car, that very soon it might have to stop running, since no tyres were obtainable on the market.

We had been, I may say, very strict about the import of tyres into Sweden, as we knew that Germany was especially hard up for tyres and was offering almost any price for them. Russia also was clamouring for tyres. Here was an opportunity to get a few transited. I replied at once that I should be delighted to help her to get whatever she wanted in the way of tyres, if she could persuade the Swedish Government to give us a transit license for a smiliar number to Russia. She said she would try and next day telephoned me that it would be all right and I sent a telegram to London accordingly, asking for license of export for so many tyres for the Crown Princess and so many for Russian transit. This was granted at once.

Some days later she again called me up.

HER ROYAL HIGHNESS : " Could you get two sets of tyres for the King ? "

I : " I am sure I could if His Majesty will obtain transit license for a similar quantity to Russia."

HER ROYAL HIGHNESS : " There will be no difficulty about that, so I can count on that ? "

I : " Certainly, Ma'am. I will telegraph about it at once."

But I could not help chuckling that His Majesty who had once spoken to me, most politely as always, for King Gustav could not be otherwise than a most courteous gentleman, about the iniquity of setting up the Transito Company, should now be brought to make use of its services in order to obtain tyres for his car.

CHAPTER XII

SWEDEN: LAST YEARS OF THE WAR

(1916–1918)

AFTER the conclusion at the end of 1915 of the unsuccessful negotiations in Stockholm for an arrangement to regulate imports no further effort was made in this direction for some time. Several important American Companies such as the leading oil companies and the Chicago meat packers had during 1915 made separate agreements with the Contraband Department of our Washington Embassy, which agreements put neutrals on a ration for lubricants and propellant oils and meat stuffs. Swedish cotton spinners were also allowed by their Government to sign a rationing agreement with us, and it was gradually dawning on the Swedish public that Herr Hammarskjöld's resistance to any agreement which resulted in a system of rationing by constant detention of shipping and forced sales of suspected contraband goods was far more onerous to neutrals than the system we had brought into operation by agreement with the Governments of Denmark, Norway, Holland and Switzerland. The result of these agreements was that the shipping of the countries that made them passed the blockade area with far less difficulty and delay than that of countries which did not.

In 1916 the system of " letters of assurance " for cargoes that would be allowed to pass the blockade area and of so-called " navicerts " for ships carrying cargoes grew up in the United States. As the American Government raised no objections to arrangements of this kind which were privately come to by Swedish shipowners, as well as others, in the United States, the Swedish Government

could hardly take exception to them against its own
nationals. To that extent friction was reduced between
the British and the Swedish Governments.

The Swedish Government did, if I am not mistaken,
send a Commission over to the United States of America
to endeavour to persuade the United States Government
to take action against this plan, but in this Mr. Hammarskjöld was unsuccessful.

The leading business men in Sweden were now becoming restive under the doctrinaire rule of the Prime Minister
and put pressure on their Government to send over to
London a delegation composed entirely of business men
to try to reach a new agreement on a purely business
basis by which Sweden might be placed on a footing
similar to Norway and the other neutral Powers adjacent
to Germany.

Negotiations regarding the terms of reference of this
new delegation lasted many months and it was not until
the end of the year that, headed by Herr Marcus Wallenberg, brother of the Minister for Foreign Affairs and an
outstanding figure in international finance, it arrived in
England. By that time the Hammarskjöld regime,
growing more and more unpopular, was beginning to
totter. Both big business and the mass of the working
people combined in opposition to it. The first did so
for economic reasons connected with the blockade and
the latter because that Government was looked upon as
the representative of Royal as opposed to democratic
authority, on account of the *coup* by which it had originally
come into power. These two elements therefore joined
to put pressure on the unwilling Prime Minister to
accept an agreement including all the rationing practices
then in vogue for neutrals. Thus rationing schedules
were included, provisions introduced for setting up
approved receiving and distributing associations, etc.
This agreement was, however, never ratified because, the
Hammarskjöld Ministry having fallen from power, a
new Ministry presided over by Herr Swartz and Admiral
Lindman (the President of the Swedish Delegation

which negotiated unsuccessfully with us in 1915) took its place. The new Swedish Government naturally wanted time to examine the agreement but in the meantime, on February 1st, of 1917, Germany began her intensive submarine campaign, which was so nearly a decisive factor in the War, a factor which Great Britain with her usual unwillingness to prepare for disaster beforehand had not taken seriously until it was upon her. There were many who blamed Germany for this as an immoral act. I cannot go so far for, as before stated, there seems to me to be no question of any special act of immorality in war. The whole business is immoral and unethical and when a nation believes itself to be fighting for its life it cannot be expected to consider niceties of this kind. I hope I may be forgiven in using the expression " niceties," but I do so because all barbarities, submarine warfare, poison gasses, blockade, in fact every act, which is not simply like sadism a kind of inhuman perversion dictated by a love of cruelty for its own sake, become legitimate in time of war, if we all accept Moltke's dictum that the most humane war is the shortest. With regard to the submarine war, therefore, I feel that, as it was a measure, an entirely new measure indeed, that was intended to achieve and very nearly did achieve an early victory, it would have been justified had it achieved its purpose. It was only because by becoming the principal factor in bringing America into the War it actually defeated its purpose that, always assuming Moltke's point of view, it became unjustifiable.

The result of the German intensive submarine campaign was naturally to stop for some time all neutral shipping whether out or in, and both Germany and her neutral neighbours suffered accordingly. In these circumstances negotiations for the regulation of neutral imports ceased and did not recommence till the Americans, having stopped all exports to neutrals adjacent to Germany, advised them that such exports would only begin again after agreements against re-export had been concluded.

The Swedes at once sent a Delegation to America,

which returned home towards the end of 1917, having, however, accomplished nothing.

The fact was that the American Government was much more intransigent than Great Britain had ever been. Their association with us in the War against Germany of course simplified the whole blockade business immeasurably.

America could attach any conditions she thought fit to the despatch of American goods. Americans then not only insisted on the most strict control over the re-export from Sweden of their goods of all kinds, but also brought into being new doctrines for contraband such as that of "*produits similaires*" and "derivative contraband." They insisted that all trade in such goods between Sweden and enemy countries should cease. Further, inasmuch as American oils and lubricants were used in Swedish mines, they declared that they would not export oils to Sweden unless the Swedes undertook to stop all export of ore to Germany. The Swedes refused to negotiate on this basis.

At this time so little was passing into Sweden that we English did not trouble ourselves any further about rationing agreements. We only went on detaining cargoes consigned to "jet black" firms. It is not surprising that by November there was a very severe scarcity of food stuffs in Sweden. Even diplomatic households were severely rationed and children over two years of age could not get fresh milk. The production of milk throughout the whole country fell, if I remember right, by nearly fifty per cent. in a few months owing to lack of oil cake and vegetable fats. We managed to obtain a little tea, coffee and sugar by the diplomatic bags, but otherwise we were kept on as short rations as the Swedes themselves.

At last, however, this scarcity and the scandals about cypher telegrams transmitted to Germany through the Swedish Legation in Washington, drove the Lindman Government from office and brought into being a Liberal and Moderate-Socialist Coalition of which the real head was the Socialist leader Herr Branting, a very able and reasonable man, who afterwards became a most highly respected personality in the Councils of the League of Nations. New Allied and Associated negotiations were begun with the Swedish Government in December, 1917. These, however, came to no conclusion till the end of May, 1918.

This delay was caused by the fact that the general situation had by that time so changed that the ends we pursued had also altered. We no longer troubled about rations, since it was clear that all neutrals adjacent to Germany would be very short of all supplies for the rest of the War. We were, however, most anxious to charter all the shipping we could to make up for losses from the submarine campaign and to collect transports to carry American troops to Europe. The Swedish Government had no objection to chartering this shipping but would not do so until they had assurances from Germany that she would not retaliate by reprisals. Strange to say the Germans gave these assurances and thus our negotiations with Sweden, which had begun in July, 1915, only resulted in an agreement in May, 1918, and that agreement was in force for about four months up to the end of the War.

So during the last weary years of the War, 1916, 1917 and the beginning of 1918, of that miserable stationary war of attrition on the Western Front, which seemed like a sort of endless hell even to us who were so far away from it, the work of our Chancery gradually reduced itself to a regular routine of answering the questions of our Contraband Department about the reliability of Consignees in order that cargoes from overseas might obtain " letters of assurance " and the ships carrying them " navicerts " and so pass the great *cordon* of the blockade.

We had little to encourage us, for though confidential reports from Germany gave us some hope as regards internal conditions, her military power appeared as strong as ever.

Russia was clearly crumbling and no reliance could be placed on her recovery, but rather the reverse.

R

The Battle of Jutland, if it was far from being the victory which the Germans with their keen eye for propaganda proclaimed it to be, was not the great victory that we British had hoped for, though it did confine the German High Seas Fleet to port until the day for its surrender. The attack on the Dardanelles missed by a hair's breadth, by the mere chance of some floating mines, being the spectacular triumph it should have been and became instead a magnificent tragedy.

Italy suffered an almost complete knock-out blow at Caporetto.

Finally the intensive submarine war in 1917 seemed to be within an ace of achieving its object and of bringing Great Britain to her knees.

In the midst of all these tremendous and terrible occurrences we continued at Stockholm our routine. Letters of assurance, navicerts; navicerts, letters of assurance day after day. Yet, as I hope I have made clear, this humdrum work was having its effect on the great German military machine. It was preparing the way for the final *débâcle*, which without it would never have taken place. But the apparent results at the time were as small, in comparison with the heroism of the men on the fields of blood and mud in France, or the Dardanelles, as the dripping of water on a rock which gradually wears it away. For this reason I have a special admiration for those sailormen who day and night, summer and winter in small boats tossed and battered about in those cold, grey, wild northern waters kept the long line which as surely as any land trenches defended the lives and independence of their people and their people's Allies from the amazing military machine of German *Kultur*.

Besides this routine work I had, however, one or two interesting side shows to deal with.

As the disintegration of Russia became more and more probable Stockholm grew to be a meeting house for the leaders of various subject races who hoped to achieve independence after the collapse of the Romanov Empire. Little by little, Poles, Finns, Lithuanians, Letts and

Esthonians began to approach my French colleague and myself with reports of their countries, their hopes for the future and above all and always their good will towards the Allied countries. As time went on and when it became clear that despite the Russian collapse as a factor in the Allied front, the final defeat of Germany was probable, all these nationalities grew bolder and their plans took on clearer shape.

Their opponents among the supporters of the old Russian régime, however, endeavoured to persuade the Allies that these nationalities were either Bolsheviks or Prussian Junkers in disguise. They could use certain plausible arguments in support of their contention, particularly with regard to the Finns, Letts, Esthonians and Lithuanians. There were persons in authority in the Allied countries who inclined to this point of view. I, however, became early convinced that these people had really a strong sense of nationality which would support them against either Russian or Prussian aggression.

Besides this, I began also to respect and to admire among the small Baltic nations especially the Esthonians and the Letts who seemed to possess a grit and courage as well as a grasp of actualities in political life which was little short of amazing, considering that they had never had any political experience at all. They were certainly not Bolsheviks, but they did look forward to the breaking up of the estates of the great Baltic barons, descendants of the German Teutonic knights who had divided up the country centuries before.

In race of course they were neither Russian nor German. The Esthonians were of a Central Asiatic stock, speaking a language akin to the Finnish, Hungarian and possibly Basque,[1] a stocky, intelligent, straightforward and apparently reliable people. I believed in their future if they were left to themselves, and I also believed in their assurance of friendship to Great Britain and their desire to establish firm commercial relations.

---

[1] The Letts and Lithuanians however belong to another stock of Indo-European origin and are ancestors of the Prussians.

I have not been disappointed.   Most people who have followed their story since they became independent will agree to this.

I always pleaded the cause of these Baltic nationalities with all the vigour I could at that time and afterwards during the Peace Conference where, however, I was not always successful.   I remember one afternoon in Paris going to see Field Marshal Sir Henry Wilson, Chief of the Imperial General Staff, in order to get him to take sufficient interest in this group of peoples to assist them in their struggle against the Bolshevik hordes that were threatening them.   This must have been in the Spring of 1919.   All he did was to say :

" Come with me to look at the map."

He pulled down a roll map of the Russian Empire on the wall and in his rather effusive Irish way threw his arm round my shoulder and said :

" Now, my boy, look at those two little plots on the map and look at all that enormous country beside them.   How can they hope to avoid being gobbled up ? "

I felt it was hopeless to convince him, but Mr. Balfour and the Foreign Office were sympathetic, and also the Navy who supplied the Esths and Letts with ammunition, which was what they really needed.   In due course General Laidoner, the Esthonian leader, inflicted on the Bolshevik army so hard a blow that the Soviet Government wisely left the two heroic little lands alone since that time feeling perhaps that they, like all other sturdy peasant people owning their own land, would be too indigestible a morsel for the Dictatorship of the Proletariat.

While I had every sympathy with the national aspirations of the Lithuanians for some reason which I could not exactly define, I felt less confidence in their grit and, therefore, in their power ultimately to protect themselves. Some appeared inclined to lean on Russia and others on Germany, and in present circumstances neither of these policies could be satisfactory.   The Lithunanian language is, I believe, like that of the Letts, a very ancient Indo-European language, different from that of the

Esthonians and having, so philologists assure us, more close kinship with Sanskrit than any other known language. Had I not been busy with so many things at that time I should certainly have taken up the study of these most interesting Baltic languages.

Of the Finnish question, which became an absorbing matter for us in Stockholm and presented its own complications, I shall speak later.

There remained the Poles. Talleyrand is said to have exclaimed when a young Pole was presented to him :

" *Si jeune et déjà Polonais !* "[1]

After meeting many Poles and hearing all they had gone through in the Great War, being forced to fight against each other for masters for whom they felt no affection, I felt more inclined to say :

" *Polonais et encore si jeune !* "[2]

For in spite of all, they almost invariably possessed a resiliancy of character which enabled them to retain their natural buoyancy even in the most adverse circumstances.

The Poles I had met formerly were mostly diplomats in the German, Russian or Austrian service, clever like most Slavs, entertaining in drawing-rooms like most Slavs, artistic, friendly, companionable but lacking something in their general make-up which made them different to other peoples.

It was not till I met Poles after hopes were again born amongst them that their country might rise anew from its ashes, after its dismemberment by Prussia, Austria and Russia in the eighteenth century, that I grew to understand that what had been lacking to them before was the sense of possessing a country to serve, and a people and a family. They might indeed serve a master in the army, in the diplomatic service, in politics at home, but in serving him they were always conscious that they might be injuring indirectly if not directly the interests of their Fatherland. Humanly speaking, Frederick the Great, that past master of cynicism, spoke that which at the time seemed a true word when he said, according to report, of

---

[1] " So young and already Polish ! "   [2] " Polish, and still young ! "

the first division of Poland which he had instigated and brought about :

" We—Prussia, Russia and Austria, should never quarrel again for we have gone to Communion together and divided the Host."

During the nineteenth century Poland had more than once tried by force of her own to break the chains which these Empires had rivetted about her. But the cunning perversion of Frederick the Great had always proved too strong for her, and after the last insurrection in 1863, it seemed as if the Polish question was dead and buried and it no longer occupied the European Chanceries.

Now, however, I found among these Polish leaders who came to see me in Stockholm that hope for their country was stirring again in their hearts. There were Russian, Austrian and even German Poles, though these, as they were still supposed to owe fealty to the Emperor William, had to be more cautious. More than one told me how in the trenches with his own regiment he would hear Polish folk songs being sung in the ranks of the enemy whom his people had to fight next day and was driven to despair by the thought that whichever side won it would be all the same for his country and for his people. Surely few people had a more tragic outlook during the first years of the War. But little by little as Imperial Russia began to decompose, as Germany's strength began to fail under the blockade, and as Austria was clearly falling to pieces, the picture of a resuscitated Poland began also to take shape in the minds of all. President Wilson in January, 1918, included among his fourteen points a reunited and independent Poland with access to the sea. Finally the Allied Prime Ministers declared publicly at Versailles on June 3rd, 1918, that in case of victory they guaranteed independence to a United Poland with free access to the sea.

After these declarations which made the resurrection of Poland, humanly speaking, a certainty I naturally did my best to study the map and history of Poland and to see what her proper limits should be. Some of her leaders remembering the great days of the Polish State from the middle of the seventeenth century up to the first partition in 1772, were inclined to open their mouths a good deal more widely than the President's point regarding self-determination would permit.   I came to the conclusion that former greatness was really a serious handicap if it made statesmen anxious to return to the glories of ancient frontiers.   Many of our difficulties later on in Paris arose largely out of this, for all the new States, instead of contenting themselves with what was unquestionably theirs by right of nationality, language, culture, etc., were hypnotised by these ancient frontiers and so set up great causes of strife and discord for the future.   This might be said of Serbia, Czechoslovakia, Greece as well as Poland.

The States which did not suffer from the incubus of a past such as the Baltic States settled down much more comfortably and fitted in fairly well with their neighbours.

All questions connected with the future of these States I naturally discussed at length with their representatives who came to Stockholm, and I reported these discussions to the Foreign Office.   The Poles I saw more than others, for they had more money to spend in advancing their cause, and so came in greater numbers.   M. Dmowski toured Europe, but besides him we met in Stockholm two Princes Lubomirski, M. Skirmunt, afterwards Polish Ambassador in London, the two Counts Wielopolski, Prince Lubecki, Count Joseph Potocki, and others.   I confess that this question of the resurrection of Poland excited me above all others in North Eastern Europe, both on account of its historical interest and the present problems involved.

The situation in Russia after the outbreak of the Bolshevik Revolution caused us the deepest concern.   By degrees it became clear that we could no longer rely on Russia takeing any further part against Germany on the Eastern front and the seal was set on this state of things by the Peace of Brest-Litovsk, which gave the Allies a sufficiently clear picture of what they would have had to expect from a victorious Germany.

Imperial Germany allowed Lenin to pass over her territory on his journey to Russia to upset the last vestiges of the bourgeois system that remained. Lenin passed through Sweden on his way, and for a hectic moment the Allied Ministers discussed whether they could not, with the help, naturally, of the Swedish authorities, hold up the arch-revolutionary on the way through. But the plan seemed impossible. It looked as if it might make the situation worse. Indeed, so far had the Revolution gone in Russia by that time that it appeared wiser to let things take their course rather than interfere in matters of which we were then practically ignorant. Who, in fact, understood anything about them ? In any case, Lenin, with the assistance of Imperial Germany, successfully established himself in Russia with the results we all know. But the end is not yet.

When the Bolshevik revolution, the Dictatorship of the Proletariat, took hold of the helm in Moscow, its sympathisers in Finland seized the helm in Helsingfors. The Finnish " Whites " under General Baron Mannerheim, a former general of the Imperial Russian Army, a Swedish Finn by birth and a first-rate soldier, took the field against them. The German Government feeling perhaps some compunction for having let Lenin loose on the world sent reinforcements to help Mannerheim, who, however, always protested that he was not fighting for Germany but only for Finnish liberties against the Red Dictatorship. The Swedish Government was pro-Mannerheim but in the Allied countries there was hesitation as to whether a man who had accepted assistance from one enemy against another should be helped. It always seemed to me that Baron Mannerheim was compelled to accept the German help he received whatever the motive that lay behind the German action.

It was only later that I learnt that the real aim of Germany was, with the help of Finland, to occupy the Russian Province of Karelia and so to become the owner, if not actually in fee simple, at least temporarily of the port of Murmansk. This was the only ice-free port the

Russians possessed. It was characteristic of the Russian Imperial Government that they had never until the second or third year of the War attempted to turn their ice-free harbour into a regular port. The advantage to the Germans of obtaining possession of this port as a flanking station for their submarines was obvious. There was no doubt a strong leaning towards Germany on the part of the " White " Finnish leaders. The Finnish Provisional Government went so far as on June 26th, 1918, under German pressure, to send me a note through the Finnish representative in Stockholm categorically demanding the withdrawal of British troops from the Murman coast.

I believe I advised my Government to take no notice of it, which they did, and no reply was sent. This was as well for it could only in the circumstances have led to complications with Finland.

It was in the early part of 1918 that the Odyssey of the Diplomatic Corps from Petrograd took place. The Bolshevik Government, in this for once showing some sense of courtesy to the Foreign representatives accredited to the former régime, allowed them all to depart in a comfortable train with enough food to take them round the Gulf of Bothnia into Sweden. Unfortunately for these poor wanderers the offensive of General Mannerheim, advancing from the north against the Reds of Helsingfors, had just begun and he was naturally unwilling to defer his military plans for the sake of a parcel of fugitive diplomats.

So the diplomatic refugee train was held up in the snow while the contending armies on either side drew nearer and nearer. Stocks of both food and fuel grew perilously low and even bridge as a means of passing the time began to pall. Messengers were sent to Helsingfors to negotiate for supplies—a little bread and coffee would have been gratefully received. The train was cold and outside it froze and snowed.

The British Chargé d'Affairs, Mr. F. O. Lindley, afterwards our Ambassador in Tokyo, was sent at considerable personal risk to himself through the White Finnish lines to negotiate a safe passage for the diplomatic train, but General Mannerheim could not grant this until several important manœuvres had taken place, and Mr. Lindley was unable to return and report to his friends in the train, so that these unhappy ones believed that they had been deceived and deserted. From what I was told they took no further interest in bridge. For want of anything better they just quarrelled, which was very human.

The Allied Ministers in Stockholm being appealed to on all sides for help, sent urgent telegrams to General Mannerheim, who, having achieved his immediate object, finally after I forget how many days allowed the wanderers to proceed. They arrived in Stockholm like people who had seen Hell and at last been allowed to enter the gates of Paradise. I have never read a good account of the last days of the old Diplomatic Corps in Petrograd or of this final Odyssey, but it certainly should be written. Unfortunately I forgot to write down all the stories I heard at the time.

From all the above it may be understood that during 1917–18 Finnish problems and difficulties gave us in Stockholm plenty to do. Most fortunately for us I made the acquaintance in Stockholm of a most friendly Finnish gentleman, Mr. Ossian Donner, who afterwards became Minister in London. He spoke English perfectly, and what was more understood the English character and did not believe German propaganda to the effect that Englishmen were the most astute and cunning liars on the earth's surface. He taught me all I knew about Finland and made me genuinely interested in the future of that Baltic country. We have remained good friends ever since and I had many dealings with him over the Åland Island question during the Paris Conference.

It may well be supposed that by the autumn of 1918 I felt somewhat stale. Four years and some months in these surroundings gave me a great desire for a rest. Up to that time feeling all that others were going through I was ashamed of even thinking of leave, but by August, 1918, the tide of war seemed definitely to have turned in our favour, so I sent Isa and the children (Esmetto and Francis having already gone to school at Downside the year before) over to England and asked for leave for myself in September. It was impossible not to feel alarm when family or friends crossed the North Sea during the intensive submarine campaign when ships might be " *spurlos versenkt* "[1] and often were, for scores of ships were torpedoed in those waters. The Admiralty passenger ship that carried passengers from Bergen to Aberdeen via the Shetland islands was never convoyed and the passage was far from agreeable. The course was always zigzag to avoid torpedoes and the ship was kept with all lights down at night. There were many other curiosities of travel at that time which made passengers realise that things were not normal.

Isa and the children were allowed to land at Lerwick on their way over and were given lunch by our Admiral and treated with customary sailor's courtesy and hospitality. The younger members of the party, Hubert, Edmund and Henry, have never forgotten their visit to Lerwick and the Fleet. The relief of getting a telegram announcing their safe arrival can be better imagined than described.

Having a presentiment that I should most likely not return to Stockholm as a diplomatic post I went to say farewell before leaving to all those with whom I had been on specially friendly terms.

For the Crown Princess of Sweden and the Crown Prince we both had sentiments of the greatest respect and of real friendship. Both had been perfect in their dealings with us during these times, which were perhaps as difficult for them as for us. The premature death of the Crown Princess was a real loss to her country and to all who knew her. I have seldom met any woman more generally beloved and respected than Margaret of England, Crown Princess of Sweden.

Next perhaps came Herr Wallenberg, the ex-Minister for Foreign Affairs, often mentioned in these pages and his

[1] Sunk without trace.

wife, who also through fair weather and foul had always been staunch friends and still remain so.

My French colleague, M. Thiébaut, was also a close friend, whom it was a relief to have in the dark years, one with whom I could talk over our mutual difficulties.

Of our other colleagues I saw most of the American Minister and his wife, Mr. and Mrs. Ira Nelson Morris, the most hospitable of American diplomats, which is saying very much. As long as America remained neutral Mr. Morris could give entertainments to both camps, and I think that he most regretted America's entrance into the War because it precluded him from showing hospitality to his German and Austrian colleagues alternating with his French, Italian, Russian and British ones. He never forgot the children, and we used to have the finest childrens' parties and Christmas trees in the American Legation at Oakhill in the Djurgården that I ever remember, and I remember these with especial gratitude, because in those days the laughter of children was the best medicine against war melancholia and trouble.

Another curious personality whom we saw frequently was Marquis Lagergren. He was a Papal Chamberlain and spent his winters in Rome, so that he always brought us back news of our freinds and relations there. He had married a rich and kindly American with whom we, to tell the truth, got on better than with him, for he was both pro-German and reactionary to the last degree, so that we often had passages of arms. One occasion I remember well. He possessed a magnificent old château called Tyresö, to which we were sometimes invited for the Sunday. I used to enjoy going there on account of the beauty of the place, which stood at the head of a long fjord surrounded by splendid trees, oaks and firs. He possessed also an excellent library, most of which unlike many owners of libraries he knew intimately and when he talked of his books, and particularly of the Ancien Régime in France, of which he was a devoted admirer, he was really interesting and often amusing.

One splendid winter's afternoon driving back from

ULLSWATER, FROM LYULPH'S TOWER

LYULPH'S TOWER, ULLSWATER

LYULPH'S TOWER, ULLSWATER

Tyresö to Stockholm in a sledge over the ice-covered fjords I cannot forget. The sun lit up the sheets of snow till they became bright orange and almost scarlet in places, while the shadows under the rocks and trees were purple and violet and blue almost shamelessly brilliant. I wanted to be quiet, enjoying the beauty around me and the bright keen air and above all forget the War. He on the other hand wanted to talk about the War and especially to attack me on the score of the iniquities of England. I replied without, I fear, the proper spirit of moderation. The argument became so heated that at last I said that if we did not stop the sledge would get so hot the ice would melt and we should certainly go through. He took the hint and left me in peace for some time, and I have always been grateful to him for the memory of that sledge drive over the fjord in the sun under a cloud-less sky and the snow around us all the colours of the rainbow.

In September I followed Isa and the children and joined them at Lyulph's Tower on Ullswater. Trains being all disjointed during the War, I arrived at a very early hour at the door of the curious old house. As I got out of the ramshackle car which brought me from Penrith, the door was flung open and all the pack of five sons giving tongue like hounds threw themselves upon me as if they would worry a fox; the chauffeur, like the good Cumberland sportsman that he was, joined in the fun and laughed so loudly as almost to drown the other noise. That was a great homecoming.

But peace was not yet, and we had been so long accus-tomed to disappointments that we did not care to dwell too much on the end of war. It seemed too good to hope for. However, here among these ancient hills whose coats of many colours were reflected in surfaces of water like polished steel which even intensified and added to the hues of their ever-changing raiment, and with the family about me I felt for a month peaceful and happy as I had not been since the day of the memorable Belshazzar's feast of July 25th, 1914, in the royal castle at

Stockholm.   For a few weeks at least I could stop thinking about blood and mud.

But the interlude came to an end.   The older boys went back to school and Isa wanted to see her family in Italy.   I got leave to accompany her for a few weeks before, as I thought, returning to my post in Stockholm.

A few days in London sufficed to give us a glimpse of London in wartime, to see my own relations, and to discuss with my Chiefs at the Foreign Office Baltic questions in which, to say the truth, they were but moderately interested.   This considering what was going on elsewhere hardly surprised me.   We left the younger children with my sister, Elsie Carnarvon, and one fine morning in October embarked at Dover for Calais on board a vessel packed with the last troops to be sent across the Channel.   It was deeply stirring to us who had read so much of these things and yet never come into personal contact with them.   The ship crowded with soldiers, many Americans among them and foreign officers, the escort of torpedo destroyers and aeroplanes and above all now the general sense of hope with an odour of victory in the air.   That was a channel crossing to be remembered.

The railway journey to Paris and beyond with its signs of the War everywhere, then Rome once more where, as usual, we put up with my brother and sister-in-law Count and Countess Colleoni in their charming Villino in the Via della Tre Madonne—delightful name—now changed alas, to Ulisse Aldrovandi.   This person was a naturalist of the seventeenth century.   He is mentioned by Izaak Walton for the discovery of a new frog or toad.   The good Compleat Angler was doubtless interested in this discovery, since he set great store by frogs as bait for pike, as those who have read his book will remember.

We had happy family meetings, and I had hardly gone the full round of relatives and friends when I got a telegram from the Foreign Office summoning me back to London at once.

I was loath to leave Rome, which was delightful to me, as always especially in its October garb and above all with the general sense of great things in store for the nation after Caporetto had been more than wiped out by the Piave. My poor brother-in-law, Carlo Bandini and his wife, however, were plunged in mourning for the loss of their much loved and gifted youngest son, Giuseppe, who had enlisted though he was under age. He was a truly delightful boy, talented, patriotic, courageous, one of the many boy heroes whom the War swept away and who would have been useful to his country during the after-math. His name is recorded in the War Memorial set up in the House of Lords to the sons of Scottish Peers.

But this was not the only blow that was to strike that unfortunate house, for shortly after the Peace Carlo's eldest and only surviving son, Sigismondo, also a most attractive and noble character, and a great favourite of mine, having served in the War and come out much weakened, was struck down by the virulent influenza of that period. So with Carlo the family ends in the male line. The War truly turned that house into a house of mourning.

Nevertheless, spring—a new spiritual spring seemed to be in the air with approaching peace. I had no idea what the Foreign Office wanted me back for, but I hoped for some small part in the British Delegation to the Peace Conference. Perhaps this summons meant that peace was near.

So I set out for Paris on November 9th, full of anticipa-tion, hope and keen interest for what was in store. I reached Paris very early in the morning. The Gare de Lyon seemed almost deserted. An old porter took one of my handbags, I took the other. We made our way slowly to the exit of the station. As we reached it he suddenly dropped my bag and held up his hand :

" *Écoutez*," he cried, " *Les Canons du Mont Valérien. Ils vont signer.*"[1]

The guns of Mont Valérin were telling the people of Paris that the Armistice would be signed that day, November 11th.

---

[1] " Listen ! The cannons of Mount Valérien. They will sign."

Many have recounted their experiences of Armistice Day but few, I think, can have been so touched as I was by that old porter with tears of emotion in his eyes. Had I not been an unhappy Anglo-Saxon suffering like all my people from inhibitions regarding the expression of emotion of any kind, I should have flung my arms round the old man's neck. As it was I dropped my bag and we clasped hands for some moments in a silence that meant much more than words. Then he told me that he had lost two sons in the War but had two more whom he surely hoped now to see again.

Driving to my hotel near the British Embassy I saw little stir as yet in the streets until I passed the statue of St. Joan of Arc with the uplifted sword near the Louvre, where some American soldiers, always the first in any business that was afoot, were already decorating it.

On that day and with the sound of the guns of Mont Valérien still in our ears that act had a peculiar significance. The Americans were right to be the first to do it.

CHAPTER XIII

PARIS: THE CONFERENCE

(1919)

" Certes, c'est un subject merveilleusement vain, divers et ondoyant que l'homme ; il est malaisé d'y fonder et establir jugement constant et uniform."—MONTAIGNE.[1]

DURING the morning of November 11th, 1918, a sense of gratitude and relief too deep for noisy expression seemed to take hold of Paris. I at least heard no note of triumph. Most of us were past the desire for triumph long ago. It was rather as if the world had been suddenly lightened of a burden intolerable but had not yet become accustomed to the relief. Streets and squares were filled and packed with crowds of civilians and of soldiers in all the Allied uniforms, but all moved quietly about as though they hardly realised what had taken place.

The statues of the French Provinces in the Place de la Concorde were decorated with wreaths and flags. Unless I am mistaken this was the first time I had ever seen the statues of Alsace and Lorraine so decorated and my heart rejoiced. In former years these statues were indeed decorated with flags hung about with crape. The absence of the crape from these monuments was the first outward and visible sign of the changes all expected to see as the result of victory.

I walked about the streets till lunch time and bought all the papers I could find being more than hungry to see the great news actually in print. How curious is the satisfaction produced by the printed word when it conveys good news. The headlines of the papers satisfied me even more than the guns of Mont Valérien.

[1] Certainly man is a creature marvellously vain, changing and uncertain, and it is not easy to build on him any opinion which is constant and uniform.

S

I lunched alone at my hotel and devoured not only the
déjeuner à la fourchette to which I paid little attention, but
also and above all the papers with accounts of the signature of the Armistice and the hectic negotiations which
preceded it. These are so graphically described in the
life of Admiral Lord Wester Wemyss[1] that I need not
say anything here on the subject. Surely few great
historical events have taken place in such strange circumstances. The hour : 5.10 a.m. The place : Saloon of
a railway carriage on a siding in the midst of a forest.
But I must leave it to Rosy Wemyss to tell his own story.
I wish I had been with him and Admiral Hope when they
walked at sunrise in the forest of Compiègne immediately
after the signature of that document which was to end the
War at the eleventh hour of the eleventh day of the eleventh
month of 1918, nearly four years and four months after
war had been declared.

After reading my papers and a short stroll in the streets
and the Place de la Concorde, I went to have tea at the
British Embassy in the Faubourg St. Honoré, where I
remembered Lord Lyons about forty years before, and
where at this date a great figure on the English stage,
Lord Derby, had recently taken the place of my old
" patron " as the saying went in the eighteenth century,
Sir Francis, now become Lord Bertie of Thame. Lord
Derby, most English of Englishmen, was yet most easy of
access even to those who like myself he barely knew by
sight.

Among others whom I met that afternoon I was delighted to see " Rosy " Wemyss, now Admiral of the Fleet
and First Sea Lord, just returned from signing the
Armistice as British Naval Delegate. It was a real joy
to meet again my old school friend on such a day and on
such an occasion and to find him just the same as ever,
as cheery and friendly as when we were boys at school.
He at once asked me what my plans were and I told him
that I was under orders from the Foreign Office to report

[1] *Life and Letters of Lord Wester Wemyss, G.C.B., Admiral of the Fleet*, pp. 385–
395.

myself there as soon as possible. He said he was leaving that night for London and had a reserved carriage to Calais. Would I travel so far with him ? I accepted with gratitude not only because of his companionship, but also I must confess because I had had experience of war-time trains when coming from Rome to Paris, and having had to spend the night sitting on my own luggage in the corridor of an extremely cold and dingy carriage did not make me wish to repeat it.

Rosy Wemyss told me of his thrilling experiences at Compiègne. On arrival at Dover he was whisked off in an official motor car with all the insignia of high official rank about it, and I saw him no more till we met from time to time at Paris during the Conference.

On arrival in London I, as usual, at once put up at my sister's house at 32, Charles Street, Berkeley Square. Early next morning I reported myself at the Foreign Office, where I was told that I was to be the head of that section of the British Delegation at the Conference which was to deal with North Eastern Europe, i.e. the Baltic and Scandinavian States, Russia and Poland.

Nothing could exceed my satisfaction at taking part in the Conference and nothing could have pleased me better than this particular job, though dealing with Russia, which was then in the throes of civil war between Russian "Whites" and Bolsheviks was not an exhilarating prospect.

I was at once assigned rooms in which to work at the Foreign Office. I had my usual luck in obtaining as assistants in my department two most helpful, able and pleasant younger secretaries in the Diplomatic Service : E. H. Carr, now First Secretary at the Foreign Office, and Michael Palairet, now Minister at Stockholm. With the help of these and of the handbooks on our special coun-tries containing historical, ethnographical, geographical and economic data which the historical department of the Foreign Office had already prepared, we started full of confidence to draft memoranda giving our views as to how best to deal with the innumerable and complex problems involved.

The world seemed very young then, though there were not wanting croakers in the Office as to the outcome of the Conference, just as there had been on before the outcome of the War. I had, however, most pleasant companions to work with and work I thoroughly enjoyed. With Isa, who presently joined me, and my sister Elsie and occasional glimpses of my boys at school and of the others who were housed I forget how, I passed as agreeable a November and December as I ever recollect.

My one great regret was that my two elder brothers, Henry and Stafford, had both died early in the War. In the excitement and stress of work at Stockholm I hardly had time to take stock of all this meant to me. But now back in England I fully realised the loss of two faces from our family circle of six members who had always lived together in complete harmony. Indeed, I never remember a word spoken in anger passing between any of us though our views on many things in life were totally different.

Some parties of our Delegation left for Paris before Christmas, but the presence of my Department not being urgently wanted, I went with Isa and all the boys to spend Christmas at Pixton with Aubrey and Mary Herbert. My sister Elsie was also there and we had a good family party. The only thing that rather spoilt my holiday was that, not having let off a gun for about five years, my hand and eye had lost such cunning as they ever possessed and I " tailored " so many of the high Pixton pheasants that in disgust I decided to give up shooting altogether. I gave my guns to Esmetto and Francis, who were now old enough to shoot, and never myself let off a gun again.

Directly after Christmas I returned to the Foreign Office, awaiting orders to proceed to Paris, but these did not come till January 2nd.

So much has been written by persons who were much closer to the working machinery of the Conference that I shall not attempt to do more than give a short account of my own personal experiences, which I can do with some accuracy as, by exception, I kept a diary of that period and of my mission to Poland during the Conference.

I had already gathered during the weeks I spent at the Foreign Office and in talking to Aubrey Herbert, who was deeply interested in the Near East and especially in Albania, and others that there were countless pitfalls ahead which it seemed impossible to avoid. Before long it was evident in Paris that the feeling between the Delegations of the victorious Allied and associated countries was often so bitter that they might have been engaged before the Armistice in fighting each other instead of fighting side by side.

Many members of our Delegation went so far as to express quite openly their hopes that certain of our Allies or associates would *saboter* the secret Treaties, Pacts or Agreements that Great Britain had herself made with other Allies while the War was in progress. Thus, if we can trust Mr. Harold Nicolson's book *Peace Making*, he sincerely hoped that America would pull the chestnuts out of the fire for us by refusing to recognise any part of the Secret Treaty of London of 1915 guaranteeing our support for the Italian *desiderata* in the Tyrol, the Adriatic and elsewhere in return for Italy's entrance into the War Mr. Nicolson expresses himself as extremely indignant with the Americans when they accepted the Brenner frontier as defined in that Treaty. His attitude and that of many of our delegation in this matter always seemed to me to be of rather doubtful honesty. We had bound ourselves to take certain action if the Italians joined us in the War. Whether the Italian policy before had been quite spotless did not affect the question. It is true they had put themselves up to the highest bidder, but we had made the highest bid and they had delivered the goods. It was certainly for us to carry out our part of the bargain however much we disliked it, and distinctly not for us to attempt to persuade others to block the way, which is, as I gather from Mr. Nicolson's book, what some of our delegation wished to do. The Italians, of course, quickly got wind of this and not unnaturally relations were strained. Personally I quite agree that it was unfortunate that a great part of Southern Tyrol, inhabited entirely by German Tyrolese, should be handed over to Italy as the result of this secret Treaty to which America was not a party. But it must be remembered that, as Mr. Lansing, the American Secretary of State, so truly says in his book,[1] in determining boundaries,

> . . . the chief object in the determination of sovereignty to be exercised within a certain territory is national safety. National safety is as dominant in the life of a nation as self-preservation is in the life of an individual.

So he classes the different factors that require consideration in dealing with boundary questions in the following order :

1. Strategic, to which are closely allied the geographic and historic.
2. Economic, affecting the commercial and industrial life of a nation, and lastly
3. Ethnic, including in the term such conditions as consanguinity, common language and similar social and religious institutions.

Now it was true that President Wilson in emphasising " self determination " (which Mr. Lansing rightly defines as but another expression for the old Liberal slogan " Government with the consent of the governed ") had reversed the order of these factors and that the more idealistic of those engaged in the Conference hoped that he would stand firm on that arrangement of them, but it must also be borne in mind that the Italians had for countless generations seen their country invaded from the north through the Alpine passes, that being realists they did not feel that the League of Nations, which was not then even in being, offered the best security against a repetition of such invasions. They therefore insisted with determination on obtaining as a frontier the crest

---

[1] *The Peace Negotiations*, pp. 91–92. Constable & Co.

line up to the tops of the passes. This may not have been in accordance with the most idealistic conceptions of boundary planning which obtained in many circles in Paris but at least it was not a reason for all the abuse that was showered on Italy at the time, and I don't feel at all sure that the British Government or the American Government would not have been equally insistent in similar circumstances on obtaining such security as a " natural frontier " can give.

In any case it was not for any members of the British Delegation to attempt to persuade another Delegation to *saboter* a Treaty which the British Government had bound itself to observe. Such an attitude, if indeed it was adopted by our Delegation, seems neither loyal, straightforward nor moral.

Another cause of dissension between the Italians and the British and American Delegations was, of course, Fiume. Here the President stood firm against Italian claims and eventually went so far as to issue an appeal to the Italian people over the head of their Government and Delegation at Paris, with the result that might have been expected by anyone having some understanding of human nature, namely that of uniting the whole people against the President in support of their Government.

Lastly the Italian Delegation felt itself slighted and treated as of little consequence during the meetings of the Council of Four, which was composed of President Wilson, M. Clémenceau, Mr. Lloyd George and Signor Orlando. The three above mentioned spoke rapidly to each other in English, which Signor Orlando did not understand, and they did not take the trouble to have their remarks translated into French for the benefit of Signor Orlando, who often knew nothing of what had been discussed. There was a story that some friend once asked him whether he had understood what had passed at the last session and that he had replied sadly that he was just beginning to understand a tale that President Wilson had told for the sixth time about a nigger in a woodpile.

I may be quite wrong in the following assumption about the bitter feeling of the Italian Delegation at Paris, namely, that it was largely due to the somewhat slighting attitude of the other Allied Delegations who were inclined to treat the Italians very much as poor relations who would have to be content with whatever was left over. There appeared to be numbers of the younger members of the Delegations like Mr. Nicolson who could find no words to express their indignation with the Italian Government for their presumption in expecting that Great Britain and France would honour the cheque they had drawn in favour of Italy in the " Secret Treaty " of 1915. But the Italians saw nothing so heinous in persisting in their demands for that security for their frontiers and for their maritime interest which was incorporated in the Treaty of London of 1915, especially as they had kept their part of the bargain.

I do not want to labour this point, but it has always appeared to me that had the British and French Governments then had the foresight to hand over to Italy, in the place of certain of her claims in Europe which clashed too violently with self determination, one or two of the many mandated ex-German Colonies, which were attributed to them and which they could well have done without, this would have saved us much subsequent vexation and trouble—possibly even the present Italo-Abyssinian war and the troubles that must ensue from it.[1] Mr. Lloyd George was recently reported in a public speech to have attributed the Abyssinian trouble to the Secret Treaty of 1915 for which as a member of the Cabinet at that time he was presumably partially responsible. He might have said with more accuracy that the trouble had arisen largely from the breaches of that Treaty for which he is also greatly responsible.

Up to the last there was a hope among the Italians that one of the smaller nations would for one reason or another refuse to sign the Treaty of Versailles and so hold up the whole chain of Treaties. Carlo Placci put it to me in his own inimitable way.

[1] This was written in November, 1935.

" You will see.   When Mr. So-and-so is called on to
sign he will advance to the table and then instead of
signing, he will shake his head violently and all the
piddocks (Carlo was always fond of anglicising Italian
words in this way and in his tongue " piddocks " are a
noxious form of insect) will fly out of his hair and scatter
on the carpet and we shall all rush forward and pick
them up as mementoes of an heroic act."

Not only was there war to the knife at the Peace Conference between Italy and the other Allied and Associated
Delegations over the Tyrol, Fiume, etc., but between the
Americans and Japanese over Shantung (vide Mr. Lansing
on this question) and difficulties between France and
England over Syria, between England on one side and
France and America on the other over Danzig and the
Polish " Corridor."   In fact there was hardly a corner
of the map where dissension and very likely a breach was
not to be expected.   Almost the only matter on which all
appeared to be fairly firmly united was in the determination to make Germany pay for the war whether she could
or not.   She was, in the picturesque language of one of
Mr. Lloyd George's henchmen during the " hang the
Kaiser Election " of 1918, to be " squeezed till the pips
squeaked."

Just as the Delegations set out for Paris full of criticism
of each other even before the Conference began, so also
different members of the same Delegations were often in
grave disagreement with each other.   Notably was this
the case in the American Delegation where it was a
matter of common knowledge that President Wilson's
League of Nations policy was vigorously opposed by
Mr. Lansing, though the extent of his opposition was not
common knowledge until the issue of Mr. Lansing's
remarkable book.   There were dissensions in the British
Delegation especially with regard to the financial clauses,
and so on almost all along the line.

Reading Mr. Nicolson's book is most illuminating,
not to say entertaining.   He was, as the head of his
Department for Balkan affairs, clearly under the influence

of my old insurgent friend from Crete, M. Venizelos, who certainly was one of the most persuasive if not of the ablest of the statesmen present at the Conference. He was particularly potent in treating of the future of Asia Minor. Nicolson tells us that after some sitting on the carving up of Asia Minor, A. J. B. (Mr. Arthur Balfour) very critical, observed " these three ignorant men (referring to President Wilson, Clémenceau and Lloyd George) with a child to lead them." Harold Nicolson adds, delightfully : " The child, I suppose, is me. Anyhow, it is an anxious child—and one who does not want to have anything to do with leadership in the matter."

We must be grateful to Harold Nicolson's refreshing candour in thus recording A. J. B.'s remark.

The final paragraph of this entry in Nicolson's diary for May 16th, Friday, says :

" The Greeks land at Smyrna. Great jubilation at the Hotel Mercedes."[1]

Looking back on it all I personally feel it was very unfortunate for the Greeks that M. Venizelos exercised such fascination over many of the Delegates at Paris.

Mr. Nicolson attributes much of the alleged failure of Versailles to the assumption by President Wilson in connection with the League of Nations of responsibilities in the face of the Senate which he ought to have known he could not discharge. There is certainly much in this, but to say that this inability of the President was the *principal* cause of the " failure " of Versailles to establish a just and lasting peace is to go too far.

The causes were far more complex and lay, I think, to a great extent in the inability or unwillingness of all the " three ignorant men " and many of their subordinates to try to understand the view points of all the different peoples whose fates were in the balance. Mr. Wilson is, however, perhaps most to blame in this respect because he failed to understand the view point even of his own people regarding whom the other Delegations at Paris

---

[1] The Greek Delegation were, I suppose, lodged at the Hotel Mercedes.

were naturally compelled to accept his opinions as representing those of his country. I am inclined to think that poor Mr. Lansing, who was treated by the President as of no account, really represented his people far more reliably. The President, apparently, represented at Paris no one but himself.

Having now endeavoured to describe with the help of others as shortly as possible the atmosphere of Paris, I will, with the help of my diary, try to give a short account of my own experience as being those of a very minor performer on the eventful stage. I might in truth almost describe my part as that of a super considering all the interest my Reports and Memoranda aroused or the influence they had on the course of events.

Foreign Office. January 2nd. Thursday.

" Departure for Paris put off again till next Wednesday. Commander Leighton, who has just returned from visiting Wilhelmshaven, Hamburg and Kiel with British Naval Mission, told me that all seemed to be going Bolshevik more rapidly than in Russia. At Hamburg there is a Republic of the Elbe with a stoker, aged 24, as President. He was very polite and offered to carry the coats of the Officers of the British Mission. Food conditions very bad. No police. All Municipal Government apparently stopped, but no rioting. German officers only allowed to wear uniform by special permit. All German bourgeois very friendly and clamouring for British occupation to save them from Bolsheviks. No mercantile ships built during the War and submarines still being feverishly constructed to keep men employed. As fast as they are ready they are handed over to British Government. Two so handed over last week ! Kiel more discipline and order but likely to go the same way very soon."

The concluding entry of this date is curious.

" Tiger (the nickname for my niece Joan Howard, who was acting as private secretary to Sir Eric Drummond, who was himself Private Secretary to Mr. Balfour, the Secretary of State for Foreign Affairs) tells me that at the Foreign Office they are again thinking of me for

Washington. I again spoke to Eric Drummond telling him that I thought Washington too important a place to be given to a Minister in a small neutral country. I suggested Lord Finlay, present Lord Chancellor. He thought this a good idea."

In this connection I might note that Lord Northcliffe sent for me about this time to Crewe House and asked me what sort of man I thought ought to go to Washington. I told him not a *diplomate de carrière* but someone better known in the official and political world. I believed Lord Bryce was probably the most successful Ambassador we had ever had in America because he was known to every American by name before he arrived, had the gift of making friends with all and sundry and was also an excellent speaker, which diplomats rarely were, not having the training. If someone like Lord Bryce could be found he would be the man.

He thanked me and we never, I think, met again. But it struck me at the time that he must have been taking my measure and agreed with my opinion that some more important person ought to be sent to America. Lord Grey of Fallodon was sent out after Lord Reading left, but, owing to some trifling objection to a member of Lord Grey's suite, President Wilson never received him during the nine months he spent in Washington.

January 3rd. Friday.

" President Wilson has gone to Rome and had a great reception.

Things seem likely to come to a head soon between extreme Socialists (Spartacus group) in Berlin headed by Liebknecht and Rosa Luxemburg on the one hand and the Ebert-Scheidemann Government on the other.

Our troops in the Rhine area seem to be settling down well.

In London great speculation as to the members of the new Cabinet. (After the so-called " Hang the Kaiser " Election).

Defeat of Mr. Asquith on the whole greatly regretted. Owing to complete disappearance of leaders of Liberal

Party, Labour leaders will occupy front Opposition Bench, an interesting novelty. There are many good men among them.

Bolsheviks still advancing in the Baltic States but not very rapidly. They now threaten Vilna."

The Russian problem with which I was to be greatly concerned in Paris had been so near me when I was in Stockholm that I naturally followed its developments as closely as I could both in London and in Paris. The opinions of the Allies as to how to tackle it are well described in *Intimate Papers of Colonel House*, Vol. III, chapter XIII, " The Russian Enigma." As in almost everything else these opinions were greatly divided, which led to complete incertitude and indecision. President Wilson on July 8th, 1918, wrote to Colonel House :

> I have been sweating blood over the question what is right and feasible to do in Russia. It goes to pieces like quicksilver under my touch.

Generally speaking the President, and also apparently Lloyd George, hoped that it might be possible to cajole the Bolsheviks into an attitude of friendship even if they refused to continue active assistance to the Allies. France on the other hand was all for assisting the " White "[1] Russians in their struggle. The Japanese wished to intervene against the Bolsheviks and occupy the Eastern Siberian Railway.

On March 11th, 1918, in response to a message sent by Trotsky, President Wilson had returned a cordial reply expressing sympathy with Russia at the moment " when the German power had been thrust in to interrupt and turn back the whole struggle for freedom " but he confessed that the United States was not " now in a position to render the direct and effective aid it would wish to render."

On March 16th the Congress of Soviets ratified the Brest-Litovsk Treaty with the German military authorities and expressed the belief that " the happy time is not far

[1] *Intimate Papers of Col. House*, Vol. III, p. 412.   E. Benn, Ltd.

distant when the labouring masses of all countries will throw off the yoke of Capitalism." The Bolshevik leader, Zinoviev, was reported to have boasted: "We slapped the President of the United States in the face."[1]

In spite of this discouraging attitude on the part of the Bolsheviks, Mr. Lloyd George clung to his belief that it would be possible to make friends with them.

January 4th (Saturday).

President Wilson was received by the Pope in Rome. His speeches were very strongly in favour of the ideas of the Fourteen Points. It looks as if he felt sure of his backing in America. I hope this is so.

According to the papers, the American public, even those who opposed the President's European journey, are struck by the enthusiasm of his reception in Paris, London and Rome which has given great satisfaction.

January 6th (Monday).

" Foreign Office. Nothing settled as to date of departure. Very aggravating as nothing to be done here. There has been some fighting in the streets of Berlin and Spartacists have seized some public buildings and newspaper offices but Government (i.e. the Moderate Socialists) are putting up a good fight. For the future much depends on whether German Bolsheviks obtain power in Germany. It will greatly complicate the Peace settlement if they do. They already talk of extending their front to the Rhine.

In the meantime the Bolsheviks' (Russian) defeat at Perm by Admiral Kolchak's troops seems larger than before believed and over 30,000 prisoners, much war material and rolling stock taken. This opens Kolchak's route to Viatka. On the other hand Bolsheviks have taken Ufa."

There is little doubt in my mind that even at this late hour if the Russian Whites had been willing to distribute land among the peasants as they went along they could still have obtained a victory over the Bolsheviks. They lost, as Trotsky says in his interesting account of the

---

[1] *Intimate Papers of Col. House,* Vol. III, p. 412.   E. Benn, Ltd.

Russian Revolution, simply because the peasants who cared only about the ownership of the land and nothing for the doctrines of Marx and Lenin got no encouragement from the Whites, and therefore remained passive and even hostile.

January 7th (Tuesday).

" Was finally told I should leave to-morrow with Hardinge and Mallet.[1]

There still seems great uncertainty about accommodation in Paris and it is possible that the Foreign Office ' personnel ' will have to be cut down to accommodate the Dominion Delegations, which are larger than was expected. There is great trouble between Alwyn Parker, who has charge of arrangements for the Foreign Office and Lionel Earle, Secretary to the Office of Works. Parker very nervous, calls up Earle on the 'phone at all hours of the day and night, declares that Astoria, which is to be our office, has been a hospital during the War, is not properly disinfected or furnished, etc., etc., Earle very indignant, declares twenty cart loads of dirt have been removed from Astoria and all is as perfect as it can be in the circumstances. Hardinge will have to make peace—this will be the first Peace Conference."

January 8th (Wednesday).

" Train left Charing Cross at 10.30 a.m., but was told on enquiry to be there at 9.45 when Military Transport Officer would hand me passports, tickets, etc. Found Mallet and others at the station. All luggage taken and booked by an F.O. clerk and tickets, etc., given us. No places reserved for Mallet and self nor indeed for anyone but Hardinge and the F.O. clerk, who had carefully reserved compartment for himself, cabin on boat, etc. One hour at Folkestone for lunch. Sea rather rough but sat on deck with Llewellyn Smith[2] and discussed ' Freedom of Transit,' one of the questions to come up at the

---

[1] Lord Hardinge of Penshurst, Under Secretary of State for Foreign Affairs, and Sir Louis Mallet, former Ambassador at Constantinople.

[2] Sir Llewellyn Smith of the Board of Trade and one of my former colleagues on the Charles Booth Enquiry into " Life and Labours of the People of London."

Conference. Ship full of officers and W.A.A.C.s, latter mostly sick. Arrived Boulogne about 4.15, and left about 5 p.m. Arrived in Paris about 11 p.m., one and a half hours late. Drove in military motor to Hotel Majestic, where we are to live—very like coming to school for the first time. Hanging about in the hall, being looked at by those already arrived as ' new kids,' picking out our baggage, noting times for meals, etc., to-morrow—very amusing. I have an excellent bedroom with bathroom and sitting room on the fourth floor and feel in clover."

I at least had no reason to complain of the harassed Alwyn Parker, who had done wonders, as also my old friend Lionel Earle and his department.

January 9th (Thursday).

Nothing was ready and it was impossible to settle down to work at once, so after visiting our offices in the maligned Hotel Astoria, which were reasonably good, I took a walk with Michael Palairet just to see what Paris looked like. Diary continues :

" In afternoon I called on Carlo Placci at 43 Rue Copernic, which is near, and afterwards on Nicoletta (my sister-in-law, Duchess Grazioli).

Carlo Placci said that in Italy there was some anxiety that the ' Roman question ' (i.e. the position of the Pope in Italy) might be raised at the Conference, and that French Clericals believed that England would do this or Americans supported by England. I told him they might rest assured that His Majesty's Government would do nothing of the kind. . . . He also said that Wilson was almost alarmed at the warmth of the reception he had in Italy and had asked someone ' What do these people think I am or can do for them ? '

Severe street fighting has been going on for two days in Berlin between Government troops and Spartacists. Latter have seized some stations and newspaper offices showing the importance they attach to propaganda."

January 10th (Friday).

" Government seem to be holding their own well in Berlin. Bolshevik insurrections have broken out simultaneously in a number of German towns—Dresden, Munich, Leipzig, Dusseldorf, etc., showing that it is intended to bolshevise all Germany at once.

It is amusing at meals at the Majestic Hotel, and rather like the beginning of a voyage on a big Atlantic liner. Little by little one makes acquaintances. One of the most interesting men here is without doubt Colonel Lawrence, who ran the Hedjaz campaign with and for the Arabs. He looks like a young boy of seventeen and is only about twenty-eight. A wonderful character.

Dined at Ritz with Count Sobanski[1] to meet M. Dmowski[2], whom I thought interesting and clever. Everyone agreed about this. He said that Pilsudski's delegation, headed by Dr. Dluski, was now in Paris and negotiating with him (Dmowski) about a Coalition Government. But he did not seem confident of success."

General Pilsudski had seized power in Warsaw with the help of his Socialist followers who had early in the War fought for the Austrians against Russia. Later he had been interned by the Germans in the fortress of Magdeburg. Released at the Armistice he returned to Warsaw and vigorously possessed himself of the Government and ejected the German troops. The more conservative elements in Poland, who were represented at Paris by Dmowski, were not at that time enamoured of Pilsudski and his followers, and it looked very much as though Poland on the very morrow of her liberation might, as in the eighteenth century, be hopelessly split. That was the view taken by many English people. Everything indeed seemed to depend on the formation of a National Government. M. Paderewski had, before the War ended, hurried from England to Poland in a British cruiser very largely with the object of preparing the way for such a Government, for he realised that without it, it would be difficult for the Allied and Associated Governments to recognise Poland as a stable and independent State.

---

[1] One of my Polish acquaintances from Stockholm and a member of the Polish National Committee.
[2] Head of Polish National Committee.

T

January 11*th.   Saturday.*

" Still very little work to do, but accommodation troubles at last settled and people beginning to arrive.

Sobanski came to see me and complained bitterly that England was doing nothing to help the Poles and that even the request he had made some weeks ago for some aviators and new planes had met with no reply.   Paderewski and Wade[1] have arrived in Warsaw and an attempt has been made on Paderewski's life.   Bolsheviks have taken Vilna but have been driven back slightly in Esthonia.

In Germany and at Berlin Moderates seem holding their own and even taking back points occupied by Spartacists.   Elections in Bavaria and Baden have gone for Moderates, even almost Conservative.

If we could only get arms and ammunition to Poland I believe that Poles would smash Bolshes in Poland and Lithuania.

Messrs. Lloyd George, Balfour and Bonar Law arrived to-day and a preliminary meeting is to be held to-morrow. Bonar Law flew over.

Had a meeting with Board of Trade people to discuss Convention for Freedom of Transit.   Very interesting."

January 12*th.   Sunday.*

" Meeting at 11.30 to discuss Freedom of Transit and agreed on text of Convention.

Dined with Carlo Placci and his sister Madame Henraux and talked till midnight about League of Nations, Italy, Yugoslavs, Roman question."

January 13*th.   Monday.*

" Again nothing to do.   It is of course very flattering to know that one has a small share in the greatest Conference in the world's history, but one would like to be doing something.

Olympians still discussing the renewal of the Armistice.

Bolshes have been definitely knocked out in Munich and Stuttgart and I think Dresden, and are trying to

[1] Colonel Wade had been detached from the British Army as liaison officer in Poland.

parley in Berlin. I think Bolshevism has failed this time in Germany.

Dined at Ritz with Mrs. Wynne of Red Cross car fame in the Caucasus and on Italian front. Ian Malcolm, H. Norman and J. Bevan besides some others. Mrs. Wynne is wonderful. After spending four years in the trenches she now appears in a gown cut in the latest fashion. She has twice had the Russian St. George for bravery and afterwards the Italian *Medaglia pel Valore*."

January 14th. Tuesday.

" At last something to do for the Conference. Eric Drummond told me to prepare a paper for the Prime Minister showing proof of the Bolshevik attack on Esthonia and to go at 2.30 to Hotel Crillon (the American Headquarters) where the Prime Minister is to meet the President. Got an excellent little Memo. by Carr ready and went off to Crillon. Presently Mr. Balfour arrived and we went up with him to Col. House's room. Told there that meeting was at Prince Murat's house, which had been lent to President Wilson.

All dashed off there. Waited in ante-room with Philip Kerr, Eric Drummond, Harold Nicolson and my E. H. Carr till past five, hearing voices and occasional laughter. Then Prime Minister, Bonar Law, Mr. Lansing, President and Mr. Balfour came out. In passing A. J. B. (Mr. Balfour) said to me how sorry he was I had had to wait all that time, especially as the last hour had been employed in comparing the characters of Napoleon and Frederick the Great. He added :

' I wish I had known you were there as I might have called you in to answer one or two questions.'

If the public only knew the immense importance of our rôle at this Conference, they would surely not grudge us our board and lodging."

January 15th. Wednesday.

" Dined last night at Ritz with Sobanski to meet Maurice Zamoyski. Diamandi, late Roumanian Minister at Petrograd, who was imprisoned by Lenin, was also there."

The only meeting that took place between Lenin and the diplomats accredited to the Czar was arranged because of the arrest of M. Diamandi. I got the following account of it from M. Caclamanos, the Greek Minister to Russia, after the diplomats accredited to Russia reached Stockholm from Petrograd in the beginning of 1918.

M. Caclamanos said that when the arrest, on some charge which I forget, of M. Diamandi, the Roumanian Minister, was reported, the Diplomatic Corps was convened by its doyen (i.e. the senior ambassador), who was at that time Mr. Francis, the American, and it was decided to ask Lenin as head of the State to receive the whole Corps in a collective audience in order to protest against this gross violation of all international custom.

Somewhat to the surprise of all the request was granted and an early appointment made. The heads of all Missions in Petrograd duly assembled in the building where Lenin's offices were situated. They were taken up stairs carpeted with the skins of sunflower seeds, which Russians eat in enormous quantities, spitting out the skins, and were shown into a long room at the end of which at a writing desk sat Lenin with armed Red Guards behind him.

The diplomats were asked to sit down on chairs placed in rows before the table.

Proceedings were opened by the American Ambassador who spoke in English. Lenin let him go on for a few minutes then held up his hand and said in French that he had always understood that French was the language of diplomacy and that he would be obliged if Mr. Francis would speak in that language for the convenience of those present who did not understand English.

Mr. Francis, not understanding French of which, Lenin was, of course, quite aware, turned to the French Ambassador, M. Noulens, and said :

" What's he say ?   What's he say ? "

M. Noulens explained and Mr. Francis said to him :

" Well, you'd better go on," and sat down.

M. Noulens then made his protest in the name of

international law and custom. Lenin listened attentively to the end. Then with a cynical smile he made a little speech in perfect French to the effect that while he knew that according to international law the persons of ambassadors and diplomatic representatives were immune from arrest, yet the Soviet Government had come to change many things and this amongst others. At which one of the Ministers present jumped up and shook his fist at Lenin, who continued to smile quite unperturbed, but the Red Guards rattled their swords in their scabbards.

" I was glad," said M. Caclamanos to me afterwards and also smiling, " that I was the junior Minister and nearest to the door because I foresaw the massacre of all European representatives taking place before my eyes, but with some hope of escape for myself."

Lenin, having ordered his guards to keep quiet, went on to say that he had found on this occasion there was no serious charge against M. Diamandi and he was glad to tell the Diplomatic Corps that he would order his release forthwith. They thanked him and withdrew without lingering unnecessarily to ask for further explanations.

Diary continued :

" Saw Robert Bacon, former American Ambassador in Paris, now with our G.H.Q. as Liaison Officer, an old friend whom I was very glad to meet again.

Zamoyski gave me a telegram from Paderewski to the Polish National Committee (in Paris) saying that General Pilsudski had charged him with the formation of a Coalition Government and would recognise the Committee as representing Polish Government in Entente countries. So it seems the breach between the Polish Parties is healed and we may hope for a really united government at last. It is the only thing to save Poland.

The Berlin Bolshevik rising seems definitely crushed. Liebknecht and Rosa Luxemburg are prisoners.

Called on Prince Lvow (ex Russian Prime Minister) at Russian Embassy. He seemed more hopeful of success against Bolsheviks in the spring. M. Sazonow (former

Russian Minister for Foreign Affairs and an old friend of Isa's and mine) comes to-morrow.

Lunched with Sidney Peel and his wife."

Mr. Sidney Peel and his wife, Lady Delia, were among the most delightful of the members of the British Delegation. He was an old acquaintance of mine, having been, with his brothers William (now Lord Peel) and George, a member of the Crabbet Club. He was on the Reparations and Financial Section of our Delegation. Being a strong Keynesite,[1] he was as unhappy as most of us were at the way in which financial affairs were being handled by the Conference and often expressed to me his indignation over the Reparations policy, which he rightly believed could but lead to general financial disaster. It also seemed foolish to me even then, but I was too much occupied with my own Department's affairs, especially with the immediate question of how to prevent Bolshevism from overwhelming all Eastern Europe and Germany then and there, to have time to study Keynes' theories or to realise how well-founded they were. The idea of " squeezing Germany till the pips squeaked " seemed to me, morally, utterly wrong, but I did not realise till later how unsound it also was economically.

January 16th. Thursday.

" Saw Esthonian representative, Professor Piip, and Lettish representative, Dr. Meierovitch, in the morning. Both want loans from His Majesty's Government, and to be recognised as belligerent nations so as to get in a delegate at the Conference.

Lunched with Consett's sister, Comtesse de Boisgelin, in a most beautiful old house behind the Invalides. The dining-room was all decorated with large lacquer panels of eighteenth century.

Even the preliminaries of the Conference have not been easy. It took two sessions to decide the representation of different Powers. Each great Power : 5. Smaller belligerent Powers : 2. Dominion Governments : 2.

---

[1] Follower of Mr. Keynes, the Economist who persistently fought the fantastic demands for Reparations made on Germany.

Language question hotly debated. Great Britain and America stood out for English as well as French as official language and Italy then said that Italian must be included. Question of publicity also raised a delicate point. President Wilson proposed that Press-men should be present but it was generally considered that unauthorised reports of debates by irresponsible Press-men would never do, only leading to wrangles and misunderstandings which is no doubt right."

January 17th. Friday.

" It appears that Liebknecht and Rosa Luxemburg have been shot at Berlin. Pompey Howard[1], whom I met in the *Majestic* just back from going with Marshal Foch and Admiral Browning to Trèves told me that Erzberger had announced ' *Sie wurden alle beide todgeschlagen*[2]—a curious expression.

The Bolshes have been further driven back in Esthonia to near Narva.

This evening we had London papers of this morning in the hotel brought by aeroplane. People are flying over daily now. It takes about two and a half hours."

January 18th. Saturday.

" To-day the anniversary of the Declaration of the German Empire at Versailles in 1871 was the opening day of the Peace Conference in Paris. The session took place at the Quai d'Orsay.[3] Not having received any invitation I went outside in the court to see the delegates arrive, but got rather late and only saw President Wilson and President Poincaré ; very little cheering. The opening ceremony consisted of speeches by President Wilson, Mr. Lloyd George and Baron Sonnino inviting M. Clémenceau to preside, which he accepted in a fine speech. I hear that when the delegates were putting on their hats to leave, Wilson, who saw Clémenceau putting on an old felt hat, said to him :

[1] Commander Henry Howard, son of Sir Henry Howard, British Minister to the Vatican and a distant kinsman of mine, acted as Naval interpreter during the War and after.
[2] Translation : " They were both killed dead."
[3] French Foreign Office.

' I was told I must wear a tall hat for this occasion.'

' So was I,' returned Clémenceau, cramming his soft felt hat over his eyes.

There is still a certain amount of soreness among the smaller nations over the number of delegates apportioned to them.

Went in the morning to call on Baron Degrand at the Quai d'Orsay to talk about Polish matters. He questioned me very closely about our ideas of Polish frontiers and especially East Prussia. I told him we considered this could not go to Poland."

January 19th. Sunday.

" Morning, visited Notre Dame and Sainte Chapelle with E. H. Carr, but windows of latter taken out to preserve them from bombs. Carlo Placci, the Zamoyskis, Colonel Bingham and Colonel Kisch lunched with me.

To-day German elections take place."

January 20th. Monday.

" Peace Conference took Russian question to-day and heard M. Noulens, late French Ambassador at Petrograd, who spoke against peace with Bolsheviks but is said not to have made a great impression. It is clear that President Wilson and Mr. Lloyd George have made up their minds somehow or other to establish relations with Bolsheviks and whatever anyone says to the contrary will have no effect."

This continued to be my impression respecting Lloyd George all the time I was in Paris, i.e. till after the signature of Peace. Whatever I proposed or suggested to help the nations adjacent to Russia against Bolshevik attacks met with a stony silence. Though I was head of the Department whose business it was to deal with the present condition of Russia and which had collected a mass of evidence on the situation, I cannot remember that I was once asked to discuss with the Prime Minister any single matter connected with Russia and her attitude to her neighbours. Whether he read any of the Memoranda and reports we sent in I cannot tell. I really wondered what use I and my excellent helpers Carr and Palairet could be in these circumstances. It was singularly disheartening never to hear even a word of criticism of our reports.

Looking back on that time it seems to me that the Prime Minister was so obsessed with making peace with Soviet Russia that it mattered nothing to him what progress the Communist ideas might make in Eastern Europe and he was willing to allow all new neighbouring States to fall into the Soviet net provided he could get the temporary respite he needed. He apparently never understood what those who knew something of Russian conditions fully realised, namely that Marxism, like a new religion, had its fanatical adherents who now believed they could sweep the world as Mohammedanism did in the centuries after the prophet's death, not by force of persuasion but by conquest. That at least was the intention of Trotsky. It nearly succeeded because Lloyd George would not support a policy of helping the new countries of Eastern Europe against the Soviet attacks and also, I may say, because our Military Delegation, dominated by Field-Marshal Wilson, distrusted the powers of these new States to defend themselves against Russia, whether Imperial or Soviet, and putting their faith in the White Russian leaders supported them with arms and munitions which would have been valuable if given to Poles, Esthonians, Letts, Lithuanians and Finns.

All these peoples had, as I read the signs of the times, a fanaticism of another kind equal to that of the Soviets, and perhaps even greater. The fanaticism of the Soviets centred only in their new doctrines which, however, had not by any means taken hold of the peasants, who were ninety per cent. of the population of Russia. On the other hand the resuscitation of a national will and of pride in their freedom among the hitherto subject nations and their hatred of Russia made a foundation on which to build that was infinitely more effective than any theories of Karl Marx on the one hand or on the other reminiscences of the Imperial Régime which was all the White Russians had to offer. If, as Trotsky explains in his book on the Russian Revolution, the moderate Socialist Kerensky Government had divided up lands in Russia among the peasants it would have swept the board. But the old Imperialists and the great landlords prevented this and from that moment a moderate Republic in Russia was doomed.

Apart, therefore, from any personal sentiment in favour of the freedom of all the subject countries above mentioned I was strongly convinced that their national spirit formed the best bulwark against Bolshevik fanaticism which, had it then gained Germany, might have swept away our civilisation, Mr. Lloyd George included. If he ever gave me a thought at all, which I doubt, he probably considered my views as unpractical and reactionary, while my military friends considered them as unpractical and revolutionary. But both were agreed that they should not be supported—and yet I feel that I was justified by the outcome. But it was sorely disheartening to go on turning out reports day after day and never even to know if they were read.

After this digression, which was necessary in order to explain the situation, I continue the entries in my Diary. *January 21st. Tuesday.*

" German election results are unquestionably satisfactory and show a large majority for the Moderate parties.

Esthonians have had a really good victory over the Bolshes ; retaken Narva and taken a large quantity of war material and prisoners.   This is excellent.

Peace Conference heard M. de Scavenius, Danish Minister at Petrograd, who testified against Bolshes and urged Allied intervention. He seems to have made more impression than Noulens but no decisive effect. It was decided to invite delegates of all Russian Governments (Soviet, Kerensky, White, etc.) to meet Allied delegates on Isle of Princes (Prinkipo) near Constantinople with a view to trying to arrange peace between them. I fear this will only result in all being caught in some Bolshevik trap. It is heart-breaking to get constant appeals (for help) against Bolsheviks and see nothing done."

January 22nd. Wednesday.

" Went to lunch with E. H. Carr and Tufton at Versailles with Major Philip Currie, a cousin of mine, who works on War Council there—a very pleasant Mess. General Studd and General Thompson[1], whom I had met in Stockholm."

January 23rd. Thursday.

" Invitation by Allied Powers to various Russian Governments published this morning. French papers are mostly furious at this truck with the Bolsheviks.

Prime Minister asked me to lunch and proposed that I should go to Prinkipo as British delegate to treat with Bolsheviks and other Russians."

Philip Kerr[2] had told me the previous day that I might perhaps expect this and I therefore was not taken aback but had my mind made up and my answer prepared when the Prime Minister, with his most ingratiating smile said :

' I think I have a job for you which you will like above all things—to go to the Isle of Prinkipo and made peace among all those warring Russian factions.'

Diary continued :

" I told him frankly that if his object was to come to terms with Bolsheviks he had better take another man, and said I thought that anything done to confirm in power Lenin, who was a great danger to British interests, especially in India where he was carrying on a tremendous propaganda, was too dangerous a policy for me to wish to see carried into effect. I said that if we could make peace with Bolshevism by eliminating Lenin and Trotsky, etc., that would be another matter. He thanked me for my frankness and said he must choose another man. I am glad not to have to go on such a wild goose chase.

Nelidoff came in in the afternoon trembling with

---

[1] Gen. Thompson was subsequently Lord Thompson, Air Minister for the Labour Government, who perished in the terrible Dirigible Balloon accident in France.

[2] Now Marquis of Lothian.

excitement to say that decent Russians would never meet Bolsheviks. I advised him to do so all the same."

January 24th. Friday.

" A terrible row in the French Press about the invitation to Bolsheviks to Conference at Prinkipo. This is generally denounced except by *Humanité*, extreme Socialist paper.

Eric Drummond told me that as I had refused to go to Prinkipo, Prime Minister had last night decided to send me on a special mission to Warsaw. The four (Allied) Powers are all sending two Commissioners. The other British Commissioner is to be General Botha, if he will accept, and we are to leave at once. I confess the idea of going to Warsaw at this time does not smile on me— but there it is.

The Conference is moving on. To-day was the second plenary Session to which the small Powers were also invited. Some of their representatives complained bitterly that they were not sufficiently consulted, especially the Belgian, M. Hymans, who had a passage of arms with M. Clémenceau. The latter said that the object of the Conference was to get on with its work and too many cooks would spoil the broth or words to that effect.

Senhor Alberto de Oliveira, my Portuguese colleague in Berne dined with me at Majestic."

January 25th. Saturday.

" I saw M. Sazonow[1] yesterday at Hotel Vendome and tried to persuade him to accept Prinkipo invitation, saying that anti-Bolshevik parties might propose such conditions as proper food distribution (i.e. no discrimination), free press, free speech, which it would be difficult for Bolsheviks to refuse. He said he and his could never meet Bolsheviks. There was not one of the White families who had not had some member brutally murdered and they would never compromise with them. Lunched afterwards with Mr. Balfour and told him about my meeting with Sazonow and asked him (A. J. B.) to see him.

Esthonians and Letts both called to ask what their

[1] Former Russian Minister for Foreign Affairs.

attitude should be about Prinkipo. I advised them to accept on condition of Armistice and recognition of their territory by the Bolsheviks. They agreed.

Dr. Holsti, Finnish delegate, also came."

January 26th. Sunday.

" Worked after breakfast till lunch as there were masses of papers I could not get through yesterday. Lunched with Palairet, General and Mrs. Studd and Colonel Lawrence of Arabia, the man who has run the Hejaz army also there. Lawrence is a wonderful little man, simplicity itself. He has done more than most men in the War and has not a single ribbon, having refused all decorations that were offered him.

After lunch went with Palairet to hear *Damnation de Faust*, by Berlioz, at the Trocadéro. It is delightful music from end to end. I had not heard it for thirty-five years. Tea with Nicoletta Grazioli and met Celere, the Italian Ambassador at Washington who, like all Italians, was very dissatisfied at the encouragement given to Yugoslavs. I do not like the situation in that part of the world. It seems to me too explosive altogether."

January 27th. Monday.

" Snowed hard last night as I walked home from the Ritz after dinner : the Place de la Concorde and Champs Elysées were full of American soldiers and sailors snow-balling each other. In fact no one else about. The walk up the Champs Elysées with rows of German big guns covered with snow in the electric light was impressive.

General Botha has accepted to go to Poland, which I am very glad to hear. Frank Lambton and young Philip Currie came to lunch with me.

Instructions to Inter-allied Polish Commission issued by French Foreign Office handed to me for observations. I find them too vague and suggested points of detail. In the afternoon Dr. Lord, the American Commissioner and I called on Baron Degrand of the French Foreign Office to discuss arrangements for departure and found they were not far advanced. Probably a lot of time will be wasted before we get off though our departure is urgent as Bolsheviks are already at the gates of Poland.

Count Wrangel, Swedish Minister in London, dined with me and talked Åland question.

Aubrey Herbert turned up to try and get a hearing for the Albanians."

January 28th. Tuesday.

" Little news about Russia except that Bolshes have attacked our Archangel force and obliged it to retire some distance. They do not seem to be advancing elsewhere.

Peace Conference. Committees have been appointed to report on League of Nations and International Regulation of Labour, the Colonial question and one or two other matters. Mr. Henderson and Mr. Thomas, of the Labour Party, are staying at the Hotel Majestic, and I spoke to Mr. Henderson about a policy for contested areas around Poland,[1] suggesting the plan of an American Commissioner who would raise gendarmerie with that object. He personally approved but wished to consult colleagues before giving a definite answer. A conflict has occurred between Czechs and Poles in the Duchy of Teschen, Austrian Silesia, where the Czechs have occupied with troops a district in the hands of the Poles. There has been some fighting. When *will* people cease fighting ? They ought to have had enough after nearly five years war.

There are stories of a passage of arms at the Conference between President Wilson and Mr. Hughes, the Australian, which was assuaged by General Botha with much tact."

January 29th. Wednesday.

" Went in morning to attend Peace Conference at Quai d'Orsay as Polish case was taken. The smaller Conference when only the Great Five (England, France, America, Italy and Japan) take part is held in the room of the French Minister for Foreign Affairs out of the Salle de l'Horloge." The following is a picture of those Conference sittings as I still see them photographed in my mind.

---

[1] e.g. Boundaries East and West of Prussia, Silesia, Teachen, Eastern Galicia, Volhynia, Lithuania, etc.

The room was panelled with seventeenth century Gobelin tapestries from the Rubens pictures, representing scenes from the lives of Henri IV and his wife, Marie de Medici, mother of Louis XIII of France.

Just opposite Mr. Balfour, behind whom I sat whenever Russian, Polish or Baltic questions were discussed, was a large panel representing, if I remember right, the apotheosis of a stout lady, Marie de Medici, dressed in black with an enormous ruff and very *décolletée*, being floated to Heaven on the shoulders of extremely fat and naked cherubs.

At a beautiful Louis XV writing table facing down the room and with the Plenipotentiary delegates in a row on his right sat *Le Tigre*, M. Clémenceau, President of the Conference, in a black jacket and skull cap, wearing grey silk (or were they cotton ?) gloves. In his right hand was a large pencil like a Field Marshal's baton. Harold Nicolson's description of his appearance, ' like an irritable, sceptical and neurasthenic gorilla,' is true to life. Considering all he had gone through this is, perhaps, not surprising, but he was certainly an alarming old gentleman when roused.

Behind him sat the official translator of the Conference : Captain Mantoux, who was surely the best translator from French into English and vice versa ever known.

The principal delegates sat in a row down a long table on M. Clémenceau's right in order of precedence. First, President Wilson ; second, Mr. Lloyd George ; third, Baron Sonnino ; and fourth, the Japanese, Marquis Saionji. After them came the respective Ministers for Foreign Affairs, M. Pichon, Mr. Lansing, Mr. Balfour, Signor Orlando, and the Japanese, Baron Matsui.

Behind each one sat his Secretary or ' expert,' a terrible attribute. I could only pray that I knew enough about my subjects—there were plenty of them—not to be caught out by my principals. With Mr. Lloyd George I should have felt fairly safe, but with Mr. Balfour one never could tell.

Fortunately Mr. Balfour never called on me to explain

any difficult problem requiring an immediate solution, though he sometimes asked questions after the sitting was over. I was therefore free to watch Mr. Lansing on our left drawing with meticulous care caricatures, hideous faces and hobgoblins, which when finished he crumpled up and threw on the ground. I at first picked them up and handed them back to him. He said he did not want them so I kept one or two for souvenirs. They were exquisitely drawn.

Opposite to us sat the Delegation whose case was being heard. It might be Poles, or Czechs, Esthonians, Letts or Finns, etc., etc. The speaker spoke in French or English if he knew either well enough. After he had spoken for some minutes, M. Clémenceau, who appeared to be asleep, suddenly woke up, beat with the end of his great pencil on the table, pointed it over his shoulder at Mantoux and said sharply : ' *Traduisez.*' Then Mantoux began at once reading from his notes the most perfect translation of what we had heard without either hesitation or error, in English or French. When he finished the speaker began again, and so it went on for two or three hours till the brain was bemused and weary and I could think of nothing but Marie de Medici and her fat cherubic supporters.

M. Dmowski, the Polish delegate, spoke for two and a half hours, translating for himself from French into English—a wonderful performance. After lunch Dmowski finished his speech and Czecho-Slovaks were heard, Dr. Benes and Dr. Kramarz.

The conflict between Poles and Czechs in East Silesia was discussed. I suggested to Mr. Balfour that the Inter-allied Polish Commission should try to settle this dispute. He put it to the Conference, which agreed.

Dined with Rosy and Lady Wemyss at the Majestic."
January 30*th*. *Thursday*.

" Had meetings morning and afternoon at Quai d'Orsay with Poles and Czechs. Both very cross with each other. However, we (the Inter-allied Commission) drew up an arrangement to be submitted to them next morning.

IMAGINARY HEADS DRAWN BY MR. LANSING, UNITED STATES SECRETARY
OF STATE, DURING A SESSION OF THE PARIS CONFERENCE, 1919

Dr. Kramarz, very energetic but not very tactful, constantly reminds us of what we owe to Czechs, as if they owed us nothing !

Poor Wade (Colonel Wade) keeps telegraphing that Poland lacks everything for her army and is starving, but no decisions are taken. It is really heart-breaking. However, if we get this arrangement with the Czechs through, Poles should begin to have arms through Czecho-Slovakia.

In the afternoon the Conference approved our draft arrangement between Poles and Czechs (but without sending Allied troops to Teschen, which both parties asked for) and we had to force it down their throats. They finally agreed ; Dmowski with good grace and Kramarz with violent protestations, though he really got all he wanted."

January 31st. Friday.

" Heard to-day that Benes[1] will not sign but do not know why.

The armistice Wade was negotiating between Poles and Ukrainians does not seem so likely to come off. Saw Lithuanian Deputation and Åland Island Deputation. Lithuanians say they have had a victory over Bolsheviks. In fact latter do not seem to be advancing in Baltic provinces or beyond Vilna for some reason.

There is little news from Germany just now and things seem fairly quiet there. Most people are depressed as to progress of Conference. The fact is we are hardly a step nearer peace with Germany than we were at the beginning and demobilisation is as far off as ever. Labour situation in England is disquieting. Belfast and the Clyde are out on strike. Prices are higher than ever and all armies anxious to get home. The position is not reassuring."

February 1st. Saturday.

" Lunched with Count Wrangel and met Messrs. . . . and . . . there. Mr. . . . told me he had seen a letter from the Queen of Sweden saying that when a deputation

---

[1] Foreign Minister of Czecho-Slovakia.

U

of Generals went to the Kaiser to ask him to abdicate he got into a fit of fury and threw his Iron Cross in the face of the nearest General. He had apparently suffered from intolerable nervous irritability for three months before the end. Ludendorff escaped from Berlin to Sweden with a false Finnish passport made out at the Finnish Legation at Berlin.

Mr. Barnes (Labour delegate) tells me that the International Labour Control scheme is getting on very well, and Robert Cecil seems pleased with progress made with League of Nations. But we are now working in such watertight compartments that I rarely hear what is happening in the other sections of our Delegation."

February 2nd. Sunday.

" After Mass went with Gulkevitch,[1] Russian Minister at Stockholm, to see poor Thiébaut[2] who is in a Maison de Santé with a broken leg. He has suffered terribly. Worked afterwards, then lunched with Madame de Saincay[3] where I met Walter Berry, an old friend of Washington days. After lunch called on M. Coromilas, the Greek delegate, and then had a long talk to Rowland Kenney[4] who had just returned from Warsaw with despatches showing that Czechs had behaved very badly in pretending the Entente Powers had authorised their attack on the Poles in Teschen. He was much disturbed by the state of things in Poland. I took him at once to see Mr. Balfour, who was exercised about Benes not signing the agreement and asked me to find out what had happened.

Salvemini[5], Kenney, Crowe, Mallet and I dined together."

[1] M. Gulkevitch was a close personal friend of Isa and of me. He had an almost too angelic disposition and was one of those really Christian-minded Russians one meets in some of Tolstoy's novels but rarely in real life. He died in poverty in Geneva trying to help those poorer than himself.

[2] M. Thiébaut was French Minister in Stockholm and also a great personal friend.

[3] Now Lady Maxwell Scott of Abbotsford.

[4] Now of the News Department of the Foreign Office. Author of *Pedlar's Pack* and other books.

[5] Well known Italian Socialist, Intellectual and Historian.

February 3rd. Monday.

" Morning taken up with Rowland Kenney and a meeting of our heads of sections with American heads of sections discussing in common our ideas about frontiers, etc. I am delighted about the co-operation with the Americans but wish it could all have begun sooner. We have wasted so much time and ought to have started all this committee work at least a month ago." (Various committees had recently been formed for special work, e.g. Polish committee, Baltic committee, which were the two to which my section was attached). " However, there may still be time to save the Conference from shipwreck, though as Salvemini says what will probably happen is that we shall go fooling on until the great public becomes really furious and then there will be a rush and everything settled in twenty-four hours.

In afternoon started on Polish-German frontier with my American counterpart, Prof. Lord, who is very well informed."

Professor Lord and I, bearing in mind the declaration of the Allied and Associated Powers of June 3rd, 1918, that Poland was to be re-established within her old ethnographical frontiers and with free access to the sea, worked out independently the frontier of West Prussia and Poland on the basis of the last Prussian census of 1910 which gave the fullest and most accurate details on every possible subject. With these facts and figures before us we came to the same conclusions, which are embodied almost without change in the Polish Western frontier and the famous ' corridor ' to-day. It is quite misleading to say that this was based on Polish data. Our data was taken wholly from the Prussian Census of 1910.

Diary continued :

" General Carton de Wiart, V.C., said to be ' the bravest man in the British Army,' who has thirteen wound stripes and has lost a hand, a foot and an eye, comes to Warsaw with us. He seems a first rate fellow.

The two Wallenbergs dined with me at the Majestic

and were greatly entertained by the dancing there after dinner.

After dinner every evening the Majestic became like a night club with all the young typists dancing like nymphs in a world that had never heard of war. They certainly needed relaxation but strangers were sometimes critical."

February 4th (Tuesday).

" Dr. Benes has signed agreement (i.e. with the Poles *re* Teschen).

Venizelos was heard yesterday and spoke with consummate art. He is generally acknowledged to be one of the biggest figures in Paris. It amuses me to think of the days when he was my antagonist in Crete as head of the insurgents.

Meeting of Polish Commission all the morning at the Quai d'Orsay.

Afternoon : Lettish Delegation. They want of course arms, money, food, but they are very satisfied with the situation. The Lettish Bolshevik regiments have gone over to the Lettish Government. Later discussed Polish frontiers with Dr. Lord till dinner, but no time to get through papers which accumulate.

Dined in Quartier Latin with Commander H. Howard (Pompey), Commander Spencer Cowper, E. H. Carr, and an American friend of Pompey's.

General Botha has decided to give up going to Poland for reasons of health. I much regret this."

This was most unfortunate as he carried much weight with Mr. Lloyd George, which neither Carton di Wiart nor I could be said to do. General Botha's absence from our councils was, therefore, a very serious loss.

As a minor matter it pleased my fancy to think that I, who had been a trooper in South Africa and a prisoner of the army which he then commanded, should now be his colleague on this interesting mission for the British Government against which he had previously fought. He was certainly one of the most absolutely sound, straightforward, reliable and unprejudiced men I ever met."

February 5th (Wednesday).

" Meeting of the Polish Commission at Quai d'Orsay all the morning.

Lunched with Caffery of the American Embassy at Cercle de l'Union. Whitehouse from Stockholm also there.

Afternoon work at Astoria interviewing various people. Worked with Prof. Lord on Polish frontiers.

Hardinge refused me a secretary from Foreign Office for work in Poland, but military section most obliging and will try to find an officer.

Very little news of Peace Conference but people are waking up to the idea that Conference is doing everything but what it ought to do, i.e. make peace with Germany, while Allies are rapidly demobilising. British troops to extent of 1,200,000 already demobilised. Meanwhile Germans are recovering strength.

Dined with Colonel Kisch to meet General Haller (Polish Army) and Sir Henry Wilson, C.I.G.S." General Haller commanded an army recruited among Polish refugees and Polish American Volunteers, which had been formed in France for service there against the Germans. The utility of this force in France being now at an end, the French Government greatly desired that these troops should be transported to Poland for service there, where organised troops were very badly needed, particularly on the Eastern front. The question of the transport of this force was one which gave rise to much discussion at the Conference, for while the Polish National Committee were most anxious for it, General Pilsudski was very uncertain about the advisability of this step for various reasons which it is unnecessary to enter into here. The actual means of transport and route to be taken were also rather hotly debated between the French and British authorities and are only worth recording at all as a further instance of the many minor difficulties which all helped to create irritation and bad will during the Conference.

General Haller and his army finally left for Posen but how and when this was accomplished I must confess I have entirely forgotten.

February 6th (Thursday).

" Work at Astoria in morning.

Railway situation bad and strikes in every direction.

Mr. Thomas on his way from Socialist Congress at Berne, going to England to try to settle strikes. He was evidently impressed by German majority Socialist arguments at Berne, saying that they were beguiled into believing that Germany was fighting a defensive war. Bernstein, he said, was first convinced of this error after reading the English White Book. Müller, a large man weighing sixteen stone, was now reduced to a scarecrow.

German Constituent Assembly has met at Weimar.

Bolsheviks have not yet replied to Allied Governments' invitation to Prinkipo except to say that they think Prinkipo too far out of the way for their purposes. Naturally they wish to make propaganda in Paris."

February 7th (Friday).

" Meeting of Polish Commission. Very difficult to get arrangements for journey, which is definitely settled for Sunday. There are difficulties as to trains, routes, passports, amount of luggage, number of *personnel*, etc. Carton de Wiart appointed to take Botha's place, and I am very glad. He is a splendid man and withal the most modest of men.

Worked on Polish frontiers all afternoon. Mr. Lloyd George left for England for opening of Parliament. Lord Milner takes his place in Paris. The League of Nations Committee is said to have almost finished its work. This is good, but peace with Germany is more pressing.

Railway strike in England continues."

February 8th (Saturday).

" German Constituent Assembly opened at Weimar.

Ebert speaks for a Federal Republic and emphasises necessity of unity. An Austrian delegate appointed to German Federal Council. There seems no doubt that Germans, taking courage on account of vacillating attitude of Allies, are determined to cede as little as possible and are beginning to say they will never sign a Peace which takes away their Colonies. In this way they hope to drive a wedge between England and America and possibly split up association before Peace is signed. Particularly will they make a great effort to retain Prussian Poland. Are we ready to insist ? I believe so. Commission met in morning and took a number of decisions with reference to Poland and settled final arrangements for journey. Packed after dinner."

February 9th (Sunday).

" Morning. Went to see M. Thiébaut. Found him better. Carlo Placci, Madame Henraux, Capt. Leveson Gower (the officer attached to me to act as Secretary in Poland) and Philip Kerr to lunch. Philip Kerr spoke to me about Prime Minister's views regarding Poland. He (the Prime Minister) fears Polish Government may not represent public opinion and therefore that there may be a revolution towards extreme Left. I suppose he does not want to be accused of helping the ' forces of reaction.' I am particularly to inquire what are the strength and the views of the Socialists, the Peasant party, etc., and how they view the present Government.

Afterwards wrote letters and finished packing.

Francesco Rospigliosi, one of Isa's nephews, arrived just before I left for Gare de l'Est. Got to station in good time and found our special train marked ' *Paris-Varsovie* ' consisting of one dining car, four sleeping cars, two ordinary carriages for orderlies and military guard accompanying us and two vans for luggage. Such a train for an International Commission must be almost unique. Left at 7.20 p.m. punctually."

CHAPTER XIV

POLAND—AN INTERLUDE

MOST Englishmen of my age at least were brought up in such complete ignorance about everything connected with Poland that before attempting to deal with the Polish question at the Paris Conference it was practically necessary to go through a course of instruction on the subject, a duty which unfortunately most of the principal delegates had not the time, if they had the will, to do. It was indeed as if Poland had even ceased to be what Italy was called before the days of Cavour "a geographical expression." Everyone with pretensions to education has a fairly accurate knowledge of the boundaries of Italy and of her history, ancient if not modern, but as regards Poland it is hardly an exaggeration to say that one hundred years after the Partition of 1772, she was wiped off the map, for the name of Poland actually does not appear in the great pre-war German atlas *Stieler's Hand Atlas*. Surely no such deliberate attempt to expunge a large country from the minds of men was ever made before. Poland indeed was like a closed and forgotten book put away on the topmost shelf. None there were except students of history who could without consulting an encyclopædia tell an inquirer what were the boundaries of Poland, that she became a great country in Europe as far back as A.D. 1,000 under Boleslas the Brave, that long before Prussia, her principal antagonist, was known, she was sought for as an ally by her neighbours or feared as an opponent, that she very early developed a system of constitutional monarchy more democratic perhaps than that of any mediæval State except Switzerland, that she had reached at the time of the Renaissance as high a degree of culture and civilisation as Great

Britain, and a higher degree of material wealth, or indeed that she has to-day a larger area than Italy and a population greater than Spain, with great material resources of every kind, both agricultural and mineral.

Why then did Poland in spite of the many fine qualities of her people and her many natural advantages fail so dismally to maintain her proper status in the ranks of the nations and finally cease to be in the minds of men even a geographical expression ? Many answers can be given to this question, which is an important one for those who wish to understand the problems of Eastern Central Europe to-day. Unless I am greatly mistaken there are few countries at the present time that will more repay careful study than this once powerful country which had by 1914 so sunk into oblivion, that there are countrymen and countrywomen of mine to-day who do not seem yet to have grasped the fact that Poland is indeed risen from the dead and destined to be a factor of the greatest importance in the political structure of Europe. This she can do if she will, owing to her geographical position, as a bridge between the East and West of our Continent, between Slav and Teuton, between Latin and Slav and help each to a better understanding of the other, provided she does not allow herself to be carried away by the prevailing gusts of ultra-national tornadoes and refuses resolutely to be tempted into the maelstrom of super-patriotic megalomania which has engulfed certain nations to-day to the danger of their neighbours and themselves.

The truth is that Poland's best prospect of surviving to play the great part that is her due lies in the realisation that, having no natural frontiers (except to the south) her best frontiers are to be found in the goodwill of her neighbours. In this way she may become a beacon light to us all and teach Europe a lesson which indeed it badly needs. Let her understand the basic truth in the angelic salutation, " Peace on earth to men of goodwill," and there is every hope that she will attain to that high place in the councils of the nations of the world to which the spiritual and the temporal gifts, with the exception of natural frontiers, that have been showered upon her naturally entitle her.

I may perhaps express the hope that my countrymen will give a little more time than hitherto to the study and understanding of Polish problems, because after having come in such close contact with Poland as I did during those weeks in 1919, when she rose from the grave in which she had lain for some hundred and fifty years, I became convinced not only that her people is capable of great things but also that its future like ours is inextricably bound up in a common aim, the maintenance of the peace of the world.

The *personnel* of the Interallied Mission to Poland in 1919 was made up as follows :

Four countries were represented on the Mission—France, Great Britain, America and Italy.

The French representatives were, first, M. Noulens, head of the Mission. He had been Ambassador to Russia during the last years of the Tsarist règime. Second, the French military representative, who was General Niessel.

The British representatives were myself and General Carton de Wiart.

The Americans were Professor Lord and General Kernan.

The Italians were Signor Montagna, Minister at Christiania, and General Romei.

M. Noulens, who had lived through the catastrophe of the Russian Revolution was, perhaps naturally, above all things anxious to avert a similar danger from attacking other European countries and regarded Poland as the first natural bulwark against Bolshevism. General Niessel was, so far as my impression goes, above all anti-German, but both were eager to see the old bond of friendship and even of political alliance between France and Poland re-established as before the partition.

I was frankly out to help Poland as far as I could to re-establish herself as a strong and independent State, not only because I was genuinely interested in the almost

miraculous resurrection of this country, which had played
a great part in European history, but also because I
hoped that Poland would with encouragement and assistance from the Allied and Associated Powers, be strong
enough to weather the Bolshevik storm herself, and to
help in beating it back from the Central Powers of Europe,
Germany and Austria, which were so seriously threatened.

General Carton de Wiart was, I think, mainly interested in the Polish problem from the military point of
view, because it offered him the chance of hearing bullets
whizzing about his head once again, a chance of which he
freely availed himself on the Eastern frontiers of Poland.

Professor Lord was interested in the rebirth of Poland
as an historian who had closely studied the history of that
part of Europe, and thought with me that the partition
of Poland by Prussia, Russia and Austria was one of the
most shameless acts of political brigandage ever per-
petrated by the strong against the weak.

General Kernan could not understand what it was all
about, and would have liked to have drawn a cordon
round all these warring peoples and let them fight it out
in peace.

Signor Montagna took the Italian view of the time that
the re-establishment of Poland as a relatively strong
Power was a definite advantage for the future of Europe,
in which I agreed with him.

General Romei was a quiet, reasonable and agreeable
soldier who, so far as I could judge, had no particular
views about this part of the world but was out to do all
he could for the pacification of it.

In addition to the principal Delegates there were also
one or two Secretaries and A.D.C.'s attached to each
Delegation.

I was particularly lucky to have attached to me Captain
Clement E. G. Leveson-Gower, who not only copied my
interminable reports but who also with Mr. Jan Ciechanowski, later private Secretary to M. Paderewski and
Polish Minister in Washington, looked after my creature
comforts and my health with all the care of a mother and

of a tutor taking a young man on his first travels. I cannot imagine what I should have done without them. I also had a typist and orderly attached to me who was invaluable, but Leveson-Gower copied confidential matter and cyphered telegrams.

The prospects of a happy, peaceful and prosperous conclusion of our mission did not seem bright at the time of our departure.

At this distance of time there are few people not actually connected with the Conference who realise the problems with which my department of the British Delegation which had to do with North Eastern Europe was confronted. The work before us did not consist so much in preparing new frontiers in any part of the territory assigned to us except between Poland and Germany, as in trying to establish order and to protect from Bolshevik encroachments the countries adjacent to Russia. There was not one of these North Eastern European countries, with the exception of the three Scandinavian States, which was not in the throes of political upheavals and in many cases of complete chaos. All these countries from Finland through the Baltic States and Poland down to Hungary and Austria, which last two were not within my province, were without any settled government. In many of them civil war was rampant. It was so in Russia where the so-called Russian " Whites " as opposed to the " Reds," were actively fighting with the Bolsheviks in Siberia under Admiral Kolchak, in Southern Russia under Generals Wrangel and Denikin, and in the Baltic States under General Judenitch. In Finland the " White " Finns under General Mannerheim were fighting the " Reds," while at Archangel the British troops were keeping that port from being seized by the Bolshevik army, and even penetrated some distance into Russia.

In the Baltic States of Esthonia, Latvia and Lithuania, which had thrown off Russian domination but were still in many places occupied by German troops who refused in their turn to accept orders from the German Republican Government at Weimar, and also occupied a considerable portion of the German-Polish province of Posen, matters were still further complicated by the so-called Baltic Barons. These were the great landowners of these provinces who were descended from the mediæval Military Order of the Teutonic Knights. Although they had been Russian subjects for generations, they still retained an hereditary affection for the land of their fore-fathers, speaking German in the family circle and being generally sent to Germany for their education. This feeling was, however, not shared by the overwhelming mass of the inhabitants of these provinces, who were neither Slav nor German but came of an Ural-Altaic, or else of an Indo-European, stock and spoke languages having no affinity whatever with those of either of their two great neighbours. These in their hearts were not on the side of any Russian, whether White or Red, but were determined to establish their own independence, not only from the Russians but also from the Baltic Barons, whom they feared quite as much and on whose account they objected strongly to anything like German domination. The Esthonians and the Letts had, how-ever, no feeling of antagonism towards the Poles, whom they regarded as equally with them obliged to defend themselves against Russia and Prussia.

Finally we come to Poland where a Socialist Govern-ment under General Pilsudski had established itself immediately after the Armistice when the German Commander-in-Chief, von Beseler, abandoned Warsaw and left the German garrison in Poland of some 50,000 men to its fate. These men were almost miraculously, considering the lack of rolling stock and coal in Poland, sent back to Germany in less than a fortnight by the organising capacity of General Pilsudski. But as may well be imagined this organising capacity was taxed to the utmost by the need of setting up without delay the necessary machinery for the maintenance of law and order throughout the whole of a country which had been divided into three different systems of Government and was now of a sudden placed more or less under his jurisdiction.

Meanwhile the authority of the Polish Government, such as it was, was being disputed on various frontiers : in Galicia by the Ruthenes who were besieging Lemberg ; in the east by the Bolshevik armies which had penetrated as far as Vilna ; by the remainder of the German forces in the province of Posen on the north-west and lastly, on the south-west by the Czechs who were resisting by force the possession of the Duchy of Teschen.

The Polish situation was still further complicated by the fact that up to the arrival of M. Paderewski at Warsaw, to which reference will be made later, the Pilsudski Government was looked on with suspicion and even hostility by the Polish National Committee in Paris which had been accepted by the Allied and Associated Governments as the representative and mouthpiece of the Polish people.

I hope that this short résumé of the conditions which faced us in north-eastern Europe at that time may help the readers of this book to understand somewhat more clearly the otherwise obscure and complicated references to these various disputed territories in the following pages.

After the above introduction which appears necessary in order to explain the situation of Poland when the International Mission arrived on the scene, I return to my diary.

February 10th. Monday.

" Arrived Bale 9 a.m. after a very cold night. Heating apparatus in our sleeper does not work. The other Delegation's sleepers are quite warm but this is a small matter. Snow everywhere and hard frost. When we got to Zurich beautiful sunshine and blue sky.

At Buchs we met a train of English, French and Belgians coming from Poland. One Englishman, Lynch by name, a *monteur* at Lodz, stated that not one factory could work because Germans had looted all copper and leather from the machinery. The whole population apparently out of work and starvation very bad. These poor people all cheered us as we left the station.

After Buchs enemy territory for the first time. People

in Switzerland and here look at our smartly-painted train
" *Paris-Varsovie* " with wonder.

A young Swiss secretary, Girardet by name, says that
the Swiss Minister, Odier, at Petrograd, is being literally
starved. A Swiss secretary who went to talk business
with a Commissary at Moscow was threatened with a
revolver. These Bolshes are the people we invite to
Prinkipo."

February 11th.   Tuesday.

" Arrive Linz about 9 a.m. Still very cold and much
snow.

At first Czech station we were greeted by a deputation
and speeches made.

Arrived Prague about 4 p.m. After reception at
station, where I was met by Cecil Gosling,[1] we all drove
up to the Castle to see President Masaryk. The Castle
wonderfully picturesque in the evening light. It was
strange to be received in one of the great rooms, hung
round with (bad) Hapsburg portraits, by the new President
of the Czecho-Slovak Republic.

M. Masaryk was rather *boutonné* but thawed towards
the end. He promised that the terms of the Paris Pact
re Teschen would be faithfully kept by the Czechs.

After reception at Hradschin we returned to the station
and continued our journey."

February 12th.   Wednesday.

" At first Polish station a deputation with guard of
honour, band, flags, speeches, etc. M. Noulens, the
French delegate, who is accompanied by his wife, made
excellent speeches. Similar greetings in our honour
occurred at each large town. One town, Novo-Radom,
enjoyed the unenviable distinction of having passed seven
times from one hand to another during the War. People
at these stations looked very anæmic, ragged and poor.
At Warsaw, where we arrived about 4.30 p.m., the station
was packed. M. Paderewski the Prime Minister came

---

[1] Mr. Gosling was a member of the Consular service and had been Consul-
General at Gothenburg during the War. He was at this time British representative at Prague.

to greet us. Allied flags everywhere and lines of old Guild flags made the station quite bright. After speeches a march past of a few soldiers, then the drive through the streets packed with thousands of people all cheering for the Allies as we drove at a foot's pace in open motors. I felt that the people looked on us as in some sense saviours. Poland was beset on four fronts by Germans, Bolsheviks, Ukrainians and Czechs. We were expected to save them and bring food, clothes, arms, etc. It is to be hoped that the Allies will decide to do something at last."

With reference to the above entry in the diary, I have a vivid recollection of the emotions which this reception by the crowds in Warsaw produced. The streets were already dark and lighted by glaring arc lamps. It was cold and the pavements were dirty and slushy. The crowds were ragged and thin and anæmic, with sunken cheeks and great hollow eyes. Nothing could have seemed more gloomy and more depressing than the picture they presented. Yet the enthusiasm of a people raised unexpectedly and almost miraculously like Lazarus from the dead and still beset with so many dangers was such that it carried me, at least, away. That slow progress through the gloomy, unkempt city, hung though it might be with flags from windows and balconies through the cold of a winter evening, became, owing to the wild joy of the inhabitants, starved and wretched though they were, more inspiring and impressive than the most gorgeous royal or triumphant procession with all possible pomp and ceremony, and the cries of the ragged urchins clinging to our motor cars like swarms of bees were far more moving than the ordered cheering of well dressed crowds. It was indeed Lazarus emerging from the tomb.

Harold Nicolson says somewhere in his book on the Conference that Mr. Balfour taught him to avoid all emotion in politics. I must, however, say that a man who could look on untouched and unmoved at the greeting of such a crowd in such a place and at such a time might as well have been dead, in fact had far better have been in the tomb.

February 13*th.   Thursday.*

" General Carton de Wiart and I are lodged in a house belonging to Prince Czartoryski and in an apartment which is leased by Baron Taube who is now in Paris. We have attached to us a young M. Jan Ciechanowski of the Warsaw Foreign Office and young Count Roman Potocki who was educated at Downside. We lunch and dine at the Club which is near and very comfortable.

At first there seems no great sign of want in the streets and food in plenty. But this is only for the rich who can get anything by paying. There are 70,000 men out of work and hundreds of beggars in the most ragged condition. The main streets of Warsaw are not attractive but are broad and well laid out.

There are five different kinds of currency in circulation in Poland : German marks, Austrian kroner, Russian roubles, Imperial and revolutionary, and Polish marks issued by Germans during the occupation. None of them are really worth anything. The financial situation is chaotic."

February 14*th.   Friday.*

" Mission met in morning and heard M. Korfanty, Deputy for Government of Posen, and in afternoon called on General Pilsudski, the ' head of the State.' He does not call himself President until confirmed by the Diet. He lives in a small summer Palace called the Belvedere built by one of the Grand Dukes, Governors of Poland, about 1835. His is a strange and fascinating personality, very simply dressed in a grey military tunic and black trousers. He has a spare figure and a small, thin, worn face, very deep set eyes and black eyebrows which meet ; a moustache which quite covers his mouth, and a well chiselled nose and chin. He has occasionally a wonderful smile. His past history is one of conspiracy and imprisonment in Russia. He comes of an old family and the Socialists to whom he belongs do not quite trust him, while the Conservatives do not trust him at all. He is fanatically Polish and patriotic.

After another Mission meeting we dined with M. and

Madame Paderewski. He made a wonderfully good impression on all the members of the Mission by his perfect sincerity. He has great gifts but not the air of mystery and power of Pilsudski."

As this entry mentions General Pilsudski and M. Paderewski for the first time I must devote a little more space to these two fascinating personalities.

Everyone of course has heard at least of Paderewski's great reputation as a musician, though I curiously enough was to hear him speak as Prime Minister of Poland before I ever heard him play the piano.

There was a story going round in Paris that when he first called on M. Clémenceau in the latter capacity the Tiger eyed his card when M. Paderewski came into the room and then said with a mischievous smile :

" *Pardon. Etes vous cousin du fameux pianiste Paderewski ?* "

M. Paderewski : " *C'est moi même, M. le Président.*"

Clémenceau, throwing up his hands : " *Et vous, le célèbre artiste, êtes devenu Président du Conseil? Mon Dieu ! quelle dégringolade.*"[1]

Apart from his genius as a musician Paderewski was also a consummate orator, speaking equally fluently and gracefully in a classical style of oratory both Polish, French and English. His speaking was perhaps just a trifle too perfect for our more debased era. But what endeared him above all to those who had the pleasure to know him was his generosity to the poor, his real love of his neighbour, his transparent sincerity, his great simplicity of character and his unselfish affection for his own people which did not prevent him from holding other nations in esteem and affection.

Paderewski's approaches to the political scene were as unusual and perhaps even more picturesque than those of Pilsudski and naturally very different. Paderewski

---

[1] Translation : " I beg your pardon, Mr. Prime Minister, but are you a relation of the famous pianist, Paderewski ? "
Mr. Paderewski : " I am he, Mr. Prime Minister."
Clémenceau : " And you, the famous artist are now President of the Council ? My God ! What a come down."

was known far and wide as one of the greatest living
musicians. He was perhaps the only pianist who could
fill with ease the largest public halls in Great Britain or
America. When during the War the Polish question
came once more to the fore, he placed his astonishing
popularity at the service of his country in the United
States, and began to give piano recitals all over the country
for the benefit of Polish sufferers from the War, and then
he would intersperse between the music short addresses
respecting the history of Poland, her treatment by her
three great neighbours and her hope of independence and
liberty after the War. These mixed performances—
artistic and political—were so popular that he came to
be recognised everywhere as the representative of the
millions of Poles in the new world. As such he met and
fascinated President Wilson and Colonel House. There
was a story current that some Senator, who no doubt
feared foreign entanglements, once went up to Paderewski
at an evening party and said :
    " I suppose, Mr. Paderewski, that every time you play
to the President on that fascinating instrument of yours
(making a gesture with his arm as if he were fiddling)
you get the promise of another Province for Poland."
    There is in any case no doubt that during these tours
he won the sympathies of a vast number of American
citizens for Poland's coming struggle for liberty and
finally in the autumn of 1918 he left for Europe to take
part in the debates in Paris as the representative of Poles
on the other side of the Atlantic. He naturally attached
himself to the Polish National Committee in Paris which
was recognised in countries outside of Poland as representing the Polish nation and therefore being the body
with which the Allied and Associated Governments would
have to deal at the Conference.
    Then at the moment of the Armistice occurred the
Pilsudski *coup* in Warsaw by which General Pilsudski
became " Chief of the State " and *de facto* ruler of Poland.
Unfortunately Pilsudski's Socialist followers and the
Conservatives who looked to the National Committee for

salvation could not agree about the composition of a united National Government by which alone Poland could be saved and reorganised as an independent State by the Allied Powers. The latter indeed were, as has already been explained, placed in a very difficult predicament as regards their future policy towards Poland since it was more than probable that any arrangements or conventions made with the National Committee would be disavowed by the government of General Pilsudski, and they could hardly treat with the latter without arousing the most violent opposition on the part of the Committee whom they had previously recognised as the representatives of Poland.

It was in these circumstances that when Paderewski went on from Paris to London to discuss the situation with Mr. Arthur Balfour, then Secretary of State for Foreign Affairs, the latter pointed out in what an unfortunate position Poland would be placed unless she could appear united at the Paris Conference table. In taking leave of Paderewski, whom he knew intimately, Mr. Balfour emphasised this point and said :

" It is your task. I want you to go to Poland to unite Polish hearts."

Paderewski at first demurred but finally agreed on condition that he travelled via Danzig on a British war vessel of some sort. This was doubtless because he realised that it would give him a certain prestige to arrive under the British flag and he did not perhaps want to appear to owe everything to France. After Balfour had had time to consult the Cabinet, Paderewski was informed that he might start with Madame Paderewska on December 21st on board a light cruiser, the *Concord*, a ship of 3,700 tons which, according to Janes' *Fighting Ships* rolled a good deal and shipped much water.

The sea was rough and the ship had to zig-zag continually on account of mines and possible torpedoes. But Paderewski did not mind. He enjoyed the society of the captain and officers and of an evening played to them on the wardroom piano which had not been tuned for years, whose hammers would not work properly and whose pedals stuck. After he had finished a piece his audience clapped and cheered and wanted more, but his hands and arms were stiff and one leg, which had to deal with the broken pedal, felt as if it had been wounded. Nevertheless he enjoyed himself on board the *Concord* and in describing that strange journey to me afterwards always spoke of it with real gusto. I fear Madame Paderewska was not quite so enthusiastic except as regards their treatment by all on board which could not, so they said, have been more considerate or hospitable.

After touching at Copenhagen, where she picked up Colonel Wade, the British Military Attaché, the *Concord* proceeded to Danzig and arrived there on Christmas Day, 1918.

A few leading Poles came to meet her at the empty docks. The German military authorities made some difficulties about allowing Paderewski to go on to Posen, but finally gave way. He was enthusiastically received by the Polish population of Posen which rose and declared a provisional Republic of Posen, until annexation to the rest of Poland could be arranged.

He passed a day or two of feverish organisation in Posen where, considering the circumstances, the Poles, after 137 years of Prussian domination and oppression, behaved with singular restraint. Many Poles of Posen told me that while the harshness of Prussian rule was odious they yet realised that the discipline and order that accompanied it had been useful school-masters.

A few days later Paderewski arrived in Warsaw and was received with exuberant enthusiasm. He saw with joy his own country's resurrected flag, the white eagle on the red ground, flying from all public buildings and soldiers in new Polish uniforms greeted him on the platform of the station, but at the back of his mind there must have been the thought, would he be able to create that union of hearts which Balfour had urged on him and which he knew was necessary for the salvation of his country.

No two men could be more dissimilar than Paderewski and Pilsudski. Pilsudski, the man of action, with his spare figure, his strange almost mystical eyes and very plain dress, looked every inch a conspirator-soldier and his silences and lack of all effort to please confirmed this impression. Paderewski on the other hand was both an artist and a man of the world, who loved, within reason, good living, good company and good talk to which he could contribute his full share.

Yet both adored their country and knew that if they could but co-operate in harmony all would be well. The question before him was could he charm the man of mystery as he had charmed President Wilson, M. Clémenceau and Mr. Balfour ? Paderewski's biographer, Rom Landau, gives a most graphic account of the first meeting of these two men whose co-operation was of such vital importance to their country and concludes :

> When both men rose after the long conversation, Paderewski knew that no understanding was possible, and not merely because of the difference of political opinions. It was as though two planets had tried to revolve in the same orbit.[1]

That same evening on his return home feeling discouraged Paderewski was informed that Prince Sapieha and some friends were preparing a *coup d'état* against the Pilsudski Government. Paderewski, however, would have nothing to do with it and left immediately for Cracow. Whatever happened he was not going to assist in creating a breach in Poland instead of a union of hearts.

The next night in Cracow he was aroused from his bed at 3 a.m. by General Szeptycki, Pilsudski's right hand man, and told that the *coup d'état* had failed, that its authors were in prison and that Pilsudski invited him to return to Warsaw and form a Cabinet as Prime Minister.

This unexpected invitation he at once accepted, begged Madame Paderewska to make a cup of hot tea for the General and ordered a special train for them all to return to Warsaw.

[1] *Paderewski*, Rom Landau. Ivor Nicholson & Watson.

PADEREWSKI

BY BURNE JONES

The union of hearts had been created just as everything seemed to be cracking and falling to pieces. I made an entry in my diary on January 15th in Paris that Poland was saved. This was perfectly true. In spite of their great dissimilarity of outlook, character, education, manner, in fact of almost everything that goes to make friendships, Paderewski's obvious sincerity had somehow charmed Pilsudski into as much of the spirit of union as was necessary for the time being.

Later Pilsudski remained on alone in Warsaw where his organising capacity was invaluable while Paderewski returned to Paris, where his services were also invaluable to his country during the remainder of the Conference.

In this way the great musician became Prime Minister.

He is indeed one of the greatest gentlemen I ever met. I have met him many times since those days of Warsaw and never had any reason to alter those first impressions of him. Great and small were alike to him. Once years after this time when I was in Switzerland with my family he asked us, boys and all, to lunch at his villa at Morges, and afterwards played the piano for an hour or more to the immense content of my boys who were mostly still at school. Unfortunately Esmetto and I, being in a clinique in Berne, could not enjoy that party, but the others have never forgotten the honour done them by, I suppose, the only great musician who has also been a Prime Minister, and that at a most critical time for his country. All those who have had the joy of his acquaintance can surely never forget this most lovable genius, who could charm thousands with his music and also as a practical statesman played a signal part in rebuilding his country from an almost forgotten ruin into an edifice which, with its growing population of peasant proprietors and advancing prosperity and liberty, is likely to become one of the bulwarks of civilisation on the eastern marches of Europe.

The story of the drawing of the head of Paderewski by Burne-Jones which appears opposite this page is a singular one. It was told me by Mrs. Henry Gaskell who was a friend of Burne-Jones and introduced me to him.

One day B. J., as we called him, rushed into her house in a state of great excitement.

" I've seen an archangel," he declared, " and I've made a drawing of him. Here it is," and he showed her the head of which this is a reproduction.

" I saw him," he said, " coming down the street towards me. Twice I went back and passed him, studying his face all the time closely, but he was so taken up with his thoughts that he paid no attention. Then I ran home and from memory breathlessly did this drawing."

It is a most beautiful thing, and it is still looked on as the finest portrait of Paderewski.

But B. J. was not satisfied to have drawn his archangel, he wanted to know who he was and to meet him.

Some days later a friend wrote and asked him if he might bring another friend of his to the studio. The request was granted, and what was B. J.'s surprise to see his archangel enter, while Paderewski was dumbfounded at seeing on an easel a portrait of himself by a man he had never seen—so far as he knew.

The other great figure of resurrected Poland, Pilsudski, on the other hand was of a very different fibre and had graduated in very different and harder schools. Coming from an ancient but impoverished Polish family of Zulow in Lithuania he had early been taught by his mother, who was an ardent patriot, to look forward to the day when freedom should again dwell in the land. He remembered the ruthless policy of suppression of all Polish aspirations which was inaugurated by Russia after the insurrection of 1863 shortly before his birth. At his school in Vilna lessons were in Russian, teachers were Russian, prayers were said in Russian, history was Russian, and his language —the Polish language—was treated as the tongue of traitors and punished as such. He entered the University of Kharkov as a medical student; but when he was only twenty years old he was expelled and exiled to Siberia on the false suspicion of being implicated in a plot to

A. s. Excellence Sir Esmé Howard.
pour rappeler notre entretien a Varsovie.
Belvedere. 29/III 1919. Piłsudski

(MARSHAL PILSUDSKI)

assassinate the Emperor Alexander III of Russia. In this hard University of Siberian exile he graduated. On his return he joined the advanced Socialists who believed in " direct action " rather than in the gradual evolution of political liberties because in the former method he thought lay the best chance of freeing his country. He founded a Socialist paper which was written, printed and sold secretly, but he was arrested again in 1901 and imprisoned in the fortress of Warsaw. By simulating madness and being sent to an asylum he managed to escape. He played hide and seek with the Russian police for a few years till the Russo-Japanese War broke out. Then he founded a band of armed guerillas in Cracow to hamper the Russian authorities in every possible way. Among other things he attacked trains carrying Russian Government money, and once he seized a convoy with 2,800,000 roubles. His object was to make the Russian Government itself pay for the war he carried on against it. He never took a penny for himself and always gave a receipt for all the money he seized.

Daszynski, the Polish Socialist leader, wrote of him :

> Two traits of his character gained him our love, his kindness and his objectivity. Infinitely patient, he could pardon men even after severe misdeeds ; he could bring together by his friendly spirit people who disliked one another. Devoted to a work which appeared at that time almost desperate, living for years a life of poverty, Pilsudski was for us the most beautiful type of a Polish saint, who hopes for victory against all hope. His contempt of death gave him power.

In 1908 he organised a secret military society, and with this at his command he joined with Austria in the Great War to fight against Russia. Russia was always the principal enemy for him. But in spite of successes with his Legionaries, for he was a great guerilla commander, friction soon arose between him and the Austrians and Germans—it could hardly be otherwise—and on July 21st, 1917, because he would not agree to exchange Russian for German domination in Poland, he was arrested and sent as a prisoner to the German fortress of Magdeburg.

On November 9th, 1918, two days before the signature of the Armistice, he was released and allowed to return to Warsaw.

Such was the man we found there as Chief of the State on our arrival on February 12th, 1919. A sort of legend had grown up around him and his life was, so to say, shrouded in mystery.

I looked forward greatly to meeting this man who was by some of his compatriots lauded to the skies as a most self-denying patriot and by others looked on with undisguised suspicion as a man who might either sell his country to German Socialists or even connive at the introduction of pure Russian Bolshevism and thus lead to civil war and the frustration of all hopes of Polish independence.

These two men on whom the eyes of all Poland were turned were both unfortunately, and yet fortunately, as fire and water. Unfortunately because their whole past lives and characters were such that it was almost impossible for them to co-operate in a really friendly spirit, yet fortunately because each possessed the precise qualities the other lacked for the special business in hand.

Paderewski in Washington was able to win the confidence and esteem of President Wilson and Colonel House and later in Paris of Mr. Lansing, while he also gradually became the friend of M. Clémenceau and M. Pichon. Mr. Balfour's esteem and friendship he already long enjoyed, but Mr. Lloyd George's reported remark when he heard that Paderewski was coming to Paris as Polish representative was :

" What can we think of a country which sends us a pianist as its representative ? "

This was perhaps characteristic. He would no doubt have been delighted to receive a soldier, sailor, tinker, tailor, etc., but an artist, however distinguished, was in his eyes absurd. Yet in the end Paderewski to some extent conquered even Mr. Lloyd George's prejudices against artists.

February 15*th.   Saturday.*

" Morning meeting of Mission. Afternoon called on Archbishop Kokowski, Monsignor Ratti[1] and other persons.

General Pilsudski returned my visit and again fascinated General Carton de Wiart and myself. He has most beautiful hands.

In the evening we all dined with Count Wielopolski, whom I met in Stockholm, and there was a party after for Warsaw Society. It was very ' pre-war.' Women all dressed like *grandes dames*, unlike the astonishing figures one sees in Paris with skirts up to their knees, bangles on their legs and gowns cut down to their waists behind.

General Pilsudski told me that General von Beseler, the German Governor, bolted in a motor boat down the Vistula as soon as he heard of the revolution in Berlin, leaving his soldiers to look after themselves. In this it must be admitted that General von Beseler but followed the example of the Kaiser and Ludendorff."

February 16*th.   Sunday.*

" Early Mass in the coldest church I was ever in. No churches heated now. Mission met after breakfast. Lunched with Countess Joseph Potocka at Palais Potocki, a very fine old house. Everything pre-war.

At 5.30, reception for the Mission at Town Hall M. Noulens made a fine speech in reply to the Mayor. There was much enthusiasm which evidently comes from the heart. At 7.30, gala performance at Opera for the Diet. The house decorated with Allied flags and all Missions fully represented. Much cheering for Allies and symbolical tableaux representing four Allied Powers with Polish children kneeling and offering wreaths, etc. Both Pilsudski and Paderewski loudly cheered."

---

[1] Mgr. Ratti, the Apostolic Delegate in Poland, became Pope in 1922 and took the name of Pius XI. His Holiness has always been good enough to remember our meeting in those agitated days in Warsaw. He played a conspicuous part in August, 1920, maintaining the morale of the inhabitants when the Bolshevik Army was at the gates of Warsaw by refusing to leave the city. He is a great man and a great scholar.

February 17th.   Monday.

" In morning Mission heard Colonel Grove of Commission for Supply on the food and financial situations.

General Carton de Wiart and Professor Lord left for Lemberg to try to effect armistice with Ukrainians (Ruthenes) who are still investing city.

Lunched with Paderewskis and was taken by Madame Paderewska to see Polish refugee camp. There were nearly one million Poles driven by Russians into Russia during their retreat in 1915, and 700,000 Poles deported to work in Germany during German occupation, besides prisoners on both sides. All these are coming back in thousands and have to be provided for and sent home. I never saw a more heartbreaking sight than these poor people all destitute and completely ragged. Thirty-five children died of cold in a train recently arrived from Germany as they are sent in unheated cattle trucks and have no warm clothes. Lord ! it's awful, and little food and no clothing in the country to give them."

February 18th.   Tuesday.

" Lunched at Count H. Potocki's and met Monsignor Theodorowitch, Archbishop of Lemberg, who told me of extraordinary Austrian intrigues to put a Hapsburg on the Ukrainian throne. Up to the last the Emperor Karl seems to have had hopes of this and for this reason Ruthene regiments were placed in Lemberg when the Austrians felt their authority going and took possession of the town. They were turned out by the students of the University and a few local Poles who fought them for a fortnight in the streets before any Polish troops could be sent to help them. There are now boys of fourteen fighting and even girls and women. It is said that a son of the Archduke Stephen is still with the Ruthenes.

Dined with General Pilsudski at the Belvedere—a dinner in honour of the Mission. He unbuttoned a good deal more than before, and told me about his being sent to Siberia as a student of nineteen while at the Vilna University. The leader of the Peasant Party, Witos, was there in his costume, a fine looking fellow."

At the dinner General Pilsudski sat by me and talked much more freely than he had previously done. One part of our conversation particularly impressed itself on my mind. He asked me what part of England I came from and whether I had any sentiment about it. I told him about my devotion to Cumberland and that I never felt really at home anywhere but there.

" Oh," he said, " then you will understand what I feel for my native district near Vilna in Lithuania. I am never really happy except there. So strong was this feeling with me that when I was a fugitive proscribed by the Russian police I never could let a year go by without seeing my own homeland, though of course the risk of capture was infinitely greater because they were always on the look out for me."

Then I began to understand why this man would never consent to separate Vilna from Poland. Men may blame his forcible occupation of Vilna as they will, but it is impossible not to sympathise with his desire to live within the same frontier as his old home. It is perhaps all wrong to allow sentiment to mix itself up with political or economic considerations, but it will sometimes, as in the case of Pilsudski and Vilna, intrude upon them. The imponderabilia are often very powerful.

After that conversation I felt Pilsudski was a real human being whom I could understand and I had a genuine fellow feeling for him.

February 19th. Wednesday.

" No news from Carton de Wiart. The Teschen affair is very puzzling. A telegram from Colonel Coulson our Commissioner at Teschen saying that Czech evacuation of town postponed pending further instructions from Peace Conference in Paris. Our Commission sent urgent telegram to Paris to order immediate evacuation as this delay is upsetting all our policy here very greatly and Poles are inclined to believe that despite our denials the Entente Powers were really behind Czech occupation. Meanwhile desultory fighting continues which is deplorable. If we cannot settle up this matter quickly how can we deal with more difficult problems like Ruthene and German armistices ?

Evening : Great reception given by Prime Minister and Madame Paderewska in Radziwill Palace, formerly Palace of Russian Governor-General. A most interesting motley crowd. One cardinal, several bishops and priests, two rabbis, numerous peasant deputies in costume, Polish and Allied officers in uniform and all the *grandes dames en grande toilette* and jewels. All our National Anthems played and one of Chopin's polonaises."

February 20th. Thursday.

" Generals de Wiart and Bartélemy and Professor Lord arrived Lemberg after being held up for two days at Przemysl. They are in touch with Pavlenko the Ruthene General, but de Wiart has not much hope of an armistice.

No change at Teschen. Armistice Commission at Trèves has imposed armistice on Germans at Posen and our Commission is charged to meet Germans at Posen to settle details. Meanwhile Germans are attacking Poles with asphixiating gases, etc., against which the latter have no appliances.

General Dupont of French Mission in Berlin expected here to discuss meeting of our Mission with Germans.

We have heard a variety of Polish witnesses *re* financial and economic conditions."

February 22nd. Saturday.

" Messenger arrived with letters from Carton de Wiart. He thinks he may be able to get a temporary cessation of hostilities but doubts about a real armistice pending decision of Paris Conference on final frontiers. Both Ruthenes and Poles want oil wells, which are one of the few available sources of revenue.

Commander Rawlings arrived after bringing an ammunition train through from Vienna. He is a splendid fellow and when the Czechs tried to stop his train on the frontier he telephoned to Prague at 2 a.m. and got the Czech Minister out of bed and insisted on orders being given to the railway officials to allow his train to proceed in accordance with Czech promises. He is a very efficient and active sailor and thoroughly enjoys these jaunts.

Big " pre-war " dinner at Countess Joseph Potocka's. All Warsaw Society at reception afterwards.

General Dupont arrived."

February 23rd. Sunday.

" After breakfast meeting to arrange instructions for General Dupont, who leaves to-night for Posen and then for Berlin. After lunch walked with M. Ciechanowski to the bridge over the Vistula called Poniatowski Bridge, which was blown up by Russians when they evacuated, then burnt by Germans and has not yet been repaired.

Meeting from 6 to 8 to decide what to do about Teschen affair. It was decided to send Generals Niessel and Romei to Teschen and Przemysl to settle up things as general effect of delay is that no one in these parts believes that Entente Governments are able to enforce their decisions."

February 24th. Monday.

" As Teschen affair seems still to be dragging the two Generals leave to-night for Teschen with Colonel Wade. General Niessel will not stand any humbug.

The Lemberg Mission met General Pavlenko at his headquarters east of Lemberg and arranged for cessation of hostilities while negotiations for armistice continue.

A huge dinner at the Commercial Club with about three hundred people at which M. Noulens, General Kernan, Signor Montagna and I had all to make speeches in our own languages. Very much applauded though probably not fifty per cent. of those present understood. As the Marshal of the Diet, M. Trumbinczki said, it was rather too much like the Berlitz School.

M. Noulens stated that he had received telegrams from Paris with the information that French, British and Italian Governments had decided formally to recognise Poland as an independent State.

M. Clémenceau has been shot at and wounded by an anarchist in Paris."

February 25th.   Tuesday.

" Meeting to discuss various current questions. Decided to leave for Posen on Friday.

Lunched with Professor Askenazi, a most able Jew historian and Professor at the University. Met General Soskonowski, Commandant of Warsaw, General Pilsudski's right hand man and a cavalry officer, with whom a great discussion after lunch as to relative strength of Bolshevik Army and best way of dealing with Bolshevik danger. They were all for intervention. I tried to explain why Allies objected to intervention from outside as being more likely to solidify Bolshevik resistance and to prevent internal disintegration of Bolshevik Russia. Some persons present believed that Bolsheviks would soon have an army of two and a half millions.

No telegram yet from His Majesty's Government about recognition of Poland, so decided to write a note to M. Paderewski with the announcement and hand it to him at dinner which he gave for members of the British Mission. Both he and Madame Paderewska much delighted."

February 26th.   Thursday.

" News has come in that Teschen to be evacuated to-day. General Niessel has put matters through to great confusion of Teschen Committee. This is the first step. We at once telegraphed this news to Lemberg to impress on Ruthenes that Entente can impose its wishes. If this had not gone through our position would have been untenable.

Telegram announcing His Majesty's Government's recognition received which I at once communicated to General Pilsudski, who was evidently much pleased. I told him that it was the most honourable and agreeable message I had ever had to give in my life. Leveson Gower came with me and was as much under General Pilsudski's charm as I. This is indeed a red letter day."

February 27th.   Thursday.

" In the afternoon saw Countess Sieradowska from West Prussia, who told me that Germans were carrying

POSEN, 1919

MARCH PAST OF POLISH TROOPS

on a reign of terror against Poles in that Province. The Councils of Soldiers and Workmen were much fairer but now the authorities were gaining the upper hand and the situation was very serious.

Ruthenes are bombarding Lemberg in spite of the cessation of hostilities.

Polish soldiers have re-entered Teschen amid (according to Polish Press) great enthusiasm."

February 28th. Friday.

" In afternoon prepared for journey to Posen. General Pilsudski came at 5 to thank me for my visit announcing recognition of Polish independence. He talked mainly about Lithuanian question which interests him particularly as he comes from Vilna. He told me his ancestors were among those who had signed the Deed of Union with Poland in the fifteenth century.

Dined at Hotel Europa with Kenney[1] and Brailsford[2] and talked over situation in Poland. Socialists whom Brailsford had seen were, he said, much exercised because they believed Entente was only helping Poland on condition Polish Army would undertake to crush Bolshevism in Russia. I told him to reassure them on this point as we did not believe that armed intervention would be of any use, but rather the reverse. Left Warsaw by special train—the whole Inter-allied Mission consisting of about fifty persons."

March 1st. Saturday.

" In Province of Posen we were received at stations by deputations, guards of honour, etc., especially at Jarotschin, a great turn out. On arrival at Posen (without washing or toilet, as no water on train) a tremendous reception. Municipality and Provisional Government at station. Streets lined with cheering crowds and town beflagged, but perfect order in contrast to Warsaw. The German domination has had its effect and Posen Poles admit this, much as they dislike Prussians. After breakfast at eleven, bath and dress. We are lodged in the Emperor William's castle, which he built some ten years ago as the seal of

[1] Of the Foreign Office. [2] The well-known Socialist journalist.

Y

German dominon in Posen.   It is an extraordinary place,
everything very heavy and Imperial eagles everywhere.
The Emperor's private sitting-rooms are remarkable for
the ugliness and discomfort of the furniture.   After
lunch, meeting to discuss our programme.   General
Dowbor-Musnicki (of the Polish Legion in Russia) now
commanding here, is present.   After dinner go to amateur
tableaux vivants for the Red Cross.   To bed very tired."
March 2nd.   Sunday.

" After church and breakfast, where we had goose fat
for butter, which did not exist in Posen at that time, we
were taken to a military parade on ex-Wilhelmsplatz, now
Liberty Square, when troops were reviewed by Generals
Niessel, Kernan and Romei (General Carton de Wiart
still at Lemberg).   Some annoyance caused by General
Niessel taking the honours with Polish General Dowbor
Musnicki.   After this drive through Polish part of the
town, great enthusiastic crowds, flags everywhere.
Reception at Town Hall, a very fine old building, dense
throng in square in front.   Speeches by members of
Posen Government and M. Noulens, then back to lunch
at Castle.   Conference to arrange meeting with German
delegates and settled to meet at Kreuz just within German
line.   Wired this to General Dupont in Berlin.   Short
walk and then gala dinner at Castle and reception for
numbers of people in the Throne Hall of the Emperor, a
fine room with walls of grey marble and frescoes.   Several
peasant women invited in curious costumes with enormous
flowered headdresses.   Met all Posen society, in particular
Countess Zamoyska, mother of the boy at Downside.
Very tired."

The Posen Schloss was a singularly unattractive building evidently erected as Baalbak was built by the Romans
to impress the nations.   The Emperor William stated at
the inauguration of the building that it was intended to
set the Prussian seal for ever on German Poland.   It was
a heavy modern Gothic building with Alt-Deutsch
decorations everywhere.   I particularly remember Imperial eagles stencilled all over the walls.   On seeing

them in my bedroom, where they were the only mural decoration, General Niessel remarked, " *Vraiment ce volatile est par trop envahissant.*"[1] Another object that struck me as particularly tactless in Posen was a gigantic statue of Bismarck, whose anti-Polish policy was notorious. This was the statue in whose fingers was placed, after the Posen *coup* that took place when Paderewski arrived there in 1918, a fourth class ticket to Berlin—the only insult offered I believe to anything German after the Poles of Posen recovered their liberty. The third monument to German domination in Posen, which was near the Schloss, was an enormous building with an inscription in huge letters, " *K.K Deutsches Ansiedlung's Ministerium.*"[2] As there was nothing which so irritated the Poles of the German Polish Provinces as the settlement policy of replacing Poles by German farmers on the land this palpable and perpetual reminder of it was not calculated to make for good relations between the two races.

Lastly there was in Posen one of those beautiful old Renaissance Town Halls built by Italian architects and workmen about the beginning of the sixteenth century, which are not infrequent in the older Polish towns, and are a testimony to the prosperity and culture of that period in Poland. The rest of the town is like any well kept modern German city."

March 3rd. Monday.

" Conference in morning to draw up agenda of our meeting with Germans. After lunch work again.

Telegram from Warsaw that the Lemberg Armistice negotiations have broken down and that Generals Carton de Wiart and Bartélemy and Professor Lord are coming to Posen to-morrow. Ruthenes have renewed hostilities.

Czechs still not carrying out Teschen agreement properly.

Invitations keep pouring in for dinners, lunches, evening parties, etc. We shall be as hard worked socially as politically."

[1] " This fowl really intrudes a little too much."
[2] " Imperial and Royal German Settlement Ministry."

March 4th. Tuesday.

" Germans will only arrive to-morrow at Kreuz.

Conference in morning to hear our three delegates from Lemberg, who describe situation there as desperate, and say that Ruthenes can cut the railway whenever they wish and isolate town, so reducing it by famine. Commission sent a strong telegram to Paris *re* Lemberg situation urging sending ammunition and if possible Roumanian intervention to save Lemberg. Carton de Wiart says Polish organisation there quite hopeless.

Petlura (head of Ukrainian Republic), they said, seemed an intelligent but very unreliable person. Ukrainian troops at headquarters were well equipped and apparently well disciplined. But no doubt in the country they are mostly armed bands of peasants. They are said to have between 30,000 and 40,000 men. Women and boys are helping in the defence of Lemberg.

Ruthenes fired on train taking our delegates from Lemberg and severely wounded two Polish officers."

March 5th. Ash Wednesday.

" Left at 9.30 in special train for Kreuz to meet German Delegation consisting of Baron von Rechenberg, Staatsminister Drews, General von Dommes, etc. Arrived about twelve and lunched in the train. German soldiers with artillery guarding line before we reached Kreuz. German soldiers and sailors lounging about the station looking very Bolshevik and untidy. Lots of people at stations staring at us, but all polite. Germans arrived about 1 p.m. and had lunch, after which we met in one of the waiting-rooms. They were all in civilian clothes, and von Rechenberg and Drews had shooting caps on, perhaps to mark the completeness of the German revolution. Sat from 2.30 to 5 p.m. and got through our programme fairly satisfactorily. Germans decided to come to Posen and continue sittings there. Got back to Posen in time for dinner.

We only raised our hats to Germans but did not shake hand."

March 6th. Thursday.

" Germans unable to arrive to-day owing to track difficulties.

Did business with Polish authorities in Posen. The state of things here is extraordinary, as hardly any change has been made in administrative offices, German officials being almost everywhere retained, with Polish controllers. When German stamps threatened to run out a short time ago Berlin refused to send any more, the Polish Posen Government then threatened to print their own and the German stamps were at once forthcoming. No change has been made in laws and German is still the language of the schools, etc. Certainly after 150 years of oppression the Poles show wonderful moderation. All German monuments are respected. The German theatre goes on giving performances in German."

March 7th. Friday.

" Germans arrived late last night and refused to come to the meeting at the castle because they are escorted by Polish officers. The Polish staff here is not so wise as the civilian Government and is acting vexatiously. After some trouble, incident was settled and meeting began at twelve. Agreed a Military Sub-Commission to arrange details of demarcation line of armistice. Arranged for a Civilian Sub-Commission to settle liberation of hostages, prisoners and reciprocal protection of Poles in Germany and Germans in Posen.

Civil Sub-Commission consists of self, Lord (American) and Montagna (Italian) ; Germans are Drews and three others. We meet in afternoon. Long discussion without much result except getting German views of what they want for protection of their people in Posen Province."

March 8th. Saturday.

" Bag in with letters from Isa and one from Metto[1] with his ideas on League of Nations which he does not believe in. Wrote to him to tell him why necessary. The draft scheme seems well spoken of by the English papers I have seen, but I have no time to read papers.

[1] My eldest son Esme at school at Downside.

Carton de Wiart and Bartélemy left last night for Paris to explain Lemberg situation to Conference. M. Paderewski arrived to-day to try and get Posen people to send troops there. General Musnicki against it because of lack of munitions. We hear trains of munitions are coming from Budapest, some of these taken from Macken-sen's army which surrendered in Rumania, but it is doubtful if they can arrive in time to save Lemberg. Polish Government much attacked by Socialists on account of Lemberg—altogether a very volcanic situation. Long sittings up to late at night with Paderewski, Musnicki and Posen Government.

Met German Sub-Committee in afternoon."

March 9th. Sunday.

"Mass in Emperor's chapel in Castle which had been provisionally consecrated for the purpose. Mass said by Father Adamski, Minister of Finance of Posen Govern-ment, a very able man. Chapel is copy of Palatine chapel at Palermo and is the best thing in the whole place. The first Mass there was very impressive.

Our Sub-Committee afterwards met Posen Govern-ment, M. Korfanty, Father Adamski, the Minister of Finance of Posen, and M. Porsjewski to discuss hostages, protection, etc. It seems very difficult to reach an agreement.

Afterwards went to country house in neighbourhood, where a big lunch was given for all the Mission by Count and Countess Zultowski.[1] Little children in costume greeted us in front of the house, and waved Allied flags and danced. We were to have a meeting with the Germans in the afternoon, but it was put off, as they had no instructions from Berlin on certain questions. Held a Commission meeting instead, and worked after dinner with Lord till twelve."

March 10th. Monday.

"Meeting at 10 with Germans in Castle. They explained about difficulties of communication with Berlin.

[1] We were given a bottle of Tokay wine which had not left the cellar since 1772 —date of the partition of Poland—and drank it to resurrected Poland. Strange to say it was drinkable.

I fear some foolish telegraph clerk cuts off communication. It is most tiresome. Shortly after sitting began an incident occurred. The German translator suddenly refusing to translate into French any more and, when M. Noulens expostulated, saying rudely he would not take any remarks from him. We got up from the table saying we would not sit with him any more. Germans retired to consider position, and on returning apologised. The young man took no more part in the sessions. We got through a number of economic questions fairly well.

Lunch at Bazaar Hotel with M. and Madame Morowski. At 4 p.m. meeting of our Sub-Committee. General von Dommes called to German Headquarters to discuss certain questions connected with military side of matter.

A man from Paris says that Clémenceau is going about with the bullet in his lungs as cheerfully as ever. He is really wonderful at seventy-eight.

I wish we had news as to how the Paris Conference is progressing."

March 11*th.   Tuesday.*

" Serious Spartacist riots in Berlin, and a widely spread railway strike in Central Germany have made matters again very critical there. Casualties in Berlin are said to amount to 1,000 and forty million marks of damage.

The German military delegates who left on Sunday have not yet returned. Letter from Headlam Morley in Paris saying that Peace Conference is about to decide Polish frontiers of Germany, and that Professor Lord's and my memoranda more or less hold the field. Danzig is the thorny question about which much ink has been spilled, but opinion is growing that it must go to Poland. I hope this is so. Anything else, as I have stated, would be an economic abnormality.

We had long sittings with German Sub-Commission on exchange of prisoners and protection of Poles and Germans, and finally won on almost all points. Our proposals agreed to by Posen Government. Germans send courier to-night to Berlin with text. Colonel Anderson, King's Messenger, arrived in morning and left to-night. A very busy day during which I never left the house."

March 12th. Wednesday.

" Spartacist movement in Berlin seems to have been quelled but still continues in Eastern suburbs. At the same time similar movements were attempted in various German towns, but without better success. This is good.

There is considerable agitation amongst Poles in West Prussia and Silesia, and an armed rising may take place as a result of continued German persecutions. It is possible that Germans will try to provoke this. No news from Paris as to our recommendations for immediate help to Poles in Eastern Galicia. I have had no news from Paris about the situation since I came to Poland except Headlam Morley's letter. The ways of the Foreign Office are incomprehensible.

A general strike is to be called by Polish Bolsheviks for to-day, but has been stopped by opposition of moderate Socialists.

Met Germans and agreed on text of economic arrangement—railways, river traffic, exchange of goods, etc. Everything now ready but the military part, and still German officers do not return."

March 13th. Thursday.

" Met a representative of Polish Foreign Office and one from Lithuania. They laid before us grievances *re* Czechs, who are not carrying out agreement of Paris. Latter told us Germans were advancing again in Lithuania and endeavouring to make trouble between Poles and Lithuanians, which is most probable. Poland is surrounded by enemies and is a network of intrigues.

Settled finally with German Sub-Commission last points *re* exchange of prisoners, and Red Cross Commission to inquire into outrages.

Baron von Rechenberg called in evening to say misunderstanding had arisen in Berlin, and he ought to leave at once to try and clear matters up. He promised to be back on Sunday. This means we are held up here for some days more.

In afternoon went to see a regiment parade which is leaving for Lemberg to help against Ukrainians. It was rather a touching sight. Many quite young boys. They have not had more than six weeks' training.

Professor Lord called back to Paris this evening and goes through Berlin. I hope he will be of use there."

March 14th. Friday.

" No meeting with Germans. In the afternoon we went to a country house belonging to Monsieur de Chlapowski where there was an old English governess, Miss Cameron, who had not seen an English paper for over three years, and was much exercised by a rumour that America was going to leave armies of occupation in France and England.

Lloyd George has come forward with a proposal that the German Army should be reduced to 100,000 men, consisting not of conscripts but the long-service volunteers. This is generally approved.

The Germans continue artillery bombardment on Posen front despite armistice.

There is news that Bolsheviks are evacuating Vilna and that Germans are advancing to occupy it.

No news from Lemberg.

Papers state that Peace Conference has decided on frontiers of Germany and Poland, giving Danzig, part of Western Prussia and Upper Silesia to latter. I wish Foreign Office would sometimes give me a hint of what is going on."

March 15th. Saturday.

" Germans returned this morning and we had a plenary session. All three Conventions : 1. Military. 2. Protection of Poles and Germans. 3. Resumption of economic relations, were gone through and practically agreed to, though Baron von Rechenberg made reservations *re* composition of mixed Commission of Appeal at Posen, and General von Dommes said High Command would not agree to withdrawal of artillery for 20 kilometres behind line of demarcation.   We said we considered these questions as settled.   I drove out to lunch with Count Schaldaki at Tsarki, passing through the little town of Schrim, where I was accorded a great welcome by people who decorated motor with flowers.

At 6 another meeting with Germans.   We decided to send them the text of three Conventions next day, and told them we should expect answer in course of day.

Evening party given by Princess Czartoriska at Bazaar Hotel."

March 16th.   Sunday.

" At 10 Baron von Rechenberg told us that Herr Erzberger proposed that third member of Mixed Commission at Posen should be named by the Pope or by the President of the Swiss Republic.   We declined.

In afternoon another long session from 3 to 8.30, at which texts of agreements finally decided, and although both Rechenberg and Dommes maintained protests, Rechenberg said that he would sign Military Convention as Plenipotentiary and that German Government would be bound by his signature.   Therefore nothing left over but question of Mixed Commission.   Were informed in evening by M. Korfanty that General von Dommes had telegraphed to German Ministry of War at Berlin that German Headquarters had ordered him not to sign, and that they would not be bound by von Rechenberg's signature ; they are therefore in open conflict with Civil Government.   They clearly intend to keep up full strength on Posen front so as to attack if necessary.

A wonderful demonstration of about 3,000 children in our honour, all waving Polish and Allied flags and singing patriotic songs in the court in front of the Schloss.   I went down among them and was nearly squashed by hundreds who wanted to shake hands and kiss my hand."

March 17th.   Monday.

" No further news from Germans, only a letter from von Rechenberg asking for further delays.   An intercepted telegram from him to Berlin proposes that as our

Commission will not give way, the three members of the Mixed Commission should be named by the Permanent Armistice Commission at Spa. I favoured accepting this if he suggested it to us. This was agreed to. We fully expect Germans will sign to-morrow.

Dinner in evening with Count Cziekowski at Bazaar Hotel, and as usual speeches.

Cold and snowy weather.

News from Lemberg better. Our Posnanian regiment has gone into action and cleared most of the line from Przemysl to Lemberg.

There is great opposition in the United States to present League of Nations proposal, and it looks as if Senate would not accept it. Senators Lodge and Knox are principal antagonists."

March 18th. Tuesday.

" Baron von Rechenberg, having received a letter from M. Noulens that unless we got a definite answer from him by midday we should leave, came round with his Spa proposal, which we accepted. He said he must submit it to Berlin to Erzberger and might have an answer anytime. We said we could only wait a few hours as we wanted to leave Posen to-night.

Waited all afternoon in vain ; in evening M. Noulens wrote that unless he received reply by midnight he should consider negotiations broken off. About 11.30 he got a letter from von Rechenberg saying that Herr Erzberger asked him (Noulens) to inquire whether Posen Government would treat directly with Germans. It is clear that Germans are only playing with us and creating delays.

After dinner met M. Seyda, Head of Polish Party in German Reichstag."

M. Seyda gave me a dramatic account of the communication to him and other Party leaders by the German Vice-Chancellor, von Payer, of a letter from German Headquarters on September 30th, 1918, insisting on the necessity of an immediate armistice. I repeated this in the following dispatch to Mr. Balfour :

British Mission to Poland,
Posen,

19th March, 1919.

To the
RT. HON. A. J. BALFOUR, M.P.,
PARIS.

Sir,

I have the honour to report herewith an interesting conversation which I had last night with Mr. Seyda, Head of the Polish Party in the German Reichstag, which is I think worth recording as a matter of history.

Mr. Seyda told me that late on the night of September 30th, 1918, he was called to a conference on the following morning at 9 o'clock by Herr von Speyer, Vice-Chancellor of the Empire, together with heads of the other parties in the Reichstag, nine persons altogether. These included Count Westarp, of the Conservatives, Herr Streseman, of the National Liberals, Herr Fischbeck, of the Radicals, Herr Ebert for the Majority Socialists, Herr Haase for the Minority Socialists and Herr Grober for one of the Parties which I cannot remember and others whose names I forget.

Mr. Seyda arrived first with Herr Grober, and found Herr von Payer alone. Herr Grober asked what was the object of the Conference. Herr von Payer simply raised his hands with a despairing gesture and went out of the room. Herr Fischbeck then came in and Herr Grober repeated the question to him. He made no reply beyond clenching his fists, raising them above his head, and bringing them down suddenly with the evident object of showing that the fall of Germany was complete.

When all were assembled Herr von Payer came back again. He stated that a special messenger had arrived the night before from the German Headquarters, stating that it was useless to continue the War and that it was urgently necessary to propose an armistice without delay. He had therefore called together the heads of the different Parties in order to hear the report of the messenger, who was Major von dem Busch, and to consult with them as to the measures that should be taken. This statement was received in complete silence. Major von dem Busch then came in and read a report to the effect that Headquarters Staff had come to the conclusion that it was useless to continue the War as all hopes of a victorious ending were now out of the question. Two factors had principally contributed to the situation. Firstly, the great number of tanks of which the Allies disposed which made it practically impossible for the Germans to be sure of holding the line in any particular place. The German battalions instead of numbering 800 men were reduced to 550 and there were practically no reserves. With the help of tanks the enemy could repeat their attacks and continually succeed in taking prisoners in considerable numbers, thus reducing almost daily the effective strength of the German Army.

Secondly, the forces of the enemy were constantly increasing owing to further arrivals from America at the rate of about 200,000 a month. In view of these circumstances the Germans might continue the War for a few months longer but the final result would be the same and it was therefore better to ask for an Armistice at once on the best terms they could obtain.

Herr Stresemann and Count Westarp both asked bitterly why the German people had been persistently kept in ignorance of the true state of things. Herr Stresemann said, " What will the people do when they know that Germany has been defeated ? They have always been told up to now that we were victorious." And he declared that the result of this sudden announcement by the General Staff must have disastrous consequences.

Herr von Payer shrugged his shoulders saying that all they could do now in the face of this message was to try and make the best terms they could. He then asked each man present his views as to the best way of presenting the request for an Armistice. After some discussion it was decided that they should state that the German Government would ask for an Armistice and declare that it was ready to discuss Peace on the lines of President Wilson's 14 points. The 14 points were then produced and gone through carefully. When they came to the point dealing with Alsace-Lorraine somebody said : " But this means that we have to give up the two Provinces to France ! " Herr von Payer again shrugged his shoulders, saying : " We must do the best we can."

When they reached the point respecting Poland, Count Westarp exclaimed violently : " But this means that we shall have to give up Posen and Dantzig." Herr von Payer again shrugged his shoulders in silence.

After hearing the opinions of the other members present, Herr von Payer then turned to Mr. Seyda, who had not spoken up till now, and asked his opinion. Mr. Seyda said that he had not intended to speak but that if Herr von Payer wished to hear what he thought, he would say that in his opinion it would be wise for the German Government not to say merely that they would take the 14 points as a basis for discussion but to declare frankly once for all that they accepted the 14 points *in toto*. He felt sure that if they simply took them as a basis for discussion this would not satisfy the Government of the United States, and would only lead to prolonged correspondence during which time Germany would continue to lose both men and material, if the report of the Headquarters Staff was correct, and that the only result would be the further useless shedding of blood ; this was in effect exactly what happened.

The meeting nevertheless decided that they could not then accept
the 14 points, and that the Government should simply propose to
agree to them as a basis of discussion.

Mr. Seyda stated that at the end of the meeting one of the members
burst into tears and that Count Westarp and Herr Stresemann were
like men turned to stone.

As for himself, he said : " My own feelings on leaving the meeting
can better be imagined than described."

I have the honour to be, etc.,

(Sgd.)   Esme Howard.

In describing this scene to me it was evident that
M. Seyda was still stirred to the depth by the memory
of it.   It seemed to me that his sympathy for the feelings
of men he knew intimately must have mingled with his
joy at the prospect of the restoration of liberty of his
country and people.   As told by him, the meeting became
one of the most dramatic scenes I had ever read of in
history or in fiction.

It is within my memory that M. Seyda also mentioned
one other cause of the German defeat as having been
referred to in the missive from the German G.H.Q. in
France (i.e. from General Ludendorff).   This was the
complete failure of the great German submarine campaign
either to end the blockade or to prevent the arrival in
France of hundreds of thousands of American troops.
It was no doubt the latter fact which so impressed German
public opinion behind the lines that, combined with the
prospect of another winter of blockade, it took the heart
out of German resistance and made a continuation of the
War out of the question.   Mr. Winston Churchill, in
The Crisis, Vol. IV, p. 454, gives the following most
graphic account of the arrival on the scene of the new
American troops :

Now suddenly the roads between Provins and the front, between
Meaux and towards Collommiers began to be filled with endless
streams of Americans.   Half-trained, half-organised, with only their
energy, their numbers, and their magnificent youth behind their
weapons, they were to buy their experience at a bitter price, but this
they were quite ready to do.   The impression made upon the hard-
pressed French by this seemingly inexhaustible flood of gleaming

youth in its first maturity of health and vigour was prodigious. None were under 20 and few were over 30. As, crammed on their lorries, they clattered over the roads singing songs of a New World at the tops of their voices, burning to reach the bloody field, the French Headquarters were thrilled with new life. " All felt that they were present at the magical transfusion of blood. Life arrived in floods to reanimate the mangled body of France, bled white by the innumerable wounds of four years.''[1]

It is no wonder that the moral effect on both sides of the line of the appearance of these new forces must have been almost overwhelming.

March 19th. Wednesday.

" Met at 10 a.m. and decided to send a letter to von Rechenberg enclosing draft Convention and stating that we considered *pourparlers* broken off and had referred the whole matter to our Governments in Paris. Germans were told politely that, as we should leave at 10 p.m. for Warsaw, they must leave before for Berlin. Left at 10 p.m. for Warsaw.''

March 20th. Thursday.

" Arrived at 9 and went straight to my room at Erivanska 12. No hot water as no gas in the town on account of lack of gas coal.

Hungarian Government has resigned on account of division of Hungary by Allies which Karolyi would not accept. Their places taken by a Communist Government which at once declared solidarity with Russian Bolsheviks and received fraternal greetings from Moscow. This has caused consternation in Poland. A speech of Lloyd George stated that peace may be signed in a fortnight— very optimistic.

Poles have had a success against Ruthenes near Lemberg and reopened communications with Lemberg.''

March 21st. Friday.

" Meeting morning and decided to leave Warsaw for Paris on 30th March.

No more news of Germans though papers say that their

[1] (From Churchill's *Crisis*, Vol. IV, p. 454.) (Last four lines from Pierrefeu.) Thornton Butterworth & Co.

delegates have been ordered to go to Warsaw to sign
Armistice Convention with us.

It has turned bitterly cold and there was a regular
blizzard with deep snow in the evening.

Reports from Eastern Province of Poland are very bad,
famine and typhus raging. No medical stores, no doctors
or nurses. All the regions east of Brest-Litovsk which
Poles have occupied are simply a desert—no cultivation,
villages deserted—only Jews left in the towns."

March 22nd. Saturday.

" Saw deputation of Mazurian Poles in morning who
ask to be annexed to Poland but said that population was
at present too much under the heel of Germany to vote
for annexation if there was a plebiscite which should only
be allowed if country had been occupied by Allied troops
for at least a year.

The Protestant Pastor very emphatic that no fear of any
persecution need be entertained if handed to Poland.

Met at Club a Count Mielowynski who said he had just
escaped from Bolsheviks at Mamel (?) where he was
imprisoned for five weeks under constant menace of
death. Food : half a pound of black bread, one plate
of vegetable soup and water per day. Released by
influence of an actress in Moscow who knew Lenin ! and
then allowed to go about town freely and look after his
affairs. Frequently dined with four Moscow Commissars
all educated men who discussed politics and said
Bolshevism would not be safe until Germany, France and
England were won."

March 23rd. Sunday.

" News from Hungary very bad. French troops there
disarmed and interned. A railway strike threatened at
Vienna.

The strike of agricultural labourers in the Lublin
Province of Poland is spreading and causing anxiety.
Kenney who has just returned from there says situation
is very bad.

Had a long conversation of two and a half hours with
Socialist leaders Morashewski and Dazcinski. Told them

we did not want Poland to invade Russia and beat Bolshevism for us. They laid great stress on necessity of defending Poland against Bolshevism and begged for arms and ammunitions but were strongly averse to any action agsinst Russia beyond confines of old Duchy of Lithuania. They were, however, strongly in favour of this territory belonging to Poland as an outlet for surplus agricultural population."

March 24th. Monday.

" Wrote reports and dispatches in morning, also letters.

Conference in afternoon.

General Kernan left for Ruthenian front under instructions from Peace Conference at Paris to try and arrange truce between Poles and Ruthenes. I don't think he will succeed as latter are intractable."

March 25th. Tuesday.

" Went in morning with Count Krascinski to see some old palaces in Warsaw, and his library which contains some 350,000 volumes and some very rare MSS, *incunabula* etc.,

After lunch, meeting at 4 p.m. to consider various questions especially date of departure as no news of departure of Inter-Allied train from Paris. Lunched with Marquess Wielopolski and several landlords at Club who discussed agrarian question. Quite interesting as showing that landlords are really alive to danger of a policy of refusing demand for land. They are ready to offer two million acres at once to be cut up into lots.

Dined with Commander Rawlings and Mr. Kimmens at ' Europe.' Rawlings a wonderful fellow. His adventures in getting munition trains through are like a page from Dumas."

March 26th. Wednesday.

" Meeting at 10 a.m. to hear Orthodox Jews, Assimilated Jews and Zionists. The former (largest Jewish party in Poland) do not care much about special political privileges but very strong for separate confessional schools. Second represent mostly professional classes

z

and most reasonable, only desiring same rights and duties
as other Polish citizens. Zionists insist on recognition as
separate nationality with special electoral privileges,
cultural autonomy and heaven knows what. Asked if
they wished their separate nationality to be considered as
subject to the Palestine Government they scouted the
idea. In fact they want to have special privileges in
Poland.

Lunched with Countess Joseph Potocka at Palais
Potocki which is really very fine. In afternoon rushed to
Diet to hear vote on Resolution for alliance with Entente
but found no vote would be taken to-day. Returned
and worked at home. General Kernan should meet
Ukrainians at Chyrow to-day to arrange armistice.

Dined at Prince Ladislas Lubomirski's—the ex-Regent
—a nice house. Great agitation about events in
Hungary."

March 27th. Thursday.

" Meeting in morning at 10.30 to hear Jewish Populist
Party, who differ from Zionists in as much as they take
no interest in Palestine but express same wants as to
Poland, i.e. recognition of Jews as a separate minority
nationality, separate elections to Diet and Municipal
Councils, separate Budget, etc. They, however do *not*
want confessional schools.

After lunch went to Diet to hear formal Resolution in
favour of alliance with Entente Powers passed unanimously
amid great ovation which MM. Noulens, Montagna and
myself acknowledged by bowing from gallery.

Dined at Club and went afterwards to a ' party ' at
Countess Rzeczrzewska's—a fine modern house and good
crowd of people amongst others, the Cardinal Archbishop,
old Prince Ferdinand Radiziwill and M. Paderewski who
thanked me for what I had said to Socialist leaders which
had made things easy for unanimous vote of Diet to-day."

March 28th. Friday.

" Quiet day—preparing reports for next bag, etc., in
morning. Decided to leave for Cracow on Sunday to
get out of the turmoil of Warsaw entertainments and

wait there for Interallied Mission train which should reach Cracow from Warsaw with French Mission about Tuesday or Wednesday next.

Lunched with Abbé Lutoslawski, a Deputy and very intelligent. Speaking of Jewish question he said *re* Orthodox Jews' desire for confessional schools supported by the State that he believed Polish Government would agree to this as it would be supported by Catholics and Protestants also.

Afternoon wrote speech for the evening's dinner and saw M. J. Diryev and a proprietor from Lublin who gave information about agrarian strikes in Lublin district which he attributes to Bolshevism. They are spreading it appears.

Dinner given by Interallied Mission in evening to Government, City Fathers, Deputies, Generals, etc. Sat next to Pilsudski, who was very cheerful."
March 29th. Saturday.

" A heavy day. Interviewed deputations from Trades Unions, High Finance, Agriculturists, Socialists, etc.

In the evening Paderewski gave a great *dîner d'adieu* at the Bristol Hotel. Sat next to Pilsudski again. Dinner lasted till 1.30. There were sixteen speeches in Polish, English, French and Italian. Witos, the peasant leader, made a great speech. The Cardinal Archbishop talking to old Rabbi Perlmutter was worthy of a snapshot. At this dinner the band suddenly interrupted Paderewski in the midst of a most eloquent speech and put him out of his stride. He remained silent for an appreciable time, then, shaking his head vigorously, he exclaimed to the delight of all present : ' *Vraiment, la Musique commence à m'embêter.*'[1]

General Kernan returned from Lemberg having failed to settle any truce."
March 30th. Sunday.

" In the morning had a long interview with Pilsudski who went over almost all the points of the Polish question—Danzig, Lithuania, of course, Eastern Galicia,

[1] " Really, Music begins to annoy me ! "

Jews, Haller's Army. He said he was rather afraid of latter because it was so highly paid and this might cause jealousy with other troops. His love for his home, Vilna, was really touching.

After Church packed, wrote, and settled accounts. At 4 p.m. went to Agricultural Institute and heard a lecture there. After dinner at Club finished packing and left with General Carton de Wiart, Leveson Gower, Ciechanowski, etc., for Cracow."

March 31st. Monday.

" Arrived Cracow about 9 a.m., met at station by City Fathers, guard of honour, etc.

Taken to Countess François Potocka's house, a fine old Italian Renaissance building, and put up there ; very comfortable. Lunch given for us at one of the Hotels. Then visited Cathedral and Castle under guidance of M. Zelinski. Most interesting tombs of old Polish Kings in Cathedral. Castle very fine, Italian Renaissance court. After dinner at Club went to Zelinski's house. He played Chopin beautifully till midnight.

Had tea at Prince Radziwill's, whose wife is a daughter of the Archduke Charles Stephen. Political atmosphere in Cracow ' Faubourg St Germain,' decidedly lukewarm towards Entente and pro-Austrian, but everyone most kind and hospitable. A great difference from Posen in the matter of national feeling, however. Very cold—deep snow."

April 1st. Tuesday.

" After breakfast went to see Prince Czatoryski's collections which are very fine. All kinds of things— books, MSS., china, arms, etc. Afterwards visited University Library with fine old courtyard.

M. Noulens and remainder of Mission arrived on International train.

Afternoon spent seeing churches, old synagogue, etc.

Dined with Prince Bishop Sapieha who is a most attractive person. Afterwards a party for Mission at Countess François Potocka's.

Have lost sight of papers and do not know what is
going on in the world."
April 2nd.   Wednesday.
  " Stayed in most of morning writing letters and one or
two despatches.
  Lunched at Count Tarnowski's who had some good
pictures.   After lunch reception at town hall or rather
picture gallery, speeches, tea.   Packed and supped with
Potocki's.   Count Potocki had arrived from Warsaw and
showed me a letter from his agent in Podolia saying that
peasants were again anxious to pay rents, etc.
  All this Society seems very *ancien régime*—" *Piccolo
mondo antico* "—but very charming though unreal in our
days.   Even Bolshevism at their doors does not seem to
have waked them up to realities.
  Left at 10.30 p.m.
  Poor old General Kernan (American) has been ordered
back to Lemberg to his great disgust to try again to
arrange a truce."
April 3rd.   Thursday.
  " Arrived Vienna about 10 a.m. and drove with
Leveson Gower to Embassy where I met old friend,
Philpots, very busy.   Saw General Smuts and Harold
Nicolson and Leeper off on a mission to pacify Budapest
and deal with Soviet Government there !   They would not
deal with Karolyi, but no sooner is there a Bolshevist
Government than they send it a Mission.
  After lunch walked round with Philpots.   Town very
depressing. People sad and apathetic. Great lack of
food.   But shops still full of lovely things.   The body of
the old *Kaiserstadt* is there but not the spirit ;   a Bolshevik
revolution is expected daily.   It looks as if all Eastern
Europe would become one vast cockpit of horrors, and
Germany will certainly end by getting her own back in
this part of the world.   Will the Allies not do something
to save the place ? "
April 4th.   Friday.
  " Spent morning visiting picture gallery at Vienna
which is still one of the finest in the world.   Many

pictures which had been originally taken from Venice have been taken by the Italian Government back to Venice. Their places are empty and a notice posted inside the frames ' *Von der italienischen Waffenstillstand-Kommission widerrechtlich weggeschaft.*'[1] Afterwards bought stamps and prints with Leveson Gower and lunched at Sachers with Prince Lubomirski and Count Hadik, latter very bitter against Karolyi. Said that Austrians were not militarily defeated.

After lunch at Embassy wrote letters. Embassy like an old furniture shop. Had tea with Prince and Princess Festetics whom Bolsheviks in Hungary had turned out of their house. On going back to train Leveson distributed coffee, cocoa, etc., from our stores to about 200 famine-stricken children. Poor Vienna ! Left at 7.0 p.m."

April 5th. Saturday.

" A lovely day passing through the Vorarlberg. Plenty of snow in Switzerland. At Zurich when I got out of the train to walk on platform I found a polite Swiss soldier who asked me to get into the train again. I asked why ? He said it was ' *auf Befehl.*' I said : ' *Was ist denn hier geschehen ? Ist die Schweiz preussisch geworden ? '* He laughed, made a gesture of despair and said : ' *Ach seit lange !* ' "[2]

At Bâle met M. Carlin, Swiss Minister in London, who asked to get into our train, which was naturally allowed.

Paderewski who was with us was much depressed by news that Spa had arranged with Germans for Haller's army to go to Poland otherwise than by Danzig. Does this mean that Danzig is not to go to Poland ?

[1] " Illegally carried off by the Italian Armistice Commission."
[2] " What has happened here ? Has Switzerland become Prussian ? " " Oh, long ago ! "

CHAPTER XV

CONCLUSION OF PEACE CONFERENCE AND SIGNATURE OF TREATY OF VERSAILLES

I DO not propose to quote so much verbatim from the rest of my diary for the remaining weeks spent in Paris at the Conference. The entries are so uniform and monotonous in their lamentations over the lack of all reasoned and consistent policy for dealing with the Russian problem and my own fear for the immediate future as a result of this lack of vision that they weary me to read and I do not like to think of the effect they might have on others. The entries before the journey to Poland are presumably enough to give a fairly clear idea of the general atmosphere of the Conference during the opening weeks. It did not change except to become even more confused as time went on until at last it may be said that the one desire was to sign almost anything and pack and go.

Occasionally there occurred some extraordinary episode, some incident which may be worth recording, some personality who stands out peculiarly vividly above the rest but otherwise it reminded me of nothing so much as a show I remember seeing in Paris in the early 1880's which was called " *Le Théatre des Invisibles.*" This was said to be the contents of a drop of water magnified many hundred times and then by means of a magic lantern thrown on to a white sheet stretched across the stage. The drop of water appeared as a sort of globe in which strange prehistoric creatures were swimming in the most lively and pleasant fashion. There were apparently dragons and pterodactyls and sea serpents—every variety of invisible animalcule which the waters of the rivers

359

near Paris, the Seine, the Marne, etc., were supposed to contain.

On one occasion when I went to " *Les Invisibles*," a stout Frenchman sitting next to me on being introduced to " *L'eau de la Seine*," was so upset that he grasped his large waist with both hands and shrieked " *Mon Dieu !* *Mon Dieu !* " Well, at first *Les Invisibles* behaved well and kindly to each other, but as the water grew warm under the influence of the lantern they began to struggle and fight ending by tearing each other to pieces, until at last the water boiled and they were all so to speak, blown to bits.

The Conference of Paris was not merely vaguely reminiscent of the Théatre des Invisibles, and there were times when one wondered whether it might not end in the same general cataclysm. Fortunately, however, the heat which was engendered from time to time more or less died down, and so we finally arrived at the moment when the curtain was rung down on June 28th, and most of us could leave the scene of the party after washing up such of the crockery as was not altogether broken and smashed beyond hope of repair.

I should, however, before starting on this impressionist sketch of our later labours in Paris, explain in justice to myself what were the conclusions I had reached some time earlier with regard to the great question of the policy which the Entente Powers should follow towards Bolshevik Russia. We were then practically all agreed that Bolshevik Russia was a danger of the same general cataclysmic character as that which threatened Europe at the time of the French Revolution, of the Moham-medan invasions, or of those of the Mongols under Genghis Khan, a danger like that of a general earthquake, flood or hurricane. If Bolshevism could produce a sufficiently great military genius we might all—given our war weariness and social unrest—expect to be engulfed little by little, State by State. It was clear that the countries near to Russia would be the first to receive the impact and if they fell their neighbours would no doubt fall likewise in regular progression. To me, therefore, it seemed essential to assist the neighbouring States, not in order to enable them to attack Russia—that we ought to guard against—but to enable them to defend themselves against Russian attack which was then definitely a part of Russian policy and so remained as long as Trotsky was Minister of War.

To safeguard Western Europe from the Russian attack, most of the Entente statesmen believed that the best policy was to support the " White " Russian armies in their struggle with the " Reds." I, however, noting the little real progress made by the " Whites " and the frequency of their defeats and losses of arms and ammunition supplied by us at great cost urged, I fear, in season and out of season, that we should assist the Finns, the Baltic States and the Poles to obtain all requisites in food and clothing, in equipment in arms, ammunition and instructors for the formation of the best possible organs of defence provided they kept within the borders traced by the Entente Powers. I preferred this line of defence rather than reliance on the " White " Russian leaders who seemed to have lost the confidence of the people in Russia especially of the peasants. These were, at first, far from being Bolshevik or Communist, and only wanted a division and distribution of land amongst themselves, and would readily have supported any party that would convince them of its determination to do this. Trotsky admits as much in his book on the Russian Revolution.

The Baltic nations and the Poles on the other hand were strong in their new-found liberty, and I believed would fight like men inspired in defence of that liberty.

In Paris I could get no one to listen to me. I was, as I wrote in my diary, a " *Vox clamantis in deserto* "[1] and a " *Vox et præterea nihil.*"[2] This was the cause of my continuous lamentations. My exasperation was ceaseless and boundless and I must have been the " compleat " bore. Everything went to the Russian Whites—little or nothing to the others. But that my diagnosis was right

---

[1] " Voice of one crying in the wilderness." [2] " A voice and nothing more."

was proved by the outcome of the battle of Narva, where
the Estonians defeated the invading Russians in the
spring of 1919, and that of Warsaw, where the Poles,
under General Pilsudski, with the assistance of the
French General Weygand, and some other French officers,
inflicted a decisive defeat on an overwhelming Bolshevik
army in August, 1920, and undoubtedly saved our
civilisation in the greater part of Western Europe.

Lord D'Abernon[1] has given a most vivid and arresting
account of this Polish victory in his book entitled *The
Eighteenth Decisive Battle of the World*.[2] If people in
England will read this book and study its lessons, they
will understand the dangers which I felt so near to us
on that Eastern front during the days of the Paris Conference. They will also understand the magnitude of the
Polish contribution to the preservation of Europe from
disaster.[3]

[1] British Ambassador at Berlin, sent on a special mission to Warsaw in August, 1920.

[2] Hodder & Stoughton, MCMXXI.

[3] Page 114 of Lord D'Abernon's book gives the following quotation from his diary : " Paris, 29th Aug. 1920. " Radcliffe's judgment (Gen. Radcliffe was the British Military Representative in Poland at the time) regarding military events is so calm and reasonable that importance attaches to all his opinions. He holds that the Polish Army has won a victory as dramatic as any in history. All honour to Poland for her achievement, the merit of which is enhanced by the fact that the battle was fought while the Polish Government was being urged by more than one friendly Power (especially it may be said in parenthesis Great Britain under Lloyd George) to accept the conditions offered by the Soviets. Radcliffe stresses the point that victory has been obtained less by hard fighting than by skill in manœuvre and by bold strategy. The Russian failure was due in a large measure to the fatal but not infrequent mistake of underrating the enemy."

To all the above any reader of Lord D'Abernon's book will agree, as well as that it was mainly owing to the skill in manœuvre and bold strategy of Marshal Pilsudski to whom was due the plan that led to the astonishing Russian defeat after a victorious advance of over 300 miles. The total number of Russian prisoners taken during and after the Battle of Warsaw was 66,000 and those driven over the Prussian frontier and there disarmed amounted to about 44,000. There was no reliable estimate of Russian killed and wounded. Polish losses were given as approximately 50,000 during the whole course of operations in 1920, including, presumably, the retreat from Kiev.

The Russians fell back into Russia after the battle and never again attempted to invade Poland. The Polish victory was therefore rightly called a " decisive battle " by Lord D'Abernon. It is perhaps worth mentioning for those who have forgotten it that Lord D'Abernon was at this time British Ambassador at Berlin and by no means specially favourable to the Poles nor particularly influenced by any Polish statesman. His verdict on these events may therefore be taken as that of an unbiassed mind.

Mr. Lloyd George's contribution to this victory was advice to Poland to accept any terms the Bolsheviks would offer, and the Russian terms communicated to the British Government by M. Kemenoff on August 10th, a week before the Russian defeat, were such that Lord D'Abernon says that they amounted to a " disastrous capitulation." I would be inclined to say more. Had they been accepted, they would have reduced Poland to a mere satellite state of Soviet Russia. There are few even to-day who realise the fate from which we were saved by that Polish victory.

I returned to Paris on April 6th, a Sunday, and found the affairs of the Conference which concerned North-Eastern Europe not going so well. I reported to Lord Robert Cecil as to the urgent economic needs of Poland, and had short conversations about the situation there with Eric Drummond and Philip Kerr, who was the right hand man of the Prime Minister.

I noted in my diary everyone was busy and very little being done. Carlo Placci called it " *Il dolce fare senza far niente.*"[1]

The general cry was for a policy dealing with Russia. How stop Bolshevism from spreading and if not, how to get into touch with the Bolsheviks of that time without too great capitulations ? If Vienna and Prague went Bolshevik, how was there to be free access to Poland and the Baltic States, unless we could count on Danzig, and if Danzig was not to be under the control of Poland nor to be occupied by Allied troops, how could we count on that port ?

It was all as confused and complicated as before the departure for Poland of the Inter-Allied Mission.

I noted on Tuesday, 8th, that I lunched with Rowland Kenney, who was at that time, a sort of free lance, and had been sent to Scandinavia during the War to help us poor diplomatists to deal pleasantly with the Socialists of those parts who were friendly to the Entente. I found him so useful in this work, that I asked that he should accompany our Mission to Poland, also where he was

---

[1] Translation : " Pleasant activity without accomplishment."

equally invaluable. My diary registered on April 8th that he was " always cheerful and good company and sane in a world generally going mad."

I dined with the Esthonian Delegation that evening and had to make a speech. " Of all things the making of unprepared speeches is the worst." That is true. It poisons life at the time and probably later, if the speaker makes a slip, especially if journalists happen to be present. On this occasion I was told that the colours of the new Esthonian flag were to be blue, black and white. Blue for the freedom of the sky, black for Russian and German domination, white for a happy future. I hoped that blue and white might dominate the picture.

On April 9th I noted, " Lunched with Mr. Balfour, who is always delightful."

Certainly I was grateful to the Conference for this, if for nothing else, that it enabled me to become more closely acquainted with A. J. B. His charm was extraordinary and quite unlike that of other men. Nothing ruffled or troubled him. He seemed quite devoid of all personal vanity. Ready always—perhaps a little too much so—to " pass the buck " if I may use an expressive American phrase taken, I suppose, from those who during a fire stand in line and pass buckets of water to each other. When, however, he was needed to give an opinion or criticism, he was always amazingly on the spot. An intellect like a rapier and a satin tongue cossetted together under an appearance of complete indifference to the world and its opinions and trotted out from time to time into the open with a benevolent irony towards the minor weaknesses of the human race, including himself—I certainly rarely met anyone of such pleasant and jocund company as A. J. B. and I wished I could as his secretary have enjoyed it continually. In any case the days when I lunched or dined with him were always red letter days for me.

Ian Malcolm of Poltalloch, A. J. B.'s private secretary, was a friend of mine of old standing from the days when I was in the Berlin Embassy. He looked so admirably after the creature comforts of his Chief that the latter appeared to be supremely happy dispensing hospitality on a small scale in his " well-appointed " flat in the Rue Nitot. I had occasionally to bring him some of my clients from different North-Eastern European countries who wished to make him familiar with their conditions, circumstances and *desiderata*. Then he sighed, lay back in his chair and with complete self-effacement left the field of discussion to others. Yet it must be admitted that he was by no means unsympathetic, but seemed perhaps for this very reason to have very little influence on the Great Four.

Meanwhile I bored not only A. J. B. but all the important people I could with importunate demands for boots, clothes, shirts and food and sometimes for arms, ammunition and money—generally without result. Having myself seen something of the misery of those parts, I longed that the Prime Minister might send for me and ask for news at first hand of these districts. I waited in vain. He never showed the slightest inclination to hear anything about these distressful countries.

To relieve my gloom about this time Eric Drummond informed me that I was definitely destined for the Embassy at Madrid, which rejoiced me exceedingly. Some time before he had sounded me as to whether I should prefer Rome or Madrid. I replied that there was of course no post which, *cæteris paribus*, I should prefer to Rome. But seeing that I was a Catholic and that the Vatican and the Quirinal were not yet reconciled, and that Isa was actually a Roman of a " black " family, I thought it would be more prudent to send me to Madrid. The Foreign Office evidently agreed.

On April 11th I lunched with A. J. B. to meet Paderewski and Sir R. Borden, the Canadian Premier, whom I had met before in Canada, and who had been very kind on the occasion of my last visit there. A. J. B. and Paderewski were old and close friends and were delightful together.

I saw General Smuts at the Astoria back from his

mission to the Bolshevik Government at Budapest. He appeared to be quite disillusioned about the glamour of Bolshevism, if indeed he ever entertained any illusions on that score.

I noted in my diary : " Thinking all day about Russia and believe only thing will be a food offensive. Telegrams from Russia state that 300,000 children there are starving."

The next day I put my thoughts about a " food offensive " for Russia on paper, suggesting that we should send food for starving people there provided we were allowed to control distribution and Bolsheviks would stop hostilities on all fronts. Curiously enough the same idea had occurred about the same time to Dr. Nansen, whom I met at dinner at Baron Wedel-Jarlsberg's next day, and he told me he had also sent in a scheme for a food offensive to the Council of Four, which was almost the same as mine. He managed to persuade the Council of Four to adopt it and, unless I am mistaken, was sent to Russia some time later to superintend the execution of it.

All this time and for weeks after the general situation was clouded by riots, threats of revolution, strikes and actual revolution in different parts of Europe, but especially Germany, Hungary and most States of Central Europe, and also even in India and Egypt. In England, however, the labour situation improved by degrees. I remember a very interesting conversation I had at the time with Mr. Branting, the Swedish Socialist Prime Minister. I had frequently met him in Stockholm, and, like all those who knew him, had learnt to appreciate highly his ability, integrity and good sense and the breadth and sanity of his outlook. While a moderate Socialist, he was as opposed as I was to the Russian brand of Communism and to the class war teaching of Marx.

On April 15th I lunched with the Lettish Delegation, and found them very interesting. I noted : " Their memorandum to the Conference is one of the best I have read." This dealt, doubtless, with their hopes and wishes for the future of their country. I was already won over to the recognition of Latvia as an independent State, but there was yet much work to be done before the Conference would agree. There were too many delegates who still believed that the Russian Empire would be re-established as before and wanted it to be so re-established.

The same day our Polish Commission completed its report respecting our Mission, on which we had been working for days. It is a very voluminous document, which may still be read at the Foreign Office. I have never heard yet that anyone has read it.

That evening I also had the honour of meeting Marshal Foch at the house of M. and Madame Noulens. He interested me greatly. A simple man, with kindly blue eyes and an open face, squarely built and thick set, absolutely without " swagger " of any kind and nothing about him to show that he had been the Commander-in-Chief of the victorious armies in the greatest war in history. A man to whom every man would naturally go for help and support. But the " Tiger," I believe, did not feel so about him.

Things were going from bad to worse in the Baltic Provinces, and I was particularly incensed because, by some carelessness apparently equally divided between the Conference and the Military Commission at Spa, an exchange of Polish potatoes against German coal which we had arranged with the Germans at Posen was never carried through on the ground, I believe, that it must wait till the signature of the Versailles Treaty which might well not take place for months more. The result of this was that a million tons of potatoes badly needed in Germany were allowed to rot and the towns and sugar factories of Posen lacked coal. I said I would not indulge in any lamentations, but in this matter of the exchange of potatoes against coal I find it difficult to refrain. Why was such an obviously good arrangement for both sides to wait for the signature of the whole Treaty of Peace ? Was there no one in authroity who could insist on having this useful purely economic deal put through ? Apparently not. It was, I suppose, not interesting enough to be brought before the Council of Four, or if brought before them to be attended to. Shortly after I learnt that another arrangement we had made at Posen for the exchange of German and Polish prisoners had been shelved in the same way.

About April 20th the difficulties with Italy over Fiume increased steadily and serious trouble threatened between China and Japan about Kiao-Chao. Disturbances in India and Egypt were still serious, but were diminishing.

The situation in Latvia and Esthonia, on the other hand, was very disquieting, as both Governments appeared to be at the end of their tether. The German Balts, i.e. descendants of German colonists in Esthonia and Latvia, had, with the help of the German troops of the army of occupation, arrested the Lettish Government and put in nominees of their own. The Entente Powers, having given the Esthonians and the Letts no help, were quite powerless to prevent these high-handed measures on the part of the Germans, and were apparently willing to rely on them to defend North-Eastern Europe against Bolshevik attack, a most humiliating position for the Allies, who were at the same time inviting the Germans to come to Versailles on April 25th to receive the terms of Peace.

April 20th, a Sunday, I went with Robert Vansittart [1] to see Napoleon's tomb at the Invalides. There were many American soldiers there, but very few British. I always noticed that the Americans with their thirst for knowledge were much to the fore at all the principal " sights," whereas the British were conspicuous by their absence.

The following day the Italian claim on Fiume and Dalmatia resulting from the Secret Treaty of London was discussed at a long private meeting between Clémenceau, Lloyd George and Orlando, the Italian Prime Minister. Everyone realised that a crisis was inevitable shortly. President Wilson, who would not recognise the Treaty of London, refused to attend this meeting of the three Premiers.

[1] Now Permanent Under Secretary of State at the Foreign Office.

As we needed a regular diplomatic representative at Warsaw, I suggested my old school friend and fellow member of the Crabbet Club, Percy Wyndham,[1] who had till recently been our Minister in Venezuela. I had become so accustomed to having no attention paid to any suggestions I made that it was a pleasant surprise to find this not only at once accepted, but immediately acted on, and Percy arrived in Paris rather alarmed at being suddenly dumped on a country which was in the chaotic condition of Poland. I tried to console him by saying that it was really much more peaceful than Venezuela, but he replied that in Venezuela there were orchids and butterflies to make up for revolutions, and that whatever might be the charms of Poland, it certainly could not provide these compensations for the minor worries of life. He asked me, however, to tell him all about the Polish situation in the two days he was to spend in Paris before leaving for Warsaw. We both worked hard at this, but when I saw him off at the station he was dejected at the prospect before him and not to be comforted, for I could not truly pretend that Poland would produce orchids and butterflies for him in April. Nevertheless, I believe he found many very charming people there to console him for the absence of the joys of the Spanish Main.

It was just at this time that Marshal Pilsudski occupied Vilna and thereby greatly annoyed certain elements in England which would much rather have seen Vilna in the hands of the Germans or of the Bolsheviks.

On April 24th my diary records: " Departure of Italian Delegation [from Paris] and publication of Wilson's declaration [about Fiume] to the Italian people has had the obvious result that anyone should have foreseen of rallying all shades of public opinion in Italy round the Italian Government and making the situation infinitely more difficult. Robert Cecil, to whom I spoke some days ago, said Italians would never go, and Mr. Barnes and others were full of praise for Wilson's manifesto.

[1] *Vide* p. 73, Vol. 1, *Theatre of Life.*

2 A

Colonel C. thought that the sloppy sentimentality at the end would appeal to the Italians. How wrong people go when they build on foundations of guesswork."

On Friday, April 25th, having been granted a week's leave to join Isa and my five boys who had gone to Arundel for Easter, I left Paris for London in company of Lord Eustace Percy, who had been in the Diplomatic Service, but had left it to go into politics, which seemed to me very regrettable because we needed badly men of his intellectual calibre and industry in our service. But he is now a Cabinet Minister, and the House of Commons gains what the Foreign Office has lost.

Arundel was a delicious change from Paris, but I missed Norfolk terribly. It was the first time I had been there since his death, and it was very different without his kindly and most lovable personality. I never met a man who so combined the character of a real *grand seigneur* with absolute sincerity and extreme natural simplicity. It is a very rare combination and a supremely attractive one. But the family party, consisting with my five boys, the Arundel children and Eric Drummond's family, of thirteen children in all, was a truly delightful change from the Hotel Majestic in Paris, where there were indeed many children, but not in years.

I had nothing to think of but to play tennis with the young people or ride with them in that lovely Sussex country in springtime. For these few days Russians, Balts, Poles and Germans no longer existed for me, and the sessions of the Council of Four and the other Councils or Committees and meetings were forgotten. It was a glorious time, and on May 6th I returned to Paris like a giant refreshed.

I motored back from Boulogne to Paris with the King's Messenger, Captain Wilton, whom I had met so often in Stockholm during the War. All along the first part of the road there were still large numbers of British troops, though they were being rapidly sent home and demobilised.

The great news that met us in Paris was that Orlando

and Sonnino had suddenly decided to return to Paris and take part in the final negotiations with the Germans.

I was told that President Wilson had said to Orlando before the latter left for Rome that he (the President) believed he had the people of Italy behind him in his dispute with the Italian Delegation. What an error of judgment and what a mistake in psychology. One wonders if the President had any advisers who at all understood Italian mentality.

On May 7th I entered the Conference vortex once more and wrote in my diary :

" The old life begins again. The situation in the Baltic States very bad. Esthonia desperate from want of money and likely to make peace any day with the Bolsheviks, which would be disastrous to us all. In Latvia German Balts have upset the Government, imprisoned members of the Cabinet and disarmed Lettish troops on the charge that they are Bolshevik. They mean, of course, to establish German influence there quite firmly.

Poles are moving forward beyond Vilna to Dwinsk or Minsk and encountering very little opposition.

Germans were handed text of Peace Treaty to-day. Ian Malcolm tells me the ceremony was not very striking, in the dining-room of the hotel. Brockdorff Rantzau (the German Representative) made a very bad impression by reading his speech sitting after Clémenceau had opened the congress standing. (I believe it was explained later that Count Rantzau was suffering from some illness of the legs which prevented him from standing.) After Rantzau's speech, which was largely an exculpation of Germany, the meeting at once ended. Germans have been given fifteen days to reply."

The following day, May 8th, the terms of Peace were published in summary form, since the Treaty itself was an enormous volume. There was such a hurry at the last over its preparation that Hurst[1] and the Legal Section were working eighteen hours a day. Finally it was said

[1] Sir Cecil Hurst, legal adviser to the Foreign Office.

that the volume had to be handed to the Germans without having been properly read over.

The members of the German Delegation were allowed to walk about in a part of the park at Versailles, which was specially fenced off and was given the name in Paris of *Thiergarten*, German for Zoological Gardens.

I noted baldly in my diary that day that " Arabian Lawrence " and Lady Muriel Paget dined with me, but unfortunately have not recorded anything he said. Presumably there was nothing worth recording.

The next day Paderewski hurried off by motor to Poland to try and stop the Diet from passing a resolution in favour of the annexation of Lithuania. He said he was not too dissatisfied with the latest Danzig arrangement (Danzig to be a free city with special privileges to Poles for free entry and export, etc.), and hoped to be able to explain it satisfactorily to the Diet. He was, however, much attacked about this when he returned to Warsaw.

I took Commander J. Gade, United States Navy, whom I had known and made friends with in Stockholm during the War and who was just back from the Baltic States, to lunch with Mr. Balfour, in order to explain to the latter all the gravity of the situation. He was, like most of us, fascinated by A. J. B.—who could be otherwise ?

The Council of Five, after discussing the Baltic situation, appointed a Baltic Commission to deal specially with Baltic affairs and report. I was the British member of this Committee. Next day Colonel Kisch of the Military Section, and a member of the Polish Ukrainian Armistice Committee, came to me in great agitation, saying that a telegram had come in from General Carton de Wiart to the effect that Haller's (Polish) army was on the point of attacking the Ukrainians. At his request I sent telegrams to M. Paderewski and General Pilsudski urging them to suspend attack and accept Armistice conditions.

Pilsudski received a tremendous ovation on his return to Warsaw after occupying Vilna.

The next day after dinner with Aubrey and Mary Herbert, I spent the evening with M. and Madame

Zyondakis at the Hotel Mercedes, the home of the Greek Delegation. Venizelos and Carlo Placci were there, and Venizelos talked much of our old days in Crete, when he was leader of the insurrection against Prince George, and we had many good laughs over our experiences of those times. He is a wonderful man—the Cavour of the Conference, and has done miracles for his country by the force of his personality. " Perhaps the only great man of the whole crowd." I made in this a great error of judgment. He was a supremely clever man but not a great one as subsequent events proved.

The next day I dined with the Russian scholar, Harold Williams and his wife, to meet a number of Russian *emigrés*, among others Savinkoff, a former active revolutionary who had the reputation of having arranged the assassination of the Grand Duke George and others, but was now *rangé*. I noted : " An interesting evening."

The food position in Riga was now so bad that even Bolshevik troops abandoned it. There was complete anarchy and about five thousand persons were reported to be marooned on an island and starving. The German troops in Latvia asked if British troops would co-operate with them in the capture of the city. This His Majesty's Government felt they could not do in the circumstances. The Council of Five appointed a sub-committee of the Supreme Economic Council under Mr. Hoover to discuss this question. Meanwhile German military authorities were disarming the Lettish troops and imprisoning notables and behaving as absolute conquerors. We could not bid them begone because there was no organised force to take their place.

A story was going the round of the Delegates that Clémenceau, having been accused of giving way too much in the Council of Three, replied :[1]

" *Mais que faire quand on est avec deux hommes dont l'un se croit Jésus Christ et l'autre se croit Napoléon ?* "[2]

[1] The Italian Representative was, of course, absent in Rome, and there had been according to report some very plain speaking at the Council Board.

[2] " But what is one to do when one is with two men of whom one thinks himself Jesus Christ and the other Napoleon ? "

On May 16th, to my great content, Isa arrived. She was not allowed to stay with me at the Majestic, though my apartment was quite large enough. This was not because the Majestic was run as a monastery, far from it, for it was overflowing with dames of all sorts, secretaries, shorthand writers, but the strict puritanism of some authority in the Foreign Office had drawn the line at wives. Some time later, however, ideas grew less srtict and wives were finally admitted for a short time before the Conference ended.

The Austrian Peace Delegation arrived at St. Germain about this time, and whatever they may have thought of the terms of their Treaty they were delighted to get to a land of white bread and butter and real coffee.

On May 17th, three American areoplanes started for a flight across the Atlantic from Newfoundland via Azores to Lisbon. Hawker, the English airman, started from Newfoundland on a non-stop flight to Ireland. Great excitement was created over these two events. Hawker unfortunately fell into the sea just before landing, but was picked up some days later.

Isa and I lunched with the Norwegian Minister, Baron Wedel-Jarlsberg and his wife, a very rich American, who lived in Lafayette's house, 20, Rue de Surenne, which they had furnished with great taste. Baron and Baroness Wedel-Jarlsberg were reputed to have the best cuisine in Paris and frequently invited Isa and me in order I suppose to win my support for Norway's claim to Spitzbergen. The assignation of that chilly island was one of the questions which the Paris Conference was expected to settle. I had made up my mind before coming to Paris that Norway ought to have it, and therefore had no scruples about enjoying Baron Wedel-Jarlsberg's hospitality. But there were interests in London who wished it to be assigned to Great Britain, and one day Ronald Graham of the Foreign Office, asked me to meet in his room a certain M.P. who was also a City magnate. This gentleman, after giving me lengthy reasons for Spitzbergen's annexation by England and finding me cold, at last burst out that if England did not get it there would be WAR. I fear I smiled and asked who would carry on the war. Still more angrily he said : " The Company," meaning his company who had pegged out mineral concessions there. I fear I smiled again and asked : " Where will the fighting be ? " He, in a crescendo of indignation replied " In Spitzbergen." Greatly relieved I assured him that I would carefully note what he had said. This passage is clear proof that I have never forgotten it.

Spitzbergen was assigned to Norway by the Conference.

On May 23rd, news of a most cheering character arrived from the Baltic States. Mr. Hoover's representative in that part of the world telegraphed to the Supreme Economic Council, which having in its hands the distribution of foodstuffs, clothes, etc., was rapidly becoming the Supreme Council of the Conference, that the Esthonians had defeated the Bolsheviks east of Narva, near the scene of Charles XII of Sweden's great victory over the Russians in A.D. 1700. This news doubly delighted me, because it checked for the time being the Russian advance into Western Europe, and also because it justified my often expressed confidence in the Esthonians and Letts to give a good account of themselves against the Bolsheviks, and greatly improved our situation in the Baltic.

My nephew, Algar Howard, turned up unexpectedly on May 24th, from the East, where he had taken part in the Gallipoli and Palestine campaigns.

The Dutch Minister, M. van Swinderen and his wife, old friends from Washington, dined at the same party with Isa and me, and he regaled me with the latest *mot* about the Conference, which was that the Peace terms contained all the germs *d'une guerre juste et durable.*"[1]

Sunday, May 25th, was a day of especial interest. At 7.30 a.m. Isa, Alda (Isa's competent Italian maid and the faithful and beloved friend of all the family, for she nursed us all in our illnesses), and I left for Rheims in a very crowded train on a very hot day. We were to carry out a long-made plan to visit that city with its glorious cathedral,

---

[1] Translation : " Of a just and enduring war."

of which now little remained but a shattered shell. We reached Château Thierry which the Germans occupied when they crossed the Marne the second time in July, 1918. Here were the first serious signs of the destruction of war ; houses, churches, etc., in ruins. But arrival at Rheims made a truly terrible impression, not so much the cathedral, which was singularly beautiful in its ruined state, but the town itself, which was literally a heap of ruins like a modern Pompeii. About fifteen houses out of sixteen thousand were said to be untouched by shell fire. It looked as if the enemy had deliberately tried to destroy the town house by house. I remember in a street which must have been in a good residential quarter a well-dressed man walking alone and unconcerned down the deserted roadway. Presently he stopped, drew out a key from his pocket, and opened the door of an apparently ruined and certainly quite roofless house, passed in and closed the door behind him. I cannot tell why this incident has remained so indelibly engraved on my mind. It was probably the unexpected discovery that a house that looked as did all the others in that street ruined beyond repair, hopeless, abandoned and deserted should be occupied by a man dressed like any other and owning a latch-key to the door. The warm spring sun, flowers coming out in the abandoned gardens, and birds singing in such trees as had survived the destruction wrought everywhere by the German shells, completed the sense of contrast, and in some way added to the sense of desolation.

We lunched in the garden of an inn which had just been reopened, and then wandered about and found some dug-outs beyond the barracks in the Boulevard de la Paix—what an irony of a name—which had been shelled almost out of existence. I picked up part of a German shell here.

We left Rheims at 4.30 feeling very depressed, and arrived at Paris at 7.30. Algar Howard, my nephew, dined with us and told us about the Palestine campaign and how he had only just failed to catch General Liman von Sanders because he had got no guide to the German headquarters at Nazareth, and Liman was warned and escaped a few minutes before. The news of the day was that Hawker and Grieve were safe, having been picked up at sea not far from the Irish coast.

I spent most of the following day translating the German reply, which had just come in. It was distributed for translation among all those who knew German well enough. The parts given to me concerned the financial clauses, and I thought it very well drawn up. The whole reply was translated and typed by midnight which, considering the length of it, was quite a fine performance.

We dined with the Marchese Imperiali, Italian Ambassador and one of the Italian Delegates. Isa and I had a long talk to Marshal Diaz after dinner. He was the Italian Commander-in-Chief at the end of the War during the victories of the Piave and Vittorio Veneto, which completed the destruction of the Austrian Army and the Austrian Empire, and may be considered as one of the first entirely decisive victories of the whole War. He expatiated on the excellent qualities of the Italian soldier. Marshal Diaz, like Marshal Foch, was a quiet dignified man utterly devoid of " swagger," just what one expects a great soldier or sailor to be.

On Friday, May 30th, there being no special work for me, Baron Wedel-Jarlsberg and his wife motored Isa and me to Versailles through the Bois de Boulogne and the Park of St. Cloud. We were shown the private apartments of Marie Antoinette and Madame Dubarry and others, and finally the Galerie des Glaces, where the German Empire was proclaimed in 1871 by the old Emperor William, surrounded by Bismarck and Moltke, the Crown Prince and various Kings and Princes of German States. Here within a few days, or perhaps weeks, we looked forward to seeing the signature of the Peace Treaty with Germany. The table for the signature had already been chosen, and all plans laid for the great day.

Next Sunday Isa and I went to Chantilly and put up at a little Inn, as the principal Hotel, the Hotel d'Angleterre,

which had served as Foch's headquarters, was still
requisitioned. After lunch we visited the Château, which
was fine but of modern restoration. It contained, however, numerous works of art, amongst which we particularly admired some forty illuminated pages by Jean
Fouquet (fifteenth century). We drove in the Forest and
picked lilies-of-the-valley and passed an ideal day, for-
getting Paris and the Conference.

We returned to Paris early next day, and I worked all
day. We dined with M. and Madame Noulens to meet
several *émigré* Russians, among others Count and Countess
Kokofftsoff. He complained bitterly and with reason
that, having supported the Entente cause for years as a
Minister in Russia, no one in authority in the Entente
countries would see him now. I thought it shameful to
turn our backs on these Russian *émigrés* who had been
our friends and Allies during the first part of the war.

There was also present at the dinner M. Kloboukoffski,
the French Minister of Information, who got on so well
with Isa that he offered to send us on a conducted tour
round the devastated areas on the following Saturday and
Sunday.

The French were glad to get members of the Allied
Delegations to visit these areas so that they might be convinced by their own eyes of the complete destruction of
all that the hand of man had created for centuries past.
Ronald Campbell, Lord Hardinge's Secretary, who had
been there, told me no one could believe it without having
seen it. So I readily accepted M. Kloboukoffski's offer
for Isa and myself, provided I could get leave for a week-
end for the purpose.

The Austrian Delegation received their Peace conditions on June 2nd, and Herr Renner made a speech which
was favourably contrasted with that of Count Brockdorff-
Rantzau and left a good impression.

June 3rd was passed in preparing memoranda on the
German reply, and with members of other Sections of
our Delegation, Mr. Paton and I called on the Prime
Minister in order to discuss various points. All the other

foreign Delegations were also hard at work preparing their comments on the German reply.

I noted : " Most people in the Majestic seem to think that German objections to financial and economic reparations clauses are to some extent well founded." It took us all years, however, to discover how true this was. Yet on the other side there were those appalling devastated areas which would require to be restored and rebuilt. The Germans had no devastated areas. Their factories could start and would start again the day after Peace was concluded, while it might take months and years before the French and Belgian factories could be rebuilt, and the Germans must pay the bill for the rebuilding, for there was no one else. It was a terrible problem. But few realised how impossible it was to make any country in the world, let alone a country like Germany which had been through four and a half years of war and blockade and had been bled white in man power, pay the fantastic sums which were being demanded of her.

On June 6th, Baltic affairs were once again in a critical state, because German and Balt troops together, having taken Riga from the Bolsheviks, were reported to be marching against the Esthonians, and refused to give us satisfaction for the arrest of British Naval officers at Libau. General Thwaites, Admiral Hope, Sir William Goode of the Economic Section and I met and together drew up recommendations to the Big Four to the effect that Germans should be at once ordered to cease advancing against the Letts and told to withdraw from Baltic States. The great difficulty of course was to know how such an order could be enforced, as the Chief of the General Staff, Sir Henry Wilson, was adamant against sending any military force there, saying that none could be spared. It seemed, therefore, that we should be compelled to allow the Germans to do what they liked there.

On June 7th, a Saturday, having obtained leave to take the week-end off to visit the devastated areas, Isa and I left early by train with M. Jules Bloch, of the French Foreign Office, who had been attached to us as conductor.

He was a most efficient and agreeable guide, though he suffered all through from a severe attack of hay fever, which is enough to make of most men both misanthropes and misogynists—especially the latter.

We reached Noyon, much devastated, at 10.30, and left at once in a motor-car for Amiens *via* Mondidier. Nearly every village was but a heap of ruins and hardly a living being along our route. It seemed hopeless from the point of view of the well-being of the inhabitants, but the country-side, which was almost completely uncultivated, was brilliant with poppies and cornflowers. Although the woods stood mostly gaunt, bare and torn to shreds among the poppy fields, yet song-birds in numbers filled them with music. It was a scene of strange and striking contrasts.

We passed many entirely obliterated villages whose names were simply recorded on a board by the side of the road, names which we had eagerly sought for on our maps whenever they were mentioned in the war news of the day.

We reached Amiens at 2.30, and after a little food went to visit the beautiful Cathedral, which had fortunately hardly suffered, only one bomb having fallen through the roof.

During this day or the next we met soldiers in all kinds of uniforms and of many races—French, English, German (prisoners working on the roads), American, Russian, Negroes, Arabs from Algeria and Morocco, Annamites and Hindus. What a War! Masses of barbed wire, piles of shells, abandoned tanks were left beside the roads. What a waste it all was ; this struck us especially and the stupidity of it all. How anybody not a lunatic can sing the glories of war passes all comprehension.

We passed Albert and Péronne, both completely in ruins, and St. Quentin, rather less so, and picked up some German helmets in the " Hindenburg Line." Among some sandy hills we came across a cave which had evidently been used as a dormitory. It had been hastily abandoned and afterwards apparently used as a cemetery, judging by the half-buried human remains which dogs had partially uncovered. The stench and, above all, countless masses of enormous flies soon drove us out of the place. " Who fills the butchers' shops with large blue flies ? " occurred to my mind, and my answer was " the Devil." It was horrible.

Poppies everywhere. So on through Cousy le Château and Clancy, both destroyed wilfully by the Germans with dynamite. The road was full of deep shell-holes, difficult for the car to avoid. Masses of bombs and grenades piled along the roadside, many still unexploded, and here and there an unburied horse, and still those red poppies. The heat was excessive, and in the midst of such destruction and horrors conversation ceased. Truly, as St. Thomas More says : " Warre and Battel is a thing very beastly."

We reached Lâon tired, oppressed and sad, at 4.30 and got back to Paris at 9 p.m. A real nightmare of a " day out." I am glad I went, however, for it determined me to do all I could in my humble way to prevent all this " beastliness " from overwhelming the world again. I hoped much from the League of Nations as a means of pumping sanity into a crazy world.

On my return I was at once plunged again into the old problems.

I noted in my diary :

" Yugo Slavs attacking Austrians at Klagenfurt and Czechs beaten by Hungarian Reds."

" On June 10th, in the morning, Messrs. Piip and Pusta, Esthonian delegates, much agitated, poor people, about German attack on Esthonia. Afternoon Baltic Committee. Heard Lettish delegates and spent from 7 to 8 with Mr. Balfour, Admiral Hope and Ian Malcolm discussing Baltic situation. All agreed Germans must be required to leave Baltic Provinces, but no one could suggest any practical way of inducing them to do so. A hopeless situation. If only people had listened to my warnings five or six months ago this intolerable mess would have been avoided."

The next day, however, the Supreme War Council accepted our recommendation that Marshal Foch might be requested to order Germans to stop their attacks on Esthonia and evacuate Baltic Provinces and Lithuania.

At 3.15 got a frantic appeal from Ian Malcolm to go round at once to the Rue Nitot, where the Esthonian delegates were interviewing poor Mr. Balfour, who hated to be alone on these occasions. They were pressing for immediate recognition of independence. They were told —in accordance with the policy at that time—that final settlement could only be with the consent of the Russians. They argued for three and a half hours !

I tore back exhausted to prepare for a dinner Isa and I were giving that night to a number of distinguished lions of the Conference, including Mr. Balfour, M. Venizelos, M. and Madame Paderewski, Princess de la Moskowa, Countess Jean de Castellane, Signor and Signora Brambilla, Carlo Placci, Ian Malcolm and Lady Malcolm, etc.

So we gradually, like caterpillars, ate our way through the Conference cabbage.

On June 12th the Council of Four adopted our recommendation for the evacuation of the Baltic Provinces by Germany. It therefore looked as if at last something might be done.

The Austrians ordered three days public mourning on account of the Peace Terms.

The Hungarian Soviet Government which had defeated the Czechs and occupied Czech territory had been ordered by the Council of Four to retire. Instead Soviet troops continued to advance, and actually threatened Pressburg.

There were all sorts of rumours that the Italian Government were supporting the Hungarian Bolsheviks and supplying them with arms. I could not believe this, and supposed that these were stories put about for an obvious purpose.

Mr. and Mrs. Morgenthau, the United States Ambassador at Constantinople, dined with Isa and me at the

Majestic. We talked at length about the condition of the Jews in Poland and alleged pogroms. He said he had been asked as a Jew to go to Poland and investigate. But as he is a strong anti-Zionist he feared the Jewish element there, especially the Zionists, would not consider him *persona grata*. I told him that I thought that while there might be some foundation for these stories of attacks on Jews in Poland they were rather the result of long civil war than of " pogroms " in the regular sense of the word.

On the 14th I had breakfast with Lincoln Steffens, the American correspondent who had just come back from Moscow, whither he had gone on a semi-official mission from President Wilson. He declared that much real national pride or its equivalent had been aroused among the Bolsheviks, who genuinely believed themselves to be defending Communistic ideals against a world of capitalists in arms. The situation was not good in many ways, he said. Lenin, whom he believed to be the greatest man the War had produced, was veering to the right, and Trotsky had made a bad impression on him.

The Bolsheviks said they could not prevent propaganda going abroad if they tried. If there was one thing certain in my mind, however, it was that they never would try.

Next day, June 15th, Francis Lindley,[1] who had just returned from Archangel, and Captain Maule from Warsaw lunched with us. The latter was nervous lest the Powers should not give Poland support in case of attack from without because the Polish Government had refused to hearken to the admonitions of the Council of Four respecting Eastern Galicia.

Lindley told me life at Archangel the winter before had not been quite so intolerable as I might have supposed. A battalion of Bolshevik prisoners had been a grand success and fought against the attacking Bolsheviks with great courage. The Polish contingent had also done well.

[1] Afterwards H.M. Ambassador at Tokyo

On June 16th, Captain Alcock and Lieutenant Brown completed the first transatlantic non-stop flight in an English aeroplane, flying from Newfoundland to Ireland in sixteen hours and twenty-seven minutes, but the papers were so taken up with the Peace signature, and the possibility of a renewal of hostilities if the Germans would not sign, that this really great aeronautic event hardly got its due. So much was this the case that some years afterwards, few persons on being questioned could say that two Englishmen, Brown and Alcock, were the first that ever flew the Atlantic in a non-stop flight. It often gave me pleasure afterwards to bring this into the conversation, and to notice the surprise of foreigners and their obvious belief that I was just bragging.

The reply to the German observations on the Treaty was handed in to them this day, and they were given one week to sign. So doubtful did the issue then seem to be that I noted in my diary : " I bet they don't sign."

We were indeed all in a state of acute nervousness, and the tension grew daily. Colonel Warwick Greene, of the U.S.A., just returned from the Baltic Provinces, reported to the effect that the Germans there were threatening to dominate everywhere. Germanism seemed to me a greater danger than Bolshevism in those parts, for we could easily create local forces to defend themselves from Bolsheviks, but though we were giving millions to Denikin in South Russia, to Kolchak in Siberia, and to the North Russian Republic, we could spare nothing for these unhappy Provinces. Yet there they are now, independent and prosperous, and where are Kolchak, Denikin and the Northern Republic ?

There was great discord in German Government circles over the question of signature, and up to the last it was touch and go. We believed that Rantzau and Scheidemann and, of course, all the old Junkers were against, but Ebert and the mass of the people were for signing. There was truly no other way out. The greatest difficulty of Europe at that time was that all countries were so physically and mentally tired that no individual could be relied on to do a full day's work, and production was being reduced by leaps and bounds, while prices went up.

This would have been the golden opportunity for obtaining a golden Peace, the Peace of goodwill, had there existed a real will to peace and confidence in security from future aggression. Unfortunately the world was not yet ready for it. The Napoleon of Peace had not yet arisen, and it will probably take many more generations of suffering and learning before the world is ready to accept him.

The Council of Five at last decided one of the principal difficulties, or rather allowed events to decide it for them. Eastern Galicia was, after all, to go to Poland with local autonomy—a change from the negative attitude hitherto adopted. There were many, of course, who objected to the Eastern part of Eastern Galicia becoming Polish against the wishes of the inhabitants. But it was a choice between this or setting up another diminutive State and " Balkanising " that part of the world still more, or joining Eastern Galicia on to the Soviet Republic, which was clearly to be the fate of the Ukraine. Largely as a result of Soviet policy in dealing with that land of peasant proprietors, some three to four millions of these perished during the famine of 1933.[1] What the treatment of peasant proprietors (*kulaks*) would be in Soviet Russia admitted of no doubt even in 1919. It was always described by the Soviets themselves by one graphic word, " liquidation." I think, therefore, that most of us felt that the Ruthenes of Eastern Galicia would probably be far more gently treated under Polish administration than if they were joined on to the Ukrainians over the border, and subjected to the gentle system of " liquidation " under the dictatorship of the Russian Proletariat, for whom " ruthlessness " was as much a necessary part of government as it was for the conduct of war by a Prussian Junker.

On June 23rd the news came from Scapa Flow that

[1] *Vide* p. 88 of *Russia's Iron Age*, by Mr. Chamberlain, for twelve years Correspondent of the Christian Science Monitor in Soviet Russia from 1922 to 1934.

the Germans had there scuttled and sunk practically the entire Fleet which they had surrendered at the time of the Armistice. Most of the officers and men were saved and then imprisoned. Our Jingo papers made a great outcry, demanding that the German Admiral should be shot. The French papers were particularly indignant, as they claimed some of these ships for France. Since His Majesty's Government had first proposed that all the ships should be sunk when they were handed over, some French papers now accused His Majesty's Government of collusion. The Germans also burnt at Berlin all the French flags which were under the Peace Treaty to have been returned to France. These different matters did not make the last chapters of the Peace Conference story any more rosy than the first or the intervening ones.

From my diary, June 23rd : " At five o'clock Tom Spring Rice [1] came to my office to tell me that the Germans after many protests had finally consented to sign the Treaty. At last it appears we are nearing the end."

At 6 p.m. an old Roman acquaintance, the Polish pianist, M. Radvan, had invited Isa and me to go to his rooms to hear him play. At seven o'clock, when the Allied troops were to have marched forward if the Germans had refused to sign, the cannons of the Invalides, which were close by Radvan's house, fired a salvo of 101 guns in honour of Peace. During the firing Radvan played the great insurrectionary Polonaise of Chopin (*Op.* 53), which is for me one of the most exultant triumphant pieces of music ever written. I never hear it now without remembering that thrilling moment and the triumph that Radvan put into the playing of that glorious music. For the moment we too shared the feeling of exultation, but it passed all too quickly, and by the date of the signature it was but a thing of shreds and patches.

" June 24th. There was yesterday not nearly so much excitement as on Armistice Day, but flags are beginning to go up on most houses.

[1] Afterwards Lord Monteagle.

" Germans are having difficulties in finding Plenipotentiaries to sign, and there are signs of trouble among
Prussian officers, who declare they will march into Holland
and deliver the Kaiser rather than allow him to be given
up to the Allies. Everything points also to Prussia making
trouble in the Eastern Provinces and refusing to give them
up. But mass of people are for peace at any price.

" June 26th. Still uncertain whom the Germans will send
to sign. The Peace Conference sends them an ultimatum.

" Scapa Flow incident is still subject of much controversy and criticism. It appears that British Admiralty
at time of Armistice asked for surrender (of fleet) and not
internment, but Americans and French opposed this.

" June 26th. Rumoured escape of German Crown
Prince from Holland. Will the Prussian Militarists proclaim him King of Prussia ? Anything is possible.

" Germans have named their Plenipotentiaries at
eleventh hour. They are to be Müller, Socialist Minister
for Foreign Affairs, and Bell, of the Centre Party.

" June 27th. Secretariat very busy with lists of
invitations for to-morrow's signature at Versailles. Crown
Prince has not escaped after all. Isa and I lunch with
Madame de Sainçay,[1] after which the Committee of Five
in afternoon. It was settled that Eastern Galicia was to
have autonomy under Poland, with a plebiscite at some
future date—so that long controversy is finally out of the
way. . . .

" June 28th. Wretched men of the Secretariat up to
5 a.m. yesterday settling invitations for Versailles. I got
a ticket for Galerie des Glaces, and Isa for the gardens
where the fountains play. After lunch I left with Crowe
and Mallet for Versailles."

I think we most of us started for Versailles on the
morning of that June 28th, 1919, with feelings if not of
satisfaction and content, at least with a sense of immense
relief that a temporary return to an appearance of what
President Harding called " normalcy " might now be
hoped for.

[1] Now Lady Maxwell Scott of Abbotsford.

The day was a beautiful one, and we were about to take part in an historic and unforgettable ceremony. I suppose nearly all of us thought of the scene on January 18th, 1871, when the conquering German Princes proclaimed the unity of Germany, and the German Empire was set up under the King of Prussia in that same Galerie des Glaces of the Château of Versailles in which we were about to witness the signature of the Treaty containing the Covenant of the League of Nations. Whatever might become of the territorial and other clauses of the Treaty of Versailles, there were not a few of us there present who felt that this Covenant, faulty though it might be in some respects, was by far the most important part of the Treaty which was to become law that day, and hoped that it constituted indeed a revolution in International Law which, by introducing the Reign of Law into the world, would really establish peace on firm foundations, and not, as some cynics openly professed to believe, contain together with all the other Treaties of Peace the germs "*d'une guerre juste et durable.*" [1] We who hoped for the Reign of Peace and Law might well have exclaimed, as the old Emperor William of Germany did in 1871, "*Welch eine Wendung durch Gottes Gnade !* " [2]

The scene was certainly set for one of the most dramatic occasions in history, but how would it all turn out ? The hall itself, I confess, smacks rather too much of the meretricious taste of the days of Louis XIV to please me greatly. How much grander and more solemn, for instance, would be the setting of a Westminster Hall for such an occasion ! Another note which spoilt the impressiveness of the scene was the lack of colour. Practically all the hundreds of men assembled were dressed in black. There was nothing festive there. I have seen many State funerals which were far less funereal. We arrived just behind the " Tiger " who, getting out and having to be photographed on the steps, looked very cross. There was a great hum of conversation while all were finding their seats and greeting

[1] " A just and enduring war."
[2] " What a change by the mercy of God ! "

each other. Then suddenly came a dead silence. The doors at the end were thrown open and the two German Plenipotentiaries entered. The Republican Guard, which had stood to attention with their swords drawn down the central gangway, sheathed their swords with military precision, and the two Germans, Herr Müller and Herr Bell, walked rapidly to their seats, looking neither to right nor to left. They seemed to me intolerably lonely. I felt then that I should have liked to get up and shake them by the hand because, after all, these were not the men who had any responsibility either for the making of the War or the way in which it was conducted. I felt then, as I have felt ever since, that had we been able and willing at that time to make friends with the Moderate Socialists who had, for the time being at any rate, ended the Junker domination which threatened Europe with its mailed fist, we should probably have laid a far better foundation of, a just and lasting peace, which was, we all said and I believe quite sincerely, what we wanted.

The Germans, having taken their seats near the table in the centre of the hall on which the text of the Treaty lay, M. Clémenceau rose, made a very short speech in his clear, incisive voice, and invited the German Delegates to sign first. They rose amid profound silence, a silence that could be felt, went to the table, subscribed their names and returned to their seats like men walking in a dream. Then began the long file of other Delegates signing in the order of the Protocol which had been arranged from the beginning of the Conference.

Besides those of the Council of Five, who naturally stood out above the others, the most remarkable men there were unquestionably Botha, Venizelos, Benes and Paderewski. These four had all exercised an extraordinary influence on the outcome of the negotiations, and all were exceptional men. Botha for his magnificent sanity of outlook, Venizelos for his brilliant mind and powers of persuasion (not always, I am inclined to think, used for the benefit of his country as things turned out), Benes for his logic and vigour, and Paderewski for his complete sincerity and desire that his country should emerge from the trials of this time strong indeed and united, but without stain and without reproach. I have never heard anyone who criticised his conduct during all the time of the Peace Conference and after, unless it was those of his countrymen who accused him of not having been sufficiently Chauvinist in pressing its claims.

The whole ceremony of signature was over in less than an hour. All that the Treaty needed was ratification. The important question in the minds of all of us was whether President Wilson's signature would be confirmed by the Senate. It was difficult to foresee what would happen if it was not so confirmed, and yet this seemed to be very likely.

The Germans were conducted again to the doors, and suddenly a bugle announced the completion of the ceremony to those waiting in the garden below, which a salute of 101 guns announced to the world outside, and the *Grandes Eaux* (the wonderful fountains of Versailles) began to play.

After the Plenipotentiaries had left there was a tremendous rush to get out into the gardens and see the fountains. All of us, the small fry, were seated on priceless Louis Quatorze benches and stools covered with the beautiful hand-work tapestry of the time. We were all eager to get to the windows and see the fountains, and many chased over these *tabourets* and *bancs*. One of the last sights I remember in the Galerie des Glaces that day was that of Mr. Balfour's long legs, not contented with steeplechasing over benches, but mounting upon them and leaping like a mountain goat from one to the other. How he came to be left behind by the Plenipotentiaries I cannot say, unless it was for the reason which he once gave me as an excuse for not knowing what had been happening at some meeting of the Council of Four—" I fear I must have been asleep."

The night of signature, Isa and I dined with Prince Constantine Radziwill to meet his daughter, the Duchesse de Doudeauville, and her family. Prince Radziwill had been marooned, so to speak, for months in Stockholm after the Russian Revolution broke out. Like many other Russian subjects, he had fled from Russia, but having got to Stockholm he dreaded crossing the North Sea. He used periodically to get the necessary permission from the British Legation for a passage in the British Admiralty steamer, the *Prince Arthur*, which was then the only ship taking passengers from Scandinavia to England, and as regularly, when the day of departure came, he was seized with influenza or some other convenient sickness, and had to go to bed. About a fortnight later he began to consider the advisability of another attempt, and would call at the Legation and consult Isa and me as to whether it was really safe. During these visits he behaved just as I remembered seeing actors at the *Théatre Francais* do when playing parts of the *grand monde* under the Third Empire, bringing into the drawing-room his top-hat, his cane and his gloves. The top-hat was placed carefully on the ground beside his chair, his gloves together were meticulously laid over the side of the hat with perfect precision, his cane between his knees and his hands resting on the handle in the most approved Third Empire style. He had a very precise way of speaking, which amused us considerably. After a precious quarter of an hour—for minutes were precious in those days—he would again cautiously approach the subject of the passage over the North Sea, telling us that this time, if I could but get him permission, he would really start. All was ready for the worst : " *J'ai fait ma paix avec Dieu.*" This being so, we encouraged him not to put it off any longer, but still he hesitated, and it was fully six months before he was finally persuaded to take the plunge.

Now in Paris, gratefully remembering Isa's and my part in speeding him across the North Sea during the German submarine campaign, he invited us to meet his daughter and her children at dinner, and it happened to be the day of the signature of Peace. The Doudeauville family were determined to celebrate it by venturing out into the crowded streets and making a demonstration before the Jockey Club, of which their father was President and where he was dining that night. The bare idea of going into the crowd on such a night as that terribly shocked Prince Constantine's ideas of what was correct and proper. He protested vigorously but was overborne, so, leaving him at home, the Duchesse de Doudeauville, Isa and I and the younger members of the family, who were full of enterprise, changed into everyday clothes and went down into the streets. At first the crowd was not difficult to pass through, but as we approached the Boulevard de la Madeleine we were blocked. Then the eldest son had a brain-wave. Joining hands and in single file, singing some popular song, we charged and pranced triumphantly through the mass of folk till we reached the building in which *Le Jockey* is situated. There we demonstrated with such success that the President of the Club at last came out on to the balcony to see what was the cause of the commotion, and was horrified to see his family at the centre of it all shouting " Papa ! Papa ! " in chorus, while others in the street joined in the fun. With the help of other members of the Club we were extricated with difficulty and taken off somewhere, hot and exhausted, to refresh ourselves after our adventure with cherries and champagne.

So ended the day of the signature for us. I was as much amused as if I had been a schoolboy at the end of a long and gruelling term, and even Isa, who does not generally like being hustled in crowds, galloped quite willingly with the rest of us. It was a great evening's entertainment.

We were not alone in celebrating the return of peace like schoolchildren set free. All about that part of Paris people were dancing and singing in the streets, dragging about cannons, pushing motor-cars backwards, etc. ; it was a good-humoured carnival—a strange end to the Pentecost of Calamity.

That was on a Saturday. The Monday following, June 30th, the daily round began again at the Hotel Astoria and Balts and Esthonians, Germans and Bolsheviks filled my mind once more. I noted with satisfaction that the German Government had dismissed the famous General Hoffmann from his East Prussian command for declaring that the Germans would never give up their Polish Provinces. This was, I presumed, the General Hoffmann who has since been credited with the plan of the great German victory at Tannenberg for which both Hindenburg and Ludendorff acquired so much glory.

An old friend of mine, Ralph Paget, afterwards British Ambassador to Brazil, who was designated as High Commissioner for the Baltic States, arrived in Paris and we had a long talk over the situation with Mr. Balfour. At the close of this, Ralph asked A. J. B. what his instructions would be. The reply was very characteristic of everything to do with that part of Europe. Said A. J. B.: " I am afraid I can't say anything more than ' Do your best ' " ! I strongly¹advised Ralph Paget not to go unless and until the Allied Governments would give credits to the Baltic States to enable them to buy what was absolutely necessary to carry on. General Gough, who was at Libau, was crying out for half a million pounds in order to carry on at all.

That evening I gave a farewell dinner to the members of the Lettish Delegation, Messrs. Meierovitch and Grossvald. They were somewhat more satisfied with the outlook in their part of the world.

The following day I was informed I was to leave Paris in a week, together with Hardinge and Mallet, Crowe only being left in charge of all. I was frankly delighted. The habit of working all day and never getting anything done was altogether too Sisyphean. I had had little to do with the actual Peace Conference work except the German Polish frontiers, which have been much criticised since by those who have never studied the history, economy and ethnology of those parts. My American counterpart, Professor Lord, and I, basing our conclusions on the admirable statistics of the Prussian census of 1910 relative to the character of the population of that area, were in absolute agreement as to the proper frontier to draw, and I have neither read nor heard anything since which has shaken my views on the subject. The point about which public opinion in Great Britain appears to be most ignorant and most misled is the so-called " Danzig Corridor." Over and over again I have heard highly educated people waxing indignant over what is called " cutting Germany in half," and the injustice to German travellers of having to cross foreign territory in order to reach a Province belonging to their own people.

I should like to remind my compatriots :

First. That the corridor is inhabited in a large majority by Poles, or people nearly akin to Poles, who wish to be attached to Poland and who speak a dialect of Polish.

Second. That it was for hundreds of years an integral part of the Kingdom of Poland until the partitions of that Kingdom between Russia, Prussia and Austria, which began in 1772.

Third. That one seaport at any rate is practically a necessity for Poland, a country with a greater area than Italy and a larger population than Spain.

Fourth. That so far from the " Corridor " forming a danger to Germany in time of war, it is rather the reverse, for it is in reality a hostage in the hands of Germany, and inclines Poland to be a friendly neighbour. As soon as Germany recovered, it seemed to me obvious that this must be the necessary corollary of the establishment of the Corridor.

In time of peace, on the other hand, there was no reason why, with the goodwill on both sides which is beginning to grow up, the Corridor should prove a serious impediment to the flow of commerce between East Prussia and the rest of Germany.

It has naturally taken some time for both Germans and Poles to reach these conclusions, but it almost seems now that they are realising that it is in the best interests of both to make the arrangement work. One thing is sure, and that is that for Germany a friendly Poland is a sheer impossibility so long as Germany bars her access to the sea all along the Baltic coast. This being so I have never —though I admit I may well be wrong, because the

GALLERY OF MIRRORS IN THE PALACE OF VERSAILLES, PREPARED FOR THE SIGNATURE OF PEACE, THE 28TH JUNE, 1919, BETWEEN THE ALLIED AND ASSOCIATED POWERS AND GERMANY

relations between nations are unfortunately not always based on goodwill or even common sense—believed that friendly relations are impossible between Poland and Germany on account of the " Corridor," but rather, if they will both look upon it from the point of view of *Realpolitikers*, that it may become a point of connection between them. The whole crux of the problem lies in the question whether both have sufficient political sense to make it so.

For the rest of my time in Paris, i.e. up to July 9th, work went on much the same as before. I used occasionally to walk in the Avenue du Bois before breakfast, and once or twice met there, and had very interesting walks and talks with, Lord Milner respecting the future development of the British Empire. I found to my satisfaction that, if I remember right, he was much in agreement with Rhodes's views tending towards a loose federation of equal and autonomous States under the Crown. We occasionally watched with pleasure a company of American infantry who paraded there every morning with their band, and an alert, quick little bandmaster who while he was marching went through the most wonderful antics with his band staff. I noted in my diary : " What a clean, quick step these men have, and how they march ! " I much regret that I could not see more of Lord Milner, and I rarely saw him again after Paris.

On July 5th I noted that the British airship R.34 had arrived over Newfoundland. This was, I think, the first time an airship crossed the Atlantic, but the journey was not the success that was expected, because she took 108 hours to reach New York, constantly battling against storms and head-winds.

I assisted at one more scene at the Conference on July 5th which is worth recording.

There was a sitting of the Council of Ten that afternoon at which I was listed to be present as an " expert," one of those who were well described as persons who knew more and more about less and less. My subject, Eastern Galicia, was not due to come up at once, so I stayed in the anteroom of the Council chamber to write up notes. After the sitting had been going on for twenty minutes or so, I heard voices raised apparently in anger through the closed doors, and was surprised to see these flung open, and all the " experts " in the room, Generals, Diplomats, Admirals, Financiers and others come dashing out like frightened sheep. It appeared there had been a great scene in the Council room, with the " Tiger " in his best form.

He suddenly woke up to the fact that there were numerous " experts " in the room and became furious. The Council of Four, he declared, had never wanted so many experts, and he had summoned none to be present. He was still more angry when he heard that there were French experts present, and he turned on poor M. Pichon, the Foreign Minister, for summoning them, and was terribly rude—so I was told—to M. Seydoux, the French economic expert. The end of it was that he drove them all out with lingual whips and scorpions, saying that all they did was to carry gossip about the town. It was no wonder they fled before him, but there came to my mind a saying of Talleyrand's after he had been similarly trounced by Napoleon : " *C'est dommage qu'un si grand homme soit si mal-elevé.*" [1]

I waited outside the closed door till the sitting ended, and then, going in for a cup of tea, found the " Tiger " still growling and snarling at poor M. Pichon, who looked at him mildly through his great round spectacles.

On July 7th my last meeting of the Baltic Commission took place. We settled a letter regarding the Åland Islands, the fate of which was left to be decided by a plebiscite and which ultimately voted for Finland. We also at last decided on a declaration of policy regarding the Baltic States.

We dined for the last time at the Majestic with Mr. (now Sir) Cecil Hurst, legal adviser of the Foreign Office. I had grown very much attached to him during these months in Paris and was sorry to say good-bye.

[1] Translation : " What a pity that such a great man should be so ill-mannered."

The following morning I said good-bye to Mr. Balfour, who was, I noted in the diary, " as kind and cheering as ever and more definite about Russia. He seemed quite in favour of the federal idea and authorised me to say so to Curzon."

We dined for the last time with Carlo Placci and his sister, Madame Henraux. The old Byzantine historian, Professor Schlumberger, and one or two others were at dinner. Comtesse de Cossé-Brissac, a most charming elderly French lady, typical of the intellectuals of the Faubourg, was also there. I noted in my diary " Carlo played Parry's music to my paraphrase of John o'Gaunt's speech which I heard for the first time. It seems a good, ringing melody, but I doubt whether the song will ever be popular."

Isa and I left Paris the following morning and had a perfect crossing, the ship being, as usual, packed with officers and men returning home. We put up with my sister at 32, Charles Street, where we found our " Tiger," my niece Joan, who had begun her work with Eric Drummond for the League of Nations at Sunderland House, which was at that time the head-quarters of the League pending the move to Geneva.

And so ended my experiences of the great Peace Conference of 1919.

CHAPTER XVI

CUMBERLAND HOLIDAYS. FAREWELL TO STOCKHOLM

(1919)

ON arrival in London I went at once to the Foreign Office, but could get no news about Madrid. This was disconcerting, and I wondered whether, perhaps, Mr. Lloyd George, as a consequence of my disagreement with his Prinkipo policy, was thinking it worth while to pay me so much attention as to object to my appointment as Ambassador. This suspicion which, I have now no doubt, was entirely unfounded, for I have no reason to suppose that he ever gave me another thought after the Paris Conference was over, did not, however, trouble me very much. I certainly wanted to go to Madrid, but I was fortunately not worried by any ambition to become an Ambassador and should, indeed, have been quite happy to end my career as Minister at Berne, which suited my tastes and needs perhaps better than any other capital would do.

In any case, for the present I was simply told to keep myself ready for some post, which meant that I could go and spend these school holidays with Isa and the boys in Cumberland, and rest there. Satisfied with this prospect, I looked no further into the future.

All the countries of Europe were in a state of furious unrest, England almost as bad as the others. Everywhere the old order was changing and the economic foundations on which it had been built were crumbling. It was impossible not to feel that the house might fall in about our ears at any time, as it had done in Russia, in Germany and in the Austrian Empire, and threatened to do in Italy. I believed I had done what I could in Paris to prevent this, but apparently without persuading anyone in power to my views as to the necessity of drawing a *cordon sanitaire* round Russia, instead of encouraging civil war in Russia itself, which seemed a hopeless plan from the first. It was one which, in truth, had never finally succeeded at any time anywhere, for the party which relied on foreign support always failed as soon as that support was withdrawn.

So for the moment the prospect of Cumberland with the family and a few weeks of *otium cum* or *sine dignitate* seemed " paradise enow."

Before the school term ended Isa and I went down to Downside Abbey, near Bath, where the four elder boys were at school. I cannot say, looking back on these parental visits to school, whether considered from the point of view of a boy or of a father, which is the more joyful.

This particular visit remains especially pleasant in my memory. It was the first time I had seen the boys at Downside. We stayed at the little guest house in the village, and we spent the evening together until the detestable school bell rang. I particularly disliked the sound of the Harrow School bell, and the Downside one was its first cousin. They represented discipline, and I have all my life only submitted to discipline with a great reluctance, at any rate in the matter of keeping regular hours. Whatever may be said in its favour, it makes life dull.

The following entry in my diary may serve to recall to the memories of the boys what a parental visit to Downside in the year 1919 was like.

" *July 13th, Sunday.*—A very fine morning. After early Mass boys came to breakfast with us at Guest House. Then High Mass in Abbey Church. About five extra guest boys to lunch, after which we went to see lawn tennis tournament and cricket, then tea for sixteen ! Benediction afterwards, and then Fathers Raymond, Lucius and Thomas to dinner.

" Father Trafford (the head master) speaks highly of all

the boys, as indeed do all the masters. Boys seem most happy and keen on work and play.

" Fortunately a very fine day, so that I could realise the beauty of Downside in summer. It is certainly a most attractive school. Boys are simple and natural, and relations between boys and masters most cordial."

To this short notice of Downside I must add a word on the Abbey Church, which is, with the American Episcopal Cathedral at Washington, possibly the most beautiful modern Gothic church I have seen, being a finely proportioned Early English structure of great harmony and simplicity and, like nearly all Benedictine churches, free from the crushing weight of gilded decorations and baroque statuary which has so disfigured many of the grand early churches of Italy and to a lesser degree of Spain. I can only suppose that these plutocratic decorations were a form of reaction promoted by the spirit of the Counter-Reformation against the spirit of severe Protestant " plainness " in church architecture which turned places of worship into " meeting houses," that might just as well have been lecture rooms or even, in the case of Wren (except only as regards St. Paul's) into buildings more suitable for town halls than for the faithful to gather for the worship of God.

The following day, July 14th, we went back to London and called on the Crown Prince and Crown Princess of Sweden at Clarence House. They had both been so kind to us during the War days in Sweden that this visit was far more of a pleasure than a duty. My diary says : " He (the Crown Prince) asked on leaving what I thought about the Kaiser's trial (which was then much discussed in certain circles in England and France). I said I had always strongly objected, and especially to a trial in England. He told me that King George and the Duke of Connaught very much disliked the whole business, which I well understood."

Personally, I must confess that I particularly disliked the proposal, not only because it was intrinsically wrong, but because I was sure that any trial would but turn the

Kaiser into a victim not only in the minds of his own countrymen but also in those of many others, and end in giving him a full measure of that limelight which he dearly loved and certainly did not deserve.

July 19th was the day of the great march past the King at Buckingham Palace of troops of all the Allied and Associated Powers in celebration of our victory.

M. Carlin, the Swiss Minister in London, was in charge of German interests and therefore, of course, of the German Embassy house in Carlton House Terrace, past which all the troops were to march on their way to Buckingham Palace. I asked M. Carlin, whom I knew well, if I might, with Isa and Elsie Carnarvon, see the troops march up the Mall to the Palace from the windows of the Embassy. He readily agreed.

My diary records the event thus :

" About 10 a.m., Elsie, Isa and I went to the German Embassy, Carlton House Terrace. From the corner of the terrace there was a clear view. Found there M. Carlin, Swiss Minister, our host, his daughter, and Count and Countess Wrangel (Swedish Minister and his wife). The march past, headed by Americans under General Pershing, hardly reached the Mall before 11.30. He was well cheered, but the greatest cheers were for Marshals Foch and Haig and the Naval Brigade under Beatty. (I remember particularly noticing, as I had done in Paris, the extraordinary precision and the quick, resilient step of the very athletic-looking Americans.) Of Allies there were, besides French and Americans, about two hundred Italians, and squads of Belgians, Poles, Czechs, Serbs, Greeks, Japanese, Chinese and Siamese, and several squads of women workers, who were much cheered. The morning was fine and not too hot, and everything went off very well. By 2 p.m. it was all over and we walked home to lunch. After lunch, Elsie, Isa and I went to Hyde Park but, beyond enormous crowds, such as I have never seen before, were unable to see anything. In the evening it rained but did not prevent fireworks in Hyde Park being very fine. I only saw one drunken man all

2 C

the day—*Mirabile dictu.* This is a real change for the better."

The next day we three motored down in the afternoon to tea at Lancy Hugh Smith's delightful house and garden, Mount Clare, Roehampton, with its view over Richmond Park—the pleasantest place in the neighbourhood of London that I know. "Isa and I tried to walk back to Charles Street through Kensington Gardens, but could not get into the Gardens which had been turned into a huge camp for the soldiers who marched past yesterday. We walked through Hyde Park, however, which was covered with a litter of paper left by the crowds on the previous day and looked horrible. I was truly ashamed that all the foreign soldiers and guests assembled for the march past should see it in this state."

After a few more days in London waiting for the boys to come from school at the end of the term, during which I at least heard that my appointment to Madrid had been approved by the Prime Minister, we all left, the last day of July, for Lyulph's Tower, on Ullswater, which my sister-in-law, Mabel, had most kindly lent us for the holidays.

Riots, strikes, civil wars and fighting of all kinds were in full swing all over Europe, and political pressure on the Government was even threatened by means of a coal strike, the first time I think that this had ever been proposed in England. There were the great riots in Liverpool, during which about £200,000 damage was said to have been done. Though this was all very unpleasant, it did not seem to foreshadow anything like a genuine revolution. I wrote : " I do not believe in Bolshevism in this country any more than in Germany, though we may have some *mauvais quarts d'heure* in the big towns. Everything seems so peaceful here in the country," i.e. on Ullswater. Cumberland was, indeed, a refreshing change. The fells round Ullswater, which I knew so well, always reminded me of a favourite couplet of Wordsworth :

> The silence that is in the starry sky,
> The sleep that is among the lonely hills.

On August 4th I noted : " Five years since War was declared. This period seems still unreal and it is impossible to believe all that has happened, though I have seen the devastated areas in France and been to Paris during the Peace negotiations."

A Police strike had also been declared in London, and though the Police Union ordered out all their men, only three hundred out of twenty thousand came out.

Denikin took Poltava, where Charles XII was finally defeated in Russia. Bela Khun's Bolshevik Government in Budapest was overturned and replaced by a moderate Socialist administration, and the usual futile searchings for the door of the Temple of Universal Peace continued in Paris.

What did all this matter to me now, however ? I was with Isa and the boys with the peace that is among the lonely hills, and I wanted nothing more.

I walked over the fells with the two elder boys and renewed my acquaintance with them.

At the back of Lyulph's Tower was Gowbarrow Fell, now fortunately the property of the National Trust, which, with Glencoyn, also a part of the Greystoke Estate, had been declared a deer forest in the time of William Rufus. Here Esmetto and Francis and I would go to stalk those red deer—without rifles, of course—just to see how near we could get to them and watch the flight of the buzzards that nested in one of the plantations. We walked over High Street to look at Haweswater from above on a glorious day of high wind, sun and racing clouds, lights and shadows. "We lunched on the Fell top and had an excellent tea when we got down at Howtown Hotel, which tasted as good as when I was a boy. Got back to the Tower in time for dinner after a hard pull against the wind."

The next day the diary says : " In the evening climbed, with Isa and all the boys, up Yew Crag (a very small matter, it must be confessed), which Isa did not like at all. Henry (aged six) was wonderful. He is tremendously strong and quite undefeated."

On August 8th the diary says : " Glorious day again, but our water supply threatening to give out. This always happens in Cumberland after a few weeks of fine weather. However, as long as the weather is hot, boys can all bathe in the lake. Metto and Francis swim well, Bimbo (Hubert) just learnt last term, Mondi and Henry do their best to learn. They make a splendid picture in the lake."

The bathing place was close to the spot where Wordsworth wrote his poem on the daffodils :

> Beside a lake beneath the trees
> Fluttering and dancing with the breeze."

There are still some wild daffodils not far off, though I fear those of the poem have joined the asphodels on the Homeric meadows of the dead.

" A fine picture " (I wrote in the diary) " I should like to have painted by Peter de Hoogh for choice (anachronistically) of the family party at breakfast with the brown panelling on the terra-cotta walls, the deer, elk and antelope horns, the old oak table with the blue-and-white china, the eighteenth century chairs and the boys and Isa."

I cannot refrain here from saying a few words about Lyulph's Tower, which from that time became the regular summer haunt of our family group and is, therefore, full of the happiest memories for me and all of us.

It was built as it now stands by Charles, eleventh Duke of Norfolk, about 1770. I at least date it (this is my own guess) from an old empty black bottle bearing the date 1772, which has stood on the mantelpiece of the dining-room from the earliest time I can remember. Whether the bottle was emptied to celebrate the first house-warming or some other event of importance in the eyes of the old Jockey of Norfolk it is now impossible to say, but, judging by the records we have of his habits and those of his times, it is very characteristic that that old black bottle should have continued for over a hundred years to preside over the dining-room of a house so intimately connected with him.

As will be seen from the illustrations of the Tower here given, it was built in the sham Gothic style of " Strawberry Hill Gothic," beloved at that time, and especially by the Jockey, and has no architectural merit except that of surpassing quaintness. Wordsworth thought little of it, and having been taken in by it when reflected in the lake and thought it was a fairy castle, dismissed it with a contemptuous gesture in his guide to the lakes as a mere " pleasure house."

No, Mr. Wordsworth, it was never that, though it has afforded much pleasure to many who have lived in it. It was built for something which some may think higher and some lower in the social scale, a shooting-box for the parties of the Jockey when he came over for stalking or grouse shooting from Greystoke, and we may surmise for the emptying of many black bottles like the one that still stands on the mantelpiece.

Besides the exceptional beauty of the site on the hill-side above Ullswater, which Wordsworth calls the noblest of the lakes, looking up towards Helvellyn to the west, down towards High Street to the east, and across towards the steep screes of Place Fell, where ravens and buzzards, peregrines and kestrels still nest, we all loved the curious old house despite of, and perhaps because of, its lack of modern conveniences. Only Isa, who ran the household, bewailed the fact at times that we were about twelve miles from our nearest shopping centre, Penrith, and over three from a telephone and telegraph. I was frankly delighted to be out of reach of a telephone.

On the 18th August, after taking the two elder boys to try for a grouse on one of the small mosses under Saddleback, I got a telegram from the Foreign Office telling me to hold myself in readiness to be sworn of the Privy Council. This was the first notification I had that my appointment as Ambassador had been approved by the King. Had the boys only bagged two or three grouse this would, therefore, have been a red-letter day, but it was a wretched year for grouse, and nothing was to be seen but old birds and these very wild, so they hardly got a shot and were much disappointed.

About this time a striking memorandum was published from the pen of Mr. Hoover, stating that only the most rapid return to normal conditions could save Europe, because the United States could not go on providing raw materials on credit indefinitely.

My sister Elsie joined our family party, to the great joy of us all, for she had badly needed a rest after her work, first in Alexandria during the War looking after wounded soldiers and since that in London. For a woman of her age her activity was amazing.

Diary on August 15th. "The poor Council of Four or Five at Paris is much exercised over the action of the Roumanians in occupying Budapest on the fall of the Soviet Government there and over the assumption of Provisional Government by the Archduke Joseph. But I think that in all things it will not control the events but merely waddle ungracefully after them."

On the 17th August, at eleven o'clock, there was a meeting of the Privy Council, to which I had been commanded in order to be sworn in. The other new Councillors were Lytton, Peel and Ralph Paget. Curzon, as Lord President of the Council, presided. What lent the whole ceremony some solemnity was the presence of the King. Otherwise there was nothing impressive about it. In a small room on the ground floor, looking out into the courtyard of the Palace, all dressed in black coats we, the new Councillors, awaited our turn while Curzon and Sir Almeric Fitzroy went through some conventional ritual or other relating, I suppose, to the Royal Assent being rapidly given to Bills which had passed Parliament. Then, having been supplied with cushions to kneel on and small Prayer Books, we were told to kneel down and hold our Prayer Books aloft. After we were on our knees I heard Ralph Paget whisper that he had no Prayer Book and ask what he was to do about it. I replied I had no idea, but seeing the eye of

the King fixed upon us wondering no doubt what the whispering meant, I hastily suggested that he should catch hold of mine. I held it aloft between us, and Ralph caught hold of it like a drowning man at a straw, with Curzon gazing sternly and the King still wonderingly at this unusual procedure. Meanwhile, Fitzroy had begun to read the oath aloud, which we had only to follow mentally, afterwards signing our names at the table. No one made any remark about one Testament being used by two Councillors, so I presume we had been quite legally sworn in. As neither of us has ever been asked to attend a Council[1] since, it would not presumably have mattered much if there had been some trifling irregularity. The scene, however, stamped itself on my mind because of the difficulty of keeping my physical balance on my knees with Ralph Paget over a yard away clinging on to the same Prayer Book.

The days passed quickly enough at Lyulph's Tower. Bicycling with the four older boys all over the country, walking over some of our little Cumberland moors with the two elder ones, trying to get a grouse or a duck for the pot, and watching birds of all kinds. One day we watched five buzzards going through extraordinary flying evolutions over the lake, rising in spirals to a great height and dropping suddenly head first. I dare say this may be a common occurrence, but I have never seen anything like it before or since.

We went to the Grasmere sports and the Patterdale sports, being entertained by that most hospitable of hosts and kindly of men, Lonsdale.[2] It is grievous to think that Lowther, following the example of nearly every other great Cumberland house, is to be shut up, and that henceforth he will live in the south of England. I have always looked on him as being fully as much a part of the Cumberland scene as Helvellyn or Saddleback, and the Grasmere and Patterdale sports without him will

---

[1] We were however summoned with all Privy Councillors to attend the first Council of the Reign of King Edward VIII, an historic occasion.

[2] Hugh, Earl of Lonsdale, the famous sportsman.

be like the play of *Hamlet* without the Prince of Denmark. The Patterdale sheepdog trials on a fine day are especially delightful. Nowhere are the surroundings more lovely or typical of Lakeland, and there were yet no great crowds there. The boys were especially delighted with one fierce old sheep which turned on the dog that was trying to herd him into the pen, and drove him off the field.

In Russia the Bolsheviks were faring badly for the moment about this time. Denikin captured Odessa, British motor-boats sank some of the largest Russian battleships in the Black Sea and practically cleared that water of the Bolshevik fleet, and Petlura, the Ukrainian general who had besieged Lemberg when I was in Poland, now turned his attention to Kiev, which we expected to fall daily. I retained a mild interest in these events, though the defeat of the sheepdog by the old sheep at Patterdale was almost more thrilling now. Ludendorff's " Memoirs," which were being serialised by *The Times*, I found enthralling.

Towards the end of the month the whole of our party went to stay at Kinharvie,[1] a visit memorable for the fact that though no less than six schoolboys, my own two included, were out grouse driving that day, it was an adult gun which shot poor Bernard Norfolk just below the left eye. There was naturally great alarm, though both he and his mother were quite calm. A surgeon from Dumfries extracted the shot the same evening, to the great relief of all. He said that had it penetrated one-hundredth of an inch farther the eye must have been lost—a merciful escape.

On August 30th we got the news of the death of General Botha, which truly grieved me, for I felt he would be a great loss not only to South Africa but also to the Empire and the world. He was a fine, great-hearted man, and in the short time he was in Paris he made himself an extraordinary position, being trusted and respected by all for his honest, straightforward and simple character. I felt him to be an eminently loveable personality.

[1]Dumfries-shire estate belonging to the Duchess of Norfolk.

After a few more happy days at the Tower my holidays came to an end, and I had to prepare to go over to Sweden to present my Letters of Recall to King Gustav, say good-bye to many friends, and pack up our belongings, which had been left at the Legation. I travelled over with the American Minister, Mr. Ira Nelson Morris, who had been at Stockholm all through the War, and we had naturally many experiences to talk over, which made the hours pass quickly and pleasantly. We sailed from Tilbury to Gothenburg on September 12th. On the fourteenth we came in sight of the Danish coast and saw a number of floating mines in the course of the day. We amused ourselves by keeping a sharp look out for these, and then running aft to watch the ship's officers shoot at the mines to make them explode. They never appeared to hit one, but it added to the excitement of the voyage and kept alive memories of the War.

We reached Gothenburg at seven, being met by the British Consul-General (Mr. Grove), and the Chaplain (Mr. Baldwin), who had sometimes taken charge of the Consulate-General. Leaving the same night at 10 p.m., we arrived at Stockholm at 7.30 the following morning, and were met by the Chargé d'Affaires (Mr. Patrick Ramsay) and all his staff. It was noble of them to turn out at such an hour.

I spent the hours up to my departure on October 2nd very busy between packing and eating, for farewell dinners and luncheons were the order of the day.

On Sunday the 21st I spent the day with my old friends the Alwyne Maudes. He had run a hospital of his own, first on the Franco-Belgian frontier, and had his place badly bombed, and later for the refugee Serbs in Corfu, so had much to tell me.

On the twenty-second I presented my Letters of Recall to the King of Sweden who, despite my having had to do very disagreeable things during the blockade times, was most affable, and spoke at length about the Åland Island question, which greatly exercised the Swedish mind at that time. We had at Paris settled that the inhabitants should decide by a plebiscite whether they were to belong to Sweden or Finland, and I could naturally not say more than that.

A big dinner was given to me at Hasslebacken, the famous restaurant in the Djürgården Park, by twenty friends, including Herren Branting and Knut Wallenburg, Baron Adelsward, Herr Axel Johnson, Alwyne Maude and others, who presented me with a gold plaque with views of Stockholm.

The Crown Prince and Crown Princess also most kindly gave me a farewell dinner, at which Herr Branting was present for the first time, I was told, at a Palace dinner. I was truly sorry to say good-bye to the Crown Prince and Crown Princess, who had shown the greatest kindness to Isa and me and to all the boys.

The next day I went to Björno, on the Nostelje Fjord, to say good-bye to Axel de Bildt and his family. He and I had gone through stormy times together over the Transito Company, but " Transito " was now passing into oblivion, and Bildt's eldest daughter Beatrice, a charming girl, was there with her fiancé, Stig Hasselrodt. This was like a Montagu-Capulet marriage, for old Mr. Hasselrodt was a faithful follower of Mr. Hammerskjöld, and was therefore a great supporter of neutral rights to make money by complete freedom of trade in time of war.

It was a glorious autumn day with brilliant sun, clear blue sky and the leaves all colours. In that dress Sweden looked its best and could compare with any country in the world.

Just at this time the general railway strike which had broken out in England and Scotland overshadowed all the other news in the Swedish press. It was looked on as a kind of test. If it was settled quietly Scandinavians believed that Europe could settle down peacefully, and that unrest would decline. If, on the other hand, it led, as it might have done, to lack of food in the towns and consequent riots and civil war it was felt impossible to foresee what the end would be in any country in Europe.

I was asked to a farewell lunch at the Palace by the

King of Sweden, who was very friendly and offered me a Swedish decoration, which I declined on account of our instructions against accepting foreign orders. He then asked if I would like his photograph, which I was truly glad to take home with me, as it seemed to me to be the outward and visible sign that His Majesty bore me no ill-will for the part I was obliged to play during the War years. I went away, therefore, feeling that all the disagreeable time was dead and buried, and that it would leave no aftermath of ill-feeling between our two countries. I believe that it may truly be said that this is so.

On October 2nd I left for Gothenburg, a number of people being at the station to say good-bye, even the Minister for Foreign Affairs, which was decidedly unusual, and again gave me the satisfaction of feeling that bitterness of any kind was past. In the gift of being able to forget past injuries or supposed injuries, the gods have given the Scandinavians and the English a treasure of extraordinary value, which is sometimes miscontrued by other people as weakness, but is really a pillar of strength. We cannot see any use in storing up ancient grudges.

I cannot close my account of Stockholm without mentioning three friends to whom it gave me real regret to say good-bye. These were Strandberg, the head Chancery messenger, who also acted on great occasions as my butler, and was invaluable ; and old Frida Andersen, the housekeeper of the Legation, who took every new Minister under her parental wing, and was beloved by all. Finally, there was M. Philippe, an old Belgian workman and a very devout Catholic, whom some of my household first met in church and used on Sundays to bring to the house for a good meal because he deprived himself of everything to send supplies and money back to Belgium. M. Philippe suffered deeply from the martyrdom of his country, and in his own quiet and humble way was, indeed, more ready to make far greater personal sacrifices for it than the most flamboyant jingo orators would perhaps have cared to make. Yet he never spoke with bitterness of the men who were trampling his country underfoot. M. Philippe in all that ghastly time maintained a serenity that is the special mark of the real saint. His example was of the greatest support to me in those days, and I was truly glad to see him once more before leaving Sweden. Soon after he returned to Belgium and entered an almshouse, from which he occasionally wrote to Esmetto, who was a particular friend of his, and also to me. Then, some time about 1926, the letters ceased, and we knew that M. Philippe had received his reward.

At Gothenburg I stayed in the house of a great collector of works of art, Mr. Conrad Pinsens. There was a lunch at the British Factory, as the British Chamber of Commerce had been called in Scandinavia and the former Hansa cities for centuries, with inevitable speeches afterwards, and a big farewell dinner to special friends at Mr. Pinsens' house.

And so the Swedish act of the drama of life closed for me on a note of kindliness which has a very pleasant savour in my memory.

CHAPTER XVII

SPAIN

(1919–1924)

" How sayest thou so ? " quoth Don Quixote. " Dost thou not hear the horses neigh, the trumpets sound and the noise of drum ? "
" I hear nothing else," said Sancho, " but the great bleating of many sheep."

The History of Don Quixote (chapter IV),

JUST before leaving Gothenburg we received information by wireless that the General Railway Strike had begun in England, and that no accommodation could be had in Newcastle, for which port our ship sailing from Gothenburg was bound. This was a cheerful prospect, but there was no use in putting off departure. It was fortunate I did not do so, for we had a splendid passage and saw this time only two floating mines in the North Sea.

We arrived at Newcastle early in the morning, to find the railway strike settled (without any political capitulations), reached the railway station in time to catch the first train to London about 1 p.m., and arrived at 32, Charles Street, about 9 p.m.

Next morning I reported at once to the Foreign Office, delivered the sealed bag with dispatches which I carried from Stockholm, and inquired when I should be expected to take up my appointment at Madrid. I was told that Sir Arthur Hardinge, my predecessor, was not anxious to leave before the middle of November, and that I should have to wait till then. This I was not sorry to do, as it would give Isa and me time to visit our relations in Rome.

On October 9th I was summoned to Buckingham Palace

and kissed hands on my appointment as Ambassador to Madrid. I noted in the diary which I still kept that His Majesty was much pleased at the conclusion of the railway strike without disorders and at the excellent organisation for revictualling London and other big towns which had been prepared well beforehand by the Government in case of a general railway strike.

The organisation was indeed most remarkable, and from the first day London was well supplied with everything, including milk. Necessary railway communications were kept moving with the help of voluntary assistance, even the older boys from the great public schools being called upon to serve as porters, etc. In this way Esmetto and Francis rendered their first service to the State, being accepted from Downside for work on the London and South-Western line, and stationed in London.

There can be no doubt that this prevision on the part of the Government saved us from a situation which might otherwise have been desperate.

It was also a very encouraging sign that though the strike lasted a whole week no disorders or sabotage to speak of occurred.

Bolsheviks all over Europe were full of hopes that this strike would be the first move towards a Communist revolution in England. There can be no doubt whatever that the determined opposition of the great mass of the English people to Bolshevism, made evident by the failure of this strike, raised all over Europe the courage of the friends of the British system of Government based on liberty combined with order, and correspondingly discouraged the votaries of the Marxist economic theories combined with the dictatorship of the proletariat. In this sense the failure of that strike was perhaps decisive not only in England but far beyond her frontiers, and the King was certainly more than justified in his satisfaction over the result.

After going to Downside to see our schoolboys once more before leaving for Rome, Isa, Henry and I, with Alda Berselli, Isa's maid and our faithful companion and support for so many years, left for Rome, where we arrived on November 2nd, putting up as usual with my kind brother-in-law and sister-in-law, Count and Countess Colleoni, at their Villino in Via delle Tre Madonne. Here nothing marred the even tenor of our ways.

On the following Sunday there was a General Election in Italy under a new system of voting—the *scrutin de liste* combined with proportional representation. The day passed very quietly in Rome.

November 17th was the anniversary of Isa's and my marriage twenty-one years ago. After Mass I took Henry up into the ball of St. Peter's dome, and in the afternoon, in memory of our honeymoon drive along the Appian Way, we took Carolina Colleoni and Henry for a drive along the same old Roman road. The day was, as then, a warm autumn day with the wonderful light of October shining through the misty vapours of the Campagna. The Campagna then still retained the old charm of loneliness almost up to the walls of the city, it was untouched by modern improvements and the hand of the builder. No one who sees it now for the first time, dotted over as it is with small villas and modern farms, can realise the extraordinary fascination it exercised in those days on the minds of those who came from countries which had been sacrificed in great part to the ruthless demands of industrial development.

The following day, having settled to go to Spain by sea in order to avoid the discomforts of railway travel, which in those days immediately after the War were considerable, I left for Genoa, where I met the nucleus of my domestic staff for the Embassy at Madrid : Alda, of course, and Virginio Lissi, our excellent Milanese cook who, with his good wife, had followed our fortunes ever since Berne, and Fioravanti dell' Agnese, who was shortly to be the head of the male staff of the Embassy. He was, indeed, a pillar of support. A young man of remarkable distinction of carriage and good looks, and about six feet two inches in height, he was also endowed with unusual intelligence and education that in other times should have given him a far higher place in life.   His father was an Italian married to an Austrian, and was employed by an Italian firm engaged on railway construction in Bulgaria, where he was brought up.   He thus acquired as a child three languages of totally different families—one Latin, one Teutonic, and one Slav.   He had used his linguistic facility to such good purpose that he spoke, when he came to me, not only the above-mentioned languages, but also French and Russian and some Swedish, and while with me he learnt to speak Spanish and, naturally, English fluently.   In addition to this, he was one of the most conscientious and hardworking men I ever met, with the manners of a grandee of Spain.

With Isa to run the house and such a household to back me, I felt I could face, socially, the rigour of any Embassy, and I hoped that the diplomatic work of Madrid would not be above my capacity to deal with.

I therefore embarked with all my traps in a happy frame of mind and with confidence in the future on board the s.s. *Teresa Tayà*, a small Spanish steamer, for Barcelona in the evening of November 20th.   The *Teresa Tayà* was not an attractive vessel.   Small and not overclean, her engines were in such poor condition that for no particular reason she was more than twenty-four hours late on a short Mediterranean voyage.

The following day, a strong northerly wind having got up, the captain of the *Teresa Tayà*, who wisely would not trust her to face heavy weather, anchored for the night in the roadstead at Hyeres.   He refused to move out of the safe anchorage till 10 a.m., though the sea had gone down so much that at 2 p.m., off Marseilles, there was a dead calm.   The sea got up again towards evening and the poor old *Teresa Tayà* creaked and groaned to such an extent that I believed she would break in two.   She made hardly any way at all.   At daybreak we were still off the French coast, but we were compensated for the discomfort of the journey by the lovely views of the Pyrenees off the Bay of Rosa and of the fine bold coast of Catalonia.   I especially remember an extraordinary sunset, the like of which I never saw before or since. The entire Western sky was of a pure and limpid violet darkening to deep purple where sea and sky met and, both being fused into one, it was impossible to say where sky ended and water began. It was well worth a cruise on the *Teresa Tayà*.

We landed at Barcelona at 9 p.m., and were much helped by our own Consul, Mr. A. Rowley, who found us rooms. There would, without his help, have been considerable difficulty about finding even beds, for there was a strike of waiters on in the town and most hotels were temporarily closed. Such were the common occurrences of travel at that time. Railway and steamer services were disorganised, both railway rolling stock and ships' engines not having been renewed or overhauled for about six years. After arriving a day or two late, it was more than probable that a traveller would find a strike of some sort at his journey's end that precluded him from getting a bed.

Despite the violet sunset, after my experience on the *Teresa Tayà* I decided that I would give up my old habit of taking the first steamer available without inquiries as to her comfort and safety.

I arrived in Madrid the morning of November 25th, and found the house practically without bedroom furniture in the bedrooms, as the new furniture promised by the Office of Works had not yet arrived. There was, however, enough for one bedroom and I decided to move in as soon as possible.

My nephew, Mervyn Herbert, was a Second Secretary at the Madrid Embassy which, as he had innumerable friends among the Spaniards and spoke Spanish fluently, was both useful and delightful for me. He and Sir Arthur Hardinge met me at the station and took me to the Ritz Hotel, where I stayed until two of the rooms of the Embassy were ready to receive me.

News from Eastern Europe that greeted me in Spain was not reassuring. The Bolsheviks in Russia were gaining ground on all fronts. They had taken Omsk, in

2 D

Siberia, from Kolchak; Kiev, from Denikin; and Yarburg from Jedenitch, thus apparently confirming my fear that owing to lack of support from the peasantry the "White" Russians were doomed to failure. Now that Trotsky had created a formidable machine in the Red Army, the Whites with the peasantry in passive opposition had practically no chance at all.

In Italy the Socialists had won one hundred and fifty seats at the recent elections, not having expected more than one hundred and twenty, while in France the Nationalists had an overwhelming success.

I was so busy getting the house in order during the first few days that I had little time to look about me in Madrid, the first impressions of which were confined to the great central avenue, the Castellana, and the neighbouring streets. At first sight Madrid struck me as a modern city of fine, wide streets, well-built houses and all surprisingly clean. The autumn days were clear and sunny and the air crisp and invigorating. My former recollections of the place, dating from 1891, were amply confirmed.

One night I dined with the Arthur Hardinges. His table talk was as brilliant as ever. At his best, he was as good a conversationalist as any I have ever met. A great scholar (he was a Fellow of All Souls) he was the least pedantic of men, and in the Foreign Office his complete disregard for clothes was a standing jest. A story was told about him in the Office that having as a young man been summoned into the presence of the Secretary of State, he was found hastily sewing a trouser button with a shoelace on to the front of his frock coat from which all buttons of any kind had long since disappeared. He was a master of all the principal modern languages, and knew well the literature of France, Germany, Italy, Spain and Portugal besides that of Persia. Latin and Greek he was equally at home with.

With all this no one could be less "highbrow." There was nothing of that sort about "the Professor," as he was called in the Service. A most unconventional, interesting and delightful companion, he yet left little behind by which he will be remembered in after years.

In a few words at dinner that night he sketched to me the political situation in Spain. I gathered more from him in this way, half by historical parallels, half by amusing anecdotes of living personages from the King of Spain downwards, as well as by a review of recent important facts presented in a masterly way, than I could have done by hours of study of Blue Books.

He gave me a graphic description of the power of the military *Juntas*, a kind of military trades union which, I was soon to learn obliged everyone in the State to dance to the tune they piped.

Two days later, indeed, there was a Ministerial crisis produced by the dictatorship—for it was little else—of these *Juntas*. I understood little of what was occurring at the time, but it appeared that the *Juntas* had taken it upon themselves to tell the Minister of War to dismiss twenty-three officers who were not *personæ gratæ* to them. The Minister of War promptly resigned and all the Government went with him. This was my first experience of Spanish politics. But no one seemed greatly interested.

Spanish politics appeared to be pursued in a spirit of amicable pleasantry which was more in keeping with the tradition of Sancho Panza than of Don Quixote, especially as the crisis ended happily two days later and all the Ministers remained at their posts. What happened to the unhappy twenty-three officers who had offended the *Juntas* I do not remember, but I am certain that the *Juntas* did not retire from the field without some *quid pro quo*.

About a week later, Arthur Hardinge having departed, I was received at the Palace by the King to present my credentials. This was a truly wonderful show, like all the great ceremonies at the Court of Madrid. As it is now a thing of the past and may never recur, it is worth a short description.

Three magnificent eighteenth century coaches, all of carved gilt and lacquer panels and great glass windows,

of the time of Louis XIV, on whose Court functions all
those of Madrid up to the revolution of April, 1931, were
modelled, drawn by six horses with plumes and harness
to match, were always sent to fetch a new Ambassador
to the Palace. Postillions were on the leading horses,
a coachman of vast girth sat on the box of each *carosse*
(the word coach seems hardly magnificent enough to
express the grandeur of these vehicles) and footmen
walked on either side all in eighteenth century royal
liveries, wigs and cocked hats. A mounted escort of
guards rode behind and a guard of honour awaited us
in the courtyard of the Palace.

For the first time I was really glad to be wearing my
gold-laced Ambassador's uniform so as not to appear a
complete minnow among these sartorial tritons. I must
admit that I was enjoying this, to me, novel mode of
progression. The introducer of Ambassadors, the Conde
de Velle, presumably seeing my satisfaction, asked me :
" What do you feel like now ? " As he was a Spaniard
and, like all Spaniards, had a sense of humour, I hazarded
the reply : " I feel as if I ought to be stuffed and put
in a museum."

In the Throne Room, a long room full of sun, were
numbers of Grandees of Spain, Court functionaries,
Generals, Ministers, etc., all in their various uniforms.
These were grouped on either side of the King, who was
seated on a throne set on a dais some steps up. I was
expected to bow three times as I walked up the room,
and the Conde de Velle kindly gave me a dig in the ribs
to remind me of this duty each time I got to the proper
spot.

Arrived in front of the King, after another bow I read
my speech containing the usual platitudes suitable for
such occasions. The speech having been previously
communicated to the Palace, His Majesty, always seated
upon the throne, replied in words which were also
appropriate to the occasion.

The solemn part of the ceremony having been now
accomplished, he came down the steps and with that

particular grace of which he was a past master he greeted me in the friendliest way and remained talking for some minutes without a touch of the grand manner that he knew so well how to assume when the occasion required. As soon as the ritual of a ceremony was ended no one knew better how to throw off the grand manner and become a human being. This was undoubtedly the secret of the charm which he possessed, especially for those who met him for the first time.

The King then shook hands with members of the Embassy staff who had accompanied me, and we returned " well pleased " to have been translated to a Pepysian atmosphere which, indeed, was perhaps more truly Pepysian than I quite realised at the time.

After this ceremony I realised that for better, for worse I had been moved up from the pit to the stalls in the Theatre of Life, and I felt far from sure that the change would be pleasant. It would, in any case, require a greater sense of decorum on my part for the future.

Isa, with my sister, Elsie Carnarvon, the four school-boys, and Henry arrived safely for Christmas on December 21st, and our family party was complete.

The record of public events in Spain for the remainder of the year was one of continued political unrest, especially in Catalonia, where political Home Rule propaganda continued with labour troubles to charge the situation with electricity.

Thus, while the National Confederation of Labour on December 1st announced a meeting to arrange for concerted action against employers of labour, Senor Graupere, Chief of the Masters' Federation, had an interview with the King of Spain at the same time, and let people know that His Majesty had said that he sympathised entirely with the employers and promised his support for measures taken to stop the then existing industrial unrest.

On December 8th trouble again arose between the Government and the *Juntas Militares*, and it seemed that the long-drawn-out struggle was coming to a head, but the Army was itself divided, as the Artillery and Engineers

Juntas did not support that of the Infantry over the question of the dismissal of the twenty-three officers. Arthur Hardinge told me just before he left on December 5th, that he had learnt that the King had asked General Primo de Rivera to form a military Government, but that the latter had declined. In view of the military dictatorship set up later by the General this piece of information became interesting at that time.

The remainder of the month of December was filled with squalls of the same kind, and strikes and Government crises followed each other with wearisome iteration, while, except for the bad feeling engendered between employers and employed, no one seemed for the moment to be a penny the worse.

I thought, however, that at the close of the year I would give an account of my first impressions of the state of Spain for what they might be worth after so short a sojourn in the country.

Judging from accounts in the press of different shades of opinion, I wrote to the Foreign Office that Spain seemed at the beginning of 1920 to be on the verge of a very dangerous crisis, which was to be attributed to three principal factors.

First.—General labour unrest, which was then almost universal all over the world and especially serious in countries where political conditions were not especially stable.

Second.—Action of officers of the Army (*Juntas Militares*) working on the Spanish Government to attain their own ends.

Third.—General dissatisfaction with the administration of the Government owing to instability of the latter in consequence of the failure of the Parliamentary system to work so as to give security of tenure to any Government for a reasonable time.

Each of these factors was separate from the other, but they were all interconnected though the connection was often difficult to trace.

As regards the first, not a day had passed since my
arrival without the front page of the papers being dedicated
to strikes, lock-outs and acts of violence arising from
them. There seemed little hope of the country settling
down quietly. The Federation of Employers openly
declared that they were out to break the tyranny of the
Syndicalists, while the latter declared equally openly
that they would not rest until they had " liquidated " the
bourgeoisie and established pure Communism.

It was difficult to say whether these various strikes
were concerted or sporadic. They did not, as a rule,
last long. Here and there public bodies, such as the
Federation of Householders, in Madrid, and the *Man-
comunidad* (Catalan Home Rule Association) of Barcelona,
endeavoured to settle such disturbances to business by
acting as mediators.

Taking it all in all, it seemed to me that the labour
situation in Spain was as serious, if not more serious,
than in any other Western European country.

The second factor of unrest was undoubtedly the
political power of the Military *Juntas*.

When these came to life again in 1917, after a period
of quiescence, they busied themselves mainly with alleged
military grievances, but in 1919, when I wrote, they were
actually supported by numbers of civilians who were
disgusted by Parliamentary Government in Spain. This
gave the *Juntas* a power in the country which they would
not otherwise have possessed, though the Liberal element
in the country was naturally quite averse to anything like
a military dictatorship.

It was rumoured that the King of Spain was chary of
opposing the *Juntas*, and that if he had given wholehearted support to certain Governments when these were
attacked by the *Juntas* and resigned from office, they
need not have done so. Even if this was not the fact,
it was widely believed in Parliamentary circles. Liberals
believed that General Villalba, the Minister for War,
at the end of 1919 was preparing to dissolve the *Juntas*,
but they thought it unlikely that he would dare to do so

in face of the opposition of the extreme Right, who looked on the *Juntas* as bulwarks of social order, and of the King, who feared to touch them, though he had asked General Primo de Rivera to form a Ministry and it was known that the General was opposed to the *Juntas*.

As a parenthesis to this résumé of the situation in 1919, it may be noted that when General Primo de Rivera did seize the reins of power in 1923, one of the first things he did was to dissolve the *Juntas*, no doubt with the approval of the King.

It was a puzzle, I confess, to me at the time and one of those paradoxes that were always cropping up in Spanish politics, that Señor Lerroux, the Republican leader, in an interview with *El Liberal*, the great Barcelona paper, went so far as to say that the Army was the body which possessed the greatest prestige throughout the country, due to its " virtues, its activities, its moral courage, and not due to force," and should, therefore, " be honoured and would itself honour whatever the superior authorities might ordain. The maintenance and strengthening of the Army is a matter which interests all those who sincerely love their country, but that which cannot be done is to make use of its name for political considerations. The Army is the guardian of national honour."

Was this, I asked myself, a bid for the support of the Army by Señor Lerroux ? And did it confirm the report of an understanding between the Republican leaders and certain of the *Juntas* ? This would account for much of the King's unwillingness to offend the latter.

The third factor of unrest was the general dissatisfaction of all parties with the working of Parliamentary institutions in Spain. It was hardly possible to read a paper of any colour without coming across references to this. Thus, the *Heraldo de Madrid* (Liberal) stated as proof of this incompetence of the *Cortes* (Parliament) that owing to frequent Ministerial crises the Chamber in 1917 only had twenty-two sessions. In 1919 the old Chamber met only twenty times.

In fact, since the disappearance of the " rotatory system," by which the Conservative and Liberal parties had arranged by means of a convenient pact to take Government in turns at almost regular intervals, Spain had fallen a victim to the fate common in all Latin countries blessed with the English system of Parliamentary Government, and was split into various factions which made Government by party majority vote impossible.

The old Parliamentarians had no idea what to advise in order to create stability. The Extreme Right prescribed a military Government, while the Extreme Left wished to adopt the Dictatorship of the Proletariat and the Soviet system. All that could be said was that Parliamentary Government as we understand it in England was becoming more and more discredited, and this naturally encouraged revolution in one sense or the other.

I ended my report as follows :

> It seems impossible that the present state of things can continue much longer, and, though one hesitates to prophesy, it may be inferred that unless a stable and well-ordered Government be set up, very serious consequences may before long be expected in this country.

The New Year, 1920, began with a fresh surprise sprung upon the Spanish public by the inevitable *Juntas* in the shape of a Royal Decree giving them official recognition in terms demanded or even practically dictated by them. At the same time the Prime Minister refused permission for presentation in the Senate of a Bill sponsored by General Ochado for the reinstatement of the twenty-three officers who had been dismissed from the Army under pressure from the *Juntas*. The Prime Minister stated in the Senate that he hoped that General Ochado would withdraw the Bill so as to save him from having to refuse permission to bring it forward.

He agreed with the General's view that the Officers' *Juntas* ought, like those of the Sergeants shortly before, to be dissolved, but that he could not do so because the remedy would be worse than the disease.

By this speech the Prime Minister admitted publicly that the Spanish Government dared not take the steps it believed to be necessary in order to shake off the yoke of these Officers' Trade Unions which often paralysed its usefulness and rendered it impotent.

A short time afterwards our Military Attaché reported to me that these intolerable Unions were trying to bring about the cancellation of the appointment of Marshal Weyler, the Captain-General of Barcelona, and to force Count Romanones, the Liberal leader, out of political life. They had, however, been for some time rather less active in politics, even almost quiescent, and this was attributed to the fact that they could not count on the loyalty of the rank-and-file of the Army, especially of the non-commissioned officers, whose *Juntas* had been suppressed while those of the Officers had been " officially recognised." Major Gandy concluded his report as follows :

> Thus you will understand that the *Juntas* (officers), though the most powerful factor in Spanish politics and affairs at present, cannot be certain of the support of their rank-and-file, and are obliged to limit their programme to less ambitious dimensions.

Nevertheless, the activities of the *Juntas* continued more or less unabated during the whole time of my sojourn in Spain, and remained a continual menace to the stability of the Monarchical régime, while pretending to be its principal pillar of support. I remember well one evening at the Opera when the King was present, that His Majesty suddenly in the middle of an act was called out of his box and remained away for a considerable time. It afterwards became known that a deputation of the *Juntas Militares* had called upon him to insist, if I remember right, on the resignation of a certain Minister who was distasteful to them, and that His Majesty after a considerable struggle finally gave way, and only returned to hear the end of the Opera after having promised to sign the decree they asked for.

I do not propose to continue mentioning the vagaries

of the *Juntas*, which were continual. It is enough to say that they were always cropping up in one form or another, and made political life in Spain quite unnecessarily " cockelty," which is a good Cumbrian word for unsteady. It had not taken me long to learn that side of it.

Meanwhile, early in the spring of 1920, a small incident occurred which showed me that foreign politics in Spain were not conducted in quite the same way as in most other constitutional countries.

In March, 1920, Major X, a representative of the British Munitions Department, came out to Madrid to negotiate with the Spanish Government for the sale of surplus stocks of munitions left over after the War.

The King of Spain expressed a wish to see him, and he was accordingly taken to the Palace and introduced to His Majesty by the Military Attaché. His Majesty afterwards saw Major X alone, and made to him the following proposition, which struck me as a very strange one considering not only the nature of it, but also, and perhaps above all, the person who made it, the person to whom it was made, and the arguments used to support it.

After speaking shortly about the real object of Major X's visit to Madrid, i.e. the sale of surplus munitions, the King turned to the international status of Tangier, always a sore point with him. He asked what *quid pro quo* Spain could receive for the friendship shown to England during the War, of which her readiness to supply the British Government with iron ore was an evident proof. His Majesty declared that for fifteen years past he had continuously worked for an *entente* with Great Britain and France, but now, after the War, it seemed that the Scandinavian States which during the War were, according to His Majesty, looked on in England as little better than German colonies, got everything they asked for, while Spain's claim to Tangier, recognised by the French Government at the time of the Algeciras Conference and set aside at that time under pressure from Germany, was now again likely to be forgotten, since France was claiming Tangier for herself and surreptitiously increasing her *tabor* (military contingent in Tangier) with Moorish troops.

(It may be mentioned that the French were accusing the Spanish Government of doing precisely the same thing.)

His Majesty then went on to speak of Gibraltar. He said he wished to see the question of the defence of the Straits studied by the British and Spanish General Staffs together, which would help to remove much of the feeling still prevalent in Spain that the British occupation of Gibraltar was both a menace and an " insult " to Spain.

His Majesty added that the British Government should recognise that Gibraltar under modern conditions of warfare was useless as an isolated fortress, but that, in conjunction with other defences which could be constructed by Spain on both sides of the Straits, Gibraltar could make it impossible for any hostile fleet to attempt to force a passage through the Straits.

The King, according to Major X's report of the conversation, stated that he would be ready to start work on these defences at once if the British Government agreed.

Major X very properly replied that he had come to Madrid to negotiate for the sale of surplus stocks of munitions and had no authority to discuss questions of this kind.

This extraordinary conversation, which Major X reported to me for transmission to the Foreign Office, gave me a first insight into the curious methods adopted by His Majesty for initiating or conducting negotiations on very delicate political questions. I was, I must confess, particularly struck by the fact that though Major X was accompanied to the Palace by Major Gandy, the Military Attaché of the Embassy, the latter was not invited to be present during the conversation.

It was clear that King Alfonso's conception of the duties of a constitutional Monarch was, as regards foreign policy at least, much more like that of the Emperor William II of Germany than that of King George V of

England. I hoped that they would not lead the King of Spain into the same difficulties and misfortunes that *his* methods had led the Kaiser.

This inclination to treat subjects of gravity by light and, if I may call it so, backstairs methods, put me early on my guard against some of the ways of His Majesty, whose personal charm and friendliness of manner were otherwise only too engaging for strangers.

On March 8th, the Conservative Prime Minister, Don Eduardo Dato, was assassinated as he was driving home in his car at night. Three assailants followed him in another car and poured a volley into the back of the Prime Minister's car, killing both him and his chauffeur almost instantaneously.

Señor Dato, if not a statesman of very outstanding eminence, was a sincere and honest administrator, an able parliamentarian, and a quiet, gentle-mannered man, against whom no one, so far as I knew, entertained any grudge. He was a good speaker, polite and friendly to all, and had perhaps achieved his position at the head of the largest party in the Chamber rather on account of these qualities than owing to any unusual intellectual power or strength of character. Yet he was a man whose sudden withdrawal from the stage of Spanish politics all who knew him sincerely deplored, because he combined honesty and moderation, two qualities which were at the time of the greatest value to Spain. It is doubtful whether he would ever have introduced any real reforms into the body politic, which was very sick, but his disappearance seemed to make some kind of radical cure more necessary than ever.

He went rarely into society, and beyond meeting him at occasional official dinner parties we of the Diplomatic Corps seldom met him. He left all foreign politics entirely to the Marquis de Lema, his Foreign Secretary.

The funeral of Señor Dato impressed itself on my mind on account of the unparalleled opportunity it offered to any revolutionary criminal to rid the world at one successful stroke of the King, his Ministers, and most of the Diplomatic Corps of Madrid.

The funeral procession, comprised of all these elements, followed the coffin on foot down the broad avenue known as the Castellana, which divides the more modern part of Madrid, and came to a halt in the great square at the end, where a religious ceremony, the Absolution, if I remember right, was solemnly performed in the open air. This lasted about half an hour, and it was during this halt that many of us felt that the Terrorists were missing the opportunity of their lives. The King stood surrounded by his Ministers, with the Diplomatic Corps a few yards on his right, while almost immediately behind him was massed a dense crowd divided from His Majesty only by a single file of soldiers.

Considering the circumstances which had brought us together there, I could not but admire the perfect coolness of His Majesty, and many others commented upon it. He appeared to be absolutely unconcerned and unaware of the existence of any possible danger. We remembered the ghastly attack on their Majesties just after their wedding, which resulted in the loss of many lives, and how they both drove out later in the day and received a great ovation and welcome from the crowd. The murder of the Prime Minister, in the circumstances in which we stood there under the bright March sun of Madrid, made it impossible not to think of that other crime only a few years ago. From that time on, remembering the complete absence of all nervousness in the appearance of King Alfonso, I have always firmly believed that whatever motive might have caused him to leave Madrid on April 14th, 1931, on his way to exile, it was not fear.

Count de Bugallal, Minister of the Interior, was appointed Prime Minister *ad interim*, pending a new shuffling of the Ministry which Señor Dato's death made imperative. Practically all felt that Spain was now really approaching a serious crisis, and that, considering the various questions of great moment which were awaiting solution, a coalition or National Government would be the safest for the country.

Señor Maura, leader of the Extreme Right, was requested by the King to form such a Party, including the old Liberal leader, Count Romanones, and the Catalan Regionalist leader, Señor Cambo. This plan was generally well received, but no sooner were the proposed appointments to the various Ministries known to the different parties in the Chambers than there occurred something like a mutiny among the Datist Conservatives, who considered they had a right to more places in the Government. Within forty-eight hours of the death of Senor Dato the Coalition Government disappeared.

A homogeneous Conservative Government was then formed, mainly by Datists under Señor Allende Salazar, who had been Prime Minister for a few months at the beginning of the year. The two most important members of this Cabinet were the Marquis de Lema, Minister for Foreign Affairs, whom I was very glad to see back at the Foreign Office, because he was like a peaceful-flowing stream along which it was at once safe and pleasant to paddle in the Embassy canoe, and Don Juan de la Cierva, an extremely able, energetic and forcible Conservative of the Extreme Right, from whom anything might be expected. He is the father of the inventor of the Autogiro aeroplane.

The situation in Barcelona, which continued to be the centre of most of the Terrorist activities in Spain, was at once the subject of various debates in the Chambers as soon as the *Cortes* met after Señor Dato's death.

As regards the debates of that time, I wrote to Lord Curzon, then Secretary of State for Foreign Affairs, that I would not trouble him :

with any résumé of individual speeches which have been both verbose and vague to a degree which has even caused comment in the Madrid press, accustomed as it is to these qualities in a Parliament in which futile eloquence is traditional. The general upshot of the debates goes to show that political parties have been stirred by the murder of Señor Dato to a feeling that something ought to be done to restore normal conditions in Barcelona, but that no one, with the exception of the Socialists and Republicans, appears to have a concrete suggestion to offer as to any radical change in the present policy of mere repression.

The debate was wound up by Señor Allende Salazar, who compared himself to an " unknown soldier " who occupied his place pending the election by the Conservative Party of a new chief. His speech does not seem to have suggested any prospect of a vigorous programme of reforms, yet I noted that it made a profound impression on all parties, because he was recognised as being a man with no personal axe to grind, who had undertaken an uncongenial job out of a sheer sense of duty.

No doubt Señor Allende Salazar's self-sacrificing attitude was worthy of all praise, but it was difficult to avoid the impression, after reading these debates, that what Spain most needed in a time of crisis was a man who would gather public opinion behind him in an effort to clean up the political life of the nation.

As another example of the different atmosphere in which Parliamentary institutions were expected to work in Spain to that of Anglo-Saxon countries, it may be excusable to give a short account of an internal dispute which, in April, 1921, almost provoked a major ministerial crisis. A Socialist Deputy, Señor Prieto, had made in the Chamber some reflections on the conduct of General Martinez Anido, the Governor of Barcelona, which the latter considered wounding to his honour.

The Governor then instructed two other generals to demand satisfaction of Señor Prieto. The first of the generals, Don José de la Vega, thought however that it was unreasonable to deny to an elected representative of the Spanish people the right of criticising the official acts of the Civil Governor of Barcelona and, his colleagues agreeing, they consulted the Captain-General of Madrid, General Aguilare, as to what they should do. He felt that the honour of all the generals was at stake, and that the attacks of politicians on the general who was Governor

of Barcelona must be stopped. The Military Governor
of Madrid backed up this opinion.

But General de la Vega still hesitated, and consulted
the head of the King's military household, who sent the
two seconds of General Martinez Anido to the Minister
of War and informed the King. His Majesty recommended that no action should be taken that seemed to
call in question the right of free speech in the *Cortes*.
Viscount Eza, the Minister of War, then suggested that,
following an earlier precedent, General Martinez Anido
might put off challenging Señor Prieto until his term of
office had expired. This, however, the Captain-General
of Madrid and the Governor-General of Madrid would
not hear of, and the Minister of War then handed in his
resignation to the Prime Minister. The Prime Minister
threatened to resign also.

Finally, after a prolonged meeting in Madrid of all
the parties involved, it was agreed that General Martinez
Anido's honour was in no way affected, and that he was
not called upon to challenge Señor Prieto. So all ended
peacefully.

The following paragraphs, while they have little direct
or immediate connection with Spain, interested me greatly
as entirely confirming the opinion I had formed before
and during the Paris Conference that whichever of the
contending parties in Russia got the apparently inert mass
of the peasantry on its side would win the Russia of the
future.

The words of Lenin to a delegation of Spanish Socialists,
reproduced by the *Socialista*, are entirely in accordance
with this view. He said :

> The peasants are opposed to Bolshevism, but more so to its enemies,
> such as Denikin, Koltchak and Wrangel, and are gradually drawing
> nearer to the Government.

There is no doubt that this was perfectly true. Trotsky
later confirmed it in his book on the Russian Revolution.
Had the Russian " Whites " but had enough insight to

understand this, we might have been spared much suffering and many errors. Unfortunately their eyes were fixed rather on the past than on the future.

The *Socialista*, of Madrid, organ of the Spanish Socialist Party, published, on January 17th and 18th, 1921, a remarkable report of two of the party's delegates to Russia in the previous November. From this report it appeared that the Russian chairman of the meeting, Zinoviev, asked mainly about the chances of the early disappearance of the capitalist system in Spain. To this the Spanish Socialist, Fernando de los Rios, replied there was nothing in Western Europe or America to warrant that view, though there was an economic crisis which gave Labour unexpectedly great power, but Labour still had a long and difficult task to perform before capitalism could be overthrown.

The Spanish delegates were later received by Lenin, and asked him the following questions, " in order to satisfy doubts caused in their minds by their own observation of life in Russia."

> How and when do you think it will be possible to pass from the present period, called one of transition and of the dictatorship of the proletariat, to a régime of full liberty for the Syndicalist press and individuals.

Lenin replied, according to the report of the *Socialista*, that :

> Bolsheviks had never spoken of liberty, but of the dictatorship of the proletariat ; they exercise this on behalf of the proletariat, which is a minority in Russia, and will continue to do so until the rest of the community submits to the economic conditions of Communism.
>
> The peasants are opposed to Bolshevism, but more so to its enemies, such as Denikin, Koltchak and Wrangel, and are gradually drawing nearer to the Government. The great difficulty which confronts the latter is the lack of manufactures to deliver to the peasantry in exchange for the products commandeered from them, but the Government has paper and printing presses, and the paper currency represents a promise to pay in manufactured articles.

Lenin added that the transition period would be long, perhaps forty or fifty years, but in industrial countries like Germany and England it might be less.

Asked by the delegates if the granting of concessions to foreign capitalists would not prolong the transition period and make another revolution necessary to seize the undertakings formed under cover of these concessions, Lenin admitted that such would be the case, but added that Russia was exhausted after three years of sacrifice and privation and could not fight against the foreign capitalism sustained by the working classes of other countries. He was convinced, however, that the world revolution had begun, though its development was slower than might be wished. Lenin spoke with enthusiasm of the electrification project, and said that as in 1917 they (the Bolsheviks) had aroused the Russian people to political enthusiasm and later to military enthusiasm, so also now would they succeed in launching them enthusiastically along the road of economic reconstruction.

It is not surprising, perhaps, that after these explanations the Spanish Socialist Party Executive Council, after having also received a communication from the Moscow Council stating the Spanish Socialists were hopelessly at sea as regards :

(1) World Revolution ;
(2) The Dictatorship of the Proletariat.
(3) Soviet Government,

and after being roundly rated for their ambiguity, vacillation, muddle-headedness and impotency, should have rejected by ten votes to three an appeal of the Moscow Council to " enter like the working-class vanguard into the Third International." The famous Moscow " twenty conditions " were also rejected by the same majority.

From the foregoing description of the situation in Spain, it will be clear that the work of our Embassy was mainly that of an observer only. In May, 1921, there were signs, however, that we might soon have commercial negotiations to occupy us, and this gave me no little satisfaction, for diplomatic life without some definite aim or object to it had a tendency to provoke atrophy of the brain.

The Spanish Government had, preparatory to the introduction of a new tariff some time previously, denounced most of the existing tariff arrangements with other countries, and we had received information from certain junior officials of the Spanish Customs Department that our existing Customs arrangements with Spain might be similarly treated and much higher duties imposed.

When I inquired of the Marquis de Lema about this he expressed surprise that our agreement had not yet been denounced, but assured us that Spain had in any case no intention of putting Great Britain in the first column of the new Tariff. This was confirmed by the Minister of Commerce, who suggested that we should send in a Note containing proposals regarding any reductions we desired on items in the new Tariff. It was only towards the end of the year, however, that the Spanish Plenary Commission for the new Tariff seemed likely to have its report ready to lay before the *Cortes*, and, therefore, beyond urging His Majesty's Government to be prepared with such proposals as they might think advisable, there was no immediate prospect of starting negotiations.

I regretted this, since, never having had anything to do with negotations for a commercial treaty, I was looking forward to being allowed to have a finger in the pie. Unfortunately, however, no serious negotiations took place in this connection before the following summer.

In July of this year a great disaster overtook the Spanish arms in Morocco. It is quite unnecessary to give here any detailed history of Spanish military operations in the Spanish zone in Morocco which had, up to 1921, been more like the efforts of a physician to deal with an incurable and chronic disease than those of a surgeon to effect a radical cure with the knife. Successive Spanish Governments, indeed, had been quite content to hold on to one or two ancient fortresses on the coast, such as Ceuta and Melilla, allowing the Riffs and other wild tribes of the interior, who were not for any practical purpose under the sway of the Sultan of Morocco, to live in their own way altogether outside the pale of modern civilisation. When, however, the Spanish zone was internationally recognised by the Franco-Spanish Treaty of 1913, and especially after the French definitely accepted responsibility for the pacification of Morocco proper, it became evident that sooner or later Spain, if she intended to make good her title to the Spanish zone—a most mountainous and difficult country inhabited by wild and warlike tribes—would have to take some definite action to establish order of a sort in Spanish territory defined by the above-mentioned Franco-Spanish Treaty.

During the Great War successive Spanish Governments were wisely content to leave ill alone in their Moorish zone, but afterwards it had become clear that some more definite action was necessary. Therefore there was started a campaign in Morocco which was destined to have a disastrous influence on Spanish politics, and to which may, indeed, be traced much of the popular dissatisfaction that led to the Revolution of 1931 and the fall of the Monarchy.

As Colonel Melvill, the British Military Attaché at Madrid, wrote at the end of 1921 :

> The whole attention of the Spanish Army is directed towards Morocco and nothing else. There are to be found the best troops, the best officers, and practically all available war material. The Army undoubtedly emerges this year with a debtor balance.

The plan of campaign adopted by General Silvestre, Spanish Commander at Melilla, in the east of the zone, was apparently to occupy with scattered garrisons the coastline westwards, while General Berenguer was doing his utmost to defeat the famous brigand Raisuli in the west. It must be admitted that both generals were severely handicapped by the lack of interest taken by the people and the politicians of Spain in their proceedings, which made it useless for the generals to ask for sufficient men and materials to carry out a real campaign of pacification of this extremely difficult territory.

The Annual disaster began on June 1st, when a small

garrison at Abaran of two hundred native troops and twenty Spaniards was attacked and killed almost to a man. This was but a beginning of many attacks against the small Spanish garrisons scattered along the coast, which culminated with extraordinary rapidity in the disaster of Annual in July, when General Silvestre, trying to relieve that place with troops from Melilla, was entirely overwhelmed.

As Colonel Melvill says, in forty-eight hours the Spanish Army of Melilla had almost entirely disappeared, and all the materials and the ground conquered after twelve years of continuous struggle was lost. Out of a total strength of twenty thousand Spaniards and five thousand natives, the losses were about fifteen thousand Spaniards while the native troops were either killed or deserted.

The world had during the Great War become callous with regard to loss of life, and outside Spain, Annual hardly created even a ripple of interest. It was, however, as Colonel Melvill described it :

> an almost incredible disaster in which chaos, confusion, flight and massacre were the predominant features. It was no wonder that Spanish papers for months spoke of little else, and that the Government and Parliament discussed it and the measures necessary to be taken to repair the damage done to the detriment of scores of more pressing needs.

Colonel Melvill attributed the disaster to four causes :

1. The system of small posts dotted over the conquered territory, inadequately defended, often some distance from water, without mutual tactical support one for another.

2. No provision whatever for any lines of resistance upon which troops could fall back in the event of an enforced retirement.

3. The ill-advised confidence in the natives which permitted thirty thousand between Melilla and Annual to retain their rifles.

4. The desertion *en masse* of the native troops, who were invariably employed in the forefront of the battle next to the enemy.

At the end of the year 1921 there were no less than two hundred thousand troops in the Spanish zone and in the harbours of the peninsula facing Morocco. The operations in the western part of the zone were fairly successful, so that by January, 1922, it was hoped that it would soon be possible to restore the *status quo ante*, to withdraw most of the troops to Spain, and undertake the pacification of the country by other than military methods, as was now being demanded by Spanish public opinion. It seemed as if, owing to the Annual disaster, Spain had at last realised that her manner of dealing with the Morocco zone needed a complete change. In fact, as Marshal Lyautey, the greatest living authority on French Morocco, had said : " Roads and sugar will do more for your country than cannon." He might also have added that they would be much cheaper.

But Morocco was yet to give Spain much trouble, and in addition to the actual fighting still required, there was the delicate question of ransoming the prisoners who had, to the number of some hundreds, survived the Annual disaster and were subjected to untold hardships at the hands of the Riff leader, Abd-el-Krim. The stories of their sufferings which reached Spain so worked on public opinion that negotiations had to be opened with Abd-el-Krim for this object, though Spanish and Riffians were still fighting each other. Abd-el-Krim refused, however, to negotiate with the military authorities and finally a Franciscan friar, Padre Revilla, who possessed his confidence, was authorised to negotiate on behalf of the Spanish Government, and succeeded in obtaining his promise to release the prisoners for a ransom of four million pesetas. The actual release of the prisoners, however, was delayed till the following January.

The number of troops in Morocco was not very greatly reduced, and continued to be a serious drain on Spanish finances. As a first step towards introducing a Civil Government in the Spanish zone a species of condominium—partly military, partly civil—was established, and resulted rather in disagreements between the Spanish civil and military authorities than in the pacification of Morocco.

In fact, the misfortunes which dogged every step taken by Spain during this unhappy period did not cease.

Some day the history of these years that led up to the grievous events of April, 1931, will doubtless be studied and analysed by some objective mind.

As for myself, I can but repeat what I wrote as my first impression of Spanish politics after a few months' residence in Madrid :

> If I had to paint an impressionist picture of Spain in 1920 for which accurate and detailed drawing was not required, I would take a large canvas and produce on it a stage in a state of chaotic welter on which various politicians would prominently figure, pulling strings in different directions and to no purpose across a background of strikes, bombs and outrages, of apparent general discontent, of committees of military officers springing suddenly into the foreground and retiring as suddenly into obscurity for no particular reason, of railway companies carrying on systematic sabotage against themselves in order to force the country and Government into raising rates. of banks and profiteers indulging in wild speculations in foreign exchanges undermining all the advantage the country obtained by her policy of neutrality during the Great War, of regionalism in an extreme form increasing in certain provinces and, on the other hand, extreme centralisation clinging to floating straws of hope of maintaining itself, all awaiting the advent of some wise, strong man to emerge on the stage to put all these tragi-comedians into their right places and allow the play to proceed to the benefit and content of the public in the playhouse.
>
> The brighter side of the picture would be the public itself, watching the tragi-comedians with a kind of amused indifference and Oriental fatalism, occasionally applauding or hissing the actors, more frequently smiling at their antics or criticising them with caustic good humour, each of the spectators being on the whole more occupied in gossiping with his neighbour, drinking and smoking, than with what takes place on the stage.

These impressions were obtained from reading the press of all parties, and while I could not but sympathise deeply

with the people on account of the faults of their Government, everything I saw around me tended but to confirm
afresh the conviction arrived at in other countries that
the British Parliamentary system of government by a
bare majority was, even if moderately successful in
Britain, utterly unsuited to the Latin temperament. I
wondered when the wise men of these countries would
begin to turn for inspiration rather to Switzerland than
to England.

CHAPTER XVIII

SPAIN *(continued)*. COSAS DE ESPAÑA

IN my last chapter I have dwelt entirely on the darker and most unlovely side of Spain after the Great War, its political conditions, which I found both unattractive and wearisome. In this chapter I shall devote myself, be it only superficially, with joy to the reverse of the medal : the real glories of the cities and country-side, to the extraordinarily engaging qualities of the inhabitants, of which their sense of humour is not the least, to the wonders of its ancient buildings, from the days of Rome, through those of the Goths, of the Moors, and of the Spanish Empire up to the present day. It would take, of course, many volumes to do justice to these things, and I have to compress my sense of it all into the compass of one chapter. That is, I know, an impossible task, and already, when I think of what lies before me, at least half the joy and self-confidence with which I started out has oozed away and left me. Before another two paragraphs have been written it will all have disappeared and I shall have arrived at the conclusion that it simply cannot be done. On the whole, therefore, I give it up and refer those interested who have no time for many volumes simply to " Murray's Handbook for Spain," written by Richard Ford and published by John Murray, London, in 1869, fourth edition. This book, written by one who was a real expert on all *cosas de España* —" things of Spain "—and a real lover of them as well, should be the inseparable companion of everyone visiting this country who wishes to know something of it beyond " doing it " as an ordinary tourist. The reader may, perhaps, on reading Ford's introductory chapter on " Tours in Spain," think that he is overdoing the praise, and may even think so after a short visit to the country, but after a sojourn of some length he will assuredly agree with almost all Richard Ford—whose guide-book is the model for all guide-books—has written.

Even what he says about the things one must not expect in Spain is still largely true. " The mere Idler and Man of Pleasure " is advised to go rather to other European lands than to Spain, for " Iberia is not a land of fleshly comforts or of social sensual civilisation." " Oh, *dura tellus Iberia*—God there sends the meat and the Evil One cooks," and this, be it remarked, is not the only similarity with England and the English.

Once started, one might quote interminably from Richard Ford's famous introductory chapter, but one sentence more I may be allowed to transcribe where, in describing the cathedrals of Spain, he writes of them— strong Protestant though he was—as places, " where God is worshipped in a manner as nearly befitting His glory as finite man can reach."

So the first thing I did on being appointed to Spain was to provide myself with three books, which I knew of old : *Ford's Guide*, Borrow's *Bible in Spain*, and, above all, *Don Quixote*, and when I grew weary and despondent over contemporary Spanish politics I refreshed myself with these, and turned whenever I could, under Ford's advice, to " mingle with the gay, good-humoured, temperate peasantry, free, manly and independent, and to live with the noble, dignified, high-bred, self-respecting Spaniard," whose sense of humour and of the absurdity of those who in this life take themselves too seriously is unfailing if appealed to in a friendly spirit.

It was on account of all these various gifts and charms that, despite politics, I soon began to be frankly in love with Spain, and even to treat their politics as most Spaniards treated them, more or less as a sort of play staged for their particular amusement.

As regards our private life in Madrid, nothing could have been pleasanter. A good house, large enough for all our needs ; a Society that was not at all exacting, so that we could spend many evenings at home *en famille* ; an excellent climate, clean, sunny and invigorating in winter, and by no means too hot in summer ; and wonderfully agreeable surroundings.   We were near enough for our boys to come to us for the holidays and for friends and relations to visit us from time to time, and, as may have been gathered from the previous chapter, not so much work as to prevent us from making excursions of two or three days in different directions, which were always not only pleasurable, because both Isa and I enjoyed the varied scenery and objects of interest—and they were many all over the country—but I could also meet our Consuls and local magnates, from whom I often obtained a different picture of political happenings from that to be got in Madrid.

Then with a motor-car we were able in a few hours to visit many places off the main railways, that would have taken us many days by rail because, as used to be said, the trains along country lines were of three kinds : those that started but did not arrive at the place one was making for ; those that arrived but did not start from the place one was leaving ; and those that neither arrived nor started.

Railway travelling was, indeed, not always smooth or pleasant, but it was generally amusing.   Thus, I remember on one occasion I had arranged with one of the Secretaries of the Embassy, Victor Perowne, who was also a great lover of *cosas de España*, to meet me at Avila, he coming from Madrid and I from Valladolid, where I had gone to visit the English and Scottish Ecclesiastical Colleges. These colleges were established after all instruction in the Catholic religion in England became a penal offence, in order to keep up a continual supply of priests for those who, despite penal laws, still maintained the practice of their religion at home.   I was hospitably received by these colleges at Valladolid, and greatly enjoyed their old-world Spanish atmosphere combined with the society of a body of twentieth-century young Englishmen, among whom one might have believed oneself in one of the

Catholic colleges in England. There was something both piquant and entrancing in the contrast. On another occasion I had taken one of my Secretaries, a Protestant, with me on business since, as the members of the college were all British subjects, the Embassy was naturally expected to give them advice and assistance in case of any little trouble arising with the local authorities regarding assessment of rates and taxes and other similar matters. I was much amused at my friend's complete bewilderment at finding himself in an old monastic establishment as one of the guests at luncheon, for the first time in his life and this in Spain. I had a feeling that he expected that if he didn't cross himself after grace, there would surely be a rack or a thumbscrew waiting for him in the cellar which, however, only produced excellent wine.

But to return to my journey from Valladolid to Avila, a distance, if I remember right, of not more than fifty miles. The train was due to leave at about 5 p.m. and to arrive some time after 8 p.m. Quite good this—only three hours and a half for fifty miles. It was November and darkness set in early, besides which there was a howling and icy gale blowing over the stony plains of Northern Castille. I was almost the only passenger in the train. It grew quite dark, and the lamps in my carriage would not light. I huddled myself in some rugs and coats I had with me ; the train, of course, was not heated. Presently it stopped in the bleakest, most inhospitable part of the plain, and the wind beat upon it with devilish fury. Looking out of the window on the lee side, I saw men moving slowly about the engine with flickering lanterns, but it was so cold that I was glad to draw back into the darkness of the carriage, shut all windows, and try to sleep. It must have been something like three hours that we stayed there buffetted by the wind, when another engine came snorting along the line, and finally carried us to Avila, which we reached about midnight. I was the only passenger in the train then, and after some search discovered an official of some kind. Leaving my luggage in his charge, I went out into the ancient streets to look for the hotel which was to be the rendezvous I had given to Perowne. After some difficulty I obtained admission, only to learn that the hotel was packed with a troop of strolling actors, some of whom were even sleeping on the sofas in the hall, that a *Señorito ingles* had indeed asked for a room some hours before, but had been told there was none, and the people of the hotel did not know where he had gone. In despair, I went back to the station. On the road, however, I ran across the *Sereno*—night watchman— of the little city, who was going the rounds with his flickering lamp. He was most polite, and when I told him of my predicament of being roofless and bedless that wild night (it was by now past 1 a.m.), he entered into the spirit of my troubles and said he would guide me to a little inn where I should probably find a night's lodging. Then I mentioned diffidently my two suit-cases left at the station, and these he offered to help me to carry. We, therefore, went back to the station, recovered the luggage and carrying it between us, slowly finding our way through the pitch-dark, narrow and winding streets by the light of his lantern, we continued our conversation, he wanting to know where I came from, what my nationality was, etc. When he heard I was English, he said, surprised, that a *Señorito ingles* had arrived that afternoon, and having failed to find a lodging in the hotel had gone to the inn for which we were bound. I felt sure this must be Perowne, and so rejoiced that I should not have to spend the next day by myself, which comforted me, for I dislike sightseeing alone almost as much as I dislike doing so with an uncongenial companion. When we got to the inn all was locked up and as dark within as without. My friend the *Sereno*, however, would not be defeated, and battered at the door until heads were poked out of windows asking angrily what the trouble was about. My friend's reply that it was the *Sereno* brought someone quickly to the door, and when the situation was explained I was told that a *Señorito ingles* had engaged a room for a friend who had, however, not yet arrived,

and I therefore took possession of it without further
ado.

The bed was clean and flealess, if in other respects
the inn was not flawless, and next morning I woke
refreshed and ready, with the pleasant companionship
of Perowne, to do justice to Avila.

The quaintness of my arrival in the old mediæval city,
the hotel filled with strolling players, the courteous
Sereno with his flickering lamp, the darkness of the narrow
streets, and the icy blasts of the gale had all prepared me
for something out of the way at Avila, but the city itself
seen in the clean sunlight of a fine November morning,
for the weather had returned to " set fair," far more than
surpassed my expectations, for the history of Spain from
the eleventh century to the present day is, roughly speaking,
written there in stone.

Since that day Avila has become for me the most
complete example of a mediæval city which is not a ruin
but still inhabited by men and women of the twentieth
century living more or less as other citizens of a twentieth
century State.

Avila is said to have been founded in 1600 B.C., but
without going as far back as that we can rest content
with the fact that the present city was rebuilt by Dom
Ramon of Burgundy in A.D. 1088, and is still surrounded
by the most perfect and magnificent girdle of granite
walls, forty feet high and twelve feet thick, having eighty-
six towers and twelve gateways.

The splendid cathedral is even built into these walls,
for its apse forms a semicircular excrescence of the same
strength as the walls themselves, and was evidently built
as much for defence as for worship, having castellated
machicolations which make it literally half church, half
fortress. The interior does not in any way belie the
grandeur of the exterior, and is pure Gothic of the end
of the twelfth and beginning of the thirteenth centuries.

I cannot attempt to describe its glories in detail, and
will only refer to an admirable book on the cathedrals of
Spain by a friend of mine, Commander John A. Gade,

now Naval Attaché to the United States Embassy at Brussels, and also at Lisbon, whom I first met in Stockholm during the War. Architect, banker, naval attaché, writer—he has written, among other things, a most interesting account of Charles the Twelfth of Sweden and a life of Cardinal Mercier—and perfect travelling companion, his book on the cathedrals of Spain is one which everyone who wishes to have more than a bowing acquaintance with these marvellous examples of mediæval art should certainly take with them and study carefully.

I venture to transcribe here Jack Gade's description of the first view of Avila :

> The cathedral of San Salvador is the strongest link in the chain that encircles the city of Avila, " *ciudad de Castilla la vieja.*" Avila lies on a ridge in the corner of a great undulating plain, clothed with fields of grain, bleached light yellow at harvest, occasional groups of ilex and straggling pine and dusty olives scrambling up and down the slopes. Beyond is the hazy greyish-green of stubble and dwarfed woodland, with blue peaks closing the horizon. To the south rises the Sierra Gredos, and eastward in the direction of Segovia, the Sierra de Guadarrama. The narrow, murky Adaja that loiters through the upland plain is quite insufficient to water the thirsty land. Thistles and scrub oak dot the rocky fields. Here and there migratory flocks of sheep nibble their way across the unsavoury stubble, while the dogs longingly turn their heads after whistling quails and the passing hunter.
>
> The crenallated ochre walls and bastions that, like a string of amber beads, have girdled the little city since its early days, remain practically unbroken, despite the furious sieges she has sustained and the battles in which her lords were engaged for ten centuries. As many as eighty-six towers crown, and no less than ten gateways pierce, the walls which follow the rise or fall of the ground on which the city has been compactly and narrowly constructed for safest defence. It must look to-day almost exactly as it did to the approaching armies of the Middle Ages, except that the men-at-arms are gone. The defences are so high that what is inside is practically hidden from view, and all that can be seen of the city so rich in saints and stones are the loftiest spires of her churches.[1]

The cathedral cannot be left without a word for the

[1] *Cathedrals of Spain*, pp. 67–68. John A. Gade. Houghton Mifflin Co., Boston and New York. 1911.

stained glass which, though late and not to be compared
with that of Leon, is gorgeous in colour.

There are numerous other most interesting churches
in and around Avila, and these and the curious, ancient
architecture of the houses, gave Perowne and myself as
much as we could do to absorb during that day. I still
remember two things, apart from the city itself and the
cathedral. The first was a curious monument set up on
a little hill to mark the place where St. Theresa de Avila,
then seven years of age, was found and brought back to
her father's house after setting out to obtain the crown
of martyrdom from the Moors.

The other is the beautiful Renaissance monument by
an Italian sculptor to Don Juan, the only son of Ferdinand
and Isabella, who died in 1497 at the age of nineteen.
Quite apart from the beauty of the monument itself, this
tomb is most impressive because the death of the young
prince who lies there must certainly have altered the
history of Europe and possibly of the world. He, the
son of Ferdinand and Isabella, being of pure Spanish
blood, would never, we may suppose, have entangled
Spain in adventures to the north and east of the Pyrenees,
like his cousin, the Emperor Charles V, Burgundian and
Austrian, who gathered half Europe and all the known
Americas under his sceptre. Spain, for the lifetime of
Charles V, ceased to look west from the Pyrenees, and
was forced to take part in the incessant wars of the Low
Countries, from which she only emerged weakened and
impoverished after a century or more of continuous
struggles to which the wars of religion added much
bitterness.

One other tomb of a young and promising Prince
which may be compared to that of Don Juan from the
point of view of the changes that might have been written
in our own history at any rate had its occupant lived to
reign over England and to found a dynasty, is that of
Prince Arthur, the elder son of Henry VII, who is buried
in the cathedral of Worcester. There is no pastime,
perhaps, quite so profitless as that of historical speculation,

2 F

but here at Avila in the Church of Santo Tomas, before the tomb of Don Juan of Castille and Aragon, and in the cathedral of Worcester, before that of Prince Arthur, son of Henry VII of England, one may perhaps be forgiven for indulging in it.

For these reasons, and for the general appearance of the city within and without, Avila and its cathedral came to symbolise Spain for me more possibly than any other place I visited in that country, and I always returned to it with increasing interest.

Once Isa and I were lent a very comfortable private house there, the owners being away, and had a most enchanting time, getting on to a more intimate footing with the little town than the same number of hours would have entitled us to had we been living in an hotel.

The adventures of my arrival at Avila by train might, perhaps, have seemed very appropriate, as though the city protested as much against desecration by rail and steam as Wordsworth did against similar desecration of Windermere. But Isa was never accustomed to roughing it to that extent, and when we made our trips together, it was a happier arrangement on such occasions to win on the swings of comfort what we might have lost on the roundabouts of romance.

To the east of Avila lies another wonderful and ancient city on which Romans, Goths, Moslems and Spaniards have all left their traces in architecture and otherwise. The grandest thing there, however, is without doubt the great Roman aqueduct, which is, perhaps, quite as magnificent as that of the Pont du Gare, in France, and worthy of the builders of Baalbek. For general interest as an historical museum Avila is possibly to be preferred, but the splendid position of Segovia, astride on a spur of the Guadarramas, with a stream on either flank and the old gold colour of the cathedral dominating from its hill miles of the plain of North Castille, gives it a special grandeur of its own.

In order to visit these northern slopes of the Guadarramas we sometimes, when the weather was warm

enough, spent a week-end at San Ildefonso, where La
Granja is situated. This latter is a royal palace built of
pink granite with French eighteenth-century gardens *à la
Versailles*, water rushing everywhere almost like that at
the Villa d'Este at Tivoli, great reservoirs and hillsides
covered with trees. It is a perfect place for refreshment
and repose in summer. The Court formerly spent the
summer and autumn here until most of the palace was
burned in the last century, after which San Sebastian
and Santander replaced it as a royal *villeggiatura*.

In my opinion La Granja was an ideal summer place,
and if it had not been necessary for the Ambassador to
go to San Sebastian or somewhere nearby because the
Minister for Foreign Affairs followed the King there in
summer, I should have preferred La Granja, with its
fountains, forests and neighbouring mountains.

Besides this, La Granja in summer time possessed a
magnet in the person of the Infanta Isabel. She was an
aunt of the King of Spain, over seventy years of age,
and one of the most adorable old ladies I ever met. Kind
of heart but sharp of tongue, with a truly Spanish sense
of humour, caring little or nothing for appearances, but
yet with an unmistakable air of a great lady whatever she
did or wore, a keen sportswoman and very charitable
withal, with a natural courtesy like that of a Spanish
peasant, which often exceeds that of a grandee, she
seemed to epitomise all that was best and most attractive
in the Spanish character.

On Sunday morning after Mass she was accustomed
to hold a little court in the garden at La Granja, in the
shade of an ancient spreading plane tree. Here an arm-
chair was set for the old lady, while a circle of lesser
chairs was set for those who wished to come and pay
their respects. She would keep the whole company
amused by the hour by the quickness of her repartees,
the piquancy of her stories, and the humour of her gossip.

In the afternoon she liked to drive a four-in-hand
herself through the woods, and Isa and I were once or
twice honoured with an invitation to drive with her.

The only others in the brake were her two ladies-in-waiting, the Señoritas Bertran de Lys. The first great event of these drives was the establishing of the Infanta Isabel on the box of the brake, which was very high, and, the Infanta being large, heavy, lame and over seventy, this was no easy matter. A stalwart coachman first climbed up on to the box ; some steps were then placed firmly against the body of the brake, the coachman on the box bent down and caught hold of the Infanta's hands, while the other two menservants pushed her up from behind until, amid laughter and cheers, in which she joined, she was dragged and pushed on to her high box-seat.   Here she was in her element, took the reins and her long coaching whip from the coachman, who sat beside her, and ordered the grooms to let the horses go.   These started off along the forest road at a canter. But before we got into the forest it was the Infanta's delight to swish round the sharp corners of the reservoirs so that the brake almost hung over the water. The ladies-in-waiting, knowing what was required of them in order to impress the guests the more, shrieked in high soprano voices : " *Señora, señora, cuidado por amor de Dios.*"[1] But the more they shrieked, the more the Infanta whipped up the perspiring horses and rejoiced to show off her dexterity as a whip. When we got home safely she was delighted to receive compliments on that dexterity, in which the ladies-in-waiting, who had done their part as a kind of shrieking chorus of Shabash-wallahs joined, praising the old lady, who was all smiles, for the marvellous accuracy with which she had swung round the most acute angles.

These drives were a great delight, and it was no wonder that they and the sporting old lady who conducted them from the box should have remained so clearly carved on my memory and will be ever connected with the enchanting gardens of La Granja.

So when we received invitations from our kind friends, the Bauers, who were the great bankers in Madrid, to

[1] " Señora, señora, take care for the love of God."

spend a week-end at La Granja with them in the summer, we never refused, one of the baits held out to us being the chance of a drive in the Infanta Isabel's four-in-hand brake. Poor Infanta—she was dying when the Revolution broke out on the night of April 14th, 1931. Yet when she heard that the King had left Madrid, she said she could not die in Spain without a King, and insisted on being taken to France. Everyone loved her because she was *muy Española*,[1] and so all facilities were granted for her journey, and a few days after crossing the boundary into France she crossed that other boundary from which there is no return.

On the way from Madrid to La Granja you pass the Escorial. Like most Englishmen of his time, Richard Ford is bitterly prejudiced against Philip II, and where he does not actually revile he holds him up to ridicule. Philip has lately fallen into the hands of writers more eager for truth for its own sake than many of those of the last century, so that while some formerly spotless heroes have been " debunked," other arch-villains have been found to be less black. Now, why I have here dragged in Ford and the Escorial is because he so strongly condemns that building on account of Philip, the designer of it, who in his eyes could do nothing right.

When he says that the edifice has " nothing in form or colour which is either royal, religious or ancient, mediæval or national," he is simply allowing his anti-Catholic prejudice to run away with him. What particularly excites his wrath is that Philip should have asked a great architect like Herrera to build him a palace, mausoleum and monastery in the form of a grid in honour of St. Laurence, who suffered slow martyrdom from the Romans on a gridiron. To this Ford elegantly refers as being " broiled by Valentianus, August 10th, A.D. 261, on a slow fire and not quickly done, *à la bifstec*." It is a pity that Richard Ford, who wrote a really remarkable book on Spain, should so often have disfigured it by cheap

[1] One hundred per cent. Spanish.

gibes whenever anything Catholic is mentioned. But
that was perhaps in the spirit of the times. What, however, is inexcusable is that he should have been so blinded
by his religious prejudices that he could not appraise at
its proper value one of the most remarkable buildings in
the world. In this I suppose any architect of to-day
would agree. I would but venture one observation on
Ford's criticisms. So far from the Escorial not being
"national," it has one most Spanish quality which is
rarely found elsewhere at that period or later, namely, the
great beauty of a very plain surface enhanced by and
enhancing the beauty of some highly decorated doorway,
window or balcony. It has, that is to say, the quality of
reserve, of refusing to be carried away by decoration for
its own sake, which is surely one of the qualities of supreme
artistry. Then, where else can one see a royal residence
built by a great monarch in which he lived for years,
occupying only a few small rooms specially designed by
himself for his own use in that vast biulding? Most
striking of all is the little plan drawn by his own hand
of his bedroom, still hanging there, with the exact spot
marked where his bed should stand, having one line
drawn from the pillow to show the line of vision through
a window to the high altar of Herrera's splendid church
—" Wretched bigot ! " Ford would say—and the other
line of vision carrying the poor invalid's sight out of the
window over the great sun-bathed plain of South Castille
which, Fleming though he really was, he came to love
more than anything else. And if Philip of Spain, like
other monarchs of his time, permitted his subjects to
be tortured, and even burned, in the name of religion, it
is difficult to see any great difference between his actions
and those of Elizabeth of England. She allowed her
subjects to be tortured and then drawn on hurdles to
Tyburn, there to be hung, drawn and quartered while
still alive, with special and nameless indignities for priests.
The only real distinction to be made between the two
systems indeed appears to be that while Philip permitted
these horrors for the punishment of treason to God, as

he believed, Elizabeth permitted them rather for alleged treason to herself.

I write these minor and interesting details regarding Philip's strange palace of the Escorial because they particularly struck my imagination, so that other visitors to Madrid may not be put off from going to the Escorial by cheap criticisms like those of Richard Ford.

The road from the top of the pass over the Guadarramas opening out as it descends from the heights on to glorious vistas of the Castilian Plain which Philip loved is, in the spring time, sweet with myrtle and cistus, laurustinus and broom and heather. So I naturally loved the Guadarramas, whether snow-capped in winter or brown and indigo and violet in summer.

Out of the many glorious buildings we visited in Spain —at Toledo, Burgos, Seville, Cordoba, Granada, Salamanca and others—I will give special mention to but one more, because it is less often visited and because it left on my mind the greatest impression of them all.

Isa and I one autumn motored home to Madrid after our summer *villeggiatura* at Zarauz, along the northern coast through Limpias with its wonderful crucifix, industrial Bilbao and the naval station Santander, past some village with extraordinary prehistoric cave pictures of animals, to Covadonga, where is a small cave in which the Christian Gothic leader Pelayo took refuge with a few followers, who swore to rid Spain of the infidel Saracens and, indeed, inflicted on them their first serious defeat after their invasion of Spain in the early part of the eighth century. Covadonga lies in a narrow rocky valley, with a swiftly-running stream full, in the days of Richard Ford, with trout. From Covadonga we continued our journey through Coruña, well known to us English from Campbell's poem on Sir John More : " Not a drum was heard, not a funeral note," and over the mountains to Leon. We reached Leon just before sunset, in time to see the last rays streaming like a flame of violet and blue and amber through the cathedral's great west window, and lighting up the whole gorgeous interior with colours that were not of this world. Some years later I read in a description of León by an American writer that to enter the cathedral when the sun is sinking is like entering into the glory of the presence of God. Truly, I have never in any church or cathedral experienced such an overwhelming sensation of beauty as there. It was literally beyond the power of words to describe.

I cannot, however, leave the Cathedral of León without one or two extracts from the book of my friend, Jack Gade, on the cathedrals of Spain.

Speaking of the plan of León Cathedral, he writes (page 99) :

It is a plan that must delight not only the architect but any casual observer in its almost perfect symmetry and in the relationship of its various parts to each other. It belongs to the primitive period of French Gothic, though carried out in later days when its vigour was waning. It has not been cramped nor distorted by initial limitations of space or conditions, nor injured by later deviation from the original conception. It is worthy of the greatest masters who planned once for all the loveliest and most expressive house for the worship of God. Erected on the plains of León, it was conceived in the inspired Provinces of Champagne and the Isle de France.

and again :

It is not until you enter a Spanish church that its power and beauty are felt. The audacious construction of León which one wonders at from the outside becomes wellnigh incredible when seen from the nave. How is it possible that glass can support such a weight of stone ? If Burgos was bold, this is insane. It looks like a house of cards ready for a collapse at the first gentle breeze. Can fields of glass sustain three hundred feet of thrusts and such weights of stone ? It is a culmination of the daring of Spanish Gothic.

. . . .

Internally, León is the lightest and most cheerful church in Spain. The great doorways of the western and southern fronts, as well as to the north leading into the cloisters, are thrown wide open as if to add to the joyousness of the temple. Every portion of it is flooded with sweet sunlight and freshness. It is the church of cleanliness, of light and fresh air, and, above all, of glorious colour. The glaziers might have said with Isaiah : " And I will make thy windows of agate and thy gates of carbuncles and all thy borders of pleasant stones." The entire walls are a continuous series of divine rainbows.

The side walls of the aisles for a height of some fourteen feet to the bottom of their vaulting ribs, the triforium, commencing but a foot above the arches which separate nave from side aisles and immediately above the triforium, forty feet of clerestory—all in glass, emerald, turquoise and peacock, amber, straw, scarlet and crimson, encased in a most delicate, strangely reckless and bold-traceried framework of stained ivory.

Is it strange that after entering into that wonderland I immediately placed León, with Chartres, as one of the six most perfectly beautiful buildings I had ever seen ? I still read at times Gade's description to remind myself of it, especially of those windows which if not all so perfect as those of Chartres nor all belonging to the very best period, are yet together, perhaps, even richer and more gorgeous in colour. I hope to see them once again before I die.

Life, as I have said before, was very pleasant at Madrid. I am not a lover of Court ceremonies as such, but those at Madrid had a flavour generally lacking elsewhere, which was perhaps due to the religious element of many of them, especially the " *Capillas publicas* "—when the King and Queen and the Infantes all on some *fiesta* attended Mass in the chapel of the palace at Madrid and walked in procession along the corridor which surrounded the principal court of the palace. This corridor was then always hung with beautiful tapestries, and we were told that there were, if I remember right, over seventy complete sets to cover the walls on such occasions.

The Holy Thursday ceremony was a noteworthy one, retaining as it did the special features of a religious ceremony, which had by the time of which I write practically disappeared from every Court.

After Mass the King and Queen, in presence of the Court and members of the Diplomatic Corps, " washed the feet " of twelve old men and twelve old women chosen from the inmates of almshouses in Madrid, in remembrance of the washing of the feet of the twelve apostles by our Lord.

The feet of these old people had, of course, been carefully washed beforehand, but the Sovereigns poured over them some warm water from a silver jug and then dried them with linen towels.

After this their Majesties served them with an excellent dinner of several courses which, however, had no sooner been placed before the aged pensioners than the plates were carried off by servants and the food sold for the benefit of the old people. Among other items of food, such as whole hams and gobbets of fish, cakes and fruit, were always large round orange-coloured cheeses, one cheese for each old guest. It invariably happened that one or more of these cheeses rolled off the plate on which the King was carrying it, and His Majesty would then run after it to retrieve it before it rolled away under a bench or table. To do this he tried at times to stop it with his foot, like a dexterous football player saving a goal. This always produced a titter among the audience.

But the old people got an excellent hot dinner after the ceremony which, coupled with the money realised by the sale of other comestibles, possibly accounted for the fact that there was never any lack of candidates for the honour of taking part in it.

One more ceremony at Court amused me not a little, this was that of the *Cubertura*, or of wearing a hat in the presence of the King by a grandee of Spain, whereby his claim to the rank of grandee was finally established.

Only grandees were actually present in the Throne Room when this took place, but outsiders were sometimes invited to stand in the ante-room from which the grandees who were to be " *cubiertos* " issued into the royal presence.

I was once so invited by an Englishman, Mr. Hussey Walsh, who had married a Spanish duchess. She had with her title also inherited the grandeeship from her father, but was unable to exercise the right of " *cubertura* " on account of her sex, and this privilege or duty devolved on her husband.

On this occasion two or three grandees were waiting

their turn to be "*cubiertos*" in the ante-room in which several outsiders like myself were also grouped.

When the King and Queen had taken their places at the far end of the long Throne Room, the doors separating them from the new grandees were opened, and a little procession consisting of the first grandee in seniority, with two supporters, walked up the central path between two rows of grandees and bowed to the King and Queen at stated intervals. When, bareheaded, he approached, the King invited him to seat himself on a tabouret just in front of His Majesty who, when he was seated, gave him permission to put on the great feathered hat of his rank. They then conversed for a time, after which the King shook hands and the new grandee rose and returned as he had come.

The doors, however, were closed after the gentlemen who were to be "*cubiertos*" had entered the Throne Room. What particularly amused me was that the friends of the "*cubierto*" assembled in the ante-room crowded to the keyhole to watch the ceremony in that way. When Mr. Hussey Walsh's turn came I was also invited to make use of the same point of vantage. This I did, and have therefore now been able to describe what I saw. There was much merriment and hustling to get to that keyhole and loud complaints if anyone monopolised it too long. The whole ceremony passed off, so far as the ante-room was concerned, with a singular lack of gravity for a people so generally supposed to be naturally solemn and formal. When, therefore, I was asked, after I had watched the performance in the manner described, what I thought of it, I ventured to say that I had found it all highly interesting, but most of all the fact that it was at the Court of Spain that I had been initiated into the art of looking through a keyhole.

The summers we generally spent at Zarauz, a small fishing village about twelve miles along the coast to the west of San Sebastian. It was a wholly delightful place, and my boys loved their summer holidays there. We had a villa on the sandy beach where we could bathe and sun bathe to our hearts' content, and there was also a small golf and tennis club where we passed the time pleasantly enough. It was here that I saw A. J. B. (the late Lord Balfour) for the last time. He came out one summer as Secretary of State for Foreign Affairs to attend the meeting at San Sebastian of the Council of the League of Nations, which at that time moved about to various capitals for its autumn session.

I naturally asked him out to lunch at Zarauz to meet one or two local magnates, and he made himself as agreeable as ever and delighted the company.

After lunch he wanted to play tennis at the club, so I arranged this for him. We walked off to the club, where the President, the Duke of Lecera, with members of the committee, was waiting on the veranda to give him a ceremonial welcome. When, however, we were at a short distance from the club, A. J. B. espied a group of shady pine trees not far off, and saying to me : " I think I will go and have a little siesta under those trees before playing," he went off and, stretching his long length out on the pleasant pine needles under the shade, he slumbered peacefully for about half an hour, leaving me to explain to the President and committee that he had acquired the Spanish habit of the siesta, and could not play tennis at all up to his proper form unless he had had his little sleep. This relieved their anxiety, for they feared he had been suddenly taken ill and was perhaps in pain. But I could tell them truthfully that having seen much of him at the Paris Conference I knew that it was his invariable custom. Afterwards he came up to the club smiling, was properly introduced, and again won all hearts. He played a game or two of tennis, charging about the court like a two-year-old.

The year 1922 was the quater-centenary of the return to Spain of Juan Sebastian de al Cano, or Del Cano, after completing for the first time the circumnavigation of the globe. This was celebrated with considerable pomp at his birthplace, Guetaria, a most picturesque little fishing port some fifteen miles to the west of San Sebastian.

Up to that time the name of Del Cano had been, for some inexplicable reason, almost entirely forgotten, so much so indeed that he is not given even a separate mention in the *Encyclopædia Britannica*, but is only referred to in the article on Magellan.

On account of the almost complete obscurity which covered the story of the great navigator, I may be excused if I give a few details of his adventurous career.

Coming from a family of substance in Guetaria which owned whalers, then a lucrative industry in the Bay of Biscay, Juan Sebastian took early to a seafaring life, and after some adventures he both owned and commanded a whaler which he lost owing to unfortunate speculations. As master of a small vessel, the *Concepcion*, he joined Magellan's famous expedition of 1519, which resulted in the discovery of the Straits of Magellan and the Southern Pacific Ocean. The story of this expedition is so well known that it is unnecessary to repeat it. It is enough to say that after the death of Magellan in the Philippines, Del Cano was elected to the command of the *Victoria*, which was the only ship of Magellan's flotilla that continued the voyage to Europe westward round the globe. After incredible hardship and adventures, recounted in the only known Life of Del Cano by one, Navarrete, he arrived at the Cape Verde Islands in July, 1522, and then returned to Seville in the *Victoria*. For this feat he received from the Emperor Charles V his very modest reward—a Spanish coat-of-arms quartering various spices surmounted by a globe with the inscription " *Primus circumdedisti me.*"[1] The object of the Magellan expedition was to find a navigable passage to the Spice Islands from the West. Thus the first part only of the voyage round the world was accomplished by Magellan. In recognition of his services, Del Cano was also granted

---

[1] The arms granted to Juan Sebastian Del Cano are still to be seen, I believe, on his house in Guetaria, and are thus quaintly described in heraldic language : " Argent three bars azure, a border of eight alternate gules, a star or, and a wolf sable, parted per fess, in chief gules a castle or, in base gules a semee of cloves, two sticks of cinnamon saltere-wise between three nutmegs proper."

I quote this delightful piece of heraldry from Esme's article, but under correction, as he was probably as ignorant as I am of that science.

a pension of five hundred ducats a year, which was never paid, and two fully-armed retainers for his protection. He sailed on another voyage in 1524 and died at sea in 1526.

It was indeed an irony of fate that the first circum-navigator's only assets at his death should have been his armorial shield and unpaid arrears for his captaincy and his pension of five hundred ducats.

However, as a consolation prize these celebrations in his honour were held four hundred years later at Guetaria, and were attended by ships of the navies of many countries, among others two light cruisers of the British Navy under the command of Admiral Nicholson who, after the ceremony at Guetaria was over, excited both the admira-tion and surprise of all at San Sebastian by bringing his flagship into the little bottle-necked harbour of San Sebastian against the advice of the Spanish pilot. The cruiser was, of course, visited by numbers who would not have gone out to see her had she been moored outside in the bay, and the admiral gave a most successful luncheon party in honour of the King and Queen of Spain.

My eldest son, Esme, who was still a schoolboy at Downside, was so thrilled by what he read in the Spanish papers about Del Cano, and so indignant at the general neglect of his achievements, that he got himself placed on the list of newspaper reporters for the occasion and wrote an article on Del Cano and the quater-centenary ceremonies which, to his delight, was accepted by one of the London weeklies. I have taken the above particulars of the circumnavigator from Esme's article.

CHAPTER XIX

SPAIN (*conclusion*)

DURING the remainder of the term of Constitutional Government in Spain, i.e. till September, 1923, when General Primo de Rivera established his Dictatorship, political life went on much as before.

The tyranny of the *Juntas Militares* and their constant interference in the political life of the country is perhaps better shown by a list of Spanish Governments over-thrown by their malign influence than by pages of reports on the proceedings. After they were reconstituted in 1917 to remove injustices in the Army, and for no other reason, they removed instead the following Governments from office :

1. Liberal. Marquis de Alhucemas. 10th January, 1917.
2. Liberal-Conservative. Señor Dato. 27th October, 1917.
3. Liberal. Marquis de Alhucemas. March, 1918.
4. Liberal. Conde de Romanones. April, 1919.
5. Conservative. Señor Sanchez de Toca. December, 1919.
6. Extreme Right. Señor Maura. January, 1922.

It will be seen from the above that the *Juntas* distributed their favours without partiality. I remember on one occasion visiting Salamanca with my old friend, Carlo Placci, who had come to stay with me in Spain, and as he had a letter for the well-known Professor Don Miguel Unamuno we went together to present it. Don Miguel, who was distinguished as a writer and had been Rector of the University of Salamanca, had been condemned, in December, 1920, during a temporary suspension of the

Constitutional Guarantees, to sixteen years' imprisonment by a military tribunal for alleged insults to the Army. He was, however, too important a person for such a sentence to be carried out, and a few days later, before the sentence was confirmed, it was quashed by some higher authority. The fact is he never went to prison at all, but military jurisdiction, which was not a favourite of his, did not grow in his esteem as a result of this episode.

As we were walking through the cathedral together, and he was pointing out its beauties, two Canons came up and saluted him in a friendly way. I asked him whether he was on good terms with the Church, as I had heard the contrary. He said, smiling :

" There used to be an ecclesiastical tyranny in Spain, but that is all over long ago. Now we are suffering from a military tyranny, which is worse. But the worst of all will come later—the tyranny of the pedants."

I have always treasured this remark because it happened to fit in with my own opinion that government by pedants —whether German Nazis or Russian Communists who, if pedantry can best be defined as living intellectually in blinkers, surely deserve this title—trying by force to pour human nature into one standardised mould, cut out on the theories either of " surplus values " or " race purity," is probably the most unattractive spectacle that can be offered to man. That, I believe, is what Don Miguel Unamuno really meant because, being a Spaniard, he would never allow himself to be poured into a mould. May not only Spaniards but Englishmen also ever remain men and not robots. I should like to see another prayer added to the Litany : " From the tyranny of pedantocracy, good Lord, deliver us ! "

In November, 1922, the then Prime Minister, Señor Sanchez de Toca, introduced a Bill dissolving the *Juntas*. Yet, though it was received amidst the plaudits of the whole Chamber, nothing was done and the *Juntas* continued their activities.

Every Government in turn tried to tackle the question of responsibility for Annual, which invariably produced a crisis. The fact was that all parties and party leaders, except the Socialists, as well as most of the generals, dreaded the awful washing of dirty linen in public that would result. In November, however, a new Liberal Ministry of Concentration was tried, with Count Romanones as Minister of Justice, and as Foreign Minister Don Santiago Alba, a most able and energetic man, though accused by his opponents of being none too scrupulous in his methods.

The greatest reform passed during the whole four years I spent in Spain under Parliamentary Government must be put down to the credit of the Minister of the Interior, the Duke of Almadovar, who at once introduced a Bill, which was actually passed, suppressing innumerable gambling establishments that had sprung up all over Spain of recent years. Only some of the older gambling houses, like that of San Sebastian, which had been given special concessions, it was found impossible to abolish at the time.

The Government also announced their intention of stopping military operations in Morocco and forming a volunteer army to keep order in the Spanish zone. A Civil High Commissioner took the place of the Military one.

Many strikes and labour troubles broke out again in the course of the year, showing that the calmer atmosphere of the previous year was far more apparent than real.

The year 1922 was an interesting one for us, since it brought with it negotiations for a new Treaty of Commerce. By the middle of 1921 it was clear that, owing to Spanish commercial legislation, unless we could negotiate a regular Commercial Treaty with Spain the *modus vivendi* on which our trade relations had previously existed for many years would be denounced, and we should be placed on the first column of the Tariff, which was called a War Tariff, because it indicated that, having no privileges of any kind for our goods, British goods imported into Spain would have to pay the highest rates under the new Tariff legislation. This was naturally a very serious matter.

During the negotiations, into which we were forced against our will, for we were quite satisfied to carry on with our *modus vivendi*, it was borne in upon me with ever-increasing force that we were terribly handicapped by our unilateral Free Trade policy for the making of Treaties of Commerce. The right of free entry into England of most Spanish products gave us no right to expect reciprocity because other countries benefited equally. It was quite useless for us to argue, as we did for a long time, that we should be treated on the "*do ut des*" principle. The Spaniards simply replied that they were authorised under their new Tariff legislation to give concessions in return for special concessions given to them. If we chose to admit goods from all countries free that did not alter the case for them. The negotiators on our side were Mr. Fountain, of the Board of Trade; Captain Charles, Commercial Secretary of our Embassy; and myself. It was in vain that we argued with the Spanish Delegation during the hot days of a very hot July in Madrid. Spain would do nothing for us unless we reduced our import duties on dried fruits and wine, which His Majesty's Government were most reluctant to do. It seemed at one time as if we should have to go empty away. However, somehow we finally mutually squeezed some concessions out of each other, and signed a Treaty in the sweat of our brows. At the very end, however, it looked as if it would fail because the Asturian coal owners made a powerful attack on the provisions concerning the quota for coal imported from Britain, in which we were most interested. Two of the most powerful Ministers in the Spanish Cabinet came from Asturias, but the Minister of Finance finally accepted what in Italy would be called "*una piccola combinazione*," by which a large subvention, amounting to some twenty-eight million pesetas per annum, I believe, would be paid as compensation to the Spanish owners. The Minister of Finance was said only to have given way on this point after great pressure had been put on him by the two Asturian Ministers.

I was truly glad to leave Madrid that August, because

my schoolboys from Downside had already arrived at Zarauz and we all looked forward to our holidays together there as the greatest treat the gods could give us.

Besides these Treaty negotiations, there was one matter which occupied much of my time in Spain. This was the arrest outside the three-mile limit by Spanish Customs cutters of feluccas, small sailing boats, and even motor launches, flying the British flag. The constant correspondence that passed between the Embassy and the Spanish Foreign Office on these cases was an education for me later in dealing with very similar arrests of bootlegging vessels in the United States after my transfer to Washington.

These smuggling feluccas flew the British flag in spite of the fact, which we knew as well as the Spanish Foreign Office, that they were actually for the most part Spanish owned. Their Spanish owners paid certain British Gibraltarian subjects to act as cover for their boats and to allow them to sail under the Union Jack so as to give them a better chance of escaping condemnation in Spain if they were caught. We always protested against the capture of these tobacco smugglers, for such they were, whenever they had been taken outside the three-mile limit. The Spanish reply invariably was that Spain recognised only a six-mile limit, and so negotiations went on interminably. But it must be admitted that we were in no hurry to see justice done too rapidly in such cases, for we saw no reason why we should make ourselves officious in pressing the claims of these Spanish smugglers masquerading under the British flag.

With poor British sailors, on the other hand, who were often held up for months for trial after having been run in for a spree on shore, we were always extremely anxious to get the trial over as soon as possible. The officials of the Spanish Foreign Office were generally sympathetic, and were often shocked to hear that for a slight misdemeanour of this kind a man should be kept in prison for many months without chance of trial. The local authorities were generally immovable. It was not until my good friend, Mr. Willard, the American Ambassador, who was always ready to put his experience in Spain at my disposal, taught me how to deal with such cases that we were able to rid ourselves of the constant correspondence and worry they gave us.   His plan was this.   Offer the local authorities a reasonable deposit on account of the prisoner, to be forfeited if he left the country after leaving the prison pending trial.   No difficulties were made if he walked on to the first ship sailing for home.   The Consul paid the small deposit, which was much cheaper than defending the prisoner at his trial, and everyone was happy but the lawyers, whom nobody cared for.

I found this system worked like a charm in almost every case.

Mr. and Mrs. Willard became our very close friends, and even almost relations, for their second daughter, Elizabeth, married in Madrid my nephew, Mervyn Herbert, of Tetton House, Taunton, who was one of the Secretaries of the Embassy.   Nothing could have been more felicitous than this marriage for all concerned, and while the Willards remained in Madrid we formed a very happy family party there.   This, unfortunately, was broken up in 1922, when the Ambassador had to leave on the defeat of the Democrats in the Presidential Election of that year.   When we were translated to the United States, Mr. and Mrs. Willard, and their elder daughter, who married Kermit Roosevelt, President Theodore Roosevelt's second son, invariably kept up the tradition of friendship between the two families.

The last Elections I was to see in Spain took place with a Liberal Government of Concentration in office, which " made " the Elections perhaps more openly and unashamedly than any previous one, if that were possible, and got their reward in a large majority.

The principal Liberal paper, *El Sol*, commenting on the open jerrymandering practised, wrote that while political institutions and among them Parliamentary Government were losing ground every day, there was in Spain an institution, the Supreme Military and Naval

Tribunal, presided over by General Aguilera, which was acquiring an authority belonging to no other public body and gaining the position of a final Court of Appeal in questions of justice and national security.

Meanwhile it became evident at each Election that the great mass of voters had lost all interest in the affairs of the State, and were wearied to the point of despair by the intrigues of politicians, or were suffering from both together.

There was one significant incident in these Elections which should not escape attention since, with others, it helps to explain the discontent of the Right as well as of the Left with the conduct of Parliamentary elections in Spain, and therefore also to explain the ease with which a few months later Constitutional Government was upset and a military dictatorship accepted by the country at large. This was the election, as one of the representatives for the Island of Mallorca, of the immensely rich so-called smuggler king, Don Juan March, who was returned as a follower of the Liberal group of Don Santiago Alba, the Minister for Foreign Affairs, and was trying to get the concession for building a railway from the north to the south of Spain. At the same time, Don Antonio Maura, Conservative, and one of the most respected Parliamentary leaders, who had also been a Mallorcan representative for many years, was defeated. This combination of circumstances naturally led the public to put two and two together, not to the advantage of Don Santiago Alba.

According to press reports, some candidates spent from £5,000 to £10,000 on these Elections.

In May, 1922, rumours reached me of a probable *coup d'état*. The plan was that troops should surround the *Cortes*, declare Parliament dissolved, and proclaim a Dictatorship under General Aguilera, the President of the Supreme Military and Naval Tribunal.

When Parliament opened in May the King's speech contained a significant reference to the Moroccan disaster, declaring that, as regards " responsibilities " for this, the

Government (which was, of course, Liberal) intended that complete justice should be done promptly, though calmly. This created uneasiness among certain Conservative leaders, since a Conservative Government had been in power at the time of that unhappy event, and many thought that some Liberal leaders were not averse to paying off old scores in this way. There were even rumours that the King himself might be drawn into this Inquiry and that it might be made a peg on which to hang an anti-monarchical movement.

The King's speech further referred to the colossal expenditure on the Morocco zone as one of the principal causes of the annual deficit which burdened the country. Numerous reforms were promised.

On May 20th the attention of the capital was, how-ever, for a moment distracted from politics by an ancient and most beautiful ceremony, the most beautiful I think I ever attended at the Court of Spain. This was the presentation by the Papal Nuncio, Monsignor Tedeschini, to Her Majesty Queen Victoria Eugenia of the Golden Rose which had been brought from Rome by a special envoy, Marchese Sacchetti.

The presentation of the Golden Rose, which is the highest honour the Pope can confer upon a Catholic Queen, highly gratified public opinion in Spain, and was unquestionably popular with all who were not definitely subversive and anti-Catholic. The latter were, however, comparatively few.

The ceremony took place in the *Capilla Real* of the Royal Palace, and was preceded by the usual formal procession round the great corridor of the court, hung, as always, with magnificent tapestries. It was conducted with unusual splendour. There were present all the Royal Family, members of the Government, grandees, military and naval officers, members of the Diplomatic Corps, all in uniform ; the ladies wearing white mantillas instead of black. It was truly the Queen's day, and she looked magnificent, tall, stately and dignified.

Monsignor Tedeschini, also tall and imposing, was

worthy of the occasion. The music of the choir was admirable. It was indeed an unforgettable sight.

Towards the end of June a petition was presented to the Senate by the Supreme Military and Naval Tribunal, under General Aguilera, asking that senatorial privileges might be waived as regards General Berenguer, Commander-in-Chief in Morocco at the time of Annual, so as to make it possible for him to be tried by the Tribunal for his share in the events of that time.

The petition was, by adroit manœuvring on the part of Count Romanones, now President of the *Cortes*, accepted by that body, General Berenguer having himself demanded to be heard before the Tribunal. At the same time the Government announced that they were considering the appointment of a Parliamentary Commission to inquire into the question of the civil responsibilities which both the Extreme Left and the Military had been clamouring for. For the moment, therefore, this burning question seemed to have been happily shelved.

It suddenly, however, leapt again into the limelight, as things had a habit of doing in Spain, on account this time of a most insulting letter sent by General Aguilera to Señor Sanchez de Toca regarding the latter's speech in the Berenguer affair. The letter ran as follows :

> Since this baseness of yours was directed against my person as President of the Supreme Military Tribunal, a baseness very much in harmony with your depraved morality, I have to inform you that a repetition of it or anything like it will compel me to proceed against you with all the vigour and energy that men of your stamp deserve.

The letter was, of course, intended to provoke a challenge. Instead, it was read aloud in the Senate by Señor Sanchez de Toca, who then handed it to Count Romanones, then President of the Senate, to be dealt with. The latter insisted on the inviolability of freedom of speech in the Senate, and when the matter came up for discussion General Aguilera declared that he had addressed it to Señor Sanchez as a man and not as a Senator, and refused to withdraw one word of it. This was badly received both within the Senate and outside.

There was reason to suppose that Aguilera and his followers had been preparing a *coup d'état* for July 5th, with the object of placing the General in power as Dictator. After his speech, however, it seemed that no one wanted him.

During the remainder of the summer further crises were threatened, but as they never came to anything, the public fell into the usual summer siesta condition of mind.

On September 13th Spain was aroused by the news that General Primo de Rivera, Captain-General of Catalonia, had the previous night declared martial law throughout his district on his own initiative, seized all communications, and invited all other Captains-General of the Provinces to support his action. He further issued a manifesto explaining that the Army had petitioned the King to remove all politicians from the Government in order to save the country from disaster. All garrisons in Catalonia at once supported him. In San Sebastian and Madrid troops were confined to barracks, but no disturbances occurred in any part of the country. The King, who was at San Sebastian, left by train for Madrid on September 14th, and, the Government having placed their resignation in his hands, His Majesty called a meeting of generals, after which he telegraphed to General Primo de Rivera, Marques de Estella, to come to Madrid and form a Government.

At that time I felt it almost incredible that King Alfonso should not have been cognisant beforehand of this *coup d'état*. Everything seemed to work so perfectly that I could not believe he had not been informed of what was to occur. He told me, however, on his return that he had been kept in complete ignorance, and the reason His Majesty gave me was one which convinced me after I became acquainted with General Primo and learnt to know his character. The King told me, and I can believe it, that Primo absolutely refused to allow His Majesty to be let into the secret because he could not allow his Sovereign to be in any way compromised in case of failure. King Alfonso gave me a long account of what occurred during these days which I repeated, at his request, to King George. It was remarkable how keenly desirous he was to let King George know that he had had no hand in the plot, showing that he realised how greatly the King of England would object to any violation of the Constitution on the part of his brother monarch of Spain.

When I next saw King George in February, before leaving for the United States, he spoke to me at some length on the subject, but I got the impression that he was not as much convinced as I that Primo had kept King Alfonso altogether in the dark about his intentions— but, then, he did not know the Spanish Dictator as I did. I was certain that he would willingly have risked his life not to compromise his Sovereign.

On September 14th, before coming to Madrid on the King's summons, General Primo issued another manifesto to the country, declaring that the time had come to free Spain from the professional politicians who were the cause of all public misfortunes and political immoralities, that the new military Government was determined to exact " responsibilities " (for Annual) and conduct Government themselves, or appoint civilians who would govern according to their ideas. A new " Military Directorate of Inspection " would be appointed, charged with the maintenance of public order, the normal work of the Government Departments and of official organisations. This manifesto specially picked out Don Santiago Alba, the Minister for Foreign Affairs, as one against whom immediate proceedings would be taken, and also the Prime Minister, who had supported and shielded " this depraved and cynical Minister."

Don Santiago, having no doubt received a timely hint of what was in store for him, brought with him to a ball, which took place at the Royal Palace at San Sebastian on the night of September 12th, his resignation from the Government. He informed the King at the same time that he was obliged to leave San Sebastian for Asturias, where his mother was dangerously ill.

Instead of going to Asturias, however, after leaving the palace he at once left in his motor-car for France, and before the Primo de Rivera *coup* was announced he was well over the Franco-Spanish frontier at Hendaye—which is only thirteen and a half miles from San Sebastian, and therefore he was able to reach French territory before orders were sent to close the frontier. Don Santiago never allowed the grass to grow under his feet, and I certainly never had to complain of his handling of our mutual business at the Ministry of Foreign Affairs on this or any other account.

As soon as I heard the news of the *coup* I started from Zarauz, taking my passport with me as a precaution, and drove the thirteen and three-quarter miles to San Sebastian, though not probably as fast as Don Santiago had driven to Hendaye. Having collected what details I could, I drafted a telegram to the Foreign Office, only to find that all telegraph and telephone offices were closed. I therefore went over the border and, having been permitted with my passport to leave Spain, dispatched my telegram without difficulty.

My new American colleague, Mr. Alec P. Moore, however, took another route. Hearing that King Alfonso was leaving by special train for Madrid at an early hour, he went down to the station and bluffed the officials in charge of the train into allowing him to get on. In this way he succeeded in reaching Madrid before any other heads of missions, which caused them some annoyance, and they complained to me as doyen or dean of the Diplomatic Corps.

When I passed on their complaints to Mr. Moore, whose unconventional ways always amused me, all he said was :

" Well, you know, I used to be a newsboy at Pittsburg, and wherever there's anything on I have to be on the spot."

I said, laughing, that this might do well for Pittsburg, but as the whole Diplomatic Corps could not be mysteriously accommodated on the King's special trains, they hoped that he would not again steal a march on them in this way. He promised he would not.

Mr. Moore was a tall, fine-looking man, clean-shaven, of course, and carefully dressed in quasi-1850 style with a high collar, black stock and double-breasted waistcoat. He was most entertaining. He told me that when he first presented his Letters to King Alfonso he had asked permission to call him " Chief," saying that he did not know where to put in " Majesty " or " Señor " or " King," and that in newspaper offices in Pittsburg the head was always called " Chief," and he was accustomed to that. The King laughingly assented, and " Chief " he remained for Mr. Moore as long as the latter stayed in Madrid.

The stories about Mr. Moore were innumerable. One of the best was that on the occasion of the opening of some memorial in a southern port town to those who had fallen in the Spanish-American War, Mr. Moore was asked to lay a wreath. This he at once accepted, and laid his wreath with becoming gravity. But when, after it was laid, the King invited him to join him in his box, Mr. Moore, who had heard rumours of bombs, looked up, wagged a forefinger at the King, and said :

" Nix doing, Chief. I hope to get back to Pittsburg."

Mr. Moore and I hit it off very well, and the first time he came over to Washington after my appointment there he took the opportunity of some press dinner to tell all the Washington pressmen gathered there that, though they might hardly believe it, I was really quite a good sort of guy and begged them to treat me kindly. I think his recommendation had considerable influence for, except for one occasion, which will be mentioned later on, I was always treated with the greatest courtesy—more, indeed, than was customarily meted out to American public men.

The Constitutional Government having resigned, the King, on September 15th, signed a Royal Decree appointing General Primo President of the Military Directorate, which contained nine other generals of no special distinction. The President was invested with the authority and powers of sole Minister with the duty of submitting to the King all resolutions of the Government Departments.

Various decrees followed each other with bewildering speed, some bringing really needed reforms, especially and at last the abolition of the *Juntas*, others, such as abolition of trial by jury, of a definitely reactionary tendency.

There was a cartoon in *Punch* about Christmas time of General Primo saying, " Yes, we have no mañanas to-day," which was based on a street song of that time, " Yes, we have no bananas to-day." This was most true of the Military Directorate, which produced legislation at a pace that had never been seen before in Spain. We found it almost impossible to cope with the various decrees that were turned out daily from this rationalised law factory.

One thing, however, was agreeable to me. Everything was speeded up generally. Cases pending in which British subjects were involved were treated with the real and plain intention to deal with them quickly and fairly. As far as politics were concerned, they were now non-existent, and this, I think, came as a relief to the Spanish public quite as much as to us, who felt that reporting home details of various political crises was a most barren occupation.

Life for the moment was, therefore, moving on more comfortable lines than it had for the past three and a half years when, one evening after the New Year, 1924, a bombshell fell on me to disturb my new-found peace.

I remember well a telegram being sent down after dinner from the Chancery, marked " Private and Confidential. Decipher yourself." This was alarming. I began to decipher, and before I had gone far I found that owing to the serious illness of Sir Auckland Geddes, British Ambassador at Washington, Lord Curzon, who was then Secretary of State for Foreign Affairs, wished to offer me the Washington Embassy.

I confess I was thunderstruck and thoroughly disturbed. I had obtained as much and more in the Diplomatic Service than I had a right to expect. I believed what I had been taught by two very dissimilar Englishmen : first, Cecil Rhodes, secondly, James Bryce, that the future of the British Empire and perhaps of the peace of the world, if it was ever to be firmly established at all, lay above every other thing in the maintenance of friendly relations, but also most decidedly in the avoidance of alliances of any kind, with the United States. I had therefore always looked upon our Embassy at Washington as being a key position. No one could say it was an easy position, for just because we spoke the same language our people and theirs misunderstood each other more easily perhaps than any other two peoples in the world. Generally speaking, I believed that the " ancient grudge," as Owen Whister calls it, still existed in America rather, indeed, in the working classes than among those who have had a wider education in history and knowledge of the outer world and, on the other hand, with us at home among the public school and university folk as well as the dwindling descendants of ancient Tories who, however, continue to possess considerable influence. Desire for friendship and understanding with the United States and British sympathy with the United States was built up on the broad basis of sympathy with democratic institutions, and therefore was found more generally among our working classes.

Apart from the difficulties arising out of these broad and basic principles on which I, following the lessons of Rhodes and Bryce, so firmly believed that British foreign policy must finally and definitely rest, I could not hide from myself that there were many difficult and prickly questions which would have to be settled in course of time. Above all, there were War Debts, and also claims arising out of the War ; the attitude of the United States Government towards the League of Nations, to which we were, in my opinion, rightly and definitely attached ; the attitude of the United States with regard to neutrality in war time, which always threatened us with a possible breach if we supported the League Covenant fully—it was useless to close our eyes to this—and, besides, many other thorny subjects rose up before my mind. Then I asked myself frankly : " Are you the man for a job like that ? " and I came to the conclusion, as I had before, that I was not.

Beyond this, family reasons urged me not to accept. To be on the other side of the Atlantic necessarily compelled much longer absences from my five sons, all of whom, except one, Henry, were now of school age, and I realised that Isa would wish to be with them as much as possible in case of any being ill. For reasons both public and private, therefore, I felt it would be wiser and better for all concerned that I should stay where I was. I consulted Isa and finding her of my mind, I replied to Curzon pointing out that a more conspicuous person than I—some man whose name was well known both in America and at home, which mine was not—would certainly be more suitable for the post, and also making an appeal on the private grounds above stated, as well as one *ad misericordiam*, because Isa was such a bad sailor that I was really alarmed every time she crossed the ocean. I added that I was writing a long letter explaining my views, which I would send by the first possible safe opportunity. All this I did, and sent my letter by a Spanish diplomat friend who was returning straight—so he assured me—to London.

Not receiving any reply, I rejoiced, only to be again thrust back into the slough of despond by another telegram from Curzon saying that, as he had not received my letter, he had sent my name in to the King for the Washington Embassy. I rarely remember receiving any message that so appalled me. But now there was nothing more to be done, and I dragged myself heavy-hearted up to bed. I had, fortunately, in those days one great gift : whatever happened, I could always sleep.

The next morning I asked what could have happened to my private messenger. On inquiry I found that he had been unable to resist the temptations of Paris, and had lingered there several days.

Having, therefore, had my name submitted to the King, it was incumbent on me without further delay to telegraph to Curzon saying that I would naturally obey His Majesty's wishes whatever they might be in this matter, and received a very cordial reply from " the Marquess " thanking me and saying that all was settled, and that my appointment would shortly be gazetted. He wrote me afterwards an amusing letter, sweeping all my objections away with his lordly hand, and saying at the end : " As to Lady Isabella's sea-sickness, she will, of course, when she crosses the Atlantic have to choose her own weather." In his magnificent way he would doubt-less have expected the winds and the waves to obey him, but she did not feel so sure of her supernatural powers.

One thing pleased me greatly over this business, which was a letter from my old friend Crowe, the Permanent Under-Secretary of the Foreign Office, not only con-gratulating me, but actually thanking me for accepting, as if in the circumstances I could do otherwise. But I felt, if I can put it so, more upholstered after that letter from Crowe.

I was actually transferred to Washington on February 2nd, 1924, just after the first Labour Government had come into office, Mr. Ramsay MacDonald being both Prime Minister and Secretary of State for Foreign Affairs. It seemed to me an act as gracious as it was unexpected on his part to confirm an appointment of this importance made by his predecessor just before leaving office.

The rest of our time in Madrid passed hectically in packing and saying good-bye to friends and colleagues, but before closing the Madrid chapter I must mention some leading and interesting personalities with whom we came into contact, especially the Duke of Alba, our most extremely Spanish friend, though his family name was FitzJames-Stuart, and his second title Duke of Berwick, for he was the lineal descendant of the great Marshal Berwick, son of James II of England. Though his

Duchy of Berwick had long ago been attainted in England, he liked to remember his English and Stuart ancestry, and had indeed inherited a true Stuart look.   He possessed one of the most attractive houses in Madrid, the Palacio de Liria, some excellent pictures, among others a famous portrait of his other great ancestor the Duke of Alba, as well as a lot of tapestries specially woven for the latter with pictures of his battles, and a variety of other possessions.   One of the pictures in the Palacio de Liria which most delighted me was a portrait by Goya of the Duchess of Alba of that date, a lady who was said to have been *au mieux* with the painter.   However this may have been, Goya had used on this canvas his peculiarly satirical brush.   She was a little lady, dressed all in white muslin with a pink sash round her waist and a pink bow in her hair, and beside her stands a little white poodle with a pink bow in its hair and a pink ribbon round its tail—a perfectly humorous picture.   The pictures of the royal family of that date by Goya, which are in the Prado, also strike the top note of satire, as does, in a minor gallery, one of Godoy, Principe de la Paz, a fat man lolling complacently on a flowered bank with a battle-piece going on behind him.   I have always wondered why these great people allowed Goya to paint them with his tongue in his cheek, as he did.   I have, however, eschewed writing of pictures in Madrid or anywhere in Spain, for it might be endless.

The principal figure connected in my mind with the Duke of Alba and the Palacio de Liria was undoubtedly his great-aunt, the Empress Eugénie, widow of Napoleon III.   She had always been a most fascinating personality in the time of my youth, and I can hardly imagine anything that would have seemed more strange to the little boy living up in remote Cumberland when he read or was told of the Empress's adventures in 1871 during the Franco-Prussian War, and her escape from the mob in Paris in the carriage of her American dentist, than that he would take her in to dinner in a Spanish house in the year 1922.   But I never met a more wholly

MADRID, 31ST MAY, 1920

EMPRESS EUGENIE AND THE QUEEN OF SPAIN

charming old lady, full of talk, and eager for information about all questions of foreign politics, and paying me, who was thirty years her junior, the compliment of listening to what I had to say about the Paris Conference and every sort of subject. One thing she would not do— that was to speak about her own past, which filled me with despair, for I, of course, could not ask her questions. Both Isa and I fell completely under her charm. She was then almost blind with cataract, but had an operation later in Barcelona which was quite successful. When the bandages were taken from her eyes, seeing the light she exclaimed : " *L'Espagne m'a donné deux fois le jour*," a pretty conceit.[1]

She died not long after.

Then General Primo de Rivera, who dominated the scene when I left, must be mentioned. A large, kindly man, who rolled in and out of the room like a friendly Newfoundland dog, he was not at all the popular conception of a dictator with an iron fist. Nor was he that. In fact, considering the usual course of such *Putsches*, his advent to power caused little disturbance and practically no bloodshed at all. He must have been greatly relieved at Don Santiago Alba's precipitate flight. But he had an unquestionable gift for Government and administrative ability, and as long as he was allowed to continue in power he managed to make straight many crooked places. I knew him but slightly, but had a great respect for his character, and whatever criticisms may be found with his régime he certainly ended the Moroccan war, which was bleeding the country white, abolished the *Juntas Militares*, so far as active interference in politics was concerned, put Spanish finances on a much sounder footing, and initiated many useful public works. He deserved better treatment than he got from his country or his King.

One more personage must be mentioned, the Condessa de Casa Valencia, whose husband had been long Spanish Ambassador in London, and had always retained an affection for England and the English without, however,

---

[1] " Spain has twice given me the light of day." She was born in Spain.

dropping any particle of her Spanishry. In her house we often met men of different political complexion as well as writers and artists and men of ability in many walks of life. Having been the wife of a diplomat, her house was thrown open much more widely than is customary in Spain, where there is still a somewhat Moorish tradition about keeping the house for the family only. She was not only hospitable, but well read, of keen intelligence and bright wit. One of the many Prime Ministers of Spain during my time once said of her that she had all the mental qualifications necessary for a Cabinet Minister. This was not, perhaps, excessive praise ; he might, I think, have said rather for a Prime Minister, and then have been nearer the mark. Her sons, of whom Don Alvaro Alcalà Galiano has written the only published account of the days of April, 1931, which led to the fall of the monarchy, were among the younger Spaniards of Madrid whom we saw most frequently, for they were all, with such a mother, intelligently cosmo-politan—a very pleasant combination.

So the day of departure drew near. We gave our last party and ate our last dinner. We were received in our last audience by the King and Queen and the Queen Mother, for whom we all entertained a most profound respect, for during her regency, while the King was a minor, all agreed that she had played both with wisdom and courage the difficult part in Spain of a constitutional monarch.

We went down for the last time to see the King play polo in his private ground in the park of the Casa del Campo, where on fine afternoons I had so often ridden with all my boys. We went to play golf for the last time in sight of the snow-capped Guadarramas, and for the last time we visited that wonderful room of the Velasquez pictures at the Prado, of which one can never tire. We said good-bye, so far as we could, to as many of the places round Madrid for which we had learnt to feel real affection.

But, above all, we said good-bye with sorrow to the

Spanish people, splendid, courteous, kindly, dignified and, when unspoiled, least avaricious, most contemptuous of money in the world, in which lies their great charm. So I will end these chapters on Spain with two or three stories of Spanish peasants.

Some friends of mine motoring in winter over the Guadarramas to Madrid, were stuck in a deep snowdrift. Presently a muleteer with a cart and a string of eight or ten mules came ploughing his way down the pass. My friends asked if he would be kind enough to hitch his mules on to their car and help to drag it to the top of the pass. He at once agreed. When they were at the top they offered him a tip which must have been like a small fortune to him, but he waved it away with an apologetic smile (as if unwilling to hurt their feelings), saying : " *El unico que pueden offrecer los pobres son los favores.*"[1]

Could that be beaten in any country or among any people in the world ?

Another time I was driving along a country road with my old friend Denbigh, who wanted to take a photograph of a very picturesque Aragonese carter with his white oxen all gorgeously caparisoned as if for a Court ceremony, but in fact only to carry home a load of hay.

I asked him if he would mind stopping for his photo, because my friend so much admired his turn-out and wanted to take back a picture to show his family in England. He immediately stopped the oxen and the photo was taken. Denbigh thought he should offer him some pesetas. Rather shyly, knowing the feeling of these peasants about tips, I took it to him, but he simply rose and bowed to us both : " *No, señores, el honor es mio.*"[2]

And yet one more personal reminiscence. My friend de Caux, *The Times* correspondent in Madrid, and I occasionally went for a day out tramping in the forests of the Guadarramas, which he knew well. One day we sat down by a spring on some turf in a high valley to

[1] " All that the poor can offer is favours."
[2] " No, gentlemen, the honour is mine."

have our lunch, when an old peasant came up the hill and asked us with much ceremony if he might sit down also by the spring ; of course, leave was given with all due form and ceremony, for a Spanish peasant can only be treated as a grandee.   Then we fell into conversation.

THE PEASANT : " Where have you señores come from ? "

DE CAUX : " We have come to-day from el Paular.   But before that from Madrid."

THE PEASANT : " Indeed ! So have I. I have a son working in a store there. A fine place. Perhaps the owner is a compatriot of yours."

DE CAUX : " Really ? "

THE PEASANT : " Yes, he's a German."

DE CAUX : " Oh, then he can't be a compatriot. I'm French."

THE POOR PEASANT (realising he had made an awful *gaffe*, rising and sweeping his hat from his head with a courtly bow) : " *Muchos años.*"[1]

De Caux tried after this to make our casual acquaintance feel quite at home again, but the conversation flagged, and he presently rose and wishing us a very pleasant holiday, went off on his way.

The recollection of these little meetings with Spanish peasants by the way has a very soothing effect on a mind tired with political controversies and the greasy oil required to make the machinery of life go round.   Every unspoiled Spaniard contains within him something of both Don Quixote and Sancho Panza.

I said good-bye sadly to both, hoping that I might some time return to quench my thirst at the fountain of good manners of the Spanish peasant when my throat was parched and dry from the deserts of the rationalisation of the surrounding world.

---

[1] " May you live many years."

CHAPTER XX

" THE AMERICAN SCENE "

(1924-1930)

INTRODUCTION

Extracts from Will Rogers's Jubilee Broadcast[1]

" Hello, England ! You have had a great week, haven't you ?

* * * * *

" I'd like to say right away, please, don't mistake me for one of those self-styled goodwill Ambassadors. You have, I know, been goodwilled to death. I know we have over here. So get me right, England. I bring you no goodwill.

* * * * *

" I am just a humble admirer of a few of your—well, in fact, of many—of your customs and a great many of your people.

* * * * *

" We will never have trouble with each other. England, you are us. We both have humour. If we started to fight, we would have to stop in the middle and start laughing at each other. I don't know—you are naturally funny to us and we are like a Mickey Mouse cartoon to you."

I HAVE headed these chapters with these quotations from Will Rogers, who was perhaps the most delightfull philosopher of the age. He may have been an optimist when he wrote " We shall never have trouble with each other. . . . We both have humour," but it is, all the same, one of the truest things ever spoken, especially if we can only remember that we are really funny to them and they can remember that often to us the American scene is like a Mickey Mouse cartoon.

He said earlier and quite as truly, " We both have manners and customs that drive each other pretty near

[1] Published in the *Canadian Moving Picture Digest*, Toronto, 1935.

crazy and an American with a mouthful of chewing-gum can get on your nerves almost as an Englishman with only one eye full of monocle can get on ours, but, after all, neither commodity contributed to the success that the nations have made."

Well, Mr. Rogers, you may not have been a good-will Ambassador, but I think you have done more than many generations of well-meaning pompous hands-across-the-sea post prandial orators to help us to understand Americans, and for that I thank you.

I wish we had your counterpart over here whom we could send to America. He mustn't be an ambassador—good will or not—but just a good, straight human being like our King George, whom you admired, with a sense of humour like yours, ready, like you, for a cheerful give and take. Then, bless us all, what fun we should have.

Starting on the last lap of this book, *Theatre of Life*, which will deal with my diplomatic life as Ambassador to the United States of America, I feel at once the impossibility of attempting to deal even superficially with the subject within the limits of a book of this size. Three to four chapters are necessarily the limit, and one might as well attempt to confine the whole essence of that largest of land mammals, the elephant, or shall I say in this case the " jackaphant " in a pill, as to give in that space an adequate idea of a country which is rather a continent than a country, of a nation which is as yet rather an unblended mixture of many peoples than one nation, of a Government which so often resembles rather a triangular duel than a co-operative organisation. How can a plain man with the limitations of common humanity hope to achieve any such purpose ? I have indeed read many books on America from Mark Twain to James Bryce, from the lives of Washington, Hamilton, Jefferson, Andrew Jackson and Lincoln to more modern delineations of American life and character contained in novels which sometimes tell the reader more than the most carefully written histories. Especially is this the case with modern American writers who have a passion for debunking themselves and their country and its institutions. I have travelled over great stretches of the United States and come into contact with men of all kinds, except unfortunately the real backwoodsmen and cowboys whom I should have liked to meet, but I have not been able to formulate in my mind any of those easy generalisations about America and Americans with which travellers from Europe who have spent a month or two there so often return home ; generalisations they can easily pack into a small " grip-sack " and offload on audiences at home eager for news of that land full of unexpected contradictions.

I left it after six years in a state of mind which so far as the conditions reigning there were concerned might be described as " visibility not good."

I feel, in fact, towards that extraordinary country very much as the American who comes to Europe for the first time and tries to understand it and leaves it bewildered and depressed.

When I get into that frame of mind which I sometimes do in pondering over America, I turn to Lincoln, the one really great statesman of the nineteenth century whom, were I allowed a half-hour's conversation with one great man, I would choose before all others of the last century or of the present day before Napoleon or Cavour who also stands for me absolutely in the front rank. And when I feel depressed I read again Lincoln's Gettysberg speech, which I wish all would read, and my most earnest hope is that all the world over men may take to heart the closing words of his second inaugural address :

> With malice towards none ; with charity for all ; with firmness
> in the right as God gives us to see the right, let us strive on to finish
> the work we are in ; to bind up the nation's wounds, to care for
> him who shall have borne the battle, and for his widow and his
> orphan—to do all which may achieve and cherish a just and lasting
> peace among ourselves and with all nations.

Therefore as when, in appraising a great artist we should always think rather of his few masterpieces than of his poorer works, so America brings back to my mind

Lincoln, and I am grateful to her for having produced one Lincoln to be a guide to us all in matters of statecraft in these days when many men are inclined to run after demagogues and pedants and even mere politicians.

There is, however, one generalisation which I will be bold enough to formulate about America now at the very beginning of this short sketch.

Wherever you go in America, wherever you meet Americans, you will always invariably find one common quality all over the continent. Everyone, man, woman and child, is continually fired by an *insatiable curiosity*, though not necessarily about everything in the world.

Mr. Coolidge once told Isa that he thought he would never visit Europe because America had everything he needed to learn, against which singular belief she, *Romana di Roma* and citizen of no mean city, in her own direct fashion and to his amusement, vigorously protested. But at least about something or other all Americans are certainly panting to know more and most often about many things. It is as if all had naturally taken to heart Kipling's verse :

> I keep six honest serving men
> (They taught me all I knew)
> Their names are What and Why and When
> And How and Where and Who.

And with that one generalisation I will leave this introduction to the last phase.

My American friends will, I hope, understand that if I do not always in these pages attempt to prove that everything in their country is—in my humble opinion—perfect, this does not mean that I shall not always be deeply grateful for all the unending kindness which I have had showered upon me, nor that I left Washington less sure that the safety of our world depends more than any other proposition on a good understanding and friendship between the United States of America and the British Commonwealth of Nations, but without capitulations on either side. In any case, if I seem

---

¹ Kipling's Chapter Headings—*The Elephant's Child.*

sometimes to criticise or to permit myself to be entertained by things I see or hear it will always be " with malice towards none."

* * * * *

I landed at New York one pleasant morning in February and shared the common fate of all things rare on such occasions, being interviewed and photographed. It was an alarming ordeal for the first time, but I imagine that nothing very serious transpired. Reporters were most gracious, and one even remarked that I looked as if I had stepped out of a band-box, though my clothes, as a matter of fact, were many years old. This was an excellent beginning.

I was met by Sir Harry Armstrong, our amazingly active Consul-General, and by our Chargé d'Affaires from Washington, Mr. H. G. Chilton (now His Majesty's Ambassador at Madrid), and others, and speedily carried off to the Pennsylvania station to take the first train to Washington.

There was no time to get any impressions of New York, but I realised that much had changed since I left in 1909. New York is many things, but is decidedly not static. Skyscrapers had multiplied and were continuing to multiply and everywhere there was much noise of riveting steel bolts, a very characteristic noise in the streets of New York and other American cities. Horse-drawn cabs had already disappeared and the whole residential area had moved up town. The nice comfortable old house, 1, Fifth Avenue, belonging to our friend Mr. Butler Duncan, where formerly Isa and I had often stayed with the children, had made way for some store or apartment house. Otherwise " Little Old New York " as New Yorkers affectionately call it, seemed to me much the same.

But the Pennsylvania Railroad Station was a surprise. Millions of dollars had been spent upon it, and one needed a compass to find one's way about. It was not necessary any longer to take a ferry-boat, for the tunnel under the Hudson River was finished and open, and so we,

Chilton and I, talking over changes in Washington, passed
rapidly through the rather dreary scenery of the first
part of the journey and finally landed in the splendid
great new white marble station of Washington. It is
certainly the finest in the world, and I, remembering
the old wooden shanty of a station of former days,
wondered whether all Washington would be so completely changed as this. Not quite yet. Driving to the
Embassy down Pennsylvania Avenue, I still noticed a
few little wooden houses, the property of coloured men
no doubt who, like Frederick the Great's Potsdam miller,
held out against every pressure and refused to sell.· I
was rather pleased to be welcomed by a few of these
landmarks. The old Embassy, anyhow, was not changed,
and as I entered its great doors I had the strange presentiment of sorrow which I remembered from previous
inhabitations of it. The entrance hall, moreover, with a
heavy wooden staircase of the type of 1860–70, was like
a too, too solid nightmare.

" Well," I said to it, " you may not like the looks of me
any more than I do yours, but we must learn to put up
with each other for a time and try to rub along."

Even a pleasant dinner with the Chiltons could not
altogether remove the nightmare feeling of ill hanging
about that large, commonplace but uncanny house.

There was a very numerous staff, some thirty-six in
all, with secretaries, military, naval and air attachés, commercial secretaries and countless typists and others, all
of course new to me, but I was glad to find there to greet
me two old acquaintances in the messengers, " Bob "
Williams (strangely enough having the same name as my
old friend from Rhodesia and Aberdeen) and " Charlie "
Brown, the most active, intelligent and reliable coloured
man I ever came across. He sent me not long ago an
admirable little history of the Embassy House and its
inhabitants, written by himself.

Little by little, with the help of Chilton and Hugh
Tennant, a secretary who had been allotted to me as
Private Secretary, in which capacity he had served with

Sir Auckland Geddes and was invaluable to me, I became acquainted with the principal members of the Government and the Heads of Missions, having, according to etiquette, to pay the first call not only on the President, but also on the Vice-President, the Chief Justice of the Supreme Court and the Secretary of State (Minister of Foreign Affairs), and on all Ambassadors, while Diplomatic Ministers and such other members of the Washington hierarchy, as wished to, called on me. My days were fully occupied.

In addition to all the social side of the duties it was necessary to learn about the routine work of the Embassy, which meant the study of masses of papers. Those who think that diplomacy is all beer and skittles would be surprised at the quantity and variety of work which confronts a new Ambassador in a large Embassy like Washington.

Among the principal personalities with whom I had to make acquaintance was, of course, first and foremost, President Coolidge. The ceremony of reception by the President was much like what it was in the time of President Roosevelt ; there was certainly, as Mrs. Leiter had described it to me, the same lack of " uniformity." But what a difference between the two men. President Roosevelt, rather careless about clothes, affecting a little the bluff heartiness of the Wild West and full of talk and knowledge of English literature. President Coolidge, smart and slim, brushed up and very carefully dressed, and with his words so compressed, they were like meat lozenges, only more so. President Coolidge did not welcome me with references to Scott and " Belted Will." To tell the truth, he said nothing I can remember, but he gave me from the first a sense of security and of a man who would never leap before he looked. He had perhaps, as someone said, the appearance of one who had been weaned on a pickle, but he had also a very humorous eye. I never saw a man who looked less like the son of a farmer, yet his father owned a small farm in a remote village in Vermont and utterly unromantic as Mr. Coolidge was, there have surely been fewer scenes more romantic, if the accomplishment of highly important events in very modest surroundings may be so termed, than the swearing-in of Mr. Coolidge as President of the United States.

He was staying at his father's homestead at Plymouth, among the Vermont mountains, when in the early morning of August 3rd, 1923, a telegram reached them telling of the sudden death the night before of President Harding in California. Mr. Coolidge, being Vice-President, succeeded automatically and under the Constitution he had to be sworn in immediately by the nearest magistrate, who happened to be his father. So there in the little parlour, by the light of an old-fashioned oil-lamp at 2.47 a.m., Mr. Coolidge senior administered the oath to his son and made him President of what is potentially the most powerful State in the world. That is an extreme example of the unexpected contradictions which suddenly in America bring up the European stranger on the curb of incredulous amazement. If this doesn't savour of romance I should like to know what does.

Mr. Coolidge's humour was of the very dry Yankee sort. When I had interviews with him I used to watch his eye, which had a peculiar gleam, rather like that in the eye of a parrot that is about to give someone a tweak, just when one of these specimens of his humour was maturing.

Once not long after my arrival Lord Cecil, who had been speaking in New York, came down to stay in Washington, and I took him, as I did most visitors of distinction, to pay his respects to the President. There was a long silence, long enough to become painful. Then I caught Mr. Coolidge's eye. The gleam was there. He put the tips of his fingers together and drawled :

" When folks come to see me I expect them to do the talking."

It was inexpressibly funny and done inimitably. I knew that I was expected to laugh, and did, which broke the ice. After that conversation flowed as much as it ever did with Mr. Coolidge.

One day the messenger from the Treasury who habitually brought Presidents their quarterly cheque, came into the room and laid one on the table where the President was writing. Mr. Coolidge paid no attention, and the messenger stood waiting for some acknowledgment. Presently the President ceased writing, then, looking up, he saw his cheque and the messenger. He nodded and said, " Come again," and started writing afresh.

The stories about him were endless. I grew to like him because I knew I could trust him completely. He would never promise what he feared he could not perform. But it was difficult to get on to ordinary friendly terms with him. Once when saying good-bye before going home on leave I ventured on a little general conversation, and said that I was glad to see, after travelling about a good deal, that what Owen Wister had called " the ancient grudge " appeared to be dying down by degrees. The President thought, and weighing his words, said :

" Perhaps you're right," then a long silence. Suddenly the parrot gleam in the eye : " I remember my grandfather, old Colonel Coolidge, never had a good word to say for the British."

I laughed, which was what I was supposed to do. What he meant, of course, was that he was not quite as bad as that, and he certainly wasn't.

I cannot leave President Coolidge without a word about Mrs. Coolidge, who won the hearts both of myself and my wife by the extraordinary simplicity and charm of her character and the ease with which she managed to receive and entertain all her guests, whether at a great reception or dinner-party or when she received us alone.

One other lady I must also mention here to whom I have referred in the pages dealing with my first sojourn in Washington. This was Miss Mabel Boardman, whom I first met when I went to Berlin in 1888 as third Secretary to our Embassy there when she was keeping house for her uncle, Mr. Phelps, the American Minister. Miss Boardman has now become a very conspicuous personality in Washington : a great administrator and organiser,

she was head of the American Red Cross and had even
been one of the three Commissioners (virtually Governors)
of the City of Washington and District of Columbia, an
honour to which I believe no other lady has ever attained.
The Boardman house was still as it had been when I
left in 1909, a centre of social gatherings of a rather
serious type, and leaders of all shades of political, industrial and intellectual life, together with a good sprinkling
of diplomats, were always to be found there. On our
return to Washington in 1924 Isa and I were received at
the Boardman house on exactly the same footing of
friendship as when we left fifteen years before.

I owe to Miss Boardman some of the pleasantest musical
recollections of my life. She was always most kind in
inviting Isa and myself to share her box when the great
symphony orchestras of Philadelphia, New York and
Boston visited Washington, which they did once or twice
during the winter. In this way did Washington become
for me a centre of my most vivid musical experiences,
more so even than Berlin or Rome. We had not only
the finest orchestras with players drawn from all parts
of the world, but also unquestionably the most magnificent
instruments that could be heard in, I suppose, any
orchestra in the world, and directing them such geniuses
as Toscanini, Stokowski, Mengelberg, Furtwängler and
Koussevitski. These afternoons given up to the Symphony Concerts were amongst the greatest of our joys in
Washington ; they would have been amongst the greatest
joys anywhere, and for these I had frequently to thank
my old friend Miss Mabel Boardman.

First and foremost amongst the few remaining old
friends and acquaintances who had been in Washington
during my first stay at the Embassy in 1907 was Mr.
Justice Oliver Wendell Holmes and his wife, who seemed
hardly to have changed at all. Their conversation was
as keen and as amusing as ever, and they still honoured
Isa and myself with invitations from time to time to share
a meal with them quite alone. He was decidedly the
Grand Old Man of the Supreme Court and a man whose

views and opinions on the most varied subjects were always interesting.

Two other of the most outstanding personalities of this time were also conspicuous during the administration of Theodore Roosevelt. One was Mr. Charles E. Hughes, who had been Governor of New York and a Judge of the Supreme Court and very nearly defeated President Wilson in the contest for the Presidency in 1916, when he was beaten by an electoral majority of only 276 to 254. It is, of course, impossible to realise what it would have meant to Europe and to the world if Mr. Hughes, who was a great lawyer—he is now Chief Justice of the Supreme Court—and a man of singularly balanced mind in all concerns of life, had been elected in the place of President Wilson. In external politics Mr. Hughes was then and no doubt still is no narrow isolationist. Far from it ; he has always worked for international co-operation and the cause of peace, but his equanimity and sound judgment prevented him from being carried away in one direction or the other by the tornadoes which swept the minds of statesmen not only in Europe, but also in America. I have often thought that many of our troubles during the years that have succeeded the War might have been avoided had he been the principal American delegate at the Paris Conference instead of President Wilson. The only difficulty would have been that had President Wilson stayed behind in Washington, given his unbending certainty in the righteousness of his own policies, it would have been practically impossible for Mr. Hughes to have influenced the deciding factor at Washington, although it is not unlikely that his influence in Paris would have been of immense value.

Mr. Hughes was Secretary of State for the first two years of my term of office in Washington, and owing to his fairness of mind and perfectly level temperament it would have been impossible to find any man with whom it was more agreeable and satisfactory to deal.

The other outstanding figure who dated from the days of Theodore Roosevelt was Mr. Elihu Root, who was Secretary of State in the Roosevelt administration. He also was very much of the same type of mind as Mr. Hughes, and though most distinctly a man, as the saying is in America, " of Presidential timber," he was perhaps too sound and too careful in his judgment of men and of things to have easily received the nomination of the Republican Party for candidature for the Presidency. He was, however, greatly in request as a speaker at big political functions on account of the invariable shrewdness and wisdom with which he diagnosed political questions. His speech was, especially for an American, extraordinarily slow, and he often waited, not in a hesitating way, but simply because, as you understood, he was ruminating in order to find the exact word to fit his meaning. He spoke almost as if he were drawing up a legal document. When the word came, however, as I have said in a previous chapter, it was wholly satisfactory, which is seldom the case with speakers whose words flow like torrents.

Both Mr. Root and Mr. Hughes were a great education for me as to the way in which public business, especially international business, should be conducted.

In 1925 Mr. Hughes retired from the State Department into private life for the time being, to my great regret. He was promoted later, on the death of Mr. W. H. Taft, to the next highest position in the United States after the Presidency, that of Chief Justice of the Supreme Court. Mr. Hughes was succeeded by Mr. Frank Kellogg, who had been American Ambassador in London.

Among these old friends must also be mentioned the *doyen* of the Diplomatic Corps, M. Jusserand, and his charming wife. His knowledge of everything to do with diplomacy and the conduct of diplomatic business was unsurpassed and a more excellent *doyen* it would be impossible to find. He was Ambassador in Washington for very nearly twenty-five years, and therefore from every point of view he was for his younger colleagues a perfect mine of information.

One of the things which most concerned me on my

arrival in Washington was the current and increasing irritation produced by British comments in the Press on the subject of the War Debts Settlement, which in America had been acclaimed at the time it was made as a true and reasonable settlement and as an example to the world of the honest methods of Great Britain in dealing with creditors.   There was no doubt that the Settlement arranged by Mr. Baldwin and the other members of the British Delegation in 1923 had made an immense impression on American public opinion and was most valuable, for, by increasing a spirit of confidence in Great Britain throughout America, it helped us to deal satisfactorily with other somewhat thorny questions.   On arrival in the United States I was frequently asked by reporters and at public dinners what I felt about the War Debts and the Debt Settlement.   I invariably made the same reply, saying that I could not, of course, answer for a great many of my countrymen, but that my own feelings on the subject were simply that I should hate to see England, who had received such enormous benefits from the loans made to her during the War, obliged to repudiate any part of those loans.   Without the various goods which we were able by means of these loans and credits to purchase in the United States and in which our allies were also able to share, it was exceedingly doubtful if we should have been able to carry on the War and to bring it to a victorious conclusion.   Whatever other people might think of the advantage of a victorious conclusion for the Allies, I certainly had no doubt that any other conclusion would have been absolutely disastrous to us.   For this reason, if for no other, I felt that it was essential for England to strain every nerve to repay the whole of the capital borrowed and so far as possible to live up to the Funding Settlement.   I generally ended by saying that if ever, as I thought was possible, America *in her own interests and those of the world at large* were to ask for a reduction of the amount due to her I thought it not impossible that the request might have favourable consideration.   This reply was generally received with laughter and cheers. For the moment, therefore, this question, apart from the criticisms that came from England, was not in the United States a pungent one.

There was, however, one matter of a somewhat allied nature which I looked forward to with particular dread should it come up, because it was replete with high explosives.

I had been warned before arrival that it was possible that the United States Government might present claims against the British Government for action taken during the first years of the War against American shipping in furtherance of the blockade of Germany. There was no doubt that many of these actions taken under British Orders in Council were not in harmony with the rules either of the Declaration of Paris of 1856, which, however, had never been agreed to by the United States, or the Declaration of London of 1909 which, on the other hand, had never been ratified by the British Government. There were flaws, therefore, in both these instruments, although it may be contended that they embodied rules of maritime law which had previously been very largely accepted. What, however, would have made the presentation of these claims a particularly bitter pill to swallow, in my opinion, was that the United States Government itself, after entering the War, had adopted practically the same methods which we had enforced, and carried them out, I think I may say, with even more vigour and rigour than we ourselves had done. The idea, therefore, that we should now be made to pay claims for interference with shipping on legal grounds which the United States Government had, it must be admitted to our great satisfaction, themselves entirely disregarded a few months later, seemed to us to be indeed a raw deal, and I felt very strongly with our Government that the presentation of these claims would really produce an explosion throughout Great Britain.

In March, 1925, I received information which I at once passed on to the Foreign Office that the American State Department would shortly present the blockade claims.

I then received instructions from Sir Austen Chamberlain to take action in the matter.

I accordingly spoke to the Secretary of State, Mr. Frank Kellogg, of the deplorable effect the presentation of these claims would have in Great Britain. The Debt Settlement, being already felt to be a terrible burden, the piling on of these further claims for measures on the ground of their illegality, which the United States Government had themselves also taken against neutral shipping after entering the War, would have an effect on the relations between the two countries which could not but be most unfortunate.

Mr. Kellogg replied that there could be no question of immediate presentation of these claims as they had not yet been looked over. As, however, this answer clearly showed that something of the kind seemed to be intended, the Foreign Office instructed me to see the President.

This I did shortly after, on November 7th, 1925, and spoke to him in much the same terms as I had to Mr. Kellogg. The President listened sympathetically, but said he thought His Majesty's Government had been unduly alarmed. He added that there was no intention of presenting these claims without previous consultation with us, and said that he attached the greatest value to friendly relations with Great Britain and did not wish to do anything that would press hardly upon her.

I have always remembered that interview with President Coolidge, as it was typical of him to say so little in his rather cold and precise way and at the same time to do his utmost, as I found out afterwards, to arrange this matter so satisfactorily that it quietly disappeared and was buried unnoticed and unwept. This result was naturally an immense relief to me, but I cannot claim any special credit for it.

After some further discussion it was decided to appoint a joint commission to examine these claims and certain old British claims which the United States Government had till then refused to consider. Of the American claims only about one-tenth were considered by the American representatives to be worth presenting in any form, and these were set off against the British claims. Thus was the whole question of War claims happily settled by an agreement signed in 1925 and passed by the Senate two years later, in the form of an exchange of notes between the two Governments after, I believe, a much more difficult negotiation between the President and certain senators. The principal credit for this happy solution lay unquestionably with the President, who proved better than his word and in whom after this I always felt complete confidence. But after him must be mentioned Mr. Kellogg and the two American members of the Commission, Mr. Olds, the Assistant-Secretary of State, and Mr. Phenix, both of them most anxious to see this possible stumbling-block well out of the way. The English members of the Commission, too, Sir Robert Vansittart and Sir John Broderick, the Commercial Secretary to the Embassy, played their parts so well that they left nothing for me to do. Sir John, who was a most able servant, was later promoted to be His Majesty's Minister at Havana, and finally, while still a comparatively young man, British Ambassador to the Argentine Republic, but most unfortunately he died suddenly before he could take up his new post. He was an extremely valuable and able member of the Diplomatic Service.

Negotiations had been begun on June 11th, 1923, at the suggestion of the American Secretary of State for a treaty to overcome the inconvenience caused to Maritime Powers by the decision of the Supreme Court that no intoxicating beverages could be carried into United States waters, even under seal. The American Draft Agreement contained among other things a provision extending the right of search to a distance of twelve miles from shore. His Majesty's Government did not, for various reasons, accept these proposals, and submitted a counter draft of their own on September 1st.

The first Article declared it to be the firm intention of both parties to uphold the principle of the three-mile marine limit for territorial waters.

In Article 2, however, the right of search and seizure was extended to the distance which the suspected vessel could cover in one hour from the coast.

A useful proviso at the end stated that :

> In the event of either contracting party being prevented by difficulties of a constitutional nature from giving full effect to the provisions of the present Treaty, the said Treaty shall automatically lapse.

With slight modifications suggested by Mr. Hughes (the Secretary of State) this Treaty was accepted by His Majesty's Government, but Mr. Chilton, the Chargé d'Affaires, was instructed not to communicate it in its final form pending the concurrence of the Dominion Governments.

This must have been the first time that the Dominion Governments had been consulted before the signature of a treaty affecting British shipping as a whole, and was therefore a proof of the solidarity of the new Commonwealth of British nations which I hailed as of happy augury.

Much of the time of the Embassy was taken up with difficulties arising out of liquor vessels flying the British flag hovering off the coast of the United States outside the territorial limits.

My opinion in regard to this question was that whatever the attitude of Americans themselves towards their laws —and it was slack enough in many cases—it was not for us to encourage British rum-runners, who were, of course, always in active co-operation with American law-breakers.

Canadian vessels were naturally also frequently involved in cases of arrest and prosecution for smuggling liquor and added to the burden of correspondence connected with these arrests that fell on the shoulders of our Embassy staff at Washington. It must, however, be stated that numberless schooners flying the British flag, whether British or Canadian, were really, like the similar smuggling feluccas off the coast of Spain, owned in this case by Americans with Canadian or British covers.

Some of our British newspapers of the good hard-shell Tory type were much concerned about any action taken to give the American authorities greater powers of search than they would possess under accepted rules of International Law, and therefore these papers severely criticised the Liquor Treaty which His Majesty's Government had signed.   Nevertheless, it seemed to me that it was only fair and right that we should not throw our cloak over this organised trade—deliberately organised on a gigantic scale for the purpose of breaking the laws of a friendly country and thus, for the sake of private profit, causing great friction between the two Governments and making the settlement of other questions such as, let us say, that of war claims infinitely more difficult.

Moreover, as regards the concessions received by the United States with respect to right of search outside territorial water limits, those who criticised these forgot that we also had by this Treaty received a considerable concession for our legitimate shipping interests by the permission to keep liquor in our ships under seal in American harbours.   Before this was agreed to our great liners had naturally continual trouble with the authorities, who wanted to seize all the liquor on board.

I feared, therefore, that if we adopted too strong a line with reference to the trials of smuggling vessels and their crews the United States might, to satisfy their ardent Drys, abrogate this Treaty which was of great value to our ships.

It may not be out of place here to give a very short account of the procedure of the liquor smugglers or " boot-leggers " whose business had now assumed vast propor-tions.   Foreign vessels engaged in this illicit trade now no longer approached within three miles of the coast, nor were their small boats used to transport liquor ashore. Instead these vessels generally lay at anchor from twelve to twenty miles from the coast out of reach of the Revenue officers.   On shore the " bootlegger " had his agents, who arranged to send out fast motor boats to " Rum Row," as the principal anchorages of the importing vessels were called. These boats picked up supplies and returned under cover of darkness to some secluded cove where the cases of liquor were loaded into motor lorries and despatched to those who had purchased the stuff. It sometimes happened that these motor-boats were chased and captured by Revenue cutters, but, generally speaking, the trade " got away with it," and was seriously afraid of two dangers only : bad weather and " rum pirates." The adventures of these latter were often worthy of a Hollywood film or a tale of the sea by Joseph Conrad. Liquor smuggling vessels lying in " Rum Row " were frequently boarded at night by ostensible buyers who, once on deck, produced automatic pistols which were turned against the crew. Cases of this sort must have occurred frequently, but rarely, naturally enough, came to the ears of the public. One such case will suffice as an example.

The captain and mate of a Nova Scotia schooner were shot down in cold blood by such liquor pirates, the rest of the crew terrorised and about fifty thousand dollars stolen. A result of this and other like incidents was that crews of smuggling vessels were by this time armed to the teeth and peaceable purchasers of " booze " or even curious visitors to " Rum Row " would be likely to find themselves covered with service revolvers and compelled to keep a respectful distance until they had satisfied the smugglers that their intentions were strictly honourable.

It was truly " Yo ! ho ! ho ! and a bottle of rum," but not " on the dead man's chest " or any other island of the Spanish Main, but *proh pudor!* often within a few miles of Boston.

The summer season was generally spent by the Ambassador and a part of the staff of the British Embassy on what was called in Massachusetts the " North Shore," a delightful stretch of rocky coast with pines and other trees coming down in places to the water's edge. Here were small coves and inlets which appeared to have been made specially for bootleggers, and I well remember one afternoon being shown over her garden with great indignation by a most highly respectable dame whose flower beds had been trampled underfoot the night before by a party of these ruffians who had dared to use her private cove for their evil purposes.

Meanwhile, however, partly on account of the Florida land boom and also of the stricter blockade by the American authorities of the Long Island and Massachusetts Rum Fleet the latter turned its attention to the coast of Florida, using not only the American islands and cays as bases, but also to a considerable extent those of the Bahamas which, as British territory, afforded them all facilities since they were mostly uninhabited, and there was practically no police force.

I had for a considerable time been exercised in my mind as to the rôle that was being played in the rum-running game by these innumerable, quite abandoned and unpoliced islands and cays of the Bahamas which form a chain of 29 major islands and 661 cays, not counting 2,387 rocks, extending over a distance of some 630 miles. Some of them are not more than fifty miles from the Florida coast, and many were unquestionably used as depots for British or American bootleggers and had become in fact a kind of stationary " Rum Row." It appeared that if this state of things was allowed to continue indefinitely, and if the British Government insisted on the strict letter of the law with regard to the inviolability of Bahamian territory while at the same time declaring themselves unable to police the islands adequately on account of the expense to the Bahamian Government, there was sure to be an explosion sooner or later when the American public learnt that some of these British isles were being used habitually as a depot for passing liquor illegally into the United States. It seemed to me that whatever we might feel about Prohibition and the Volstead Act, which I had always considered an impractical proposition, we British, *mutatis mutandis*, whether the goods so smuggled were rum-bottles or pork pies, would in similar circumstances have protested vigorously if only on account of the extra expense caused to the public purse for this item of law enforcement.

I was informed by the Governor of the Bahamas in April, 1925, that United States Revenue cutters made a practice of anchoring off Gun Cay, a semi-desolate islet in the Bimini district belonging to the Bahamas. These cutters sometimes interfered with British vessels lying at Gun Cay, and this naturally caused complaints to be made to the Government. As a general rule no intimation was sent previously of the intention of these Revenue cutters to call at Gun Cay or to operate in British territorial waters. It was the desire of Sir Henry Cordeaux, the Governor of the Bahamas and his Government that these visits should cease without delay.

I spoke in this sense to the State Department, but without much result. While I was in London during 1925, having discussed the question with members of the Foreign and Colonial Offices, I obtained permission to visit the Bahamas that winter in order to endeavour to bring about a working arrangement with the Bahamian Government that would, by permitting United States Revenue cutters to visit and inspect certain unpoliced islands and cays, relieve that Government and indirectly His Majesty's Government from the reproach of reaping financial benefit from this state of things. It is perhaps unnecessary to explain that the smuggling business brought many dollars to the island of New Providence, on which the capital, Nassau, is situated, and to other islands of the group.

On December 9th, 1925, I therefore left for Nassau, the capital of the Bahamas, to spend Christmas there with my two youngest sons, Edmund and Henry, who were at school in America, and my majorduomo, Fioravanti, who liked nothing better than travelling, was the best of couriers and took all worries of travel off my hands.

We arrived at Miami, Florida, at the beginning of the end of the great Florida land boom. The main street of Miami was a long row of estate agents' offices and banks, which were but haunts of speculators and gamblers in land values. For many miles before the train reached Miami, while we were still out in heather and pine-covered wastes, wide asphalted roads left the great main road which ran alongside the railway and "ribbon building" was in full swing. The country was dead flat, with sandy soil and not, in my eyes, specially inviting. Here and there a wooden house had been put up alongside one of these roads and a palm of some sort had been planted to vary the natural vegetation which consisted almost entirely of heather, pines and palmetto scrub. Remembering the glowing paradisian descriptions of the country which appeared by hundreds in the advertisements of real estate agents all over the length and breadth of the United States, I began to think that the old saying that there are three classes of lies, namely " Lies, damned lies and statistics," might be modified by substituting " advertisements " for statistics.

But the boys and I enjoyed our day at Miami. The whole atmosphere was so entirely novel and, to say the least, exotic that every moment was packed with interest and fun. The culminating point which the boys never forgot was perhaps when we were all three invited to a sumptuous luncheon by the Mayor of " Coral Gables," one of the most recent suburbs of Miami, in order specially to see the great new hotel, not yet open, built in the style of the Doge's Palace in Venice and surrounded with artificial canals brought up from the lagoons at great expense, on which were plying real Venetian gondolas rowed by real Venetian gondoliers and carrying Venetian singers with guitars.

Having admired all this, we were entertained at a luncheon at which champagne flowed, and the Mayor, after making a most friendly speech of welcome and proposing my health, raised a glass with " beaded bubbles winking at the brim " and said in a voice of conviction, the sincerity of which none could dispute :

" I, Mr. Ambassador, am all in favour of putting liquor down," and he put it down, very effectively.

I felt rather a traitor in the camp, going as I was on a mission to make it more difficult for my kind host to put it down in the way he clearly preferred.

We were taken for a drive round Miami before embarking for Nassau. The curiosity which most impressed me at Miami was a lagoon the bottom of which had already been sold for building sites to speculators who resold them to farmers or small store-keepers in the Middle West, who again resold them to others or exchanged them. I was told a story at Miami to illustrate the way in which these land values were constantly changing. A man enters the club, beaming.

"Say, you fellows, I did a fine deal this morning. I sold my hound dog for a thousand dollars."

"Good for you. Did you get cash?"

"No, I can't say I got cash, but I got two five-hundred dollar cats."

That story was so illustrative of the way in which exchanges of villa sites in swamps or in sandy places were effected in those days that I have never forgotten it. And with every exchange the price went soaring up higher and higher. It was not surprising that early next year that house of cards known as the Florida Boom fell to pieces.

We embarked the same evening and arrived early next day at Nassau.

The Bahamas are very pleasant, but only, after all, the gateway to the West Indies. Still, for those who have no time or inclination to visit the more southerly groups and especially Dominica, the most beautiful of all, the Bahamas, which are but low-lying coral formations, have numerous attractions. Above all, the bathing and sea fishing are a continual delight. The tropical vegetation in the gardens and the birds, especially the humming birds, were a joy for the boys, who enjoyed their Christmas holidays to the full.

The little work I had to do with the Governor, Sir Henry Cordeaux, was completed without difficulty, and His Majesty's Government and the Bahamian Government shortly after gave permission to United States Revenue cutters to visit without previously asking permission certain remote and unpoliced islets and cays, though they were not permitted to arrest ships in Bahamian territorial waters. This, however, sufficed to make the escape of rum runners carrying liquor into Florida so difficult that it almost broke the back of the trade, and no doubt resulted in making Bahamian waters much more " wholesome " for law-abiding citizens.

The Christmas Midnight Mass in a little church almost entirely filled with coloured folk, the women in cotton gowns of many colours, with the altar decorated entirely with crimson poinsettias and lighted with candles in glass globes to safeguard them from the sea breezes that rushed through the open doors and windows, was very satisfying and unforgettable.

The afternoons were spent in a boat through the bottom of which a funnel with a glass end could be let down so that we could see in that astonishingly clear water many feet below us, in rifts in the coral, the brilliant fishes and seaweeds most beautiful moving slightly with the movement of the water. We had also picnics on some of the little coral islands near Nassau.

It would have been a perfect Christmas holiday for a fortnight or so for all of us if all had been well with Esmetto, but he was under the care of doctors in Switzerland and Italy with his mother, and the two elder boys spent their holidays there. So this separation threw a grievous shadow over our pleasant Bahamian days.

I dined with the Governor and we went to a tennis party at Government House ; we explored the old derelict fort, an inevitable adjunct to every West Indian island that respects itself, and finally left Nassau with sincere regrets and pleasant memories.

If anyone desires to escape completely from the world and yet be within a few hours of civilisation I can imagine nothing more agreeable than a tornado-proof house on an uninhabited Bahamian island.

So we all returned to Washington well pleased with our holidays, the two boys going to their school at Lakewood, New Jersey, and I alone to the dreary old house on Connecticut Avenue.

Among the many public ceremonies it fell to my lot

to attend as British Ambassador was one which gave me singular pleasure.

In June or July, 1925, I received an invitation to attend the 340th anniversary of the first British Settlement on the North American Continent at Roanoake Island, off the coast of North Carolina. I accepted this invitation with joy because it offered the opportunity of seeing an interesting and rarely visited stretch of the Atlantic coast of the Southern States and also because naturally the site of this first British settlement, the name of which I had actually never heard before, excited my curiosity.

The story of the settlement is a very slight one, but as it is connected with that great hero of Elizabethan romance, Raleigh, it deserves to be more generally known.

In 1584 Raleigh, fired by the example of the Spaniards, sent out two sea captains, Philip Amadas and Arthur Barlowe, to search for a possible site for a colony in North America. They followed the coast from Florida up to an inlet between Albemarle and Pimlico Sounds in North Carolina. These are lagoons of vast extent containing many islets and divided from the sea by a long strip of sand.

As a result of this expedition Raleigh sent out the following year a first shipload of colonists under the famous Sir Richard Grenville. These in 1585 established themselves on the island of Roanoake, which thus rightfully claims the honour of having been the first British settlement in North America. They, however, quarrelled with the local Indians, found no gold and threw up the game of colonisation, quitting the island with Sir Francis Drake when he visited it the following year.

Other attempts at settlement were made in succeeding years, but were no more successful, Roanoake being completely abandoned. No further effort was made at British colonisation till 1607, when Jamestown in Virginia was founded. Having attended the Jamestown Tercentenary celebrations in 1907[1], it was but fitting that I should now go to Roanoake.

Commander Knothe, assistant Naval Attaché, accom-

[1] pp. 124—127, Vol II.

panied me as we were offered an American destroyer for the journey.

After the usual pleasant voyage down the Potomac to Hampton Roads, we entered the canal which cuts through the Great Dismal Swamp of Virginia. This name had for years past possessed an extraordinary fascination for me. I felt it ought to have inspired a poem by Edgar Allan Poe or a drawing by Rackham. This was, therefore, the first object of interest. For several hours we steamed through the Great Dismal Swamp. It was decidedly great, dismal and swampy, but for some reason did not live up to its name. We had, however, a cheery lot of sailors on board the destroyer who entirely compensated for any failure of the Swamp to come up to my romantic imaginings. Their cheerfulness may have contributed to my disillusionment. It might perhaps have been less great had I had to travel alone on foot through those woods of dead trees with whitened trunks covered with dark green poison ivy, having an undergrowth of large-leaved swamp plants, all intersected by slow muddy streams containing presumably alligators and snapping turtles while, perhaps, in the interior of the Swamp there would have been wild Teddy bears hanging from every other leafless branch.

In due course we came out of the Swamp into Pimlico, or Albemarle Sound, I forget which, and finally towards sunset anchored off a low green island within sound of the Atlantic ocean breaking tumultuously on the great sandbank to the east. Within the lagoon all was calm. It was a delightful place.

After a perfectly peaceful night we rose early and prepared for the usual programme on such occasions. A short round of sight-seeing after breakfast, followed by a big luncheon and speech-making after, of which I was of course expected to do my share. I fell in love with Roanoake at first sight, and this feeling was heightened after the landing. A small, very primitive community of fishermen and sailors, a village of wooden houses set round a " campus " of tropical green with a little church and diminutive courthouse and a few straggling streets radiating from this central hub. A number of fine old trees and shrubs, a deep green being the general colour tone of the place, sandy tracks for roads, the brown lagoon and the distant booming of Atlantic rollers on the sand-bank under the shelter of which we lay—such is my now rather hazy but pleasant memory of Roanoake Island.

We visited the old earthworks hastily thrown up by the first British settlers against Indian marauders. We inevitably compared the place in our minds with New York City, the final issue of that early colonial adventure. It would surely be impossible to find two places more dissimilar; frankly, if I were compelled to choose one or the other in which to pass the rest of my natural life, I believe I should choose Roanoake.

Next came a copious luncheon with the thermometer soaring up into very high temperatures, and speeches, after which, having talked incessantly for hours with many new acquaintances, eaten more than was good for me and made a speech on top of all, I asked to go back to the ship, and there I collapsed and lost consciousness. I merely mention this because it was the first time it had happened to me, and it was to recur more than once until at last, after a tour in the Western States and Western Canada in 1928, this culminated in complete loss of memory for about forty-eight hours and necessitated my being hustled back to Washington like a bale of goods.

I was clearly not intended by Providence to be a public speaker and have always avoided, so far as possible, per-forming as such on festive occasions. But unhappily for my audience as well as myself it was occasionally necessary to do so because it was expected of the British Ambassador.

In spite of this misadventure, however, that trip to Roanoake remains a pleasant memory very largely on account of the happy time I spent on board the cruiser, where I could not have been better looked after had I been the President himself.

As to Commander Knothe, I would have given him a certificate as a Red Cross nurse on the spot.

CHAPTER XXI

APPOINTMENT OF FIRST DOMINION MINISTERS

A QUESTION OF PRECEDENCE

THE KELLOGG PACT

ONE great change in the structure of the British Empire, or rather, as it has now come to be called with more accuracy, the British Commonwealth of Nations, took place during my tenure of the Embassy at Washington. This was the appointment by certain British Dominions of their own Diplomatic representatives.

Their right to this new confirmation of their status as equal, independent and Sovereign States bound together with the Mother Country by the sole link of the Crown could no longer be disputed by anyone. Being as I was still a disciple of Cecil Rhodes in regard to the natural development of the British Empire, it gave me great satisfaction to see that development gradually working out to its only possible and logical conclusion if the Empire was to continue to exist at all. That those who hated the British Empire—and there were many—should frankly and openly hail this new step forward in natural growth as a sign of the Empire's approaching dissoluton neither surprised nor caused me anxiety. That they would do so was obvious. The only thing that rather worried me was the question—an important one for our Embassy—as to how the first arrangements regulating the appointment of Dominion Ministers and the relations between them and the Embassy would be decided.

As usual in England nothing was decided beforehand at all. The " Protocol " was completely absent, in fact non-existent, and it was left to me and the new Ministers to work this out on the spot in the way that seemed most suitable for each case.

The first Minister from any Dominion to be appointed was the representative of the Irish Free State, Professor Smiddy.

There had been some hints in the Press that this appointment was to be made but nothing from the Foreign Office, and I saw no reason why I should not accept an invitation from Mr. Morgenthau, former American Ambassador to Turkey, whom I had frequently met at the Paris Conference, to stay with him to attend the opening of the Democratic Convention in June, 1924.

I had seen a Republican Convention in Chicago years before[1] and felt I might excuse my absence from Washington on the grounds that it was necessary for an Ambassador to keep the balance even.

The Convention promised to be a lively one as between Governor Smith (Catholic, wet, Radical) and Mr. McAdoo (Protestant, dry and Conservative), at any rate as far as Big Business was concerned. In fact, the different alignments of policy in the Democratic family criss-crossed to such a degree that it was difficult to understand what it was all about until one realised that the fight was really one of persons rather than of any Party principles.

I had two interesting days at the Convention and heard Mr. Franklin Roosevelt speak there for the first time. He made, as he must do on almost everyone who hears him, the effect of a most magnetic speaker which was enhanced by seeing this man, of magnificent physique naturally, having to drag himself up to the Speaker's table on crutches.

The opening of the Convention was much quieter than the Republican Convention of 1908 had been, so far as I remembered it, but it was easy to feel that the atmosphere was charged with electricity, and it took many days and many votes before a candidate could be chosen. In the end, as had happened before, the two Democratic

---

[1] pp. 136–138, Vol. II.

armies were so evenly divided and so fierce that neither of the leading candidates, McAdoo or Smith, was chosen, and wearily the delegates turned to Mr. John W. Davis, a great lawyer and a cultured gentleman known in London through having been American Ambassador to Great Britain from 1918 to 1921.

To return, however, to the appointment of Dominion Ministers. It was just as things were beginning to grow warm in the great hall in Madison Square in New York, where the Democratic Convention was being held, that I got from the Embassy an urgent summons to return to Washington, and found there instructions from the Foreign Office to hand a note to the Secretary of State, Mr. Hughes, saying that His Majesty's Government considered it would be desirable, if the United States Government agreed, that an Irish Free State Minister should be accredited to the United States for the handling of matters exclusively relating to the Irish Free State. This Minister's credentials would enable him to take charge of all such affairs, while matters of Imperial concern such as affected other Dominions would be handled as before by His Majesty's Embassy. These arrangements did not denote any departure from the principle of the diplomatic unity of the Empire. The Irish Minister would not be under the control of His Majesty's Ambassador, neither would the latter be responsible for the Irish Minister's actions. In concluding the Note, His Majesty's Government expressed the hope that the above proposals would promote good relations, and that the United States Government would concur in the appointment of an Irish Minister on the above footing.

Mr. Hughes stated in reply that the United States Government were quite in agreement with the Note and would receive the Irish Minister with pleasure. Both the Note and the written reply of Mr. Hughes were published by agreement on July 24th, and on August 9th the Secretary of State signified the agreement of the United States Government to the appointment of

Professor Smiddy, of Dublin, as Irish Minister. He thus not only became the first Irish Minister but absolutely the first Minister of any Dominion under this new dispensation.

In due course I received Professor Smiddy's credentials, which, of course, he would have to present to President Coolidge, and on arriving in Washington towards the end of September he called on me. I supposed that he would probably have received some instructions as to the ceremonial to be followed when he presented his credentials to the President, but neither he nor I had received any orders on this head. It was obviously a matter that would require careful handling, for any false step at the outset would very likely result in a newspaper controversy, since the Irish Republican element would have been only too ready to seize on any excuse to make it appear either that the new Minister was to be only a creature of the Embassy or else had been treated with scant courtesy by the Ambassador.

As soon as I saw Professor Smiddy I realised that we should be able to understand each other and so, explaining my difficulties frankly, I said that I was quite uncertain how the ceremony of presentation was to be carried out. I felt that if the British Ambassador accompanied him to the White House he might perhaps be made the object of attack amongst some of his nationals in the United States, and therefore I would leave it entirely to him to decide whether he should go alone or whether I should accompany him. He thought it over and then said that if it was all the same to me, he considered that it would really be better that he should go alone. So it was done, and no one either in America or England commented on the fact. I handed to him his credentials and forwarded to the Secretary of State the duplicate copy as is always done in these cases.

The presentation went off very well, and from that day up to the end of his tenure of the Irish Legation, Professor Smiddy and all his family were on the most friendly terms with us and the members of the Embassy

Our work seldom brought us together, since the Embassy had not volumes of Irish business to deal with as it had Canadian, but in all social gatherings, whether at the Embassy, at the Irish Legation, or elsewhere, there never was the slightest ruffling of the smooth waters that dated from that first meeting.

After the appointment of Professor Smiddy as Irish Minister to the United States it was more than natural that the Canadian Government should seriously consider the appointment of a Canadian representative also.

The affairs of Canada supplied the Embassy with fully one-third of its work, which is not surprising when it is remembered that the United States and Canada have a common frontier of some 3,000 miles, that they are almost each other's best customers, both for exports and imports, and that during the days of prohibition the number of liquor-smuggling cases between the two countries was very large. But besides these were questions of boundary waters, transit, fishing, and many other matters which soon led me to the belief that the establishment of a Canadian Legation was actually overdue. It would, I felt, be certainly far more satisfactory for us to have Canadian questions treated by Canadians, because however much time and trouble the Embassy might give to the negotiation of these matters, there were sometimes Canadian critics in the Press and elsewhere who thought that if Canada did not get all she believed herself entitled to, this was due to carelessness or indifference on the part of the Embassy.

Now that Canada was on the road to becoming a Great Power, and had many men who were as capable as any in the world of conducting diplomatic negotiations with regard to any subject, it was surely in the interests of all concerned that she should take on herself the responsibility of this work.

So when I went to Canada, and was obliged to reply either to questions from reporters or in public speeches as to my views on the advisability of the establishment of a Canadian Legation in Washington, my reply was always that this was not a matter upon which I could properly give any opinion as it concerned the Canadian and British Governments. But this I could say : that all were now agreed to Canada's right to establish a Legation at Washington ; that as long as the Canadian Government preferred to be represented there by the British Ambassador, I should, of course, be proud to continue to act in that capacity for Canada, but that if ever the Canadian Government thought that the time had come to appoint a representative of its own I should welcome him there and be delighted to assist him in any way in my power.

This answer fully satisfied my Canadian audiences, and while representing my own feelings in the matter, also perfectly described what actually happened when Mr. Vincent Massey was appointed Canadian Minister to the United States in 1927. As in the case of Professor Smiddy, I left it to him to decide whether he wished to go alone to the White House, or would prefer me to be present for the ceremony of the presentation of his credentials to the President. He chose that I should be present and I went gladly to mark the solidarity of the senior Dominion and the Mother Country.

All through the remainder of my sojourn in Washington that solidarity was firmly established, not only between Mr. Massey and myself, but between the members of our staffs. We of the Embassy, I think I may say, were able to help the Canadian Legation not a little at the beginning of its operations, and the members of the Canadian Legation were constantly in and out of the Embassy, as there were many Canadian files in our archives which they naturally took over at once.

It was just the same with Mr. Massey and myself.

I shall never forget the satisfaction with which, after discovering the Canadian registry of a rum-running schooner, *I'm Alone*, which had been fired on and sunk by an American Customs launch many miles outside territorial waters on the justification of " hot pursuit," and which threatened to become a case of international renown of interminable length, I packed the papers in a parcel and with them under my arm marched in triumph to the Canadian Legation.

When I was shown into his study Vincent Massey, who was writing, looked up, and said :

" I know what *you've* come for. You've come to pass the buck."

" You've said it," I replied, and plumped my large case of correspondence on to his desk with a sigh of deep relief.

Nothing illustrates better perhaps than that little episode the terms on which we were and on which we worked together. The Canadian Legation was without doubt of the greatest assistance to us, and it was a pleasure from beginning to end to work with them.

The last days Isa and I spent in Washington were passed in the Masseys' hospitable house, and they invited a farewell party of all colleagues to bid us good-bye.

I must not, however, forget that actually the last dinner we attended, together with the Masseys, was at the house of our South African colleague, Mr. Eric Louw, appointed only in 1929, who had gathered for this occasion all the representatives of the Empire in Washington, i.e. the Canadian Minister, the Chargé d'Affaires of the Irish Free State, Mr. Macaulay, who had worked for a considerable time in our Embassy before changing his quarters, and myself, for Great Britain. There was also an American present who, seeing us such a happy party, said that he began to think George Washington had made a mistake. I hoped that this, our last dinner in Washington, might prove of happy augury for the future, as it has proved a very pleasant memory for me.

I need hardly say that it was with the greatest joy that Isa and I welcomed our friends, the Masseys, to London when in the winter of 1935 he took up his duties as Canadian High Commissioner here.

Professor Smiddy was transferred to London in 1929, and was succeeded by Mr. M. McWhite, who carried on the same tradition in the Irish Legation.

*　　　*　　　*　　　*　　　*

As an example of the curious incidents with which the *Doyen* of the Diplomatic Corps occasionally has to deal, I may be allowed to recall here a great struggle over a question of precedence which convulsed Washington society and indeed society all over the United States for a short time after Mr. Hoover and Mr. Curtis, who was elected Vice-President at the same time, were inaugurated in their respective offices in March, 1929.

Mr. Curtis was an interesting personality and had had an interesting career. He was half-Indian and had, I believe, started life while still quite a boy as a jockey somewhere in the Middle West. He then studied law and made a success of it, went into politics, and was elected to the Vice-Presidency principally because of his record as a perfectly upright, square-dealing man who had, so far as I know, not an enemy on either side of the Senate, of which he was a member.

Mr. Curtis was a widower, and when he became Vice-President he called to help him in attending to the social entertainments which were expected of a Vice-President his half-sister, Mrs. Gann, of Kansas City, who lived in Washington with her husband. Mrs. Gann considered that as " hostess " to the Vice-President she should have in Washington society the precedence of the wife of the Vice-President not only at home but also abroad. For some time the Diplomatic Corps only heard distant rumblings as of an approaching earthquake with regard to Mrs. Gann's claims which were strenuously opposed by all the ladies in Washington society who had a definite status according to the then existing protocol. This, I believe, had been drawn up in the days of President Roosevelt when old European ideas with respect to the difficulty that exists in any society of permitting more than a certain number of people to pass decorously at the same time through one door had already begun to be recognised. There was then set up in the State Department, as in most European capitals, a department to deal with questions of precedence and etiquette which required adjusting to these ideas. To this department Mrs. Gann appealed and we diplomats understood that the decision given was that in her house she should naturally have the position of hostess and therefore the place which the hostess would occupy, but elsewhere she could not aspire to the precedence of the wife of a Vice-President.

The Corps Diplomatique breathed again, hoping it might be freed from the possibility of being embroiled in a serious social conflict, but Mrs. Gann not being willing to submit so easily, appealed to Cæsar in the shape of the President who, I believe, said that he had never heard of a department in the State concerned with such questions and therefore did not wish to endorse its decision.

The newspapers, of course, began to plunge into the fray, many of them declaring that anything like a European protocol was unthinkable in the spacious atmosphere of the United States.

Then, to my horror, I heard that as no decision could be obtained from the White House or the State Department, Mrs. Gann had made a direct appeal to the Diplomatic Corps to decide the question in Diplomatic houses, at any rate.

As *Doyen* of the Corps I felt that we had now come to so serious a situation that the whole Corps Diplomatique would have to be convened in order to decide the issue. This was done, and two or three times the big ballroom of the old Embassy House in Washington was filled with the heads of Missions, who in Washington numbered over sixty or more, in order to discuss this much debated question which was sometimes taken seriously, especially in the Kansas City papers, and sometimes, I regret to say, with a very improper levity.

One Kansas City paper I remember—which was of course sent to me—declared that it was a public scandal that a number of old foreign blackbirds (the blackbird in America is, I may say, not our tuneful songster, but a disagreeable, rather disreputable, drab and dingy-looking creature of the grecco tribe with a bill something like that of a parrot) should be allowed to sit and chatter

RATIFICATION OF THE KELLOGG PACT, JANUARY, 1929

(*Left to Right*) Nobile Giacomo de Martino (Italian Ambassador); Sir Esme Howard (British Ambassador); F. W. von Prittwitz Gaffron (German Ambassador); Secretary of State, Frank B. Kellogg; William J. B. Macauley (Chargé d'Affaires, Irish Free State); Ferdinand Veverka (Czechoslovakian Minister); Hon. Vincent Massey (Canadian Minister)

about the proper place of a good, honest Kansas City lady.

Well, after much discussion we finally decided, wisely taking the line of least resistance, that as we were all anxious to comply with the wishes of the Vice-President of the United States, for whom we had a sincere respect, and as we were unable in this particular matter of official precedence in the United States capital to obtain any lead from official sources we were naturally only too pleased to comply with Mr. Curtis's wishes and give Mrs. Gann in diplomatic houses the precedence she desired, though we could not pretend in any way to establish a precedent for houses outside the diplomatic circle.

The result of this was, of course, that before inviting Mrs. Gann to our house we had always to inquire whether there was any lady to whom we were issuing invitations who would refuse to accept an inferior position, and there were many of them.

*   *   *   *   *   *

The Pact of Paris, commonly known as the Kellogg Pact, which was signed in Paris on August 27th, 1928, originated as follows.

At the beginning of 1927, Franco-American relations were none too amicable, and France, who had always looked upon herself as the privileged friend of the United States, was somewhat sore at being treated with no more consideration than the rest of the world in the matter of War debts.   I was told by my former colleague in Madrid, Mr. Alec. P. Moore, who was a good judge of feeling in the Middle West, that when certain Middle-Western regiments returned from France they marched home, singing :

> We've paid our debt
> To Lafayette
> And who do we owe to now ?

Whether this was quite true I cannot say, but it certainly seemed to be the case that the warmth of the old Franco-American union of hearts created by Lafayette and Rochambaud was cooling down. France's rejection of the Coolidge proposal for a Naval Limitation Conference did not improve matters, but in March, 1927, France agreed to pay off ten million dollars of her War debt. This produced a more friendly spirit, relying on which M. Briand threw out a feeler through the Press that France would be willing to subscribe publicly together with the United States to a mutual engagement " tending to outlaw War as between their two countries." Later, on June 20th, 1927, M. Briand submitted to Mr. Kellogg, Secretary of State of Mr. Coolidge, the draft of a Treaty in this sense.

In reply to an inquiry from me as to what line the United States Government proposed to take with regard to this proposal, Mr. Kellogg stated at once that he would be glad to support the plan of adhering to any such Treaty if it was of a general nature, but that he could not favour signing it with one country only, because this would be, in his opinion, tantamount to an indirect alliance by depriving the United States of its liberty of action in case of that country being at war with a third party.

After carefully considering the question for six months Mr. Kellogg finally replied to M. Briand by suggesting that instead of renouncing war between France and the United States only—

. . . we join together and try to persuade all the principal Powers of the World i.e. Great Britain, Germany, Italy, Japan, France and the United States to renounce war as an instrument of National policy.

As it stood, this suggestion did not altogether commend itself to M. Briand, who explained that France was bound by the Locarno Treaties and by sundry military " defensive " alliances to go to war with an " aggressor " nation.

M. Briand made, however, further counter proposals in the following year, which ultimately led up to the signature of the Pact of Paris for the Renunciation of

War by the following Powers on August 27th, 1928 : the United States of America, France, Belgium, Czechoslovakia, Great Britain, together with Ireland, India and the British Dominions beyond the seas, Germany, Italy, Japan and Poland. By the Pact of Paris these countries all agreed in the most solemn and categorical manner, under Article 1st, that they condemned recourse to war for a solution of international controversies and *renounced it as an instrument of national policy in their relations with one another.*

By Article 2nd the *settlement or solution of all disputes or conflicts of whatever nature or of whatever origin they may be*, which might arise among them *should never be sought except by pacific means—*

Article 3rd stated that the present Treaty should be ratified by the High Contracting Parties above named and should take effect as between them as soon as all their several instruments of ratification had been deposited, etc.

It was one of my duties in 1929 to sign, on behalf of my Government, the ratification of the Treaty in Washington on January 17th. It seemed to me at the time that the Pact of Paris was not taken very seriously, either in America or Europe. At least, although the Press everywhere hailed it as a further step towards the Reign of Peace, there appeared to be considerable doubt among the out-and-out supporters of the League of Nations as to whether this further Instrument was not simply a work of supererogation, and among those who did not support the Covenant as to whether it was not quite frankly mere eye-wash.

Personally I took no such cynical view of the Pact, especially after it had gathered under its wing practically all the nations of the earth, including even most of those who, like the United States, were outside the pale of the League. I believed that the fact that this Pact, even though lacking any articles for the application of Sanctions on account of a breach of its obligations, gained so much by its universality that I hoped that intending lawbreakers would think twice before flouting the good opinion of the whole world. I was frankly ingenuous enough to think, in the first place, that nations great and small would not dare to sign such a moral condemnation of recourse to force with their tongue in their cheek, and, secondly, that if any among their number later on gave evidence of having done so, the rest would surely not rush in to play the old part of *Tertii gaudentes* and to make profit by selling to belligerents goods necessary for the conduct of war. Yet this has happened, both in Manchukuo and in Abyssinia.

The nations of the world have still to learn their lesson, that, while it may be in the interest of particular individuals to supply belligerents with the wherewithal for the conduct of war, it can never be so in the interests of whole national communities.

Until they choose to learn this elementary lesson it is to be feared that any *Machtpolitiker* who fancies his neighbour's goods will " take them if he has the power and keep them if he can."

Meanwhile the Pact of Paris, even more than the Covenant, seems to be suffering from a total eclipse.[1]

---

[1] Written 9th May, 1936, after Signor Mussolini's declaration of the annexation of Abyssinia.

CHAPTER XXII

ESMETTO

I CANNOT write of him—nor can I leave him out of this book, which was originally begun for his amusement when he was lying near the end in a clinique in the pine forest above Neufchatel, in October, 1926.

From the day he was born in the little house in the Via Gregoriana, which looked out over Rome to the Dome of St. Peter's, till the day he died in the nursing home at Hampstead on a bleak November day twenty-three years later, he was in truth the centre of the family round whom all revolved, not only the family, but also good old Alda, who assisted at his birth and at his death, and the others who served under our roof and loved him.

Though he must have been suffering agonies daily and nightly all his last term at Oxford, he held on and passed his examinations because he did not wish me to be disappointed.

But it was only when he arrived in America for the summer holidays in 1924 and joined us at Pride's Crossing, near Boston, that we realised that something serious was amiss. It was there the doctor told me one afternoon that there was no hope.

I had been away on business at Ottawa, and when I was overwhelmed by the unexpected blow the doctor said that he had already told Isa two or three days before. She had never betrayed anything to me either by word or sign, not wishing to disturb my work, and yet her grief must have been as immeasurable as was her love for him. She could be truly spartan. This, more than all else, gave me the true sense of what she was, and she had imparted her character to him.

I will not attempt to write about those two years, except to say that, despite the doctor's diagnosis, which was confirmed by all others, I was able to carry on only because I could not despair, and Isa wrote me encouraging letters from Italy and from Switzerland, where most of those two years were passed.

The summer holidays of 1925 we all spent with him at Mürren. Those were the last days he was able to walk a little, and he and I had occasional strolls to a seat from which he could drink in the great white purity of the Bernese Alps. We would sit in silence, which was better than words, for it brought us nearer together.

He made friends with guests at the hotel, particularly with Miss Ruth Draper, who would sometimes come up to his room and rehearse some new piece, to his great delight. He was busy completing an anthology of poems on music, which he called " Music in the Poets," which was published shortly after his death.

He occupied himself designing book-plates for friends and making sketches of birds and flowers. He was never idle for a moment as soon as he was out of pain.

In September we returned to Berne, and the two younger boys and I to America, where they were at school. I felt the parting less, perhaps, than he, for I was still convinced that some way would be found to save him, and for a few months reports received from Isa were not discouraging, so that Edmund, Henry and I went to the Bahamas that Christmas in a fairly happy mood. But from the spring onwards it was clear that he was failing, till in September, 1926, I got a telegram from my sister-in-law, Cristina, telling me to lose no time in coming.

Of the rest I cannot write, except that we still had in the Clinique at Neufchatel, among the pines, some happy hours, but he could no more walk with me. So as a last hope, Guy's Hospital, for special treatment, and, finally, for a rest, to the Nursing Home at Hampstead, where the end came on November 27th.

We were all together in England, except poor Francis,

who was at Harvard after taking his degree at Cambridge. This was grievous for him, as they had always been specially united.

I will not attempt any description of Esmetto—the loss is still too great. Yet, in order to show what others felt, the two following papers will help those who never knew him to understand something of what he was to those who did. The first is a letter from that great Preacher and Priest, the late Father Bede Jarrett, O.P., written only a few weeks before Esmetto's death ; the second is a poem written by his friend and ours, Jock Balfour, one of the Secretaries in the Embassy at Washington after his death.

Sept. 8th, 1926.

DEAR ESME,

Really you shouldn't have written though it was a real pleasure to see your writing and to have those words.

You really must have had the grinding stones well over you and under you during all those weary months and years that your long-drawn agony has lasted. But it certainly has not been wasted since it has brought you into that bleak and barren place where at last all is seen " to be nought compared to the excellent knowledge " of Our Lord. It's easy enough to preach it but no one can really know it to be true who hasn't had to buy his wisdom at that long price.

In a way you have had it for years. I think of you always asking to find your way there early enough. You weren't a gamester. You hadn't quite the hearty amusements of the other boys, you had chosen rather for your interests the beauty of the arts and of language, the finer emotions of the soul. Well, these when followed in school-days make their worshippers rather aloof from the crowd. They have not only to seek alone but they tend to be avoided by the rest.

Was Oxford so very much easier ? I often wondered when I saw you. You seemed not unhappy ; but you looked as tho' at times you felt your isolation.

Nothing isolates like sickness, so that I think, my dear, that you have been pushed further and further into the lone places. Of course your loved ones have been with you and crept into your heart but your isolation no one can take from you. You would pain them too much if you told them all you had gone through, and so the secrets of the King have to be kept secrets, much as in one way you would be relieved by telling someone of them, yet in another way you could never dare tell them all. How could they bear it ? How could you bear it really even to tell them, for to tell these things is to live them thro' again. You could not do that.

So it has been a progress in loneliness, despite all the affection shown, even because of it. It was so delicious you could not bear to hurt it. And that's the worst terror of life : witness the Garden of Olives and the cry Eloi.

But you have come to that blessed meeting-place where the isolation diminishes again. Alone ? No, I am not alone, for the Father is with me. " When my Father and Mother deserted me (how could they help it when you slipped out from them ?) Thou hast taken me up." " Though I go down into the valley of the shadow I shall have no fear because Thou art with me." Thus a sufferer comes at last to the bleak heights, bed of pain and a weariness of the soul, and finds that the barrenness of the hills has this advantage, it hides now to the eye of faith none of the contours of God. It seemed to be growing darker, really you were walking towards the light.

He will help you, dear Esme. At my Mass I think of you and Him ; find your friendship in His, the disciple not above the Master, blessed when he's as the Master. As the Master ? Alone, naked, crown of thorns, cross. Yes, you answer, blessed to be as the Master, bearing crowns of thorns, and alone, for I'm sure you have real peace in your dreadful sleeplessness and your pain. God bless you always.

Affec.
B. O.P.

To
E. J. H. S. H.

Others whom poets sing and men remember
Dying have writ their name in honour's roll ;
Soldiers who made no bargain with existence
But gave their lives and gladly paid the toll.

Because you too when called, obeyed the summons
And fought your young life's battle to the end
Bearing a martyr's cross of pain in patience ;
You leave to us who loved you as your friend

The treasured memory of your example,
The faith and splendid courage which were yours,
Deeper assurance of the life hereafter—
Belief confirmed in Beauty which endures.

JOCK BALFOUR

CHAPTER XXIII

" THE AMERICAN SCENE " (*continued*)

NAVAL ARMAMENTS

IT would be impossible for me to attempt to give any account of the many and extraordinary happenings which filled the public Press and the public mind during the six years in which I occupied the British Embassy at Washington, from February, 1924, to February, 1930. As is usual, they did not seem so extraordinary at the time. Blériot's flight over the Channel perhaps arrested my imagination even more than Lindbergh's over the Atlantic on account of the future consequences for England implicit in it.

As to the Teapot Dome scandals, the famous " Dayton Monkey Trial," the vagaries of Big Bill Thompson of Chicago, who feared King George's " snoot " might penetrate and denature the 100 per cent. Americanism of his great city, the wild period of speculation and the beginnings of gangsterism, the number of tons, carefully reckoned, of ticker-tape showered upon Lindbergh from the windows of New York to welcome him on his return from his great adventure, the changes in social customs and the introduction of hip flasks and petting and necking, vocational versus liberal education, all these and many other things that have wrought complete changes in Henry James' " American Scene "—are they not fully recorded in Mr. Frederick William Allen's most illuminating and entertaining book, *Only Yesterday*, dealing with that strange period of such rapid evolution in all directions that it was impossible to realise in which direction the world, and particularly the American world, was heading.

But of one or two matters with which I was to some extent personally connected I may be allowed to write as they appeared to me. The rest I can safely leave to those who were more familiar with their intricacies and surprises.

Of all the outstanding changes, however, that happened in America in the post-war period, the almost incredible diffusion of wealth was the most extraordinary. As evidence we need but take the figures of assets of Life Insurance Companies amounting, in 1924, to over sixty-four thousand millions of dollars. These were, according, I believe, to official statistics, the property of some fifty million persons, who were thus real owners of the vast investments held by the Companies in real estate, mortgages, State, Municipal and Farm Loans, Railway Bonds and Industrial securities, the value of which was continually increasing as the demand for such investments increased.

These enormous sums thus gathered for investment helped to produce speculation and partially caused the appalling crash which, in 1930, followed the fat years of the Coolidge Boom. Yet between 1924 and 1930 few even considered the possibility of bad times to come, and they sincerely believed that the great Prosperity Band Wagon would go rolling on for ever in the United States while Europe, as a fitting punishment for general wickedness, would remain stuck in the mire of its own sinful incompetence.

This point of view, however, was of course not that of those who realised the economic interdependence of all countries of the world, but it may, I think, be admitted that it was held by the vast body of the uninformed.

In one matter, however, a great change had come over public opinion. This was as regards the necessity for an increase in the development along modern lines of the Defence Services.

It is not publishing a secret to say that many of our leading Naval experts, while accepting loyally the principle of parity on water for British and American capital ships established by the Washington Convention of 1922, could not understand why the United States Government should need so large a Navy as Great Britain. During the Naval Disarmament conversations and negotiations that followed the Washington Treaty they almost subconsciously tried to prove that actual equality was not necessary for the United States of America. This irritated the American Great Navyites, who, by every kind of Press and platform propaganda, sought to excite public opinion against Great Britain as endeavouring to prevent America from having her acknowledged due. There was indeed for months and years a prolonged Press controversy between the extremists on both sides. The Washington Treaty had agreed to " parity " in the matter of capital ships and aircraft carriers, and the American naval experts were insisting clamorously on recognition of parity for all classes of ships. The British argued, on the other hand, that in view of the " far-flung " nature of her possessions Great Britain must have greater tonnage in cruisers of all types and of smaller vessels. This was really at that time the principal issue between us, for many naval experts argued that Great Britain must build, taking into account not only the naval power of European and Asiatic countries, but also of America as well, and therefore, unless we could come to an arrangement with America, by which she would take all British arguments into account, we should be compelled to add immeasurably to our burden in naval armaments. This was, very shortly, the crux of the matter.

As already stated, there was a tremendous propaganda started in the American Big-Navy-Press, one of the principal contributors to which later brought an action for a heavy sum against certain wealthy armament firms for not paying him the promised fees after he had delivered the goods. I forget how the action ended and it matters little now, but it helped not a little to discredit the value of this propaganda campaign.

What, however, struck me most about the campaign

was that it was carried on with extreme violence in order, above all, to persuade Congress to pass the Naval Construction Act of 1929, providing for fifteen new 10,000 ton cruisers and one aircraft carrier to be built within three years. This was opposed by the Pacifists of course and those who, on principle, preferred economy to security. There ensued a fierce battle of words, both on the platform and in the Press, though no member of the Government, so far as I remember, ever specifically dragged in Great Britain. On the contrary, nothing could be fairer than the attitude of President Hoover and his Secretary of State, Mr. Stimson, but the difficulties of calculating " parity " by tonnage only and of finding a " yard stick " whereby to measure exact and precise parity in ships of equal tonnage but different ages and entirely different gun calibres, etc., became so evident that it was almost impossible for naval construction experts, still less Admirals, to reach any agreement as to what really established parity.

Each side was convinced the other was trying to get not an equal deal, but the best of the bargain.

I remember Mr. Dwight Morrow, for whose judgment I had as great a respect as for anyone I knew, once saying when we were discussing privately this apparently insoluble problem of determining parity :

" Of course if we leave these things to the Admirals we can never hope to reach an agreement. I should have no opinion of an American Admiral who did not try to manœuvure so as to get the sun into his opponent's eyes, or, for the matter of that, of an English Admiral either."

Personally I had long before reached the stage where I believed all this manœuvring for " exact and precise parity " was waste of time on our part.

I could not pretend to answer for America, but I was certain that as far as England was concerned, war with America was out of the question, if for no other reason than because it inevitably meant the break-up of the Empire. Assuming this, it was surely wiser for us not to take the American fleet into account at all in preparing our Naval building programmes. Our policy, I held, must always be such that we should be compelled, even at great sacrifice, just as at the beginning of the Great War, to avoid real danger of a break with America. I saw no chance of hostilities occurring between us unless they were forced on us against a League of Nations blockade by some intransigeant supporter of Neutral Maritime Rights in time of war. As I could not believe that the success of any blockade policy could be pushed to such extremes as to endanger the maintenance of our British Commonwealth of Nations, I refused to admit the possibility of such a breach. Like Will Rogers, it seemed to me that it would be so ludicrous an act of folly that both of us would have to stop in the middle to laugh at ourselves.

I did not naturally hide my views from the Authorities in writing home privately that our best course was simply to leave the American Fleet out of our calculations altogether. Then we need never compete in naval construction with America since she was not to be considered as a possible enemy and we could not hope in any case to build successfully against a country of such immeasurable potential wealth. As far as the United States was concerned a frank and good understanding in this as in other matters was likely to be far more successful as a policy than competition in armaments.

I do not wish to suggest that in recent years any British Government has questioned the right of the United States to parity with the members of the British Commonwealth of Nations in any category of ship. Our authorities may have considered that the naval requirements of the United States, particularly in cruisers, were, in practice, not as great as our own, but it was recognised that this was a matter primarily for decision by the United States themselves. Since Sir Austen Chamberlain first recognised in 1928 the principle of parity in respect of all categories of ships, there has been no tendency in any quarter to go back on this declaration. Since 1928 the difficulty has been, not to agree on the theoretical question of the right to parity, but to find an answer to the two following questions :

1. On what standard or basis is parity between the two countries to be measured ?

2. At what level of naval strength should this parity be established ?

The answer to the first question did not present serious difficulties, but the second raised a more difficult issue. The United States Government were at first inclined to argue that parity should be fixed at a level suitable to American requirements, i.e. that our own naval strength should be reduced as part of a Disarmament Treaty. We, on the other hand, maintained that while we were prepared to limit our naval strength *pari passu* with other Powers, parity with the United States must be calculated at a level which we considered necessary for the defence of our own vital needs.   A compromise on this question was embodied in the London Naval Treaty of 1930, which for the first time limited all classes of fighting ships, and latterly there has been no disposition on either side to question the right of the other to parity or to seek to impose on the other limitations which might prove embarrassing or even dangerous.

This was an incalculable step in advance and another cause of friction between the two great English-speaking countries has been eliminated.

But to return to 1929.

In order to understand the situation that led up to the much-discussed visit of Mr. Ramsay MacDonald to Washington in the autumn of 1929 it will not be amiss to give a very short account of the negotiations between the British and AmericanGovernments which preceded it.

Both Governments at the beginning of 1929 were sincerely anxious to prepare the way for co-operation in the discussions to be held at Geneva that autumn which were to precede the larger Naval Disarmament Conference that was due to be held in Geneva in 1931.

Hence conversations began amongst " experts " early in that year.

As far as America was concerned the moment seemed propitious. After the American Bill for the construction of fifteen 10,000-ton cruisers was passed and received President Coolidge's signature on April 12th, there was a noticeable reduction of anti-British propaganda in the Big Navy Press in the United States of America. It had served its purpose and could now be dispensed with.

This confirmed my conviction that whenever a Party or statesman wishes to put through a policy which is believed, rightly or wrongly, to be opposed to that of some foreign power, there is no such certain way of carrying the electorate with them as to accuse that foreign power of bad faith and malicious intent.

By this process a state of mind approaching hostility is quickly engendered on both sides, leading on to mob mentality in which reason plays no part. Bismarck with his Reptile Press was a past master of this gentle art, and Hitler, Mussolini and Stalin with their servile Press are all showing themselves to be apt pupils.

One can but wonder how soon it will be before public opinion in all countries is sufficiently educated to take Press statements with caution. In England members of the public are generally just as ready to swallow anything published by the Press of that Party to which they belong, but at least there are generally two or three sides to choose from.

In any case by May, 1929, the Big-Navy-Press turmoil had largely subsided and both the new President, Mr. Hoover, and his Secretary of State, Mr. Stimson, were ready to co-operate for reduction in Naval Armaments with the Conservative Government then in office in Great Britain, where Mr. Baldwin was still Prime Minister and Sir Austen Chamberlain Foreign Secretary.

After some preliminary discussions His Majesty's Government was informed on April 20th that the United States Government agreed that " as an expedient for gaining the time necessary for the United States and

British Governments to attempt an accord and understanding upon their own Naval disarmament, the suggestion of an introduction of programmes to be agreed upon at a final Conference merited careful consideration." The Secretary of State added that, in the event that no progress could be made at Geneva along orthodox lines, the United States Government would be glad to consult with His Majesty's Government with a view to evolving some plan for the avoidance of controversies (I read this as meaning competition in armaments) between the two Governments. He went on to say that for the United States Government the essential thing was that an understanding should be reached by the principal Naval Powers regarding the ratio in which and the extent to which they were to reduce naval armaments, but the United States would be prepared to discuss with His Majesty's Government the possibility of a limitation of the naval types not covered by the Washington Convention (i.e. all but capital ships and aircraft carriers) which would take into account the relative value of ships of varying unit characteristics such as displacement, gun calibre and age.

The United States Government had been making careful studies of this question and were convinced that it would not be impossible to find a solution not incompatible with the views of His Majesty's Government as to special British naval needs.

His Majesty's Government replied that they were most grateful for this friendly communication.

On April 6th, 1929, President Hoover had issued a statement to the Press pointing out that while the Preparatory Commission at Geneva was concerned not with the actual limitations of armaments but with the preparation of a formula as a basis for the future International Conference, the principal problem for him was to find a method for the evaluation of fighting strength (in other words the famous " yard stick "). This was not merely a matter of tonnage (as many American papers continually proclaimed) but also of speed and age.

This was, I believe, the first attempt made by the

American authorities to enlighten their public and make them understand that in trying to measure " parity " something more was required than the consideration of mere ton for ton equality.

On April 22nd Mr. Hugh Gibson, the American Representative at Geneva, in a speech laid down as a fundamental principle of United States naval disarmament policy that naval needs are relative (i.e. dependent on the strength of other fleets). He also proposed the consideration of some new method for the evaluation of the fighting strength of different types with a view to more accurate adjustment of parity or of other ratios than was possible if tonnage only was to be taken into consideration.

I was instructed to inform Mr. Stimson that His Majesty's Government entirely reciprocated the spirit of Mr. Gibson's declaration and agreed that the problem should be investigated along these lines.

Mr. Hoover being, as I have already stated, apparently most anxious to put Anglo-American relations on the friendliest possible footing, Mr. Gibson next suggested to our representative at Geneva that it would be useful if, as soon as His Majesty's Government were prepared to move in the matter, a British Cabinet Minister could meet Mr. Hoover and discuss the whole matter with him. His Majesty's Government informed Mr. Gibson that they viewed this suggestion very favourably.

At this point the General Elections intervened in Great Britain and the second Labour Government was returned to office.

This was naturally expected not to lead to any change of policy in London as regards reduction of naval armaments except perhaps to a quickening of the *tempo* in the negotiations.

These therefore continued uninterruptedly and by the end of August had been brought to a point at which we could request the United States Government to be good enough to let us have a definite statement showing what they would consider to be " parity " as regards cruisers after the latest British scrapping programme, which had just been communicated to them, had been carried out.

We waited for this statement until well in September. The Prime Minister's visit, which could not be delayed later than some date early in October, had already been announced as probable and was the subject of much speculation.

I was therefore instructed to ask President Hoover if sufficient agreement had not yet been reached to justify the settlement of a definite date. The President replied that he thought the visit would be well worth the risk of even partial failure. At the same time neither he nor the Secretary of State was willing to incur the responsibility of actually inviting Mr. MacDonald to come. Yet they considered that the visit would be most desirable in order that public opinion should not be discouraged.

The day after I had this conversation with the President the American statement respecting cruiser requirements was cabled to London and both the President and Mr. Stimson informed me that it was not only desirable but also " safe " for the Prime Minister to come to America.

Still there was no definite invitation.

According to the American statement the difference between our requirements had been reduced to 30,000 tons for cruisers and a question of whether United States cruisers should mount eight inch or six inch guns.

The visit, however, still hung fire, the President being unwilling to send an invitation until an agreement had been reached on all points, and the British Government unwilling to propose a visit unless a definite invitation was forthcoming. It was not unlike the situation at the time of King Edward VII's visit to Pope Leo XIII which I have narrated in my first volume.[1]

About the middle of September we gave up hope.

Robert Vansittart[2] who had been sent out to prepare

[1] pp. 327–329, Vol. I.
[2] Sir Robert Vansittart, my friend from Stockholm days, was now Private Secretary to Mr. MacDonald.

for the visit, took his passage home from New York, and I, thinking there was no more to be done at the moment, left one stuffy September afternoon to join Isa at Bar Harbour, one of the most refreshing places I know, to spend a few days in coolness and peace after our grilling summer in Washington. Isa had gone up there a week or two earlier as the guest of a great friend of ours, Mrs. Edgar Scott of Philadelphia, and her two delightful daughters.

It was already dark when I reached the Pennsylvania Avenue Station in New York, and I was preparing to turn in when a message was brought me from the station-master to say that our Consul-General, Sir Harry Armstrong, wished to speak to me on a most important matter.

There were only ten minutes to spare before my train started, but I begged it might be kept for me a few minutes more and dashed to the telephone. There I heard the voice of Lady Armstrong who told me that the Embassy had just telephoned that a very important telegram had arrived from Mr. MacDonald which I ought to answer myself at once and that I should therefore return to Washington without delay.

I saw all hopes of refreshment, light and peace at Bar Harbour dashed to the ground and, regardless of Lady Armstrong's feelings, I used strong language down the telephone. She, however, understood and at once forgave, " *Tout comprendre c'est tour pardonner.*" I asked her to let the Embassy know I was returning by the next train, tore back to my Pullman car, bundled my luggage out on to the platform, caught the next train to Washington and reached home soon after midnight.

There the telegram awaited me. It was from the Prime Minister saying, if I remember right, that as no definite basis of agreement had yet been found, the President was hesitating about inviting him to visit America though he would be glad to see him if he wished to come. In other words the President did not want, in case of failure to reach an agreement, to be saddled with the responsibility of having brought the Prime

Minister across the Atlantic to no purpose. So Mr.
MacDonald concluded by asking my advice as to what
he should do.

I told my Private Secretary, Michael Wright, whom
I consulted in all things, that we had best sleep over
the question, to which he, nothing loth as the hour was
then well advanced towards morning, agreed.

On thinking it over it appeared to me that nothing
could be more disastrous in such circumstances than to
appear to shirk the issue. That was an attitude that
would never help in America. I felt that we had the
goodwill of the President and of the Secretary of State.
I knew Mr. MacDonald personally for he had stayed with
me before in Washington, and I was sure he would be a
persona grata with the President and others with whom
he would come into contact. If the visit was a total
failure and I was to be blamed that would be unfortunate,
but so far as I was concerned I could risk taking the
blame.

I discussed the question with Michael Wright next
morning and told him my point of view. He agreed and
so did Ronald Campbell, Acting Minister (the next in
command after the Ambassador in Washington has the
rank of Minister) and John Broderick, the Commercial
Councillor whom I summoned to the conference.

So a telegram was sent off to the effect that I believed
that personal contacts would in any case be of real use
and advised that the visit should take place. Upon that
Mr. MacDonald decided to come and instructed me to
inform the President and the Secretary of State that if
the United States Government were agreeable he would
start very shortly and be in Washington before the end
of September.

They both appeared to be frankly pleased at the Prime
Minister's decision.

As soon as this decision became known the situation
cleared up as if by magic. The two Governments were
after all going to arrive at an agreement. Enemies were
silenced and friends were jubilant. So clear indeed did

WASHINGTON, 1927

(*Left to Right*) Lady Isabella Howard, Mr. Ramsay MacDonald, Miss Ishbel MacDonald,
Sir Esme Howard

the sky suddenly become that I decided to take after all a run up to Bar Harbour and bring Isa back to Washington in time for the Prime Minister's arrival. I had a craving to see Bar Harbour again before leaving America and I was not disappointed.

Two or three days there after a long journey of nearly thirty-six hours in the train seemed perhaps too short a recompense, but it was well worth it. I was not disappointed in the astonishing symphony of keen sea air, of the pine forests and of the mountains. It is a delicious place, especially in such pleasant company as that of our friends the Scotts. After the heat and worries of that summer in Washington it was a perfect and comforting sedative.

However, back to Washington we had soon to go to prepare for the Prime Minister's visit. There was great interest in the event. It was the first time a British Premier had visited America and he was the first Labour Prime Minister. Everyone was agog to see how he would get through the difficult task before him, for quite apart from his negotiations and conversations with the President and Mr. Stimson, it was settled that he should speak to the Senate, the Pilgrims' Club in New York, and on one or two other occasions. All agreed he would have no easy ordeal to face.

I had already entertained Mr. MacDonald as my guest in the Embassy for two or three days at Easter when he came to the United States in 1927 after the fall of the first Labour Government. Both Isa and I found him then a most welcome guest, pleasant, cultivated and above all not " superior," which I rather feared. Miss Ishbel also by her frank and straightforward ways won golden opinions from all. So both Isa and I looked forward with great satisfaction to seeing them again as our guests at the Embassy, though this was an occasion of greater solemnity and even gravity, for much might depend upon the issue of this visit.

The programme was soon arranged with the American authorities. I forget exactly what it contained, but I

know that the first night in Washington on arrival was
to be spent at the Embassy quietly after the tumult and
commotion of landing at New York. Then a lunch at
the Embassy and presentation of the staff, reception at
the White House, a trip by motor-car up to Rapidan
Camp in the Virginia Mountains, where President Hoover
spent his summer vacations. Here it was thought the
two statesmen could indulge in quiet talks over naval
armament questions for two days. Then they would
return to Washington and, after some further entertainments at the White House and the Embassy and more
conversations with experts, an address by Mr. MacDonald
to the Senate, a visit to Mount Vernon and the Lincoln
Memorial, and the Washington sojourn would come to an
end.

The welcome accorded to Mr. MacDonald on arrival
in New York was truly spectacular. I had never seen
one of these modern civic welcomes, still less assisted at
one. This certainly took my breath away. Mr. Mac-
Donald was reported by one newspaper to have had
" roses, roses all the way." This was not strictly true
for I saw nothing but the modern and highly characteristic
substitute for roses, namely, ticker tape.[1] Yet it was
very impressive. The Prime Minister could not have
had 1,800 tons of this stuff thrown on him out of the
windows like Lindbergh but he may perhaps have competed with the Armistice celebrations which only reckoned
155 tons so used in their honour.

I of course followed in a second automobile after the
Prime Minister, who naturally drove first with the great
American officials and the Mayor of New York, but we
in the second car collected enough ticker tape to last us
a lifetime.

There was a reception at the Mayor's office, and then
to the Pennsylvania Railway Station and comparative
quiet for the evening at the Embassy.

---

[1] For the benefit of the uninitiated it must be explained that ticker tape consists
of the narrow strips of paper on which Stock Exchange prices are typed every
minute of the day in Banks, Clubs, Offices, etc.

Mr. MacDonald was accompanied by Sir Robert Vansittart, his Private Secretary, and Mr. Craigie of the Foreign Office. Also Lord Arnold, a member of the Labour Party, and Mr. Thomas Jones, Deputy Secretary to the Cabinet, a most genial Welshman.

In the afternoon following arrival Mr. MacDonald and those he desired to accompany him left for Rapidan, and the conversations with the President and American officials began at once.

The visit passed off most successfully, and the Prime Minister's speeches were generally considered master-pieces of the art of fine speaking, both as to matter and manner.

The apparent concrete results of the negotiations were perhaps small, but the Prime Minister left behind him an atmosphere of real friendliness, having given everyone to understand that Great Britain was definitely not out to compete with America in the matter of armaments. This was in no small measure due to a very courageous step. When thanking the members of the Senate for his reception on the floor, he said :

" What is all this bother about parity ? Parity ? Take it, without reserve, heaped up and flowing over."

It had been the custom for distinguished visitors to avoid any reference to political topics in the Senate and to confine their remarks on such occasions to a graceful, if conventional, expression of thanks. But this bold break with tradition was thoroughly justified in the event, and created a most favourable impression. The visit, I felt at the time and still feel, helped not a little to improve relations and to bring nearer a general under-standing of the naval armaments problems as between our two countries at any rate.

Finally, as Mr. Stimson said, the agreement between Great Britain and the United States of America establish-ing parity in principle for all classes of vessels was an immense step forward. At the Washington Conference Great Britain had agreed to parity as regards capital vessels and aircraft carriers only. Now Mr. MacDonald had carried this agreement further, so as to cover all classes of vessels. It might be, as Mr. Stimson said, futile, in the military sense, to attempt to make two fleets mathematically equal, but the doctrine of parity was one of statesmanship ; it did not look to future combat between navies, but had exactly the opposite purpose, namely, to prevent them from building against each other and to accomplish instead a reduction of their respective naval power. It was the only doctrine by which two independent nations like Great Britain and the United States could agree to be free and to eliminate the thought of war.

Two matters other than the actual relative strength of the navies were touched upon at the meetings of the President and the Prime Minister, i.e. Neutral Rights in time of war and British Naval Bases in the Western Hemisphere.

As regards the second, the American Navy Department gave a declaration that these bases did not in their opinion constitute a menace to American security.

As regards the first, President Hoover was especially anxious that food ships might be immune from seizure in war-time.

To this Mr. MacDonald showed himself very favourable, and it is much to be hoped that, should the subject be brought up again, it will be supported by His Majesty's Government at any future Conference, not only on the obvious humanitarian grounds but also for reasons of high policy, because there is no doubt that a food blockade whether by sea or land, especially when applied to noncombatants, leaves behind it a poisonous sting which years of conciliatory remedies will not suffice to extract.

As the latest development in Anglo-American naval negotiations I append here copies of the letters exchanged between Messrs. Norman Davis, Principal American Delegate at the Naval Armaments Conference in London in 1935–36, and Anthony Eden, His Majesty's Principal Secretary of State for Foreign Affairs and Representative at that Conference.

March 24th, 1936.

On the eve of the completion of the work of the Naval Conference and of our departure from London, I desire to express on behalf of the entire American delegation appreciation for the many courtesies extended to us during our stay here. I also want to record our appreciation of the patient and untiring efforts of the United Kingdom delegation and of their contribution to the success of the Conference in reaching the various agreements which are incorporated in the Treaty we are about to sign.

There is one thing further I should like to mention. In view of the fact that the new Treaty does not provide for a continuance of quantitative limitation as established by the Washington and London Treaties, which are to expire at the end of this year, Admiral Standley and I have had, as you will recall, some discussion with the United Kingdom delegation during the course of the Conference with regard to maintaining the principle of naval parity as between the fleets of the members of the British Commonwealth and of the United States of America, which was fixed by those treaties and which has now become a well-established principle acceptable to the peoples as well as to the Governments of our respective countries. As a result of the conversations on this subject, it is our understanding that we are in agreement that there shall be no competitive naval building as between ourselves and that the principle of parity between the fleets of the members of the British Commonwealth and of the United States of America shall continue unchanged.

Sincerely yours

(Sgd) NORMAN DAVIS.

Foreign Office, S.W.1.

March 25th, 1936.

The First Lord and I very much appreciate the kind references which you make in your letter of the 24th inst. to the efforts of the United Kingdom delegation to bring about a naval agreement.

I can assure you that the friendly relations which have prevailed between the United States and the United Kingdom delegations have been a source of pleasure to all of us and we are greatly indebted to yourself, Admiral Standley and the other members of your delegation for your wholehearted co-operation throughout the difficult period of negotiation which now lies behind us.

I am glad, furthermore, to be able to confirm the correctness of your understanding in regard to the maintenance of the principle of parity. We are in full agreement that there must be no competitive building between our two countries, and that neither country should question the right of the other to maintain parity

2 M

in any category of ship.　I can indeed go further than this and say that, in estimating our naval requirements we have never taken the strength of the United States Navy into account.

ANTHONY EDEN.

Mr. MacDonald and those who accompanied him may, I think, now be congratulated on the work they accomplished in Washington in 1929, which laid the foundations for this further advance towards a complete accord with regard to this vital matter.

CHAPTER XXIV

"THE AMERICAN SCENE" (*continued*)

A WESTERN TOUR

(1928)

TWO places stand out vividly before my mind's eye of all those I saw in the United States. The impression they made has never dimmed with passing years—they remain fresh and clear-cut in my album of memories.

These were the Grand Canyon and the Wawona Grove of giant sequoia trees.

In the spring of 1928 there being nothing of urgent importance to keep me in Washington, I decided to ask leave of the Foreign Office and make a rather extended tour in the Southern and Western States, to which I had already received various invitations.

In this I was only following the example of two of my predecessors, Lord Bryce and Sir Auckland Geddes. There are some who think that the British Ambassador's absences from Washington should be restricted to New York and Boston, and possibly Philadelphia as regards cities, and Newport, Long Island and Palm Beach as regards " resorts." Lord Bryce, who knew his United States as no one else, always taught me that a knowledge of the Eastern States only was proof of a very superficial education in regard to American conditions. I early realised this, but had no chance before 1928 of completing my education in this respect.

So, having received the permission of Sir Austen Chamberlain, I prepared to make a tour including the principal cities of Louisiana, California and Oregon,

as well as a visit to British Columbia. Isa came with
me, of course, and also my Private Secretary, Henry
Hopkinson, without whom I could not contemplate such
a programme of receptions, public luncheons and dinners,
at all of which speeches would be expected. Each of
my Private Secretaries in turn : first, Hugh Tennant
(now, alas, dead), second, Henry Hopkinson, and, third,
Michael Wright, on these occasions most successfully
played the part of tutor and guardian to keep me in the
straight and narrow way when dealing with public
invitations and public speeches, which were the price
I had to pay for travel in the United States.

I have always intensely disliked speaking in public,
well knowing that I had no facility therefor, and I rarely
ventured to touch on anything but generous platitudes,
with a funny story thrown in for a sauce or *hors d'œuvre*.
However, I got through these ordeals without any serious
disaster largely owing to the advice and assistance of my
constant counsellors above-mentioned. Not only, however, did I rely on them for advice in the tricky business
of speech-making, but also for keeping my papers in
order, and seeing that I did not deliver to the Daughters
of the American Revolution an address intended for the
Rotarians, or one meant for the English Speaking Union
of Boston to the students of some Vocational College in
the Middle West.

So Henry Hopkinson was not only a companion, but
a real necessity on a trip of this sort.

Thus, in the spring of 1928, we set out on our grand
tour of the States, beginning with New Orleans. The
papers had written much of the great Mississippi floods
and the immense damage they were doing. It was not,
however, till we reached New Orleans that we realised
the very precarious state of the city, which is protected
from floods by high banks or levées. On our arrival we
found the waters of the great river, which gives the
sense of a huge continent behind it and is quite as impressive as even the Amazon, were up to a foot or so of
the top of the banks, and there was real fear that they

might break through the levées and carry away a great part of the city.

One of the things I most remember about New Orleans was being taken for a trip in a motor-boat up and down stream and looking into the windows of the second floors of the houses, which were on a level with the top of the levée. We found, to our surprise, that we were acclaimed in the Press almost as heroes for having ventured to visit New Orleans at such a time. But during our stay all danger was averted by blasting big breaches in the levées below the city, which naturally enabled a large volume of water in the river bed above to escape without flooding any part of the town. There was something peculiarly sinister and malignant in that chocolate-coloured, slowly-swirling flood winding its way through the great town on a level with the roofs of many of the lower houses and negro shanties.

The floods above and below did many millions of dollars of damage, but that may be considered as part of the price Americans have to pay for inhabiting a vast Continent. Such great natural scourges at least we avoid in our small European island. The troubles we suffer from are rather man-made and should therefore be more easily controlled, yet how often does the truth seem to be exactly the reverse.

We were able to admire some beautiful gardens in New Orleans and avenues of tall magnolias, yet the flood dominated the scene.

I need hardly dwell on the friendly hospitality shown to us, which is indeed the same all over the United States, wherever a British traveller goes with introductions. I, at least, have never discovered any difference between North, South, East or West in this respect.

Our next move was to the Grand Canyon.

I confess I was not prepared for the wonderful and overwhelming impression created when one first looks over the abrupt edge of that mighty rift in the crust of the earth. To describe it is impossible, but I wrote to my sister Maud in Cumberland that if she could imagine to herself a sudden chasm about as wide as the space between Saddleback and Crossfell—say fifteen miles across—falling abruptly from 5,000 to 6,000 feet, and formed as it descended into great rocks, pinnacles and towers, bastions and ramparts of brilliant colours, red and orange, yellow and brown, with bright green shrubs and trees growing in the crevasses, she might form some sort of conception of the tremendous grandeur of the scenery. At the bottom of the Canyon flows a rushing river which from the rim looks like a mere trickle, but which, when one is down beside it, is not unlike the wild flight over the rocks of the Rhine at Schaffhausen, though there it was not the same beautiful clear green water of the Rhine.

Henry and I decided at once that we must ride down to the bottom and spend a night there. So with the help of a kind officer of the United States Army, who was stationed at the Canyon, we hired a guide and two mules and started down the precipitous path, cut out from the side of the rocks in many places.

It was a splendid ride, wild and dramatic and fantastic, with all the sulphurous colours of the rock like a Blake illustration of Dante's *Purgatorio*. In all my travels I have rarely seen anything so impressive. Most tourists just " stop off " at the Canyon Station between trains, look over the edge of the rim, buy some souvenirs from the Indian half-castes who make Indian toys for strangers, and then depart again. But the only way to taste the full savour and aroma of the Canyon is doubtless to ride or walk down to the bottom and spend a night at the little rest-house near the bridge that spans the torrent. In this way you may see the gorgeous changes of colour as the sun goes down, from orange and ochre and red and burnt siena to purple and prussian blue, and watch the same transformation at sunrise. I could have wished to stay for days in and about the Canyon, but two days were all the time we could spare. So, in the freshness of the morning, we rode up again, and after lunch took a car and drove out to a point where, in that clear atmosphere, we could look away from the Canyon over the Painted Desert for more than a hundred miles of sand in coloured stripes. Out of this every here and there arose a great flat-topped rock of basalt like the sacrificial altar of a race of giants, standing up black and dark blue out of the striped carpet of red, yellow and orange sands at its foot. That also is an unforgettable landscape, and there are those who think it more impressive than the Canyon itself. Formerly not a few trekking westwards to California in covered wagons lost their lives in this desert. Now it can be crossed in a few hours in motor-cars. But even modern invention, which can almost abolish time, will not for generations be able to take away from the Canyon or the Painted Desert their primeval grandeur and solemnity.

From these glories of nature to Hollywood was one of those sudden transitions to which the tourist in America has to accustom himself, and which indeed are rather exciting to the palate. We did not, however, go to stay at Hollywood itself. The change might have been too highly spiced to be quite digestible. We did not even go to Los Angeles, which resembles many other American business centres of comparatively recent growth. We chose rather to stay at Pasadena, an agreeable suburb of Los Angeles, a sort of Garden City, where Mr. Huntingdon has built an attractive home for his magnificent collection of masterpieces of the English school, all those pictures of Reynolds, Raeburn, Lawrence, Gainsborough, Romney, Hoppner and others of that period, which we had known from childhood from illustrations and copies and which have found here what may be presumed to be their final resting-place. It is well worth a visit to Pasadena to see them. Yet I suppose there are many travellers who go to Hollywood and pass them by. I certainly generally feel, on seeing many pictures of that school and time together, a slight sensation of having dined off *crème à la Vanille*. Yet the examples collected here are so much superior to any other collection of pictures of that period that we must all be grateful for them. There is moreover nothing of *crème à la Vanille* about the great landscape painters, or indeed about Hogarth, who has, till recently, been considered inferior to the others.

In Mr. Huntingdon's collection at Pasadena even the most critical might, without patriotic prejudice of any kind, exclaim that here was something outstanding in the world of art. We at least spent a very happy day in the Huntingdon House at Pasadena.

Besides that we had the usual great dinner, with speeches, at Los Angeles, where, I confess it with shame, I distinguished myself by being introduced to the " World's Sweetheart," Mary Pickford, without ever realising my good fortune. This seems incredible, but it was nevertheless true.

We also spent a day—a most fascinating day—at Hollywood. We were kindly taken over one of the great studios, and were present at the making of a film by John Barrymore and others, and learnt how this gigantic power for good or ill or perhaps only for trivial amusement worked from inside. Having seen so many films wholly devoted to what, if I may use Freudian slang, is now called " sex appeal," and very common " sex appeal " at that, I confess I was prejudiced rather against than for the films. But I have since seen so many most beautiful and pleasantly instructive films on all kinds of scientific and other subjects of which I was hopelessly ignorant, that I am sure the cinema can and will become, when it is properly used, a great power, not only for wholesome amusement, but also for " reading without tears."

Well, we not only saw John Barrymore doing some little scene over and over again till I felt all naturalness must have been squeezed out of him, like the juice out of a lemon squeezed till the pips squeaked (though I admit this may have been an entirely wrong conclusion), but we also were ourselves put on the film with Miss Marion Davis and Mr. Conrad Nagel, in a scene in a play called, if I remember rightly, " Quality Street." That was a real adventure for a member of so pompous a profession as Diplomacy is generally supposed to be. I must, however, hasten to reassure my readers. Nothing will appear on that film, if it is ever shown, but what would be approved by Queen Victoria and even Prince Albert.

In spite of the perfect propriety of the proceedings, we left Hollywood feeling that we had really done something to complete our education, and enjoyed the pleasant meals there to which we had been invited.

From the highly sophisticated atmosphere of Hollywood we plunged again into the primeval world of the Wawona Grove of giant sequoias, where we passed a memorable night many thousand feet above the sea before descending into the famous Yosemite Valley.

Motoring on the way up we moved through miles of forest destroyed by the greed of man thinking only of profit, and we expected to meet with a grisly disappointment such as often happens when approaching some far-famed spot. Here was ragged secondary growth out of which stood up now and then, to show what had been, not so long ago, the gaunt, bare stumps of magnificent trees which must have been as the courtiers guarding the approaches to the throne-room of the real Kings of Wawona. This scene of destruction and ruin without beauty was indeed depressing, but when we reached the narrow valley of the Wawona Grove depression gave way to wonder. The sun was setting and its slanting rays caught the almost crimson trunks of the great trees, whose branches spread from the trunks one hundred and more feet above our heads, where their dark and solemn foliage cast an everlasting twilight. There was little undergrowth, nothing but a carpet of brown needles, soft and silent to walk on, and here and there some giant which had fallen from age but which still refused to submit to the common fate of rotting and putrefaction. It was difficult to take in the fact that according to accepted figures, based on the rings of trunks that had been cut down for investigation, some of these trees were over three thousand years old, and that several more were well over three hundred feet high and over one hundred and twenty feet round.

Indeed they seemed to dwarf the pyramids which they rivalled in age and infinitely surpassed in colour. It was impossible not to be confused and awed by their grandeur. There was no sound but the song of the streams in the valley below and the rustling of the branches high above us. Isa and I wandered quite alone in this Court of the gigantic Kings of all forests, the oldest living things in the world, while the setting sun gradually moved up their crimson trunks and darkness slowly conquered the vale.

It was one of those places where words have no meaning. It explained the urge felt by pagans for the setting-up of altars to their gods in groves of noble and ancient trees. I felt like building an altar there and then.

There are few of these groves of giant sequoias left, not more than twenty or so, I believe. If I am not mistaken, the world owes their preservation and that of many other splendid areas of forest and natural growth to Theodore Roosevelt who loved these masterpieces of the work of God, when men were only out to destroy in order to create swollen balances in banks in the cities, and do the things that men mostly do with swollen bank balances.

If " Teddy " had done nothing more he would deserve our eternal gratitude for having saved these trees.

Isa and I were fortunate in being quite alone in that grove and being able to enjoy it in silence. We returned to our car chastened in spirit by the magnificence of what we had seen.

Next morning we thought of returning, but fearing to spoil the impression made we started down the hill into the Yosemite Valley.

The valley is undoubtedly most beautiful, but it lacks the grandeur and the awfulness of the Wawona Grove and the Canyon. The high precipices surrounding it, down which waterfalls tumble a sheer two thousand or more feet, losing themselves in the air, are like those of

some Norwegian fjords but without the sea water at
their feet.

Yet these splendours have been described again and
again and need no description from me. One peculiarity,
however, of these Western tourist resorts must be noted,
for it pleased me greatly. This was the so-called " Camp "
in the place of the usual great caravanserai hotels which
obtain in Europe.

Gathered round a large central hall where all dine
together are numerous small chalets scattered about
under the natural trees which have not been disturbed.
These chalets, for three or four persons, with a sitting-
room, contain comfortably a small party with that privacy
which is lacking in great hotels, though all meet in the
big barnlike dining-hall for principal meals.

No arrangement in such a climate as that of California
could be more pleasant. Small deer came to our doors
in the early morning to ask for bits of bread, which
added to the charm of the camp. We both of us left the
camp, delighted with this feature of travel in the Far
West.

The section of a great sequoia cut off about six feet
above the ground which we saw in the Yosemite Museum
impressed us and even increased the awe we felt for
these Kings among trees. For many of the rings of the
tree were marked with a little flag giving the date of
each, and enabling the stranger to form an idea of the
age of the tree.

A flag with the date of the foundation of Rome, of the
conquest of Britain by Julius Cæsar, of the Birth of Our
Lord, of the destruction of Jerusalem, and so on, up to
our own times certainly increased our respect for the
living specimens we had seen the day before in the
Wawona Grove, if anything was needed to do that.

We continued our Western tour without anything
occurring of special note. The natural beauties of San
Francisco are of course as well known as are those of
the country round.

We began to realise that we were not only in point of

distance but also in general mental outlook thousands of miles away from the Atlantic coast.

Isa put it very tersely to some reporter who asked her if she found a great difference between the East and the West coast of the United States.

" Well," she replied, " I have been looking for news of Washington in the San Francisco papers this morning, but all I could find was that the President had been sent to bed, not because he was a naughty boy, but because he had a cold in the head."

" Well, yes," admitted the interviewer, laughing, " there is not much contact between East and West in this country, especially in the West."

Once one is on the other side of the Rockies it is easy to understand this, for the Far West is more cut off from all European interest than even the Middle West, and its windows definitely look out on to the Far East which has long since ceased, after hearing the legions thundering past, to plunge in thought again.[1]

The Far East occupies—so far as foreign affairs are concerned—the attention of the Far West practically to the exclusion of all other matters. This makes the Far West undoubtedly self-sufficing in the matters of news, and also as a result necessarily somewhat provincial in outlook. But it is none the less delightful for that, for those who are satisfied with the great charms of climate, scenery and vegetation.

From San Francisco we took the train to Portland, Oregon, a very pleasant city lying in the beautiful valley of the Columbia River, along the banks of which we were taken for some miles over a magnificent motor road so that we could get an idea of the country and its great fruit farms. We regretted that our stay there had necessarily to be cut short, but we were all now very

---

[1] " The East bowed low beneath the blast
In patient deep disdain
She let the legions thunder past
Then plunged in thought again."
                                   MATHEW ARNOLD.

" Obermann once more "

anxious to get a glimpse at least of the Canadian West and of the Canadian Rockies before returning to Washington.

A short and lovely passage across the Straits of San Juan de Fuca brought us to Victoria, the capital of British Columbia, situated at the extreme southern end of Vancouver Island. Here we were all most kindly entertained at Government House by the Lieutenant-Governor, Mr. Bruce, and his daughter and were allowed rather more rest than would have been considered quite correct on the other side of the border where, if refreshment, light and peace may be considered desirable for souls of the departed they are certainly not looked upon as suitable for the stranger that is within their gates.

The view across the Straits of San Juan to the snow-capped mountains of the Olympic range in Oregon, over 9,000 feet high (of which I had never heard before I went to those parts) is one of the most satisfying I know anywhere, and the golf course along the top of a cliff looking out over the sea is enchanting except that the golf balls seemed to be as much attracted by the view as the players.

All things considered I felt that if for some reason I was compelled to pass the rest of my natural life away from England I should certainly choose Victoria as a final resting-place. I believe not a few British have had the same idea. The enchantment was all the greater at that season of the year because masses of English golden broom were in flower and formed the foreground to the silver blue sea and the snow-capped peaks of the Western Olympus beyond.

From Victoria we went across the Straits again to Vancouver city where we saw the sights and were entertained at a large luncheon. There I made the last speech I was to make on my Western tour. It proved too much for my exhausted speech-making capacity, for that afternoon while " saying a few words " to a ladies' association that was entertaining Isa to tea I suddenly realised that my memory had completely gone.

THEATRE OF LIFE

The doctors found that it would be impossible for me to continue the tour, and the Canadian Pacific Railway Company having most generously placed a large car at our disposal I was sent with all the party straight back to Washington, so missing Banff and that part of the Canadian Rockies which I had been looking forward to as the final *bonne bouche* of our journey.

I recovered my memory, however, before getting to Washington and was fortunately able to deal again with the business of the Embassy before many days had elapsed.

CHAPTER XXV

CONCLUSION OF " THE AMERICAN SCENE "

JUST a few more vignettes or rapid etchings of people and things in America sketched in without order as they occur to my memory, and this already over-burdened presentment of the American Scene must end or it will become a volume in itself.

I have already spoken of the Government proposal to build a new Embassy house in Washington. I had inherited from Mr. Bryce the conviction that the old house on Connecticut Avenue was no longer suitable for the purpose for which it was built in the eighteen-seventies. Connecticut Avenue was being rapidly com-mercialised. A double tramline ran under the Embassy windows and made work and conversation equally difficult in the ground floor rooms where the Ambassador's study was situated. The offices of the Chancery had been put up roughly during the War, and would have to be entirely rebuilt and their site in summer was terribly hot—in fact, there were endless drawbacks to set against one real asset which was that it was a first-rate house for entertaining on a large scale.

The moment was a good one for selling the site which had risen greatly in value, and also for buying rather farther out some other building lot or lots giving the new house a garden, which is of great importance in Washington. As soon as the Office of Works authorised me to do so I selected three possible sites among those offered, of which that of the present Embassy on Massachusetts Avenue Extension was one. There was one feature of it that pleased me greatly. The ground was covered with low secondary scrub and as I pushed my way through this the first time I went to inspect the site I put up a covey of about a dozen quail. I remembered old stories which aged warriors told in my youth about their having spoken to men who had shot snipe in Belgrave Square, and I then determined that the quail on the site of the new Embassy should be recorded for the future.

After some correspondence Sir Lionel Earle, Secretary to the Office of Works, came out and stayed at the Embassy. We had many pleasant walks together and finally chose the present site out of the three I had first selected. He had an eye for landscape gardening, and I have no hesitation in saying that he made the best choice. Those who worked in the Embassy in future would be far enough back from the main road to escape the noise and petrol gases of the main avenue.

I owe to the new Embassy building my acquaintance with Sir Edwin Lutyens, a man who like all true artists can see visions and dream dreams. He grasped at once the possibilities of the site for the house, garden and chancery. When I complained, because I could not see visions, that I thought it would be considered curious in Washington that the offices should be put facing the Avenue so as to hide the greater part of the Embassy House he replied :

" In England we don't like to put all our goods in the shop window," and he certainly did not. There are not a few who, I know, criticised the design, but I saw when it was up that he had been quite right in getting the best view of the house, which is a fine and stately building, from the garden, thus looking rather to the pleasure of those who lived in the house and their guests and turning, so to speak, the cold shoulder to the inquisitive public. There is something *signorile* in this attitude of indifference to the public which is unusual in our day, and especially perhaps in America, where I remember Henry James, in his " American Scene," describing the houses in some famous summer resort, speaks of them as apparently only panting to " fly to the highest pinnacle of publicity and flap their wings there."

The building of the house gave me so much interest and so much occupation for the last three years of my sojourn at Washington that I wish I had been able to see it quite finished before I left. Now it is unlikely that I shall ever do so. It is one of the changes in that magnificent city that I fear I must be content to see only in dreams.

*   *   *   *   *

The last year of my incumbency of the Washington Embassy I made what most of my friends thought was a *faux pas* which, though of itself of little or no importance, reverberated so ridiculously in the Press both at home and abroad, much to my annoyance, that if my term of office in Washington is ever remembered hereafter it will probably be as the result of this particular action. Whether it was ill-advised or not I do not now feel sure, but I hope it may act as a warning to budding diplomats (if indeed any should read this book) never to act under the influence of irritation. Lord Lyons's advice to diplomats quoted in my first volume, " Always avoid an incident," would possibly have been useful for me to remember in the circumstances I am going to relate.

The attacks of the Prohibitionists or Dry Party against the Diplomatic Corps for continuing to avail themselves of the permission granted to its members by the Federal Government to import wines and spirituous liquors for their own consumption under special license were frequently renewed in the Prohibition Press throughout the country. The Drys had at the beginning of 1929 been particularly active, individual members of the Senate having even charged the Diplomatic Corps openly with being little better than a gang of bootleggers. It was indeed a cheap way of acquiring merit with certain elements of the Electorate. The State Department had of course no representative in the Senate or the House who could take up the cudgels for the Diplomatic Corps, and there was no one—owing to the peculiarities of the

2 N

American Constitution—who was specially authorised to answer attacks of this sort on behalf of the Secretary of State.

The result was that among certain 100 per cent. American senators diplomat-baiting became at times as pleasant a sport as bull-baiting in Madrid, the only difference being that the sorry diplomat had no means of defence whatever, for if he complained to the State Department the reply was always the unanswerable one that while much regretting the attack made, etc., it was impossible in view of the sanctity of the doctrine of freedom of speech and of the Press in the United States to intervene in order to protect any person whatever from such attacks, whether in Congress or in the Press.

Generally these attacks meant little. Some electoral steam was blown off in this way, and the matter was forgotten the next day. But the extreme Prohibitionist section of the population was already beginning by 1929 to feel the ground slipping from under its feet. There could be few plans for keeping alive interest in maintaining Prohibition more popular than a continued campaign against foreigners and accusing them of breaking the law of the land. Nothing lent itself so readily to such manœuvres as an attack on the privileged position of the Diplomatic Corps in the matter of importing spirituous liquors.

I had, I fear, allowed myself to become somewhat restive under the lash of Press articles of this sort which were sent me by the Press-cutting agencies from time to time, when one morning, while I was working in my study, one of the messengers rushed in and asked me in considerable excitement what he should do.

A lorry had just arrived from Baltimore with a consignment of wine which some of my secretaries expected from Bordeaux, for they clubbed together to import their supplies for the year at one time which the State Department permitted if the head of the Mission made himself responsible for such imports.

" There are at least," said the messenger, " thirty reporters and photographers standing on the kerb-stone on the other side of the street waiting to report all the cases of wine that are off-loaded into the cellar and to take snapshots of them as they are carried into the house, and the driver of the lorry wants to know what he's to do."

I was frankly annoyed, but there was nothing to do about it.

" Treat them all," I said, " as if they were dead, or as if there was no one there at all, and get all the stuff into the cellar without wasting time."

The one thing I did not want was a scene of any kind in the street before the Embassy.

I heard no more of the matter for two or three days, when Press cuttings with picture headlines began to come in from different parts of the country : " Booze for the British Embassy," etc. This irritated me still more, but my cup of wrath was filled to the brim and running over when letters reached me enclosing cuttings—one particularly asking if it was not a scandal that members of the Diplomatic Corps should avail themselves of a special privilege thus openly and publicly to break the law of the land.

I made the mistake of answering this correspondent, and told him that this privilege had been willingly conceded by the United States Government, but that if the United States authorities wished to withdraw the privilege I naturally should accept their decision without demur, or words to that effect.

I don't know whether or not I marked my letter " private," but in any case it was at once published in a number of papers, and some hinted that I had written this in order to embarrass the Government.

The long and the short of it was that I went to see the Secretary of State and told him the whole story.

I said I was not coming to lay any complaint or make any protest because I knew that he was powerless to prevent such acts evidently done with the intention of throwing discredit on the Diplomatic Corps. I knew perfectly well that the State Department could do nothing to remedy this state of things so far as the Press or speeches in Congress were concerned. But I felt that it was impossible for me to continue to avail myself of the privilege kindly allowed us by the Federal authorities, if this led to such scenes as that outside the Embassy, as this was really not compatible with the dignity of H.M. Embassy in Washington, and I therefore should ask for no more licences to import wines, etc.

Mr. Stimson, as always, most courteous, polite and friendly, said he much regretted what had happened, but that he was not in a position to prevent its recurrence.

I said I knew this only too well. I hoped, however, that my action might have the effect of checking the latitude which some of these gentlemen of the Press allowed themselves in dealing with strangers who could not defend themselves.

It did, indeed, have that effect, for I never again heard of any of my colleagues being similarly treated. Meanwhile, however, I became for a time very unpopular with my colleagues of the Corps. Some English papers announced that I was trying to make the British Embassy " bone dry," and my friends in England gave me to understand that I was a foolish fellow. As I knew this already it did not greatly trouble me. I had fortunately enough wine left in the cellars to suffice for the last great party at the old Embassy House which was given in honour of Mr. Ramsay MacDonald, the first British Prime Minister to visit the United States.

But I got great amusement and even satisfaction out of a paragraph from some book on Washington Society of that period for a reference it contained to me stating that I had given out that Prohibition was to be strictly observed in the Embassy during the remainder of my term of office. The author summed up the incident in some such words as the following :

> Poor old Sir Esme, however, got none of the credit he expected from the Prohibitionists when they found out that the Embassy cellars were so well stocked that there was plenty of wine to last his time.

So are our noblest actions often misinterpreted and

travestied. Yet if thus we are spared the fate of complete oblivion which we deserve, have we any cause for complaint?

*   *   *   *   *

I have already noted that one almost universal characteristic of the citizens of the United States is an insatiable curiosity to learn, to find out, to make new scientific discoveries and to apply such discoveries to the uses of everyday life.

Three great examples still stand out in my memory. The Research Laboratories of General Motors at Detroit, with which I in my mind connect also Mr. Henry Ford's works in the same city. Second, the great *Chicago Tribune* building in Chicago, and lastly the research department of Eli. Lilly & Co., of Indianapolis.

It may be that something like the laboratories of General Motors exists in Europe, but in my ignorance I have never heard of it. In any case, this palace of research at Detroit made, like the Ford works there, an unforgettable impression on my mind. A great building of some ten or twelve stories, if I remember rightly, in which each story, divided into many laboratories, was dedicated to the discovery of some new invention or the perfection of old ones. Improvements in metals, alloys, woodwork, rubber, paints, varnishes, textiles, in fact anything that enters into the make-up of a motor-car, nothing was forgotten here, and highly paid metallurgists, chemists and experts of various kinds worked there ceaselessly day by day, as I say, to discover and improve by application to practical use any new discoveries, wherever made.

At the Ford works I met Mr. Ford himself, and after a short conversation he was good enough to take me on a personally conducted tour.

Great steel works always interest me, but these are very much the same everywhere. What, however, really almost left me speechless was the shop where the motor is assembled and fitted together. I shall not attempt to reproduce this from memory—I should doubtless make absurd mistakes—but this I can say : side by side with Mr. Ford I walked along the continuous chain, following one car from the moment the naked chassis was put on the chain to the moment that it was driven off apparently complete. The whole operation took, by my watch, I think about fifty minutes, and every five minutes a new car was being driven off at the finishing point complete. Let those who are interested in this miracle of organisation read a full account of how it is accomplished. Mr. Ford himself explained everything as we went along so lucidly that I left with a reasonably clear notion of the various processes. But, as usual in life, the man interested me more than the machinery.

Here was a rather ascetic, frail-looking man, evidently a good deal of an idealist, looking indeed more like a thirteenth century saint than a great American manufacturer, who had by sheer organising power and quickness of perception combined with mechanical genius built up for himself one of the greatest industries in the world, of which he remains still supreme dictator. I found him most interesting and sympathetic. I had wanted greatly to meet him, remembering the sad fiasco of his great Peace Ark full of enthusiastic young men and women, with no previous knowledge or understanding, who set sail for Stockholm during the Great War with the object of " getting the boys out of the trenches before Christmas," and I thought I understood how a great industrialist may be at once completely practical as a competent business man and completely unpractical in the affairs of State.

The workshop in which new models were designed also filled me with admiration. Like a great cathedral of steel and glass whose roof was supported by square steel pillars, it was all one vast open space, dedicated to light and air.

Here there were, so to speak, side chapels, shut off from the rest of the building, in one of which Mr. Ford had his own office.

The floor of the great hall was of planks as clean and

polished as those of a ball-room. In fact one part was used at regular intervals for dances for the employees. No spot of dust was allowed to settle anywhere in this great hall. The temperature was always kept equable and the air at the same time fresh by a system of heating and ventilation carried up through the steel pillars that supported the roof and so carefully regulated that the temperature could be controlled to a degree. It was indeed a wonder palace of industry, and the brain of it all, the man who had created it and kept it going, was moving through it all, conversing as pleasantly and unconcernedly as if it was of little account. I do not believe he ever mentioned himself during the hour and a half or two hours which he was good enough to dedicate to my instruction.

It is not to be wondered at that his personality impressed itself on my memory.

As regards the *Chicago Tribune* building and my visit over the works of that famous paper, I will but say that at the invitation of the owner, Colonel McCormick, whom I had met during the War at Stockholm, Isa and I, during one of our visits to Chicago, or rather to the ever-hospitable house of Judge and Mrs. Goodwin on the shores of Lake Michigan some miles out of the city, spent the best part of a day in examining the whole process of building up a daily newspaper from start to finish.

We began by being interviewed (and photographed, of course) on the roof of the famous *Chicago Tribune* sky-scraper of I forget how many stories. There a brilliant reporter produced an interview of several columns out of some platitudes with which I endeavoured to acquit myself of my duty as the victim of an interview and of my debt of gratitude as the guest of a friendly proprietor of one of the greatest papers in the United States.

We went down story by story examining how page by page the paper grew. Half-way down, in Colonel McCormick's office sitting-room, we found an excellent luncheon ready for us, and then began once more to visit the various workshops. By the time we reached the bottom my interview in a special edition was ready for distribution to the public.

There were no flies on the *Chicago Tribune*.

Finally I specially remember the research laboratories of Eli. Lilly & Co.—first manufacturers of insulin [1]—over which I was shown without any reserve whatever, this being also characteristic of American methods. These laboratories were equally thorough, practical and, no doubt, efficient.

As I see it the difference between English and American methods of industry is that while the former often regard any new thing or even the idea that there may be any new thing under the sun with the deepest suspicion, in America the mere hint that there may be a new method of producing some article at once creates a tingling desire to try to see whether it is not better than the one in use.

I will conclude my American reminiscences with a few personal sketches.

Mr. Herbert Hoover, whom I had met and looked up to at the Paris Conference as the great organiser of supplies to the starving or destitute during and after the War, I met again in Washington, first as Secretary of Commerce in Mr. Coolidge's administration, afterwards as President of the United States. Here he played a considerable part in helping to stem the great Mississippi floods of 1928 and to organise relief for those in need. He was recognised on all hands as a great organiser, and the Republican Party hoped that he would be an irresistible organiser of victory and that the Coolidge boom would continue indefinitely under his care. But Mr. Coolidge, the most prudent of men, was undoubtedly wise in 1928 when he declared, " I do not choose to run again." (It is surely characteristic of the United States that candidates for any elective post over there " run " ; they do not " stand," as in England. Nothing is static in that land of perpetual motion.) Mr. Hoover was swept into office on the crest of the boom, but from that moment, for no fault of Mr.

---

[1] Insulin was discovered by Banting, a Canadian working in Toronto University, and was first used clinically in the Dominion.

Hoover's administration, the great wave of prosperity began to subside and continued so to do throughout his term of office and well into that of his successor. He certainly was most unfortunate, but I think it will also be generally admitted that he lacked the power of establishing contacts with fellow human beings and he had little or no knowledge of what Mr. Kent has called " the Great Game of Politics." He was master neither of the Glad Hand nor of the Good Smoking Room Story, nor of Mr. Coolidge's peculiar mordant humour. He had not the art of swimming successfully against the tide.

It was quite untrue that he was either anti-English or anti-European. He was, if I read him aright, definitely out to help the world to recover prosperity if he could do so without sacrificing American interests. Yet I found him, without exception, the most difficult American to know whom I have ever met. This failure was no doubt owing to my own incapacity, and I put it down to my being unable to interest him. But I have been told since that Mr. Hoover is by nature extremely shy, and that it is difficult to win his confidence except for those who actually work under him and for him. Some of these I knew well, and they were certainly devoted to him.

For Mrs. Hoover both Isa and I always felt the highest respect and the most friendly feelings.

One more scene is vividly photographed on my mind. The place : the Morgan Library in New York ; Dramatis Personæ : Mr. J. P. Morgan, Junior, Mr. Owen Young, Mr. T. Lamont and myself. Subject under discussion : The American Delegation for the Paris Conference, which was summoned for the consideration of what we fondly hoped would be the final settlement of the German Reparations question, and which did in fact produce the " Young Plan."[1]

I was only present as an interested observer to inform my Government at once as to the persons finally chosen to represent America on this occasion.

---

[1] The " Young Plan " was the outcome of the meetings of the Second Committee of Experts appointed by the Reparations Commission and the German Government, 1929.

This preparatory conference remains particularly impressed on my mind, first because of our meeting in a room like the Morgan Library, full of priceless treasures of art, rather than at the famous bank in Wall Street. This reminded me of Lorenzo de Medici, great financier and patron of the Arts in Florence four hundred years or more before, who might well have met his friends and done much of his business in a similar magnificent setting.

Secondly, I was greatly impressed during this my first and only meeting with Mr. Owen Young. There are men who so impress us we hardly know why ; but I carried away with me a strong belief that Mr. Young was a man who could easily attain to the highest place in any walk of life he might choose to follow. He had, it seemed to me, a sureness of touch and a rapidity of decision that singled him out as a great man.

Mr. Pierpont Morgan, after working closely with Mr. Young in Paris, confirmed this view by what he told me of that Conference. I remember he put it in this way :

" All that the rest of us had to do at Paris was to hold up Owen Young's hands as the Children of Israel held up the hands of Moses during the battle of Rephidim against the Amalakites and the battle was won."

Three other personalities, I feel, require special mention.

M. Claudel, the French Ambassador at Washington, who was probably the greatest mystic poet of our time— a curious combination, that of mystic and diplomat—and Miss Ruth Draper, that great comedian, tragedian and satirist who, with a light touch or an inflection of the voice and with no artificial help of any kind, can transform herself from one to the other by sheer understanding of human nature as I never saw any other artist do.

The last was Lindbergh, the young Lohengrin, who came suddenly out of the sky, as it were, and was transformed in twenty-four hours into a popular hero and remained withal just as unspoilt and simple as when he " hopped off " for France for the first solo non-stop flight across the Atlantic.

I am glad to have known, and I hope I may say made

friends with, all these three very different but very attractive characters, each of whom, in spite of genius and success, managed to retain that fundamental simplicity of outlook which is surely one of the greatest assets in life.

As to all the innumerable friends who showered kindnesses on my family and myself during our stay in the United States, how can I thank them enough ? I can but say that I left Washington filled with a sense of profound gratitude to them and to their country, and with an ever-increasing hope that with the passing of the years the British Commonwealth of Nations and the United States of America may be drawn together in good will and good fellowship for the peace of the world and the benefit of all.

CHAPTER XXVI

TOBAGO REVISITED

(1930)

BEFORE leaving America I had long desired to pay a farewell visit to the West Indies, and especially to Tobago. The Foreign Office gave me leave after the Prime Minister left Washington early in October, 1930, and so Francis and I left together for Bermuda, where we arranged to take one of the Canadian " Lady " ships for Trinidad.[1]

While waiting for our steamer we spent three or four days delightfully at Government House and Admiralty House, Bermuda, as guests of the Governor, Sir Louis Bols, and Admiral Sir Cyril Fuller. The Bermudas, however, like the Bahamas, are but so to speak the gateways of the real West Indies, and have not the full Antillian flavour of the isles farther south. Perhaps the most interesting event of our visit was a lecture by Professor Beebe on his experiences at hitherto unexplored depths of the ocean in his diving ship, from which he was able to examine strange submarine creatures at thousands of feet below the surface.

The aquarium at Bermuda is one of the most interesting in the world on account of the variety of shape and colour of the fish of those waters.

The islands have what in these days has come to be considered a rare merit : no motor-cars are allowed upon them, and though many inhabitants would like to see them introduced, visitors from the United States object so strongly to having this haven of rest disturbed by

[1] For those wishing to visit the West Indian Islands and the Spanish Main, the *Pocket Guide to the West Indies*, by Sir Algernon Aspinall, C.M.G., C.B.E., published by Sifton Praed & Co., London, 1927, may be heartily recommended.

the hoot of the car, and their likes and dislikes are financially of such importance to the islanders that hitherto the prohibition against motors has been steadily maintained. Long may it continue.

From Bermuda our ship took us to St. Kitts and Nevis, where the real Antilles begin.

St. Kitts was a constant bone of contention between the French and English in the seventeenth and eighteenth centuries, when sugar was almost as precious as oil is to-day. It possesses a magnificent specimen of eighteenth century fortification, now ruined and abandoned, which must have seen much fighting in and around it. It remains almost unchanged and full of interest. These seventeenth or eighteenth century forts add much to the romance of the West Indian landscape.

Nevis is notable mainly as the birthplace of Alexander Hamilton, and a tumbledown house is shown as the scene of his birth. There is, however, considerable doubt as to the authenticity of this site, or American admirers of the great man would surely have subscribed the small sum required to restore the house and garden.

At Nevis there also are still the remains of an eighteenth century watering-place, where wealthy planters from neighbouring and distant islands came to take the waters after living too well in a tropical climate.

Francis and I, after a swim in the sea, having tasted the mineral waters, were refreshing ourselves less medicinally on the terrace in front of the old hotel with a lovely view across to St. Kitts, when two old and blind negroes, one with a violin, the other with a concertina, came up to the terrace and began to make music. They played and sang American songs of the day, and received their reward from our fellow tourists.

Then suddenly, without warning but with immense energy and vigour, the old violinist occasionally beating time with his bow, they struck up " Rule, Britannia." Both musicians sang it with a patriotic enthusiasm which was at once pathetic and inspiriting. As they beat time with flat and naked feet on the terrace, with the sun setting behind them in gorgeous splashes of crimson and orange, it flashed across my mind that Britannia had just agreed to " parity " on the sea, and could no longer expect to rule the waves as of yore. It was left to two poor old, blind West Indian negroes to sing the old song with the enthusiasm of Nelson's day.

Sic transit. They, however, got the reward they looked for.

From St. Kitts it was a short night's journey across to Antigua, where I was taken off by the Governor, Lieutenant-Colonel St. Johnston,[1] to visit the famous dockyard at English Harbour from which Nelson started on the long trail in pursuit of the French fleet, which pursuit ended only in Trafalgar and established British supremacy at sea for generations.

The dockyard had been little changed since his day, and it is a memorial of great historical value. There are the sheds and the graving-docks, the winches and the windlasses of Nelson's time still in their places, but they are rotting rapidly. It is a thousand pities that nothing is done to preserve this most interesting historical relic. There also is the house Nelson lived in, and Clarence House, where lived Admiral the Duke of Clarence, afterwards King William IV, who commanded the dockyard and naval station at Antigua. It is still easy to reconstruct the scene as it must have looked before Trafalgar when Nelson was refitting there.

The Governor, who kindly drove us over from St. John's, the capital of the island, was most anxious that a committee should be formed in England to make a public appeal to preserve this fine Nelson relic. I promised I would do what I could to help when I returned to England. An influential committee was formed, but no one could spare the time to take the matter up seriously, and it petered out. It is much to be hoped that it may be taken up again.

From Antigua the steamer went on to Dominica, that most unspoilt and most beautiful, perhaps, of all West

[1] Now Sir Reginald St. Johnston.

Indian islands, where we spent the day and had time for a ride to some falls up a valley behind the little capital of Roseau. Thence one more night's journey, and we anchored at St. Lucia, the last of the Leeward Islands ; away again during the night to Barbados, which, of course, I knew well from previous visits and so on, touching at the principal Windward Islands, each seeming more beautiful than the last—St. Vincent and Granada—at which we were kindly entertained for the day by the respective Governors and Administrators, until at last we passed through the Bocas del Dragon, which divide Trinidad from the mountainous mainland of Venezuela, into the Gulf of Paria and cast anchor, as I had done so often before, in the roadstead off Port of Spain. Here we were welcomed by the Acting-Governor, Mr. (now Sir) S. Grier, and his most kindly and hospitable consort, who at once carried us off to Government House, where we spent two or three days in great comfort before leaving for Tobago.

I hardly ever had a more enjoyable journey than that out with Francis down the whole length of the Leeward and Windward Islands, which are like a most glorious chaplet of pearls of great price. The thought now occurs to me as I write that it was like saying the joyful mysteries of the rosary.

Our " lady " ship, moreover, was perfect in every way for us. We were given a large cabin on the front of the saloon deck and could keep our large windows—no portholes here—open day and night, and the welcome breezes carried into our cabin every sort of pleasant scent from the islands we passed. The " lady " ship was excellently run, and it would be really impossible for anyone to ask for a more enchanting holiday after a rather gruelling period of work than a cruise from Bermuda down to British Guiana and back (we had to miss out British Guiana for the sake of Tobago) in one of these Canadian liners.

With Francis I visited my old haunts in Port of Spain and played the cicerone to my satisfaction. The Cathedral, where I had been received into the Church, and the Botanical Gardens, where, with Sir Rowland Biffen and Mr. Hart, I had worked on rubber ; the first being the one great success of my life ; the second ending in conspicuous failure.

The journey to Tobago is now much easier than formerly. All luggage was shipped overnight in the small steamer that served as the link between the two islands, and next morning we took a motor-car to the north-eastern corner of Trinidad, at Toco, where we joined our steamer, and after a rather choppy crossing caused by the Trade winds at that time of year, we anchored off Scarborough,[1] Tobago's minute and delightfully West Indian capital.

Wars, conferences, revolutions, and all the changes which had so altered life elsewhere, had enchantingly passed Tobago by, and life here had to me a special savour that it could never know in Piccadilly or Connecticut Avenue, the Rue de la Paix, or even the Piazza di Spagna.

My dear old friend, Thorleif Orde, had come down from Louis d'or to greet us, and welcomed me as though it was but yesterday that we parted.

I stayed a night in Scarborough to have the joy of attending Mass the next day and receiving Holy Communion in the little church by the sea under the rustling coco-nut palms where I had first been privileged to do so. It was all as I remembered it, and very satisfying.

But then, instead of the old, long ride over the windward road, we motored in an ancient Ford which, however, approached as nearly as could be to one of the old broken-down West Indian ponies of yore, and so we drove in state up the hill to Louis d'or House.

Any man who returns after many years to some places which held all the ambitions and dreams of his youth, and sees them all crumbling and disintegrating before

---

1 These places have all been described in Vol. I, pp. 221-222, 247-259, and therefore need no further mention here.

THORLEIF ORDE   SELF

TOBAGO, NOVEMBER, 1929

his eyes, will realise what I felt in revisiting these plantations to which such high hopes had been attached. To
others who cannot realise these things it is useless to
attempt to describe my sensations. It is enough to
repeat what I have said in a previous chapter, that
returning after what, I suppose, to many men would
appear to be a fairly successful diplomatic career, I
realised more than ever that I would gladly have
sacrificed it all for a measure of success in building
up a new planting industry—rubber or any other—
in the West Indies, and so bring back prosperity to
the islands which had such an immense attraction
for me.

I had been fascinated as a young man by the theme (if
I read it aright) chosen by Goethe for the second part
of " Faust " that a man's sins may be forgiven if he
devotes himself to work for the welfare of others. I
hoped, therefore, with the naiveté of youth, to combine
the price of my redemption with work which I
enjoyed and also a little temporal benefit to myself.
A pleasant programme, but hardly a truly spiritual
one.

Now, however, I saw this dream of my youth withering
before my eyes, and realised only too clearly that I should
never be able to say as Faust wished to say :

> " Zum Augenblicke dürft ich sagen
> Verweile doch du bist zu schön !
> Es kann die Spur von meinen Erdetagen
> Nicht in Æonen untergehen."

Faust, Part ii, Act V.

Translation :

> To the speeding moment would that I might say :
> Stay but a while for that thou are so fair.
> The footprints left of this my earthly Day
> Through endless æons ne'er shall pass away.

2 O

I said good-bye to Thorleif and his family with the most sincere regret. The end of my visit to Tobago was made sad by the news of the death of my sister Maud, the last of my generation and the special friend of my childhood. My eldest sister, Elsie Carnarvon, who died in the spring of 1929, had literally worn herself out like so many other women during the War looking after the wounded and invalids, at first in Alexandria, and later, at the end of and after the War, helping to make conditions in Albania a little more tolerable. This last she undertook for the sake of her son, Aubrey Herbert, who had for years devoted his energies in Parliament and out to assisting that strange and romantic people. After her seventieth year she took to flying in Albania, finding it a much easier method of locomotion than carriages or carts among the wild Albanian mountains. A friend of hers who knew her well in those days in Egypt told me that she was known among the British troops stationed in Alexandria as the " Harbour Master," because she regularly met incoming troopships to see if she could be of service to any invalids on board.

The manner of her death was pleasant and greatly to be envied. In the spring of 1929 she was at her Villa Altachiara, at Porto Fino, which stands on a high and precipitous rock looking out over the Mediterranean. She was just finishing her day's correspondence which, always voluminous, she dealt with in the morning in bed. Suddenly she said : " I think I will go out a little into the sun," and, falling back, lost consciousness. Those were her last words.

My sister Maud died, as I have already stated, when I was in Tobago at the end of 1929. She also, as she would have wished, at her home in Cumberland. For years she never left Cumberland for more than a week at a time, except once in order to go and help her sister at Alexandria during the War, and a second time to keep me company in Massachusetts while I was there alone. She was the most uncompromising Cumbrian I ever met.

It is the penalty, I suppose, that the youngest of a family must often pay that at the close of life there is no one left with whom to tell over old tales together.

I shall not dwell much longer on the West Indian voyage. Francis and I returned to Port of Spain after about ten days in Tobago, and having spent a few more days quietly with the Griers, we embarked for Jamaica via certain ports of Central America of which I remember especially Port Limon de Costa Rica. Here, having twenty-four hours to spare, we risked being blocked by landslides, which were frequent on the railway up to the capital San José. This lies in a rolling, down-like, cattle-ranching country about four thousand feet above the sea. Here we came in for a most sumptuous wedding in the cathedral by which two rival families, the Montagues and Capulets of Costa Rica, were joined in holy matrimony, and were almost suffocated by the crowd, mostly of Indians and half-castes, during the ceremony. It was all highly interesting and brilliantly exotic.

Rocks and earth fell on to the roof of our railway carriage as we went up, but the line was cleared before our return, and we happily caught our steamer to Jamaica. There a few days at Government House as guests of Sir Reginald Stubbs and an excursion to the beautiful northern shore kept us agreeably occupied.

I was pleased to discover under the base of a brass lectern in the old Cathedral at Spanish Town the tombstone of the ancestor of my mother's family, Samuel Long, of Netheravon in Wiltshire, who went out to Jamaica with the expedition that conquered the island in Cromwell's time.

We returned to the United States via Cuba, landing at Santiago and crossing the island by train—a somewhat dull journey for those who like us had come from the glories of the Leeward and Windward Isles.

In Cuba we were the guests of the British Minister and his wife, Mr. and Mrs. Morris, and we were much struck by the extraordinary modern developments of Havana.

Thence across to Key West over the immense causeway that joins that most southerly point of the United States to the mainland of Florida, and so home to Washington in good time for our last Christmas on American soil.

A few weeks of farewell feastings, in addition to our usual family and Embassy merry-makings at Christmas time, brought my diplomatic experiences to an end.

It was hard work to say good-bye to so many friends knowing that probably we would see few of them again. Leaving any post where we had spent happy years was always a wrench, and because we had spent six years of our diplomatic life at Washington, leaving it was the greatest wrench of all. But I had a feeling of real satisfaction at the end, for the last few days were spent in the house of our friends the Vincent Masseys,[1] and our very last dinner in Washington was, as already stated, given by Mr. Eric Louw, the South African Minister, the other guests being the Vincent Masseys, Mr. Macauley, the Irish Chargé d'Affaires, and one American from the State Department.

A great number of colleagues and American friends were at the station to bid us farewell, and farewells did not cease until our ship left New York.

One farewell, however, I particularly insisted on celebrating myself, for the other party cared little whether I stayed or left. This was to the great " skyline " of New York. So I travelled from Washington to New York by a Baltimore and Ohio Railroad train in order to get a last view of that impressive skyline across the Hudson River. Most of those who make that journey prefer to take the Pennsylvania Line, which passes under the Hudson in a tunnel, from which, of course, none can get an idea of the magnificence of that skyline. I often took the " B. and O." simply for the pleasure of crossing the river by ferry and enjoying the movement and the

[1] Canadian Minister at Washington.

bustle of the ships and launches and ferries in the port of New York, all backed by the incredible towers of that unique city. I could not leave New York without seeing that view of it again.

CHAPTER XXVII

THE HOLY LAND

(1931)

WE did not stay very long in England after landing from America, but as soon as all necessary formalities had been accomplished we left for Italy and spent the first joyful month of our release from official life peacefully and pleasantly in Rome. It was truly a most agreeable change to know that officially it mattered not the least whether one was alive or dead. It is one of the greatest advantages of diplomacy that once on the shelf one is allowed to vegetate in peace and enjoy one's *otium cum* or *sine dignitate* as one pleases.

One land I was determined to visit before giving up travel altogether, and so I persuaded poor Isa, who disliked all forms of locomotion and would never have moved from the neighbourhood of Rome if that could have been avoided, to accompany me on a pilgrimage to Palestine.

At the end of April, 1931, we sailed in a Japanese ship from Naples to Port Said. The ship was so clean and comfortable and the food so excellent, that we did not feel like genuine pilgrims. All I can say in our favour was that we really carried so few changes of raiment that we could not accept the kind invitations we received from Sir Percy Loraine and his wife to stay at the British Legation in Cairo, or from Sir John Chancellor, the British High Commissioner in Jerusalem, to stay with him while there. We, however, accepted invitations to dinner provided I might be allowed to come without a tail coat and white tie. To go attired in a black tie and jacket would, I felt, not be altogether incongruous even in a modern pilgrim, so I had not packed the other luxuries

582

when setting forth, and they were kindly and most hospitably dispensed with.

Cairo was, of course, intensely interesting—the Mosques, the Pyramids, the Tombs of the Kings, and the glimpse of the real desert and the museum. But these things were not the true aim of our journey and need no description here. Like others, I had read of them superficially and knew something of their interest in a general way. One of the sights, however, I did not expect, and it came, therefore, as a special and unusually pleasant shock to find that there were beautiful stained-glass windows dating, I believe, from the tenth century, in one or two of the mosques. These had, of course, no representation of figures of any kind, and were merely arranged in geometrical patterns and set in plaster tracery so thick that looking at the window from a side angle the glass was invisible. It was thus almost impossible to obtain a general view of the colour and design of a large window from any particular spot. But this had a special beauty of its own, which I remarked later in the great Mosque of Jerusalem, known as the Dome of the Rock, in that it produced certain kaleidoscopic effects as one moved about the mosque.

It was no doubt very ignorant of me not to have known about these windows, but no traveller had ever mentioned them to me, and I did not remember ever having read a description of them. They were not, indeed, the windows of Chartres or Beauvais or Leon, but they had a real charm of their own and fitted in wonderfully with their surroundings like the carved and painted woodwork.

A night's journey brought us from Cairo to Jerusalem. The first sight my eyes met in Palestine was at the station of Gaza, which evoked memories of Samson and the Philistines, where I looked out of the window of my sleeping-car in the light of a somewhat chilly and rainy dawn. The only moving object in sight was a stout Jewish dame in patent leather button boots and the shortest of Parisian skirts then in fashion, picking her way delicately among the puddles of a very muddy road.

So this, I said, is Palestine. I had been warned that I should be grievously disappointed in the Holy Land, but I did not expect this. At any rate, nothing could be more disillusioning than this first introduction, and with that comforting thought, I drew the curtain of my window and, saying good-bye to Samson and the Philistines, I plunged in sleep again.

I have not been back there to disturb that first impression of Gaza, but I found that such incongruities are not altogether unusual in Palestine, as in other parts of the world of which we have formed our own preconceived ideas. There is only one way of dealing with such unharmonious sights and sounds, which is simply to treat them as if they were not there.

I understand people who are quite lacking in this useful art complaining that the Holy Land, and especially Jerusalem, do not in all things come up to the picture which their fancy has painted, and which is probably something akin to the print of a Gustave Doré picture of the Flight into Egypt. Yet I cannot but feel sorry for those who criticise everything, let us say, in the Church of the Holy Sepulchre, that does not come up to their peculiar standard of perfection in religious cults, forgetful of the fact that millions of men and women from all parts of the earth have, whatever certain sceptics may say about the authenticity of the Holy Places, hallowed them by their prayers since the days of the Empress Helena, that is, for sixteen centuries at least.

Is this to count for nothing ?

It always seems to me little short of presumptuous for Professor This or Doctor That, on the grounds of some new archæological discovery, or even theory of his own generally declared by his disciples to be based on profound study, to question the traditions of that time so near to the century of the Gospels.

For this reason I have never felt much patience with those who tell us that it is better not to go to Jerusalem because : " Of course, my dear sir, all those traditions about the holy places are pure fabrication, and the forms

of worship followed there are often really too shocking."
Therefore, we cannot too often remind ourselves that
these places have been hallowed by Christian worship,
even if that worship is not always identical exactly and
is not always conducted with that particular decorum
which might be expected in a church or chapel in other
lands.

There were places in Palestine where I felt the sanctity
of the spot to an especial degree, even more, perhaps,
than in the Church of the Holy Sepulchre. Such were
Jacob's Well, where our Lord had His marvellous colloquy
with the woman of Samaria; the synagogue at Capharnaum,
where He so clearly enunciated the doctrine of the Blessed
Sacrament; the village of Bethany, where He performed the mighty miracle of the raising of Lazarus;
and, lastly, the stable of the Nativity at Bethlehem,
which, though much decorated, yet enables one to reconstruct it in imagination in its original state, and thus
gives us a very realistic picture of the cave-stable of an
inn of that time.

Perhaps these sites may appeal more to us than that
of the Church of the Holy Sepulchre itself because they
are more withdrawn from the world. They are also less
covered with that cheap decoration which often offends,
though on second thoughts it may attract by the very
simplicity of the faith which it expresses.

It was comforting to hear His Holiness Pope Pius XI
express much the same views when on our return from
the Holy Land he admitted us to a private audience.
This he has always done when we returned to Rome,
remembering, perhaps, the critical days of 1919 when he
was Nuncio in Poland and I was the British representative
on a Special Mission. At this audience in 1931 he
naturally talked much about the Holy Places, and asked
for our impressions. Isa replied that with all reverence
it was yet sometimes difficult to preserve a proper feeling
of that complete devotion which the place should evoke
during Mass when there was at the same time a Coptic
service with strange singing going on at the back of

the Sepulchre, and perhaps a Greek service in the Greek chapel in front of it.

His Holiness said that it was, of course, difficult not to feel disturbed and distracted by these unaccustomed sounds and curious music. But we should dwell, rather, on the wonder that for century after century thousands had gathered there from all parts of the earth, braving all difficulties and even dangers in order to worship our Lord and celebrate His Passion and Death on this spot. This thought should rather give us cause for rejoicing than for any otherwise natural criticisms.

This is undoubtedly the true answer to those who try to belittle the Holy Places and scoff at them because they are not exactly what such critics would have them to be.

Having unburdened myself on this subject of scoffers and critics, whether ignorant or learned—and there are many of both categories—I need not again return to the subject. I will only say that if travellers to Palestine start in that sort of spirit they will probably obtain little spiritual help from their visit to the Holy Land, and will come home disillusioned and disappointed. Those, on the other hand, who ask humbly at these shrines for spiritual riches and strength will surely find what they seek.

It was still raining and chilly when we arrived at Jerusalem, and our first impressions—a modern station and the modern streets outside the walls—were not satisfying. We put up at a good, clean but unpretentious German hotel close to the Jaffa Gate. It was but a few steps through the narrow streets and bazaars of the Eastern city to the Church of the Holy Sepulchre, so that it was easy for us to visit it daily and attend Mass either at the chapel of the Sepulchre itself or at one of the chapels of the Latin rite within the Basilica. I do not propose to give any description of this strange building with its conglomeration of adjacent chapels, of which it is truly difficult without careful study to grasp any connected plan. The present edifice is the Church of the Crusaders, begun in 1130 and consecrated in 1149. It was constructed on the ruins of the Basilica set up by the Emperor

Constantine to mark the site judged by the Empress Helena, his mother, to be that of the Crucifixion and of the nearby sepulchre of our Lord. The first church of the Holy Sepulchre was consecrated A.D. 335, and remained standing till A.D. 614, when it was destroyed, like all the shrines built by the Empress Helena in the Holy Land, by the Persian invasion under Chosroes who, however, for some reason spared the Basilica of the Nativity at Bethlehem.

So much I may say of the site and antiquity of the Church of the Holy Sepulchre in order to give those readers who have not some superficial knowledge of its origins a slight acquaintance with its story. Those who are interested in following that story will find it concisely but graphically told in the admirable French guide-book, *La Palestine*, compiled by professors of *Notre Dame de France* at Jerusalem, and published by the *Maison de la Bonne Presse*, 5, Rue Bayard, Paris. This guide-book we found invaluable during our journey. It contains excellent descriptions and maps not only of Jerusalem and the whole of Palestine, but also of Syria, Cairo and Egypt, with Constantinople and the Eastern Mediterranean.

Having visited, with all care and devotion, the various points of interest in the Church of the Holy Sepulchre—except, I regret to say, the curious Abyssinian community on the roof—and the other Christian buildings and memorials as thoroughly as time would permit, we were greatly impressed by the sheer beauty of the architecture and decorations of the great Dome of the Rock, otherwise known as the Mosque of Omar, which is surely one of the most magnificent places of worship in the world. It was built in the seventh century after the conquest of Jerusalem by the Khalif Omar, in the form of a circle in imitation of the domed circular church which then covered the Holy Sepulchre

Although the mosque was built by order of an Arab prince, Abd-el-Melik—begun A.D. 688, and finished A.D. 691—it followed the design of Byzantine, or, more exactly stated, of Syrian ecclesiastical architecture of that period, both the architect and the decorators being almost certainly Christian (according to the authors of *La Palestine*). In 1016, at the time of the Crusades, an earthquake caused the original Dome to fall in, and when this was rebuilt the present glorious mosaics were set up. It became a Christian Church after the conquest of Jerusalem by the Crusaders in 1099, and they added various decorative features. Less than a hundred years later, when Jerusalem was reconquered by Saladin, it returned to its original use as a mosque, having been " purified " from its Christian perversions by the sprinkling of rose water brought from Aleppo on the backs of twenty camels by the sister of Saladin.

The Dome is supposed to cover the actual rock on which Abraham prepared to sacrifice Isaac, and is supported by two concentric circles of columns of precious marbles, porphyry, verde antico, etc. Mosaics of the most wonderful colours and designs cover the interior of the Dome and every part of the supporting structure. Whatever portion of the building is not covered with precious marbles or agates or rich mosaics is resplendent with carved or painted cedarwood, while round the Rock under the Dome is a high gilded railing of wrought iron dating from the time of the crusades. To complete this feast of colour which, strange to say, is perfectly harmonious throughout, are stained glass lights somewhat like those of the Cairo mosques but far more beautiful, dating from the reign of Suliman the Magnificent, while fine Oriental carpets lie on the marble floors round the Rock. All this beauty has been well described by M. de Vogué, and no doubt many others, but I have heard so few travellers among those who visited Jerusalem draw attention to the overwhelming splendours of this shrine on the site of the old Hebrew temple, that it is to be feared that many leave the Holy City without giving it the attention it deserves. Short as our time was, we felt compelled to return and revisit it. I wrote it down on my mental tablets beside the half-dozen most beautiful buildings I know : St. Mark's, Venice ; St. Apollinare in Classe, at Ravenna ; the Cathedrals of Chartres and Leon ; York Minister and the Parthenon. The exterior, however, it must be confessed, though beautiful, does not leave such an impression behind it.

As to all the many holy places and objects of interest in Jerusalem which are connected with the Life, Passion and Death of our Lord, these are so numerous and so profoundly impressive that I cannot attempt to give any description of the emotions they excite. It may, however, be noted that the traveller who takes with him some volume describing clearly in chronological order the events of the tremendous drama of our Lord's Passion and Death cannot but come away with a new sense of the truth of that Tragedy so unlike anything else recorded in history, and yet so vivid and completely alive in the perfect simplicity of the narrative.

After I had seen these places, two books helped me to understand this more than I had ever hoped would be possible : a little book, carefully compiled and graphically written, called *Who Moved the Stone?* by F. Morison, was the first. The second is a far greater work in three volumes by Archbishop Goodier, S.J., who is both a scholar and a vivid writer. The first two volumes are entitled *The Public Life of Our Lord Jesus Christ*, and the third *The Passion and Death of Our Lord Jesus Christ* (Messrs. Burns, Oates & Washbourne, of London). These bring home with astonishing vividness both the thoughts and manners of the various actors in the great drama and also the tremendous matters at issue which the apostles themselves so little understood. Unfortunately, I only read this book after my return to England, for after reading it much which seemed so misty and improbable as to be almost legendary suddenly became not only natural but even so inevitable that it was clear the events recorded in the Gospels could hardly have happened otherwise. On the other hand, having visited the places described before reading Archbishop Goodier's book was of the greatest help in understanding the events of that night of tragic despair for the Apostles whose actions and very words are often so difficult to explain. In its pages they become really human, and we feel as though we know them personally. I wish now that I might go back once more and follow the Passion again hour by hour and step by step.

While at Jerusalem we visited the traditional site of the Baptism of our Lord in the Jordan and of the ministry of John the Baptist, and the ancient city of Jericho, now being excavated and explored. Another day we went to Bethlehem and were shown the original Basilica of St. Helena, of which I have already spoken, and the stable-cave in which our Lord was born. This latter did not cause me surprise because I had seen many such still in use in Spain, especially near Granada. We saw also Hebron, where all the tombs of the Patriarchs of Israel are held in the greatest veneration by the Mohammedans, but where, shortly before our visit, a massacre of Jews by Arabs had suddenly and most unexpectedly taken place. In fact, not only every day but every hour of our stay in Jerusalem was fully occupied, and all these sights are engraved upon our memories.

Of the ten days we passed in and around Jerusalem, the most impressive, apart from those given up to the city itself, was certainly that spent on the excursion down to the Dead Sea past Bethany and the Inn of the Good Samaritan through a rocky tract increasing in barren wildness until at the shore of the Dead Sea itself, where the mountains descend to the sea, the landscape exceeded for sheer unfriendliness anything I had ever seen. The Kalahari Desert, in South Africa, and the Painted Desert of Arizona were festive in comparison with this comparatively small tract. All those who have taken that road have been impressed by this feature of complete desolation in the region around the Dead Sea. This gives it its grandeur and solemnity, and no doubt that spiritual quality which attracted to it so many prophets, hermits and saints.

I regret that we never visited the lonely monastery of St. Sabbas, which lies between the Dead Sea and

Jerusalem, and for the sake of which I would gladly have sacrificed time spent at the little Zionist Community Cattle Farm somewhere on the road to Jaffa, but which Isa and I are glad to have seen. As we were both anxious to see something of Zionist activities, we visited a Zionist farm settlement in company with Colonel Kisch, a friend from Paris Conference days. He was then a member of the military section of our Delegation, and we found him again here at the head of the Zionist organisation in Jerusalem. It was not one of the " show " places, only a small stock and chicken farm, but it was run on the most modern scientific lines and was doing much to improve the breeds of cattle, sheep and chickens of the district. So much was this the case that many neighbouring Arabs came regularly to learn from the Zionist instructors. This was the more extraordinary because shortly before there had been serious Jewish pogroms at Hebron and other places ; yet in this little valley no ill-feeling had been manifested.

Judging by the increase of agricultural production in Palestine since the Zionists started work, there can be no doubt that much of that long-neglected country can, with proper scientific cultivation, once more be turned into a land flowing with milk and honey. It was really surprising to see how young Jews from the cities of Russia, Lithuania, Poland and other unlikely parts had put their backs into the work and were apparently making a success of it against all forecasts. It should not be impossible for two races of similar origin to settle down to work peacefully side by side, but, as I admit, I have no knowledge of the Near East nor of the Arabs, I am quite unqualified to form any opinion of prospects for the future.

To return to the Dead Sea and its terrific desolation, it was naturally here that we were met on arrival at its shores by one of those violent incongruities which from time to time do give the wayfarer in Palestine electric shocks, destroying for the moment all sense of the solemnity and sacredness of the spot. We had hoped to lunch quietly on the shore, but this was not to be.

A small shanty, roofed with corrugated iron and shaded with palm branches, had been put up just there by two Arabs who sold beer and mineral waters. Against this we could not complain, we even benefited by it. But when presently a wheezy gramophone began diffusing jazzy music, we prepared hastily to move away—not, however, soon enough to avoid seeing a stout Teutonic person in a very tight bathing garment of many colours enter the water and, being unable to sink, float away like a gigantic toy balloon.

This was too much—and we, so to speak, gathered our pilgrim skirts about our knees, re-entered our car, and fled to less denatured parts. It was tragic, but also comic, and the vision of that brightly-coloured balloon floating away over a sapphire sea set in mountains of jasper is more profoundly impressed on my memory than many beautiful or historic scenes.

One night before leaving Jerusalem I went out for a stroll with an English acquaintance[1] who had lived in Egypt and the Near East for years. We both wanted to walk along the ramparts of the Roman wall of the city for as far as we could go, in the clear, brilliant moonlight of Judea.

We entered at the Jaffa Gate by the so-called " Tower of David," which is really of late Roman construction, and after wandering for some way along the narrow street which followed the city wall, we came to a stair leading up to the ramparts. There was not a soul to be seen and the whole city was lit with a fantastic whiteness which, of course, accentuated the blackness of the shadows. Roman walls and ramparts, domes of churches and minarets, and the great level space on which the Temple had stood and where the Mosque El-Aksa and the Dome of the Rock now took its place—all was spread out before us while beyond rose the ridge of the Mount of Olives and below to the east the Brook of Kedron and the Garden of Gethsemane.

[1] Mr. Robin Furness of the Anglo-Egyptian Civil Service.

Even if, I thought, all in the city had changed beyond recognition from the days of the Gospels, the great natural features remained just as our Lord saw them, and the very path by which He had descended from the city into the dry torrent of Kedron and then climbed again up the other bank to the Garden on the night of the Passion, perhaps on just such a moonlight night as this, was without doubt hardly changed, for there is scarcely a new house on that side of the city. Here, then, it was not difficult to reconstruct the scene of the little band of Apostles, after the Last Supper, descending that rocky path with our Lord leading the way.

It would have been worth the journey to Jerusalem only to have taken that walk round the ramparts in order to get, as I did more than once, an almost overwhelming realisation of walking amidst scenes which we saw much as He must have seen them. Every now and again, but especially on this occasion, the sensation of the reality of the great drama became almost overpowering.

If ever the utilitarians wish to " develop " that eastern side of Jerusalem for the sake of profit, I can but hope that there will be such an outcry from all those who still care that nothing short of another Crusade will be the result. In such matters, the Prophet of Islam is indeed much to be preferred to the profiteers of our time.

We left Jerusalem early one cool April morning with our guide, George Sahlar, a Syrian Christian educated in a Protestant school, and the chauffeur, a Moslem, both excellent men who did their work to our complete satisfaction during the whole of our tour. Taking the road north towards the Sea of Galilee, we first made a halt in Samaritan territory to see the Well of Jacob where our Lord met the Samaritan woman. Here for the first time we could positively say that we might actually be drinking from the same well He drank of on that historic occasion, for here no one disputes the authenticity of the site. It is recognised, unless I am mistaken, by Jews, Samaritans, and Moslems ; by Catholics, Protestants, and all the Eastern Churches. Bishop Germanus, a contemporary of Constantine, built here a Baptistry about A.D. 333, over which was erected, in A.D. 380, the Church of St. Saviour, which was destroyed and rebuilt more than once. The Russian Church was engaged in building a new Basilica over the ruins of the last—a Benedictine edifice—when war broke out. At the time of our journey it had not been finished, and like many other churches built to mark some holy place, it rather detracts from than enhances the devotional character of the spot. Nevertheless, this Well of Jacob remains in my memory as one of the outstanding places in Palestine which had a direct and intimate connection with the public life of our Lord, not only on account of its extreme antiquity and un-undoubted connection with patriarchal history, but, above all, on account of that most revealing discourse of our Lord with the woman of Samaria, the inner meaning of which was only made clear to me later by Archbishop Goodier's book.

But we were anxious to get on to Nazareth for lunch. I feel it is bold of me to write these words, " Nazareth for lunch," but such was the fact, and it is not part of my purpose, as some readers will have already gathered, to suppress these homely details. It may, indeed, interest some to know that it is easily possible to motor from Jerusalem to Nazareth in a few hours. Facts of this sort will bring home to them the astonishing diminutiveness of the land which has played so incalculably great a part in the history of mankind. It is one of the lessons of this country, indeed, that mere size goes, or should go, for little or nothing.

So we sped on through Nablus (the ancient Sichem), between the sacred Samaritan mountains of Gerizim and Habal, across the Plain of Esdraelon, that famous battle-field which is now becoming a great garden under Zionist ploughs and spades, and up the hills on the northern side, with a glorious view to the south and west out to Mount Carmel and to the sea towards what is now the modern city and port of Haifa.

We were disappointed in one thing during the journey.

We had heard so much of the glory of the wild flowers in Palestine in April, but the spring had that year come before its time, and anemones and bulbs were, unfortunately, all over. Only a few wild hollyhocks and other common flowers, convolvuli, daisies, etc., gave us some satisfaction. But I saw here bee-eaters in their splendid coats of irridescent green sitting like swallows in rows on the telegraph wires beside the road, and more of the gorgeous rollers than I had ever seen together before. The flight of the bee-eaters, moreover, so resembled that of swallows that without seeing their resplendent colours one might well have been deceived. They made up to me for the absence of flowers.

We did not stay long in Nazareth, which has been overbuilt with churches, convents, schools of all denominations, and therefore made little impression on us as a city. It was the surroundings, those hills and valleys, those wide views over the plain, all of which our Lord must have seen much as we saw them, that have remained impressed on my mind's eye.

The fact that we were in Galilee became from now on ever present in our thoughts : in Galilee, the scene of our Lord's first public ministrations and from which He gathered the band of His first Apostles.

In spite of the number of religious institutions, however, the Nazarenes have to-day scarcely any better reputation than they had in the days of our Lord. They are said to be turbulent and vexatious, according to my guide-book, *La Palestine*.

The principal church is the Sanctuary of the Annunciation, which forms part of the hospice of the Franciscans and, according to tradition, covers the site of the ancient Basilica, which was of Byzantine architecture. This was almost completely destroyed and a new church of no great architectural interest was erected in its place in 1730. The Cave of the Annunciation is a part of the house. This consisted, like many houses in Nazareth to-day, of a little chamber built in front of and leaning against the rock in which was a cave which formed the back chamber.   This was cut out of the soft rock and was the principal living-room of the house.   Such dwelling-places were, I believe, common in many Mediterranean countries from the earliest times, and are still to be met with. Such was, therefore, doubtless the home of Our Lady.

The Fountain of the Virgin, which is still the water supply for the village, is specially interesting, for there Our Lady must have gone to fetch water for the family, like the crowd of women who still go daily with their pitchers on their heads, walking with the noble carriage of Eastern women accustomed to balance these heavy pitchers in this way.

This spot, perhaps, pleased us more than any other in Nazareth, for it had been so little spoilt.   No church had been built over the well, only a simple Gothic baldacchino, so far as I remember.

We had but time for a short walk about the village and a climb up the hill to the south-west, from which we got a glorious view over the plain and the sea and the promontory of Carmel, and then the road again, for we wanted to be at the Rest House of Tabghah on the Sea of Galilee, before nightfall.

Tabghah had been much recommended to us by friends. It was simply a rest house for pilgrims near the ruins of Capharnaum, kept by an old German Benedictine Father (I am ashamed to say I forget his name).   It lies alone at the north-west end of the lake, and is one of the most enchanting places I have ever stayed at.

As one descends from the high lands of Galilee, which are, like most of the Palestine plateaux, stony and harsh with pockets of cultivation here and there in the limestone rock, the valley of the Lake of Galilee which, like that of the Dead Sea, lies below sea-level, presents a green and most enticing aspect.

Tabghah was just what we wanted, a small, spotlessly clean pilgrims' hostel with just that amount of lack of modern comforts to persuade one almost to believe that one was a real pilgrim.   Bath-rooms there were none, but the temperature was sub-tropical, and a short distance

away there was a hot spring on the shore which warmed
the waters of the lake to an agreeable temperature for a
bath.   Our most kind Benedictine host had in the course
of years planted round his settlement a delicious garden
of temperate, tropical and sub-tropical fruits : figs, grapes,
pears, cherries, date palms, oranges, lemons and bananas
vied with each other for the mastery, the bananas, I
should say, winning.   From this enchanted spot we
looked out over the beautiful Lake of Galilee, on whose
waters walked our Lord Jesus Christ, and we could not
have been far from the place where He called His first
Apostles, and were certainly near the scene of many of
His miracles.

Wonderful also to relate, with the exception of one
great modern church at Capharnaum, three or four miles
away, there was nothing to disturb and distract the
attention.

The following day was perfect.   Isa and I heard Mass
in the little chapel of Tabghah and wandered about the
shore of the lake in the morning.   In the afternoon there
was a good breeze for sailing, so with some other visitors
I hired a fishing-boat to sail the short distance from
Tabghah to the ruins of Capharnaum.   Isa, who can
never be persuaded to go by water if land is available,
took the car, but I would not have given up that little
sail on the Sea of Galilee for anything less than real
peril to life.   To sail in a fishing-boat on those waters
seemed to bring me closer to the Gospel story and to
the Apostles than almost any other experience of that
time.   Those that have imagination and read the passages
of the Gospels relating to our Lord's public life around
Capharnaum and the Sea of Galilee will easily understand
this.   To others, no explanation will suffice.   The scene
itself is most beautiful.   Tiberias, a white city on the
other side of the bay, still stands.   Its destruction was
not foretold by our Lord, but the three doomed cities—
Capharnaum, Bethsaida, Corozain, which, in spite of all
the wondrous deeds that He performed and the glorious
words that He spoke in their midst, failed to understand

and finally rejected Him—these have disappeared as if they had never been. But yet, of the old synagogue of Capharnaum enough remains to give the wayfarer and pilgrim that peculiar sense of standing upon holy ground which we can still vividly evoke among the few remaining ancient olives of the Garden of Gethsemane, in the Church of the Holy Sepulchre, in the Cave of the Nativity, at Jacob's Well, at the Pool of Siloam, at Bethany, and some few other spots which can still be definitely connected with His life on earth.

So I am profoundly grateful for having been permitted to approach Capharnaum as He must so often have done over the water, and to spend a morning in and around the ruins of the synagogue where He taught and worked miracles. Where, above all, He enunciated that " hard saying " of His Body and His Blood which has given comfort and consolation to millions and has also been a stumbling block to many who cannot resign themselves to accept it, though it was spoken by the Son of God Who could not err.

As one letter writer put it to me : " Faith is believing what you know is not true." And he went on to argue, as so many have argued before him, that the words of our Blessed Lord spoken in that synagogue at Capharnaum and recorded in the fourth chapter of St. John's Gospel were false. At least he declared, and it amounts to the same thing, that what the Catholic Church teaches, following those divine words emphatically repeated, is falsehood, and that what we Catholics believe is a lie. This was the verdict of his own very fallible senses, and therefore to him and those who think like him it must be so. In that brilliant book, *Edmund Campion—Jesuit and Martyr*, by Evelyn Waugh, we find that during Campion's trial almost precisely the same accusations were used against him by his judges. It would seem, therefore, that the central question at issue between the Catholic and the " Reformed " faith resolves itself into the one simple query : Are we to believe what Christ said or not, and, if we believe Him to be what He declared

Himself to be, namely the Son of God, how can we suppose it possible for Him to speak anything contrary to the truth or to deceive those whom He was teaching the Way of Life ? This doctrine He repeated many times, and those who preferred to leave Him rather than accept it He permitted to depart without any explanation, only saying, " Doth this scandalise you ? If, then, you should see the Son of Man ascend up where He was before ? It is the spirit that quickeneth, the flesh profiteth nothing. The words that I have spoken to you are spirit and life " (John vi, 62–4).

Now, this discourse was spoken probably within those very walls of the synagogue at Capharnaum where we actually stood. The steps mounting up to the floor of the synagogue may probably have been trodden by His feet. How was it possible not to be deeply moved at having been allowed to come to the very spot where they were spoken ? It is true He also performed miracles on that spot, but that stirred me less. The miracles were for an age that would not believe unless it saw signs and wonders. But these words were for us ; they were for our own blind, stubborn, self-sufficient, proud, ignorant, limited reason to take or to leave. Well, standing there where they were spoken could I, reasoning from His first lessons up to this final climax of His philosophy, which so far transcends any other, ancient or modern— could I do other than accept even this " hard saying," with mind and heart and soul, and there at Capharnaum, on the ground where He taught these things, say humbly " Lord, I believe. Help Thou my unbelief " ?

Therefore, Capharnaum remains to me a specially sacred place, as well as a beautiful one, full perhaps more than any other, except Jerusalem itself, of the greatest memories of the Son of Man.

Isa and I made our adoration together to the " Bread which cometh down from Heaven " in the neighbouring church of the Franciscan Fathers. This new building has, fortunately, not been erected over the ruins of the synagogue, which have been left open to the sky, and it is far enough from the synagogue not to disturb the venerable atmosphere which clings to those ruins.

I wandered back alone along the shore to Tabghah, for it was still too hot for Isa to go on foot. Benediction in the little chapel, a simple supper, half-an-hour's conversation with our wholly delightful host, the tall, soldierly-looking German Benedictine, who among the turbulent and litigious natives performed with success all the functions which the League of Nations and the Hague Court are trying to perform among the nations of Europe, and whose conversation was most interesting and instructive. Then one more walk after dark with Isa now, for it was cooler, along the shore and in the garden lighted by enormous fireflies and scented with datura and orange blossom to the not inharmonious croaking of many frogs. And so ended an unforgettable day.

Next morning, after early Mass in the little chapel and breakfast with our host, with whom we were now on terms of friendship as if we had known him for years, we started off again on our way to Damascus, and with Mount Hermon covered with snow before us, we bade good-bye to the Sea of Galilee and Tabghah and Capharnaum, and left behind us the Holy Land of Palestine. We had, indeed, had a most glorious journey, and once again I can but reflect that only those either grossly ignorant or devoid of any historical sense, apart from religious interests, can visit that marvellous little country without being stirred to the depths by the scenes and thoughts it must evoke.

We continued on our road to Damascus, lunching on a turfed bank by a spring opposite the grand, snow-capped ridge of Hermon. Crossing various streams and torrents, and passing through ever more fertile country which becomes a veritable garden of olives and figs, oranges and lemons and date palms, with running water everywhere, we reached Damascus itself early enough to settle down in our hotel—what a change was here after the beloved Tabghah—and do a little sight-seeing before dinner.

I do not intend to describe Damascus. The Mosque

naturally impressed us and the memories of St. Paul in
the city are of deep interest to the Christian, yet even
these, profoundly interesting as they are, must be less
moving than those places we had just left behind us.
The Bazaar at Damascus pleased me greatly. It was the
greatest Eastern Bazaar I had seen since visiting Fez
nearly forty years before, but in comparison it struck me
as much Occidentalised. Nevertheless, it was full of
interest. We allowed ourselves one more day at Damascus
and then drove over the Antilebanon to Baalbek.

Here, indeed, was a stupendous piece of masonry by
which those great master-builders, the Romans, wished
to set for ever the seal of their dominion on the East.
At least they left nothing shoddy behind them.

To give an idea of the magnificence of the scale on
which the combined fortress and temples of Baalbek were
planned by their Roman builders, it need only be said
that in the surrounding wall there are three vast stones,
hewn and carefully put in place, which are known as the
Trilithon. They were taken from a neighbouring quarry,
and the largest measures sixty-five feet by fourteen feet
by eleven feet. The others are only slightly smaller in
length and each weighs over eight hundred and eighty tons.

These figures will give some notion of the vast scale
on which the builders of this temple-fortress worked. It
is said they intended the whole surrounding wall to be
on the same scale, but after setting three stones in place
found this plan too grandiose to carry out, and were
compelled to reduce the size of the monoliths used.
Nevertheless they are so large as to strike the visitor
dumb with amazement. All these huge blocks are most
perfectly joined together and set with unerring accuracy
in their places. They seem, indeed, to be built for
eternity. It is no wonder that Robinson, an English
archæologist, writes of Baalbek, in his *Biblical Researches*,
quoted in *La Palestine* on page 609 :

By the grandeur of their plan and by the fineness and delicacy
of their execution these buildings seem to surpass all others in Western

Asia, Africa and Europe. Like those of Athens in delicacy, they surpass them in grandeur; vast and massive like those of Thebes, they surpass them in their grace and proportions.

I at once set down Baalbek as among the really great and unforgettable buildings that I had ever seen.

And all this stupendous work must have been constructed by slave labour, no matter at what cost to human life. Nothing appears to have daunted these sublime builders, and the lives of slaves presumably counted less than those of oxen. There is one column of pink granite from Assouan, twenty-three feet long, which must have been brought by sea from Egypt and then rolled up over the Lebanon from Beyrouth and down on the eastern side into the valley of Baalbek or Heliopolis.

We had but an afternoon and morning to spend at Baalbek, and then we had to follow—but in a good car and on a wonderfully engineered road built by the French over the Lebanon range—the reverse journey of the great pink granite column we had left behind at Baalbek.

It is a glorious journey, and we actually caught glimpses of one or two groves of cedars of Lebanon which have survived the attacks made on them for centuries past. Even the *Sequoia gigantea* of the Rockies has been more fortunate, and the Lebanon is to-day far more barren than, it may be hoped, the Californian Rockies will ever become.

Of Beyrouth there is little to say, and we sped on next day past Sidon and Tyre to Haifa under Carmel.

We did not visit either Sidon or Tyre, preferring to lunch in the open air by some rock-hewn tombs, about a quarter of a mile off our road, which, apart from having been rifled years ago, were in perfect condition.

At St. Jean d'Acre we stopped for tea and also to examine the few ruins, still remaining after many sieges, of the Crusaders' Castle and the more modern fortress now tenanted by English soldiers, who have made a charming flower garden in the courtyard. And we remembered Napoleon, whose dreams of an Eastern Empire were finally wrecked here in 1799, and Admiral Sir Sydney

Smith who, with the Turkish commander, defended the place so gallantly by means of the heavy cannon he had taken from the French at sea, some of which were still to be seen in the fortress.

From Acre we continued to Haifa, passing over the brook Kishon, famous for the slaughter of the priests of Baal by the followers of the prophet Elijah. We visited the monastery of Carmel, where a congress of Carmelites from all parts of the world was in progress, and admired its glorious position on a spur of Mount Carmel stretching out into the sea.

The following day the Italian steamer that was to take us back to Italy arrived in the half-finished new harbour of Haifa, and the day after we left the Holy Land, praising God that we had been privileged to make even this brief acquaintance with the cities and places of the Gospel drama. There was not one moment we spent on that soil which we grudged, and I would gladly return there, not only to see again with more leisure the things we saw so much too rapidly, but also to spend if possible more time at Tabghah and renew acquaintance with our Benedictine host of the Rest House there.

On our way home we called for a day at the port of Famagusta in Cyprus, and drove to Larnaka, in the extreme east of the island, to see the thirteenth century cathedral built there by Guy de Lusignan, King of Cyprus, and now, unfortunately, a mosque. It seemed to me, looking on the lie of the land north of Larnaka, that if Great Britain ever needed a naval base in the Eastern Mediterranean, one might be constructed in the neighbourhood, which could be better defended than Haifa. It would not be surprising if, after recent events in the Mediterranean,[1] Cyprus might at last become a possession of supreme importance.

The part of Cyprus we saw was neither fertile nor very attractive. The beautiful parts are, I believe, the northern and western coasts and the inland valleys.

From Cyprus our ship continued via Rhodes, where,

1 Written in June, 1936.

unfortunately, we did not call. This was strange, as she
was an Italian ship, but we passed near by so as to enable
us to get a sight of that fascinating island. Leaving
behind the many barren and rocky islands of the Dodeca-
nese, we entered the Corinth Canal early next day.

I had been many times along the Gulf of Corinth by
train from Patras, but never through the Gulf by sea. It
is most beautiful from the train, but seeing it as we did
that bright May morning, with snow-capped mountains
on either side and southern vegetation along its shores,
like a Norwegian fjord suddenly become meridional, we
thought that morning's steam down the Gulf of Corinth
as perfect from every point of view as could be imagined.
It was not only the extraordinary beauty of scenery, but
also the classical and historical reminiscences which gave
it interest at every turn and made the passage all too
short.

At Brindisi we left our comfortable Italian-Lloyd
steamer, and the next day we were back in Rome.

I cannot end this story of our journey to Palestine
without an account of one of the most interesting interviews it has ever been my fortune to have.

Not long before we left Rome that spring in order to
return to England, my former friend from Crete, Ronald
Graham, now Ambassador in Rome, said to me that he
thought it would be proper for me to ask for an audience
with the Duce. I said it would interest me extremely
to have an audience, but it had always been a rule of
mine never to thrust myself upon busy people, who
probably had no wish whatever to see me.

" Well," said Ronald, " let us ask for an interview.
I think it would be the proper thing, and the Duce likes
to see people like you who have known Italy for many
years."

I said that he might certainly ask, but that I should
quite understand if the answer was negative.

Very shortly after I got a note from the Palazzo Venezia,
the Duce's office, saying that His Excellency would
receive me, I think about midday, two or three days

later at the Palazzo Venezia. Naturally I replied that I
should be honoured.

I had not been in the Palazzo Venezia since I had known
it so well as the Austrian Embassy to the Vatican in the
years before the War. Many things were now changed,
and I found it difficult to recognise the old place except
that the cortile, with its statues and fountains and trees,
naturally remained the same, and made me feel at home.

I had not long to wait, and was presently shown into
the vast room which the Duce occupies as his office.
He was writing, and did not get up or shake hands, but
motioned me to a chair on the other side of the great
writing-table. I waited till he had finished. Then he
looked up and asked me where I had come from lately.
He asked me the usual questions as to what I had seen.
Among other things, I told him about the Zionist farm.
That awoke a glimmer of interest. When I said I had
visited it with Colonel Kisch, whom I had known in
Paris :

" Yes, yes," he said, " I know. The head of the
Zionist organisation in Jerusalem."

Well, I thought to myself, he is certainly well informed.
The conversation flagged.

Then he asked me with a somewhat bored air :

" How long have you known Italy ? "

I felt something drastic must be done if I was to awaken
some spark of interest.

" I believe," I answered, " I knew Italy before Your
Excellency was born."

The arrow hit the mark.

DUCE : " Indeed. Then you can speak Italian ? "

I : " Fairly well."

We had been speaking French up to that time.

DUCE : " Then let us go on in Italian. Now, if you
have known Italy so long, tell me what are the principal
changes you see in the country now and before the War ? "

When the Duce asked me what changes I had observed
in Italy since I knew it first, I guessed at once what he
wanted to know was what changes I had observed in

the country since the Fascist régime had taken charge. I fully expected the question, so my answer was ready.

" I have motored many hundreds of miles in Italy," I said, " since the War ended, and there is one great change which particularly rejoiced me. In parts which I knew formerly, such as the Roman Campagna, where I used to hunt ; the Pontine Marshes, where I used to shoot ; and other parts that I knew simply from travelling through them by train or carriage, and which formerly were wild, abandoned and often the home of brigands, I see now crops of wheat growing luxuriantly and all kinds of vegetable crops such as beans, artichokes and potatoes. There are many other changes for the better I have noticed, but that is the principal one."

Then suddenly his whole demeanour changed. His eyes, which had been those of a man rather bored, flashed as he sprang up and began walking up and down the room motioning me to remain sitting. I had clearly struck a responsive chord.

" That," he exclaimed, " is the work that interests me most. I hope naturally to be able to develop the industries of this country, and with electricity and the water power at our disposal we shall go far. But I want, above all, to avoid the mistakes your country made in the last century when you had such an advantage over all countries in the world by being first in the field with steam power and on account of your wealth in coal. Your economists allowed you, encouraged you, to sacrifice your agriculture to your industries and mines without any Government control. Government control, in fact, of any kind was anathema. The result has been that your economic system is all lopsided. Your agriculture has been allowed to become little more than a *passe-temps* for rich men, and enormous cities like ant-heaps have sprung up which you will now never be able to control so as to make the country balance the town. This is all important, not only economically but for the physique of the inhabitants of any country, and this is what I am aiming at. This is why I am draining marshes and cultivating barren places.

That is why I am building market towns in the Pontine Marshes, and in the Maremma, which will be surrounded by peasants cultivating their own lands, the aim being that every farm or holding should be sufficiently near for the children to get easily to school and the housewife to market, and the men to go in for relaxation after their day's work and see films or learn what is going on in the world, and hear good music on the radios. Each of these market towns must have its church, its school and its hospital, its public library and its theatre. There," he said, " I've told you shortly what I'm aiming at. But I also want to do what your economists look upon as heresy—which is to make my country as far as possible self-supporting, so that it will never be easy to starve us out in wartime. We can be, and must be, self-supporting as regards all necessaries such as foodstuffs, wool and many fibres. I hope we shall soon be independent of foreign supplies of wheat and of meat, which we need less than you do, and, when our electric power is developed, to a great extent of coal and oil. Then we shall also have a more healthy population of men and women more physically fit than your countries that developed under the old now moribund system of *laisser-faire*."

I kept a memorandum of this discourse of Signor Mussolini, but have not got it by me. Nevertheless, I believe I have given the gist of it all. He spoke with extraordinary vehemence, and his eyes flashed as he spoke, but there was little gesticulation. He continued to walk up and down incessantly. As he talked of draining the Pontine Marshes I remembered the conclusion of the second part of Goethe's " Faust."

On the other hand, his conviction of his own infallibility and his certainty for the future success of his plans, which reminded me of Rhodes, made me feel that here again I was in the presence of a master of men. One may disagree both with his political ideals and his methods of putting them into execution, but no one capable of judging men at all could come to any other conclusion. I left the Palazzo Venezia persuaded that here was a man whose path it would not be convenient to cross. He would be, as the French say, "*pas commode*." In so far as many of his economic ideas coincided entirely with my own I certainly wished him well for the development of his country along the lines he had sketched out to me.

There was one great change that he had worked in the habits of his countrymen which filled me with admiration, but which I dared not mention because it might have seemed to him that I was jesting. But, as I have already stated in this book, in arriving at an appreciation of a country or of a man nothing is too small to count, nothing should be overlooked.

In the pre-Fascist days Italy was unpleasantly conspicuous for the spitting habit. Wherever you might be—in the street or in railway carriages, in theatres, even in churches—you had to watch your step all the time. Nothing surprised me more than to find that, so far south as Rome, at any rate, this habit had practically disappeared. It struck me that for one man to have been able to eradicate from a whole people a habit of generations was little short of miraculous, and I sincerely and seriously gave him all honour for that.

In any case, my one interview with Mussolini remains as definitely impressed on my memory as my solitary meeting with Bismarck, as my talks with Rhodes, and my audiences with Leo XIII.

" Very different people," you will say.

Quite so, but all of them masters of men.

CHAPTER XXVIII

OF TWO GREAT MEN, BIRDS, LAKES AND " TERTII
GAUDENTES " ONCE MORE

Of Two Great Men

I HAVE in the last chapter had occasion to refer to
" Masters of Men," who are by popular acclaim
generally accepted as " great." Yet great men need
not necessarily be " great " in the vulgarly accepted meaning of the word. It is more than sufficient if they are great
because of qualities which render them conspicuous in
the service of their fellow men. Men may be most
brilliant intellectually, and most successful in the affairs
of the world, they may alter the course of history, yet
if their lives will not pass the acid test of willing service
for their fellow men of all sorts and kinds, which is
indeed the basis of Christian philosophy, they cannot be
truly great.

Two men whom I have had the honour to meet, both
in the highest ranks of public life, two men utterly different
in character and, indeed, in almost every personal quality,
nevertheless achieved this greatest of all distinctions :
that of utterly subordinating themselves to the call of
duty and service for others, always doing what they truly
believed to be the moral obligation of their calling.

I met both only rarely, but I venture to bracket their
names together in this way because, unlike as they were
in almost every other respect, they shared to the nth
degree this peculiar quality of greatness.

They were Pope Pius X and King George V.

Pope Pius X has always had a special place in my
memory as coming nearer to the ideal type of Christian
charity than any other man I ever met.

King George, on the other hand, appears to me, looking back now on the most difficult circumstances of his reign, to be the quintessence of all that a constitutional monarch should be.

I believe that neither of them in their actions ever thought for a moment of themselves. Personal vanity or ambition simply did not enter into the intellectual or spiritual make-up of either.

Unfortunately, I never met Pius X before he became Pope, but all that we heard of him before that event pointed to a character entirely unself-seeking, utterly devoid of personal ambition. Who in Rome has not heard the story of his setting out from Venice for the Conclave in Rome at which he was elected Pope, with a second-class return ticket in his pocket and his regret that he would not be able to use it ! Who has not heard of his extreme unwillingness to accept the grave responsibility which that Conclave placed upon him, while at the same time cutting him off from all hope of ever returning to the Venice which he loved and which loved him ?

There are many such stories of his complete simplicity. He was of humble origin—his father, indeed, like the foster-father of our Lord, was a village carpenter. He was like our Lord in his unaffected love of small children. With them he let himself go, and I have few pictures so imprinted on my memory as those of the visits we paid, Isa and I and our small sons, to the Vatican in the time of Pius X. He always wished to receive us in private audience every time we went to Rome, and evidently rejoiced in the company of the children. Despite the strange surroundings, the great halls with crowds of waiting pilgrims in black, the attendants and the Swiss Guard in mediæval costumes, the Monsignori in purple silk, and lastly the Holy Father himself, dressed in white kerseymere robes, seated in a high-backed carved chair before a table whose only ornament was an ivory crucifix, despite all this, he could with his fatherly smile set the children at once at their ease. He would take them one at a time on his knee, and they immediately chattered to him in their broken Italian with as little timidity as if they were talking to their mother. Little children were always, and at once, his friends, and this is, I feel, one of the signs of a real, natural Christianity. In fact, it may be said that in all things he was the quintessence of Christian charity, one who could not entertain a bitter thought against any man, and children understand this at once.

The outbreak of War in 1914 was more than he could bear, and a few weeks after he died, as much of a broken heart as of any physical illness.

If Pius X was the type and quintessence of Christian charity, King George V was the quintessence of duty as a constitutional monarch and as a man. It was this I think, above all, that the people recognised in him at the time of his jubilee in 1935. He had the qualities that the English chiefly admire : clean family life, steadfastness, unselfishness, devotion to truth and duty, and sound common sense. These carried him through the almost overwhelming difficulties of his reign. We may well ask ourselves whether, had there been on the throne a man of the political inadaptability of Charles I, the throne could have weathered the storms of the post-War period.

It is said that he exclaimed after the tremendous ovations received when he drove through the London streets with the Queen at the time of the Jubilee :

" What can the people see in such an ordinary fellow as I am ? "

What they saw in him were just those qualities above mentioned, and these endeared him to them and to all who came in contact with him.

There was also one other quality, a rare one indeed, that both these two great men shared.

Neither of them ever did or said anything for effect. In fact it may be doubted, such was the simple sincerity of their characters, that the idea of producing an effect ever crossed their minds in anything they either said or did. This was one of their most striking qualities, which was in vivid contrast to the histrionic gifts or talents for which many others in high places have been remarkable, and which have too often ended by making them ridiculous.

So this man who thought himself " just an ordinary fellow," found his way not only into the hearts of his own subjects, but even to an incredible degree into the hearts of American citizens, and when he died the void he left was felt all round the world.

Though I have been present at many stirring public ceremonies, I have never attended any that has stirred me so profoundly as the bearing into Westminster Hall of the coffin containing the body of King George V.

Members of both Houses of Parliament and the judges and some high officials were gathered there to receive the King for the last time. It was growing dark, and there was complete silence in the hall. Presently trumpets sounded. The King was coming. The great doors were opened and words of command were heard coming from the courtyard without.

Then the Queen and the Princes came in and took their places.

The heralds in their splendidly embroidered tabards, almost the only splash of vivid colour there, marched up the hall.

Lastly the coffin, covered with a Union Jack on which rested the sceptre and the crown, was borne in by sailors and placed on trestles in the centre of the hall.

All was done without a sound, for a thick grey carpet which deadened every footfall had been spread over the pavement. This complete silence produced a sense of something ghostly and unreal in the scene before us. The magnificence of the vast hall with its historical traditions, the black garments of all present, the one splash of colour in the centre—the Union Jack, on which the jewels in the crown sparkled under the few lights, and the emblazoned tabards of the heralds—all these things gave together an impression of splendour and restraint such as nothing I have ever seen before or probably shall ever see again could equal. Splendour and

Restraint. These were fitting tributes to the man whose body lay there in our midst.

Then the Archbishop of Canterbury, a fine and venerable figure, read some simple prayers. The choristers of Westminster Abbey and St. Paul's Cathedral, with their fresh English boys' voices, perhaps the most beautiful in the world, sang a hymn ; all present, beginning with the Queen and the Royal Family, made obeisance and said a prayer before the catafalque ; the great doors were opened and all filed out into the darkness of the courtyard. The ceremony was over.

* * * * *

Presumably every man whose life has been a fairly busy one and who suddenly finds his employment at an end, after the first thrill of complete freedom feels the need of some occupation to prevent time from hanging on his hands. I knew it would be so with me, in any case, before long, and therefore had already made up my mind to devote myself to bookbinding.

I chose bookbinding for three reasons : firstly, that I was fond of many of my books and, as Venizelos said of Crete, long ago, wished to see them with a good coat to their backs ; secondly, because it combined manual labour, which I believe to be the greatest relaxation in the world, while at the same time giving its devotees a certain scope for exercising their artistic fancy which no other pursuit I could think of would do in the case of one who, like myself, was a singularly poor draughtsman ; thirdly, because it did not require too much room, machinery or implements.

The summer of 1931 and one or two following summers spent at Lyulph's Tower, and winters in London, were to a large extent happily thus occupied under instructions from Mr. McLeish, of the Central School of Arts and Crafts, who was an excellent instructor and not too sarcastic over my incompetence.

I should have been glad to have continued quietly sewing books, cutting leather, pasting it on to boards and feeling exceptionally happy when we reached the critical point of designing the decorations and stamping them on to the leather, for all this I learned to do more or less thoroughly. Accurate lettering, however, was, and always will be, beyond me. My letters leaned towards each other like happy couples engaged to be married or away from each other like the same couples later making for the Divorce Court. Bookbinding alone, therefore, would have sufficed to keep me busy and happy had I not been compelled for my own peace of mind to take part in certain matters of public interest, and—for conscience makes cowards of us all—thought it my duty to interest myself in these until they ended by swamping my poor books completely.

Of Birds

The first of these public matters which took all my time for nearly two years, to the exclusion of almost everything else, was Birds. I had no claim to be considered an ornithologist. I belonged to no scientific society having to do with birds. I knew a good many common birds by sight, and that was all. But all my life, in many countries, I had loved watching them just for the pleasure their movements, and especially their flight, gave me.

Have you ever watched the flight of swifts round an old tower in the evening, or of buzzards grandly sweeping over the tops of fells, or great squadrons of starlings all circling together as at some word of command, or of the most diminutive, such as golden-crested wrens and certain humming birds, and stopped to consider that these exquisite little creatures fly thousands of miles when they migrate ? Two verses of Goethe's " Faust " had always a peculiar fascination for me :

" Doch ist es Jedem eingeboren
Dass sein Gefühl hinauf und vorwarts dringt,
Wenn über uns im blauen Raum verloren
Ihr schmetternd Lied die Lerche singt.

" Wenn über schroffen Fichtenhöhen
Der Adler ausgebreitet schwebt,

Und über Flächen über Seen
Der Kranich nach der Heimath strebt." [1]

There are some verses—hardly consciously learned in our youth—which never drop out of our minds, though we should often be glad if they would. But these lines from " Faust," learned when I was a boy, still gave me pleasure to repeat and—who can tell—perhaps urged me to start a campaign in Parliament which ended with the British Wild Bird Protection Act of 1933.

It began in this way.

About Easter-time, 1931, Isa and I had motored from Rome to Siena, where we were to meet our four sons, who were coming out from England for their Easter holidays. All of us naturally delighted in Siena, but as I had never been to San Gimignano and wanted greatly to see that city of mediæval towers with its churches and frescoes and primitive pictures, we gave up a day to get, at any rate, a bowing acquaintance with it.

I have never tried to compete with competent critics in giving descriptions of artistic objects, and will merely say that every minute spent at San Gimignano is well worth while. But the reason why it remains particularly fixed in my mind is not so much on account of its fine old walls and towers, or of its frescoes and churches and palazzi, as because when we walked down the main street it happened to be a time of day when the sun beat pitilessly down on one side of the street, and on nearly every other house were bird cages hanging against the wall containing for the most part native wild birds : goldfinches, linnets, chaffinches, etc.

There may be people who think that these small birds enjoy sitting in the sun, but no one with the smallest

[1] " Yet all men feel an inborn pleasure
    In striving up and onward day by day.
  When high o'erhead, lost in the boundless azure,
    The Lark pours forth his thrilling lay.

" When o'er some lofty pine-clad height
    With wings outstretched the eagle soars,
  Or when the crane in homeward flight,
    Floats over plains and lakes and moors."
        Translation by W. H. van der Smissen.

knowledge of their habits and their love of shade would think of putting birds out to hang in the sun without a chance of escape. Yet here were hundreds of these poor little fellows panting and gasping in the glare of a warm Italian spring sun and giving every sign of acute distress.

This gave me food for thought, and I decided there and then to take up the matter with some friends of mine in Rome, and especially my friend from Stockholm, Axel Munthe, to see if this form of quite unconscious cruelty could not be stopped.

Then I went further, and realised that these " pets," kept in small wire cages without room to exercise their wings, could in no circumstances ever lead their natural life, of which flight was such an essential and necessary part. Even when their owners really cared for them and looked after them, there must always be times when the cage bird would be at the mercy of such circumstances as sun, overheat, cold, draughts, even lack of food and water, if the owner forgets to change its position according to conditions or has to be absent for a day. Considering all these things, it seemed to me that it would be better to get at the root of the matter and prevent, at once, if possible, the capture of these wild birds and their confinement in cages.

So I made up my mind to see what the author of *San Michele* would say about it when we got back to Rome.

I also, however, determined not to attempt to start any campaign in Italy on these lines until I was certain that our record in England was a perfectly clean one. I felt sure that if I mentioned the birds of San Gimignano in a London drawing-room, I should be told : " Oh, of course ; but what *can* you expect in Italy ? " I had suspicions that I should find matters with regard to the treatment of caged pets much the same at home. And so it proved.

Axel Munthe was, of course, most interested and sympathetic when I talked to him on the subject, but as he was at that time threatened with complete loss of sight he was naturally not able to assist very actively

in the work. But he gave me introductions to leading
Italian ornithologists such as Prince Chigi of Castelfusano,
where there is an important scientific establishment for
catching, ringing[1] and releasing birds passing in spring
and autumn between Italy and North Africa. These,
like our ornithologists at home, fully realised the danger
there is of the destruction of many species of birds by
bird-catchers working with modern nets and other instruments and with modern means of transport. Like all
those who have studied the question at all, they know
the value of bird life to the agriculturist in every country
for keeping in check the innumerable insects that prey
on vegetation of every kind necessary for the life of man.
The French authority on insect life, M. Henri Fabre,
has indeed stated that if bird life were wiped out in
any country and the insects gained the upper hand, human
life would not long survive the disappearance of birds.
The preservation of bird life is, therefore, speaking without
exaggeration, a matter of the highest economic importance,
but many farmers and gardeners, unfortunately, wage
unlimited war on birds, seeing them at work taking
their toll of fruit and cereal crops, and not realising the
good they do at the same time in keeping down the far
more deadly insects.

As regards the capture alive of wild birds to be kept
in captivity, many who objected to this being put a stop
to, argued that the few birds so kept could not possibly
make any serious difference. The reply to this is that
it is not, indeed, the few so kept. In England, as a
result of the propaganda of the sellers of bird foods,
of the Cage Bird Society, and of prizes offered for singing
bird contests, for plumage, and even for keeping alive
in captivity, such species as golden-crested wrens, my
particular friends, the dippers—about which Lord Grey
of Fallodon has written so eloquently—and even swallows

[1] For those who may not be acquainted with present methods of investigation
of the migration of birds, it should be explained that " ringing " means affixing
a light metal ring to the leg of a bird so caught and afterwards released. In this
way it has been possible to establish scientifically the regular routes and distances
traversed by many migratory birds.

(perhaps because that seems impossible), our common wild birds were being literally decimated in the neighbourhood of great towns by the regular bird-catchers. These, armed with every modern device (some legal, some illegal) to facilitate capture, would start on a Saturday night, hire motor-cars, and going to some bird-frequented spot, such as certain Surrey commons or Epping Forest, would capture, at certain times of the year, scores, or even hundreds, of wild birds. These were placed in large boxes for sale at some bird market on the first available day. As may be imagined, the percentage of those that survived was low. Even bird fanciers admitted that, quite apart from rough handling on capture, many, especially the more delicate birds, particularly nightingales, very often refused food and pined away.

I made up my mind to look into all this business, and as I returned to England I took it up at once with one or two personal friends who were leading lights in the Royal Society for the Protection of Birds, such as Lord Grey of Fallodon and Lord Buxton. Both were most sympathetic, but both were doubtful about the success of any attempt to pass through Parliament legislation to stop this growing abuse of bird catching. They said the Society had already attempted to introduce legislation of this kind, but could not make headway against the " vested interests," which always stand in the way of all reforms.

Nevertheless, I thought I could but try again and, quite apart from the fact that, owing largely to help from unexpected sources, the campaign ended with a considerable neasure of success in the Bird Protection Act of 1933, I am glad that I did, for it gave me an insight into the method of presenting a private Bill to Parliament which I could not have acquired in any other way.

I do not wish to trouble readers with the long story, which covered a period of over two years from 1931 to 1933, but very shortly, for my own satisfaction I may record the principal steps along a path, blocked by indifference, ridicule and hostility, which led to the final fairly saitsfactory conclusion.

First, to make myself acquainted with the conditions of the place where wild birds were sold, I visited one Sunday morning in June the principal market of London, known as Club Row, in Bethnal Green. I was accompanied by an exceedingly enthusiastic member of the office staff of the Bird Protection Society, Miss Barclay Smith, who knew the ropes, and for whose intelligent assistance I was most grateful. All along I may say it was the women who carried this little measure through against the persistent indifference, ridicule and hostility of many of the men. Among them, Mrs. Lemon, the honorary secretary of the Royal Society for the Protection of Birds, should be particularly singled out as deserving the gratitude of all English wild birds. Indeed, I derived the impression that if you want to put through some overdue reform, the surest and quickest plan is to enlist the sympathy of the women, and on this occasion Women's Institutes all over the country were pillars of support.

The result of my visit to Club Row was to convince me that if things might be bad in Italy and other foreign countries as regards the trade in live wild birds, conditions were no better in our own country, which always prides itself on being so far advanced over the rest of the world in its treatment of animals and birds. That visit settled my determination to try and end this trade.

This is what I saw.

A comparatively wide street with shops on either side given up mainly to the sale of live poultry, dogs, cats, etc., to which, provided these animals were not kept too long in the small cages in which they were temporarily confined, no special objection could be raised.

In the centre of the street, however, were many trestle tables, each carrying a pile of four-inch cages, the limit exacted by law as large enough to allow a bird to stretch its wings. Making a rapid calculation of the number of tables and the average number of cages, I came to the conclusion that there must be upwards of two to three thousand wild birds displayed for sale.

There were crowds of men and boys, evidently " cage-bird " fanciers, peering into these cages and examining and discussing the points of the occupants. When a sale was arranged the bird-catcher took the bird out of the four-inch cage and transferred it to a paper bag, as if it were a bun. Then, plunging his hand into a covered box with a " stocking " over the only opening, he drew out another wild bird to fill the cage again. Owing to these covered boxes, the contents of which could not be seen, it was impossible to calculate how many more birds there were above the numbers displayed in small cages.

I wrote a brief account of my experiences in Club Row in *The Spectator*. Public sympathy was considerably roused, especially by the paper bags, which for some unaccountable reason appeared to offend the public conscience more than anything else, and the editor of *The Field*, the great country gentleman's paper, at once joined the movement and wrote most valuable articles.

I took Axel Munthe down to Club Row that year, and he was also naturally roused to indignation. I shall never forget towing him through a rough but not unkindly crowd on a hot Sunday morning in July, his tall figure bowed to peer into the little cages which he could hardly see, let alone their captives ; his indignation over the indignity of the paper bags ; his pulling out of his pocket a portfolio bulging with pound notes, and his bargaining with the owners of linnets and chaffinches in English which, however fluent and correct, was yet clearly that of a foreigner ; the crowd he attracted by his wealth and his obvious incapacity to see what notes he was dragging out of his pocket—all this created a situation which made it highly desirable to get him out of Club Row as soon as possible. But he always wanted to buy one more wretched, frightened, fluttering captive. I was much relieved when Miss Barclay Smith finally drew him away, and with our burden of paper bags full of birds, we were able to take a train to Victoria, from which the birds were to be taken to the country. They all flew away at once on being released.

This visit had a useful sequel, for " Tiberio," as his

friends call Axel Munthe, because his villa of San Michele is built on the ruins of Tiberius's villa at Capri, wrote one or two letters to the press describing the scene, which were widely read as coming from the author of *San Michele*, and produced a considerable effect.

After talking the matter over with friends who knew the difficulties of introducing, and still more passing, private legislation of any kind, it was nevertheless decided to introduce a Bill into the House of Lords, where there would always be time for its discussion. The main difficulty was who was to introduce it. I was most unwilling to do so, because I was ignorant of Parliamentary practice and procedure, and was also too deaf to take effective part in any debate.

For some time I could find no one who would undertake this essential duty. But at last, having been told that the late Lord Buckmaster, a former Lord Chancellor and recognised as one of the greatest speakers in the House, was deeply interested in bird life, and had already piloted one or two Bills for the preservation of birds through the House of Commons, I took my courage in both hands and asked him if he would take charge of this Bill also. After hearing what I had learnt of the trade in wild birds in England, he at once accepted enthusiastically, though he was naturally an unusually busy man. I am grateful, indeed, to Lord Buckmaster and also to the Bill which introduced me to him. He was a man who threw himself whole-heartedly into any cause which engaged his sympathies, and never spared himself. His death while comparatively young was a very great loss to the country. I will not discuss here the, to me, curious processes by which this humble little Bill finally won its way to the Statute Book. This, however, I may say : that when the Government spokesman, in reply to Lord Buckmaster, suggested the appointment of a Select Committee of the House to consider the Bill and report to the House when it came up for the second reading, and when Lord Buckmaster accepted the suggestion my heart sank within me, for I had been given to understand that reference to a Select Committee was generally the equivalent of decent and quiet burial. But Lord Buckmaster knew that in a case of this sort an unanimous and favourable report by the Committee was the one chance of getting the Bill a hearing in the Lower House.

So, by throwing overboard some of the less vital clauses, we managed, owing mainly to the tact, moderation and sympathy of the late Lord Buxton, who had been from the first most helpful and was invaluable as a member of the Select Committee of the Lords, to obtain an unanimous report in the Committee in favour of the Bill, after which it passed the Upper House without further difficulty.

There was naturally a more serious fight in the Commons, where again we were most fortunate in obtaining the help of Mr. John Buchan (now Lord Tweedsmuir and Governor-General of Canada), who consented to introduce the Bill and father it generally. We had three such distinguished men : firstly, in the Lords, an ex-Lord Chancellor and great speaker ; and, secondly, a former Cabinet Minister and Governor-General of South Africa ; and, thirdly, in the House of Commons, one of our most gifted writers and the future Governor-General of Canada, that it would have been, quite apart from other considerations, little short of a scandal if the Bill had been rejected in either House. In the Commons also, however, it managed to scrape through the all-important second reading, in spite of strong opposition from some private members on the Conservative side and a few Labour members, who represented it as class legislation by rich men who wished to deprive the poor of one of their pleasures.

I was alone in the Peers' Gallery of the House of Commons when the result of the vote was read out— almost two to one in favour of the Bill. I had been much alarmed as to the result, because nearly all the speakers had opposed the Bill. This, however, was explained afterwards by the fact that those in favour were sure of their majority and did not want to take up the time of the House at an hour when most members wished to get home to dinner.

So the Bird Bill of 1933 became law, and I went home to my dinner rejoicing with the satisfaction of feeling that what I had seen at San Gimignano, if it had not helped those captives in Italy, had at least improved things for our own wild birds.

Two years later " Tiberio " and I again visited Club Row on a Sunday morning in June. The bird market was in full swing, but we saw no wild birds for sale on the trestle tables in the middle of the road, and only found one small boy with a linnet he was hawking about in a tiny cage. On being told that he was committing an illegal act, he asked innocently : " But I may sell guinea-pigs or mice, mayn't I ? " After this we had to buy and liberate his linnet.

Like all improvements for the preservation of our country life, this matter of the protection of birds is only a question of better edcuation. We no sooner point out to our people the many good reasons there are for protecting birds and animals, than the majority—except, of course, those who have vested interests to protect— are quickly won over to support the movement. They go naturally where their humanitarian instincts lead them, and generally err only in such matters through ignorance.

Of Lakes

The Theatre of Life has, as may have been gathered from the preceding pages of this book, many side shows, of which now one, now another may capture our attention as they appear to be attractive, interesting or important. One of these, the suppression as far as possible of the trade in wild birds, which seemed to me to be a kind of secondary slave trade, I have dealt with shortly above.

The following paragraphs deal with a matter in a sense perhaps quite as urgent and equally important, because the harm done can never be repaired. We, therefore, owe it to future generations as well as to ourselves that this harm shall not be done if by any means it can possibly be prevented.

From the above it will already have been made clear that the following pages will not be a scientific disquisition on the formation of lakes or on the question of water supply or other equally important matters. They contain merely a short record of some work done in the Lake District which may be of interest to those engaged in campaigns now proceeding in all parts of England for the preservation of our country from the hands of others who would sacrifice everything for the turning of a doubt-less perfectly honest penny, in other words, of the " Utilitarians," to whom nothing is beautiful, nothing holy, which stands in the way of the increase of wealth.

" Good Lord ! " I hear any reader, if he has got so far, exclaim. " This fellow is really a congenital crank. He has told us about his absurd and impractical views for the establishment of peace between employers and employed, of peace between nations, of the wrongs of the trade in live birds, and now he is going to talk to us about the ' amenities ' of the Lake District and Words-worth and Fell[1] and Force[2], and all that rot."

Well, to those to whom such subjects are " rot," I am and must remain a congenital crank, and I am quite willing to let it rest at that. But let me say that you have guessed quite rightly if you deduct from what I have said above that I am going to talk about the pre-servation of the Lake District, and Wordsworth and Fells and Forces and Footpaths, though as shortly as possible, so that if this chapter does bore you I hope that part of it will be left unread, for the worst thing the supporter of any cause can do is to bore his neighbour.

Perhaps it will be said in reply, and said justly : " Well, for goodness' sake get on with what you have to say, and don't talk about yourself." I will take the hint.

The Lake District for all those who come from those parts represents something apart. I hesitate to say

[1] " Fells " : Mountains in English north-country dialect.
[2] " Forces " : Waterfalls in English north-country dialect.

" unique," for that adjective is now applied to every suburban villa by every house agent. We Lakelanders admit that others may have a real affection for their birthplace, but we cannot believe it can equal the affection we feel for ours, which accounts, perhaps, for our rather excessive zeal at times in defending the Lake District against the attacks of the " Utilitarians." In excuse we can but urge that we are defending the most precious jewel in the crown of England and in the possession of its people, and that if others consider with indifference the breaking up of that jewel, we feel we are but doing our duty by king and country if we defend it with might and main.

It was two or three years after the end of the Great War that I noticed the havoc which the new arterial roadways of England and the increase of motor traffic were rapidly causing in the country districts. I began to notice this on the Great West Road, over which I travelled for the first time by motor to my great delight when going from London to Thornbury, in Gloucestershire, along the old coach road. It seemed thrilling nearly one hundred years after the introduction of railways to be travelling again along that Great West Road which my father must so often have taken in his carriage, but which I had never before seen. It was good to know how to get out of London by road and to see fields and woods so soon after leaving Turnham Green. My enthusiasm for this modern improvement in locomotion has, however, been short lived, so far as travelling in southern England is concerned. For miles along the Great West Road, now almost as far as Camberley, or at least as far as Egham, the road is flanked by factories and ribbon building, and the country-side as my father saw it before the advent of railways has disappeared. When later I realised these changes, I began to wonder how soon it would be before all the satellites of modern arterial roads invaded Cumberland, and especially the Lake District, and how soon we might expect modern conveniences such as tea houses, bungalows and filling

2 R

stations to jostle each other not only over the Shap road, but on the roads between Grasmere and Keswick, between Keswick and Buttermere, or even—if this new traffic was to catch us in its iron clutch—over passes which had hitherto been reserved for riders or walkers, such as Wrynose and Hardknott, where the Romans built one of their last outposts, and, horror of horrors, over Styhead, where to date there was not even a cart track.

Whatever happened, I felt that the Lake District must be preserved as far as possible for our children to see as Wordsworth and Gray and Coleridge and Southey and many other famous men had seen it, and that in those little valleys the sense of remoteness which is one of their greatest charms, and is so difficult to find nowadays in " this England," must be preserved for future generations of those who can enjoy our Lakeland in the spirit of the poets, whom it inspired, and not in that of the noisy holiday-makers, who can seek their pleasures elsewhere.

Among the fells and lakes and dales the " time of the singing of birds " must not be allowed to degenerate altogether into a time of the buzzing of cheap gramophones, and the " voice of the turtle " give way in our land to the toot of the motor.

Many others beside myself had been attacked by the same fear, and also filled with the same determination to preserve what we could before it was too late.

Two societies were formed with this object : " The Lake District Safeguarding Society " and " The Friends of the Lake District."

There was, not long ago, a threat of danger that the small mountain passes of Styhead, Wrynose and Hardknott would be awakened from " the sleep that is among the lonely hills." But this has fortunately been averted by the good sense of the local authorities and the petitions of these societies. We may not, however, relax our efforts in this matter, but must remain ever on guard against such changes.

In one way or another, attacks on this small district will be continued again and again by the " Utilitarians," and those who believe that the growth of bank balances should be the main purpose of life. Yet even these cannot understand their own interests in this question.

Not long ago I was given a lesson by that most practical and most popular of Englishmen, Lord Derby, who is well known on both sides of the Atlantic and whose support always carries weight for any cause. I went to ask him for his support for a petition to the Government Forestry Commission which the Friends of the Lake District were getting up, asking the Commission to desist from their plan of planting mainly with fir trees two of the most beautiful Cumberland dales : Eskdale and Duddondale, the latter of which has given its name to Wordsworth's famous " Duddon " sonnets. Having already obtained the willing support of Lord Lonsdale and Mr. Le Fleming, of Rydal, the Lords-Lieutenant of Cumberland and Westmorland, respectively, we naturally wished greatly to obtain the signature of Lord Derby. His reply was that he would sign the petition, not as Lord-Lieutenant of Lancashire but as President of the Travel Development Association, because the Lake District was one of the greatest attractions England had to offer, and anything likely to alter the character of its scenery or detract from its beauty would certainly diminish the number of visitors not only to the district but also to this country. So he signed.

That is the solid practical truth. The " utilitarians " will not admit that beauty, tradition, history, literature, painting or *imponderabilia* of any kind should ever stand in the way of an " improvement," being quite unable to realise that only too often in their race for wealth and the increase of " utilities," they are but killing the goose that lays the golden eggs. If you could transplant a portion of one of our great manufacturing towns into the Vale of Keswick and Bassenthwaite, or another so that it covered the country between Windermere and Kendal, some landowners on the spot might benefit, but the country generally would be the loser for reasons too obvious to mention.

There are no doubt many who will see the force of the argument from this practical go-getting side, but who would treat as the mere emotional outburst of cranks an appeal for the preservation of the special charm of the Lake District, which if once destroyed or even damaged can never be replaced. It seems to me that the best criterion for judging the constantly recurring conflicts between the above-mentioned *imponderabilia* and the " utilities," should be the question : " Is this particular utilitarian improvement so vital or of so great an importance as to outweigh the importance of this or that historical monument, of this or that special beauty spot, and, in any case, can it not be carried out elsewhere ? " To settle conflicts of this kind it would be very desirable that the final decision should not be left in the hands of the Government Department concerned, which, naturally and properly, considers such questions mainly from its own point of view, but to set up a Government Commission *ad hoc* to whom such matters can be referred, and whose decision could only be upset by Parliament, which must, of course, remain the supreme arbiter of the requirements of the nation.

Then, at least, Parliament would hear both sides of the question, which at present it does not, the Houses of Parliament being guided by the Government for the time being, which again, in such questions, is always certain to take the views of the Government Department concerned.

As regards the matter of afforestation in the Lakeland valleys, one or two words must be said.

There is an idea abroad that the Friends of the Lake District oppose the afforestation of Lakeland valleys because we object to afforestation as such. This is not at all the case. For my own part, being well aware of the real need of native-grown timber in the country—I will not go into the reasons for this, but anyone who has studied the question must agree—I am entirely on the side of those who wish to see the areas of forest land as largely extended as possible. Further, I am willing to admit that those who would wish to see these little open Lakeland valleys turned into miniature Black Forests or dark coniferous Scandinavian woodlands, and think they would be beautified thereby, have, of course, every right to their own opinion. It is of no use arguing on matters of taste. But this at least they, on their part, must admit : that any planting of conifers on such a large and conventional scale as Government afforestation necessarily implies, will change altogether the character of the scenery, and this is what we, the old lovers of Lakeland as it is, are determined to stop if we can.

The petition for Eskdale and Duddondale was signed by eleven thousand five hundred persons all over the country, many of them being most influential, especially amongst educationists, showing that this movement for the preservation of the Lake District is happily growing in strength throughout the country. Although the Lake District is only some fifty miles long and thirty or thirty-five across—at which I can imagine some of our American friends raising their eyebrows in surprise when they think of their enormous National Parks—this movement of ours will have to be taken into more serious account than heretofore by future Governments. We may be thankful that we have the leaders of education with us, for this, like the protection of birds, is just a matter of education.

With regard to one of two measures of Lakeland preservation that have been carried out by voluntary effort during the last few years, we may truly praise God.

The first and foremost is the preservation by and for the " National Trust "[1] of certain areas of the district, either by direct purchase by the Trust or by the action of private individuals with public spirit, who have placed their properties so far under the Trust that no buildings may be erected without the consent of the Trust. Among

[1] The National Trust for the preservation of Places of Historic Interest or Natural Beauty, 7, Buckingham Palace Gardens, London. A voluntary Association which deserves the greatest support.

these areas, the Lakes of Buttermere, Crummock and Loweswater form one of the most beautiful pieces of scenery in the whole district. I especially rejoice of the safety of Glencoyn Park, at the head of Ullswater, which Wordsworth calls " the noblest of the Lakes." This has been recently saved by the generosity of Sir Samuel Scott, of Windermere, who has acquired the property, giving similar guarantees respecting building to the National Trust. The men who do these things are indeed bene-factors of the nation. There are now not a few, amongst whom Professor G. M. Trevelyan must be placed at the head of the list. He is a man who has learnt to love the Lake District by walking all over the mountains. That, or riding on a sure-footed fell pony, and not motoring, is the way to get to appreciate it. But we Lakelanders must also not forget the late Canon Rawnsley, who was to a large extent responsible for the formation of the National Trust itself and was the pioneer of the Trust in the Lake District.

I have so far carefully avoided giving any description of Lakeland's special beauties. I have not myself the literary gifts necessary for this, but I feel I cannot leave this subject without a favourite quotation from Hugh Walpole who has, in my opinion, *pace* my Wordsworthian friends of Grasmere and Rydal, caught the astonishingly fleeting spirit of the beauties of that country perhaps more truly than any other writer. I will, therefore, end with one quotation in the hope that some stranger reading these pages may be fascinated by the glowing words and help in the good work of preserving Lakeland for future generations :

> The blue, cold sky ranged like a sea infinitely high and remote from change, the tops of the larch and birch and firs suddenly if they were high enough struck a hard stainless light and were edged like cut paper, but so soon as the feathery vapours of mist rolled curtain-like across the scene, colour so rich and varied began that the sky seemed to belong to another infinitely remote existence, unactual, and planets away.
>
> The mist was neither ascending nor descending in clouds, it was not stiff enough for form, it only caught the sunlight and transmuted

it, and that sunlight, joyfully enclosed, glowed within an imprisoned fire. It is the quality of this country that with a structure of rock, naked fell and dark, grim water, it has the power of breaking into an opulence of light and colour. So the lake that could be cold as driving snow, harsh like shadowed steel, fierce with white foam as a bird's feathers are blown angrily by storm, now was streaked and veined with shadows of the grape that trembled as though a hand gently stroked its surface. This trembling was not cold nor windswept, but burned with the sun-filled mist. . . . And yet, with all this dimness, the hills were strong, striking deep into the lake, and where they topped the mist hard-ridged against a chill sky. And on Skiddaw there was a sudden flame-shaped crest."[1]

Of " Tertii Gaudentes " once more

I will ask my readers to imagine themselves for a few moments in the junior class of a council school in the year A.D. 2000.

The subject of the lesson just over was the history of Europe in the first half of the twentieth century.

The teacher had passed rapidly in review the events leading up to the War of 1914–1918 (no longer spoken of as the Great War), of the destruction of life and of cities and villages. This, however, was as nothing compared to the losses inflicted on the whole of Europe during the war that followed only twenty-five years later, which converted whole countries into shambles, and provinces and cities into areas of starvation and misery.

Then the teacher asks the class if any pupil has questions to put.

One small boy holds up his hand.

" Please, teacher, why, after the first war, didn't the nations see that just cutting each other's throats wouldn't help anybody to be happy."

TEACHER : " Well, for a few years after that war they were impressed by the lessons it taught, and they did try to get together in order to prevent another war from breaking out."

SMALL PUPIL : " Then what prevented them from doing so ? "

[1] " The Fortress," pp. 767-8. Hugh Walpole (MacMillan, London, 1932).

TEACHER : " It's a long story, but I will try and tell you in a very few words. There were, of course, at the root of it the two old evils—the desire for power, whether in a nation or in a man ; or the more vulgar desire, whether in a nation or a man, to surpass others in possessions. This was generally at the root of all trouble, and led those who felt that they had not received their full share of this world's goods to coveting the possessions of their neighbours, and determining to redress the balance by force if necessary. This was naturally resented, and led to war."

PUPIL : " But why did not all the neighbours join together to stop them ? "

TEACHER : " Well, they tried, but they could not understand that unless all, or as many as possible, acted together and took measures that would make it very difficult, if not impossible, for those who started wars to win either the so-called glory or great possessions by their wars, persons would always be found to believe that they could make themselves or their country great and famous by having recourse to fighting and so winning possessions or military glory."

PUPIL : " But, teacher, could they carry on a great war such as you have told us about without help from others ? "

TEACHER : " Now, my boy, you have got to the kernel of the whole matter. They certainly could not. There was not one country in the world that could carry on a great war, or even a minor one, in those later times when warfare was a very complicated job, without many commodities and raw materials imported from abroad."

PUPIL : " And the other countries let the nations that were fighting obtain these goods and materials from them ? "

TEACHER : " They not only allowed them to do so, but looked on it as their right to supply those who were fighting with all they wanted, and resented any interference with this right because it deprived them of what they called their legitimate trade profits."

PUPIL : " Then they helped wars to go on in order to make a little money themselves ? "

TEACHER : " That is just what they did do."

PUPIL : " And were themselves destroyed or made poor in the end by the war they helped to keep going ? "

TEACHER : " Yes."

PUPIL : " Then they were no better than prize idiots."

TEACHER : " You are perfectly right, but it took them years to see that in order to prevent a major disaster they must be ready and willing to make a little sacrifice themselves." Then (*soliloquising*) : " Out of the mouths of babes and sucklings . . ."

SMALL BOY (*sharply*) : " What's that, teacher ? "

TEACHER (*hastily*) : " Oh, nothing, nothing. I was only quoting something said hundreds of years ago."

Those who have read the first chapters of this book will, perhaps, remember that in chapter X I dubbed those nations the *Tertii Gaudentes*, or " Rejoicing Third Parties," who, following the then established principles of International Law, not only remained neutral—against which no one, indeed, could cast a stone—but took advantage of their neutral condition to supply for their own profit belligerent nations with the commodities necessary for the conduct of war. Thus they became not indirectly but directly responsible for the continuance of war till one or other belligerent was completely knocked out. I believe I ventured then to apply to their attitude the adjective " unsavoury." That chapter was, of course, written months before the Italo-Abyssinian War broke out, but of all I wrote then I take back nothing. I frankly have naught but a feeling of repulsion for those who under the shelter of International Law seek to protect commercial rights which can but prolong war to the detriment of all but those engaged in buying, selling or transporting goods which are required by the belligerents.

Practically all goods which belligerents will buy in wartime are, if not of prime necessity for the conduct of war, at least very valuable for that purpose, because nowadays belligerent governments will see to it that money does not go out of the country except for that all-consuming purpose.

There are, however, certain minerals without which it is impossible to carry on war under modern conditions.

These are all enumerated in a most valuable little book by Sir Thomas Holland, Principal of the University of Edinburgh, formerly president of the Indian Munitions Board, past-President of the Institutions of Mining and Metallurgy and of the Geological and Mineralogical Societies of London. This booklet, for it has only ninety-three pages in all, is called *The Mineral Sanction as an Aid to International Security*.[1]

I look upon it as by far the most illuminating contribution I have yet read to this most urgent and vital question of what sanctions are to be applied by neutral countries to belligerents who, in spite of their pledges not to have recourse to war, still do so not in self-defence but in order to further some national aim or policy.

I cannot, naturally, attempt to give even a short summary of this book, but it is to be hoped that all those who are interested in the subject may give it their closest attention, for Sir Thomas Holland is a man who knows what he is talking about. On page 8 he gives a list of twenty-one mineral substances of special and vital importance in war.

None of these mineral substances have any non-mineral substitutes, though some of the all-important hardening metals may doubtless be replaced by other hardening metals, though with less effectiveness.

Of one substance, however, we may say with absolute certainty at once that no country which does not possess it and cannot import it would be able to carry on war for a day once its stocks were exhausted. This is mineral oil, whether for motor power or lubricating purposes.

As regards lubricating oils, I have already pointed out how nearly Germany was brought to her knees in 1917 by lack of this. For lack of it hits both a mechanised

[1] Oliver & Boyd, London.

army in the field and mechanised industry at home. No country to-day can exist without it.

Sir Thomas Holland points out rightly on page 37 that the establishment of the League of Nations after the War ought to have made it possible to eliminate the sinister action of neutrals or *tertii gaudentes* in prolonging war by the sale or transit of these raw materials. The League should have fundamentally altered the position of so-called neutrals, since the Covenant provided for no neutrals and it was assumed that all Great Powers would before long become members of the League.

As Sir Thomas says, the only nation outside the League that could seriously endanger the success of the imposition of the Mineral Sanction is the United States of America. He points out, however, that the Briand-Kellogg Pact of Paris would enable the United States to join in a General Convention to stop mineral supplies to *belligerents*. One of the principal points of his scheme is that it would enable all nations to join in a special Mineral Sanction Pact against "an aggressor" as a proposition quite independent of the provisions of the League Covenant.

With this proposition I am, indeed, entirely in agreement, except that for the following various reasons the word "aggressor" should be replaced by the words "persistent and intractable belligerent."

The reasons for this change in the interpretation of the Covenant, which will practically involve the recasting of the greater part of Article XV, are nevertheless so evident that it is incomprehensible that while other Articles, such as X, XVI and XIX, have been singled out for criticism, Article XV has been hitherto spared.

The greatest objection to retaining in the League any reference to the "aggressor" is, in my view, that the League was founded for the great purpose of preventing war and not for the purpose of sitting in judgment upon other nations and delivering verdicts of a moral character. Like verdicts delivered by any other human tribunal, these verdicts may be based on false evidence and, even more than in any ordinary tribunal, be influenced by political prejudices and passions of the moment, for they have necessarily to be delivered at moments when political passions run high. It is indeed almost impossible to expect an unprejudiced verdict from such a tribunal.

Assuming that a mistake in a League verdict were to be made in the future, we must all surely agree that such a mistake, which resulted in the imposition of effective sanctions and in the subsequent defeat of the party against which such sanctions had been imposed, would be the greatest imaginable disaster for the credit of the League and for the future of Peace by Collective Action. In fact, it might well be a setback from which the League would never recover. This supposition of the possibility of a mistaken verdict by the League as to the " aggressor " is no fanciful supposition. The public opinion of the world has already on two occasions in my lifetime been completely misled in contemporary verdicts respecting aggression, and I cannot believe that the League, sitting in judgment in either case, would have proved more infallible.

I refer to the famous Ems interview between the then King of Prussia (afterwards Emperor William I of Germany) and Benedetti, the French Ambassador, in 1870, the account of which was deliberately falsified by Prince Bismarck in order to inflame French public opinion. This succeeded so well that it led to the declaration of war by France, who thus, in the eyes of the world, became the " aggressor."

The other case is that of the sinking of the American battleship *Maine* in the harbour of Havana in 1898, which all men at once concluded was the work of a Spanish torpedo, and which thus led to the war between Spain and the United States. It was found after the war was over that the explosion which sank the *Maine* was from within the ship and not from without, and therefore that, as far as this incident was concerned, the Spanish authorities were innocent of all blame.

Now, let us suppose that the League had been in existence in 1870 or 1898, what line would the Council

have taken in either case and where would it have placed
the " guilt " of aggression ?

Truly, if there was any guilt of aggression, it might
have been attributed to either side, or both, and so it is
with almost every war. In most cases it is practically
impossible to attribute the guilt of aggression wholly to
one side or the other, and the most grievous injustice
may easily be committed in trying to do so. The League
Council is far from infallible. It is composed of gentlemen with the same national and political prejudices as
other ordinary men. We cannot suppose, for instance,
that in the event of Germany and Italy collaborating
again with the League, and of their representatives and
those of Russia sitting side by side on the Council bench
to decide a question of war guilt, that any of them would
be able, even if they wished, to divest themselves entirely
of their little political prejudices.

That, then, is the first reason why we must eliminate
the search for the " aggressor " from among the duties of
the League, and why Article XV of the Covenant should
be rewritten without delay if the League, not being infallible,
is not to run the risk of wrecking itself in the future.

The second reason for the alteration of this Article is
almost equally important. It is said that before certain
action can be taken to impose sanctions against an alleged
" aggressor," the whole machinery of a tribunal must
necessarily be set in motion, and in such a supremely
important matter as this that machinery, like the mills of
God, must, if its verdicts are to be respected, grind
slowly. A Council of the League sitting in judgment on
two belligerents in a manner which may alter the whole
course of history cannot be allowed to jump rapidly to
conclusions. Yet, if its action is to be efficacious it must
do so, for from every point of view time is of the very
essence of success for the ending of a war once begun.

Here, therefore, we are face to face with two absolutely
fatal defects in the machinery of the League for the
prevention of war and for the ending of war once begun.

What, then, it will be asked, do you propose should take the place of the procedure established by Article XV for " finding the aggressor " ?

The answer is really not difficult to find.

Let the League look to its own origins.

Let it strike direct at WAR without examining into the causes of the war. WAR is a breach of the clauses of the Covenant, of the Briand-Kellogg Pact, and of numerous subsidiary Pacts. War or fighting actually in progress is as near to being definite, unquestionable fact independent of inference as anything can well be. It does not require the great and the learned to decide upon that, nor does it require months, weeks, or even days, to reach a decision on the subject.

The Council of the League, then, when fighting is in progress, need only take note publicly, formally and officially of the fact and notify all belligerents that unless they, or any of them, at once declare their willingness to cease fighting and submit their case to a suitable tribunal for peaceful settlement, certain definite sanctions, agreed to beforehand and published for all to know, will be applied at a fixed and early date to persistent and intractable violators of their pledges.

I do not pretend here to say what these sanctions should be, though Sir Thomas Holland's mineral sanction appears to be the most practical and effective.

This, however, I may say, that by taking immediate action on these lines the League will be brought back to its original purpose of regarding WAR as the enemy. From this it has, as I understand the issue, been entirely led astray by the will-o'-the-wisp of " finding the aggressor."

It is, of course, to be understood that if *both sides* in a war reject an armistice and a peaceable solution, both must have sanctions, whether mineral or other, applied to them as being persistent and intractable belligerents, and therefore violators of their solemnly-pledged word given in the Briand-Kellogg Pact and in the League Covenant never to have recourse to war except in self-defence.

Post scriptum.

LYULPH'S TOWER,
ULLSWATER,
PENRITH,
CUMBERLAND.
5th July, 1936.

TO FRANCIS, HUBERT, EDMUND AND HENRY :

Carissimi,

Just two years ago in this house I began the first volume " Theatre of Life as seen from the Pit," primarily for your entertainment and possibly also a little for your instruction, for the desire to play the pedagogue grows with the years.

I am glad to have been allowed to finish the second volume, " Life seen from the Stalls," in the same place, for purely sentimental reasons, because more and more I feel that I belong to Cumberland and to the Lake District.

I am glad to have finished the book, for whatever it may be worth. The Theatre of Life has been full of interest, sometimes sad, sometimes cheerful, and the interest has grown constantly as the years passed.

Life, when I was a boy in the eighteen-seventies, was in England at least a quiet and placid stream, rather muddy in places, but still often blue and white with reflections of the sky. Now it is still muddy and turgid but broken with cataracts and whirlpools leading us—whither ?

You will have noticed that I have ended the second volume with an attack on the *Tertii Gaudentes*, who are those who continue to supply the wants of persistent and recalcitrant belligerents. I am convinced that the *Tertii Gaudentes* are in our days of mechanised warfare at the root of the evil of war. If the principal nations, who are producers of raw materials needed for the conduct of war, could agree to refuse to such belligerents both the materials and the credits necessary for war, war could not be carried on after accumulated stocks had been exhausted, but would wither and die like a plant without water, and thus the Reign of Law might at last be established.

I will not elaborate this theme, of which I have already written enough in the body of the book.

If you have read the book through you will remember that during my visit to the devastated areas in France during the spring of 1919 I made a mental vow to do what little I could to help forward the cause of Peace.

This book, then, is probably my final contribution to that cause.

Without measures to enforce law between nations, international law will but remain what it has always been in times of crisis, a broken reed.

I have, unfortunately, been unable so far to fall in with many who understand the vital part played by the *Tertii Gaudentes* in making war not only a possibility but a probability in the near future, for they deliberately and directly encourage recourse to force in others, even to their own hurt and maybe ultimate destruction.

Education is required to bring the nations of the world to realise that only by acting together in sufficient numbers can they hope to be powerful enough to bring the necessary pressure to bear on persistent belligerents who are, in truth, the enemies of all.

I cannot in the course of nature have much more time before me to take part in this work of education.

So I leave it to you and others who have eyes to see the lightning in the sky, and ears to hear the approaching thunder, to carry on the campaign of education for the cause of Law and Security, which are the only two true supports for Justice and Peace against Force.

But I would remind you that these will be but as sounding brass and tinkling cymbals unless they are welded together and strengthened and hardened, as iron is strengthened and hardened with ferro-alloys, by that greatest of all the alloys—Christian charity and understanding of our fellow-men.

Your very affectionate,

FATHER.

APPENDIX A 1

SECOND-LIEUT. ANDERSON to CONSUL-GENERAL HOWARD

Canea, Crete, June, 1906.

Sir,

I have the honour to make the following report on the Elections held at Aios Joannis on the 27th May, 1906.

At sunrise on 27th ult., I placed a guard under a sergeant over the house where the Elections were to take place, and sent a patrol to conduct the voters from the village of Garazo into Aios Joannis. This patrol returned bringing a party of about thirty men from Garazo into Aios Joannis who, I discovered, were of the Government party. I then personally returned with this patrol and took up a position about one and a half miles down the road to Garazo, with a view to meeting the Venizelists of Garazo and conducting them safely to the Polling Station. I waited there some time till I heard a fight in progress on the hills to the west of the Garazo road. I took the patrol there and saw a party of 200 or 300 men at least who were running over the hills all armed with heavy sticks and throwing showers of stones at the villagers of Aios Joannis who had come out to prevent their entry into Aios Joannis. I intercepted the two parties and disarmed a large number of men of their heavy sticks which I broke up.

I then went towards the village where I was informed that there was another fight in progress in the olive trees north of the village. I went there, and as I arrived a shot was fired which was shortly followed by another. These shots were fired by a man probably from Aios Joannis and at the voters from Garazo who were entering the village . I was then met by a party of eight men sent by the sergeant at the Polling Station to stop the fighting. They had picked up the gun from which the shots had been fired and which the man had dropped in his flight.

Joining parties I went through the village to the Polling Station which faces the village square. I found there a large and very excited crowd and was informed by the sergeant at the Polling Station that, as soon as the two shots above mentioned were fired, the crowd got very excited and quite beyond control and commenced to produce knives and sticks and stones. I also found that the Brigadier of Gendarmes, whilst trying to arrest a man who was throwing a stone at another, had received a blow on the back of the head from a large stone ; he had been taken into a house to be bound up. The crowd were running for their knives which they had secreted under stones, etc., all around the square unnoticed by us. About a dozen knives and a pistol were found in about five minutes ; five prisoners were taken, three of whom had knives ; one was caught in the act of throwing a stone on another man and the fifth was the man who had injured the Brigadier of Gendarmes. The crowd was getting more excited and quite beyond control and would not commence voting, so I closed the Elections in accordance with the Proclamation of the Consuls-General.

I then drove the people of the other villages out of Aios Joannis. I am of the opinion that several of the crowd would have been wounded and also the Gendarmes if the Elections had not been closed by me as all the crowd appeared to be armed. One of the prisoners taken had on his person a large number of voting pellets which he had also used to load a pistol with. About 9.30 a.m. as all was very quiet, I decided to reopen the Elections and sent a notice to that effect to all the villages concerned. The voting then proceeded in a quiet and orderly manner.

The leader of the Venizelists at Garazo sent me a letter that the Venizelist party would not vote as there was no time and also because they were unjustly treated by the Government party.

The excuse of time was obviously absurd as they received the meassge at about 11 a.m. and were informed that the polling would be continued till 9 p.m. and the village of Garazo is only two hours' march distant.

In consequence of this no Venizelist votes were given in.

I left Aios Joannis at 6.15 a.m. on the 28th ult., after the counting of the vote had been completed.

I have the honour to remain, etc.,
(Sgd)   A. C. ANDERSON (Second Lieutenant)
2nd Royal Sussex Regiment.

APPENDIX A 2

ACTING CONSUL-GENERAL GRAHAM to SIR EDWARD GREY
Canea, Crete, Sept. 27, 1906.

Sir,
I have the honour to transmit to you herewith copies in translation of Proclamations addressed by Prince George to the Cretan people announcing the appointment of M. Zaimis as his successor and bidding them farewell.

The *Psara* with a Greek Admiral on board arrived early on the 24th instant in company with His Majesty's ship *Barham* and proceeded to Suda Bay. Owing to the presence of numerous bands on the neighbouring hills and consequent alarm here, I asked the *Barham* to remain off Canea for the night. She played her searchlight on the town and hills, and in the small hours of the morning landed a series of patrols. In view of the ostensible reason of her presence here discretion was observed in these operations. She left for Suda at daybreak on the 25th instant.

The Consuls of the Six Powers represented here were received in farewell audience by the Prince on the 25th at midday. His Royal Highness, who looked pale and worn, addressed a few words to the Austro-Hungarian Consul-General. He then turned to the Consuls of the Four Powers and asked whether we were aware that from 2,000 to 3,000 demonstrators against his departure had gathered on the Suda road many of them armed. He had sent M. Koundouros, the First Councillor and the Metropolitan of Candia to them to speak to them and bring them to reason, but he could not answer for what might or might not happen.

I seized the opportunity of giving His Royal Highness a farewell message from Colonel Panton and the Royal Sussex Regiment, which appeared to please him.

As I had the honour to report by telegram, the arrangements for the Prince's departure, settled by the Officer Commanding the International troops in communication with His Royal Highness, were that it should take place from Suda Bay. All the International forces were to be drawn up round the Palace at Halepa to form a guard of honour, and there were to be no troops between there and Suda. At the quay at Suda were to be placed the Corps of Gendarmerie in order that they might have a last farewell of their Chief and guards of honour from the ships of war.

The change in the point of departure from Suda to Canea appears by some unaccountable means to have become known (to the insurgents) on the hills round Suda long before the ships getting up steam in the bay or movements of troops could have given them any indication. They at once marched on Halepa. At about 3 p.m. they reached the outposts of international troops near the new waterworks to the south of the town. They were summoned to stop but refused.

The French and Italian troops then appear to have discharged a volley firing into the air, but two unnamed persons were slightly injured. Some of the insurgents returned the fire ; others dispersing in small bodies ran down the streets and lanes under cover of the stone walls into Halepa. As I reached the Russian Consulate-General some of these issued from an alley into the main road about two hundred yards off, and one man fired two shots at the Italian Guard of Honour lining the road from the Palace for the Prince's departure. The Italian, French and Russian Guards of Honour at once opened out and general firing began both sides taking cover behind the stone walls of the Consulate Garden and the surrounding vineyards. The two Russian cavasses stood to arms to repel a possible attack ; one of them remained at the window of the study in which were M. de Bronewsky and myself.

I had just been pointing out to my Russian Colleague some insurgents firing from behind an outhouse, when a heavy fire was suddenly and quite unexpectedly opened on the Russian Consulate itself at from under 100 to about 200 yards.

One of the first bullets, probably from a sporting rifle, struck the cavass at the window between those at which my Russian Colleague and I were standing, blowing off the top of his head ; he only lived for a few minutes. M. de Bronewsky, who was but a few feet from him when he fell and was not unnaturally moved at the incident, produced a revolver from his pocket and accidentally discharged it, the ball striking a stove within a yard of my knee. I hastily imparted to him a rudimentary knowledge of how to handle these unreliable weapons. In the meantime a company of Russian infantry had doubled up to the defence of the Consulate, and they beat off the insurgents in about half an hour. The shooting on both sides was remarkably bad as, in spite of the short range, the casualties only amounted to one Russian non-commissioned officer wounded on the one side and one man killed and two or three wounded on the other. A good many bullets penetrated the walls of the house happily without further damage to anyone. The insurgents gradually, firing as they went, drew off to the south of the town and gathered with other bands on the hills commanding Halepa.

My Italian Colleague would only permit the Carabinieri[1] to be present on condition that this naval protection was afforded them, the attitude of the rank and file of the Gendarmerie at such a moment of excitement being doubtful.

These arrangements were much criticised by my Colleagues as being inspired by considerations of effect rather than of safety ; but in a stormy meeting at which Colonel Lubanski was present I supported his view that, unless the Consuls were prepared to dictate the arrangements themselves and accept all responsibility, the matter must be left in his hands. All the demonstrators would, moreover, be at Suda at such a moment.

My Colleagues were a good deal perturbed by the warning conveyed by Prince George as to the number of armed men on the Suda road. They considered that in the circumstances His Royal Highness should be invited to leave from Canea. I opposed a change of plan as unnecessary, but being in a minority of one agreed that we should consult His Royal Highness on the subject. In the light of what subsequently took place I believe it is not impossible that the Prince would have been carried off to the mountains ; I do not, however, think that any acts of violence would have been committed.

We returned to the Palace and Prince George, on being consulted through his Aide-de-Camp, at once consented to leave from Canea.

[1] Italian Gendarmerie officers.

Arrangements were changed accordingly, and a cordon of troops thrown round the town. But the military authorities seem to have had no idea of what their duties were to be, or whether they were to repel the advance of armed men by force or to allow them to pass. Colonel Lubanski was at first inspired by the latter idea, but certain incidents completely changed his point of view and he demanded an audience of Prince George, at which he accused His Royal Highness of having prepared a *guet-apens*.

I was visiting Colonel Lubanski immediately after this regrettable incident, in order to settle with him as to the disposal of the landing party from his Majesty's Ship *Barham* after her return from Suda to Canea when a servant rushed in to say that the insurgents had attacked the outposts to the north of the town. Colonel Lubanski at once hurried to the scene requesting me to inform the doyen of what was taking place. I proceeded to His Majesty's Consulate-General into which refugees on hearing the firing were beginning to come and seeing that all was safe in the hands of Mr. Vice-Consul Lascelles and a small guard of the Royal Sussex Regiment, I proceeded with a cavass to the Russian Consulate-General in order to warn my Colleague and assist him to concert any measures that might seem necessary.

At about four o'clock my French and Italian Colleagues, who had been cut off in endeavouring to establish communication with their ships at Suda Bay, arrived on the scene. In the light of fresh information they supplied as to the position of armed bands menacing the road to Canea, and in view of the approach of darkness and the danger of street fighting in the town at night, we resolved to seek a collective audience of Prince George, and to respectfully suggest that, in order to prevent possible collisions and further bloodshed, he should have a boat sent in for him from the *Psara* under the back of the Palace and leave for the small landing-stage there.

Our interview with the Prince was very distressing. His Royal Highness, who was labouring under strong emotion and excitement, appeared to deeply resent the suggestion. He turned to my Russian Colleague and myself and said that he had nothing against us personally but the behaviour of the Consuls and of their Governments was responsible for the present mess (*gâchis*). He then addressed my French and Italian Colleagues in the most scathing terms both as regards their personal and political attitude. He said he was being driven from Crete with a broken heart against his will and that of the Island owing to a series of diplomatic intrigues, but that his forced departure would be the signal for a state of affairs which nothing but his return could pacify. He particularly enjoined me to say that, in spite of the promises made to him, he had been hunted from the Island like " a thief and a criminal." We begged His Royal Highness to remember that we had merely made a respectful suggestion, and that if he decided to leave from Canea his wishes would of course be met, but he replied that this was an attempt to saddle him with a responsibility for what might occur which he could not assume. One of my Colleagues then suggested that the Prince should remain till the following morning when, with daylight, arrangements could be made to preserve order. His Royal Highness hesitated but I ventured to urge him to leave at once and he concurred. I believe that his continued presence at Helepa during that night would have produced a situation of extreme danger. At 8.30 p.m. the salute of His Majesty's ship *Barham* and the other ships of war at Canea announced the departure of His Royal Highness.

In the light of subsequent information I am not clear as to how far the attack on the Russian Consulate was due to accident or design. There is no doubt that the majority of insurgents deplore the incident. They allege that the Russian cavass on the lower floor, shooting from the window, killed the man who fell in the street below some 500 yards off and that this drew their fire. The man was certainly killed from the Consulate but at a later stage of the fight. Bullets struck the other Consulates, including that of His Majesty, but there were plenty in the air at the time owing to the cross firing, and they were probably purely accidental. I am inclined to think that the attack on the Russian Consulate was only an afterthought, when the insurgents found access to the Palace barred by the fire of the Guards of Honour.

On the other hand, the family of the murdered man have received a message from the insurgent who claims to have killed him and has fled into the interior, expressing regret, as the shot was intended for M. de Bronewsky. There is no doubt that, owing to false reports circulated by the instigators of the movement, which appear confirmed by the manner of the Prince's departure, and also, I fear, messages left by his entourage, the responsibility for His Royal Highness's departure is fixed on the Consuls and the resentment is centred on them.

The main body of the bands has now withdrawn to Malaxa, some eight miles away, where they will probably await the arrival of M. Zaimis and then reappear to make a demonstration rather, I hope, with a view to impressing him than with any hostile intentions. I understand that their collision with the International troops and the some half-dozen casualties they sustained have had a sobering effect. Small bands, however, remain on the hills round Halepa and sniping of an innocuous kind continues day and night. The Consulates are guarded and there are elaborate services of patrols both at Halepa and Canea, in which the landing parties from H.M.S. *Barham* are conspicuous. It would be difficult to speak too highly of the indefatigable energy shown by these parties. Their services are in constant request day and night but they always meet the calls upon them with alacrity and good will. Colonel Lubanski has referred in conversation with me to the services they are rendering. A day and night signal service from the balcony of the Consulate to the *Barham* had been established.

A reinforcement of twenty-five men is arriving from Candia for the Royal Sussex detachment quartered here, which has at the present moment only some dozen men available.

Although it is no doubt necessary to observe all precautions, I do not personally feel the least apprehension that the Consulate will again become the object of attack.

In conclusion I would venture to repeat that the insurgents in no sense represent a national movement—they only number from 300 to 500 armed men in all. The largest band, which penetrated right up to the Palace at Halepa, is led by MM. Milonoyannakis and Discalojannis, as to whose proceedings I had the honour to report in a previous despatch. These two leaders had entirely declined to obey His Royal Highness's summons to return here, and have been gradually recruiting fresh adherents. A second band, the one which attacked the Russian Consulate-General, was under one Xivas, a Lakiote Chief, in touch with the Government officials here; a third was led by the Prince's own cavass on horseback, wearing His Royal Highness uniform and monogram. This man was met by the Italian Consul-General who had him seized by the Italian Carabinieri and made prisoner.

Speaking with due deliberation I must express my conviction that the whole of the recent agitation, which has culminated in the present deplorable incidents, is due to the Palace and to the three Cretan Councillors, by whom it has been deliberately fostered during the unfortunate delay which attended Prince George's departure from Crete.

On the other hand I take pleasure in stating that, so far as I can ascertain, MM. Michelidakis and Logiades and the moderate wing of the Government party, having once acquiesced in the situation, have maintained a loyal attitude and are in no way responsible for recent events.

I have (etc.),

(Sgd) RONALD GRAHAM.

APPENDIX B 1

NAVICERT No. 1166

1916.
25th November.   Sir Cecil Spring Rice telegraphed application for thirty-five consignments for SWEDEN :
Automobiles, marine hardware, timber, paraffin wax, sugar, caustic soda, malleable iron, motor-cycles, cotton goods, woollen goods, sewing-machines, tobacco, sheet and pipe lead, blotting paper, smoking pipes.

Decision :   Three items *Accipe* (malleable iron, smoking pipes, blotting paper).

Two items *nolo* as shippers were parties to blockade breaking scheme.

One item *nolo* as consignee under suspicion.

One item *nolo* as H.M. Government cannot give facilities for these goods (lead) at present ; on rationing principle enough had already been sent.

All other items *Pendens*, referred to Sweden.

2nd December.   Paraffin wax released on condition it is not delivered until 1917.

12th December.   Guarantees for fifteen *Pendens* items considered satisfactory and goods released.

21st December.   Shipper of sugar (*nolo*) advises that he is informed that the Committee is prepared to reconsider their decision. Committee answered that he is mistaken and that it is proposed to impose an embargo on sugar for Sweden.

1917.

3rd January.   Shipper of an *Accipe* item wishes to increase his consignment : referred to Sweden for guarantee—received later and goods *Acciped*.

10th January.   Guarantees received for six items and goods released.

NAVICERT No. 741

1916.

7th September.   Sir Cecil Spring Rice telegraphed application for twenty consignments for DENMARK :

Pig-iron, motor-cycles, leather, glucose, cotton shirts, forges, lathes, sisal twine, cotton-piece goods, starch, tobacco, air-compressors, automobiles.

Three items refused outright (twine and two of starch) as H.M. Government cannot give facilities for these goods. (Rationing system.)

One item (leather) referred to Denmark.

3rd November.   One *nolo* decision reversed, with no reason given.

16th November.   Chamber of Manufacturers reply that consignee of leather has made proper arrangements and has no connection with some dark grey firms. (*Acciped*.)

21st November.   Application from a *Pendens* firm for release of their goods. Reply that no facilities can be granted until Prize Court proceedings on other consignments to the same firm are concluded.

23rd November. Danish Chamber of Manufacturers now come
forward and give assurances with regard to one
of the *nolo* consignments and the *nolo* is withdrawn.

RUBBER NAVICERTS

R. 83   SWEDEN :
29th Nov., 1916. Three items (raincoats, armlets, garters). *Acciped.*

R. 93   SWEDEN :
3rd Jan., 1917. One item (high-pressure jointing) *nolo* as the
consignee is on Class " B " of the Black List.
One item (raincoats). *Acciped.*

R. 94   DENMARK :
3rd Jan., 1917. Sir Cecil Spring Rice telegraphed application for
three items of suspenders, corsets and garters.
Acciped.

R. 99   DENMARK :
10th Jan., 1917. Corsets and hose supporters. *Acciped.*

APPENDIX C I

British Mission to Poland,
26th March, 1919.
Warsaw.
Despatch to the RT. HON. A. J. BALFOUR, M.P., Paris.

Sir,

I wish to place on record the impressions I have gained rapidly and
naturally somewhat superficially in the short time that I have spent in
Poland. Before doing so, however, I should like to give a brief
account of the different phases through which I have passed with
regard to the Polish question since I first came into close contact with
Poles at the Legation at Stockholm.

While there and under the influence of conversations with various
Poles from Congress Poland, Galicia and German Poland I became
convinced of the strong national feeling existing in the country, and
of the great advantages that there would be for the European settlement after the war, of a strong and united State of Poland to act as a
buffer State between Germany and Russia. I may also add that I
felt a strong sympathy for the Polish people, divided as they were between

three of the great belligerent Powers, forced often to fight against each other in interests which were not their own, for countries which had committed against them a great act of injustice in the past, and that these sympathies considerably strengthened the opinion that at the Peace Conference it would be necesasry to restore to Poland her unity and liberty. As regards the internal problems of Poland, such as the agrarian question or the Jewish question I had at that time very little information.

It was with these rough impressions that I reached London and began my work in preparing memoranda on the Polish situation for the British Peace Delegation. In London I found a somewhat different atmosphere. There was a strong feeling against the work of the Polish National Committee, which perhaps unfortunately, but owing to the circumstances over which the Polish people had little or no control, had taken upon itself the representation of Polish interests in the Allied countries, and had been more or less formally recognised as the Representative of the new Polish State that was to be. The Polish National Committee was considered to be working rather in the interests of the reactionary forces in Poland, and of the great landlords than of the great masses of the Polish people, and there was a feeling that if Poland were assisted with the supplies she required after the Germans had evacuated the country, this would be bolstering up a reactionary government, and might be contrary to the interests of the Polish population as a whole and even contrary to their desires. In fact, the prevailing opinion which to a great extent influenced me at the time seemed to be that to do anything the Polish Committee asked for would be to fasten upon Poland a regime of wicked landlords who spent most of their time in riotous living, and establish there a Chauvinist Government whose object was to acquire territories inhabited by non-Polish populations. At the same time there was undoubtedly a strong desire to see Poland re-established as a united and independent country, both from the point of view of righting an old injustice and of establishing a buffer between Germany and Russia, and a bulwark against the Bolshevik invasion from the East. These two conflicting points of view caused a considerable hesitation in forwarding to Poland the supplies of arms wanted in order to enable the Government to defend itself against the probable invasion of Bolsheviks on the East and the knowledge that the Polish Government was without these supplies undoubtedly encouraged its various neighbours to take offensive military action against the Poles on different fronts.

The situation of Poland during December, January and February was therefore most critical on account of the weakness of the Polish Government and the apparent unwillingness of the Allied Powers to come to its assistance ; this critical situation though now rather improved is far from being at an end. It was further believed in London that the Polish workmen and peasants were to a great extent inclined to Bolshevism owing to the desire of the peasants like those in Russia to obtain their own land, and owing to the lack of food and clothing and general unemployment amongst the industrial classes, which was the result of four years' war and foreign occupation. A certain fear was therefore no doubt entertained lest if help were given to Poland as desired, it might only be used against the Allies in the interests of Bolshevism.

On arrival in Poland and after hearing the views of almost all classes of the population, either personally or through the help of Mr. Kenney and others who were able to get into touch with the working classes, I found that the one principal factor which dominated everything else was unquestionably the national spirit which united all in favour of the re-establishment of their country. The Polish workmen have undergone untold hardships, and the thousands of absolutely destitute refugees who have arrived daily both from Russia and Germany since the Armistice was signed, have seriously complicated the problem of unemployment in this country. Nevertheless, in spite of an organised Bolshevik agitation they have hitherto refused to be led astray, and have behaved with astonishing calm and moderation. In the same way I have been convinced that while there is a strong demand amongst the landless peasants, and those who occupy holdings too small to maintain their families, for obtaining suitable holdings to enable them to settle on the land, there is amongst the great majority of them no demand for confiscation of property in their favour, nor any apparent likelihood that they would take the law into their own hands as in Russia, and divide the larger properties up among themselves. The Socialists generally state that the wish of the average Polish peasant is to obtain a good title to his land by paying for it, and if the Government and Diet can bring forward legislation which will provide for a sufficient number of peasant holdings to be brought into the market within a reasonable time, they have no doubt that the acuteness of the agrarian agitation will die away.

The landlords themselves have seemed to realise the necessity of acting without delay, and have resolved at a meeting held in Warsaw to place two million acres, or about 20 per cent. of all the holdings in Congress Poland and Galicia exceeding an area of 200 acres, at the disposal of the Government for sale in small lots, the terms of the sale to be fixed between the Government and themselves. While there is no doubt a small percentage of large landlords who own enormous estates and were very frequently absentees, the majority of the Polish landlords seemed to have lived on their estates, and in accordance with the economic conditions prevailing to have treated their peasants reasonably well. There was besides between the two classes the bond of nationality as against the Russian or German oppressor which went far to give them a common sympathy and to prevent anything like the bitterness of feeling which existed between the Polish landlords and the Ukranians to the east of the Bug river. Provided therefore the peasants feel their cause is being favourably considered there would seem good hope that any serious peasant rising against the landlords with destruction of life and property, will be avoided in this country.

The question of industrial unemployment is a most serious and pressing one, and naturally creates a feeling of great unrest in the towns. It is impossible to better it unless the Allies will shoulder the responsibility of providing the raw materials necessary, as the country owing to the great depreciation of its coinage is quite unable to meet the expense of importing at the present time the goods required. Two things are therefore immediately needed in order to remove the dangers of disorder resulting from unemployment ; one is the re-establishment of Polish currency at something like its face value, which can only be done with the help of the Allies, but will inevitably take some time, and the other is the immediate supply of raw materials required by the Allied Governments on easy terms. If measures of this sort are taken in time there seems no doubt that the national feeling of the people will overcome any tendency to Bolshevism which might arise out of the existing famine and want.

As regards the Jewish question it seems to me that the accounts of persecutions which have appeared in many Allied papers have been grossly exaggerated, if not devoid of foundation. It is unfortunately impossible to deny that attacks on the Jews have occurred, as, for instance, in Lemberg, and in Kielce and possibly in some other places, usually owing to the state of disorder generally existing at the time in these places, and to the lack of authority of the Central Government. But there is absolutely no proof whatever that the Central Government at any time encouraged these regrettable proceedings, and indeed latterly since they have been stronger they have done everything in their power to put a stop to any attacks on Jews in the provinces. In Warsaw itself no such attacks have taken place, even immediately after the German evacuation when everything was in a state of flux. This is really remarkable owing to the fact that a great number of these Jews unquestionably sided with the Germans and openly declared their anti-Polish and anti-National sentiments. Their main object indeed seems to have been to destroy the possibility of a Polish State, and it is largely owing, I am inclined to think, to their propaganda that the belief in the Poles as a persecuting race has sprung up. I noticed in an article in the *Manchester Guardian* of the 19th March, for instance, the following question : " Who dreams that Poland of her own motion will do aught but continue to persecute her Jews ? " Whatever anti-Jewish propaganda there has been in Poland has been carried on by the National Democrats only, and so far as it has been effective has taken the form of establishing Polish co-operative stores in country villages in order to take the place of the ordinary Jewish storekeeper which has been construed as a sort of general boycott. As far as I can understand, however, in the trades and industries in which Jews are employed in the towns, there has been nothing in the shape of a general boycott against them, but the anti-national line taken by many Jews both during the Russian and German occupation has not unnaturally exasperated the Poles themselves. The National Democrats also during the elections and in their Press have certainly endeavoured to excite the people against the Jews, but they do not represent a majority of the Polish nation and even among them the serious leaders recognise the danger of promoting pogroms or persecutions.

There are numbers of professional Jews, lawyers, doctors, professors, etc., against whom there is no feeling whatever, and the general view even amongst the National Democrats is that the Jews should have equal civil and religious rights but not more than the Poles. So far as I can judge there is every prospect that Poland will become not a reactionary but a liberal and a democratic country, and this being the case so long as the Jews abstain from anti-Polish and anti-National agitation and propaganda and content themselves with receiving the same treatment as other Polish citizens, there is I am convinced no fear of any religious or civil persecution.

Nothing has surprised me more than the moderation of the Poles of Posen towards the Germans. Considering the violence of their dislike of the German domination and the contempt with which they have been treated for generations by the Germans, one might have expected that when they threw off the German yoke some disorders or excesses would have taken place. On the contrary, everything seems to have proceeded with the greatest possible order. The German employers were maintained in their posts, not a German monument has been harmed, the German language is freely spoken in the streets of Posen, German stamps are in use at the post office, and German invalided and disarmed soldiers walk about the streets in German uniforms. The German schools are maintained with their teachers, the only difference being that the Polish language is expected to be taught for two or three hours in the day, and the children walk about with the names of German ships on their caps and post cards of " Hindenburg Befreier des Osten " are freely sold in the German shops. These are small matters but they indicate I think to what extent confidence may be placed in the fairmindedness and moderation of the Poles.

As regards the Jewish question I have only to add that there are several divisions amongst the Jews in Poland. There are first the " assimilated " Jews who are openly pro-Polish and desire no privileges, these are mostly of the upper and professional classes ; next the orthodox Jews forming nearly one-half of the Jewish population, who while they desire special Confessional Schools do not want any other special privileges ; lastly come the Zionists and the Party of the Jewish Bund whose desires range from a sort of educational autonomy down to having their own budget, their own police and their own military. It is these latter who have invariably sided with the foreign domination in Poland, and who are now agitating against the re-establishment of Poland as an independent country. Many of the latter have also Bolshevik tendencies.

Further, on arrival in Poland I believed there was a great gulf fixed between the Conservative bourgeois elements on the one side, and the Socialists on the other and it was impossible for them to work together for the re-establishment of their country. While no doubt there has been and is a very strong political feeling between the two, and while it is possible that certain more extreme elements may at any time take ill-considered and violent action such as the attempted *coup de main* by Prince Sapieha in December when he tried to seize and imprison the Socialist Government, yet all things considered it is remarkable with what moderation they have since the Diet has been elected acted together in many matters of material importance such as the re-election of General Pilsudski as Head of the State by a unanimous vote of the Chamber.

My general impression then is that while Poland unfortunately lacks almost altogether the trained men necessary to put her house in order rapidly and satisfactorily, the elements of sound political sense and moderation are certainly there, and that if she can be assisted with technical advisers by the Allied countries in her military, financial, and economic affairs, the Polish State ought successfully to be built up on sound democratic lines within the next few years ; no country has ever perhaps been in so difficult or intolerable a position as Poland during the last few months ; the very division of the country into three parts under three different systems of government have necessarily made it more difficult to amalgamate the men coming from these different parts of the kingdom into one central scheme, and these difficulties will probably continue for a generation.

If we add to this the devastation caused by the war, the chaotic condition of the currency, the problem of hundreds of thousands of destitute refugees suddenly returning home, the question of how to supply the unemployed with the necessaries of life, and finally, the necessity of carrying on some sort of hostilities on no less than four fronts at the same time, if we take all these into consideration and yet find that during these winter months the people of Poland have on the whole remained quiet, we may I think fairly come to the conclusion that there is good stuff in the country out of which to build a solid and prosperous State.

I have (etc.),
(Sgd) Esme Howard.

INDEX

A

Acre, 602, 603
Adams, Henry, 113
Adamski, Father, 342
Aeranthal, Count, 145–147
Aghia Moni, 48, 56
Åland Islands, 266, 305, 396, 409
Alba, Duke of, 479, 480
Alba, Don Santiago, 465, 469
Albania, 303
Alcock, and Brown (Airmen), 384
Alda, 29, 375, 525
Alfonso XIII, King of Spain, 419 *et seq.*
America and Americans, 101–142, 253, 255, 256, 272, 350, 351, 374, 485–571, 580
American Blockade Claims, 498, 500
American Debt Settlement, 497, 498
American Press, 120, 475, 520, 562, 563
Amiens, 380
Anderson, Frida, 204
Anido, General Martinez, 432, 433
Annual, Morocco, 437–439, 473
Appenzell, 195
Apponyi, Count Albert, 164, 165
Apponyi, Count Alexander, 164, 165
Archangel, 383
Archduke Charles Stephen, 356
Archduke Franz Ferdinand, 210
Armistice, 271–274
Armstrong, Lady, 539
Armstrong, Sir Harry, 489
Arnold, Matthew, 106
Arundel, 370
Askanazi, Professor, 336
Asquith, Rt. Hon. H. H., 284
Asturias, Prince of the, 185
Austria, 144–146, 184, 209, 211, 212, 215, 239, 382
Austrian Peace Delegation, 374, 378
Avila, 445–450

B

Baalbek, 601
Bacon, Hon. Robert, 140, 293
Bahamas, 504, 505, 507, 508

Baldwin, Rt. Hon. Stanley, 197, 535
Balfour, Rt. Hon. A. J., 260, 282, 290, 291, 303, 324, 364 *et seq.*, 460
Balkan Conference, 183, 200, 209
Balkan League, 182
Baltic States, 260, 296, 316, 367, 379
Banat, 154, 155
Bandini, Prince, 271
Bar Harbour, 539, 541
Barnes, Mr., 306, 369
Barthèlemy, General, 334 *et seq.*
Barton, Mrs., 185
Basset Moore, 227
Bell, Herr, 389
Benes, Dr., 304–306, 308
Berchtold, Count, 21
Berenguer, General, 471
Berne, 167–201
Beseler, General von, 331
Beyers, General, 181, 182
Beyrouth, 602
Bildt, Axel de, 249, 250, 410
Biliotti, Sir A., 14, 25
Blériot, 159, 160
Bloch, M. Jules, 379
Blockade, 226, 227, 230, 234–258
Boardman, Miss Mabel, 116, 493, 494
Boardman, Mr. and Mrs., 112
Boisgelin, Comtesse de, 294
Bolsheviks, 264, 285, 286, 289, 290, 293, 295, 298, 301, 303, 306, 310, 319, 336, 337, 353, 357, 358, 366, 371, 372, 383, 390, 393
Bolshevism, 414
Bolshevism in Spain, 433–435
Bonar Law, Rt. Hon., 290, 291
Bookbinding, 613
Borden, Rt. Hon. Sir R., 365
Borkum, 171
Bosdari, Count, 154
Bosnia-Herzegovina, 144, 153, 210
Botha, Rt. Hon. General, 300, 301, 308, 389
Bouffides, M., 87, 88
Brailsford, Mr., 337
Branting, Herr, 257, 366
Brest Litovsk, 263, 285
Briand-Kellogg Pact, 521–524, 638
British Delegation to Sweden, 243